DATE DUE

#360098076	4/11/99

Elements of Human Performance:
Reaction Processes and Attention in Human Skill

Elements of Human Performance:
Reaction Processes and Attention in Human Skill

Andries F. Sanders
Free University, Amsterdam, The Netherlands

LEA LAWRENCE ERLBAUM ASSOCIATES, PUBLISHERS
1998   Mahwah, New Jersey   London

Lawrence Erlbaum Associates, Inc., Publishers
10 Industrial Avenue
Mahwah, New Jersey 07430

Library of Congress Cataloging-in-Publication-Data

Sanders, A. F. (Andries Frans), 1933–
Elements of human performance : reaction processes and
attention in human skill / Andries Sanders.
        p.   cm.
    Includes bibliographical references and index.
    ISBN 0-8058-2051-5 (cloth : alk. paper). — ISBN
0-8058-2052-3 (pbk. : alk. paper)
    1. Reaction time. 2. Attention. I. Title.
    BF317.S34 1997
    152.8'3—dc21
                                        97-19997
                                        CIP

Printed in the United States of America
10   9   8   7   6   5   4   3   2   1

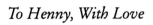

To Henny, With Love

Contents

Preface

This book focuses on two core topics of human performance theory, namely reaction processes and attention. These were chosen for three main reasons. First, both fields are neglected in texts on cognitive psychology. Reaction processes are not discussed at all, perhaps because reaction time tends to be viewed as a dependent variable rather than as an area of research. As is argued, it has unique properties that deserve consideration in their own right. Attention is usually not fully ignored but gets a few pages in a chapter on perception, presumably because attention has been most often identified with perceptual selection. This does not reflect present-day views in which attention is related equally to central processing and to action. The main function of attention appears to be control and coordination of processes at these various levels of processing. At the same time, the information flow from perceptual to central processes and from central to motor processes is the main ingredient of a reaction process; therefore, the fields are fully intertwined.

The second reason was a wish to describe the present state of the art in the principal areas of the original "Attention and Performance" symposia (Sanders, 1967a). Some main topics in 1967 were reaction time, dual-task performance, selective attention, visual search, and vigilance, all of which are therefore prominent themes in this book. Some have flourished and shown a lot of progress during recent decades; others suffered from a loss of interest during the 1970s and 1980s but tended to come back in recent years. I was an active researcher throughout these years, so the review is biased in favor of my own research and the research of those with whom I had frequent contacts. In other words, there is a bias in favor of Dutch contributions, which may actually be of interest to those who are mainly exposed to American literature.

The third reason was probably the main one and evolved from a growing concern about the increasing discrepancy between basic and applied research. Almost all basic research derives from what may be labeled small and simple laboratory paradigms (Sanders, 1984), artificially created laboratory tasks carried out by human participants with the aim of uncovering and describing elementary mental processes. Their advantage is that they allow a systematic variation of parameters that is indispensable for a more detailed analysis. However, performance theory has also traditionally been interested in complex everyday skills, such as typing, driving, flying, monitoring radar or sonar, and controlling industrial processes. The extent to which evidence from small paradigms may be generalized and applied to real-life tasks, and from there to human-factors research, is quite urgent. A few decades ago, this was not felt to be a problem: The contacts between applied and basic research flourished, and one may rightly say that at that time, the basic questions about reaction processes and attention evolved from applied problems.

Since then, increasing doubts have been expressed about the value of laboratory research to real life (e.g., Flach, 1990). There is the spreading conviction among applied investigators that basic research is irrelevant to their purposes. On the other hand, basic researchers have tended to treat applied problems with some disdain, perhaps stimulated by the anti-industrial political tide during the 1970s. Researchers who have tried to keep up in both basic and applied research experience radically different worlds. One consists of detailed experiments aimed at testing equally detailed hypotheses about human performance; the other consists of solving human-factor problems in evermore complex systems. The applied problems are usually much more composite than the basic ones that are based on more elementary laboratory tasks. I worked for many years in a setting that encouraged a combination of basic and applied research. It used to be traditional policy of most applied laboratories to have a mixture of applied and related basic research whereas from the 1970s and 1980s onward, a clear distinction has developed between a basic and an applied type of investigator. Thus, I found it shocking to hear basic research characterized as "journal research" somewhere during the mid-1970s. The research programs of most applied laboratories have now drastically changed. They largely exclude basic research, and some openly aim at a less academic attitude. What has happened? Is it merely the shortsightedness of desiring short-term applied success at the cost of in-depth investment in basic research, or does it reflect something more serious?

Basic and applied research have different perspectives that may be labeled process orientation versus task orientation (Schmidt, 1987). An applied problem asks for a solution without bothering too much about theoretical underpinning . In contrast, basic research asks for experiments relevant to designing and testing models on the underlying processes. An applied problem arises from reality; a basic one from theory. Applied issues ask for widely applicable theoretical concepts, whereas basic problems are concerned with the microstructure of a process. It is evident that these differences may easily lead to a schism. Do basic and applied research really need each other? In the natural sciences, there are various examples of technological discoveries that had little or no underlying basic theory, yet there are as many examples in which basic science identified key constraints, unlocked progress with modest effort, or provided new ways for conceptualization. In fact, basic and applied approaches need each other because they become empty when practiced in isolation. Moreover, both have their own position, value, and potential that should not be blurred by designing studies in the middle as a compromise between basic and applied research. Such attempts usually fail to serve either a basic or an applied goal. It is a prerequisite for basic research to abstract from reality, which means that experimental conditions do not aim at simulating a real-life situation. In contrast, applied research needs a simulation of reality, but usually has little theoretical rationale. Valid as this all may be as a metastatement, there remains the issue of the ecological validity of the small behavioral paradigm. The concern is that the small paradigm represents nothing but an artifactual situation that has little or nothing to say about the richness of reality. If this were the case, the schism between basic and applied research would obviously be quite serious.

Most chapters are devoted to basic research and theoretical issues on reaction processes and attention. Whenever it makes sense, the applied spin-off is discussed on completion of a theoretical argument. In the last chapter, the emphasis is task oriented and deals with real-life skills and major applied techniques in system design. Indeed, this is a radically different world. To what extent do the applied techniques rely on or need basic research results? Is it possible to bridge the gap? These questions are discussed within the context of issues on reaction processes and attention.

ACKNOWLEDGMENTS

The original plan of reviewing these themes became more concrete when I had the opportunity of spending a sabbatical at the Netherlands Institute for Advanced Studies (NIAS) at Wassenaar during the academic year 1994 to 1995. I am grateful for the highly stimulating atmosphere at NIAS, with the result that I left Wassenaar in the summer of 1995 with a first draft. Then, individual chapters were sent to various reviewers for critical comments. I wish to thank them for their highly relevant comments that led to considerable revisions of most chapters. The reviewers remarks came from the Cognitive Psychology Unit of the Department of Psychology of the Free University, namely Sander Los, Mieke Donk, Paul Kess, Dirk Knol, and Floor van der Ham; from the Psychology Department of the University of Amsterdam, namely, Jo Sergeant, Maurits van der Molen, and Harold Pashler (on leave from UCSD); and from the TNO Institute for Human Factors, namely Herke Schuffel, Wim Verwey, Jan Theeuwes, and Hans Korteling. I am particularly grateful to Eric van Rossum, who did a splendid job with respect to the artwork. During the final phase I also had much support from the secretarial staff— Alies, Heleen, and

Til—who did their share of checking and rechecking. Finally, I wish to express special gratitude to my wife Henny, who not only endured all the hardships evolving from "a husband writing a book," but who also played a very important part in shaping the final product. After all revisions had been made, she sat in front of an Apple Macintosh for some 100 evenings, working on grammar and style. She never pretended to rewrite my amateur version in proper English, but only I know what her contribution has been to make the book accessible to an English readership. It is with gratitude that I dedicate the book to her.

Introduction

The research fields of reaction processes and attention aim to describe the interplay of elementary mental processes. They belong to those classical topics of experimental psychology that have witnessed considerable fluctuations in currency. Although very much alive in Wundt's Leipzig laboratory in the 1880s, they suffered from an almost total neglect from the 1920s to the late 1940s but had a strong revival during the 1950s. Following a "golden age" during the 1960s, interest waned during the 1980s but has risen again in recent years. Such swings are invariably related to methodology and to theoretical concepts and outside questions. Here, it may suffice to note that the golden age was strongly fostered by applied issues and new theoretical tools. A growing distrust about the ecological value of the small and simple paradigm (Allport, 1980a) was among the reasons for the decline in the 1980s. In addition, the theoretical tools of the 1950s proved to be limited. Each of these elements, that is, the applied roots, the empirical approach, and the theoretical tools of the 1950s are discussed by way of general introduction. The more recent comeback may be due to the advent of neural network models and to the recent advances in brain-imaging techniques. Research on brain and behavior needs behavioral paradigms, and those on elementary mental processes may be a promising sparring partner; this justifies a brief statement about the level of analysis on which research on attention and reaction processes is thought to be based.

APPLIED ROOTS

Many questions about skilled performance in semiautomatic systems during and shortly after World War II were due to problems about operator performance that could not be solved by the dominant traditions of neobehav-

1

iorism and gestalt psychology. Behaviorism had been primarily occupied with direct stimulus–response (S–R) relations and tended to consider processes between stimuli and responses as unobservable and mentalistic. Gestalt psychology had dealt primarily with issues of perceptual organization and had little interest in the functional aspects of perception, such as visual search and visual discrimination, which are of prime relevance to performance. Both traditions had ignored the selective aspects of human behavior and, therefore, had no theory of attention. Indeed, around 1940, research on attention had virtually disappeared from the scene (Paschal, 1941).[1] Nevertheless, issues on attention were at the very center of many applied questions. Consequently, the new performance theory faced the task of drafting a theory on attention, and that is what it did (Broadbent, 1958).

Questions on Attention

One question concerned watchkeeping in sonar and radar operations. Newly installed submarine detection systems required constant alertness in order to detect infrequent, near-threshold signals. Experiences aboard ship suggested that there were frequent detection failures, despite self-evident interests of the operators on duty. These failures motivated research on alertness in watchkeeping, which flourished for at least two decades. A related concern was the sensitivity of alertness to abnormal environmental and internal conditions such as heat, noise, drugs, and sleep loss, which inspired a flurry of research on the effects of such stresses on performance. Another question was related to messages from air-traffic control that are meant for a particular pilot. How may one distinguish relevant from irrelevant messages? The problem is even more complex when different messages that are on the same frequency may overlap. This elicited a lot of research on selective listening. A related question concerned perceptual–motor load when doing several tasks at once. This has been an active research area ever since.

Questions on Reaction Time

Other applied questions concerned the speed of mental processes. Many newly developed technical systems asked for increasingly fast (re)actions in critical conditions, which required data about time limits of human performance. The study of reaction time had been a classical research topic (Donders, 1868; Exner, 1873) that aimed at measuring the time taken by hypothetical intervening processes such as discrimination, choice, and sensory and motor conduction. This early research did not fit the interests of the Behaviorists or the Gestaltists, with the result that from the 1920s on, little progress was

---

[1]Aspects such as involuntary capturing of attention and reactive inhibition were actually studied but in theoretical disguise so as to avoid being labeled as mentalism (Lovie, 1983).

made. Processing speed in discrete reactions as well as in continuous manual tracking became important themes in the 1950s. One issue concerned manual tracking of targets in antiaircraft gunnery systems, which inspired Craik's (1948) theory of the human operator as an intermittent servosystem. This was at the basis of the influential single-channel theory of information processing. Other applied questions concerned the design of optimal displays and controls and their mutual correspondence. Proper displays and controls had proven to be highly relevant in the Cambridge cockpit simulation of a spitfire, but correspondence or compatibility between displays and controls was even more important to prevent unduly slow reactions and consequent errors in time-critical conditions.

The previous section stressed applied questions on attention and reaction time. Other applications were concerned with limits of signal detection and of short-term memory. For instance, there was the problem of detecting faint targets under noisy conditions, as in camouflage. Short-term memory proved to be particularly relevant in situations with temporary peak load. Is it possible to store critical stimuli for a brief period of time so that processing might be delayed until the peak has passed?

The theoretical relevance of short-term memory research was that it served as a bridge between the new performance theory and existing notions on verbal learning and forgetting (Sanders, 1975a). There were many other applied questions on, for example, illumination, adaptation to acceleration, and physical load, which had their background in sensory perception and in stress physiology and, therefore, did not affect the new performance theory. Still other applied issues also failed to affect the new performance theory, although they should have had more impact. Examples are perception of optical flow and perceptual–motor interactions that are at the basis of the ecological theory on perception and perceptual–motor interaction. Indeed, the initial impetus for Gibson's (1950) analysis of the visual world was based on optical flow while landing an aircraft or driving a car.

All of the aforementioned applied questions belong either to skill-based or to rule-based types of behavior. Rasmussen (1986) proposed the term *skill-based behavior* as a label for well-practiced and largely automatic activities. In contrast, *rule-based behavior* is more under attentional and strategic control. It relies on the choice of a proper behavioral rule from a set of available if–then rules, that is, production rules that apply to the problem at hand. As a third category, Rasmussen proposed *knowledge-based behavior* that is invoked when standard solutions fail to solve a problem and an individually tailored solution has to be found. Applied questions on knowledge-based behavior gained relevance because human industrial tasks have become more and more supervisory. The machine does the work, and people are left with the tasks of supervising the machine and of solving any problems when the machine fails. The related applied issues concern human limits in diagnosing, decision making, problem solving, reasoning, and knowledge representation, which together define the higher mental functions.

These issues caused a new cognitive revolution during the 1970s. Performance theory of the 1960s had trouble coping with knowledge-based questions, just as Behaviorism had trouble coping with the earlier described questions. The problem was that in essence, it still relied on the S–R research model. Even when allowing for effects of a variety of intervening variables, the S–R model remains concerned with the analysis of input–output relations. In other words, it cannot cope with performance in tasks without clearly defined stimuli and responses, as in problem solving and in decision making. There are no clearly defined stimuli and responses when playing chess or maintaining supervisory control. The proper methodology for analyzing higher mental functions is still very much a matter of debate. Relevant as they are, the higher functions are not discussed in this book, which deals with reaction processes and attention. Yet, interest in the higher functions led to the previously mentioned decline of interest in reaction processes and attention during the 1980s.

FULL SIMULATION VERSUS THE SIMPLE PARADIGM

The Simple Paradigm

The new performance theory faced the problem of how to approach the applied questions. Although there were exceptions, such as the Cambridge cockpit, it was usually not feasible to simulate complete tasks or to carry out sufficiently controlled experiments in an operational setting. The obvious alternative was a controlled and manageable but simplified laboratory study that resembled reality in some respects. This led to simple and small paradigms, typical examples of which are the clock test for measuring decrement in alertness (Mackworth, 1950), the dichotic listening-paradigm for limits of selective listening (Broadbent, 1952), the memory span for short-term memory deficits (J. Brown, 1959), the psychological refractory period for performance limits at a single moment (Welford, 1952), and the "five-lights test" for evaluating stress effects (Wilkinson, 1969). It is interesting to note that these references are all to British investigators who had been inspired by Sir Frederic Bartlett. The small-scale paradigms played a major role in subsequent basic research and were quite satisfactory in the early years as a basis for application.

The hope was that besides simulating relevant aspects of real-life tasks, the simple paradigms might also serve as yardsticks for underlying mental functions such as sustained attention, selective attention, working memory, and so on. It was an attractive thought that such functions might have both a specific brain localization and a prominent role to play in complex performance. In this way, the small paradigm would be a bridge between brain functioning and behavior in complex tasks that would be an ideal mode of interaction between basic and applied research and of obvious interest to both human-factors research and neuropsychology. It is fair to say that problems arose on either side, which eventually led to the alienation between basic and applied research. In retrospect, the original aspirations were probably somewhat naive.

The first problem was that the simple paradigm was never a complete simulation of a real-life task. The failure to accomplish a more detailed simulation was obviously due to technical limitations. Simulation of raw radar or sonar is still a formidable problem, yet this was not felt to be a stumbling block because the simple paradigm was viewed as satisfactory as long as it covered intuitively relevant aspects of the complex task. For example, in the study on sustained attention, participants had the task of detecting incidental deviant stimuli such as a change in brightness of a light source. Transferring the conclusions of the results under these conditions to sonar observation was seen as legitimate; this was initially supported by some successes. Correct detections decreased as a function of time on task, which was in line with observations of detecting sonar signals at sea. The possibility of situation-specific effects was largely ignored in the early days of the new performance theory. I vividly remember the embarassment when E. Elliott (1957) reported results of an auditory vigilance study that did not show an effect of time on task. There appeared to be situation-specific effects so that the problem was not as simple as originally believed.

This example can be supplemented by many others. Together, they show that one should be careful when generalizing from a specific, small paradigm to a real-life task and that generalization is sometimes very misleading. For instance, one cannot build a predictive model about how people play the piano or type a letter from evidence from responses to stimuli presented in rapid succession. Evidence from this paradigm—the psychological refractory period—shows that a response to the second stimulus is delayed when it is presented during the response to the first stimulus. The delay in reaction time to the second stimulus suggests severe performance limits when dealing with rapid sequences of stimuli and responses, yet such limits are not found in expert typists or pianists. Moreover, there are cases in which two complex tasks can be carried out together without a noticeable performance loss in either one (Allport, Antonis, & Reynolds, 1972).

Thus, the simple paradigm met with the reproach that it is concerned with artificially created laboratory situations, irrelevant to real-life performance and to system design (Allport, 1980a; Newell, 1974). It did not fare well either as a yardstick of elementary mental functions that would enable the use of simple paradigms as ready-made tests for neuropsychological assessment. Simple tasks appeared to reflect composite activity of a set of mental functions, even in the simple case of a reaction to a light flash and of the detection of a sensory stimulus. Paradigms that claimed to measure a simple function led to various "demise" verdicts (Haber, 1983; Crowder, 1982).

The objections should be taken seriously because a lack of applied potential raises doubts about the prospects of small paradigms in basic research. Without connections with real life, basic research is merely engaged in artificial forms of information processing without any wider perspective. However, the situation may be less gloomy than depicted previously and less bright than originally thought. First, there are simple paradigms with an applied success story, so a simple condemnation of the small paradigm does not do. Rather than categorically reject the total class of small paradigms, it may be better to determine the constraints and the limits of the domain to which a particular paradigm may be applicable. Second, direct application of a small paradigm may not be a fair requirement. It is quite possible that evidence cannot be immediately transferred from the laboratory to a real-life task, yet there may be an indirect profit in that relevant, applied implications may be derived from theory arising from small paradigms. Such theoretical models may have a limited domain as well. Hence, it is relevant to delineate the limits of their theoretical domain by determining the conditions under which a model applies and the reasons for its failure in other conditions. This is a long-term goal that links up with the back-to-back approach to be discussed later.

Task Simulation

As an alternative to the small paradigm, one might focus only on complex, real-life tasks. This may be even more attractive because, in the meantime, the computer enables the design of quite complex environments. Back in the 1960s, it was common that experimenters built their own special-purpose electronic equipment. This allowed the presenting of a limited set of simple stimuli and the recording of equally simple responses that fit the needs of a particular, small paradigm. At present, there are standard software solutions for a wide range of simple paradigms. In addition, simulation of much more complex environments is possible, and task simulation and virtual reality have become passwords. Simulation may be defined as a technique of substituting a synthetic environment for a real one, so that it is possible to work under laboratory conditions of control (Harman, 1961).

One example is the simulation of a wide field of regard, which is a prerequisite for many complex tasks such as driving a car, maneuvering ships, controlling air traffic, and engaging in air-to-air combat. A conventional solution in the 1970s and 1980s was a panoramic visual display produced by several projection screens in a closed-circuit TV. At present, head-mounted displays are becoming common. They use optical bundles from remote computer image generators to relay bright, high-resolution, high-contrast, and large-angle images to each eye. They give a convincing experience of "being there," which is, of course, the major objective of a simulation. It is possible to reduce the costs of a simulator by using less expensive imaging systems, which are usually limited in brightness and field of regard but which may be equally appropriate in many circumstances. In navigation or flight, the simulation of a visual scene goes together with auditory engine noise and foghorn sounds. Some recent simulations even have speech recognizers that interpret verbal questions and commands.

It should be noted that simulation of many tasks is much less complex than depicted in the aforementioned examples, in particular when the interface between the person and the task is a computer screen. Examples are synthetic radar and sonar, bookkeeping, and process control in automatized technical systems such as chemical plants or high furnaces. In such cases, the simulation simply consists of a screen with simulated information that fully corresponds to what occurs in a real situation. Indeed, simulators are now used in a wide variety of settings, for example, aircraft flight, specialized military tasks such as antiaircraft gunnery and tank maneuvers, air-traffic control, space walks, automobile driving, ship navigation, radar and sonar, supervisory control in nuclear and chemical plants, or command and control in operational, industrial, and military settings. These developments pose challenges to human-factors research that are far beyond the issues of the 1950s. It is not surprising that the present-day questions are on the much more composite level of how to design displays in a nuclear plant—to forego accidents, how to design a user-friendly text-processing program, and how to design a training program for driving a tank. Why bother about simple paradigms, which did not fulfil their promises anyway, when one may study the present-day human-factors issues directly through total-task simulations?

Yet, as is elaborated later (chap. 10), total-task simulation also has its drawbacks. First, simulation usually requires an existing system. It is much harder to simulate a system that is still in design, in particular when there are still many undecided options. Furthermore, simulators are often poorly validated and have deficient output measures that make it hard to assess performance quantitatively. Their complexity usually allows only a global performance evaluation. The problem is that a real-life task often comprises too many variables to allow detailed analysis. Scientific analysis always aims at isolating effects of individual variables, whereas, almost by definition, real-life performance consists of a combination of variables. As is shown in chapter 10, many applied techniques draw on insights from small paradigms. This argument may not impress the applied researcher, yet even if one is merely interested in application, experiments with total tasks or skills appear to have problems. Thus, during the 1950s and 1960s, extensive studies were carried out on issues of training and design of real-life tasks, such as air-traffic control. The results were either disappointing or trivial. For example, the main conclusion of one megastudy on air-traffic control was that feedback enhances skill (Parsons, 1972), an insight that had reached us a long time ago from some of the most simple paradigms. Again, even if one succeeds in evaluating an existing system through precise simulation, the question of how shortcomings of the system may be repaired has not yet been solved. Thus, the results of task simulation tend to serve short-term applied aims without gaining more detailed insights about the principles of information processing in a complex system.

In addition, due to technical as well as financial limits, a full simulation of the reality is not always feasible. A current trend is the so-called "low-cost simulator," which aims at a partial simulation but is still capable of handling training and design issues (Sanders, 1991). The problem of a partial simulation is to decide which aspects of a task are essential and which can be omitted. If the idea of full simulation is abandoned, the situation basically becomes similar to that of the simple paradigm, which also claimed to be something like a partial simulation. It should be realized that decisions about what is needed in the partial simulation require a wel¹-developed performance theory.

A Way Out?

In summary, the Scylla and Charybdis are (a) a simple paradigm, manageable, easy to analyze, and of theoretical interest, albeit potentially artifactual and (b) a full simulation, ecologically valid, and of direct applied significance but hard to analyze. How will they ever meet?

A promising approach toward bridging the gap may be the back-to-back research strategy proposed by Gopher and Sanders (1984). The idea is that the results from simple and more complex activities are compared in regard to correspondences and divergences. This strategy links up with the earlier remark that it is relevant to determine the limits of the validity of a model. It is likely that most performance models have a limited scope and will not qualify as a general framework for describing human information-processing. The first step, then, is to establish where and how their domain is limited. Thus, the interpretation of evidence obtained in a simple paradigm may lead to hypotheses about what may happen in a more complex environment. A model gains weight when its principal predictions, as derived from a simple paradigm, generalize to a more complex environment or are consistent with theoretical statements about that more complex environment. If predictions deviate, the question arises as to which aspects of the more complex environment are responsible for the divergence. Sometimes, an extension of the model may allow wider generalization, but on other occasions, a model may not address phenomena beyond its original limited domain.

The back-to-back approach has two main aspects. The first was addressed earlier and concerns generalization of theory by way of searching for correspondence among theoretical statements from narrow and wider domains. The other side is purely empirical and concerns generalization of experimental results. As an illustration, the simulation of keeping a straight course in traffic might be accomplished by a traditional pursuit-tracking task, a fixed-base simulator, a moving-base simulator, and an instrumented car. The back-to-back approach proposes a comparison of the performance data on each of these four levels. If the results observed at a more simple level deviate from those at a more complex one, the conclusion should not be that the simple level was "false" or "ecologically invalid." Rather, the question should be raised as to what caused the divergence. Which relevant aspects were missing or different in the simple setting that brought about a change in performance? Such comparisons may contribute to bridging the gap between small paradigms and real-life tasks.

So far, very few back-to-back studies have been carried out with the explicit intention of studying possible changes when going from the simple to the complex. There are other studies, though, whose results might be compared along the lines of the back-to-back strategy. Moreover, there is the back-to-back comparison among theoretical statements. They are a main theme in the final chapter, in which the prospects of reconciling the worlds of basic research and application are considered again.

THEORETICAL TOOLS OF THE NEW PERFORMANCE THEORY

The pressure from applied questions was not the only determinant of the success of the new performance theory. Neumann (1991) wondered why investigators did not turn to evidence from earlier research. He noted a review by Henning (1925) in which applied research was summarized on dual tasks, on performance in monotonous situations, and on a number of other problems that are all reminiscent of the aforementioned applied issues. Henning also proposed an elaborate theoretical framework, which failed to elicit much interest. Besides the fact that Henning's work was published in German and, therefore, inaccessible to the Anglo-Saxon world, the high tide of Behaviorism and Gestalt psychology may have precluded any impact. This situation was different in the 1950s due to three main theoretical developments. They all stemmed from engineering and shaped the information-processing model as the dominant conceptual framework for the next few decades, that is, information theory, signal detection theory, and control theory. The combination of urgent applied problems and the availability of new theoretical tools enabled the progress that could not be achieved by Henning and his contemporaries.

Information Theory

This theory was formulated by Shannon and Weaver in 1948 as a quantitative description of the accuracy of transmitting messages in a telecommunication system. It had two notions that were highly attractive to performance theory. The first was that the efficiency of transmitting information does not merely depend on stimuli that are actually presented. This was expressed by Broadbent (1959) in his statement that "S–R theorists have used as their central variable the occurrence of stimuli, past and present. Gestaltists have considered the pattern of stimuli present at any one time. But neither of them has talked about the effect at any moment of the stimuli that might have occurred but did not" (p. 114). The second notion was that a communication channel has a limited capacity for transmitting information. When more information is presented than the channel can handle, the overflow is simply ignored, which has the effect of a loss of accuracy.

During the 1950s, the limited-capacity transmission channel became the ruling metaphor for human performance. Loss of information in the case of overload provided a theoretical starting point for a theory on attention because overload forces people to select some stimuli and ignore the remainder. Redundant messages contain less information and, therefore, take less capacity. For example, natural language has strong sequential dependencies, rendering it highly redundant, and moreso in a simple message than in a complex one. As a consequence, the capacity limit might allow listening to two simultaneous simple messages but not to two simultaneous complex messages.

Initial Successes

During the 1950s, a considerable amount of research was devoted to the question of whether a limited-capacity channel is a valid expression of human performance limits (Attneave, 1959; Garner, 1962). The approach could boast of considerable successes in at least four areas: language processing, pattern perception, absolute judgment, and reaction time. The initial enthusiasm was fostered by the fact that data from such widely different fields seemed to allow a simple quantitative description in terms of transmitted information. As already mentioned, the main emphasis in language processing was on sequential constraints in word and letter order, which could well be expressed in terms of redundancy. As an example, there were various studies on the effects of approximation of a text to real language and its effect on reading speed and memory retrieval (Attneave). Approximations were accomplished by taking a word at random from a natural language text as well as the next few words following that word. The final word of this sequence, then, served as the first word for the next sequence taken from a different part of the text. The number of words in a sequence defined the level of approximation to real language. The higher the level, the faster the reading speed, which ultimately led to now-dated, finite-state models of language processing (G. A. Miller & Selfridge, 1950).

With respect to pattern perception, the regularities of gestalt-like patterns seemed to allow quantification in terms of information transmission. Thus, a good pattern has high redundancy (Attneave, 1955). For some time, researchers were led on in the hope that information theory might provide a quantitative basis for pattern perception. Although formal systems for describing patterns have been quite successful (Leeuwenberg, 1971), they deviate considerably from original information theory. Research on absolute judgment showed a capacity limit of somewhat less than 3 bits of information, which proved largely, albeit not fully, independent of dimensions such as visual brightness, length of a line, auditory loudness, or pitch (Miller, 1956). The usual design of the studies was to present a value (e.g., a tone with a certain pitch) and to ask participants to mention a number as response (e.g., from 1 for the highest tone to 8 for the lowest tone in the case of eight alternative pitches). In one of the early experiments, Hake and Garner (1951) studied the effect of the number of possible marker positions on the accuracy of reproduction and found a limit of about 3 bits. Participants could easily reproduce some six to eight alternative marker positions but failed to transmit more information when the number of possible alternative marker positions increased beyond that number.

It is possible to increase information transmission by adding an orthogonal stimulus dimension. For example, a stimulus may vary in pitch and in loudness (Pollack, 1952, 1953). In that case, participants respond step by step. First, they assign a number to the value of each dimension separately, whereupon they combine both numbers into a final response. In the same way, more marker positions can be distinguished on a two-dimensional circular display than on a one-dimensional horizontal or vertical display. These and other results are still at the basis of the design of the optimal number of alternative stimuli in coding or in call systems. A current interpretation of the limits on absolute judgment is given further on in this book.

A final success of information theory was the discovery that choice-reaction time increases as a linear function of the amount of information contained in the stimulus. Thus, the increase in choice-reaction time was about the same when going from two (1 bit) to four (2 bits) equiprobable stimulus alternatives as when going from four (2 bits) to eight (3 bits) stimulus alternatives (Hick, 1952). The same linear relation still held when stimuli were redundant due to differences in their probability of occurrence or due to sequential constraints. Finally, the phenomenon of speed–accuracy trade-off, that is, a faster choice–reaction time at the cost of more errors, fit the description in terms of the amount of transmitted information. More errors meant that less information was transmitted, but choice-reaction time became faster (Hyman, 1953).

Information Theory Fails

The successes nothwithstanding, the constant human-channel capacity in terms of transmission (bits) or rate of transmission (bits/sec) proved to be a fiction. With regard to reaction time and absolute judgment, the problems are discussed elsewhere in this book. The general problem was that information theory described input–output relations but considered neither internal processing mechanisms nor feedback. Moreover, a telecommunication system is a static tool, incapable of learning and incapable of strategic adaptation. Human intervening-processing mechanisms are sensitive to learning, the effect of which determines their potential for modulating input. The research shows that performance limits are not fixed but depend very much on practice. This is at odds with the notion of constant transmission capacity.

Signal-Detection Theory

The traditional view of signal detection used to be in terms of a sensory threshold. A stimulus is only detected when the threshold is exceeded. The threshold varies due to neural noise, which explains the usual sigmoid-psychophysical function. In this way, threshold theory ascribed hits and misses to the sensitivity of the sensory system, which had the problem that false alarms were not accounted for. Threshold theory solved this problem by assuming two states: If a stimulus exceeds the threshold, it enters a *perceived state* that guarantees an error-free hit. If a signal fails to exceed the threshold or if no signal is presented at all, the response depends on *response bias*. At one extreme of the bias, participants report only a detection when they are in the perceived state, which excludes false alarms. At the other extreme of the bias, participants always respond positively, which has the effect of 100% hits as well as 100% false alarms. Usually, the bias will be somewhere between these two extremes.

The signal-detection model was introduced to psychology by Tanner and Swets (1954). Its main feature is that the dichotomous threshold—a stimulus is either perceived or not perceived—is replaced by a sensory impression on an intensity scale. If the impression exceeds a critical intensity, the presence of a stimulus is reported, whereas a stimulus is reported absent when the impression is below the critical intensity. Thus, in threshold theory, a sensory border is exceeded whereas a response criterion (β) is passed in signal-detection theory. The same sensory impression may come either from a "noise" or from a "signal plus noise" distribution. Ultimate detection performance in terms of hits and correct rejections depends on how far apart these distributions are (the sensitivity parameter d').

Threshold theory and signal-detection theory stem from different empirical traditions. Threshold theory has its roots in classical psychophysics, the standard paradigm of which is to present sensory stimuli in order to establish the limits of detection and discrimination. In psychophysics, noise is a matter of neural noise and does not usually refer to a noisy physical environment in which stimuli might be embedded. A noisy physical environment is more common in real-life signal-detection tasks such as detection of a radar or sonar signal, a deviation in an EEG recording, or a tumor on an X-ray picture. Such situations belong to the category of information-processing tasks and, hence, ask for an information-processing model rather than for a sensory model.

The theoretical relevance of signal-detection theory is that both perception and decision contribute to the response. After the failure of information theory, the signal-detection model became the fashionable trend. For example, reaction time was described in terms of a statistical decision following a random walk (Edwards, 1966), and selective attention was discussed in terms of modulation of sensitivity (d') and criterion (β) (Broadbent, 1971). Moreover, the impact of signal-detection theory went far beyond reaction processes and attention, extending, among others, to recognition memory and to social or clinical interaction. People may emit signals of distress that may be received or missed; in this context, a false alarm means that one erroneously feels that a signal of distress has been emitted.

Control Theory

Control theory had its main impact in the analysis of sensory–motor performance in tracking a dynamic system. This dealt with an important set of applied problems, in particular because manual control was still the dominant mode of operation during World War II. The information and signal-detection models were, first and foremost, S–R models that described single input–output relations. In contrast, feedback and feedforward were passwords of control theory as relevant principles in skill acquisition and motivation. According to control theory, information processing is a matter of correcting errors that arise from a deviation between a desired state and an actual state. A stimulus is not merely a fixed outside entity, but it consists of a perceived deviation from an optimum.

Research on manual tracking flourished (Poulton, 1974) but due to the automation of most manual systems, it virtually stopped during the early

1970s. This is a striking example of interaction between basic and applied research. The more recently developed optimal-control model stresses internal control strategies and an internal mental model in order to be suitable for describing supervisory control. In this last type of task, a human operator simply monitors an automatic system and only interferes when unacceptable deviations are detected. The optimal-control model has been applied to supervisory control but remains an engineering model, with minor impact on the main stream of psychological theorizing. The reason may be that the engineering language is unsuitable for describing cognitive activities in strategic decisions and in establishing mental models of the environment. It is needless to say, though, that the principles of feedback and feedforward are of great basic and applied value.

COMPUTER METAPHORS

Of the three theoretical tools previously mentioned, information theory had the greatest impact on the new performance theory, which was largely due to the attraction of the capacity concept. Despite the failure to establish a constant capacity in bits or bits/sec, the capacity concept remained unchallenged. The reason was that a new metaphor had emerged, namely, the limited-capacity digital computer, which could handle some of the problems of information theory. In this context, information-processing capacity is still constant and limited, but the efficiency of information processing may vary. The efficiency depends on how clever the system has been programmed, with an unduly complex program requiring much more capacity than a simple one. Learning is a matter of streamlining programs, which leads to considerable savings in capacity. It is impossible to estimate the capacity of the human processor from behavior in the same way that it is impossible to calculate the capacity of a computer from its operations (N. Moray, 1967).

It is useful to draw a distinction between two major views on capacity (or *resources* as it is sometimes called) that may be labeled *resource volume* and *resource strategy*. The first has task invariance as its main axiom, which means that a task is always performed in the same way, irrespective of how much capacity is devoted to that task. When performing two tasks simultaneously, one may reallocate capacity from one task to the other. This has the effect that one does less of one task and more of the other task, but the nature of the processes involved in either one does not change as a function of the allocated resource volume.

Although a resource-volume view is found primarily in studies on dual-task performance, a resource-strategy view has been more fashionable in research on adverse environmental or organismic conditions. The resource-strategy notion proposes that operations may undergo important qualitative changes as a consequence of load, processing priority, and adverse conditions. Both resource-volume and resource-strategy models put heavy emphasis on the allocation policy, that is, strategic principles underlying the distribution of limited capacity over different activities. The resource-volume view limits the strategic effects to relative allocation of resources to tasks; in contrast, the resource-strategy view is primarily concerned with tracing qualitative changes in performance control.

The Nature of Capacity

Questions about the nature of capacity are irrelevant from the perspective of a simple computer metaphor because all processes consume the same undifferentiated capacity (Norman & Bobrow, 1975). Yet, the capacity concept has also been shaped by other influences, most notably stemming from neuropsychology (Hebb, 1949). Basically, Hebb built on a neobehavioristic perspective by drawing a sharp distinction between structural (habits) factors and energetic (drives) factors. Behavior is a joint function of habits and drives (Hull, 1943). Energetics were fully neglected in the metaphors of the new performance theory—a telecommunication system and a digital computer are not affected by motivation—but were stressed in Kahneman's (1973) capacity concept and in Sanders' (1983) cognitive-energetic model. More recently, the role of energetics in capacity models has been discussed by Wickens (1991).

Parallel Distributed Processing

It is interesting to note that all theoretical tools of the new performance theory stemmed from engineering. This reflected a general feeling that physiology, with its strong ties to behaviorism, was of little value in solving the applied problems. Nevertheless, the metaphor of the digital computer has the problem that its architecture is very different from that of the brain (e.g., Ballard, 1986). The popularity of the more recent connectionist approach (Grossberg, 1987; Rumelhart & J. L. McClelland, 1986) may be due to the fact that it claims to offer a better approach to the study of brain and behavior via parallel distributed processors that have a virtually unlimited capacity. The new metaphor is a connectionist network consisting of mutually activating and inhibiting units among and within various levels of processing.[2] From this perspective, processing limits are due to interference, confusion, and cross-talk among elements of a neural net and not to capacity constraints.

---

[2]Besides similarities, there are also important differences between a connectionist network and the cerebral cortex. Smolensky (1988) defended the position that the new connectionism lies between the neurological and the conceptual levels of analysis. In this way, it may serve as a modeling tool for the functional level of analysis. A consequence of this position is that biological plausibility is not a primary claim of connectionism. Other investigators, such as Grossberg (1987), emphasized the construction of connectionist models with more biological plausibility.

The implication is that performance limits are much more provisional than assumed by a limited-capacity model. When activities interfere, the network will develop defenses to overcome the interference. The main reason for the enormous human processing-capacity is that a stimulus such as a word or a concept is not represented by an individual cell but by a combination of cells. This combination has many potential states, depending on which are activated or inhibited. In this way, a combination of cells may host a number of representations, which implies a much more efficient use. One advantage of this approach is the neural language of the metaphor, which enables a comparison with physiological models.

Capacity Versus Processing Stages

Two conceptualizations dominated research on attention and reaction processes. One is the limited-capacity view that was outlined in the previous section. The other emphasizes modularity of the processing system, with the aim of delineating and describing hypothetical processing mechanisms involved in the information flow. Along these lines, a reaction process is conceived of as a sequence of processing stages. For example, a stage view is implicit in signal-detection theory—an accumulation of evidence followed by a decision—and in the sequence of transfer functions in optimal control theory.

The capacity and stage approaches have their roots in earlier concepts. One is the contrast between equipotentiality and mass action of brain structures (Lashley, 1929) and localization of specialized brain mechanisms. Whereas capacity notions stress composite strategic aspects of setting priorities and performance regulation, the stage concept emphasizes the operation of specialized mechanisms. In the early studies on reaction time, the contrast between the two approaches was evident in the opposite views of Donders (1868) and Külpe (1905). About a century later, the stage concept became popular again through Sternberg's (1969) additive factors method. Originally, stages were conceived of as a simple, discrete, and serial sequence of processing mechanisms, but they have gradually expanded to include various alternative mental architectures.

The two conceptualizations represent different research traditions and tend to focus on different areas: Delineating elementary mechanisms has been particularly popular in the study of reaction processes, whereas outlining performance or capacity limits has been the main theme in research on divided attention and dual-task performance. In the latter areas, capacity and attention have even been used as synonyms (Kahneman, 1973). However, the conceptualizations are also competitors that have enjoyed various degrees of popularity during the past decades (Gopher & Sanders, 1984). It should be added that neither capacity nor stage concept contains elaborate process descriptions. Rather, they are limited to simple statements that need much more body to qualify as a theory. This restriction notwithstanding, the approaches have still inspired a considerable amount of research, the results of which have provided more detail to the rough initial statements. Most of this book deals with a description of this research.

As long as the limited-capacity digital computer was the ruling metaphor, the Zeitgeist particularly favored a capacity framework. As outlined earlier, this has changed with the advent of the parallel-distributed processors that have virtually unlimited capacity. Connectionist networks do not automatically lead to stage-like thinking (Massaro, 1988). Indeed, connectionist brain-style models are sometimes depicted as competitors for simple computer-style stage models, yet they are not inconsistent either because a network may consist of a set of stage-like subnets (e.g., Norris, 1990). An analysis of the relative merits of the stage approach and capacity approach to attention and reaction processes runs like a continuous thread through the book; the outcome is evaluated at the end of chapter 9. It is concluded there that a stage approach is the heuristic with the better prospects. There remains the question as to how the views are related to those on other levels of enquiry, in particular neurobiological foundation and mental processing on a higher conceptual level, as in language and problem solving.

CONCEPTUAL BACKGROUND

This introduction concludes with a statement about the conceptual background of performance theory. It is common to distinguish two levels of behavioral analysis, namely, the physiological level, which views psychology as an obedient servant of physiology (e.g., Churchland, 1981; Kosslyn & König, 1992) and the representational view (e.g., Fodor, 1975), which considers the mind in terms of propositionally encoded representations as the conceptual basis for studying higher, knowledge-based processes. The popular metaphor of the representational theory is the difference between physiological hardware and representational software. Although ultimately dealing with the same "subject," the data sets of hardware and software of a computer are very different and cannot be deduced from each other. Thus, it is impossible to reconstruct a program from the state of the individual hardware units, and it is equally impossible to reconstruct the state of the hardware units from the program. Psychology deals with software.

The physiological approach takes issue with the view of the brain as a programmable processor, in which the hardware is first available in an empty state and gradually loaded with software. In contrast, physiological evidence suggests that hardware gradually develops along with its software; an example is neuronal sprouting as a result of learning. This means that the computer metaphor of a programmable processor is inadequate. It is desirable to drop the distinction between hardware and software in favor of a common "wetware." The physiological approach has gained currency in recent years due to important methodological developments in brain physiology. Examples are CAT, PET, and MRI scans of brain activity and new methods in EEG analysis such as the magnetic EEG that enables a better localizing of brain centers that are active in various forms of mental activity. Fascinating as these developments are, they run the risk of a new reductionism, judging by philosophical statements such as the mind is what the brain does (Kosslyn & Koenig, 1992). Reductionism always denies the existence of other, usually higher, levels of analysis, which has the effect that phenomena belonging to those higher levels are ignored. The result is that the scope of a field is whatever the reduced level permits.

One awkward consequence of reductionism in psychology is that current concepts in brain research become the standard for the legitimacy of psychological theorizing. From a reductionist perspective, any psychological theorizing is first subjected to a neurophysiological test and may only continue if that test has been passed. Moreover, reductionism has the danger of proposing pseudopsychological theories in neurophysiological disguise. One should be careful, though, and be reminded of a similar Zeitgeist at the beginning of this century. At that time, the dominant physiological metaphor was that the brain is passive unless stimulated. This led to the behaviorist revolution, which proved to be a dead end.

This emphasizes the danger arising when related disciplines impose constraints on one another. The opposite case, that is, the prerequisite that neurophysiological theory should be constrained by psychological notions, is equally dangerous. In the context of the Gestalt movement, this led to the assumption of physical Gestalts in the brain, which turned out to be equally fruitless. When pushing a theory beyond the limits of its domain, the risk of a category error is imminent (Neumann, 1991). A category error is committed equally when a physiological model is suddenly supplemented by a functional or representational notion or when physiological notions suddenly crop up in a functional model. The category error is dealt with in the introduction to attention. In fact, attention is among the most abused concepts in this regard.

It is more adequate to consider the neurophysiological and representational approaches as complementary perspectives, each with its own methodology and potential. In addition, a functional level of analysis has been proposed between the physiological level and the representational one. The functional level mainly focuses on behavioral aspects of performance and emphasizes schemata and levels of control in the organism–environment interaction (Looren de Jong & Sanders, 1991), which are between a physiological and representational level of description. Most issues discussed in this book relate to this functional level. In discussions about plans and intentions, the functional level borders the representational one. In contrast, lower levels of control reach down to a neurophysiological description. A similar functional level has been suggested by Smolensky (1988) as the typical domain of the subsymbolic-connectionistic modeling approach.

Thus, although ultimately referring to the same individual, each level has its own way of theorizing. One obviously hopes to see converging evidence, yet a specific level remains most suitable for analyzing and describing phenomena typical for that level. For example, behavioral data usually have little to say about functioning of the brain, except for fairly rough hypotheses, and physiological data usually do not lead to models about behavior, again with the exception of some rough hypotheses. Physiological data seem even less relevant when issues of intentions, attitudes, and beliefs are at stake. In turn, physical symbol systems and production rules (Newell, 1980) aim at addressing higher mental functions such as problem solving and concept formation and add little to physiology.

This is not to say that the three levels are fully independent entities. Indeed, at least rudimentary elements of all three levels are present in any experiment. As an example, Neumann and Prinz (1987) noted that a description of intentions, even as simple an intention as obeying an instruction in a choice-reaction experiment, is usually not included in traditional performance models. Apparently, intentions are felt to be outside the realm of performance theory and tend to be neglected. The representational level has better concepts for describing intentions, but it does so in a way that does not fit the description at the functional level. These warnings against category errors and the imposition of mutual constraints are not meant to imply that the levels should ignore each other's results and suggestions. Yet, the primary merit of a theory is not whether it is consistent with the results of a related discipline but whether it opens interesting experimental avenues in the domain that it means to address. Dissociating views are more stimulating than servile obedience.

As already mentioned, the physiological level used to be closely tied to behaviorism, which did not have much to say about performing real-life tasks. As a reaction, the new performance theory relied foremost on engineering and not on neurophysiology, with Hebb's (1949) work on neuropsychology as a notable exception. Neuropsychology has always been interested in performance analysis, concerned as it is with the relation between brain and behavior; from there, it addresses questions about rehabilitation following brain damage. For some time, neuropsychology was the main link between brain and performance. There remain tensions, though, between the brain–performance connection on the one hand and the performance–real-life connection on the other hand. The problem for performance theory is that it is expected to serve either side. The human-factors type of applied problems ask for a more composite systems approach, whereas neuropsychology asks for a more molecular approach to establish relations between specific performances and brain functioning. The challenge is to bridge this gap.

CHAPTER ONE

Introduction to Reaction Processes

PRELIMINARIES

Time Versus Judgment

Reaction time is commonly defined as the time elapsing between the onset of a stimulus and the initiation of a response. Actually, time and judgment are the only behavioral variables in cognitive psychology. Some may add concomitant psychophysiological measures, but albeit of great value, they are not behavioral. Time and judgment concur in a choice reaction that always consists of the time taken by a judgment that is classified as either correct or incorrect. In other areas of psychology, such as social or clinical psychology, judgments express opinions or experiences through subjective evaluation, which cannot usually be considered as correct or incorrect.

Psychological measurement theory is only concerned with judgment as the most important behavioral measure. During the early days of experimental psychology, however, reaction time became more than a measure, but a research area in its own right. It regained that status in the new performance theory, probably due to its distinct feature that it reflects the time properties of the information flow through the organism on a single trial basis. It is self-evident that more processing time is needed as a reaction becomes more demanding and the question arises as to what is going on during the additional time. This accounts for the attempts toward inferring mental processes on the basis of the relative time taken up by different types of reactions. In contrast, an incorrect judgment, an error, reflects that something went wrong somewhere in the process. Some mental processes may be more error prone than others; therefore, error analysis is relevant, but judgments do not reflect the time course of the information flow.

The contrast between measures of time and judgment should not be overemphasized. Thus, reaction time may have a psychophysical counterpart that is fully based on judgments. As a psychophysical threshold requires a longer presentation time, reaction time is usually longer as well in a satellite study with time as the dependent measure. Presentation time reflects what can be achieved within a given time period, which reflects reaction time. Reaction times are of little value in the case of near-threshold stimuli. They tend to become highly variable, thus reflecting uncertainty and hesitation about what is going on. Reaction time is only useful when it fully reflects the time required to meet the processing demands.

Reaction time also has the advantage that it is measured with an absolute zero point and a standard unit, thus permitting the most powerful statistical techniques. In contrast, most judgments do not exceed the rank order level. For example, error proportions may suffer from floor and ceiling effects, which implies that differences are unreliable near either extreme. It is evident, though, that reaction time is only measured on a ratio scale when it is really conceived of as elapsed time. Thus, it is not on a ratio scale when (mis)used as a measure of some hypothetical construct such as fatigue, attention, or capacity. It is clearly unwise to conclude that fatigue has doubled when, as a consequence of sleep loss, reaction time in a certain condition becomes twice as long.

It is no problem nowadays to measure reaction time to the nearest msec. More precision is not required, given the inaccuracy of defining the moment when a stimulus is presented and a response is triggered. The rise time of a stimulus is usually not reported but can easily amount to 20 msec on a standard PC screen. A response often consists of pressing a key. This interrupts a circuit and stops a time counter. Interruption of the circuit requires a force and a movement path, both of which are also seldom reported and the effects of which have hardly been studied (Abrams & Balota, 1990). Force and path vary among experiments and probably also among response keys within an experiment, thus adding to the lack of measurement precision. Moreover, many PCs, which are presently in use as experimental equipment, cannot measure reaction time to the nearest msec. Hence, a more realistic accuracy is in the order of csec, which suffices for most practical purposes.

Pachella (1974) presented a detailed account of the many technical factors affecting reaction time and of the many sources contributing to its variability. For instance, the cumulative distribution (CDF) of reaction times is usually positively skewed, and it becomes more normal and less variable as a function of practice. The larger variability in early practice may be partly due to insufficient skill in responding, although the bulk is probably due to sequential effects. The point is that unpracticed participants usually fail to adopt and maintain a constant speed–accuracy criterion during a block of trials. When the participants commit an error, the next few reaction times in a block of trials are relatively long, which has an obvious effect on the upper tail of the distribution.[1] Committing a couple of errors at the beginning of a block of trials may even cause a semipermanent shift of speed–accuracy to a slower level. In addition, a choice-reaction often takes less time in the case of a repetition than in the case of an alternation at successive trials; this effect is also most pronounced in early practice.

Sequential effects are often not the primary concern of an experiment. On the contrary, it is often implicitly assumed that each new trial is a new, unbiased event, independent of earlier events, thus enabling a sample of independent estimates of the "true" reaction time for the specific condition of interest. However, sequential effects are too strong to be ignored, and much practice and many precautions are needed to get more reliable data. A sufficient interval between successive trials and a warning stimulus preceding each new stimulus are among the precautions that reduce but do not eliminate sequential effects. Individuals may be asked to report atypical reactions resulting from momentary absentmindedness or failures to press the key to the full, but this introduces the problem of subjective criteria. Outlyers are a real problem because they increase the mean, inflate the variance and, more generally, change most measures of the distribution function. Separating outlyers from real reaction times is a complex issue (Ratcliff, 1993). Using some simple cutoff rule is questionable and may obscure real effects, particularly when studying effects of motivational variables.

How much practice is required for ascertaining reliable data in an experimental condition? Chocholle (1940) continued practicing until the standard deviation was less than 10% of the mean. If this criterion is satisfied, most of the positive skew has vanished. Yet, Chocholle's work was concerned with simple reaction time: In choice reaction time (CRT) a 15% to 20% criterion seems more realistic. It is of interest that during practice, instructions should not stress speed by feedback about speed. Rather, they should aim at minimal variability by informing participants about the $C(RT)^2$ range in a block of trials. Some experimental variables have more effect on variability than on mean C(RT). Thus, monotonous, long-term performance may bring about brief periods of inefficiency. Therefore, a variability criterion can only be fed back during practice sessions but not during the experimental ones. This further illustrates the danger of skipping outlyers which may have the effect of altogether eliminating the effect of monotony on C(RT).

Many studies report only mean C(RT) and variance for all experimental conditions. Moreover, the reported means are often grand means obtained

---

[1] It is often believed that mean choice reaction time for correct responses in a block of trials decreases as more errors are made, but the sequential effects suggest that that may not generally be the case.

[2] C(RT) will refer to the union of RT and CRT.

by averaging mean data from individual participants. This is common practice, despite the undisputed merits of considering individual CDFs (e.g.,
Heathcote, Popiel, & Mehwort, 1991; Luce, 1986). The main problem concerns the acceptable size of an experiment. A reliable CDF requires some
200 to 300 reactions that can only be collected after sufficient practice in
order to avoid sequential effects. Hence, measurement of CDFs requires
long sessions that due to monotony, may introduce the artifact of increasing
the upper tail of the density function. One may consider saving on the
number of conditions. There is the problem, though, that C(RT), as a function
of any independent variable, always depends on a number of other independent variables. The interplay of the various variables in shaping C(RT)
is usually the main issue of interest, so a larger number of conditions is
required. The implication is that an analysis of CDFs is only feasible for
highly limited conditions that have proven to be of utmost relevance in
earlier studies on means and variances.

As a final comment, the legitimate question may be raised whether interpretation of a C(RT) is really meaningful. The analogy is the reconstruction
of a computer program on the basis of its duration (Luce, 1986). This is
virtually impossible, but the chances may still be best when the program is
small and not time consuming. For that reason, CRT is seldom of interest
when exceeding 2 secs (Sanders, 1993b). Moreover, C(RT) is usually not
the only dependent variable. There are error proportions and event-related
psychophysiological measures—in particular heart rate and brain potentials—to support the interpretation.

VARIABLES AFFECTING CRT

At this point, it is useful to introduce some major experimental variables
affecting C(RT). They are merely introduced, awaiting more extensively treatment in forthcoming chapters. The first main subdivision is between RT and
CRT. A simple reaction consists of a single stimulus and a single response,
whereas a choice reaction always has more than one stimulus and response.
A choice reaction usually refers to traditional information conservation, in
which each element of a set of n stimuli is uniquely connected to an element
of an equally large set of m responses. There are also choice reactions in
which several stimuli are mapped onto the same response (information
reduction $n > m$), and in theory, one might have more than one response
for each stimulus ($n < m$; information creation; Posner, 1964).

Presentation of an imperative stimulus is almost always preceded by a
warning stimulus or is at a specified interval after the previous response,
which defines the foreperiod. A simple reaction runs the risk of anticipation,
that is, responding prior to the arrival of the stimulus, or of timing, in which

case the arrival of the stimulus and the moment of the response are synchronized. To avoid anticipation and timing, the stimulus may occasionally be omitted (catch trials), or the moment of presentation may be less predictable by varying the foreperiod from trial to trial. Yet, such measures have their own effects because RT is affected by the proportion of catch trials as well as by foreperiod duration and its variability. Major variables affecting RT are (a) stimulus intensity, usually measured in cd/m^2 or in dB for visual stimuli and always in dB(A) for auditory stimuli; (b) stimulus contrast, which refers to the ratio of the luminance of the stimulus and its immediate background; (c) retinal location, that is, the degree of eccentricity at which a visual stimulus is presented; and (d) stimulus modality, that is usually visual, auditory, or tactile. On the motor side, the variables include exerted force to the key, travel time of the key, instructed muscle tension, and differences in limb, usually different fingers.

The aforementioned variables play a role in CRT as well, but choice reactions are affected by a large number of other variables. Thus, it is not surprising that CRT depends on the number of alternatives. As mentioned, the logarithmic relation between the number of alternatives and CRT belonged to the initial successes of information theory. Other variables are stimulus quality and stimulus discriminability. Stimulus quality can be manipulated for visual stimuli by degrading the stimulus by superimposing a grid, by inserting visual noise, or by omitting elements. Stimulus discriminability refers to the similarity among stimuli that may differ quantitatively when stimuli consist of, for example, line lengths, or qualitatively when they consist of alphanumeric symbols, words, colors, or geometric figures. Another interesting stimulus variable is mental rotation, in which case tilted stimuli are presented. The response may consist of naming the tilted symbol or of deciding which stimulus format (normal, mirror) has been presented (Cooper & Shephard, 1973).

Other relevant choice–reaction variables are concerned with further processing of identified stimuli. One example is target classification, in which case some stimuli are defined in advance as targets and others as nontargets. The task is to respond by pressing a target or a nontarget key. A conceptually related case is a same–different reaction. Here, two stimuli are presented at the same time or in succession, and the task is to carry out a same or a different response, depending on instructions about which stimulus features should be the same or different. Word frequency, the occurrence of words in the language, and relative stimulus frequency—the actual probability of stimuli and responses in a particular experiment—are both concerned with the probability of occurrence of a stimulus. S–R compatibility is concerned with how "naturally" stimuli and responses are related to each other and with the correspondence between a display and a participant's mental model of a situation. For instance, naming digits is highly compatible because stimuli and responses match perfectly. In contrast, the rule of adding "three to each digit"—responding "7" to the digit "4"—makes the relation much less compatible, whereas it is highly incompatible when the relation between stimuli and responses is fully random. Again, when the stimuli consist of a row of lights and the responses consist of a row of keys, the choice reaction is only compatible when the keys are located in the direct vicinity of their corresponding stimuli.

There are several response-related variables that only apply when the responses are more complex than naming or key pressing. For instance, a response may involve a movement or a movement sequence of some sort. In that case, there is usually a home key on which the finger or a pen point rests before stimulus arrival. On presentation, the home key is released, and the movement is carried out. Sometimes, it is a simple aiming movement, the direction of which depends on stimulus location. On other occasions, a sequence of aiming movements may be required, and on still other occasions, the instruction may ask for a continuous movement such as writing a letter. Other motor variables include instructed speed and distance of the movement, movement specificity,[3] the number of movement elements and, finally—in the case of a writing response—required pressure, size, and muscle groups.

There are also variables that are related to procedures rather than to S–R properties. One is sequential constraints across trials such as repetitions or alternations that may concern individual stimuli and responses but also categories such as digits and letters. Others are relative emphasis on speed and accuracy, and blocked versus mixed presentation of conditions. In blocked presentation, a particular variable, for example, intact versus degraded stimuli, is kept constant within a block of trials so that participants know about stimulus quality in advance of each trial. In contrast, when conditions are mixed, intact and degraded stimuli occur at random within the same block so that participants have no advance knowledge about stimulus quality. A final procedural variable is paced versus self-paced presentation. In a paced task, the equipment prescribes the speed with which successive stimuli are presented so that stimuli arrive at a constant rate regardless of whether earlier responses are completed in time. In self-paced task presentation, the next stimulus is contingent upon completion of the previous response.

A final class of variables is concerned with motivation and refers to effects of the general conditions under which a task is carried out. Examples are prolonged performance, in which case a reaction task is carried out unin-

---

[3]Movement specificity refers to the specificity of an aiming movement. For instance, two alternative movements are highly specific when one is to the left and the other is to the right. In the case of little specificity, both aiming movements might be forward, but one has a little inclination to the left and the other a little inclination to the right.

terruptedly for a longer time period, sleep loss, time of the day, noise, heat, and psychotropic drugs. Motivational variables are particularly relevant to alertness. Given the many determinants of CRT, the layman's conviction of "reaction time" as a mere individual constant is far from the full story. Yet, despite the many variables affecting CRT, there is a well-established, individual speed factor in that some participants are consistently slower and others faster across experimental conditions (Fleishman & Quaintance, 1984).

HISTORICAL ROOTS

Helmholtz (1850) was among the first to measure RT in order to determine the speed of peripheral nervous conduction. His attempt was unsuccessful because, as Helmholtz himself noticed, most of the RT was taken up by central processing. This conclusion was shared by Donders (1868), who further suggested that central mental processes might be inferred from C(RT) observed in different types of reaction. He defined three prototypical reactions, one of which, the *a*-reaction, was the simple reaction. The second, the *b*-reaction, was a choice reaction with two stimulus and response alternatives, and the third task, the *c*-reaction, had two alternative stimuli and only one response. In the *c*-reaction, participants carried out or withheld the response, depending on which alternative was presented. Donders proposed the so-called subtraction, or pure stage insertion, principle. The *a*-reaction was thought to merely reflect peripheral sensory and motor processes, whereas the *b*-reaction included stimulus discrimination and response choice as well. Because there is only one response, Donders felt that the *c*-reaction requires discrimination but no choice. In this way, choice time is estimated by subtracting *c* from *b*, and discrimination time by subtracting *a* from *c*. Donders found that a *b*-reaction took longer than a *c*-reaction, which took longer than an *a*-reaction, whose results were used for estimating discrimination and choice time. In this way, Donders was the first to launch a processing-stage approach to C(RT).

The subtraction method was criticized by Cattell (1886), who argued that the *c*-reaction also has a choice component, that is, the choice to respond or not to respond. As a solution, Wundt (1883) proposed the *d*-reaction, in which case there are two alternative stimuli that always require the same overt response. The idea was that the *d*-reaction requires stimulus discrimination but really no response choice. Unfortunately, except for Wundt and his research assistant, the *d*-reaction and the *a*-reaction were never found to differ systematically. As Berger (1886) already remarked, the *d*-reaction lacked control whether participants really discriminated the stimuli before responding. Some properties of the *a*-reaction were studied by Lange (1888), who distinguished between sensory and motor set. Participants were asked to concentrate on either perceiving the stimulus or on carrying out the response. The results were inconsistent, which led again to the question whether instructions about sensory or motor set are properly obeyed. There is no precise definition and, again, a lack of control. Studies on other properties of the a-reaction were more successful, in particular the work on effects of stimulus intensity (Pieron, 1920), retinal location (Poffenberger, 1912), and sensory modality. The typical 180 to 200 msec for a visual RT and the 140 to 160 msec for an auditory RT belong to the classical findings. There was also some early interest in response variables such as finger tremor (Travis, 1929) and anticipatory muscle tension (Freeman, 1940; Freeman & Kendall, 1940).

During the high tide of Gestalt psychology and Behaviorism, C(RT) research flourished only in the border areas of sensory and motor processes, and the b- and c-reactions were hardly studied. One reason was the disappointing results of Donders' (1868) subtraction method, which raised doubts about the prospects of analyzing C(RT). This was expressed most eloquently by Külpe (1905), who argued that the different C(RT)s in Donders' a-, b-, and c-reactions are due to qualitative differences in task demands rather than to the number of processing stages. Thus, a change in stimulus-processing demands might also alter the demands on response organization, and vice versa, which reminds of the controversy between processing stage and capacity views.

A second reason was that the aim of stage analysis, that is, discovering mechanisms between stimulus and response, was unpopular, in particular to behaviorists. Even Woodworth (1938) was not impressed by C(RT), as witnessed by his remark that ". . . we cannot break up the reaction time into successive acts and obtain the time of each act, of what use is the reaction time?" (p. 83). From a present-day perspective, the most serious methodological objection to Donders' classification was that the hypothetical processing stages of stimulus discrimination and response choice were simply postulated and assigned ad hoc to specific reactions.

As mentioned previously, the new performance theory had a renewed interest in C(RT). Merkel (1885) found that CRT increased as a logarithmic function of the number of S–R alternatives, but at the time, there was no interest in this result. The situation was different when Hick (1952) replicated Merkel's results and noticed that CRT increased linearly with the amount of transmitted information and suggested serial dichotomization as an explanation. Hick assumed that stimulus processing may consist of a sequence of information-reducing steps until correct identification is achieved. In this way, CRT reflected the rate of gain of information—the time taken by an information-reducing step—and, hence, the information-processing capacity in bits/sec.

Serial dichotomization did not fare well. One problem is that as the number of alternatives increases, the probability of an S–R repetition decreases. When deconfounding these two variables, the phenomenon of faster repetitions than alternations proved to account completely for the effect of the number of alternatives (Kornblum, 1969). Moreover, there are conditions in which CRT hardly increases with the number of alternatives. Examples are naming digits, letters, or words (Mowbray & Rhoades, 1959; Seibel, 1963) and, more generally, all cases of highly compatible S–Rs. The implication would be that there are no limits to information transmission in the case of compatible S–R relations.

The final problem for information theory concerned the effect of stimulus discriminability on CRT, which proved to be much larger than originally anticipated (Crossman, 1953). Without proper precautions, discriminability decreases as the number of alternatives increases. Information theory is only concerned with the number of discrete alternatives per se and has no provision to explain effects of stimulus discriminability.

SETTING THE STAGE

The preceding sections laid the groundwork for the next chapters. C(RT) is, first of all, a dependent variable that is affected by a wide variety of experimental variables. There are many models of reaction processes in terms of a single set of principles with a great deal of mathematical sophistication. C(RT) is conceived of there as a stochastic, random variable so as to enable application of mathematical probability theory. In chapter 2, the basic features of the most important single-process models are outlined. The reasons for presenting a nontechnical summary are twofold. First, it does not make sense to merely repeat because a full coverage is provided by Townsend and Ashby (1983) and by Luce (1986). More importantly, single-process models are neglected by many experimenters who find them impenetrable and not stimulating to further research. A qualitative presentation of their main underlying assumptions might add to their impact. On the other hand, however, it is argued that single-process models have limitations, in particular with respect to the limited set of variables they address.

In chapter 3, the main emphasis is on the revival of Donders' (1868) notion that a reaction process consists of a sequence of processing stages, albeit with a completely different conceptual and experimental approach (Sternberg, 1969). The stage notion has dominated research on CRT ever since Sternberg's paper and has evoked a lively debate about some of its premises, in particular the issue whether information processing proceeds in discrete steps or in a continuous flow. This discussion is followed in chapter 4 by a review of the experimental evidence on the effects of the major variables affecting CRT, divided into the traditional categories of perceptual, decisional, and motor variables.

Chapters 2 to 4 address traditional C(RT), but measures of processing time are much more widely used. A recent count in the *Journal of Experimental Psychology: Human Perception & Performance* shows that about 40% of all articles have C(RT) as a major dependent variable, whereas very few papers are concerned with traditional C(RT) literature. Some are concerned with attention, which is discussed in chapters 6 to 9, but CRT is also highly relevant to research on memory and cognition. For example, CRT is popular in studies on recognition in which a sequence of stimuli is presented, and it is decided each time whether a stimulus is "old" or "new." An example of a CRT paradigm in cognition is sentence verification, in which a statement is presented and participants respond with a true–false reaction about the validity of that statement.

Most of that research is beyond the scope of this book, engaged as it is with specific issues on memory and cognition that do not directly bear on reaction processes as such. It is admitted, though, that this is an arbitrary criterion. An information-processing model on, for example, recognition or sentence verification may well be relevant to more general aspects of reaction processes. There remains, then, the problem that discussing the total variety of C(RT) studies is prohibitive. In chapter 5, only some issues are discussed beyond traditional C(RT) in view of their direct relation to the area, namely, target classification, same–different responses, and the duration of a visual fixation. Chapters 2 and 3 are primarily process oriented and concerned with basic issues. Applications are mentioned in chapters 4 and 5 because they bear mainly on concrete effects of experimental variables aimed at a direct simulation of reality rather than on conceptual and theoretical description.

Reaction Processes:
General Properties and Models

Most CRT models describe a single process between a residual of afferent and efferent peripheral conduction. They are usually inspired by the notion of a reaction process as a statistical decision. The serial dichotomization model failed to account for CRT, which had the effect that the capacity concept was no longer significant in CRT models. The emphasis of the decision models in this chapter is on stimulus detection and discrimination, on speed–accuracy trade-off (SAT), and on sequential effects on CRT. Due to an aversion to Behaviorism, motor processes are usually not emphasized.

MODELS OF DETECTION AND DISCRIMINATION

It can be safely said that mathematical modeling has a stronghold in single-process models. The wide variety of sophisticated suggestions are all discussed in the thorough but somewhat impenetrable accounts of Townsend and Ashby (1983) and Luce (1986). Most models start with a buildup of information after a stimulus has been presented, although information is usually replaced by activation, impulses, or evidence, whose rate of accrual is thought to depend on a range of stimulus variables. C(RT) reflects the time needed to acquire sufficient evidence in order to pass a decision criterion, thus marking stimulus detection or identification. In the case of an a-reaction, the presence or absence of a stimulus is detected, whereas in the b-reaction the decision bears on stimulus identification and, occasionally, on response selection. Most models are limited to two-choice reactions. With regard to more alternatives, Luce characterized the existing models as highly unsatis-factory.

Some models only describe RT, others deal with both RT and CRT, and still others are specifically meant for two-choice CRT. In order to account for the variability and the distribution of C(RT), they are all stochastic, which may apply to the rate of activation, to the criterion setting, or to both. In some models, the positive skewness in the C(RT) distribution is supposed to be due to a convolution—that is, a combination of times taken by different processes at each particular trial—of a normal and an exponential distribu-tion, the so-called ex-Gaussian (McGill, 1963). The exponential component might reflect the accrual of evidence, whereas the afferent and efferent residuals are thought to be normal. For instance, Hohle (1965) ascribed the effect of foreperiod to the efferent component of the residual, that is, motor tension. Hence, foreperiod duration should only affect the normally distrib-uted component.

All single-process models consist of further specifications of these general principles, molded into a mathematical description to allow precise quanti-tative predictions. The present discussion is concerned with "modal" versions because most vary on details.

Runs Model (Audley, 1960)

As with most single-process models, the runs model assumes that accrual of evidence derives from a train of successive, discrete impulses emitted by a stimulus. Stimuli emit impulses in different proportions. Thus, stimulus A1 may emit 60% impulses α and 40% impulses β, the proportions of which may be reversed for stimulus A2. Thus, impulse α is more typical for stimulus A1 and impulse β for stimulus A2. The runs model assumes that identification of stimulus A1 or A2 is based on an uninterrupted run of k identical impulses; therefore, a run of k α's means that the participants decide in favor of stimulus A1. Smaller runs are abandoned and do not contribute to the de-cision. The probability distribution of obtaining a run of k identical elements determines the CRT density function.

Recruitment Model (LaBerge, 1962)

This model also assumes that impulses are emitted in different proportions, but it differs from the runs model in that any individual impulse contributes to the accrual of evidence. Accrual continues until a fixed number (r) of a particular impulse type have been recruited. If a stimulus has a proportion p of a particular impulse type (α) and $1-p$ of the other impulse type (β), the probability that m impulses are needed to recruit r impulses of the same type in a two-choice situation has a negative binomial distribution:

$$P(m \mid r) = \frac{(m-1)!}{(r-1)!\,(m-r)!}\, p^r (1-p)^{m-r}$$

from which the CRT density function can be calculated. Each impulse is supposed to take a constant time; consequently, CRT at a particular trial consists of the sum of m impulses and the afferent and efferent residual.

Problems. The recruitment model and the runs model face similar problems. First, they imply that a normal distribution is approached as more impulses are needed to pass the criterion. This can be avoided by assuming that impulses differ in amount of evidence. Some may convey little evidence and others more, according to a Poisson distribution, which leads to a positive skew (Pike, 1973). Yet, this is a convenient post hoc mathematical trick rather than a psychological insight. Second, either model has the property that evidence about a correct response accrues faster than evidence about an error. Given stimulus A1, the probability of getting a run of k β-impulses is less than that of a run of k α-impulses. Similarly, the probability of getting r impulses of the β type is less than getting r impulses of the α type. The result is that either model predicts that error CRT is longer than correct CRT, and that is atypical. The problem may be avoided by assuming trial-to-trial variation in criterion (r), errors occurring on trials in which the required r happens to be low (Pike).

Accumulator Model (P. L. Smith & Vickers, 1988)

Similar assumptions are found in the accumulator model, which elaborates on the recruitment model. Any fixed stimulus feature—intensity, length, or orientation—leads to a distribution of emitted activity. Similar to the impulses from the recruitment model, activity samples are drawn from the presented stimulus and compared to a sensory referent. For example, stimuli may consist of a line segment, the average orientation of which deviates either to the left or to the right of the vertical. The task is to indicate the direction of the deviation by a two-choice key-press response. The accumulator model assumes that the vertical acts as sensory referent, with each sample providing a certain value to the left or to the right of the sensory referent. The values are computed and added to counter A or counter B, depending on whether the value is to the left or to the right. Sampling continues at equally spaced intervals until one of the counters passes a criterion, C(A) or C(B), whichever is reached first. At this point, the process stops, and the winner is responded to. The stochasticity of the activity implies that a stimulus with an orientation to the right may also deliver values to the left, and vice versa. Given assumptions about the distribution of the activity, conditional upon the stimulus and on the values of the criteria, density functions can be determined with respect to the number of steps needed to pass a C. The main difference from the recruitment model is that a value is not fixed but has more impact when reflecting a larger deviation. As Pike (1973) suggested for the recruitment model, criteria may vary as well and may differ between stimuli A and B.

P. L. Smith and Vickers (1988) found that errors took longer than corrects when stimuli were poorly discriminable, whereas errors were faster in the easiest condition. They adopted Pike's (1973) suggestion that errors are faster on trials in which C is set low, which is most likely to occur when stimuli can be easily discriminated. They also found evidence for the so-called fixed-point property, referring to the finding that when two stimuli were poorly discriminable, the lower tail of the CRT density function was much less affected than its variance. This is at odds with an accumulator model with fixed criteria, which expects much more counterevidence from poorly discriminable stimuli. Hence, passing C would require more impulses, which means a shift of the whole CRT distribution to a higher value. Smith and Vickers showed that this problem may be solved by assuming that C varies among trials, yet the fixed-point property follows more naturally from Ratcliff's (1978) stochastic diffusion model. In another form, it is discussed again in the section on SAT.

Variable Criterion Model (Grice, 1968, 1972)

This model was first and foremost meant to account for RT, although it has been extended to CRT (Grice, Nullmeyer, & Spiker, 1982). As with the previous models, it assumes that information about stimuli accumulates until exceeding C. The main difference is that a linear and noise-free accrual of evidence is assumed. in that stimulus, A1 emits only α and stimulus A2 only β in a fully bottom-up fashion. The rate of accrual varies as a function of variables such as stimulus intensity and discriminability (Fig. 2.1a), but this is a matter of the frequency of impulses and not—as in the runs and recruitment models—of differences in proportions of impulse types. Moreover, some of the earlier models had a constant C, whereas in the variable criterion model, C is the main source of variance and is sensitive to factors affecting preparatory and motivational state. In contrast to a bottom-up accrual of evidence, C is top-down controlled.

The variation in C was originally assumed to be normally distributed. This means that RT should be normally distributed as well, which is at odds with the data. Grice (1972) proposed that as in J. L. McClelland's (1979) cascade model, the rate of accrual is alinear in that it decreases as the level of activation approaches its asymptote. In this way, the positive skew of the C(RT) density function can be accounted for. Moreover, Luce (1986) showed that alinear accrual predicts that the hazard function decreases at the upper tail of the density function, which is in line with RT data. The variable

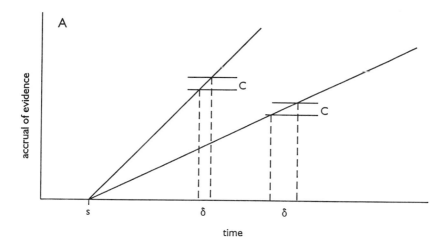

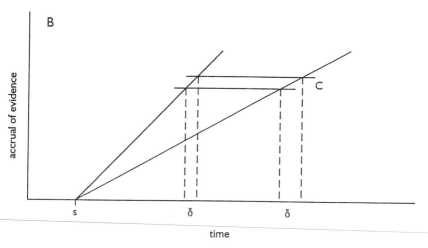

FIG. 2.1. Variable criteria for responding. The variation (δ) in RT is a matter of random variation of C within a block of trials. C is also supposed to vary among blocks of trials (panel A). For example, C may be lower in the case of weak stimuli, which have less rapid accrual. This is a strategic effect that cannot occur when strong and weak stimuli occur randomly within a block (panel B).

criterion model can easily account for the finding that errors take less time than corrects. As C is lower, responses are faster, but at the cost of sampling less evidence. In an RT study errors are always responses to catch trials, which can be equally well ascribed to the variation in C. A serious problem for the model is its prediction that the effects on C(RT) should interact when one of two variables affects accrual rate while the other affects C. For example, an interaction of the effects of stimulus intensity and block type on

CRT is predicted because the effect of stimulus intensity is prototypical for accrual rate, and block type is prototypical for a criterion-based variable. Yet, as is discussed elsewhere, this interaction is not uniformly found, not even in RT (Sanders, 1977).

A Race Between "Change and Level" Detectors (Luce, 1986)

This RT model starts from physiological evidence that some sensory neurons, when stimulated, fire transiently, whereas others show sustained firing (e.g., Marocco, 1976). Transient cells respond in the case of abrupt stimulus presentation and are also sensitive to temporal change over time, as in flicker. In contrast, sustained cells respond when the stimulus either rises gradually or is stationary, so that they reflect a steady-state level. In addition transient cells appear more sensitive to low, and sustained cells to high, spatial frequency characteristics of stimuli. Thus, a combination of a low frequency and an abrupt onset activates transient neurons, whereas a combination of gradual onset and high spatial frequency, as in a sharp edge, activates sustained neurons (Tolhurst, 1975). Luce argued that both transient and sustained cells may be active in the case of intermediate spatial frequency and intermediate rise in stimulus onset. In that case, a race develops between two stochastically independent processes, the winner of which determines RT.

Most evidence for transient and sustained neurons stems from psycho-physical contrast sensitivity functions (A. B. Watson, 1986). Effects of temporally changing stimulus features such as flicker have been widely studied in psychophysics, whereas in RT studies, stimuli are almost always viewed as a stationary, stochastic process. However, change and level detectors have a different hazard function. It follows from the transient characteristics of change detectors that the hazard function is peaked, followed by a rapid decline to zero, whereas the hazard function of level detectors rises gradually. Thus, their convolution sum rises in the beginning, followed by a gradual decline. This is consistent with Luce's (1986) summary of the experimental evidence on RTs, which suggests a gradually decreasing hazard function at the upper tail of the density function for abruptly presented ("change"), high-frequency ("level") a-reactions. In the same way, P. L. Smith (1995) found a high-peaked hazard function for detecting a low-frequency abrupt onset patch and a gradually increasing hazard function for a high-frequency, gradually rising patch. Smith extended the notion of transient and sustained neuronal activation to an accumulator single-process model in which both channels contribute stochastic evidence to the decision system.

Random Walks

Random walk models explicitly ascribe the variation in response times to a combination of accrual and C. The main difference with runs and accumulator models is that the accrual at some particular moment in time reflects the difference between the number of impulses α and β. In the case of a two-choice reaction, each new impulse pushes the total available evidence into the direction of the C of either A_1 or A_2. In its simplest form, each new impulse shifts the odds with a constant step.

Both the step size and the setting of C vary as a function of experimental factors. Step size depends on the diagnosticity of an impulse (I) that refers to the likelihood ratio $(P(I|A_1) \div P(I|A_2)$ that I belongs to either stimulus A_1 or A_2. Diagnosticity is less as the values of $P(I|A_1)$ and $P(I|A_2)$ differ less because A_1 and A_2 are harder to distinguish. For example, when stimulus A_1 emits 90% α impulses and 10% β impulses and stimulus A_2 emits 90% β and 10% α, impulse α is considerably more diagnostic than when the proportions amount to 60% and 40%. According to Bayes' theorem, the posterior odds (Po) of A_1 and A_2—that is, the odds after I has been taken into account $[(P(A_1|I) \div P(A_2|I)]$—are equal to the product of the likelihood ratio (L) and the prior odds (Pr) of A_1 and A_2. Pr, or "prior" in Fig. 2.2, refers to the odds when I has not yet been taken into account $[(P(A_1) \div P(A_2)]$. After taking the logarithm: log Po = Log L + Log Pr. Thus, Log L determines the step size of the random walk, whereas the desired value of log Po determines C. An optimal C may be calculated in terms of costs and benefits of correct and incorrect responses under the assumption that individuals truly optimize expected value (Edwards, 1966).

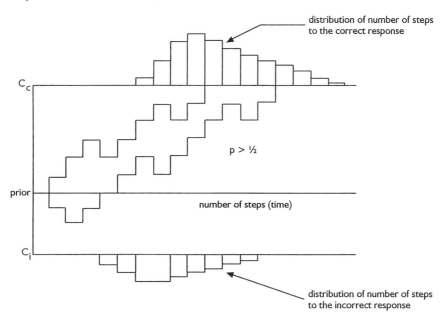

FIG. 2.2. A discrete random walk with biased prior odds (prior). C_c and C_i are the criteria for emitting the correct or the incorrect response. The CRT distributions are determined by the number of steps in the random walk.

A response is carried out when a C is exceeded (Fig. 2.2). An error occurs when the evidence happens to go into the wrong direction and passes the incorrect C (C_i). It is commonly assumed that the random walk starts between the two alternatives, although variables such as uneven stimulus probability may bias the starting point, that is, the "prior," in the direction of the more probable stimulus. Alternatively, Laming (1968, 1979) studied the possibility that participants anticipate one of the stimuli by way of a number of virtual impulses. Some variables may affect Pr, and others may affect the degree of anticipation. CRT is relatively fast when the bulk of the evidence happens to go toward one C and becomes longer as there is more contradictory evidence (Fig. 2.2).

A simple, discrete random walk has the problem that CRT should be equal for corrects and for errors. This can be evaded again by assuming a bias in the starting point (Fig. 2.2) or by assuming asymmetry in the location of the two Cs. It should be noted that the random walk accounts nicely for the finding that SAT is a linear function of log (%correct ÷ %errors) which is the same as log Post (Pew, 1969). It is of theoretical interest that log odds has a better fit to the shape of the SAT function than some of its competitors, such as transmitted information (T) and d'.

Stochastic Diffusion (Ratcliff, 1978, 1985)

The random walk becomes more complex when evidence about A_1 and A_2 does not accumulate with a fixed amount but with a normally distributed randomly varying amount (Fig. 2.3). As in the discrete random walk, the accumulating evidence ultimately passes a C. The value of each new piece of evidence is determined by signal-detection analysis. At regular, small intervals, a new "goodness of fit" value is calculated from the input during that interval that is interpreted as favoring either A_1 or A_2, depending on the signal-detection criterion β. In turn, this pushes the random walk in the favored direction, the strength of the push depending on the quality of the fit. For example, given the setting of the signal-detection criterion in Fig. 2.3, the value s is taken as evidence for A_2. However, if the criterion had been more to the left, the same value might have been considered as slight evidence for A_1.[1] Other parameters are the random walk criteria C and Pr (prior), the original starting point of the random walk. β, C, and Pr are strategical parameters that can be freely set by the participant. The signal-detection parameters, d' (discriminability) and the variance η^2 are stimulus determined. A continuous random walk is approached as successive goodness of fit values are calculated for smaller intervals. The continuous case

---

[1]There are several versions that have slightly different assumptions (MacMillan & Creelman, 1991), although all based on signal-detection theory. They are particularly relevant to the analysis of psychophysical judgments and are beyond the scope of this book.

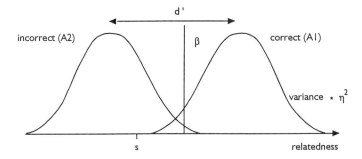

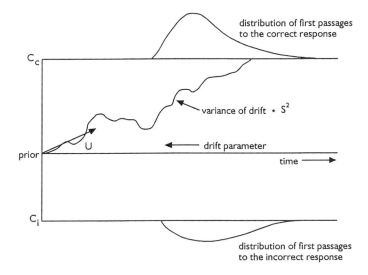

FIG. 2.3. The stochastic diffusion model. From Ratcliff, R. (1988). Continuous versus discrete information processing: Modeling accumulation of partial information. *Psychological Review, 95*, 238–255. Copyright © 1988 by the American Psychological Association. Reprinted with permission.

has drift (U) and variance of drift toward A_1 or A_2 as parameters, which derive directly from the signal-detection distributions (Fig. 2.3).

The stochastic diffusion model has been successfully applied to stimulus discrimination, to target classification (target–nontarget), and to same–different judgments (same–different). The model applies in particular to the latter two for which it provides a quantitative description of observed means and distributions of CRT and errors. It is the most elaborate single-process model, with the interesting feature that it has separate perceptual (the signal-detection part) and decision components (the actual random walk); therefore, it is not strictly a single-process model.

SPEED–ACCURACY TRADE-OFF (SAT)

SAT is a highly relevant element in single-process models, and there are even some models that fully focus on SAT, which is sufficient reason to consider them in more detail. There appear to be various issues at stake. First, there is Pachella's (1974) important distinction between macro- and micro-SAT. *Macro* refers to SAT effects between blocks of trials, and *micro* refers to variations of SAT within blocks of trials. There are studies that focus exclusively on micro-SAT, but otherwise, it is usually not experimentally controlled. Moreover, SAT refers primarily to conditions in which participants commit more errors as they react faster. As already noticed, this is only found with clearly discriminable stimuli.

A modal macro-SAT function is shown in Fig. 2.4, in which CRT is plotted as a function of the proportion of correct responses and as a linear function of log [%correct ÷ %error] (Pew, 1969). The slope of the linear function depends mainly on practice, in that better accuracy takes less time as participants become more practiced (A). An inverse relation between speed and accuracy is roughly in line with the deduction-from-information theory (Hyman, 1953) that more errors means less information transmission. However, the hypothesis that the SAT function reflects the time taken by transmitting information has been shown to be wrong. The point is that much time is saved by allowing a few errors—that is, a little loss in transmission—and almost no additional time is saved at higher error rates, neither in choice–re-

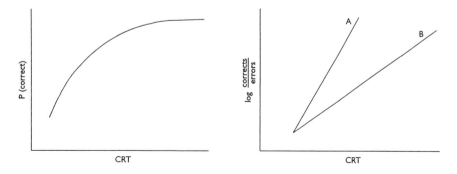

FIG. 2.4. A modal SAT function. CRT as a function of proportion correct responses (left panel) is linear when plotted as a function of log odds (right panel). Function A depicts a more practiced choice reaction than function B.

actions (Fitts, 1966) nor in typing (Seibel, 1972). As mentioned, a discrete random walk and a stochastic diffusion model do much better because they predict the observed linear function between CRT and log odds.

Measurement of SAT

The simplest technique of measuring SAT is by varying instructions, such as react "somewhat faster and more risky," "somewhat slower and more accurate," "fast and not bothering about errors," and "avoid any error." This has the advantage of being unintrusive, but the problem is that participants are fairly insensitive to changes in instruction. Even when connecting different monetary rewards to speed and accuracy (Edwards, 1961), participants usually dislike errors and fail to comply in a way that permits construction of a SAT function. An alternative is to categorize trials post hoc as errors and corrects. This creates the problem that an unduly large number of trials is needed to obtain reliable error proportions for different CRT intervals. Moreover, post hoc categorization addresses microtrade-off, which appears to differ from macrotrade-off (Fig. 2.5B). One reason is that a microtrade-off function includes sequential effects that increase the variance of CRT. Consequently, the slope of a microtrade-off function is not as steep (Wood & Jennings, 1976).

Other techniques are more intrusive but also more effective. Thus, a SAT function is obtained most easily by imposing time deadlines. Briefly, upon

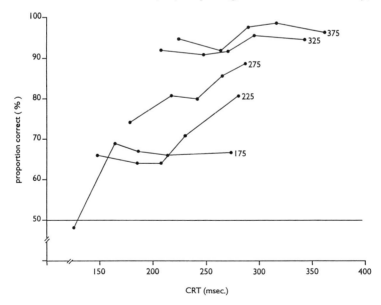

FIG. 2.5. The relation between CRT and % correct responses for different deadline intervals (in msec). The figure continues on p. 41.

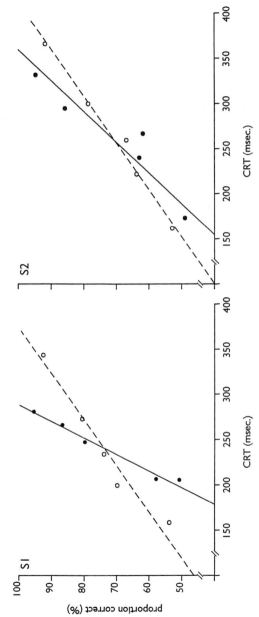

FIG. 2.5. (*Continued*). Macro-SAT (solid) and Micro-SAT (dashed) for two subjects (S_1, S_2) calculated from the same data sets. Micro-SAT and macro-SAT appear to be two distinct functions. From Wood, C. C., & Jennings, J. R. (1976). Speed-accuracy trade-off functions in choice reaction time: Experimental designs and computational procedures. *Perception & Psychophysics, 9*, 93–102. Reprinted by permission of Psychonomic Society, Inc.

presentation of an imperative signal, another signal, usually a tone, indicates that the deadline for responding has passed. The tone is not presented if the response is completed prior to the deadline. In fact, participants are instructed to respond fast enough to beat the tone. The deadline interval is varied between blocks, and participants receive some practice at the start of each new block to adapt to the new deadline. A macrotrade-off function is obtained between blocks of trials defined by a time deadline (the numbers in Fig. 2.5A), whereas a microtrade-off function can be constructed within each block. Figure 2.5A presents examples of these two time deadline functions that are not simply aligned.

A still more intrusive variant of the deadline method is the response–signal technique. A response signal is presented briefly after the imperative stimulus; it instructs participants to interrupt processing and to respond without any delay. The interval between presentation of the imperative stimulus and of the response signal (I–R) is varied in order to permit variation in the amount of processing of the imperative stimulus (Dosher, 1981; Schouten & Bekker, 1967). The problem is that it is uncertain whether the participants actually interrupt processing. Moreover, there are trials in which I–R is longer than the normal processing time, which leads to a delay of the response. The question is how to interpret such a waiting interval.

Fast Guessing

This model fully focuses on SAT (Ollman, 1966; Yellott, 1967). It holds that mean CRT reflects a mixture of fully analyzed stimuli, with an almost perfect level of accuracy, and of guesses that are basically unaffected by the stimulus. A SAT function, as seen in Fig. 2.4, is supposed to consist of a mixture of either response category. Deadlines and speed instructions increase the proportion of fast guesses, whereas a variable such as relative stimulus frequency imbalance biases guessing in that the more probable response is more often guessed. In line with this view, Harm and Lappin (1973) found that a correction for SAT eliminated the effect of relative stimulus frequency on CRT; yet the same result is also predicted by a random walk or by an accumulator model. According to fast guessing:

$$p_c CRT_c - p_e CRT_e = k(p_c - p_e).$$

where p_c and p_e refer to proportions of correct and incorrect responses. CRT_e is mean CRT for errors—which reflects guessing—and CRT_c, the "correct" CRT, is composed of both a guessing and a full analysis component

The fast-guessing model has a strong prediction in view of the property that the density function of the guessing component does not change with the proportion of guesses. This leads to the earlier mentioned "fixed-point property," namely, that the density function of CRT for guesses and for fully analyzed stimuli intersect at a constant point, provided that they overlap at all.

There are some data that support the fast-guessing model when stimuli are highly discriminable and when the participants are pressed to respond quickly. Thus, the linear relation between time and accuracy, as implied by the aforementioned formula, held in Yellott's (1971) deadline studies, and Swensson and Edwards (1971) also found evidence for a dual strategy, as implied by fast guessing. Sanders and Rath (1991) found support for fast guessing in a study on SAT for visual fixation times. At the start of a trial, participants fixated the stimulus location. They were instructed to shift their eyes to another location as fast as possible upon stimulus presentation in order not to miss a second stimulus that was briefly presented at that other location. The task was to report the identity of both stimuli. The results show that the participants either left the first location too soon in order not to miss the second stimulus, or they analyzed the first stimulus relatively long, with the effect that the second stimulus was missed. The results of this study are relevant to the issue of discrete versus continuous processing of information. Discrete transmission is in line with mixture models of SAT—either no processing or full stimulus processing—whereas continuous processing is more in line with the notion of evidence accrual followed by crossing a C.

In line with fast guessing, some SAT data suggest a bimodal CRT distribution. There is the potential problem that occasional errors still occurred when reactions belonged to the full analysis distribution, but one may hold that a fully analyzed stimulus does not preclude an error. A more serious problem for fast guessing concerns Pachella's (1974) inference that the distribution of CRT_e should not depend on the processing demands of the stimulus. Yet, CRT_e usually increases with stimulus demands. There is also the issue that besides a random component, the CRT variance of fully analyzed stimuli should be small because fast guessing does not assume criterion variations in the case of full analysis. This prediction is at odds with the pronounced sequential effects on CRT. Thus, more than a two-state model of guessing and full analysis is needed (Luce, 1986).

A Three-Stage Model

Could there be something between guessing and full analysis? Falmagne, Cohen, and Dwivedi (1975) considered a three-stage model consisting of a guessing state, a prepared state, and an unprepared state. The latter two states belong to the full analysis category but differ in that a prepared state implies a bias toward responding to one of the stimulus alternatives. On entering the prepared state, CRT for the prepared response is less than CRT for the unprepared one. Moreover, participants easily emit the prepared response, which creates an additional source of errors.

Deadline Model

Both the fast-guessing model and the Falmagne et al. (1975) model assume either guessing or full analysis. In contrast, the deadline model assumes that participants react to speed stress by adopting a shorter, subjective time deadline. Processes of stimulus discrimination end either when completed (case 1) or when passing the deadline (case 2). In case 2, participants carry out a best guess, much in the sense of the SAT decomposition model of Meyer et al (1988). A fixed, subjective deadline is unrealistic, because it predicts a peak in the upper tail of the CRT density function, which peak represents all trials in which case 2 occurred. This problem may be met by permitting both random and strategic variation of the deadline. For example, when instructed to respond accurately, the deadline may be set somewhat longer. It is evident that, in contrast to an accumulator and a random walk, the deadline model refers to elapsed processing time and not to accrued evidence. Ruthruff (1996) recently proved and tested that

$$F(ES) [t] < F(EA) [t] + F(HS)[t], \text{ for all } t \text{ (the deadline model inequality)}$$

where the symbols refer to an easy (E) and a hard (H) perceptual condition, and to speed (S) and accuracy (A) instructions. The inequality states "that the proportion of responses faster than t msec in condition ES should always be less than or equal to the sum of the proportions of responses faster than t msec in conditions EA and HS" (1996, p. 58). The argument is that CRTs in condition ES come partly from case 1 and partly from case 2 trials. Case 1 is supposed to occur more often in EA than in ES because the deadline with an accuracy instruction is presumably set a little longer. Again, case 2 should occur more often in HS than in ES, and in particular when participants are unaware of the difficulty of discrimination (E or H) at each particular trial. Thus, when pooling F(EA) and F(HS) the inequality should hold. Ruthruff falsified this prediction in two studies, one on brightness discrimination and one on lexical decisions, and concluded that a time deadline is unsatisfactory as an account for SAT. Perhaps with the exception of some extreme conditions, as in the Sanders and Rath (1991) study, C appears to be based on accrual of evidence and not on elapsed time.

SAT Decomposition

There remains the intriguing question whether incomplete stimulus analysis can be used for making a sophisticated guess. This bears directly on the issue of discrete versus continuous processing, as studied by SAT decomposition (Meyer et al., 1988), which resembles the response–stimulus technique. The difference is that a response stimulus is only presented on a certain proportion of trials. On its presentation, participants should either complete processing the imperative stimulus or interrupt and respond directly, whichever is faster in that particular trial. This creates three types of responses, namely, (a) "regulars" in trials without a response signal, (b) "regulars" in trials with a response signal where completion of the regular process was faster than interruption, and (c) "sophisticated guesses" in trials where interruption and direct response won the race. Guessing is supposed to be more sophisticated as more evidence becomes available about the imperative signal (full access assumption). Other assumptions were (a) that the guessing process starts as soon as the response signal appears, (b) that regular processing and sophisticated guessing run off in parallel and without "cross-talk" (temporal independence assumption), and (c) that CRT is fully determined by the process that is completed first (winner takes all). This model is more elaborate than fast guessing because it has the additional feature of considering partial outcomes of a reaction process.

A particular merit of the Meyer et al. (1988) paper is that it has tests for assessing the validity of the assumptions. The CDF of response times at trials in which no response stimulus is presented is compared with the CDF in which it is presented. The fastest responses should take about the same time in either case because they occur at signal trials in which the regular process is likely to win the race (Fig. 2.6A). As a regular process runs off slower, the probability increases that sophisticated guessing will be faster; therefore, the two CDFs gradually diverge due to the increasing contribution of sophisticated guessing. The variance of the sophisticated guesses should be less than that of the regulars, which follows from the assumption that guessing reflects an immediate reaction. The assumption that the time taken by sophisticated guessing is faster than by most cases of regular responding is in line with the assumption that guessing starts immediately upon arrival of the response signal.

Another test concerned the effect of the I–R interval on the CDF, made up of sophisticated guesses. As I–R is longer, there is more time for regular processing so that a larger proportion of regular responses will win the race. Hence, the distribution of sophisticated guessing responses should shift to the right, but because the guessing process remains unchanged, its slope should not change as a function of I–R (Fig. 2.6B).

Meyer et al. (1988) found the previously mentioned predictions confirmed in a complex lexical decision task. Participants saw two-letter strings and responded "yes" if both strings were words or nonwords and "no" if one of the strings was a word and the other a nonword. The evidence was less clear in a simpler condition in which a single-letter string was presented and then followed by a simple lexical decision. In this study, the slope of the sophisticated guessing distribution flattened as I–R increased, suggesting more cross-talk from the regular process at a larger I–R. Hence, the temporal

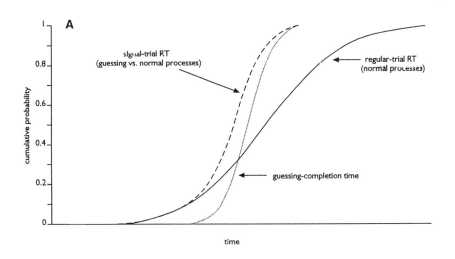

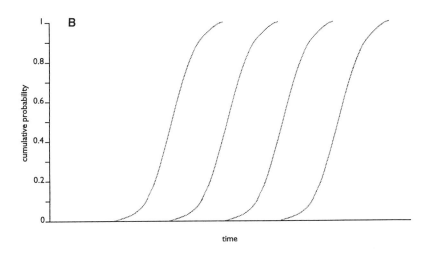

FIG. 2.6. A. Hypothetical cumulative distribution of regular trials and signal trials. The difference between the two functions reflects the distribution of guessing completion time. B. Hypothetical cumulative guessing completion distribution as a function of the interval between the imperative and the response stimulus. From Meyer, D. E., Osman, A. M., Irwin, D. E., & Yantis, S. (1988). The dynamics of cognition and action: Mental processes inferred from speed-accuracy decomposition. *Psychological Review, 95,* 183–237. Copyright © 1988 by the American Psychological Association. Reprinted with permission.

independence hypothesis was not uniformly confirmed. The validity of the temporal independence hypothesis was also questioned by De Jong (1991), who argued that a response stimulus might speed up regular responses by enhancing response readiness, thus violating temporal independence as a basic axiom for decomposing sophisticated guesses and regular processing. If temporal independence is invalid, a proportion of regularly processed correct responses is likely to be classified as sophisticated guesses.

Meyer et al. (1988) assessed the full access assumption by considering response accuracy for trials in which sophisticated guessing won the race. If partial information becomes continuously available, accuracy should gradually increase as a function of the I–R interval. In contrast, if accumulating evidence is not continuously available but limited to stage outputs, accuracy should be insensitive to the I–R interval. This is of particular interest to the debate on discrete versus continuous processing of information. The SAT decomposition method is discussed here as an example of a more elaborate fast-guessing model of SAT.

How Essential Are SAT Functions?

Most CRT studies only report mean CRT and standard deviation for individual conditions. In addition, mean error proportions are often reported, usually followed by the conclusion that SAT did not significantly affect the results. This procedure was severely attacked by Wickelgren (1977), who argued that a mean CRT cannot be properly interpreted without knowing its position on the corresponding SAT curve. Even in the case of small variations in error proportion, CRT may be seriously affected by SAT. Indeed, Fig. 2.4 shows that CRT may shift without a noticeable effect on errors, in particular at a relatively high level of accuracy.

The validity of Wickelgren's (1977) argument nothwithstanding, there is the problem that his recommendation renders CRT studies virtually impossible; the number of conditions required for measuring the SAT functions is simply prohibitive. The same can be said with regard to CDFs. The sheer number of trials needed to obtain a CDF exceeds the acceptable size of an experimental session. Other methodological problems relating to monotony and motivation would arise when implementing Wickelgren's plea. The best strategy may be to construct a SAT function and a CDF in a limited number of conditions that are of particular theoretical interest (Dosher, 1979).

SEQUENTIAL CHANGES IN SPEED–ACCURACY

CRT_c is usually relatively fast and is followed by a much slower CRT at the next trial, whose effect dissipates during the next few trials, depending on which stimuli are presented (Laming, 1979). The sequential changes are less pronounced and last less when the *same* stimulus is presented in trial $n+1$, as in the incorrect trial n, than when the alternative stimulus is presented (Fig. 2.7; left vs. right panels). Another finding is that the probability of committing a new error is much lower during trials $n+1$ to $n+5$. Accurate participants slow down more than less accurate participants (Maylor & Rabbitt, 1989).

The data from Fig. 2.7 were obtained at response–stimulus intervals (RSI) over 500 ms. Much stronger slowing—some 200 to 300 ms—has been re-

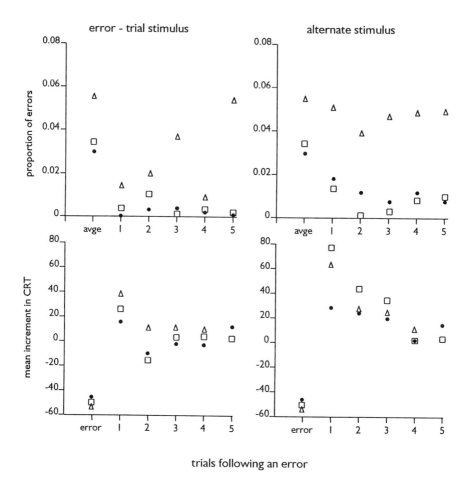

FIG. 2.7. Error proportions and mean increments in CRT on five trials following an error in three experiments indicated by, respectively, dots, triangles, and squares. In the left panels the error stimulus was repeated and in the right panels, the alternate stimulus was presented. Reprinted from Laming, D. R. J. (1979). Choice reaction performance following an error. *Acta Psychologica, 43,* 199–224. Copyright © 1979, with kind permission of Elsevier-Science-NL, Sara Burgerhartstraat 25, 1055 KV, Amsterdam, The Netherlands.

ported at a RSI of less than 100 ms (Rabbitt & Rogers, 1977), but again, the effect was less pronounced when the same stimulus recurred at successive trials. Moreover, the probability of a new error rose sharply when the next stimulus required the response that was incorrect on the previous trial. What may explain this pattern of results?

One possibility is that participants readjust C in the context of, for example, a random walk or an accumulator. Contrary to common practice, this makes sense only if C refers to response choice rather than to stimulus identification. Thus, one may hold that when an incorrect response B is given to stimulus A, the decision to carry out response B in trial $n + 1$ requires more evidence, and the C for deciding response A becomes more lax. Accurate participants may be more drastic than less accurate ones with respect to their C.

The problem with this explanation is that it does not account for the effect of RSI. Why would the readjustment be more pronounced at a small RSI? It does not explain either that CRT returns to its normal level at trial $n + 3$, or so, whereas error proportions remain below average until trial $n + 7$ (Fig. 2.7). To meet these difficulties, Laming (1979) proposed the operation of an additional factor in the random walk. Normally, participants start "stimulus sampling" before a stimulus is presented, which could reflect aspecific preparation. He proposed that anticipatory stimulus sampling might speed up CRT without affecting the probability of an error. Following an error, early sampling is stopped, which leads to the general slowing of CRT, but it gradually returns after each new correct trial. The main problem for Laming's theory is the finding that the effect of an error on subsequent CRTs is more pronounced at a small RSI. It is hard to imagine anticipatory stimulus sampling at a small RSI because one should still be occupied with the previous response. The time course of preparation appears to take some 200 ms, whereas preparation does not develop while responding to a previous stimulus. Hence, if a specific preparation is excluded at a small RSI, it cannot play a part in the aftereffect of an error either.

It might be held that anticipatory stimulus sampling is sensory rather than motor. Even then, additional ad hoc postulates are needed to account for the finding that aftereffects of an error at a small RSI are much stronger than at a large RSI. Indeed, Laming (1979) connected stimulus sampling to evidence from the "preexposure field," thus relating aspecific preparation to sensory processing. On other occasions, he contended that it may well be response related, which illustrates the problem that single-process models have in addressing the issue of localizing a potential process in the information flow.

Rabbitt and Rogers (1977) proposed that following an error, for example, response B to stimulus A, participants detect and correct the error covertly, that is, they carry out a covert response A. Overt error correction, and in particular overt error detection, appears to take much less time than a normal

CRT (Rabbitt, 1968). P. S. Bernstein et al. (1995) reported evidence for a negative shift in the ERP occurring soon after the first sign of an incorrect response, that is, peripheral muscle activity in the incorrect finger. Moreover, the negative shift was stronger when responses were more similar than when stimuli were more similar. This suggests that when the participants committed an error, (a) perceptual identification had been correct, (b) the choice of the incorrect response was rapidly fed back, and (c) immediate covert correction occurred as soon as the error was noted. Covert correction particularly delays the next response when RSI is small because one is still busy correcting the error when the next stimulus arrives. The correction hypothesis predicts that the next response will be particularly delayed when it is response B, that is, the error at the previous trial, in view of a bias against the previous, erroneous response. In contrast, response A has the advantage that it coincides with the covert correction. Indeed, this belongs to the standard pattern of results (Fig. 2.7; right panels). At a longer RSI, the effect of covert correction should be less because the correction has been completed before the next stimulus is presented. There remains, then, the issue of the gradually dissipating bias in favor of response A and against response B, which Rabbitt and Rogers ascribed to adjustment of the decision criteria. In addition, following an error, aspecific preparation might be weaker and add to the longer CRT. However, the suggestion of covert error correction is the main new element in explaining the relatively large effect at a small RSI and the imbalance of the delay of the responses A and B.

In a more recent publication, Rabbitt (1986) elaborated a tracking model to account for changes in response bias following an error. This model assumes that individuals actively track their SAT value in an attempt to obey the usual instruction to "respond as quickly and accurately as possible." The common strategy is to increase speed until committing an error, which is followed by adjusting the amount of evidence required to respond. The tracking model is a dynamic SAT model that requires a more detailed analysis of errors than a simple construction of a traditional SAT function. The tracking model has been applied to effects of alcohol on CRT. It has an exclusive emphasis on strategical resource allocation in determining CRT, which makes it an explicit alternative to the stage models, which are discussed in the next chapter.

SEQUENTIAL EFFECTS

Intertrial sequential effects on CRT refer to the effects of repetitions and alternations in a sequence of trials. The basic phenomenon is that CRT is faster on trial n when a stimulus, a response, or both are the same on trials n and $n - 1$ than when they are different (Bertelson, 1961; Eichelman, 1970;

Kirby, 1976a). The repetition effect is larger in the case of a small RSI and poor S–R compatibility (Bertelson, 1963). Again, the effect increases with the number of alternative stimuli and responses (Kornblum, 1975) and diminishes with practice (Rabbitt, 1968). In a two-choice task—but not in a multichoice task—the repetition effect turns into an alternation effect when RSI is sufficiently long (Kirby, 1976a; Fig. 2.8). CRT decreases steadily as a function of the number of successive repetitions and increases as more items intervene between two repetitions (Kornblum, 1969). Repetition effects are not limited to traditional choice reactions. Thus, Marcel and Forrin (1974) found an effect of category repetition (letters, digits) in a speeded naming-task. In the same way, Koriat and Norman (1988) observed a repetition effect in mental rotation. Rotation was considerably faster when successive stimuli consisted of the same symbol and of the same image (mirror vs. normal). The relevance of sequential effects to CRT theory was clear from Kornblum's (1969) result that when controlling for the probability of a repetition, the effect of the number of alternatives on CRT vanished entirely, a result that provided strong evidence against the information–theory-based serial dichotomization model.

As mentioned, sequential effects appear to increase with the number of stimuli (N. H. Kirby, 1976a; Remington, 1969), which is illustrated in Fig. 2.8 for a two-choice task. The data show a repetition effect at an RSI of 50 ms that turns into an alternation effect at the longer RSI of 2 seconds. The common interpretation suggests two factors, that is, automatic facilitation and subjective expectancy (Vervaeck & Boer, 1980). Automatic effects prevail at short RSIs, whereas a longer RSI enables cognitive expectancy about the next stimulus, leading to the well-known "gambler's fallacy" (Soetens et al., 1985). The main single-process description of the repetition effect is undoubtedly Falmagne's (1975) Markov chain model of prepared versus unprepared state which was already briefly outlined. The Markov chain describes the transition probabilities at discrete moments in time from (a) guessing to processing, and vice versa, and (b) from prepared to unprepared processing, and vice versa. Stimulus repetition increases the probability of entering or maintaining a prepared state for a particular alternative.

Most research on the repetition effect has been devoted to assessing its loci in the information flow. As usual, the initial attempts (Bertelson, 1965) merely distinguished between stimulus and response effects. For instance, Bertelson assigned the digits 2 and 4 to one response key and the digits 5 and 7 to another one. In this way, stimuli may differ despite the fact that the response is repeated. This procedure may be used to find out whether the repetition effect is due to stimulus repetition or to response repetition. The results of this experiment suggest that it was primarily a matter of response repetition. However, in the case of other stimulus pairs that shared a common response, for example, a red 1 and a green 2 versus a green 1

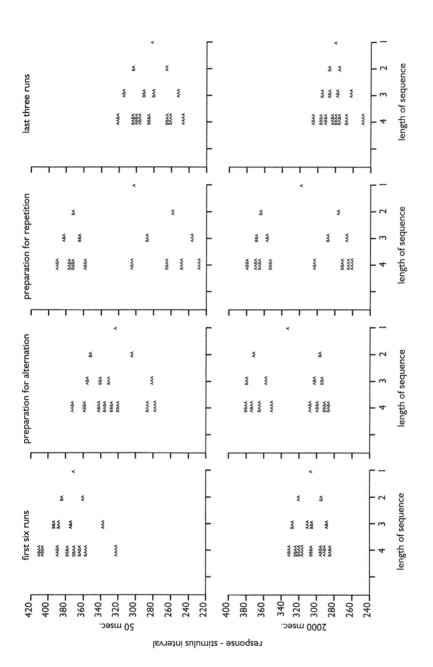

FIG. 2.8. Intertrial sequential effects as a function of instruction (prepare for alternation, prepare for repetition) practice (first vs. last runs) and response–stimulus interval (50 vs. 2000 msec). From Kirby, N. H. (1976). Sequential effects in two-choice reaction time: Automatic facilitation or subjective expectancy? *Journal of Experimental Psychology: Human Perception & Performance, 2,* 567–577. Copyright © 1976 by the American Psychological Association. Reprinted with permission.

and a red 2, the evidence suggested that stimulus repetition was decisive. It could be that the participants categorized Bertelson's digits as odd versus even or as low versus high so that response repetition was derived from a common category.

Pashler and Baylis (1991b) described various possible loci of the repetition effect based on the hypothesis that automatic activation means reusing the same processing path. Thus, the effect may originate in perceptual processing and may arise from using the same routes between preprocessing and identification. This predicts that a repetition effect occurs only when the same physical stimulus is repeated because using the same perceptual processing paths requires identical stimuli. Second, the effect might be localized in the process of stimulus categorization—letter, digit, and so on—in which case the repetition effect should extend to cases in which successive stimuli come from a common category. Third, the pathway from a category to its response might leave a transient trace (the highest link), or alternatively, a repetition might enable a shortcut from the last processed 'specific stimulus to the response (the shortcut). Finally, the effect might be localized in response programming and execution (Fig. 2.9).

To test the alternative options, Pashler and Baylis (1991b) used Bertelson's (1965) information-reduction paradigm in which more than one stimulus was mapped onto the same response. Digits, letters, and symbols such as & and # served as three stimulus categories, and three alternative responses were either mapped or not mapped to the elements of a specific stimulus category. In the first experiment, an unsystematic mixture from the stimulus categories, not permitting any category mapping, had a common response, whereas categories and responses were systematically mapped in the second study. In the third study, three alternative letters that varied in case (G, g, A, a, Q, q) were presented. Irrespective of case, specific letters (e.g., G, g) had their own responses. All three studies showed a stimulus-specific repetition effect that was the strongest when successive stimuli had the same physical appearance. Response repetition only had an effect when stimuli and responses had a categorical mapping. In a fourth study, the upper case letters (G, A, Q) were presented in different colors, but irrespective of color, each letter had its own response. In that case, response repetition was decisive. Hence, these results suggest that the repetition effect has a predominantly perceptual locus. This was tested in a final study in which odd trials required vocal responses and even trials required manual responses. Thus, a repeated stimulus asked for a different response. This manipulation had the effect of entirely eliminating any repetition effect that clearly argues against a perceptual localization. In that case, a change in response modality should not have an effect.

It emerges from these results that information reduction, that is, mapping more than one stimulus onto the same response, does not simply reflect

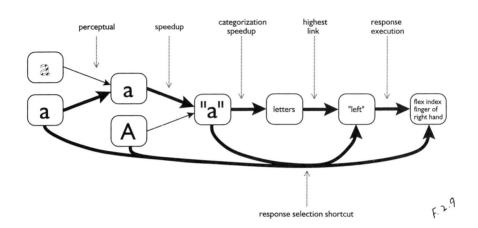

FIG. 2.9. Possible loci of the repetition effect in a task in which participants make a left key response to any letter (irrespective of letter, case, or color) and a right key response to digits and other symbols. The question is which factor elicits a repetition effect: color, case, identity, stimulus category, response category, or response. From Pashler, H., & Baylis, G. (1991). Procedural learning: Intertrial repetition effects in speeded-choice tasks. *Journal of Experimental Psychology: Learning, Memory & Cognition, 17,* 33–48. Copyright © 1991 by the American Psychological Association. Reprinted with permission.

stimulus or response effects. The results on processing stages, to be discussed in a subsequent chapter, suggest that the primary locus of the repetition effect is response selection: The repetition effect interacts strongly with that of S–R compatibility (Bertelson, 1963), whereas it is additive to that of stimulus quality (Hansen & Well, 1984) and of signal intensity (Niemi, 1981). Yet, Pashler and Baylis (1991b) also arrived at the conclusion that the repetition effect is neither due to encoding nor to responding but resides in response selection. In their view, the last S–R connection has direct access, which favors the shortcut hypothesis. Direct access of a response eliminates the need to search for the correct response, which is particularly beneficial when connections are incompatible.

    Campbell and Proctor (1993) argued that Pashler and Baylis (1991b) might have underestimated the contribution of response repetition, in particular, in light of Bertelson's (1965) strong evidence thereof. They compared repetition effects of categorizable and noncategorizable stimuli and replicated Pashler and Baylis' results that stimulus repetition has a sizeable effect in either case and that response repetition only had an effect when stimuli from the same category (letters, digits, symbols) were mapped onto the same response (Fig. 2.10). Hence, there is evidence for higher order repetition effects suggesting at least some contribution of Pashler and Baylis' highest link.

Campbell and Proctor (1993) also studied a condition in which responses changed on alternating trials. Responses were always manual, but on odd trials, the reaction was with the index, middle, and ring finger of the left hand, and on even trials, it was with the same fingers of the right hand. The spatial position of the fingers was varied among conditions. In some, the fingers of both hands had the same relative spatial position—that is, vertical alignment—and in other conditions, the fingers of the two hands had a different spatial position—that is, horizontal alignment. In one con-

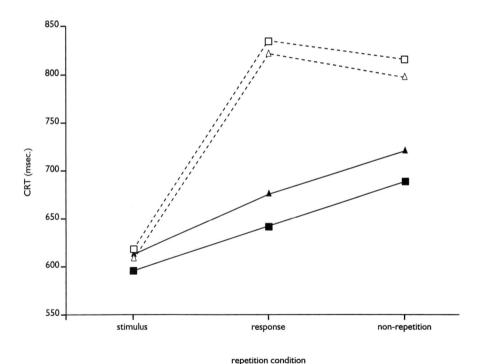

FIG. 2.10. CRT as a function of repetition condition (stimulus repetition, response repetition, nonrepetition), categorizable (solid) and noncategorizable (dashed) S–R combinations, and RSI interval (100 ms: triangles, 1,000 ms: squares). From Campbell, K. C., & Proctor, R. W. (1993). Repetition effects with categorizable stimulus and response sets. *Journal of Experimental Psychology: Learning, Memory and Cognition, 19*, 1345–1362. Copyright © 1993 by the American Psychological Association. Reprinted with permission.

dition, stimuli from the same category corresponded to the same finger of either hand at the same relative spatial position. In other conditions, either the relative spatial position of the finger or the finger itself alternated beween trials, and in a final condition, both the finger and the spatial position alternated. In this last case, the repetition effect vanished completely, as it had in the Pashler and Baylis (1991b) study. However, as long as the responses of the different hands still had one element in common, either spatial position or finger, alternating responses between hands produced about the same repetition effect. Campbell and Proctor's results argued against a peripheral motor locus of the repetition effect. In that case, it should have been eliminated by any change in effector. On the other hand, repetition of a category, for example, a letter, without any overlapping salient response feature or dimension, is not enough to obtain a repetition effect.

Pashler and Baylis (1991b) complemented the principle of pathway specific speedup (Fig. 2.9) with the weakest link principle that asserts that the most susceptible pathway is the weakest one in the information flow. This principle sheds new light on the conclusion that response selection is the primary locus of the repetition effect. It suggests that response selection is not the locus of the repetition effect per se but that it merely happens to be the weakest link in most experiments. This implies that other types of repetition effects should emerge when, for example, compatibility between stimuli and responses is high, and some other element in the information flow is the weakest link.

This view finds support in the earlier work of Marcel and Forrin (1974), who used four digits and four letters as stimuli and naming as responses. They found a considerable category repetition effect that may be duly ascribed to associative priming. It is widely assumed that letter and digit symbols have abstract internal codes organized in associative networks. Upon stimulus presentation, the level of activation of its corresponding code may be raised and may spread to nearby codes of related stimuli. Thus, codes of stimuli from the same category as in the previous trial have a heightened activation. Other intertrial repetition effects concern repetition of irrelevant perceptual stimulus aspects. For instance, Sanocki (1988) presented four-letter strings tachistoscopically and instructed participants to make a forced choice about the letter identity of each position of the string. When the strings had the same font throughout a block of trials, detection performance was better than when two different fonts alternated between trials.

Related repetition effects have been found in studies on priming, the usual format of which is that two stimuli are presented in rapid succession and then followed by a response to the second stimulus. The first stimulus serves as prime and consists either of a stimulus with some correspondence to the second one or of a neutral warning stimulus. Effects of identity or similarity between prime and imperative stimulus do not belong to the category of intertrial sequential effects. However, they are returned to in the discussion on same–different responses and on automatic versus controlled processing.

COMMENTS

The main differences among the single-process models concern the details of the assumptions about information accrual—for example, independent counters versus random walk, deterministic versus probabilistic buildup, and constant versus variable increments—and about how C behaves, that is, constant or variable. All models have in common that C(RT) is based on a combination of accrual of evidence and of setting C. An experimental variable affecting C(RT) is supposed to affect either accrual (stimulus bound), C (response bound), or both. As an exception, the sensory and motor residual may be affected, although most models are not explicit about the role of this rest.

Although accrual and C are distinct elements, CRT is determined by their joint effect, which means that effects of experimental variables should usually interact. Yet, as is shown in the following chapters, interactions are far from universal. A conception of CRT as the result of an interactive or an additive combination of stimulus and response factors is actually the main distinction between single-process and stage models.

Another objection to most single-process models is that without auxiliary hypotheses, some aspects of SAT and CDF are not properly accounted for. Thus, with respect to SAT, the models fail to explain error recognition. They assume that an error is triggered once the incorrect C has been passed, but it remains obscure how participants are aware of the fact that an error was committed. In the case of near-threshold stimuli or when a stimulus really consists of a train of pulses evolving over time (Sanders & Terlinden, 1967), errors remain actually unnoticed, but they are always detected when stimuli are above threshold. The most plausible interpretation is that errors remain undetected in the case of perceptual misidentification, but they are noticed in the case of incorrect response selection (Rabbitt & Vyas, 1970). However, this view involves "stage thinking," which is beyond the evidence–criterion scheme of the single-process models. With respect to the interpretation of the CDF, additional assumptions are needed to account for sequential effects. Thus, the long CRTs following an error add considerably to the upper tail, whereas intertrial repetitions and alternations add to the variance of the CDF. Both factors are at odds with the implicit assumption of most single-process models that trials within a block provide independent estimates of C(RT).

Single-process models address only a limited set of phenomena. In the aforementioned sections, the emphasis was on stimulus identification, SAT, repetitions, and the CDF. It is paradoxical that at the same time, the models are not very specific. Thus, it is striking that the most elaborate ones, such as stochastic diffusion, are used for describing two-choice CRTs, target classification times, and same–different response times, despite pronounced differences in processing demands among these tasks. This underlines that the models lack specific psychological content but have their starting point in convenient mathematical principles. Their level of detail and mathematical sophistication nothwithstanding, they have emanated little to related fields. Thus, they have hardly any impact on the domains of perception, response selection, and motor processes, which were among Donders' (1868) original components of a choice reaction. Moreover, they did not inspire much experimental research beyond their limited domain and have not led to noticeable applications.

However, their value and contribution should not be underestimated either. In the next chapter, the discussion focuses on decomposition of choice reactions into processing stages, each of which has its specific function in the information flow that is in need of a process model of its own. Viewed from that perspective, the single-process and the stage approach may turn out to be complementary. The scope of a single-process model is limited and concerned with a certain set of convenient statistical processes. On the other hand, stage analysis is limited to classifying clusters of related experimental variables without having much to say about specific processes that may take place within a stage (e.g., Pieters, 1983). Here, single-process models might play a relevant part. Second, they issue valuable warnings with respect to any oversimplified theorizing. Mathematics has the advantage of a more precise specification of differences among theories and of unmasking imaginary differences of equivalent theories.

Reaction Processes:
Stage Analysis

As mentioned previously, the late 1960s saw a revival of the classical view that a reaction process may consist of a sequence of processing stages. It was realized that Donders' (1868) hypothesis had never been subjected to a serious experimental test. Most importantly, Sternberg (1969) launched a completely new approach to the issue, that is, the additive factors method (AFM), which differed considerably from Donders' stage insertion and which became a highly influential, albeit not undebated, technique.

The present discussion begins with recent attempts to apply Donders' (1868) subtraction method. Although occasionally successful, its axioms remain highly questionable, so the method fails as a systematic approach to the analysis of processing stages. This is followed by a review of the axioms of the AFM, of the objections that have been raised, and of more recent elaborations. The next section reviews the main experimental evidence. One hotly debated issue, which evolved from the AFM, concerns the question whether a choice reaction process may be conceived of as a sequence of discrete stages or of processes in a continuous flow. A discrete-stage view holds that with the exception of advance presetting of parameters, processes within a stage can only start when those of the previous stage have been completed. In this way, the output of the earlier stage serves as input for the next one. In contrast, continuous flow asserts that processes are continuously passed on from one stage to the next. While stage-specific processing unfolds, the evidence is continuously transmitted. Pertinent models, experimental evidence, and arguments are discussed. The experimental evidence centers mainly around the question whether, even though still incomplete, a stage-specific process affects processing at the next stage. Besides behavioral research, there is relevant psychophysiological evidence stemming from evoked brain potentials, the discussion of which concludes the chapter.

DONDERS REVISITED

A basic assumption of Donders' (1868) subtraction notion was stage invariance, namely, the properties of the stages involved in a reaction remain the same regardless of whether further stages are inserted or deleted. In order to test this assumption, tasks that differ in one, and only one, stage should be designed. Donders viewed the *a-*, *b-*, and *c-*reactions as promising candidates.

Some studies have addressed the assumption that the *b* and *c* reactions differ only with respect to the involvement of response selection. For example, Broadbent and Gregory (1962) found that the difference between the *b-* and the *c-*reaction time is larger when S–R compatibility is poor. Donders (1868) might have argued that incompatible S–R connections impose more load on response selection, which should affect the *b-*reaction but not the *c-*reaction. However, it is hard to explain the additional finding that when S–R compatibility was high, the *c-*reaction took longer than the *b-*reaction. This was reported by Forrin and Morin (1966), who used the digits 1 through 8 as stimuli and instructed participants to respond to the digits 2 and 8—or to the digits 2, 4, 7, and 8 in another condition—by vocal naming and to refrain from responding when one of the other digits was presented. Their results were confirmed by G. A. Smith (1977) and have been ascribed to the fact that the *c-*reaction requires withholding a certain subset of responses. This has the effect that unlike the *b-*reaction, participants cannot simply produce the compatible response but are faced first with the decision to respond or not. This supports the classical objection that both the *c-* and the *b-*reactions demand response selection. More generally, the *c-*reaction appears to be much more complex than Donders had envisaged. Thus, the fact that overt responses determine performance in the *c-*reaction may elicit a bias toward overt responding (Forrin & Morin, 1966). This may be counteracted by instructions, but still, it renders the *c-*reaction sensitive to variations in SAT and, hence, to strategical rather than structural factors that render the *c-*reaction unsuitable for studying processing stages.

The problems with the *c-*reaction do not mean that Donders' (1868) assumption of stage invariance is necessarily wrong. In fact, stage deletion was supported by Gottsdanker and Shragg (1985), who presented an "informative" stimulus, one from a set of alternatives, followed by an imperative stimulus that merely signaled to carry out the response to the informative one. The interval between the two stimuli was varied. The results showed an obvious decrease of CRT as a function of the interval between the informative and imperative stimulus (ISI) with RT as asymptote. More importantly, when CRT was measured as the time elapsing from presentation of the informative stimulus to response to the imperative stimulus, CRT was unaffected by ISI as long as ISI was less than the time to discriminate and decide among the alternatives of the informative stimulus. Thus, along the lines of Donders' assumption, the *b*-reaction simply reduced to the *a*-reaction when discrimination and choice were eliminated. It is interesting that this result was obtained by a comparison between the *b*- and the *a*-reactions, but the *c*-reaction did not play a part.

An instance in which a stage was successfully inserted rather than deleted stems from Wickens, Moody, and Vidulich (1985), who had participants perform a Sternberg (1969) memory search task. The instructed target set and the imperative stimulus were either presented in direct succession or separated by a 12 secs interpolated task, that is, counting backward by 3s. The interpolated task had the effect that CRT increased with a constant, regardless of whether the target set consisted of two or four items. It has been well established that an interpolated task has the effect of removing items from working memory so that they can no longer be directly accessed but need to be retrieved from long-term memory (LTM; Baddeley, 1986). The finding that the interpolated task merely added a constant to CRT might indicate that an additional process was inserted—retrieval of the target set from LTM, regardless of the number of targets in the set. Another successful instance of stage insertion stems from Theios and Amrhein (1989), who wondered why reading words usually takes less time than naming pictures. In their view, picture naming takes longer because it involves determining a verbal label as additional process; in word naming, the label is supposed to be directly available so that mapping the word to a response is the only action.

Despite these successful instances, there remains the serious problem for the subtraction technique to define proper tasks in order to isolate a processing stage. The point may be illustrated by a study from Ilan and Miller (1994), who attempted to insert mental rotation as an additional process in a traditional choice reaction. They found that CRT to the positioning of an upright alphanumerical symbol, normal or mirror, was less when all symbols in a block were upright than when upright and tilted symbols appeared at random in the same block. They concluded that the extra operation, mental rotation, was not merely an additional stage because it did not leave the operations on upright stimuli unchanged. Yet, this conclusion may be too hasty. The occurrence of tilted symbols in the same block as upright stimuli may have added mental rotation as a new operation to which all stimuli, tilted as well as upright, are subjected. Thus, the results of Ilan and Miller could be an example of the effect of blocked versus mixed presentation of stimuli. It argues against the simplistic view that only stimuli with an additional characteristic, that is, being tilted, are subjected to the processes of the inserted stage.

THE ADDITIVE FACTOR METHOD (AFM)

Sternberg launched the AFM in 1964 at the Psychonomics meeting in Niagara Falls and elaborated it at the Donders' Centennial Symposium at Eindhoven in 1968. It was said to aim at "extending Donders' method" but in fact, it introduced a totally new approach toward analyzing processing stages. Like the subtraction method, the AFM has the starting point that CRT consists of the sum of the times taken by a set of sequentially ordered and independent processing stages. Its basic notion is that if two experimental variables—for example, stimulus quality and S–R compatibility—affect different processing stages, their effects on CRT should be additive (Fig. 3.1). This applies to mean CRT but when the time durations taken by the stages are stochastically independent, variances and convolution sums should be additive as well. In the same way, an interaction of the effects of two variables implies that they affect at least one common stage (Fig. 3.1, Panel 1). It is obvious that either variable may affect other stages as well. It also follows that a second-order interaction of the effects of three variables means that all three affect at least one common stage (Fig. 3.1, Panel 3).

Interaction and correlation are related concepts that suggest an analogy between the AFM and factor analysis as tools for isolating mental processing mechanisms. Neither technique has anything to say about the nature of the processes during a stage nor do they prescribe a particular temporal stage sequence. However, there are also differences. Thus, factor analysis applies factor rotation in order to obtain the most meaningful factor structure. In

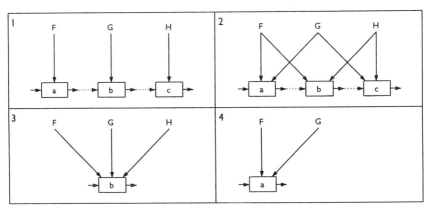

FIG. 3.1. The additive factor logic. Additive effects of variables (F, G, H) suggest separate stages (1), whereas interactions suggest at least one common stage (2, 4). A second-order interaction means that all three variables affect one common stage (3). From Sternberg, S. (1969). The discovery of processing stages: Extensions of Donders' method. *Acta Psychologica, 30,* 276–315. Copyright © 1969 with kind permission of Elsevier Science-NL, Sara Burgerhartstraat 25, 1055 KV, Amsterdam, The Netherlands.

the same way, one might consider some transformation on CRT's before conducting the ANOVA, which could turn any main effect into an interaction, and vice versa. This is not permitted, though, because the AFM is concerned with processes in real time and not with a transform. Another difference is that the AFM is only concerned with time durations of a set of stages, which limits the experimental variables to those in which time is measured. In contrast, in a factor analysis, factors can be derived from tasks, the performance of which may be evaluated with quite diverse measures. Of course, this does not mean that outcome of the AFM and that of factor analysis might not converge.

Some main differences between the AFM and the subtraction method are that (a) stages are not postulated a priori but inferred from observed relations among experimental variables, (b) experimental variables may affect more than one stage, and (c) the aim is to delineate stages and not the time taken by a stage. In fact, the time taken by a stage depends on the joint effects of the experimental variables affecting that stage. In this way, the experimental program, which originated from the AFM, was aimed primarily at delineating the mutual relations among effects of experimental variables.

More recently, Schweikert (1985) extended the AFM logic to the analysis of error proportions. Suppose that two stages, A and B, are involved. Stage A has a probability $P(A)$, and stage B has a probability $P(B)$ of producing a correct output. If a response is correct when the output of both stages is correct and if both stages are independent, then the probability of a correct response is $P(CR) = P(A) \times P(B)$ or $\log P(CR) = \log P(A) + \log P(B)$. Thus, experimental variables affecting separate stages should have additive effects on $\log (CR)$.

Another interesting recent development is the multiplicative factors (MFM) principle proposed by Roberts (1987) for describing results on response rates produced by animals. Roberts argued that many variables affecting the response rate (r) of animals have multiplicative effects in the sense that manipulating one variable has a proportional effect on response rate, depending on the level of another variable. As an example, the variables density of reward (d) and food deprivation time (f) have multiplicative effects in that $r = f * d$. It is obvious that a longer period of food deprivation increases response rate, but it does so proportionally stronger as the reward is more dense (Clark, 1958). Roberts proposed that this multiplicative relation can be explained by two successive distinct processing stages. The first generates pulses, and the second serves as a filter, with a response occurring whenever a pulse passes the filter. The suggestion is that deprivation time increases pulse rate, whereas reward density affects the transmission characteristics of the filter. Together, these result in a multiplicative relation of the effects of the two experimental variables. Roberts showed that multiplicative effects of experimental variables on response rate are common in animal behavior and argued that the AFM and the MFM basically refer to the same principle. The AFM deals with time, and the MFM deals with time intervals, which accounts for the difference between additive and multiplicative relations. The analogy between the AFM and the MFM broadens the perspective of analyzing the information flow in terms of distinct processing stages.

Axioms and Problems

Various objections have led to heavy attacks and even to discredit of the AFM logic. One concerns reversal of logic because the statement "if two variables affect different processing stages, their effects are additive" is changed to "if two variables have additive effects they affect different stages" (Prinz, 1972). The point is that two variables may have additive effects but still happen to affect the same stage (Pieters, 1983). What should be concluded in the case of a small, insignificant interaction? This leads to the related problem that inference about stages requires accepting the null hypothesis and neglecting the type-2 error (e.g., Theios, 1973). The fact that the AFM does not permit transforms on CRT means that it cannot compensate for heterogeneity of variance among conditions, which violates a basic premise of the analysis of variance. Other statistical objections have been raised by Pieters, including the difference between individual and group distributions of CRT. Pieters argued that although the AFM may have heuristic value in the sense of preliminary classification of experimental effects, it will never reach the status of a CRT process model because it has nothing to say about what happens during a stage.

Other problems of the AFM concern two highly dubious premises, that is, that reaction processes are unidimensional and serial. The information flow has only one direction, without internal feedback loops or parallel feedforward routes. The point is that as soon as processes can recur or can flow along parallel routes, CRT does not consist of the sum of the times taken by a series of successive processing stages (Schweikert & Townsend, 1989). In the same way, the AFM relies on discrete processing. One stage should complete its "work" before passing on its product to the next stage. Stage overlap violates the assumption that CRT equals the sum of the stage durations. Moreover, it is essential that a stage has a constant output (the constant stage output axiom). An experimental variable may affect the time taken to complete one or more stages but not the quality of their outputs.[1] The point is that if the quality of a stage output varies, the input to the next stage varies as well, which means that the stages do not operate inde-

---

[1]Constant quality does not refer to a correct output. Incorrect and correct codes should have the same quality. Quality is related to the "level of activation" or the "evidence" as defined in the single-process models, which is also unrelated to whether a response is correct or incorrect.

pendently. It has been objected that due to the constant stage output assumption, the AFM cannot account for effects of SAT. Finally, the AFM is a data-driven, mechanical processing system, void of strategical top-down control, in which a next stage passively awaits the input from its predecessor (Rabbitt, 1979, 1986).

COMMENTS ON THE OBJECTIONS

The aforementioned list of objections led to a negative evaluation of the prospects of the AFM (e.g., Broadbent, 1984; Pieters, 1983). Yet, the method appears to provide a successful summary of a large amount of experimental data (Sanders, 1980a, 1990), which justifies some comments to the objections. First of all, incidental additive effects on the same stage may indeed be fortuitous or due to neglect of the type-2 error. In fact, incidental additivity may well occur when two variables have minor effects on CRT. A small effect of an experimental variable—the values may have been too close to allow a clear effect—biases against an interaction. However, such additive effects are not robust and may easily turn into an interaction when the values of the variables are further apart. Yet, the very possibility of incidental additive effects issues a clear warning against interpreting observed relations among experimental variables too hastily. It has also fostered research on stage robustness. When two variables repeatedly show an additive effect, that additive effect should not turn into an interaction when the two variables are studied together with a third one, the effect of which interacts with either or both of the first two.

Most research on the AFM has been restricted to mean CRT and has ignored changes in variance. It is evident, though, that additive mean CRT's are not always accompanied by additive variances and convolution sums, which may be due to confounding (Sternberg, 1969). Thus, participants may prepare a response by advance "presetting" certain stages. The prepared response is carried out faster at the cost of CRT to an unprepared alternative, which, in turn, leads to violation of stochastic independence.

The next issues concerned serial and unidimensional processing. Unidimensional processing without internal feedback or feedforward can be easily shown to be wrong, in view of longstanding evidence for multiple processing routes in the information flow, one along direct cortical pathways and others through indirect stimulation via the limbic system and the reticular formation (Hebb, 1955). Theoretically, the effect of parallel routes can be nicely analyzed by way of a PERT network (Schweikert, 1978). A relevant issue for the AFM is the occurrence of critical points in the net that divide processing into "what must precede" and "what must follow." The AFM only deals with units separated by critical points. Hence, processes may run in parallel or overlap within stages, but a critical point is at stake when going from one stage to the next. It is of interest that when concurrent processes are involved, the typical result will be an underadditive interaction of the effects of the variables. An example of an underadditive interaction, which actually suggests concurrent routes, is discussed in the following chapter. The reason for the underadditivity is that prolonging a process can be selectively compensated by slack in the network. In the same way, overadditive interactions are obtained when two sequential processes are affected within a stage. In that case, the effects of two variables both add to the critical path.

Evidence for internal feedback comes from studies on the time taken by error detection and correction (Rabbitt, 1968), both of which take less than a normal CRT. This suggests an internal feedback loop in which the codes of the actual responses and of the correct response are compared. The only option for the AFM is that despite the evidence for concurrent routes and internal feedback loops, there is a sufficiently broad range of conditions in which CRT is not affected by these factors, and it functions as if processing were unidimensional and open loop. This may be more likely as CRT becomes less; therefore, application of the AFM is dubious when CRT exceeds, for example, 2 secs (Sanders, 1993).

It was already mentioned that only those variables qualify for AFM that can be reasonably assumed to affect the processing duration of a subset of stages. Other variables may affect CRT as well but do not apply to the stage structure. For example, stimulus modality (e.g., visual vs. auditory presentation) is inappropriate because visual versus auditory stimulation is not concerned with the time taken by a subset of stages but with qualitatively different stages. In the same way, the a-, b-, and c-reaction do not qualify as a variable because they refer to different tasks. With regard to some other variations, it is unclear whether they are appropriate. For example, it is known that CRT increases as a function of age. This might be due to a longer processing duration of some stages while leaving the stage structure unaltered, in which case the effects of age can be localized in terms of stages. Alternatively, age might bring about qualitative changes in the stage structure, in which case the AFM will render inconsistent results (e.g., Kail, 1991; Salthouse, 1991).

The issue might be further illustrated by some studies from Logan (1978, 1979, 1980). He varied the number of items to be memorized for later reproduction and inserted a rehearsal period between presentation and recall of the items. During the rehearsal period, participants carried out a choice reaction to a presented stimulus, some variables of which were systematically manipulated. The aim was to obtain a pattern of additivities and interactions of the effects of the stimulus variables and of the effects of short-term memory load, with the aim of determining the potential loci of short-term memory load in the information flow. Unfortunately, the results were unsystematic, which was viewed by Logan as evidence against the axioms of the AFM.

The question is whether short-term memory load really modulates the time taken by a subset of stages or whether it affects CRT in a different way. The answer to this question depends on the process model about what is going on during the dual task of rehearsing items and carrying out a choice reaction. One option is that rehearsing the items has to be interrupted on arrival of the stimulus. Interrupting rehearsal may be more damaging for recall as more items are rehearsed. Hence, it may take longer at a larger memory load to avoid recall failures. If this were valid, the only effect of increasing short-term memory load would be a general increase of CRT, which should always be additive to that of any choice–reaction variable. The situation is more complex when interrupting rehearsal of a set of memorized items is more damaging as the choice reaction takes longer. A longer CRT might require a longer interruption of rehearsal, thus increasing the risk of forgetting, in the case of a high memory load. If this were valid, the effects of short-term memory load and choice–reaction variables would interact whenever a choice–reaction variable has a substantial effect on CRT. The result would be unsystematic interactions and additivities, with variables affecting different stages, which was actually what Logan found. The problem is that from the perspective of potential process descriptions, short-term memory load does not modulate the time taken by a subset of stages but has the more general effect of affecting the moment that one may safely interrupt rehearsal.

This type of problem may well be the main reason why the AFM has been unsuccessful in the analysis of dual-task performance (Whitaker, 1979; Wickens, Derrick, Gill, & Donchin, 1981). Apart from the issue of shifting between tasks, a second task might interfere with the information flow of a choice–reaction process. This could violate the constant stage output axiom of the AFM. As well, the AFM has problems when applied to reactions to multiple and multidimensional stimulus displays.

The assumption of discrete serial processing has evoked considerable debate between proponents of discrete transmission and continuous flow of information. With respect to the AFM, the issue has become less relevant because, given some constraints, continuous flow models arrive at about the same interpretation of additive and interactive effects of variables. Hence, it is argued that discrete transmission between stages is not essential to the AFM. The essential premise is constant stage output, that is, the effect of an experimental variable should refer to time demands and not to a change in quality of an output code. This premise is clearly at odds with the variable criterion model as well as with other single-process models permitting a change in C. Constant stage output also implies that the AFM cannot be used in the case of near-threshold stimuli. For example, Bootsma (1988) found inconsistent effects on CRT in a study in which the participants saw pictures of a soccer player who was getting ready to take a penalty. The task was to indicate the area of the goal where the ball would arrive by pressing one of four response keys. CRT was unreliable and variable for the simple reason that the participants were uncertain about the correct response. Application of the AFM is clearly unsuitable in such conditions.

It has often been argued that a constant stage output is at odds with SAT (e.g., Wickelgren, 1977), but that is questionable. Thus, the AFM is consistent with fast guessing because the output codes of the stages—incorrect as they may be—are still supposed to have a constant quality once the fast guess has been made. In the same way, constant stage output is consistent with ill-considered or anticipatory processing, which is likely to lead to incorrect output codes and, hence, to errors. Yet, any "winner takes all" principle means that the incorrect output code still has a constant quality.

Some have proposed correcting CRT on the basis of observed error proportions. However, there are various issues that should not be confused, which all relate to Pachella's (1974) distinction between macro- and micro-SAT. As already discussed, micro-SAT has systematic and random sources that, together, always damage the reliability of central tendency measures, which are the data on which the AFM is based. For example, a sudden, semiperma-nent shift in SAT during a particular block of trials will cause a "curious" individual data point that may completely spoil an experiment. Such uncon-trolled changes in micro-SAT are not only harmful to mean CRT but affect variances and distributions as well. In the same way, stimulus detection measures are frustrated by a change of C within a block. They are not simple to trace, but when occurring, they strongly affect the estimate of d' (Wagenaar, 1973). CRT studies have the advantage that data can be analyzed on a trial-by-trial basis, which enables detection of uncontrolled changes in C. As argued earlier in this chapter, sufficient practice is the main way of avoiding the unwanted effects. Uncontrolled variation should be distinguished from shifts in macro-SAT that merely express an effect of an experimental variable. In that case, variation of SAT is controlled. Thus, Harm and Lappin (1973) found that the effect of relative S–R frequency imbalance on CRT was completely due to a shift in SAT. Their data showed faster reactions to frequent stimuli and more errors to infrequent stimuli, suggesting a bias toward the more frequent response. Correction for SAT meant that the difference between frequent and infrequent stimuli disappeared, thus artificially eliminating the effect of a powerful experimental variable.

The next issue concerns the alleged data-driven nature of the AFM (Rab-bitt, 1986). This is valid in that information is supposed to flow unidirec-tionally from input to output and that processing during a stage depends on the input of the previous stage. However, it does not mean that a stage is passive as long as no input is received from the previous stage. Strategical control is actually possible through presetting a stage on the basis of ex-pectancies, payoffs, and instructions. Processing will be faster when input from the previous stage and presetting of the present stage correspond, and both are slower and more error prone when they do not correspond. The extent of presetting may vary among stages and is actually an interesting issue for research. It is evident that the AFM has nothing to say about the control mechanisms responsible for presetting or for anticipatory activity. This leads to the final reproach that the AFM is void of psychological content. This objection is well taken. The AFM shares this problem with factor analysis and with multiple-resource theory. It is evident that given an outline of the stage structure of a reaction process, one should aim at process descriptions of each particular stage. Stage analysis only aims at describing clusters of variables in order to indicate where process descriptions are needed.

In sum, the axioms of the AFM are certainly invalid when conceived of as general principles of information processing. They may apply, though, to a limited set of conditions within a fairly strict domain. The question is how far this domain stretches. When the AFM fails, does it occur in an interesting way? This is a matter of experimental evidence to which we now turn.

EXPERIMENTAL RESULTS

General. Throughout the years, a considerable number of studies have aimed at the discovery of processing stages. The initial research (Sternberg, 1969) included a study on the relation between the effects of stimulus quality, number of alternative stimuli (visually presented digits), and S–R compatibility. The effects of stimulus quality and S–R compatibility proved additive; there was a strong interaction of the effects of the number of alternatives and of S–R compatibility and, although less pronounced, of the effects of the number of alternatives and of stimulus quality. These relations have been repeatedly confirmed (e.g., Frowein & Sanders, 1978; Sanders, 1980b) and define two stages that may be labeled feature extraction and response selection. Other studies have reported additive effects of visual stimulus intensity and stimulus quality (Everett et al., 1985) that was accomplished by inserting noise elements from a surrounding frame. The effect of stimulus intensity appeared additive to that of S–R compatibility (Biederman & Kaplan, 1970) and to that of the number of alternatives (Posner, 1978).

This last finding is of particular interest because the effects of the number of alternatives and of stimulus quality are often found to interact, suggesting that stimulus contrast affects an additional stage, labeled preprocessing, which presumably precedes feature extraction. Besides stimulus contrast, preprocessing may be affected by retinal location, a variable that should be handled with care, though, in view of the rapid decline of visual acuity in the visual periphery (Bouma, 1978). The result is that peripheral stimulus discrimination is dubious, which, in turn, prohibits application of the AFM. There is probably a third perceptual identification stage, first suggested by

Shwartz, Pomerantz, and Egeth (1977), who found additive effects of quality and discriminability of letters, but their finding conflicts with the interaction reported by Logsdon, Hochhaus, Williams, Rundell, and Maxwell (1984). The latter investigators also found an interaction of the effects of discriminability, stimulus reversal (normal vs. mirror), and stimulus rotation, whereas the effects of these last two variables were additive to that of stimulus quality. Additive effects of mental rotation and stimulus quality were also observed in experiments by van Duren (1994) and by Ilan and Miller (1994). Taken together, these results suggest two perceptual stages, one affected by stimulus quality and the other by mental rotation, whereas both are affected by discriminability. Finally, Ilan and Miller found additive effects of mental rotation and of length of the response sequence, that is, responses consisting of either one key press or of a sequel of three key presses. Thus, the effect of mental rotation does not bear on the motor stages; still, rotation might affect response selection. That relation is one of the missing elements in the structure of Fig. 3.2.

Most of the aforementioned studies used simple letters or digits, and some used words as stimuli. For instance, Meyer, Schvaneveldt, and Ruddy (1975) found an interaction of the effects of word priming and stimulus quality and of word priming and word frequency, whereas the effects of word frequency and stimulus quality proved additive. Additive effects of stimulus contrast and stimulus quality on the one hand and word frequency on the other hand were reported by Becker and Killion (1977) and by Stanners, Jastrzemb-sky, and Westbrook (1975), whereas word length and word frequency had additive effects on fixation duration (Carpenter & Just, 1983). Together, these results suggest two stages, one of which might be engaged with features and the next one with prototypes, or logogens, in order to identify the percept as a whole (Chase, 1986). Still, almost all research has used words, alphanumeric symbols, or spatial locations, whereas most research on the accumulator model of perceptual identification studied ambient differences among stimuli, such as line lengths or spatial orientation. One future research task is to determine the degree of generalization over stimulus categories.

The next stage, response selection, is based primarily on the additive effects of stimulus quality and S–R compatibility. As the label suggests, this stage plays the part of finding a response code that corresponds to the identified stimulus code. One concern, which was addressed by D. D. Larish (1986) in a study on the relation between the effects of S–R compatibility and movement precuing, has been the level of detail with which a response code is selected. The response consisted of a combination of an arm to be moved, a direction, and an extent of a movement, all of which corresponded to a particular imperative stimulus (Rosenbaum, 1980). Any of the three response components may be precued in advance of the imperative stimulus. The effect of precuing appeared to interact with that of S–R compatibility

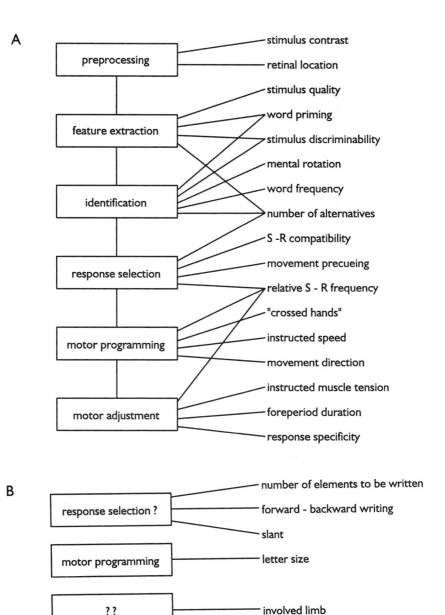

FIG. 3.2. The stage structure for traditional choice reactions, in which each stimulus has its own unique response. In Panel A the scheme is based on observed patterns of additive and interactive results. Panel B depicts results from studies on handwriting. From Sanders, A. F. (1990). Issues and trends in the debate on discrete vs. continuous processing of information. *Acta Psychologica, 74,* 1–45. Copyright © 1990 with kind permission of Elsevier Science-NL, Sara Burgerhartstraat 25, 1055 KV, Amsterdam, The Netherlands.

in that precuing had more effect when S–R compatibility was poor. The interaction was interpreted as evidence for a detailed response code at response selection. This may be too hasty because precuing also has the effect of reducing the number of alternatives, the effect of which is known to be tied to that of S–R compatibility (Spijkers, 1990).

Spijkers and coworkers (Spijkers, 1987; Spijkers & Sanders, 1984; Spijkers & Steyvers, 1984; Spijkers & Walter, 1985) approached the level of detail of response selection by studying the relations among the effects of S–R compatibility, instructed movement speed, movement specificity, and foreperiod duration in choice reactions with an aiming movement as response. With respect to speed, CRT was faster when participants were instructed to move fast rather than to move slowly (Klapp & Erwin, 1976). With respect to movement specificity, CRT was faster when alternative response movements shared a common vector rather than when all responses had their own specific direction (see Fig. 3.3A). From the perspective of stage analysis, Spijkers found additive effects of S–R compatibility and instructed movement speed that argues against the hypothesis that movement velocity had already been determined during response selection. It is not surprising that movement speed and stimulus quality had additive effects—the effects of a typical motor and perceptual variable should be additive—but it is relevant that the effect of movement speed was additive to that of foreperiod duration. The effects of foreperiod duration and S–R compatibility were additive as well (e.g., Sanders, 1980a), which suggest the operation of three motor stages: response selection, affected by S–R compatibility, and two further stages affected by, respectively, movement speed and foreperiod duration.

Sanders (1980b) found an interaction between the effects of foreperiod duration and instructed muscle tension. When instructed to be passive at the time of responding, that is, not showing any electromyogram (EMG) activity in the extensor and flexor muscles of the forearm, which was trained by biofeedback, CRT took longer when foreperiods were small and predictable, whereas instructions to be passive hardly had any effect when foreperiods were long and variable. This suggests that a passive motor attitude frustrated motor preparation, which is most harmful at brief and regular foreperiods. Moreover, Spijkers (1987) found an interaction of the effects of foreperiod duration and movement specificity (Fig. 3.3A; Semjen, Requin, & Fiori, 1978). Together, this pattern may define a motor adjustment stage, affected by foreperiod duration, movement specificity, and instructed muscle tension (Sanders, 1980a). Finally, Spijkers found an interaction of the effects of instructed speed and movement direction, suggesting motor programming or parameter specification between response selection and motor adjustment.

The implication is that at the time of selection, response codes are abstract and need specification of parameters such as direction, speed, size, and force. This is consistent with the finding that effects of S–R compatibility and of

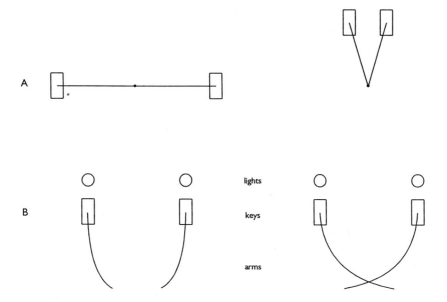

FIG. 3.3.   A. Illustration of movement specificity. The response consists of an aiming movement from a home key in the middle, to the left or to the right key. In the panel on the left the response alternatives have no common vector and are specific; in the same way, the responses are little specific in the panel on the right. B. Illustration of key-press responses with the arms in a normal and in a crossed position.

"crossed hands" proved to be additive. The crossed-hands variable refers to the situation in which participants carry out a two-choice key-press reaction—with the keys located in the horizontal plane—one corresponding to the left and one to the right hand. The hands are either normally positioned or crossed (Kornblum, Hasbroucq, & Osman, 1990; Fig. 3.3B). CRT was slower when the hands were crossed. It remains to be seen whether the effect of the crossed hands is related to motor programming, which predicts an interaction with effects of variables such as instructed speed and movement direction.

The preceding discussion was fully concerned with key presses or aiming movements as responses to alphanumerical stimuli or spatial stimuli that were presented at different spatial locations. It is interesting that a similar stage structure emerged from research on writing movements (Fig. 3.2B). Van Galen and Teulings (1983) varied instructions about forward versus backward writing as well as letter slant and letter size. They found an interaction of the effects of forward versus backward and of slant as well as an additive effect of these variables with that of letter size. This led them to suggest two stages, namely, an abstract program retrieval stage and a parameter specification stage. It is attractive to connect abstract retrieval to response selection, and specification to motor programming, although more evidence across experimental paradigms is certainly needed. In a line-drawing task, Meulenbroek and van Galen (1988) found additive effects of (a) movement size, (b) limb (wrist vs. finger) and (c) the number of successive line elements (1 or 2), which was interpreted as additional evidence for (a) abstract program retrieval (number of elements), (b) parameter specification (movement size) and, finally (c), program loading (involved limb). A program-loading stage between parameter specification and motor adjustment was also suggested by Spijkers (1987), but his evidence for this stage was scant. It is interesting to compare the evidence for a potential program-loading stage, as suggested by Spijkers and by Meulenberg and van Galen for single movements, with the evidence from studies in which the responses consist of movement sequences.

Interactions

So far, the emphasis was on additive effects, from which stages are usually inferred. In contrast, interactions are of interest in regard to which variables constitute a cluster and which affect more than one stage. This is particularly relevant for determining the loci at which an experimental variable has an effect. For instance, the effect of the number of alternatives appears to interact with that of stimulus quality and of S–R compatibility and to be additive with that of foreperiod duration (Alegria & Bertelson, 1970). Along the lines of Fig. 3.2, this means that the effect of the number of alternatives has one locus at the perceptual stages and another even stronger one at response selection but does not affect the motor stages.

In contrast, the effect of relative stimulus frequency imbalance interacts with those of S–R compatibility and foreperiod duration (Sanders 1980b), whereas the effect of foreperiod is usually additive to that of stimulus quality (e.g., F. De Jong & Sanders, 1986). Thus, the loci of relative stimulus frequency imbalance may include response selection as well as the motor stages. It is interesting that the effect of the number of alternatives vanishes when stimuli can be easily identified and when responses are highly compatible, as in naming digits or words (Mowbray & Rhoades, 1959). Under such conditions, the effect of relative stimulus frequency imbalance is also smaller but does not disappear altogether (Mowbray, 1962; Sanders, 1970b). Thus, with minor demands on perception and response selection, the probability of an S–R combination continues to affect CRT, due to its role in the motor stages.

Response Sequences

The response may consist of pressing a sequence of keys rather than a single one. Based on an extensive survey of the literature, Verwey (1994a) argued that a sequence of responses requires an additional stage, sequence construction, between response selection and motor programming. Its major task is to translate the selected abstract response code of the sequence into a more elaborate sequence representation in a motor buffer. An effect of a movement sequence (the complexity effect) was first described by Henry and Rogers (1960) but appears to be of limited generality. Thus, it vanishes as movement sequences become more familiar and well practiced (van Mier & Hulstijn, 1993). Verwey argued that practice has the effect that a sequence is transformed into a single motor chunk; therefore the sequence construction stage is no longer needed. Hence, the effect length of the sequence disappears. It is of interest that sequence construction may also be omitted when a sequence is entirely unpracticed. In that case, the first selected element of the sequence is immediately executed, followed by selection and execution of the next element, which is repeated for each further element. It is evident that this eliminates the effect of sequence length on CRT while it remains on the interresponse times.

The notion of a sequence construction stage is consistent with data suggesting that movement force and response timing are separately controlled (e.g., Ivry, 1986; Zelaznik & Hahn, 1985) and, more generally, with evidence that sequence configuration and kinematic specification have independent effects on CRT (e.g., Rosenbaum, 1991; Zelaznik & Franz, 1990). It was already mentioned that Verwey (1994a) made the highly relevant suggestion that sequence construction is inserted between response selection and motor programming without affecting processing in these stages. In fact, the evidence suggests two further stages related to producing a sequence, namely, retrieval, that is, search through the motor buffer followed by retrieval of the desired element, and unpacking, that is, recruiting the appropriate motor units for executing the retrieved element (Sternberg, Knoll, Monsell, & Wright, 1988; Sternberg, Monsell, Knoll, & Wright, 1978). Sternberg et al. (1978) found additive effects of foreperiod duration and single versus repeated execution of individual elements of a sequence—the variable relevant to unpacking— suggesting that motor adjustment remains unchanged, although it might be relevant to the first element of the sequence (Fig. 3.4).

An interesting feature of Verwey's (1994b) survey is his detailed analysis of effects of practice on executing a movement sequence in response to a stimulus. Thus, if a sequence consists of a well-established motor chunk, parameter settings may occur by default (Cordo, Schieppati, Bevan, Carlton, & Carlton, 1993), which has the effect that motor programming can be bypassed as well. Default parameter settings may well be an essential aspect of skill acquisition. Verwey's sequence production model derives from the AFM but at the same time, it marks conditions in which the AFM breaks down. The point is that the AFM is concerned with CRT. Hence, as long as participants program the complete sequence prior to executing the first element, the properties of programming will be reflected in CRT. However,

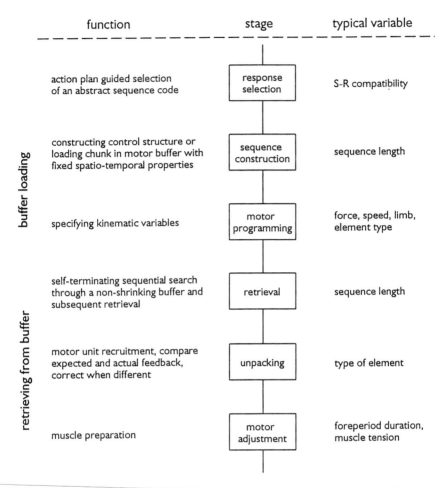

FIG. 3.4. A stage model for choice reactions, consisting of a sequence of movements instead of a single aiming movement or key press. From Verwey, W. B. (1994). *Mechanisms of skill in sequential motor behavior.* Doctoral dissertation. Amsterdam: Free University. Reprinted with kind permission of the author.

the AFM has obvious problems when programming the next movement of a sequence occurs during execution of an earlier one.

Target Classification

The stage structure of Fig. 3.2 addresses traditional choice–reactions that are characterized by information conservation. However, as is clear from Stern-berg's (1969) studies on target classification, the AFM is not limited to the conservation paradigm. Sternberg found additive effects of stimulus quality,

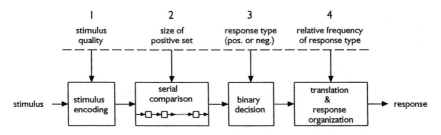

FIG. 3.5. A stage model for binary classification tasks. From Sternberg, S. (1969). The discovery of processing stages: Extensions of Donders' method. *Acta Psychologica, 30*, 276–315. Copyright © 1969 with kind permission of Elsevier Science-NL, Sara Burgerhartstraat 25, 1055 KV, Amsterdam, The Netherlands.

size of the target set, and the binary decision, suggesting three successive stages (Fig. 3.5). These results are discussed in more detail in chapter 5. The issue is whether target classification leads to insertion of a special memory search module while leaving the other stages unchanged. The additive effect with stimulus quality suggests that target classification is a postperceptual affair, the result of which is not fed back to the preceding perceptual analysis. The relations between target classification and the response stages have not been sufficiently researched to answer the question whether memory search leaves the motor stages unaffected.

Practice

Practice reduces the main CRT parameters of mean, variance, and skewness, and the question, obviously, is whether practice has particular loci in the information flow. Are all stages affected, is the effect of practice limited to particular stages only, or is there a change in stage structure? Thus, there is abundant evidence that the effects of S–R compatibility and practice interact (Welford, 1976), suggesting that response selection is among the stages that are affected. Response selection may actually be bypassed with highly compatible S–R relations such as naming alphanumerics. In the same way, Verwey's (1994a, 1994b) work on motor chunks suggested bypassing of motor stages after practice. In target classification, there are dramatic practice effects when the same target set is consistently used during many experimental sessions, but there is hardly any effect of practice when a new target set is presented at each new trial (Shiffrin & Schneider, 1977). This research is discussed in greater detail elsewhere. Here, suffice it to note that the main effect of practice is that the "work" to be performed in some stages vanishes until those stages can be fully bypassed, which is obviously relevant to the notion of automatic processing.

Recently, Pashler and Baylis (1991a, 1991b) examined the loci of practice by means of transfer of training. They reasoned that if practice affected a peripheral motor stage, it would be harmful to change the hand with which the key-press responses are carried out because responding with the other hand had not been practiced. In contrast, if practice affected only central processing stages, training should transfer from one hand to the other. Similarly, if the locus of practice were at response selection, shuffling a practiced relation between stimuli and responses should strongly disrupt performance. Finally, if practice affected perceptual identification, adding items of the same stimulus category to the S–R ensemble should selectively affect the new items for the simple reason that they had not yet been practiced.

The results showed near-perfect transfer of training in the first and last case but not when reshuffling practiced connections between stimuli and responses, which confirm that response selection is a main locus of practice. It should be noted, though, that the Pashler and Baylis' (1991a, 1991b) studies used small ensembles of familiar stimuli and responses. One may be reminded of Verwey's (1994a) practice effects on more complex motor responses. Similarly, effects of practice have been observed when stimuli are unfamiliar or degraded. Thus, Sanders, Wijnen, and van Arkel (1982) found a clear interaction of the effects of stimulus quality and practice. Pashler and Baylis may be correct, though, in their conclusion that peripheral sensory and motor stages—preprocessing and motor adjustment—are relatively insensitive to practice.

Stage Robustness

A decisive question about the AFM is whether additive and interactive relations are robust. When studied in combination with a third variable, observed additive effects of two variables should not turn into a higher order interaction. If they do, it follows that the original inference of two separate stages was incorrect. The point is that in the case of a higher order interaction, all three variables affect the same stage so that the initially observed additivity proved incidental. In line with Külpe's (1905) criticism of the stage concept, it could turn out that in the end "everything interacts with everything" which, consistent with a capacity notion, would support the view of the information flow as a single, complex interacting structure (Broadbent, 1984). However, except for a few failures, most studies have reported stage robustness. The evidence is discussed in turn.

A first instance stems from the work of Wertheim (1979), who studied CRT during ocular pursuit. Participants were instructed to follow a moving white dot in which an imperative stimulus was presented. The demands on ocular pursuit were varied by manipulating frequency, velocity, and predictability of the course of the moving dot. Additional variables were stimulus

quality and foreperiod duration of the imperative stimulus, which have usually been found to be additive (Frowein & Sanders, 1978; Stoffels, van der
Molen, & Keuss, 1985; Fig. 3.2). Wertheim found a second-order interaction
of the effects of motion frequency, motion predictability, and stimulus quality, as well as an interaction of the effects of motion velocity and foreperiod
duration (see Fig. 3.6A). He concluded that the first two variables have a
perceptual locus, presumably by frustrating fixation of the moving dot, and
that motion velocity has a motor locus by affecting preparation to respond
to the imperative stimulus. The stage structure of Fig. 3.2 was robust in that
irrespective of the demands on ocular activity, the effects of stimulus quality
and foreperiod duration remained additive.

Stage robustness was also reported by Stoffels et al. (1985), who found
a pronounced interaction of the effects of S–R compatibility and of an irrelevant spatial cue as part of the imperative stimulus (Simon effect). Yet,
this modulation of the effect of S–R compatibility did not affect the additive
relations of S–R compatibility, stimulus quality, and foreperiod duration.
Another instance stems from van Duren and Sanders (1988), who studied
the effects of mixed versus blocked presentation of conditions on the size
of the effects of stimulus intensity, stimulus quality, and S–R compatibility.

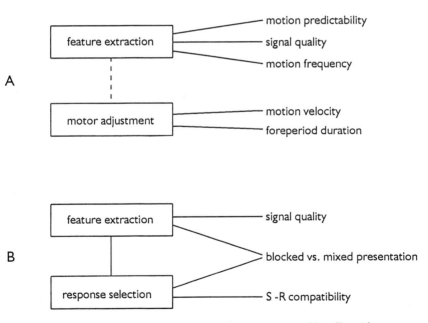

FIG. 3.6.   Two instances of stage robustness. A. Motion variables affect either
feature extraction or motor adjustment but do not change the additive relation
between feature extraction and foreperiod duration. B. Blocked versus mixed
presentation affects feature extraction and response selection but does not
change the additive relation between S–R compatibility and stimulus quality.

The effect of block type interacted with those of stimulus quality and S–R compatibility in that the effect of either variable was larger when presentation was blocked than when it was mixed. Yet, the relation between stimulus quality and S–R compatibility remained additive (Fig. 3.6B). Again, van der Molen et al. (1987) found that additive effects of stimulus quality, number of alternatives, and foreperiod duration did not alter when conditions were mixed. Stoffels (1996) varied stimulus discriminability (black–white vs. dark–light grey-colored arrows) and S–R compatibility (spatial correspondence between response key and arrow) in blocked and mixed compatibility conditions. The results show that the effect of compatibility was more pronounced in the blocked than in the mixed case, but the interaction did not affect the additive effects of discriminability and S–R compatibility.

A final example of stage robustness stems from research on the effects of sleep loss on CRT (Sanders et al., 1982; Steyvers, 1987). A considerable interaction was found of the effects of sleep loss and stimulus quality, whereas the effects of sleep loss and S–R compatibility proved additive. Sleep loss brought about a considerable number of response failures to the degraded stimulus, which is returned to when discussing the cascade model. Despite the interaction of sleep loss and stimulus quality, the effects of stimulus quality and S–R compatibility remained additive.

Failures of Stage Robustness

Stage robustness may seem quite general by now, but there are exceptions. One is the relation between the effects of stimulus quality and the number of alternatives that is sometimes additive and sometimes interactive. Van der Molen et al. (1987) observed a second-order interaction of the effects of stimulus quality, number of alternatives, and shock threat—that is, a mild electric shock that might occur during a block of trials. Without shock threat, the relation between the effects of stimulus quality and the number of alternatives was additive. It turned into an interaction when in the wake of a shock, suggesting an instable relation between stimulus quality and the number of alternatives. Another instability concerns the relation between relative S–R frequency and foreperiod duration. Bertelson and Barzeele (1965) observed an interaction, Holender and Bertelson (1975) found an additive effect, and both effects were reproduced by Sanders (1980b). Additive effects were found when individuals had been trained to be passive—defined as the absence of EMG activity in the relevant muscle groups—whereas an interaction occurred when they were optimally prepared, again in terms of EMG activity of the relevant muscles.

An interaction of effects of relative S–R frequency and foreperiod duration may be taken as evidence for selective preparation: A more probable response is selectively prepared at the cost of a less probable one (e.g., Posner

& Snyder, 1975). Preparation appears to be most effective at a short and constant foreperiod and to decline rapidly as the interval increases. Hence, CRT should profit most from selective preparation at a brief and constant interval, yet participants should really prepare! It is not surprising, therefore, that selective preparation vanished when participants were instructed to be passive. Bertelson and Barzeele's (1965) participants might have been more actively preparing while Holender and Bertelson's (1975) might have behaved passively.

These failures of stage robustness do not really damage the AFM but add to specification of the operations contained in a particular stage. It is reasonable that selective preparation depends on whether one is actively preparing. Similarly, an interaction of the effects of stimulus quality and of the number of alternatives may only occur when the demands on feature extraction exceed a critical level. There are other failures, however, which suggest real limits to the AFM.

Immediate Arousal

Thus, it would be worrying when the effect of a variable located at the input side of the information flow interacted with one located at the output side. Yet, this was the case in studies of Sanders and Wertheim (1973) and of Sanders (1975a, 1977), who found an interaction of the effects of auditory stimulus intensity and foreperiod duration in an a- or c-reaction. The effect of foreperiod duration was much less when the stimulus was a loud (80 dBA) rather than a weak (35 dBA) tone. A similar interaction was not found with visual stimuli of different intensities nor in the cross-modality condition of a light flash and a weak tone. The interaction with foreperiod duration was found, however, when a visual stimulus was accompanied by a loud accessory tone—presented together with the visual stimulus but irrelevant to the response (Sanders, 1980a). The interaction suggests that a decline of preparatory state, as presumably occurring at a long foreperiod, is restored by a loud auditory stimulus, irrespective of whether that stimulus is imperative or accessory. Thus, Bernstein et al. (1973) varied foreperiod duration and foreperiod variability in the presence or absence of an accessory auditory stimulus and found a greater effect of the accessory as response readiness was less. Nickerson (1973) concluded that the evidence on intersensory facilitation is properly explained by improved preparation.

From the perspective of the AFM, there is the compelling problem how the effect of an input variable, auditory stimulus intensity, may interact underadditively with that of an output variable, foreperiod duration, which strongly argues against a unidimensional sequence of linear stages. However, in line with a PERT network, the underadditive interaction may suggest two concurrent processes. Given a specific set of conditions, input and output may be connected by a shortcut. The first condition is stimulus intensity because the interaction of the effects of intensity and foreperiod vanished when the auditory stimulus intensities were all below 70 dBA. The interaction has been incidentally observed with visual stimuli but only at really high intensities (Niemi & Näätänen, 1981). In contrast, the interaction may occur most easily with tactile stimuli, irrespective of their intensity (Fig. 3.7). Thus, the interaction may not be related to auditory stimulation per se but rather to stimuli evoking "immediate arousal" that activates the shortcut and by-passes the cognitive information flow (Fig. 3.7). The consequence is that immediately aroused responses are ill-considered and, therefore, liable to be incorrect. Indeed, in the case of a c-reaction to loud auditory tones—that is, react in the case of a high tone and inhibit response in the case a of low tone—individuals tended to inhibit responses more poorly when the tones were relatively loud (> 75 dbA).

Immediate arousal reminds of the orienting reaction, and one may wonder whether it can be eliminated. This was studied by Sanders and Andriessen (1978), who measured CRT to auditory stimuli—high versus low tones—while also varying stimulus intensity, S–R compatibility, and foreperiod duration. The results showed evidence for immediate arousal—an interaction of stimulus intensity and foreperiod duration—when compatibility was high but not when it was poor. In this last case, the effects of auditory intensity and forepe-riod duration were additive, suggesting that immediate arousal is suppressed in the case of demands on response selection. Converging evidence for

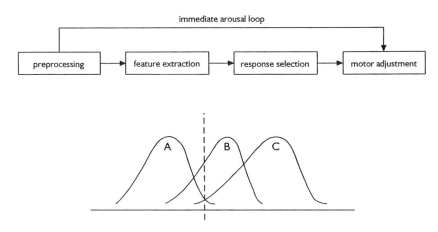

FIG. 3.7. The immediate arousal loop from preprocessing to motor adjust-ment. The suggestion is that immediate arousal is elicited when a stimulus exceeds a critical value (the dashed line) on a hypothetical intensity dimension. Visual stimuli (A) are supposed to be at least intense, tactile stimuli (C) most intense, and auditory stimuli (B) occupy a middle position.

suppression of immediate arousal in the case of incompatible choice reactions was reported by van der Molen and Keuss (1981), who found that RT diminished steadily as a function of stimulus intensity. CRT diminished as well but increased again when a critical intensity level was exceeded.

In conclusion, research on immediate arousal suggests the operation of a second dimension, the shortcut, which limits application of the AFM, albeit in a specific and interesting way. One may conceive of the AFM-defined stages as a cognitive, computational processing chain that is connected to energetic mechanisms and control structures (chap. 9). In most other cases, the AFM has been doing surprisingly well. It is good to note, as Roberts (1987) did, that there are only a very few instances in which such a simple relation as perfect additivity generalizes over such a broad spectrum of situations. This consistency has been viewed as support for the basic axioms of the AFM, such as discrete processing between stages. However, this deduction may be premature, as is shown later in this chapter.

Extensions to Neuropsychology and Gerontology

Individuals who suffer from brain damage as a result of closed-head injury react more slowly, an effect that appears to be more pronounced on CRT than on RT (Ponsford & Kinsella, 1992). Van Zomeren, Brouwer, and Deelman (1984) found that CRT of closed-head-injury patients increased more when S–R compatibility was poor and as the number of alternatives increased. This suggests a specific effect on response selection, but it does not exclude general proportional slowing either. This last hypothesis suggests that slowing of CRT following closed-head injury is proportional rather than bound to a particular processing stage. According to the general slowing hypothesis the injury causes a global effect on the total assembly of processes and should, therefore, interact with all variables affecting CRT.[2]

The alternative to the general slowing hypothesis is that closed-head injury prolongs CRT by a constant amount. In that case, the effect of the injury should be additive to that of all variables affecting CRT, which means that no specific stage is affected.[3] Contrary to van Zomeren et al. (1984), constant slowing was found by Stokx and Gaillard (1986), in that the effect of closed-head injury was additive to those of stimulus quality, S–R com-

---

[2]An alternative is that a specific disorder affects constant stage output. In particular, if the disorder has the effect that the stage output becomes suboptimal, one should expect spurious higher order interactions.

[3]Additive effects to all variables could mean that yet another, thus far undiscovered, stage is involved. At some point, this can be considered as unlikely. An alternative is that the effect is due to factors beyond the AFM logic, for example, a strategical check on correctness, which might take an additional constant. Another strategic possibility is that due to a specific disorder, participants may become particularly sensitive to sequential effects—for example, response times following an error. Such effects are all beyond the AFM.

patibility, target classification, and time uncertainty. Some of their patients consistently showed specific interactions, though, which could mean that the group of closed-head-injury patients lacked homogeneity. A more specific effect of closed-head injury was recently reported by Schmitter-Edgecombe et al. (1992). As did van Zomeren et al., they also found interactions of the effects of closed-head injury and those of stimulus quality and S–R compatibility but not with the effect of target classification. Van Zomeren and Brouwer (1994) constructed a complexity function, in which CRT from many studies was plotted for control participants and for closed-head-injured patients, the general trend of which was consistent with proportional slowing (Fig. 3.8). As argued, however, results on closed-head injury are easily bedevilled by the problem of homogeneity of patient groups. Alternatively, the same critical subset of stages may have been involved in all tests

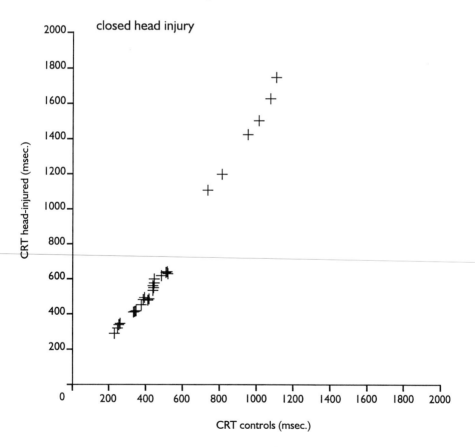

FIG. 3.8. Proportional slowing of head-injured patients. From van Zomeren, A. H., & Brouwer, W. H. (1994). *Clinical neuropsychology of attention.* Oxford, UK: Oxford University Press. Reprinted with kind permission of the publisher.

(Bashore, Osman, & Heffley, 1989). Taken together, the issue of specific versus general effects of neurological disorders on CRT appears unsettled. It will be returned to in chapter 9 where the effects of energetic deficits on CRT are discussed; they are shown to be more consistent in showing specific rather than general or proportional effects.

A complexity function and analogous global slowing have been thought to apply as well to the effects of age on C(RT). The general finding is that C(RT) increases with age and this has been ascribed to destructive processes in the brain. Neurons may be randomly disrupted with a constant probability (Cerella, 1990) which predicts proportional slowing as embodied in the complexity function. There is the problem, though, that the available evidence is not very homogeneous, with some studies showing sizable effects and others hardly any effect of age. The problem is that the interindividual variance increases strongly among older people. As a result, there is a problem of defining age as an experimental variable.

The results of some recent studies (Smulders, 1994) suggest specific loci of age effects, among which are peripheral sensory processing and response selection. Smulders found additive effects of age, stimulus quality, central motor programming, and motor adjustment. A further interesting result is that the effect of age was additive to that of stimulus quality in the case of single letters or digits, whereas older individuals took relatively longer to identify degraded words. This suggests that stimulus discrimination, that is, integration of perceptual evidence, is sensitive to age. Another finding concerned stage robustness because irrespective of age, effects of stimulus quality and S–R compatibility were additive. Hence, the increase in CRT seems not to be due to a change in processing strategy.

DISCRETE VERSUS CONTINUOUS PROCESSING

The Cascade Model

Sternberg's (1969) AFM model explicitly assumed a sequence of discrete linear stages. In contrast, J. L. McClelland (1979) developed a continuous cascade model, in which accumulating evidence (activation) is continuously passed on to the next stage. Along the lines of the connectionist view, activations are based on linear integration of excitatory and inhibitory outputs of units from the previous stage. For example, one stage may analyze physical features, whereas the next stage may be concerned with letter shapes. A particular letter stimulus may first be subjected to feature analysis, which means that the corresponding feature units are activated and noncorresponding feature units are inhibited. Next, the feature units activate corresponding letter shapes. Presumably, the shape that corresponds best to the stimulus letter will be activated the most, but competitors are also somewhat activated as they become more similar to the correct stimulus letter. On the other hand, the base activation state of dissimilar shapes is inhibited. The model assumes that the asymptotic activation of the winning shape depends on the extent to which competitors are activated. The more activation the competitors get, the less there remains for the winner. A further assumption is that all competing units at a certain stage reach their asymptote at the same time (Fig. 3.9A).

The discrete and continuous models are illustrated in Fig. 3.9B and differ in some important ways. In the discrete model, the effects of experimental variables are exclusively on the time taken to complete a stage until constant stage output has been reached, whereas in the continuous model, an effect may be on activation rate or on the asymptotic level. Activation rate is characterized by a rate constant (k), which, for reasons of simplicity, was assumed to be constant for all units within a stage. The rate constant may differ considerably among stages, though, which is analogous to differences in processing time taken by stages in the discrete model. Variation of the asymptotic level of activation reflects the property of the continuous model that experimental variables may not only affect processing speed but also

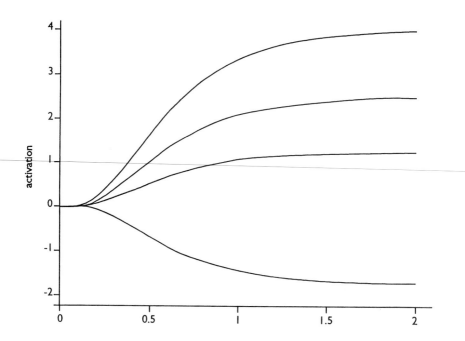

FIG. 3.9A. Features of the cascade model. Illustration of activation functions of different units at the same level—for example, feature extraction—some of which have a positive or a negative asymptote. All units reach their asymptote at the same time.

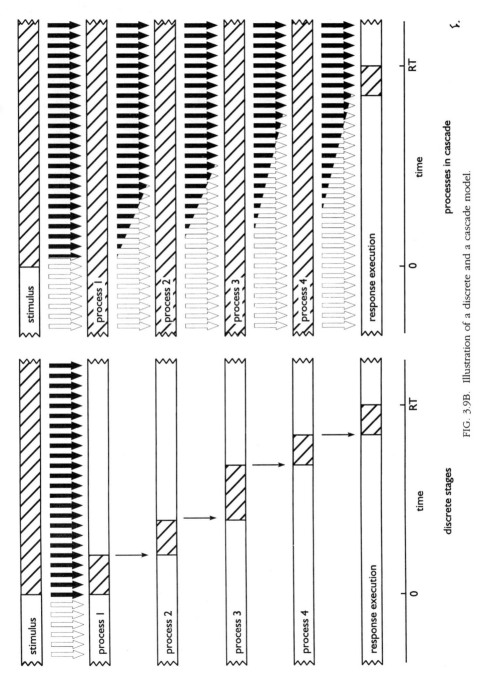

FIG. 3.9B. Illustration of a discrete and a cascade model.

87

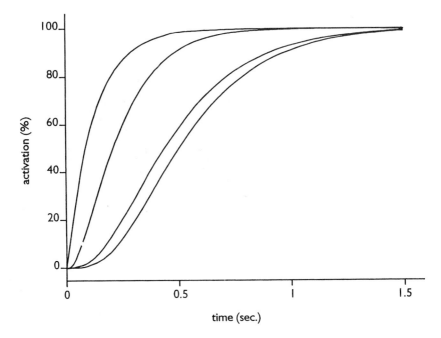

FIG. 3.9C. Illustration of accrual of activation at four successive levels of processing. Stimulus onset is at time $t = 0$. The rate constants are 8.0, 8.1, 4.0, and 16.0, respectively. From McClelland, J. L. (1979). On the time relations of mental processes: An examination of systems of processes in cascade. *Psychological Review, 86*, 287–330. Copyright © 1979 by the American Psychological Association. Reprinted with permission.

output quality, as is evident from Fig. 3.9A. The final stage has a response criterion that is set at a certain level of activation. Another central assumption of the cascade model is that the marginal rate of activation of a stage depends on the difference between the input $\{a_{a-1}(t)\}$ from the previous stage and its activation level $\{(a_i(t)\}$, both at time t, weighed by the rate constant (k).

$$\frac{d}{dt}(a_i(t)) = k\{a_{i-1}(t) - a_i(t)\}; \quad a_{i-1}(t) > a_i(t)] \tag{1}$$

The consequence is that however fast a subsequent process may be, it can never overtake a previous slower process because its level of activation cannot exceed that of the previous stage. In turn, this means that activation of a stage can only reach its asymptote when the total activation of the previous stage has been taken into account. The slowest stage is called rate limiting because its rate limits the buildup of activation at the next stages. The stimulus usually consists of a step function, so the first stage reaches its asymptote as a negatively accelerated exponential function. The second stage will start more slowly because it has to await the gradually arriving input from the first one. In particular, a rate-limiting stage will slow down activation of the next stages (Fig. 3.9C).

Regarding the AFM, it is relevant to trace the consequences of the cascade model for relations among the effects of experimental variables. What happens when two experimental variables affect the (k) of two different stages? J. L. McClelland (1979) carried out computer simulations and found almost perfect additivity (Fig. 3.10A) and in the same way, an interaction was found when two variables both affected the (k) of the same stage (Fig. 3.10b). These relations broke down, however, when one or both variables affected the asymptotic level of activation rather than (k) (see Fig. 3.10b). From the perspective of the AFM, this is not surprising because an effect on the asymptote means an effect on stage output, the constancy of which was shown to be essential. However, the cascade model has the interesting feature that as long as the asymptote is constant, the features of continuous flow and response criterion do not prohibit application of the AFM. It should be noted, though, that all McClelland's simulations used a constant-response criterion over conditions. If the response criterion were allowed to vary, the quality of the stage output would no longer be constant, and the AFM analysis would fail.

The fact that with the aforementioned restrictions in mind, the AFM is consistent with the cascade model is due to the property that all activation of a stage has to be used by the next stage. Other properties of the cascade model and, in particular, its process dynamics appear to be less essential. Thus, J. Miller, van der Ham, and Sanders (1995) simulated several variations on Equation 1 that all showed near-additive effects when different processes were affected, again provided that the asymptotic level was constant and that the response criterion was within reasonable limits. In some variations, the rate of activation of the next stage increased or decreased as a function of absolute rather than relative activation of the input $(a_{i-1}(t))$ from the previous stage (Fig. 3.11A, B). In another one, transmission between stages occurred only when exceeding a threshold (Fig. 3.11C), while in still other variations, activation increased in two quanta, that is, a first rapid increase to an intermediate level, then to a final asymptote (Fig. 3.11D). The only case in which additive effects broke down was when the activation level of the next stage was allowed to overtake that of the previous one (Fig. 3.11E). For example, one might imagine that a response is carried out while the perceptual processes have not yet been completed. In that case, the AFM logic fails because this is another example in which the constant stage output is violated.

Is constant asymptotic activation a reasonable assumption in a cascade model? Theoretically, it is no problem because a constant asymptote is accomplished by simply replacing the principle of distribution of activation among competitors by a "winner takes all" principle. The assumption that

90

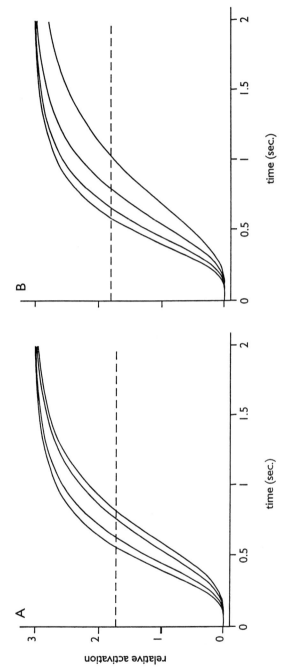

FIG. 3.10. The effect of joint manipulation of variables affecting the rate parameter (k) of two different processes (A) and of the same process (B). Figure continued on next page.

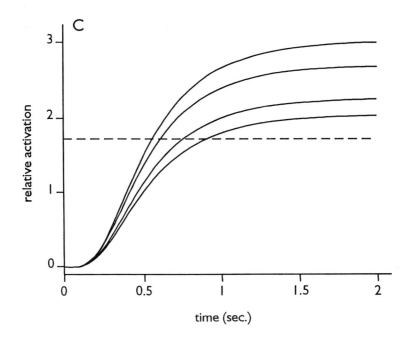

FIG. 3.10. (*Continued*). The effect of joint manipulation of variables affecting the asymptotic activation of different processes (C). From McClelland, J. L. (1979). On the time relations of mental processes: An examination of systems of processes in cascade. *Psychological Review, 86*, 287–330. Copyright © 1979 by the American Psychological Association. Reprinted with permission.

experimental variables may affect the asymptotic level of activation has also the serious complication that as the asymptote gets lower, a considerable increase of response failures is expected (Ashby, 1982). Yet, except for threshold conditions and some extremes, such as performing after sleep loss, response failures are uncommon in C(RT) tasks, which seems to exclude the occurrence of significant variation in asymptotic activation.[4]

Thus, the analysis of the cascade model shows that the AFM relies much less on discrete processing than originally thought; therefore, successful application of the AFM cannot be used either as an argument in favor of discrete processing. J. Miller (1988) extended the discussion on discrete versus continuous processing by describing three instances in which the issue may play a part, namely, processes within stages transforming input into output, the nature of a stage output code, and transmission between

---

[4]Sanders et al. (1982) argued that response failures, observed when performing after sleep loss, are also at odds with the hypothesis that the effect is due to lower asymptotic activation.

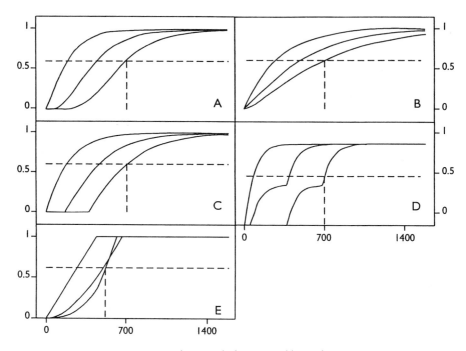

FIG. 3.11. Variations on the cascade function: Additivity between processes is never seriously affected except when activation of a next process does not depend on the state of activation of a previous process. In that case, a later process may overtake an earlier one (E). From Miller, J., van der Ham, F., & Sanders, A. F. (1995). Overlapping stage models and the additive factor method. *Acta Psychologica, 90*, 11–28. Copyright © 1995 with kind permission of Elsevier Science-NL, Sara Burgerhartstraat 25, 1055 KV, Amsterdam, The Netherlands.

stages. Any may be discrete or continuous, although not all combinations are logically possible. For example, discrete transformation, that is, transforming input into output by a single step, precludes continuous transmission between stages. The AFM has nothing to say about the nature of transformations within stages. Regardless of discrete versus continuous processing, unidimensional versus more dimensional processing, and potential feedback loops within a stage, there is only the prerequisite of a constant output code. In terms of a PERT network, stages should be bordered by sequential portions of the net, whereas concurrent processes may prevail within portions. Discrete transmission of information between stages has been traditionally considered to be an essential prerequisite for applying the AFM, but given the results on the cascade model, this is no longer a critical issue.

The output code of a stage may also be discrete or continuous, which may depend on the type of stimulus. Thus, it is intuitively plausible that a digit has a discrete perceptual stage output code, and, for example, a line length has a continuous one. The AFM requires a constant quality that may be precarious when the output code is continuous. The reason is that a continuous code may lack stability. For instance, the original assumption of the cascade model that the total available amount of activation is distributed over various competitors may well apply to stimuli with a continuous output code. It would be interesting, therefore, to compare relative stage robustness for stimulus types that are likely to have a discrete or a continuous output code. In conclusion, a discrete output code is certainly desirable for the AFM, perhaps more so than discrete transmission.

C. W. Eriksen's Continuous Flow Paradigm

The notion of continuous flow gained currency due to research by Eriksen and coworkers on focused attention. In a typical study, a group of symbols is presented and individuals have the task of reporting the identity of a central symbol while ignoring the adjacent ones. For example, the group may consist of the letters SSHSS, in which case the H should be reported vocally or by a key press, but the Ss are to be ignored. This appears difficult to do when the S may also appear as target (HHSHH). CRT in this conflicting case is compared with CRT in the congruent condition, (HHHHH, SSSSS), and in the neutral condition in which S or H is surrounded by nontargets, that is, letters that are never presented in the center, such as XXHXX (B. A. Eriksen & C. W. Eriksen, 1974; C. W. Eriksen & Schultz, 1979).

The C. W. Eriksen paradigm is returned to elsewhere. For the present purpose, it is relevant that *grosso modo*, the results on the paradigm, suggest that flankers primarily affect response selection. This is evident from the finding that CRT in the case of neutral flankers hardly differs from that of congruent flankers. This argues against the possibility that perceptual disentangling of targets and flankers is the main issue. Moreover, there is physiological evidence that conflicting flankers have "late" effects. Thus, in a study by Coles et al. (1985), participants responded by squeezing one out of two zero-displacement dynamometers with either the right or the left hand. In order to register an overt response, the squeeze force had to exceed 25% of its maximum value. The authors also measured the EMG and the course of the squeeze activity of either hand. In the conflicting condition, many trials showed muscle activitity in the incorrect hand. Moreover, the stronger the muscle activity in the incorrect hand, the longer the interval between the start of EMG activity and of actual squeezing with the correct hand. In other words, the activity of the incorrect hand hampered the development of activity of the correct one, a result that favors an explanation in terms of response competition between the hands. In addition, measurement of the difference between the lateralized readiness potentials (LRP) showed first a trend toward incorrect central response activation followed by a deflection toward correct response activation (Coles & Gratton, 1986). A more extended discussion of psychophysiological studies to the issue of discrete versus continuous processing is found in a later section of this chapter.

The usual view of the C. W. Eriksen paradigm has been that processing takes place in two broadly defined stages, namely, stimulus evaluation and response selection. During stimulus evaluation, all letters of a string are processed in parallel, and the accumulating evidence is continuously passed on to their corresponding response codes. The response codes corresponding to potential targets are in a sensitive state. As a result, they can be activated by either a target or by a flanker, typically leading to response competition in the conflicting condition. This view seems to argue against discrete processing with a constant stage output. In a discrete model, conflicting flankers and neutral ones as well might take extra time on the perceptual level in order to identify the relevant character amidst irrelevant ones. This would lead to a constant perceptual output, namely, the code of the relevant character. Therefore, response stages would not get involved in the conflict. The finding that the response stages are involved has been interpreted as favoring continuous flow of information from the individual letters. Ridderinkhof et al. (1995) showed that effects of target set size and S–R compatibility were additive when a stimulus was presented singly but turned into an interaction when the stimulus was surrounded by flankers that signaled the same response. This means a violation of stage robustness and, consequently, a failure of the AFM.

Asynchronous Discrete Processing

It has been countered, however, that the previously mentioned evidence imposes the unreasonable demand on discrete processing that a total letter string is encoded as a single unit and functions as a single stimulus (J. Miller, 1988; Sanders, 1990). The question is what constitutes a stimulus in the information flow—a single letter, a word, or a functional unit, depending on which internal representations are available? Is it the total of all presented stimulation, such as target and flankers in the Eriksen paradigm? Again, a single stimulus is composed of elementary features. May an individual feature be treated as a stimulus, in that its output can be passed on to the next stage before evidence about other features has been completed (e.g., Treisman 1988), or does discrete processing refer to the "full" stimulus only?

The results on the Eriksen paradigm suggest continuous and parallel flow of individual elements. The same is suggested by results on the redundant target paradigm, in which some stimuli are designated as targets and the individual is to make a certain response when one or more targets appear in a display and another response when no target is presented.[5] The general

---

[5]This is the divided-attention version of the Eriksen paradigm. The paradigm reminds also of visual-memory search to be discussed later.

phenomenon is that CRT decreases as the number of targets increases, which has been considered as evidence for parallel processing in the sense of a race between the stimuli (e.g., Mordkoff & Yantis, 1991). In one study (Townsend & Nozawa, 1995), a dot was either presented or not presented to the left eye, to the right eye, or to both eyes. The participant was instructed to respond by pressing the "yes" key whenever detecting a dot and by pressing the "no" key otherwise. The redundant target situation arises when both dots are presented. In addition, Townsend and Nozawa varied the brightness of the dots. Both dots could be bright (b,b) or dim (d,d), or the left dot could be bright and the right dot dim (b,d), and vice versa (d,b). The authors were interested in the contrast between the effects of brightness and eye position in the case of redundant targets.

$$CRT(d,d) - CRT(b,d) - CRT(d,b) + CRT(b,b) \qquad (2)$$

They proved that this contrast should show an interaction when the positions are processed in parallel and should be zero (additive) when they are serially analyzed. The results showed an overadditive interaction—the (d,d) case was relatively slow so that the contrast was positive—which suggests a parallel self-terminating analysis of the two dots. Such results argue strongly against serial, discrete processing of units from multiple-stimulus displays. As is argued elsewhere, serial or parallel processing of a multiple-target display may depend on the extent to which processing occurs automatically.

On the level of a single stimulus, there is also ample evidence for partial information transmission, in that information about features of a stimulus may be passed on to the next stage. Thus, the letter "S" may require a left-hand key-press response and the letter "T" a right-hand one, whereas the size of the letter determines which finger has to be used. For instance, a larger letter may require pressing the index finger, and a smaller letter pressing the middle finger. If conditions are created in which the letter code is completed earlier than the size code, the letter code may be transmitted and may activate the appropriate hand prior to the completion of the slower size code (J. Miller, 1982). This phenomenon has been confirmed in various other related studies (Miller, 1987) and has led to the notion of asynchronous discrete processing. A stimulus is thought to be composed of various features, all of which have their own output code that upon completion, are individually transmitted to the next stage. A response is carried out when all features have passed through all stages. Note that a strictly discrete model would postulate only one feature, whereas a fully continuous model assumes an infinite number of features. CRT corresponds to the slowest flow through the stages, as illustrated in Fig. 3.12, by way of a critical path in a PERT network (J. Miller, 1993). The smaller the "grain size" of the features, the more the evidence suggests continuous flow.

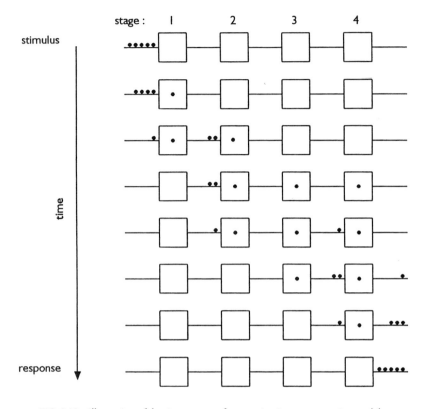

FIG. 3.12. Illustration of the time course of processing in a queue-series model in which each dot represents a component of stimulus information that can be separately processed. From Miller, J. (1993). A queue-series model for reaction time with discrete stage and continuous flow models as special cases. *Psychological Review, 100,* 702–715. Copyright © 1993 by the American Psychological Association. Reprinted with permission.

Hence, the question is which stimulus properties qualify for separate transmission.[6] They might be quite elementary but could just as well be more complex stimulus aggregates. Again, asynchronous discrete components may not be fixed but may depend on the characteristics of the total stimulus. The most widely accepted view is that asynchronous processing is possible with separable stimulus features but not with integral ones. The distinction between separable and integral stimulus features is discussed elsewhere. Here, it suffices to say that separable refers to features that can

---

[6]The assumption is that a response is triggered by identification of some but not of other features. Alternatively, participants may have control over the use of partial information so that the use of available evidence would depend on "willingness" to do so (Gratton, Coles, & Donchin, 1992). This hypothesis is in line with resource strategy and at odds with stage notions.

be changed without affecting the state of other components of the stimulus, whereas integral features are not on their own.

Asynchronous discrete transmission violates AFM logic because the stimulus as a whole lacks constant stage output. According to the logic of a PERT network, concurrent processing of stimulus attributes turns additive relations into underadditive interactions. A particularly striking example of such a change stems from an experiment by Steyvers (1991) on the combined effects of sleep loss, stimulus quality, and S–R compatibility on CRT. Steyvers used two alternative digits as stimuli that were responded to by a key press with the index and middle finger, respectively. The digits could be either intact or degraded by noise elements and were presented on a computer screen at either the left side or the right side of the visual meridian. In the compatible conditions, individuals reacted with the left hand when the digit was presented at the left and with the right hand when the digit was presented at the right side of the screen, a relation that was reversed in the incompatible condition.

In this way, the stimuli had two distinct separable attributes, that is, quality and spatial location, which is a perfect case for asynchronous discrete processing. When participants had had a night of normal sleep, Steyvers (1991) found the usual additive effects of stimulus quality and S–R compatibility (Fig. 3.13A) that turned into a pronounced underadditive interaction when participants suffered from a night's loss of sleep (Fig. 3.13B). The most striking result was that following sleep loss, the effect of S–R compatibility virtually disappeared when the digits were degraded. When the responses were compatible, sleep loss affected CRT for the degraded stimulus but not when the responses were incompatible.

This counterintuitive result is actually consistent with asynchronous discrete processing, which holds that identification of a digit and its spatial location proceed in parallel. There is evidence that sleep loss selectively increases the effect of stimulus quality on CRT in that it takes longer to identify a degraded digit after a night's loss of sleep than after normal sleep. In contrast, the effect of S–R compatibility is not affected by sleep loss (Sanders et al., 1982). This means that after sleep loss, the correct hand may have been determined, irrespective of compatibility, whereas completing the response awaits the delayed identification of the degraded digit. In other words, Steyvers' (1991) results are likely to represent an example of relative slack in a PERT network in which encoding location and digit identity proceed along parallel paths.

Utilizing Incompletely Processed Information

In regard to discrete or continuous processing, it is of interest whether incomplete evidence about a feature at one stage can be used by the next stage. A discrete processing model excludes using incomplete evidence

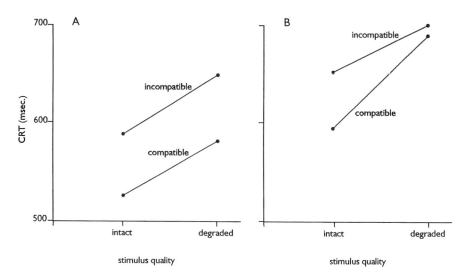

FIG. 3.13. A second-order interaction of stimulus quality, S–R compatibility, and sleep state in the case of asynchronous discrete processing. Panel A shows CRT after normal sleep and Panel B after a night of sleep loss. From Steyvers, J. J. M. (1991). *Information processing and sleep deprivation: Effects of knowledge of results and task variables on choice reactions.* Doctoral dissertation. Tilburg, The Netherlands: Tilburg University. Reprinted with kind permission of the author.

because it is supposed to be lost. In contrast, continuous transmission of information holds that all evidence, both complete and incomplete, will affect the next stage. One approach to the issue is through precuing. A precue provides advance information about a forthcoming imperative stimulus. This has the effect that processing the precued stimulus is facilitated at the cost of inhibiting reaction to an alternative stimulus (e.g., Posner, 1978). Discrete transmission predicts that only a fully analyzed precue is effective, whereas continuous flow expects that the effect of a precue develops gradually. These predictions were studied by Sanders (1971), who presented a horizontal arrow pointing either to the left or to the right. The arrow precued the location of an imperative stimulus light (left or right) that was responded to by pressing the spatially corresponding response key. The results show the expected facilitating effect of the precue when the stimulus onset asynchrony (SOA) amounted to 200 msec or more, but no effect whatever at a smaller SOA. Thus, the effect did not grow gradually but had to await full analysis of the precue and the ensuing response preparation that amounts to some 200 msec.

Hence, the results are consistent with discrete processing of the precue. This conclusion was confirmed in later studies by Gottsdanker (1975) and Meyer et al. (1985). In the latter study, the precue was either an English word, a nonword, or a row of four Xs, which served as a neutral control precue. The imperative stimulus followed the offset of the precue and consisted of an arrow pointing to the left or to the right that was to be responded to by pressing the spatially corresponding key. A meaningful word was always followed by an arrow pointing to the left, and a nonword by an arrow pointing to the right. The results showed a considerable reduction in mean and variance of CRT when the precue was presented sufficiently far enough in advance to allow identification of the verbal information and preparation of the connected response (700 msec). The most interesting was the condition in which the precue was only briefly presented. This meant that identification of the word or nonword was occasionally achieved but incomplete on most trials. Discrete transmission suggests that the distribution of the response times is a mixture of the distributions of fully prepared responses and of the neutral condition in which there is no preparation at all. The point is again that preparation should be either fully successful or completely absent. In contrast, continuous transmission predicts a single intermediate distribution, reflecting the effect of partial identification and preparation. Some results are shown in Fig. 3.14 and in support of discrete transmission.

More recently, Meyer et al. (1988) applied their response–stimulus method (chap. 2) to study the issue. A response–stimulus may arrive while one is busy processing the imperative stimulus. It demands an immediate response that initiates a race between a normal and a sophisticated-guessing process. Guessing is sophisticated because it is supposed to use all information available at the time that the response–stimulus is presented. Discrete transmission predicts that the useful information is limited to outputs of completed stages and not to incomplete processes. Continuous flow, on the other hand, assumes that all available evidence, complete and incomplete alike, adds to the quality of sophisticated guessing. Meyer et al. reasoned that accuracy should be better as more evidence can be utilized. Continuous flow, then, expects a gradual rise in accuracy of sophisticated guessing as a function of SOA between the imperative and the response–stimulus. In contrast, discrete transmission expects accuracy to increase only when a new completed stage output becomes available. Therefore, accuracy should increase stepwise with plateaus in between. In the study outlined here, Meyer et al. found accuracy plateaus, as suggested by discrete processing.

The problem with this conclusion is that Ratcliff (1988) showed in simulations that a similar stepwise increase of accuracy follows as well from a discrete random walk and from stochastic diffusion (chap. 2), which are prototypical continuous flow models. With regard to the random walk, it is reasonable that at the moment the response–stimulus is presented, the emitted response depends on the state of the walk. If negative, the response is negative—an error—and if positive, the response is positive—a correct. The random walk of fast, correct responses is usually positive at any time—otherwise the response could not be fast—whereas the walk of slower correct

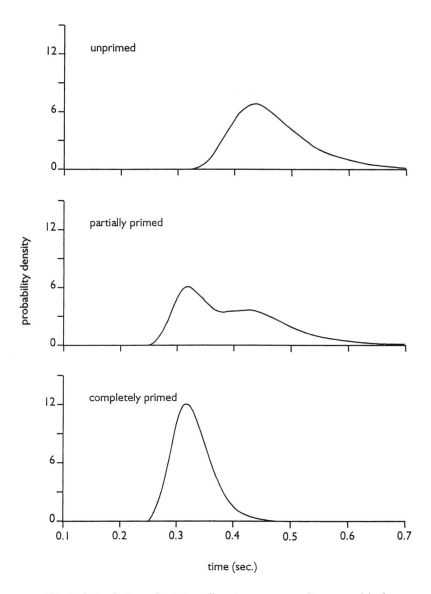

FIG. 3.14. Predictions of priming effects in a two-state discrete model of response preparation. The effect of priming appears to be all or nothing so that the partial priming distribution is composed of contributions from the unprimed and completely primed distributions. From Meyer, D. E., Yantis, S., Osman, A. M., & Smith, J. E. K. (1985). Temporal properties of human information processing: Tests of discrete vs. continuous models. *Cognitive Psychology*, *17*, 445–518. Copyright © 1985 by Academic Press, Inc. Orlando, Fl. Reprinted with permission.

responses is likely to linger around a zero state for some time. Fast, correct responses, therefore, cause a rapid rise in accuracy at a short SOA. This levels off at somewhat longer SOAs because the conditional probability increases that there is a negative count at the moment the response–stimulus is presented. This is even more so as SOA increases, in which case only a few, very slow responses have not yet been completed.

Sanders (1995) proposed still another approach to the question whether incomplete evidence can be used by a later stage. He used the paradigm of the functional visual field, in which participants first fixate and inspect a stimulus presented at the left side of the visual meridian, then shift their eyes to a stimulus at a symmetrical location at the right side of the visual meridian, and complete a trial by a same–different response. There is ample evidence that individuals do not start the saccade from the left to the right stimulus before the left stimulus has been identified (chap. 5). In itself, this is consistent with discrete transmission because completion of perceptual processing may trigger the saccade to the right stimulus, and participants cannot freely vary the moment of initiating the saccade. In line with J. Miller's (1993) asynchronous discrete processing view, Sanders found that a saccade can be triggered by a stimulus component such as color or size.

This enabled a condition in which the left stimulus consisted of two features, one of which was processed faster than the other. For example, stimuli could have the similar-shaped letters E and F as a slowly processed feature and a large difference in letter size as a fast feature. When instructed to base the same–different response on the fast feature only and, hence, to leave the left stimulus as soon as the fast feature had been identified, the slower feature usually had not been completely identified at the start of the saccade. The question is whether the incompletely processed slow feature affects the ensuing same–different response. Discrete transmission does not predict an effect because incompletely processed features are supposed to be lost. Continuous flow assumes gradual transmission of information, thus predicting an effect of an incompletely processed feature on the same–difference response. The incompletely processed feature failed to affect the same–different response, which confirmed the prediction of discrete transmission. In another condition, the slow dimension was the relevant one for the same–different response. In that case—and in line with much other evidence (chap. 5)—the irrelevant fast dimension had a pronounced inhibitory effect on the same–different response time.

Statistical Analysis of Discrete Versus Continuous Processing

In summary, the outcomes from studies on using incompletely processed information are largely consistent with discrete transmission. A similar conclusion was reached by Roberts and Sternberg (1993), who tested some detailed statistical predictions from the discrete stage and the cascade model.[7] One test concerned the means and variances of response times derived from the value of the rate constants (k) of cascade processes. As a process is slower, its variance increases, but the question is how much more variance does the cascade model permit? A general statistic for the relation between mean (M) and variance (σ^2) is the "variance change characteristic," in which the symbols (11, 22) refer to the state of two

$$\sigma_{22}^2 - \sigma_{11}^2 / (M_{22} - M_{11})^2 \tag{3}$$

experimental variables. A comparison between simulations of the cascade model and data from four studies showed that when mean CRT increased, σ^2 increased less in the data than in the cascade simulation. The point is that continuous transmission permits the occurrence of very rapid CRTs, namely, when the buildup of activation of all processes happens to be relatively fast together with a low response-criterion (Fig. 3.3C). In the same way, CRT can be quite slow when the buildup of all activations happens to be slow along with a high criterion. This can be avoided by imposing restrictions on the variation in response criterion and by inserting thresholds that limit transmission to a next process (e.g., J. Miller et al., 1995), but these are steps into the direction of discrete processing.

EVIDENCE FROM EVOKED BRAIN POTENTIALS

EP Components and Information Processing

The main rationale for research on the relation between evoked brain potentials (EP) and CRT has been that EPs may reflect an online view on what happens during a choice reaction. This has led to much literature on the effect of choice–reaction variables on EP components. For example, the amplitude of the N1 component appears to depend on abrupt changes in energy impinging on the sensory receptors. N1 is largest at the onset of a tone, and a smaller N1 is evoked by its offset (Davis & Zerlin, 1966). It follows that the N1 amplitude is larger for auditory stimuli than for visual stimuli and is sensitive to intensity (Picton, Goodman, & Brice, 1970). N1 is considered as an exogenous component because it depends primarily on stimulus features, whereas later EP components are endogenous.

---

[7]A so-called "alternate path model" was also considered, which assumes that a particular reaction task is either accomplished by process A or process B, with a certain probability. Experimental variables, then, could selectively affect the duration of process A or B but not their probability of occurrence. The predictions of this somewhat farfetched model failed on all tests.

The N2 peak, which has been related to transient arousal and to the orienting response (Näätänen & Gaillard, 1983), has proven to be most pronounced when a sequence of expected stimuli is interrupted by a deviant one. The N2 wave has a strong association with the ensuing P3a, the combination of which is sometimes referred to as the N2–P3a complex, whereas the N2 latency is supposed to be related to the time taken by stimulus encoding (e.g., Frowein, Gaillard, & Varey, 1981; McCarthy & Donchin, 1981). Yet, the evidence on the N2–P3a latency is not convincing. For instance, Mulder et al. (1984) varied stimulus discriminability and found a large effect on CRT—500 msec—but only a marginal 17 msec on P3a latency. Kok and Looren de Jong (1980) failed to find an effect of stimulus quality on P3a, whereas Rösler et al. (1986) found the latency of the P3a to depend on stimulus complexity. Curiously, the more complex stimulus had a shorter P3b latency. Finally, Kok (1986) found a complex interaction of the effects of stimulus quality and go/no–go responses on P3 latency in a c-reaction task.

Effects on P3 amplitude are most clear when participants have the task of detecting a rare stimulus or a rare omission of a stimulus amidst a train of expected stimuli. P3 is virtually absent when expected stimuli appear, but it is very pronounced in the case of a rare stimulus, its amplitude decreasing as the probability of the rare stimulus increases. The latency of the P3 in choice–reaction tasks seems to depend foremost on postperceptual processing demands such as target search, target classification, and the filtering of incongruent flankers (Brookhuis, Mulder, Mulder, & Gloerich, 1981; Mulder et al., 1984; Smid, Mulder, & Mulder, 1990). Briefly, the P3 has been characterized as expressing surprise, context updating, and stimulus evaluation, but not response selection or any other response-related factor (Donchin & Coles, 1988). This last inference is based primarily upon failures to find an effect of S–R compatibility on P3 (McCarthy & Donchin, 1981).

It has been well established that central motor processes are reflected by the LRP. For example, Osman et al. (1988) found that with incompatible S–R relations, the LRP went first in the wrong direction, which delays its buildup in the correct direction. R. De Jong et al. (1988) concluded that the evidence on the LRP supports selective response preparation when a precue precedes the imperative stimulus and response competition from incongruent flankers in an Eriksen paradigm (Smid et al., 1990; Fig. 3.15). Smulders et al. (1995) found that a degraded stimulus quality delayed the latency of the P3 as well as of the LRP, whereas response complexity, that is, pressing a single key or a combination of keys, did not affect either latency. Response complexity may only play a part after LRP onset.

Although the LRP is a main index for central motor processes, the EMG, recorded from the muscles activated prior to a response, has proven to be a sensitive index for peripheral response activation. In the case of incompatible S–R relations, the EMG of the incorrect hand may be activated without

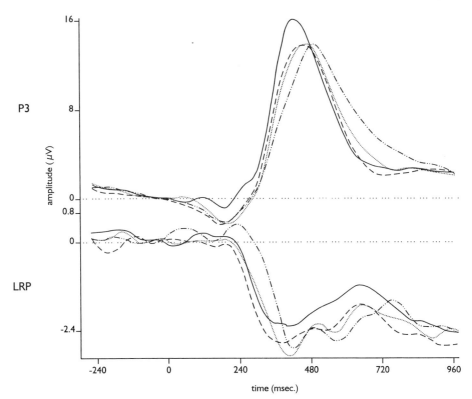

P3

LRP

FIG. 3.15. P3 and LRP components, obtained in an Eriksen flanker study. _ _ _ _ = no flankers; .... = neutral flankers; - - - - - - = congruent flankers; - ·· - ·· - ·· = incongruent flankers. P3 latency increased when adding a flanker and when the flanker was incongruent. LRP latency was also sensitive to flanker incongruence. Note that the LRP starts with a deflection in the incorrect direction. From Mulder, G., Smid, H. G. O. M., & Mulder, L. J. M. (1993). On the transfer of partial information between perception and action. In D. E. Meyer & S. Kornblum (Eds.), *Attention & Performance, 14*, 567–588. Copyright © 1993 by the MIT Press, 55 Hayward Street, Cambridge, Mass. Reprinted with permission.

actually leading to an incorrect key press. Moreover, CRT is longer because there is more "incorrect" EMG activity in a particular trial. Yet, CRT is also longer when there is no incorrect peripheral but only incorrect LRP activity, suggesting that activation of the incorrect response may either continue all the way to the periphery or be stopped earlier (Osman, Bashore, Coles, Donchin, & Meyer, 1992).

It is obvious by now that psychophysiological evidence is highly relevant to the debate on discrete versus continuous processing. Indeed, various tests have been carried out in recent years. Thus, in line with asynchronous discrete processing, Osman et al. (1988) and Smid et al. (1992) found the LRP to develop faster when a different well discriminable and separable stimulus feature, for example, a red versus a green color, should be responded to by different hands than when different hands were connected to a hard feature, such as distinguishing l (el) from 1(one). Interestingly, P3 latency was not affected, which seems to argue against the suggestion that the P3 reflects stimulus evaluation. Osman et al. (1992) presented stimuli with two features. The easy feature (spatial position) instructed participants about the hand to respond with, whereas the hard feature (letter identity) instructed participants either to respond or to inhibit response (the Osman paradigm). The results of this study showed, among others, LRP activity on "stop" trials, which suggests that the spatial position had activated the response before the letter had been identified. Similar results were obtained by J. Miller and Hackley (1992).

Smid et al. (1996) asked individuals to respond to certain global shapes, conditional upon the presence of a specific local element. In line with the previously mentioned evidence, the LRP was activated on the basis of the global shape, which activity was suppressed when the local element did not comply. EPs suggested that the global shape was available earlier than the local element, which is consistent with the idea that the global shape acted as a separable dimension. In another condition, participants responded only in the case of a conjunction between a global shape and a specific color. In that case, the LRP activated the response only when the color was correct, despite the fact that the EPs showed that evidence about the global shape was available earlier than evidence about the color. Thus, Smid et al. found that the LRP was activated by the global shape when the shape determined the response in isolation but not when it determined the response in conjunction with the color. This was interpreted in terms of strategic control whether or not to transmit the shape code to the response system (Gratton et al., 1992). Interesting as these results are, this last conclusion may be premature, in particular when "strategic control" is understood as freedom in setting a decision criterion along the lines of a single-process model. Indeed, the codes of the two features appear to be jointly transmitted when they are combined into a single response. However, strategic control would mean that the moment of response activation can be freely affected by instructions, and that remains to be seen.

Earlier, Smid et al. (1991) argued that the notion of asynchronous discrete processing had a problem in studies on the effect of feature similarity on CRT in an Eriksen paradigm. If flankers and potential targets had common features, for example, N and Q are targets, and "MMQMM" and "CCNCC" are among the stimuli, the "M" and "C" did not function as neutral flankers but delayed CRT as if they were incongruent flankers (Yeh & C. W. Eriksen, 1984). An obvious explanation is that processing a neutral similar flanker (M) activates the response to the "N." In turn, this implies that the "grain size" of information processing is on the level of a letter feature, that is, on an integral rather than on a separable aspect of the stimulus. This is at odds with the basic premise of asynchronous discrete processing.

Smid et al. (1991) carried out a study in which a target (Q, H) could either occur alone or was surrounded by flankers that were physically similar to the presented target (DCGQ, NWMH) or to the alternative one (DCGH, NWMQ). The results confirmed the finding that P3 latency increases when the target is surrounded by flankers but P3 latency was insensitive to the similarity of the flankers to the target. In contrast, LRP latency was sensitive to the similarity of the flankers to the target, starting earlier when features of the flankers were similar to the presented target than when they were similar to the alternative one. Yet, when flanker features were similar to the alternative target, they activated the LRP and even the EMG of the incorrect response, thus suggesting transmission of integral flanker features rather than of total identity to the response selection system. Transmission of integral features is not expected from asynchronous discrete processing, which led Smid et al. to argue in favor of continuous flow. Yet, in his later work (Smid et al., 1996), the evidence was against continuous flow.

In brief, the picture is far from complete and is the subject of an ongoing discussion. For instance, flankers that are similar to the alternative target might be identified as a potential target, thus causing the same response competition as really incongruent flankers. The fact that the target usually wins the competition from the flankers may be primarily due to the fact that the target has the correct location, but flankers do not. The relevance of localizing a target amidst noise will be the main issue in chapter 7 on focused attention.

An Interim Evaluation

It is beyond doubt that EP and EMG measures add substantially to the analysis of CRT and that research on the functional significance of the EP components is highly relevant. Yet, there is a danger of too-far-reaching inferences, usually in the sense of unwarranted generalizations. One danger concerns the conception of P3 latency as a measure of perceptual analysis, of LRP latency as a measure of central response activation and of EMG latency as a measure of peripheral response initiation (Mulder, Smid, & Mulder, 1993). For instance, there is evidence for at least three distinctly different types of units in the primary motor cortex, the activity of which is reflected by the LRP. These units are perceptual neurons, accepting relevant stimulus information; motor neurons, driving the movement; and sensorimotor neurons, which connect perceptual and motor neurons (Requin, Riehle, & Seal, 1993). The evidence of J. Miller, Riehle, and Requin (1992) on single-cell stimulation suggests that the primary effect of partial information transmission, as studied in the Osman paradigm, is on the perceptual neurons. This may be hard to reconcile with the notion that the LRP is an exclusive reflection of central response activation. In the same way, there are reasons to doubt an exclusive perceptual locus of the P3. For example, there are conditions under which S–R compatibility appears to affect P3 latency (Bashore, 1990; Ragot, 1990) or some related positive wave (e.g., Falkenstein et al., 1993). Thus, although P3, LRP, and EMG certainly differ in their main points of application in the information flow, one should be careful to consider a selective effect on either measure as a definitive proof of the locus of that effect.

As an example, Coles et al. (1985) and Smid et al. (1990) found a difference in P3b latency between congruent and incongruent flankers in an Eriksen paradigm. Starting from the assumption that P3 is a measure of perceptual analysis, they concluded that flanker congruence has a perceptual locus. Smid et al. found that congruent flankers delayed P3 latency relative to that of a single target. This was interpreted as indicating that congruent flankers lead to a more profound perceptual analysis. They also found that relative to a single target, CRT was not affected by the presence of compatible flankers. This divergence with the P3 was taken as evidence that components of the reaction processes are not reflected by CRT; consequently, CRT would not be a reliable indicator of the perceptual information flow. Yet, this conclusion starts from the axiom that P3 latency is a pure index of perceptual processing. In the same way, the previously discussed data on the effect of flanker similarity on the LRP (Smid et al., 1991) posed only a potential problem for asynchronous discrete processing when the LRP is viewed as an exclusive reflection of response activation.

Another basic issue is whether EP waves are indeed online manifestations or reflect derivatives of the processes involved. For instance, it has been suggested that the P3 reflects control of perceptual processing rather than perceptual activity (Sanders, 1990). This suggests that P3 and CRT might only covary when controlled processing dominates the perceptual information flow and not when perceptual analysis proceeds automatically. This could explain the finding that P3 latency is more sensitive to postperceptual variables such as target classification and search than to perceptual variables such as stimulus quality and discriminability. A related issue is whether the latency of the EP components are direct markers of the information flow or reflect an aftermath. The point is that most EP components develop relatively slowly. Thus, the peak of the N1 at around 100 msec cannot be taken as evidence that peripheral stimulus processing takes 100 msec. In the same way, the P3 may reach its peak only after a response has been actually completed. This has sometimes been taken to imply that individuals react to incompletely processed information. For instance, the ratio between P3 peak latency and CRT was proposed to reflect the proportion of completed perceptual processing (Coles & Gratton, 1986). In the same way, the LRP develops long before the peak latency of the P3 has been reached, which has been taken as evidence for continuous flow of information from perception to central motor activation. Such inferences make sense only when EP components are indeed a direct reflection of the processing times and not when they are an aftermath. The discussion of the behavioral research throughout this chapter renders it quite unlikely that EP components are pure online manifestations.

SUMMARY

This chapter aimed at summarizing the trends in research on stage analysis. It was concluded that although occasionally successful, Donders' (1868) subtraction method did not lead to a systematic analysis or discovery of processing stages. Despite its various, strong theoretical premises, the AFM did surprisingly well. It seems that as long as the total CRT is less than 2 secs, many choice–reaction processes run off unidimensionally and without internal feedback loops, at least not between stages. Moreover, the AFM may be less strictly bound to discrete transmission than originally thought. Provided there is a constant asymptotic activation, continuous flow and the AFM did not seem to conflict. Constant stage output, that is, utilizing all available information produced by a stage, seems the major real constraint of the AFM.

It is of interest in this respect that the AFM cannot be applied when a task permits asynchronous discrete processing. There is ample evidence that separable stimulus features can be independently processed, which should warn against any uncritical application of the AFM. Finally, the developments on relations between reaction processes and brain potentials proved highly relevant. They clearly exceed the study of choice reaction processes. In the wake of newly available techniques such as magnetic EEGs and other brain imaging techniques, the impact of neurophysiological correlates of performance will continue to grow (e.g., Mulder et al., 1995). However, as yet, it may be too early to assign a definitive locus in the information flow to EP components such as the P3 and the LRP.

It has been repeatedly emphasized that the discovery of processing stages has primarily classificatory value. Nothing is said about what is going on during a particular stage, nor is it clear whether the results on stage analysis are relevant to more complex tasks to which the AFM cannot be applied. In other words, it remains to be seen whether the stage structure of choice reactions constitutes a reliable starting point for the analysis of more complex skills. The alternative is that Külpe (1905) was correct in his suggestion that more complex activities are characterized by qualitatively different processing structures. In that case, the value of the analysis of choice–reactions would be limited to the small domain of a set of artificially created laboratory tasks that would undermine most of the argument in this book and deprive it of most of its applied claims. The issue of generalization will continue, therefore, to be a central theme of the book, embodied in the notion of back-to-back analysis.

Besides generalization to complex skills, successful delineation of processing stages in standard laboratory choice–reactions is likely to be a major behavioral paradigm with regard to the rapidly developing techniques of brain imaging and localization of mental functions. Generalization in this direction opens other avenues for application, in particular to the fields of neuropsychology and brain dysfunctioning. Thus, although still indirect, stage analysis is likely to have promising applied spin-offs.

Reaction Processes:
Effects of Variables

One conclusion from the previous chapter is that the AFM may define stages in terms of clusters of interacting variables but has nothing to say about the processes in a particular stage. The present chapter revisits the stages, with an emphasis on processes within stages, which is done by considering theoretical notions on the effects of prototypical, experimental variables, many of which appear to have applied significance as well. Figure 3.2 depicts three major categories that presumably are concerned with perception, response selection, and motor aspects. The perceptual group consists of three stages that are concerned with early processing (preprocessing), the analysis of stimulus features (feature extraction), and the interpretation of a stimulus as a meaningful entity (identification). On the motor side, motor programming and motor adjustment were distinguished, and a further sequencing stage was called upon in the case of composite motor responses (Fig. 3.5). The stage structure is the organizing principle of this chapter, but the discussion is not limited to AFM-related research because much of the pertinent research emanated from other theoretical arguments. Hence, the forthcoming sections are not rigidly coupled to the stages of Fig. 3.2.

Consideration of the processes that may underly individual stages meets the problem that the discussion may easily extend to central problems in perception and motor behavior, which are beyond the scope of this book. Thus, research on psychophysics, pattern perception, word recognition, motor control, movement patterning, and movement sequencing is only discussed with the aim of positioning the CRT results into a somewhat wider perspective. Hence, this chapter is not to be read as, and, indeed, is far away from, a treatise on perception and motor behavior. It is rather a matter of *capita selecta*, some of which are indeed related to perception and action, whereas others are actually neglected topics in texts on perception and motor behavior.

PREPROCESSING

Stimulus intensity, or better stimulus contrast,[1] is listed in Fig. 3.2 as a prototypical variable affecting preprocessing. This stage presumably refers to peripheral afferent conduction, perhaps extending to registration in the sensory projection areas. In the context of stage analysis, stimulus contrast may well have gained the status of prototypical because it is one of the few areas of sensory research in which C(RT) has been really relevant. The basic finding is that RT decreases as stimulus intensity increases until an asymptote is reached. Pieron (1920) proposed

$$RT = \frac{a}{i^n} + k \qquad (1)$$

as a functional relation between RT and intensity (i), where k is an irreducible minimum, a is a time constant, and n is an exponent determined by sensory modality. As i increases, the first term approaches zero, leaving k as the ultimate limit of RT. This has been viewed as a physiological limit, but as Luce (1986) noted, k equally reflects differences in measurement among laboratories. Luce also discussed the problem that the value of the asymptote k depends on the exponent n. The point is that asymptotic RT is faster for auditory and tactile stimuli than for visual stimuli. This implies that the impact of stimulus intensity depends on sensory modality. With this restriction in mind, reasonable fits have been found to Pieron's (1920) Equation 1, in particular for auditory stimuli (e.g., Kohfeld, Santee, & Wallace, 1981). RT decreases rapidly as intensity increases in the lower regions of auditory and visual intensity. On a dB scale, some 50 msec may be gained when intensity is varied between 50 dB and 110 dB, at which level the asymptote is reached.

In the visual domain, RT appears to vary more strongly in the range of low intensities than predicted by Pieron's (1920) equation. This may be due to the fact that cones are less sensitive to light. Below a certain intensity, the rods are fully responsible for sensory processing, which may be reflected by an additional increase in RT (Kohfeld, 1971). In line with this suggestion, RT proved to be relatively fast for rod-sensitive blue light in the case of

---

[1]The ratio between the luminances of a stimulus and its background is referred to as contrast. When referring to "intensity," it is assumed that the luminance of the background is constant and at least moderate. Luminances of stimuli and background depend on the reflectance of objects.

low-luminance stimuli, whereas at a higher luminance, RT was faster for cone-sensitive red light. Size and duration of a visual stimulus also have some effect on RT, which, albeit much less clearly, mimics the psychophysical effects of spatial and temporal summation on the sensory threshold. The effect of stimulus duration is small but in line with temporal summation; it is mainly found when stimulus duration is less than 100 msec (Mansfield, 1973). Similarly, RT is slightly faster as a visual stimulus occupies a wider area (e.g., Teichner & Krebs, 1972). In view of the rapid decline of visual acuity in the periphery, it is not surprising to find an interaction of the effects of stimulus contrast and retinal eccentricity on RT. In the case of auditory stimuli, RT appears sensitive to the relation between loudness and pitch; thus, at a constant dBSPL, RT is longer as pitch is lower (Woodworth, 1938).

The aforementioned discussion shows that RT reflects various main properties of sensory processing. However, behavioral research on sensory functions is almost completely dominated by psychophysics, probably due to the suspicion that the study of sensory processes will not gain from RT beyond what can be derived from psychophysical evidence. This is not unrealistic because the transition from detecting to not detecting is essential for assessing sensory performance limits, and, moreover, C(RT) is unreliable for near-threshold stimuli. On the other hand, C(RT) certainly adds to the understanding of sensory processing. For example, it shows that once above threshold, processing efficiency is not immediately optimal but continues to improve as stimulus intensity becomes stronger (e.g., van der Molen & Keuss, 1979). Analysis of above-threshold stimuli has not been a major issue in sensory perception but is actually quite relevant to creating optimal sensory conditions in real-life tasks.

Along the lines of signal-detection theory, most single-process models of C(RT) have stressed the distinction between sensory effects and decisional effects in the relation between stimulus intensity and RT. For example, the variable criterion model (chap. 2) proposed that C(RT) is a joint function of the rate of accrual of sensory evidence and the level of the response criterion (Fig. 2.1). Indeed, there is ample evidence from physiological recordings in the retina, from single-cell recordings in the ganglion cells, and from the early components of the EP that stimulus intensity affects the rate of firing (Näätänen, 1992; Nissen, 1977), which agrees with the notion of accrual of sensory evidence.

As argued, the variable criterion model predicts that effects of variables affecting accrual should interact with those affecting the criterion (Fig. 2.1). Such interactions have actually been found on various occasions. For example, Loveless and Sanford (1974) found that RT in the case of a low-intensity stimulus suffered more from a perceptual set instruction than a high-intensity stimulus. A perceptual set should raise the criterion, so most effect should be on RT for the weaker signal. The model equally predicts the finding that the effect of speed or accuracy instruction and the effect of the proportion of catch trials interact with that of auditory stimulus intensity (Grice, Hunt, Kushner, & Morrow, 1974). In the same way, auditory stimulus intensity proved to have a larger effect in mixed blocks than in pure blocks (Grice & Hunter, 1964; Murray, 1970). Grice (1968) proposed that due to uncertainty about stimulus intensity at each particular trial, individuals raise their criterion in mixed blocks.

The variable criterion model can also account for the observed interaction of the effects of foreperiod duration and of auditory stimulus intensity (Sanders, 1975a; Sanders & Wertheim, 1973) by assuming that due to less readiness to respond, the criterion is raised at a long foreperiod. However, the model has a problem explaining that the effect of block type (mixed–pure) and of foreperiod duration were additive to that of stimulus intensity (1) when auditory stimulus intensity ranged from 30dBA to 70 dBA and (2) when visual stimulus intensity was varied some 3 log units (Niemi, 1979; Sanders, 1977; van Duren & Sanders, 1988). This finding cannot be ascribed to non-linear accrual of sensory activation near the asymptote. In that case, the interaction of effects of stimulus intensity and of variables affecting the criterion level should be even more pronounced.

A stage model of RT (Fig. 3.2) predicts additive effects of stimulus intensity as a typical input variable and foreperiod duration as a typical output variable. In other words, the stage model adheres to independent effects of d' and β, as assumed by signal-detection theory. Yet, a stage model has an obvious problem accounting for the previously described instances of interaction. As a solution, it was suggested that at a certain range of intensities, stimuli are immediately arousing, which has the effect that the stage structure is bypassed (chap. 3). As with the variable criterion model, immediate arousal implies that the effect of stimulus intensity on RT is not merely due to accrual of information. However, the additional factor is supposed to consist of a bottom-up activation of the response system rather than of a top-down change in criterion setting.

Stimulus Modality

Given a normal intensity level, visual RT is some 40 ms faster than an auditory RT. This could be due to faster auditory peripheral conduction, although it has also been seen as reflecting a difference in stimulus energy (R. Elliott, 1968; Niemi & Lehtonen, 1982). Thus, normal visual stimuli might contain less stimulus energy than normal auditory stimuli. However, single-cell recordings and EP measures have shown relatively slow processes in the retina, suggestive of genuine sensory differences in peripheral conduction time. When the effect of stimulus modality on RT is sensory, it should not be affected by variations in central processing. Indeed, the differences between visual and auditory RT and CRT are about the same and do not appear to change when varying central processing demands such as S–R compatibility (e.g., Neumann, Tappe, & Niepel, 1995).

It is noteworthy that studies on perceived temporal order have shown that an auditory stimulus and a visual one are subjectively simultaneous when the auditory stimulus is presented slightly before the visual one (Neumann, Niepel, & Tappe, 1994). This could argue against a faster auditory–sensory processing speed. Alternatively, the effect may be due to processes involved in simultaneity judgments that override the effect of faster auditory, peripheral conduction. In a two-choice reaction task, Neumann et al. (1995) presented individuals with a precue[2] briefly in advance of each trial, instructing them about the S–R mapping that was required at that trial, that is, compatible or incompatible. The results confirmed that irrespective of compatibility, CRT for auditory stimuli was faster than for visual stimuli, but this was only found when the interval between precue and imperative signal (SOA) exceeded 500 msec. When SOA was less than 170 msec, visual as well as auditory CRTs increased, which may reflect a lack of time for implementing the instruction. In addition auditory CRT was longer than visual CRT at a short SOA, which suggests that the central process of implementing the S–R rule was overriding the peripheral effect. This might be related to the phenomenon of visual dominance, which will be discussed elsewhere. The results of Neumann et al. (1995) demonstrate that RT measures have their own merit in the analysis of sensory processes.

Applications.   Almost all applications of research on sensory processing stem from psychophysics, which is beyond the scope of the present discussion. Yet, there are a few occasions in which C(RT) measures are of additional interest. For instance, it is trivial that low contrast implies poor visibility and deficient detection, but it is less evident that above threshold, an effect of lower contrast still persists in C(RT). Thus, in one study, the speed of checking digits was measured as a function of their luminance and their reflectance (gray vs. black ink on white paper), both in above-threshold conditions. At a low luminance (<10 cd/m^2), contrast had a considerable effect on processing speed, whereas, irrespective of contrast, a luminance of 100 cd/m^2 always showed maximal processing speed (S. W. Smith & Rea, 1979). In some other tasks, maximal speed was only reached at an illumination level of 100 to 1,000 lux, depending on required precision and discrimination of fine detail (C. Bennett et al., 1977). Maximal response speed is obviously relevant in tasks such as driving or flying, in which rapid responding is essential. Thus, the relation between C(RT) and stimulus contrast adds to the evidence from psychophysical research. In this regard, it is not surprising that C(RT) data have played an important part in the debate on the optimal

---

[2]The results of this study proved not to be affected by the modality of the precue.

level of workplace illumination. Estimates from earlier psychophysical studies had proven to be unreasonably high (Boyce, 1981), mainly due to unwarranted generalization from threshold data to real life. Measures of processing speed suggest much lower levels of optimal illumination. These have now been commonly implemented (Sanders & McCormick, 1992).

The relation between C(RT) and stimulus contrast should not be taken to imply that a high contrast always leads to faster and more reliable responses. Thus, in the visual domain, there is the well-known problem that high illumination causes glare. In the auditory domain, van der Molen and Keuss (1979) found CRT to decrease as a function of intensity, but CRT increased again when intensity exceeded 90 dBA. In contrast, RT continued to decrease at high intensities. The negative effect of a high intensity on CRT may be due to an effect of counteracting immediate arousal elicited by a loud auditory stimulus, which is particularly harmful in the case of choice reactions (Sanders, 1977). High-intensity warning stimuli may well be equally harmful. For example, a loud horn signal in traffic is likely to elicit an ill-considered response rather than a warning to potential danger. When both loud and weak auditory warning stimuli occur, responses to weak stimuli slow down or tend to be missed (Grice et al., 1974), so one should avoid variations in loudness when using different warning stimuli.

The basic literature provides various guidelines for visual or auditory warning stimuli. Auditory stimuli are detected faster and with greater accuracy. Aside from faster sensory transmission, auditory stimuli have better sensory coupling, which refers to the link between the source of stimulation and the sensory receptors. In addition, eye blinks and movements of eyes and head increase the probability that a visual alarm will be missed. On the other hand, auditory warning stimuli have the disadvantage that they may arouse and distract, so they should be fairly rare. Auditory and visual warnings also differ in specificity. One cannot use more than a couple of alternative auditory stimuli as an index for relative urgency without running the risk of affecting workload or of eliciting a startle response (e.g., Sorkin, Kantowitz, & Kantowitz, 1988). Thus, auditory alarms are always less specific than visual alarms. As a result, a combination of more aspecific auditory and specific visual alarms may be best. Localizing a visual target among many other visual stimuli is easily achieved by stroboscopic or intermittent presentation, conditions that are insensitive to the loss in acuity in the periphery.

FEATURE EXTRACTION

It is commonly known that Gestaltists stressed perceiving a "whole" and the priority of the whole over its parts (Köhler, 1947). Yet, there are many reasons to believe that analyzing features is essential to perceiving and identifying objects and patterns. One concerns focused attention, where feature analysis of objects through activation maps is a prime assumption (e.g., Treisman, 1993). Feature analysis is also an important stage in models on word and letter perception (e.g., Rumelhart & McClelland, 1982). Again, research on visual search (chap. 7) and on asynchronous discrete processing (chap. 3) has provided ample evidence that stimulus analysis may be restricted to feature analysis and that a stimulus need not always be encoded and identified in full. What, then, remains of the Gestalt adage that the "whole precedes its parts"? Two lines of evidence may be of interest in this regard, namely, Garner's (1974) distinction between separable and integral stimulus features, and the research on the forest and the trees, initiated by Navon (1977).

Separable Versus Integral Features

Are there specific stimulus features that are functional units in the sense that they can be separately processed? This question was at the basis of Garner's (1974) distinction between separable and integral stimulus features. Two features are separable when the level of one feature can be changed without affecting the level of the other. For example, a change in color does not affect the shape of a stimulus, and vice versa. Again, a horizontal line and a vertical line, both radiating from a dot, are separable because the length of one line can be specified without affecting the length of the other. In contrast, two integral features cannot be changed without the one affecting the other. Examples are height and width of a rectangle (Fig. 4.1) and color and brightness of an object. As discussed in chapter 3, J. Miller (1982) found that variation of size and shape of a letter—that is, separable features—elicited an independent, partial response of the hand with which the response should occur. In another experiment, Miller (1982) varied visual similarity among letters and letter shape. The stimulus alternatives were {M,N,U,V}; visual similarity (MN vs. UV) indicated whether the response should be carried out with either the left (MN) or the right (UV) hand, whereas letter shape (e.g., M vs. N) indicated the finger to respond with, namely, the index (M) or middle (N) finger. The results showed that in these conditions, a partial response of the hand was not independently elicited. This was taken to imply that in contrast to shape and size, letter similarity and letter shape are integral features that cannot be independently transmitted to the next stage.

Garner's (1974) original studies on separable versus integral features were carried out with card sorting. For example, participants were instructed to sort cards on the basis of the height of a rectangle, but its width should be ignored. One finding was that when height and width were redundant, that is, correlated, rectangles were sorted more rapidly than when height and width varied orthogonally (Garner & Felfoldy, 1970). When correlated, the

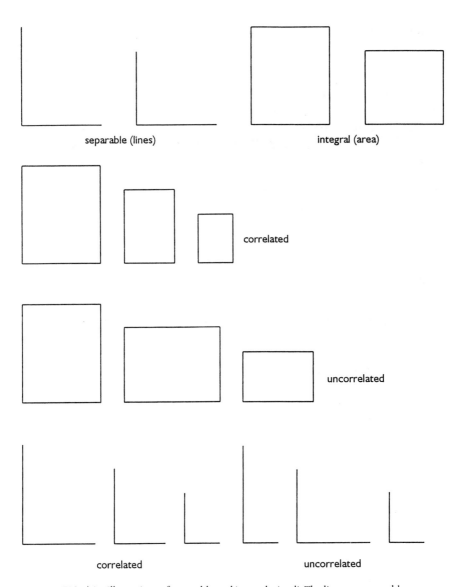

FIG. 4.1. Illustrations of separable and integral stimuli. The lines are separable because one may be changed without affecting the other. The areas are determined by a combination of two lines so that a change in one line affects the total area. Correlation between components has a strong effect on integral, but not on separable, stimuli.

irrelevant feature supported the relevant one, whereas the irrelevant feature distracted in the orthogonal case. This is a clear illustration that integral features cannot be selectively ignored or analyzed on their own. Indeed, the whole rectangle precedes and, therefore, clouds the constituent parts. In contrast, a separable, irrelevant feature can easily be ignored or gated (Posner, 1964), which is not unexpected when they are separately processed. The result is that an irrelevant, orthogonal, separable feature does not distract, nor does an irrelevant, correlated, separable feature aid. Separable features only gain from redundancy when they are degraded or difficult to perceive otherwise. In that case, correlation among separable features is beneficial for the fairly trivial reason that one may rely on a correlated, irrelevant feature when a relevant one happens to be missed.

With respect to integral features, it is essential to distinguish positive and negative correlations of features. The point is that a positive correlation of, for example, height and width of a rectangle means that the shape remains the same, whereas its size varies (Fig. 4.1). Alternatively, a negative correlation brings about different shapes, even though the total surface remains the same (as seen later in Fig. 4.3A). Changes in shape are said to create a new emergent property that adds to the discriminability of the rectangles and, hence, to speed in card sorting. Emergent-form properties depend on identity and arrangement of all parts and cannot be derived from a single feature (Pomerantz, 1986). Thus, given integral features, an emergent property may either arise or not arise, depending on how shape or size change. Emergent properties are particularly relevant in regard to the design of object displays (Carswell & Wickens, 1996).

This fairly simple picture is complicated by the fact that integrality versus separability of features is a continuuum rather than a dichotomy. Features may be more-or-less separable or integral (e.g., Carswell & Wickens, 1987). Yet, as for the discussion on the relative role of the whole and the parts, separable features function quite independently in that they may be processed without identification of the total pattern. In contrast, integral features are intrinsically related to the total pattern. They may aid identifying the total pattern but are not processed in isolation.

Applications. Data presentation in process control is still often a matter of separate displays about all measures. This means that operators have the task of integrating the evidence in order to diagnose the status of a process. Yet, an error is often characterized by a set or syndrome of deviations that is not readily derived from individual displays. Thus, at the time of the crisis at the Three Mile Island nuclear power plant, the values of some 40 to 50 displays were in disorder, a myriad that is very hard to integrate. A solution may be to construct an integral display in which a set of measures is represented by a single shape that is diagnostic for a certain error. One example of an object display (Fig. 4.2B) stems from Barnett and Wickens (1988). It illustrates the case in which two variables are displayed as separate bar graphs or as an integrated unit in which the surface of the integrated unit shows the product of the two variables. If the product is the relevant variable, the surface is obviously a better display than two bar graphs.

Figure 4.2A shows another example of an object display that has been proposed for a nuclear control room (Woods, Wise, & Hanes, 1981) and for a representation of a physiological profile in intensive care (C. A. Green, Logie, Gilhooly, Ross, & Ronald, 1996). It displays a number of variables as spokes on a polygon. The processes are in their normal state when all spokes have the same length, but a pattern of deviations reflects a specific problem. Coury and Boulette (1992) studied the polygon display when individuals were under time stress and found it superior to separate displays when a specific configuration was connected to a specific error. It was inferior, though, when configurations could be between potential error sources. The problem was that when ambiguous, an object display loses the advantage of a direct signature of the error. Hughes and MacRae (1994) varied the number of spokes of the polygon from 4 to 20. They found no evidence for slower fault detection in the case of a larger number of vertices, which suggests that the complete pattern was holistically processed. However, Hughes and MacRae asked only for global detection of any deviation from an otherwise regular polygon. RT increased as a function of the number of vertices in the case of an irregular polygon in which the individual vertices were important. This implies that the polygon display has the most potential when the number of spokes is limited (Greaney & MacRae, 1996).

Along the same lines, Wickens (1992) stressed that object and configural displays are not always satisfactory because the values of individual variables are perceived less well. It is easy to imagine that one wants to avoid clouding individual parameter values while, at the same time, retaining the diagnostic properties of the total pattern. One compromise might actually be a variant on a traditional bar graph. Bar graphs are separable, but when positioned sufficiently close together, the lengths of the bars may constitute an object-like pattern (Fig. 4.3B). Yet, a function-like representation is clearly superior in regard to perceiving general trends. It is more integral, whereas individual data points are not clouded. Another option is to stress individual elements by increasing their perceptual salience through color coding or inserting incidental number values in the configuration.

Another issue with respect to diagnostic displays is that their quality depends on how well the display corresponds to the operator's mental model, or domain semantics (Woods, 1991), of a process. For example, fault diagnosis on the basis of deviations from a regular polygon bears little relationship to an operator's mental model of the processes in a nuclear power plant. Recently, K. B. Bennett, Toms, and Woods (1993) presented a case study on

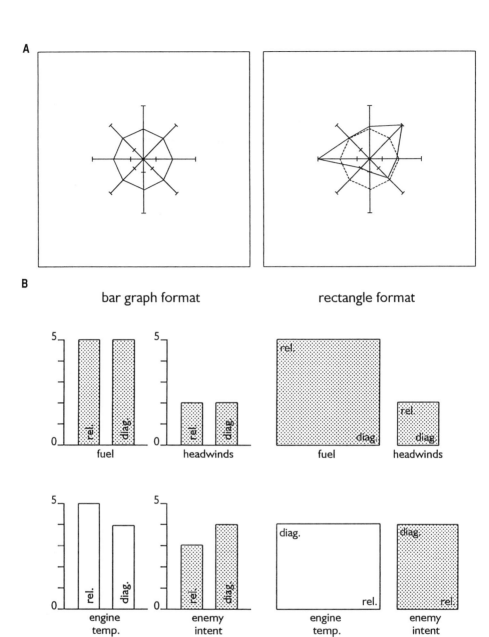

FIG. 4.2. Illustrations of integral displays. A. Polygon diagnostic display. From Woods, D. D., Wise, J. A., & Hanes, L. F. (1981). An evaluation of nuclear power plant safety parameter display systems. *Proceedings of the 25th annual meeting of the Human Factors Society*. Rochester, NY. Copyright © 1981 by the Human Factors and Ergonomics Society, Inc. Reproduced by permission. B. Bar graph and rectangle displays. From Barnett, B. J., & Wickens, C. D. (1988). Display proximity in multicue information integration: The benefit of boxes. *Human Factors, 30*, 15–24. Copyright © 1988 by the Human Factors and Ergonomics Society, Inc. Reproduced by permission.

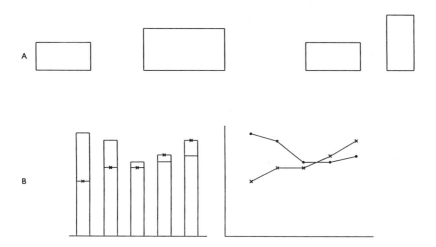

FIG. 4.3. A. Positively and negatively correlated integral dimensions. B. A separable histogram representation may be best for reading individual components. The integral graph representation is preferred for general trends.

the correspondence between a configural display and the domain semantics of how to manually control the water level in a boiler during the start-up of a power plant. Part of that problem was that (a) a correct control action showed an initial effect in the wrong direction, and (b) implementation of a control action took a considerable time, so its effect was not immediately visible. The emergent property of a newly designed configural display highlighted the future effect of a control action on the regulation of the water level. Thus, the impression of an ineffective action was eliminated.

Three-dimensional (3-D) object displays have interesting features. For instance, Ellis, McGreevy, and Hitchcock (1987) proposed a 3-D representation of air traffic, thus providing pilots with a greater situational awareness of surrounding traffic. The 3-D display had altitude as its third dimension and proved far superior to the traditional 2-D display in which symbols indicated the altitudes of other aircraft (Fig. 4.4). Again, Veltman, Gaillard, and van Breda (1995) found a 3-D "inside-out" radar display superior to a traditional 2-D display when participants had the additional task of focusing on a specific target in a simulated flight. Similarly, Sollenberg and Milgram (1993) found that a 3-D rotational display was superior in regard to pathfinding in neural brain imaging. The general superiority of 3-D displays reflects proximity compatibility (Wickens & Carswell, 1995) that refers to displays with mutually related components, emergent properties, and correspondence to an underlying mental representation of a situation or a process. Carswell and Wickens (1996) showed that both mutual relations and emergent properties contribute to the level of proximity compatibility. This is returned to later in this chapter when discussing compatibility.

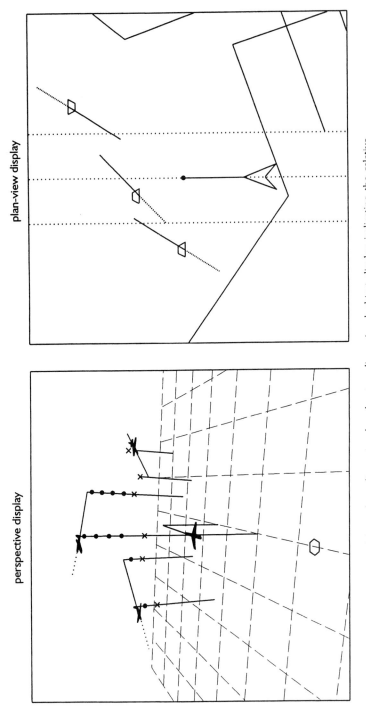

perspective display

plan-view display

FIG. 4.4. A three-dimensional and a two-dimensional object display indicating the relative positions of aircraft. From Ellis, S. R., McGreevy, M. W., & Hitchcock, R. J. (1987). Perspective traffic display format and air pilot traffic avoidance. *Human Factors, 29,* 371–382.

Forest and Trees

Navon (1977) presented individuals with a large global letter stimulus consisting of smaller local letters that were either corresponding, neutral, or conflicting (Fig. 4.5) with respect to the large one. The main finding was that CRT was longer when participants responded to the local letter than when they responded to the global letter, in particular when global and local letters conflicted. In line with the Gestalt axiom, Navon assumed global precedence, that is, the whole precedes the parts. Local elements are parts of an object, but they do not define it. Thus, the small Hs in Fig. 4.5 may together form either a large S or a large H. How does this result relate to the presumed role of feature analysis in stimulus identification?

The Navon (1977) study was followed by a flurry of research meant to delineate the conditions in which a global advantage is found. For instance, Lamb and Robertson (1988) varied the location in which a stimulus might appear and found that the global advantage effect was sensitive to attentional set. When the stimulus could appear in any of three locations, CRT was slower than when it was always in the center. More importantly, the increase in CRT was more pronounced for local letters than for global letters. This is consistent with the zoom lens notion (chap. 7) that attention may be divided over a larger area when letters may appear in different locations. Divided attention, though is particularly inefficient for detecting small local elements. Robertson, Egly, Lamb, and Kerth (1993) always presented letters in the center and precued either global or local letter identification with a .8 validity. When incorrectly cued to identify a local element, CRT to the

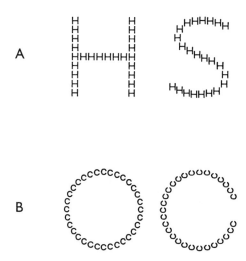

FIG. 4.5. Global and local perception of form. In Fig. 4.5B the role of eccentricity is controlled by using Landolt rings.

global stimulus increased, suggesting that the zoom lens had been set too narrow to allow rapid identification of the global form. On the other hand, an invalid global cue had less effect on identifying a local stimulus, suggesting that a little wider setting of the zoom lens still had enough resolution to identify a local stimulus without inflicting a delay in processing.

The global advantage also depends on perceptual properties of the stimuli. Thus, it is related to letter size in that it occurred only when the visual angle was less than 10°. However, Navon and Norman (1983) argued that as letter size increases, the global letter extends more to the periphery of the visual field, whereas some of the local letters can be perceived centrally. After deconfounding the effects of letter size and eccentricity, global advantage occurred, irrespective of visual angle. In this study, participants identified either a global circular letter, O or C, or the local constituent that consisted of small Landolt rings (Fig. 4.5B). The advantage of Landolt rings is that they minimize response conflict with the global letter. The global stimulus required letter naming—O or C—but the local one required indicating the position of the opening in the Landolt ring. In a control condition, a single local stimulus was presented at the same eccentricity as in the experimental condition. CRT proved about equally fast in either case, whereas CRT to the global letter was always faster, irrespective of visual angle. Hence, Navon and Norman concluded that the global advantage effect is perceptual and reflects that perceptual processing of a global shape is completed first and, therefore, leads to a faster CRT. Along the same lines, G. L. Shulman et al. (1986) suggested that lower spatial frequencies may dominate global letter, whereas higher spatial frequencies may dominate local letter processing. Together, the results on the "forest and the trees" do not suggest that feature extraction is a prerequisite for identification of a total pattern.

The generality of global letter advantage and its presumed perceptual locus have not remained undebated. For example, some studies have reported response conflict between letters, such as in a Stroop task. Naming a local letter might suffer from the presence of a conflicting global letter, whereas naming a global letter might suffer hardly from a conflicting local letter, although this does not preclude a perceptual locus of the global advantage effect. Kimchi (1992) argued that it is hard to differentiate between a perceptual locus and a decisional one because both stages play a part in the CRT.[3] She suggested that delineating the boundary conditions of the effect would be more promising than debating the locus in the information flow. In her subsequent research, she convincingly showed that the global advantage depended on how patterns had been structured. Patterns composed of many small elements were perceived as an overall form, with the local elements merely serving as texture. In contrast, patterns composed of

---

[3]The paradigm of the functional visual field (chap. 5) may be an interesting way of experimentally separating perceptual and decisional factors in the "forest and trees" paradigm.

a few relatively large elements were perceived as the sum of the figural parts. Thus, in the few-element patterns of Fig. 4.6, the local parts dominate, and global shape dominates in the multielement pattern. In support, Kimchi found that different-size, multielement patterns were judged as more similar when variations in size were brought about by changing the number of identical local elements. On the other hand, different-size, few-element patterns were considered as more similar when keeping the number of elements the same and increasing the size of the local elements. The transition from "many to few" elements appeared to occur at some seven units. Moreover, Kimchi found that the local and global features of few-element patterns behaved as integral dimensions, whereas those of multielement patterns behaved as separable dimensions. In a multielement pattern, one may

FIG. 4.6. Global or local perception is determined by the number of constituent elements. From Kimchi, R. (1992). Primacy of wholistic processing and global/local paradigm: A critical review. *Psychological Bulletin, 112,* 24–38. Copyright © 1992 by the American Psychological Association. Reprinted with permission.

change the global shape without affecting the texture. However, in few-element patterns, the global shape cannot change without changing the building stones. In other words, identifying parts in a multielement pattern is basically irrelevant, but it is essential in a few-element pattern.

The "forest and the trees" paradigm offers an interesting perspective on the role of features in perception. Local elements in a multielement object are not irrelevant but have the role of perceptual primitives, or physical material, of the total object. This means that in order to identify the object, they have to be processed but need not be semantically identified. The point is that feature extraction may occur on a physical–textural level but not on a semantic level, a contrast that will frequently recur in the discussion of visual selective attention (chap. 7). The situation is different in a few-element object. Here, each element is actually a total in itself, the sum of which makes a supertotal.

Applications. The previous discussion may be relevant to the construction of synthetic displays, for example, in air-traffic control, which always lack space for accommodating all relevant information. The results show that the elements of a symbol function as texture when consisting of more than some five or six smaller parts. In that case, an element can be perfectly identified, but it takes more time in comparison with the global symbol. Thus, a composite symbol, in which both the global shape and the local elements convey information, may be constructed. When the information contained in the global shape has priority over what is represented in the local elements, the number of local elements should be relatively large. In the case of equal priority, the number of building blocks should be reduced in order to obtain an equilibrium between global shape and local element. A further reduction would create priority of local elements.

Stimulus Quality

Research on feature extraction in the AFM tradition has been mainly concerned with variations in stimulus quality. In his original experiments, Sternberg (1969) degraded alphanumerics by superimposing a grid, whereas in other studies (e.g., Stanovich & Pachella, 1977), stimuli were degraded by blurring. However, these manipulations confound effects of luminance and stimulus quality. This may be prevented by using dotted stimuli surrounded by a dotted frame. Degradation is achieved by moving some dots from the frame to locations near the symbol. This has the effect that the stimulus is degraded, but the total luminance of the area remains the same. Thus deconfounded, the effects of stimulus contrast and stimulus quality were additive (Sanders, 1980a). The effects of stimulus quality and number of alternatives have often shown a small interaction, the size of which may depend on the actual number of alternatives. When a critical number of, for example, five or six alternatives is exceeded, it may be impossible to keep the mental representations, or logogens (Morton, 1969), of all alternatives simultaneously active. This, in turn, may render the situation more sensitive to stimulus degradation (Sanders, 1980a). Wertheim's (1979) finding that when participants track a moving stimulus with the eye, the effect of stimulus quality interacts with those of the frequency and the predictability of the moving stimulus, suggests that the effects of stimulus quality and retinal locus interact. The effects of stimulus quality and stimulus discriminability have been also found to interact, an effect that seems more pronounced when stimuli are harder to distinguish (Logsdon et al., 1984).

Van Duren and Sanders (1988) found an underadditive interaction of the effects of block type—blocked versus mixed presentation—and stimulus quality in that the effect of stimulus quality was less in the mixed condition than in the blocked condition (Fig. 4.7A), mainly due to poor performance in the case of intact stimuli. A similar underadditive effect was observed for the effects of block type and S–R compatibility, whereas the effects of block type and visual stimulus contrast were additive. Van Duren and Sanders proposed a dual-pathway model in which intact stimuli are processed along a fast holistic route, and degraded stimuli along a more time-consuming analytic route (Fig. 4.7C). In the mixed condition, participants opt for the analytic path because, albeit at the price of a loss in speed, intact stimuli may be processed along the analytic route, but degraded stimuli cannot be processed along the holistic route.

Los (1994) tested this view by presenting individuals with different types of stimulus degradation in pure and mixed blocks. One way of degrading was by adding dots in the way as described previously; another one was by omitting dots from the symbol. Adding dots depends on high-spatial frequency analyzers, whereas omitted dots may depend on low-spatial frequency analyzers. It is relevant in this regard that high- and low-spatial frequencies have been found to correspond with different neural structures in the visual cortex (e.g., DeValois, Yund, & Hepler, 1982). Los found evidence for two types of participants. One type responded faster when dots were added, and the other type was faster when dots were omitted. Either type showed the aforementioned underadditive interaction of stimulus quality and block type in that the speed of responding to the individually easier degradation suffered when mixed with the individually more difficult type in the same block. Los argued that this result cannot be explained by van Duren and Sanders' (1988) assumption of one efficient holistic route and one time-consuming analytic route. The point is that either degradation pattern, the added as well as the omitted dots, appeared to require its own analytic processing route. Thus, added dots cannot be processed along the route suitable for omitted dots, and vice versa (DeValois et al., 1982).

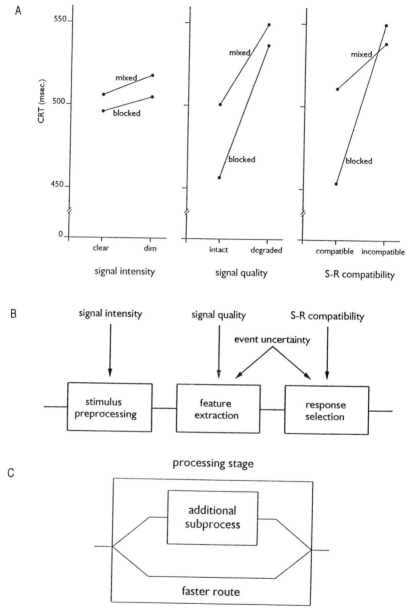

FIG. 4.7. A. Interactions of the effects of block type (mixed vs. blocked presentation) and those of stimulus contrast, stimulus quality, and S–R compatibility. B. The AFM interpretation of these results. C. The dual route explanation of the interactions of block type with stimulus quality and S–R compatibility. Reprinted from van Duren, L. L., & Sanders, A. F. (1988). On the robustness of the additive factors stage structure in blocked and mixed choice reaction designs. *Acta Psychologica, 69,* 83–94. Copyright © 1988 with kind permission of Elsevier Science-NL, Sara Burgerhartstraat 25, 1055 KV, Amsterdam, The Netherlands.

Los (1994) showed that using a processing route is not related to difficulty of discrimination. He varied difficulty by adding or omitting more or fewer dots and found no evidence for an interaction of the effects of difficulty and block type. This result suggests that as long as the same degradation principle is used, for example, added dots, all stimuli are handled by the same route, although somewhat slower as the stimuli become more degraded. In summary, Los' data show evidence for different parallel processing routes, each bound to a specific way of stimulus degradation, that is, adding versus omitting dots. The routes may be related to different spatial frequency analyzers, with some individuals doing better with the one route and some participants with the other.

When the processing routes for added and omitted dots are mutually exclusive, the underadditive interaction of block type and degradation type (added–omitted) remains to be explained. Los (1994) suggested that at the start of a trial in a mixed block, the slower route, that is, the one fit to handle the most difficult degradation pattern for that individual, has priority over the faster route, that is, the one fit to handle the easier degradation pattern for that individual. If the easier pattern is presented at that trial, a time-consuming shift is needed to the faster route, which explains why responding to the easier degradation type suffers more in the mixed trials condition. Usually, the effects of block type are ascribed to a strategic effect such as choosing a route (e.g., Sperling & Dosher, 1986). In contrast, Los argued in favor of a stimulus-driven view. The most recently used route may persist, more so as processing has become more complex. This view is related to evidence on mental inertia from studies on shifting-task set, which is discussed in chapter 8 (Allport et al., 1994).

Applications. Degradation is found in a variety of real-life conditions. Objects may be intentionally degraded, as in camouflage. On other occasions, as in brightness amplification or when driving in fog, blurred objects have to be identified. There have been attempts to determine the minimal number of lines or the amount of required visible detail on a screen needed to identify a stimulus, but these attempts have not led to unequivocal results. The problem is that correct identification of a degraded stimulus, for example, a camouflaged armored vehicle, depends on small, object-specific details. The consequence is that no general prescription can be formulated about the minimal line density aside from the trivial statement that degradation is likely to be less as line density is higher.

Alphanumeric Discrimination

Research on feature extraction is particularly concerned with the nature and the relevance of features that, together, constitute a stimulus. For instance, legibility of a Gothic letter is poor because it has many irrelevant curves. In order to improve discrimination, the differences between letters with similar features, such as *i*, *l*, and *c*, *e*, should be stressed. For the same reason, the stroke and tail length of ascenders and descenders should be at least 40% of the total letter (M. Sanders & McCormick, 1992). Letter features consist foremost of straight and circular segments that may have a horizontal, a vertical or an oblique orientation and that may also differ in size, for example, in lowercase and uppercase letters. The confusion matrix of Fig. 4.8 illustrates that letter discriminability is inversely related to the number of common features.

Numerics may be easily discriminated when presented singly, but they lose that property when presented together with other digits. Thus, 4 and 7 share only a few features, but they do much less well in the context of a larger group of identical digits (e.g., 384 vs. 387). Again, there is unanimous evidence that reading text in lowercase is faster than in uppercase (e.g., Poulton, 1967), presumably because lowercase letters have more distinct features (e.g., dog, cat vs. DOG, CAT). The superiority of reading lowercase letters has been established for text as well as for road signs.

IDENTIFICATION

Discrimination, identification, recognition, and mental rotation are among the variables that affect identification. The final product of holistic processing may be a match of a perceptual code to its representation in memory.

Discrimination

Research on stimulus discrimination belongs to the classical realm of psychophysics and is at the basis of signal-detection theory. Discrimination is also a key issue in pattern perception (e.g., Garner, 1974). In regard to CRT, stimulus discrimination is prominent in single-process models. Thus, in chapter 2, the role of SAT in easily and poorly discriminated stimuli was a recurrent theme, and the relation between discriminability and CRT was different for for near- and above-threshold stimuli. When stimuli are near threshold, CRT was found to vary linearly with the absolute difference in similarity among the alternatives, whereas the relation was logarithmic when the stimuli were sufficiently above threshold. The point is that once stimuli are discriminable, a further improvement does not speed up CRT.

Most studies on perceptual discrimination in a single-process context varied in a physical dimension such as line length (Shallice & Vickers, 1964) or line orientation (P. L. Smith & Vickers, 1988). Such stimuli may depend less on prototypical representations in memory and, therefore, less on holistic processing (Posner & Keele, 1968). If this were valid, single-process models would be concerned with feature extraction rather than with stimulus iden-

Response

S	A	B	C	D	E	F	G	H	I	J	K	L	M	N	O	P	Q	R	S	T	U	V	W	X	Y	Z
A	.633	.006	.002	.002	.004	.008	.006	.020	.016	.040	.052	.013	.005	.027	.006	.007	.004	.065	.011	.005	.001	.004	.008	.024	.007	.024
B	.018	.393	.007	.053	.013	.002	.150	.014	.001	.010	.007	.002	.002	.010	.037	.012	.064	.092	.087	.002	.009	.002	.007	.000	.002	.004
C	.002	.002	.712	.006	.049	.014	.101	.001	.006	.002	.003	.018	.000	.003	.017	.007	.013	.011	.007	.009	.003	.003	.000	.001	.002	.006
D	.004	.035	.006	.680	.004	.003	.010	.003	.006	.043	.002	.002	.002	.008	.042	.060	.023	.018	.014	.003	.016	.002	.004	.001	.006	.007
E	.004	.042	.022	.006	.350	.183	.034	.021	.038	.008	.020	.029	.002	.016	.007	.055	.008	.067	.023	.032	.007	.004	.002	.003	.010	.007
F	.011	.010	.011	.002	.057	.367	.013	.032	.052	.018	.021	.018	.008	.017	.003	.185	.002	.069	.007	.050	.008	.004	.007	.002	.013	.013
G	.007	.029	.050	.018	.018	.002	.599	.009	.002	.004	.001	.004	.001	.009	.051	.009	.103	.034	.023	.007	.013	.003	.002	.000	.000	.002
H	.015	.018	.002	.010	.007	.011	.008	.414	.035	.032	.015	.013	.101	.108	.007	.012	.006	.067	.004	.023	.018	.006	.052	.002	.013	.003
I	.002	.003	.011	.002	.015	.025	.002	.008	.608	.082	.004	.068	.002	.003	.002	.007	.001	.004	.007	.093	.006	.004	.001	.004	.016	.020
J	.008	.004	.003	.005	.002	.007	.004	.026	.078	.647	.012	.024	.005	.013	.004	.007	.007	.007	.006	.021	.046	.013	.015	.006	.018	.018
K	.002	.002	.009	.002	.008	.023	.002	.010	.014	.015	.385	.011	.011	.014	.000	.015	.001	.047	.005	.021	.006	.022	.022	.173	.114	.063
L	.008	.005	.013	.004	.019	.004	.001	.022	.147	.052	.014	.537	.005	.011	.005	.008	.005	.008	.009	.045	.022	.010	.014	.004	.011	.016
M	.005	.011	.005	.003	.006	.009	.004	.151	.006	.012	.055	.003	.437	.072	.006	.018	.005	.052	.006	.024	.014	.007	.039	.027	.021	.002
N	.019	.012	.001	.006	.001	.002	.004	.022	.005	.008	.108	.013	.027	.494	.001	.004	.003	.108	.013	.006	.005	.020	.026	.060	.028	.003
O	.001	.016	.098	.092	.002	.004	.153	.001	.004	.009	.001	.003	.000	.004	.383	.020	.142	.013	.023	.003	.014	.002	.002	.001	.004	.003
P	.018	.023	.017	.032	.018	.084	.015	.022	.002	.008	.005	.005	.006	.003	.015	.567	.007	.088	.021	.006	.013	.004	.005	.003	.006	.007
Q	.005	.014	.106	.083	.001	.003	.183	.003	.001	.011	.002	.007	.001	.002	.252	.004	.249	.011	.028	.000	.016	.003	.004	.001	.003	.006
R	.022	.022	.015	.019	.015	.036	.046	.040	.000	.006	.013	.002	.005	.023	.023	.131	.042	.444	.044	.011	.008	.002	.007	.007	.013	.003
S	.007	.068	.043	.010	.074	.020	.204	.006	.013	.010	.015	.008	.002	.013	.016	.017	.027	.101	.301	.018	.006	.004	.002	.003	.004	.009
T	.004	.002	.003	.002	.004	.069	.002	.013	.168	.036	.007	.031	.004	.012	.002	.025	.001	.011	.002	.520	.007	.013	.002	.006	.032	.022
U	.004	.003	.012	.013	.002	.002	.037	.011	.004	.028	.005	.021	.012	.025	.021	.007	.014	.005	.002	.006	.628	.049	.082	.002	.006	.000
V	.001	.002	.002	.005	.000	.013	.004	.004	.025	.021	.018	.007	.002	.025	.006	.013	.002	.015	.003	.013	.047	.528	.043	.017	.182	.001
W	.041	.014	.001	.005	.003	.007	.006	.068	.004	.013	.157	.009	.089	.083	.007	.020	.007	.127	.008	.002	.013	.005	.187	.100	.013	.010
X	.002	.001	.000	.001	.002	.005	.002	.002	.009	.016	.086	.007	.005	.023	.001	.003	.000	.022	.004	.013	.002	.037	.011	.503	.211	.034
Y	.002	.001	.000	.002	.000	.023	.000	.005	.020	.023	.012	.004	.003	.016	.001	.022	.001	.007	.002	.031	.004	.027	.007	.059	.657	.074
Z	.009	.001	.002	.002	.007	.006	.002	.003	.011	.028	.015	.013	.001	.004	.002	.003	.001	.007	.010	.014	.002	.006	.003	.027	.058	.760

Note - S = stimulus

FIG. 4.8. A confusion matrix of letters. From van der Heijden, A. H. C., Malhas, M. S. M., & Roovaart, B. P. (1984). An empirical inter-letter confusion matrix for continuous line capitals. *Perception & Psychophysics*, 35, 85–88. Reprinted by permission of Psychonomic Society, Inc.

131

tification. This would actually agree with the notion of accrual of evidence. In contrast, AFM studies usually varied in similarity among alphanumerics and words, both of which are likely to depend on memory representations. For example, the shape of visually similar symbols—for example, the "A" and the "H"—may be manipulated to render them more-or-less discriminable. The results suggest that discrimination affects both feature extraction and identification. This suggests that analytical as well as holistic processes play a part.

Letter Identification

Letter identification is more than integrating a set of features. For instance, LaBerge (1973) found that irrespective of advance information about whether to expect a letter or a nonsense symbol, participants could always efficiently identify the letter symbol. In contrast, a nonsense symbol was processed more efficiently when participants knew in advance that a nonsense symbol would be presented. LaBerge concluded that letter identification relied on stable memorial representations, or templates, whereas templates of nonsense symbols were constructed ad hoc before stimulus presentation. The effect here is that the nonsense symbol benefited from advance information.

Different codes have been found to develop in parallel when participants identify a verbal symbol. Thus, the speed of matching two letters is faster when the match is based on physical identity (a,a) rather than on name identity (a,A), which, in turn, is faster than category matching (a,e; both vowels). Posner (1978) argued that these results cannot be explained by a sequence of stages, for example, an orthographic followed by a phonological followed by a categorical stage. The problem is that variables affecting the time to establish the orthographic code should affect the name and category identity matches as well because a delay of the first orthographic stage would propagate through the remaining stages. Yet, the effect of visual stimulus similarity did not affect the speed of name–identity matches, suggesting parallel development of orthographic and phonological codes. From the perspective of stage analysis, the three codes refer to processes within a single stage.

The Word-Superiority Effect

Letters are more than a bundle of features and in the same way, words are more than a bundle of letters (Wickens, 1992). It has been known for some time that letters in a word can be identified more accurately than letters in a random sequence, a situation that might reflect postperceptual memory processes rather than word perception. Once a word is known, its constituent letters can be reconstructed from memory. This is impossible in the case of a random letter sequence. A phenomenon that seriously suggests a perceptual effect, however, is the word-superiority effect, first described by Reicher (1969). Reicher asked participants to make a forced choice about a particular letter (e.g., an *r* or an *n*) as (a) part of a tachistoscopically viewed word (e.g., ha*r*d or ha*n*d), (b) part of a nonword, or (c) a single letter surrounded by asterisks (e.g., **r*, **n*). The letter was identified with more accuracy when it was part of a word than when it was surrounded by asterisks. Inference of the letter from memory is excluded because *hand* and *hard* are both frequently used words. Reicher's finding proved to be independent of word shape (lowercase and uppercase), to extend to pseudowords, and to occur irrespective of letter constraints (J. C. Johnston, 1978). The word-superiority effect appears to be stronger when a word is presented on a high-contrast display followed by a pattern mask than when a word is presented in low contrast followed by a blank mask.

An influential model on letter perception in words was formulated by J. C. McClelland and Rumelhart (1981) and Rumelhart and McClelland (1982). The model was inspired by the connectionist notion that processing a word occurs in levels, each of which consists of an activation pattern of elementary processing units. The Rumelhart and McClelland model has three processing levels dealing with features, letters, and words. Activations are passed on and fed back between levels. Thus, units defining the letter /c/ at the letter level have an activating connection to units defining the word /cat/ at the word level, but activation is also fed back from /cat/ to the individual letters. In this way, information flows bottom-up from feature extraction to word identification and is propagated top-down from word meaning to feature level. Therefore, identification is determined by the joint effect from both bottom-up and top-down processes.

A simplified impression of the model is given in Fig. 4.9. Units between levels activate each other, so /t/ does not only activate /time/ but also many other word representations containing a /t/. Connections within a level are largely inhibitory in order to decrease activation of competing units (J. L. McClelland, 1987). The point is that perceptual stability requires that only one representation should win the race. The total input to any individual unit is the weighted average of all activations and inhibitions. Its activation is determined by the product of the sum of the inputs and the difference between the maximal (or minimal) activation of that unit and its present activation. Thus, if a unit is already near its maximum, further activation has little additional effect (the δ rule). The various activations and inhibitions are integrated over time until a certain pattern has become sufficiently dominant to qualify as the presented word.

The word-superiority effect is due to the fact that letters within a word benefit from feedback from the winning word to the letter level. This feedback drives the individual letters of that word to a higher activation level

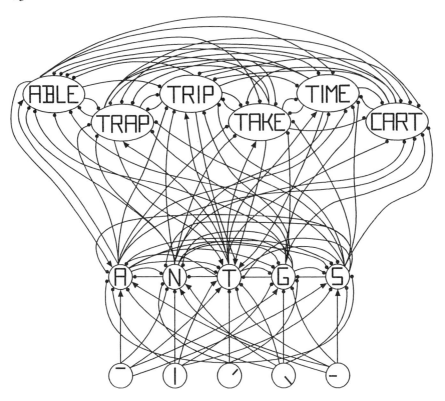

FIG. 4.9. A connectionist type of model on letter and word perception. Processing flows bottom-up from feature extraction to letter perception and from letter perception to word perception. It flows top down from word to letter perception. Arrows activate and dots inhibit. From Rumelhart, D. E., & McClelland, J. L. (1981). An interactive activation model of context effects in letter perception. Part 2: The contextual enhancement effect and some tests and extensions of the model. *Psychological Review, 88,* 375–407. Copyright © 1981 by the American Psychological Association. Reprinted with permission.

in comparison with that of an isolated letter. When disrupted by a pattern mask, the letter level is faced with spurious activations that disrupt the normal buildup of activation and rapidly deactivate the activation pattern, thus reducing the probability of correct letter identification. A word is encoded on a higher level and is, therefore, affected somewhat later by the pattern mask. Therefore, the word level can continue its feedback to the lower levels a little longer. This delays the deactivation of the letters and enhances the probability of correct letter identification. In conditions of low contrast and a blank mask, the quality of all information is poor. Hence, activation will build up slower at all levels. Hence, there is less feedback from the word level and, consequently, less word superiority.

The Rumelhart and McClelland (1982) model neither assumes that a word consists of the sum of its constituent letters nor, as held by whole-word notions, that a word is only indirectly related to its constituent letters. The decisive process in word recognition is the interplay among bottom-up and top-down processes in a continuous, interactive feedforward–feedback loop. In this sense, the J. C. McClelland and Rumelhart (1981) model is clearly beyond the AFM. Still, the basic levels, that is, feature extraction and iden- tification of letters and words, occur equally in the stage structure of CRT. This suggests that at least for word perception, some of the basic stages that were "discovered" by the AFM continue to play a part, which sounds like good news for the back-to-back approach.

The preceding convergence nothwithstanding, there is ample evidence for a complex interplay among orthographic, phonological, and semantic word properties about which the Rumelhart and McClelland (1982) model has nothing to say. The interplay shows a much more varied picture than merely mutual activation and inhibition of units on the levels of feature extraction, letter identification, and and word identification. For example, some investigators (e.g., Coltheart, Cutris, Atkins, & Haller, 1993) distinguish direct lexical effects of a letter string, either via orthography or phonology; and sublexical effects of letter-to-sound correspondence rules that enable pronounciation of nonwords such as *nust* and *mave*. Similarly, more recent neural network models (e.g., Seidenberg & McClelland, 1989) have ortho- graphic letter patterns as input and phonological word codes as output. The network learns how to pronounce regular and irregular words on the basis of a single translation derived from the weights of the connections between units. Massaro and Cohen (1994) countered that in contrast to the afore- mentioned network architecture, orthography and phonology contribute in- dependently and not interactively to letter and word recognition. Along the same lines, Grainger and Jacobs (1994) defended a dual-readout model of the word superiority effect in which a letter is correctly reported when either its own single-letter representation or the pseudoword representation in which the letter is contained exceeds a critical level of activation. The main difference between the Massaro and Cohen and the Grainger and Jacobs views on the one hand and the connectionist models on the other hand is that in the former views, letter and word representations are thought to develop independently rather than interactively through feedforward and feedback. Thus, there is evidence that the word-superiority effect depends on whether a word can be correctly pronounced. This does not follow naturally from a connectionist model. This brief sketch merely illustrates the ongoing discussion about the relative merits and prospects of connectionist and rule types of models on word recognition (e.g., Forster, 1994), a dis- cussion that is largely beyond the AFM because it presumably centers around mechanisms that operate in parallel and that are qualitatively different. An

AFM perspective has nothing to add when these mechanisms all bear on a single processing stage; in that case the discussion is fully concerned with what is going on in that stage. Alternatively, the AFM may contribute to the discussion when the variables involved can be meaningfully assigned to more than one sequential stage such as feature extraction and identification.

Lexical Decision

Many studies on word recognition employ a lexical decision paradigm in which participants are asked to indicate whether a letter string is a word or a nonword. The extensive literature on lexical decisions is beyond the scope of this book; therefore, the discussion is limited to a concise, simplified impression. There is evidence that participants carry out two tests when making a lexical decision. In the first, a letter string is rejected when its orthographical or phonological properties deviate fully from a word. Once it passes this test, a letter string might still be a word or a pseudoword, something that is decided in the second test. Part of the evidence for two tests stems from the finding that unpronounceable letter strings can be rapidly rejected much faster than pronounceable strings are accepted or rejected (Carr, 1986; Carr, Posner, Pollatsek, & Snyder, 1979).

CRT in lexical decision studies cannot be simply interpreted along the lines of the AFM either because the pertinent variables cannot be supposed to affect the duration of stages. Still, the AFM stages of feature extraction and identification may converge with the two lexical decision tests. The activation (feature analysis)-verification (identification) view on word perception (Paap, Newsome, McDonald, & Schvaneveldt, 1982), formulated at about the same time as the Rumelhart and McClelland (1982) model, also fits this picture.

The relevance of the state of the underlying word template at the time of presentation is best illustrated by the effect of context priming on word perception. Thus, Schvaneveldt and McDonald (1981) found that a context prime, for example lion, had the effect that participants more easily identified a tachistoscopic presentation of the word "tiger" and were also more inclined to accept *tigar* as word. Lexical decision time (CRT) for words (tiger) was equally reduced by a context prime (lion), but the time for rejecting a nonword (tigar) was unaffected. From a stage perspective, this divergence between tachistoscopic and chronometric data suggests that in the case of context-primed tachistoscopic word presentation, participants select a response (word–nonword) on the basis of incomplete feature analysis of the stimulus. In that case, the context prime may induce a response bias toward deciding word rather than nonword. It is of interest that a response bias is not found when, as in the chronometric case, a word or nonword can be completely processed. The word frequency effect is also viewed as due to the relative ease of matching a word to a template, and, hence, to identification rather than to response selection. Word frequency has been found to affect lexical decision time but to vanish in a tachistoscopic experiment, suggesting that a word-frequency effect occurs only when analysis of the stimulus features can be properly completed (Paap & Johansen, 1994). The effect of word frequency may be related to the relative availability of word templates. When a low-frequency word is repeatedly presented, its availability is enhanced and consequently, the word-frequency effect vanishes.

Applications. Research on visual discrimination has been widely applied to the design of words and symbols. One example of visual discrimination in symbol design concerns the brake lights in cars. Front-to-rear-end collisions account for a considerable proportion of traffic accidents (McGehee, Dingus, & Horowitz, 1992) due in part to the traditional location of brake lights next to the rear lights. The two lights are poorly discriminable, which prolongs RT. Hence, a brake light is now mounted in the center of the rear window at eye level. This change appears to have reduced accidents (Malone, 1986; Theeuwes, 1991a). Experimental studies on the road showed that the positive effect of a central braking light was less when participants were aware of the aim of the study, which confirms that deficient visual discrimination can be compensated by focusing attention (McKnight & Shinar, 1992). The positive effect of the central brake light may be further enhanced by using a meaningful icon such as an exclamation point or a danger icon.

The quality of discriminability follows from the Gestalt laws; it is particularly poor when too many unrelated patterns are presented. This situation allows the effect of hiding important features of any individual pattern. With respect to legibility of text, it is easy to demonstrate the relevance of presenting words separately and in well-known print. Reading is strongly hampered when spaces between words are omitted or when words are presented in AlTeRnAtInG case. Broadbent and Broadbent (1980) discussed the potential role of wordshape in reading and suggested that word perception may be equally based on spatial frequency analysis and on letter-by-letter analysis, as in the Rumelhart and McClelland (1982) model. Yet, the contribution of wordshape to reading is probably limited to small, frequent words—articles and endings—which is in line with the finding that printing errors occur most often in small words and endings.

It was already mentioned that reading is faster in lowercase than in uppercase, an advantage that vanishes and may even reverse when reading a single word (Philips, 1979). However, letter size and letter case may be confounded in single words. A capital subtends a larger visual angle and can be detected more rapidly; therefore, this may offset a disadvantage of less distinct features. When both factors are deconfounded, a single lowercase word may also be more legible. Detecting a SINGLE uppercase word among many lowercase words is a different story because the capitals pop out, a phenomenon that is discussed in chapter 7 in more detail. Fast detection can be reached equally well by a single lowercase word in **bold**, which has the advantages of pop out, as well as more distinctive features.

The effect of of feature analysis on reading is clear from the poor legibility of older, low-resolution VDT screens that consisted of fairly rough dot matrices and portrayed alphanumericals simply as straight lines. Again, searching or reading text from a low-resolution monitor was much slower than from a paper-printed copy. The problem has been solved to some extent with the present-day, high-resolution screens (Harpster, Freivalds, Shulman, & Leibowitz, 1989). Besides letter shape, there are other differences between reading from paper and from a screen, which include spacing of lines, size of the characters, typeface, contrast ratio between characters and background, viewing distance, amount of flicker, and the fact that turning pages on a screen usually occurs by scrolling. The general finding that reading from a computer screen is still somewhat slower, although comprehension seems equally good, may be due to a combination of these factors (Barber, 1988). Present-day text processors offer a variety of options in font, size, color, format, and style, despite the fact that there are wide differences in the efficiency of reading fonts. The wealth of choice, therefore, is not a sign of better ergonomics but of deficient research implementation.

Vocal naming of a printed word has sometimes been found to be faster than naming a corresponding icon (e.g., Fraisse, 1969), whereas in other studies, both were about equally fast (Potter & Faulconer, 1975). Fraisse suggested that words are read faster because they are less ambiguous. Even a fairly simple icon, such as a house, may elicit competing responses that delay CRT. This view predicts that the difference in CRT should disappear when icons are really unambiguous. Alternatively, naming a picture, however unambiguous, may always be more time consuming. Compare, for instance, Posner's (1978) physical and name matching, in which case a printed word would remain advantageous. It is interesting, in this regard, that icons are often superior to words in traffic signs, even when the issue of language comprehension is not being considered (e.g., Kline & Fuchs, 1993). The reason may be that the legibility of traffic signs is largely determined by the distance at which a sign can be read. When properly designed, the identification distance is greater for icons than for words because icons are usually larger, have a wider variety of features, and contain fewer fine details. The advantage of pictures, then, stems from the fact that letter discrimination requires some 10 to 12 minutes of arc and that feature detection is a primary prerequisite for discrimination (J. C. McClelland & Rumelhart, 1981). At the same time, it is clear that superiority of icons is only guaranteed when they contain little detail, are sufficiently distinct in shape, and are unambiguous.

With respect to 3-D objects, Biederman (1987) proposed the existence of a limited number of geons, that is, templates of perceptual primitives that are supposed to represent elementary building blocks of 3-D objects. There are four dimensions in which geons vary: edge (straight–curved), symmetry (symmetric–asymmetric), size (constant–expanding), and axis (straight–curved). A cube is an example of a combination of a straight edge, a symmetrical form, a constant size, and a straight axis; a cone is curved, expanding in size, has a straight axis, and takes a symmetrical form. It would be interesting to use geons for constructing 3-D icons. At present, however, most icons are 2-D, and its basic features should be based on Gestalt laws about a "good" figure. These laws coincide partly with Biederman's 3-D dimensions—symmetry, edge, and size—and further include closure, clear figure–ground distinction, clear borderlines, and avoidance of too much detail (Easterby, 1970; Fig. 4.10, upper panel).

Unambiguous meaning is the prerequisite of an icon. It should correspond to an unambiguous stereotype, for example, the crossed fork and knife and the bed for a restaurant and overnight accommodation. When an icon is designed for a new type of situation, there may simply be no stereotype available. Poorly understood icons are fully unacceptable. A common criterion is that 75% of a participant's sample should interpret the icon correctly (Sanders & McCormick, 1992; Fig. 4.10, lower panel).

Verbal abbreviations on information displays are usually inspired by lack of space. The problem is that abbreviations are often incomprehensible and always require much practice. Computer programs and military messages are known for their poor abbreviations. If absolutely unavoidable, a truncated abbreviation (abbrev.) is preferable to a contracted one (abrvn.), which follows naturally from the evidence on redundancy of letter sequences in a word.

Mental Rotation

The AFM structure (Fig. 3.2) ascribes effects of mental rotation to the identification stage. In most studies, individuals are asked to judge whether a rotated alphanumerical is presented in its normal shape or in its mirror image. In other studies, two rotated pictures or rotated 3-D shapes are presented, with the task being to determine whether they are the same or different shapes (Fig. 4.11). A common finding is an almost linear increase in CRT as a function of the angular departure from the upright (Fig. 4.11), which is taken to imply that participants mentally shift an image of the stimulus back into its upright position, followed by a decision about the shape of the stimulus, such as normal versus mirror (e.g., Cooper & Shepard, 1973). The mirror–normal decision is usually regarded as a response selection preceded by a perceptual rotation process.

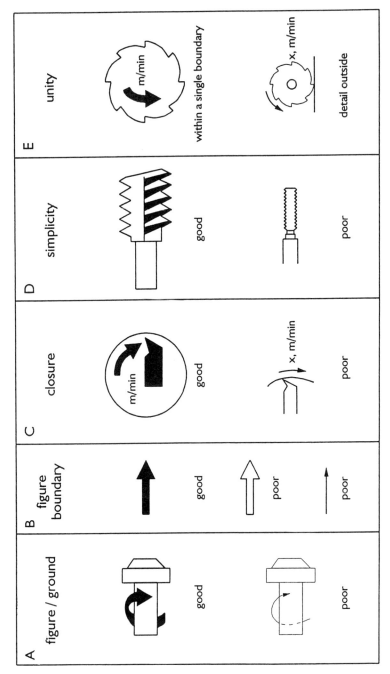

FIG. 4.10. Upper panel: Perceptual principles, relevant to the design of icons. Figure 4.10 is continued on p. 141.

140

FIG. 4.10. (*Continued*). Lower panel: Potential icons for an exit with their measured error proportions. From Sanders, M., & McCormick, E. J. *Human factors in engineering and design*. Copyright © McGraw-Hill. Reproduced by kind permission.

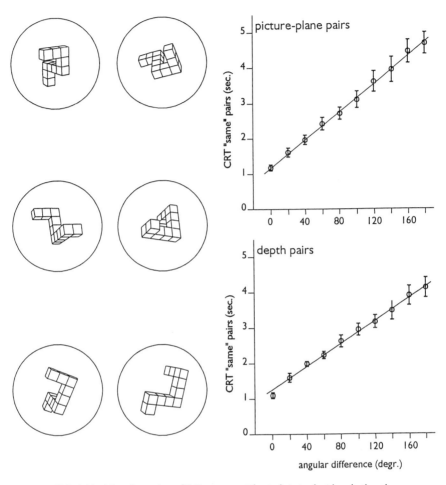

FIG. 4.11. Mental rotation of 3-D patterns. The task is to decide whether the patterns are the same or different. CRT increases as a linear function of the angular difference between two figures. From Shepard, R. N., & Metzler, J. (1971). Mental rotation of three-dimensional objects. *Science, 171*, 701–703. Copyright © 1971 by the American Association for the Advancement of Science. Reprinted with permission.

   With the exception of additive effects of mental rotation and stimulus quality, relatively little is known about the relation between mental rotation and other variables affecting CRT. It is imaginable that in addition to identification, mental rotation affects response selection. However, the usual, binary mirror–normal response hampers assessment of the loci of mental rotation within the traditional choice–reaction process. A binary response is used because mere naming of rotated alphanumericals appears to have a marginal effect on CRT (Corballis, Zbrodoff, Shetzer, & Butler, 1978; van

Duren, 1994), in particular when familiar symbols are used. A familiar symbol may be matched to its template without need for a time-consuming rotation to the upright, whereas complex figures (Fig. 4.11) require rotation. Yet, the CRT effect of naming rotated, familiar letters appears to increase as a function of the number of possible deviations within a block of trials so that AFM studies on naming rotated stimuli may still be feasible.

Mental rotation has been viewed as a continuous process based on a holistic stimulus representation (Cooper & Shephard, 1973; Corballis, 1986). This may be the case with simple letters and familiar shapes but with more complex patterns, deviations may be computed from the propositional representations of the pattern in a normal position (Just & Carpenter, 1985). Thus, a shape may be analyzed in terms of individual features rather than of its whole form. A rotated representation may consist of propositions about individual features corresponding to the major axes of the pattern segments.

Provided there are reasonable bounds, variations in pattern complexity affect the intercept and not the speed of rotation (Carpenter & Just, 1978). This result can be accounted for by both holistic rotation and analytical computation. The computational view suggests that as a pattern becomes more complex, it takes more time to determine which features should be rotated in order to compare the pattern with an internal standard. This leaves the speed of computing each particular feature unaffected (Just & Carpenter, 1985). In contrast, Cooper and Podgorny (1976) precluded rotation of features by presenting perturbations of a standard pattern. Under these conditions, they failed to find an effect of pattern complexity; they suggested that the whole pattern is rotated but that it takes longer to start rotating a more complex pattern. Finke and Shephard (1986) concluded that familiar stimuli are always rotated as a whole, whereas holistic processing and feature processing are options when stimuli are unfamiliar or multidimensional. What is done depends on individual differences as well as on stimulus properties. For instance, when using dice-type of stimuli, measurement of eye fixations has shown frequent checking and rechecking (Just & Carpenter), which suggests a feature-by-feature comparison process. In order to foster rotation of the whole stimulus, the task should preclude that rotation of parts leads to success. In the context of the AFM stage structure, mental rotation processes have been exclusively concerned with simple and familiar stimuli.

Applications. There are pronounced, individual differences in spatial skills that extend to rotation. Irrespective of skill, however, rotation is always time consuming and should be avoided whenever possible. It is a common requirement when reading a map, while driving, or when finding one's way in a building. The point is that most maps have a world reference, usually north up, when held in an upright position. The disadvantage is that one has to internally rotate the map until it is in line with the direction of the desired course. Wall maps of a building should preferably have an egoreference, that is, their orientation should be aligned with that of the user. In car driving, an egoreference is harder to achieve, although there are electronic egoreference aids available. Yet, the use of verbal route-guidance instructions at each decision point is probably superior to any map. Egoreference displays are now frequently used in flight navigation. It can be done by continuously adjusting the orientation of the map to the course of the aircraft. The drawback, though, is that the reference lacks stability. Aretz (1991) portrayed a changing egoreference map within a wider, fixed world reference map, a combination that seems to eliminate either disadvantage.

RESPONSE SELECTION

Response selection refers to the translation from perception to motor action. The notion of a translation between perception and action was controversial in behaviorism. Instead, the issue was whether the locus of an experimental variable was perceptual or motor as the only options. This was studied by LaBerge and Tweedy (1964) in regard to the effect of relative stimulus frequency imbalance on CRT. Four alternative lights were potential stimuli (a, b, c, d), one of which had a probability of .55 (a) and the others .15 each. Participants had two alternative key-press responses, one of which corresponded to both (a) and (b), with a probability of .70, and the other to both (c) and (d), with a probability of .30. The relevant comparison was between (b) and (c or d), which are all cases of infrequent stimuli corresponding to either a frequent (b) or an infrequent (c or d) response. If CRT to (b) and (c or d) were about equal, stimulus frequency would be decisive. In contrast, response frequency would be most relevant when CRT to (b) were faster than that to (c or d) and about equal to (a). LaBerge and Tweedy found that the effect of relative frequency was bound to the stimulus, but results from other studies were less clear, some even suggesting a response-bound effect (Dillon, 1966; Sanders, 1970b).

Contradictory results usually mean that there is an overriding constant variable, which, indeed, turned out to be the case in this paradigm. The effect of relative frequency on CRT may be neither perceptual nor motor because CRT for (b) relative to that for (a) and for (c or d) appeared to depend on S–R compatibility. Thus, Sanders (1970b) used the letters E (.55), A, O, and U (all .15) as stimuli. In some conditions, both E and A required the vocal response / es /, which is incompatible with the infrequent A and compatible with the frequent E. In another condition, the required response was / as /, which is compatible with the infrequent A and incompatible with the frequent E. Similarly, O and U required / os / in some and / us / in other conditions, which, in Dutch, is compatible with one and incompatible with the other infrequent stimulus. The results show that when the response to the infrequent-stimulus–frequent-response (A) was compatible / *as* /, CRT for A was much faster than CRT for the cases of compatible infrequent-stimulus–infrequent-response (O & U). However when the response to A was incompatible / *es* /, the CRT for A was equally slow as the CRT for the cases of incompatible infrequent-stimulus–infrequent-response. The conclusion was that the relative speed of responding to A depends on whether the instructed response can or cannot be rapidly selected. When it can be rapidly selected, response frequency counts, whereas stimulus frequency is decisive when it cannot be rapidly selected. The conclusion is that assessing relative S–R frequency in terms of a stimulus or a response effect leads to an oversimplified picture. The S–R translation appears to be decisive. The same paradigm with respect to the locus of the repetition effect was discussed in chapter 2.

S–R Compatibility

S–R compatibility probably has the most pervading effect on response selection. Since the work of Fitts and Seeger (1953) and Fitts and Deininger (1954), it refers to the degree of natural or overlearned correspondence between stimuli and responses. Spatial adjacency is a prototypical example in that when stimuli consist of a row of lights and responses of a row of keys, S–R relations are the most compatible when their spatial locations are identical. In the same way, Leonard (1959) found perfect S–R compatibility when individuals reponded with the tactually stimulated finger. Another example is when directions of perceived and executed movements converge. Vocal repetition of auditorily or visually presented alphanumerics or words is still another case that is often labeled *symbolic compatibility*. The correspondence is thought to be between auditory or visual codes (perceptual) on the one hand and articulatory codes (motor) on the other hand (Adams, 1971), both of which do not correspond naturally but have highly overlearned relations. It was already mentioned (that effects of compatibility diminish as a function of practice (e.g., Mowbray & Rhoades, 1959; Welford, 1976).

S–R compatibility has often been viewed as a reflection of population stereotypes on which response belongs to which stimulus or vice versa. The concept of a mental model is often used as a reference for hypothetical, internal schemes about S–R relations that are thought to be at the basis of stereotypes. The internal schemes vary from simple rules, for example, should the switch be up or down in order to turn the light on?, to a complex scheme about how a system works in order to enable appropriate actions based on the state of the system (e.g., Eberts & Posey, 1990). Stereotypes may be either acquired or innate and may also be more-or-less pronounced. As a consequence, S–R compatibility is not a dichotomy but a matter of degree. For example, in the case of two-choice reactions, with two lights and corresponding keys, Simon and Wolf (1963) found CRT to increase as the angle between the row of stimuli and responses increased from zero to 180°. In other cases, the increase of CRT appears to depend on the nature of the instructed rule that connects S–R sets. In the case of responding to alphanumerics, one may instruct participants to "add one"—that is, to respond with "three" when the numeral 2 is presented or with "b" when an "a" is presented. In this case, S–R compatibility is still better than when connections are completely random. The involvement of response selection is usually derived from the slope of the function relating CRT to the number of alternative S–R relations. In the case of perfect compatibility, the slope approaches zero, which justifies the conclusion that the response selection stage is bypassed. The idea is that response selection is not needed when a response directly reflects the identified stimulus. As S–R compatibility is less, the slope increases to the point where the correct response cannot be retrieved at all (Brainard, Irby, Fitts, & Alluisi, 1962). There is the problem that as yet, there is no general metric, so relative S–R compatibility cannot be independently assessed.

Most theoretical views on S–R compatiblity assume that stimulus identification elicits a corresponding response code, regardless of whether this code agrees with the instructed response. CRT is fast when the elicited and the instructed responses are identical, whereas CRT is slow when the elicited code has to be replaced by the instructed one. This view was proposed by Sanders (1967a), who presented participants with one out of six lights located in a 2 × 3 matrix. The instruction was to carry out two successive key-press responses, first a compatible response followed by an incompatible one (Fig. 4.12). In control conditions, participants carried out only the compatible or the incompatible response. The results show no systematic differences between the two conditions, suggesting that the incompatible response took no additional time when preceded by the compatible one. Nor was the compatible response delayed when followed by an incompatible one. These results may simply be explained by assuming that compatible S–R reactions are based on independent associations between individual S–R codes, whereas incompatible reactions require search among the various alternatives. A compatible and an incompatible response to a single stimulus do not interfere when both processes are carried out in parallel.

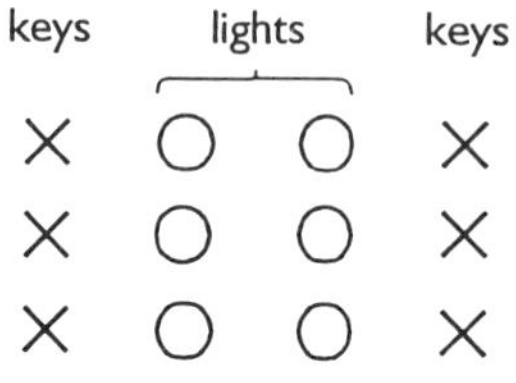

keys   lights   keys

FIG. 4.12. The display of lights (O) and response keys (X) in Sanders (1967). In a trial one of the lights was presented. The task was to produce two successive responses, namely a compatible response, the key adjacent to the light, followed by an incompatible response, a key from the opposite column that had no spatial relation with the presented light.

The aforementioned view is on the *individual element level,* which cannot account for effects of the total set of stimuli and responses. Effects of the total set may be illustrated by results from studies on block type (blocked vs. mixed) and compatibility. In prototypical studies (e.g., Duncan, 1978; Morin & Forrin, 1962) compatible and incompatible S–R relations were either presented in separate or in mixed blocks of trials. In a mixed block, some stimuli required a compatible response and others an incompatible response. As already mentioned, compatible CRTs suffer strongly in mixed blocks, whereas incompatible CRTs remain relatively constant or may even decrease (Fig. 4.7).

Duncan (1978) proposed that in a mixed condition, participants first determine the appropriate S–R transformation rule—compatible or incompatible—for the presented stimulus. Thus, a first, time-consuming selection is between the compatible and incompatible ensembles. In the incompatible cases, the ensuing increase in CRT is offset by the fact that in the mixed condition, the number of incompatible S–R alternatives is only half of that in the blocked condition. The compatible S–R alternatives are relatively insensitive to the number of alternatives, so the full effect of selecting the appropriate transformation rule is felt. The emphasis on the transformation rule concerns the ensemble level rather than the level of the individual items. The relevance of the ensemble is also underlined by results from Dornier and Reeve (1996), who showed that, when precuing a subset of stimuli in advance, the nonprecued subset still affected response selection and remained part of the mental representation, on the basis of which participants decided.

As an alternative to Duncan (1978), van Duren and Sanders (1988) extended their dual-pathway notion that was proposed as an explanation of the effect of block type on stimulus quality to response selection. A fast route may be taken when automatically elicited compatible responses are always appropriate; the slow route determines the correct response by searching among the alternatives (Fig. 4.7c), which is compulsory in the case of incompatible S–R relations. In a mixed block, participants opt for a worst case scenario by always taking the slow route because this is the only route to success when selecting an incompatible response. The automatically activated compatible response is inhibited and has to await the outcome of the slow route as well. Recent results by Stoffels (1996) and De Jong (1995) tend to favor this view above Duncan's.[4]

---

[4]As in the case of mixed stimulus qualities and mixed foreperiods, the mixing effect could be top down, reflecting a strategic bias toward the compatible or incompatible routes. In line with Duncan (1978) the bias would mean that participants first determine which route is correct and then choose the correct one, either the fast or the slow one. Instead, a bottom-up account assumes suppression of the compatible route (van Duren & Sanders, 1988). De Jong (1995) deduced that a bias hypothesis should predict an effect of the relative frequency of compatible and incompatible responses within a block of trials. In fact, no effect of relative frequency was found, which argues against the bias hypothesis.

Overlapping Dimensions

This theory (Kornblum, Hasbroucq, & Osman, 1990) considers stimuli and responses in terms of specific values on a set of dimensions, a subset of which is used in any particular ensemble of stimuli and responses. An example of a dimension is the set of horizontal–spatial locations, but a dimension may also be abstract and indirect, as in the case of symbolic stimuli and responses. As S–R dimensions of a particular ensemble have more overlap, compatible S–R relations are defined more easily. Without any dimensional overlap, it is impossible to establish compatible relations. Actual S–R mapping is on the element level.

Like Sanders (1967a), the model assumes that response selection proceeds along two parallel routes (Fig. 4.13). In the upper one, a stimulus automatically activates its most compatible response code on the element level (r_j), irrespective of the nature of the required response. The lower route has a confirmatory function and is on the ensemble level (r_k) because it only specifies the response rule. The time for determining the correct response on the lower route can vary from quite fast, when the rule is actually the most compatible one, to very slow, when S–R relations are totally random. The response must await the identity check between r_j and r_k. If r_j and r_k merge, the compatible response is carried out; if not, r_j is aborted and r_k is carried out.

A combination of full dimensional overlap and a compatible mapping rule is called ideomotor compatibility (Greenwald, 1970). A relation is ideomotor when motor movements and their feedback are directly guided by perceived events. An example is direct imitation, as in the case of vocally repeating an auditorily presented word or letter, but it can also be less direct, as in motor reactions to rhythm and movements in dance (e.g., Prinz, 1987). When stimuli and responses have dimensional overlap, CRT is facilitated to the extent that salient values on the stimulus dimensions correspond to salient values on the response dimensions (Reeve & Proctor, 1990). Salient values refer to the relative ease with which stimuli can be related to responses. For example, when precuing two out of four horizontal stimulus locations in advance of a target stimulus, CRT appeared to benefit most when the precues indicated the two locations furthest to the left or furthest to the right. It benefited least when the precues indicated alternate locations, as the first and third. Salient values also play a role when mapping alphanumericals onto spatial positions or when mapping spatial locations onto vocal responses. Thus, the vocal response, "one," and the most left position are a more salient combination than the response, "three," and the third position.

Given full dimensional overlap of a set of stimuli and responses, the relations are most incompatible when the pairings are random; they are less incompatible in the case of a fixed but incongruent rule—for example,

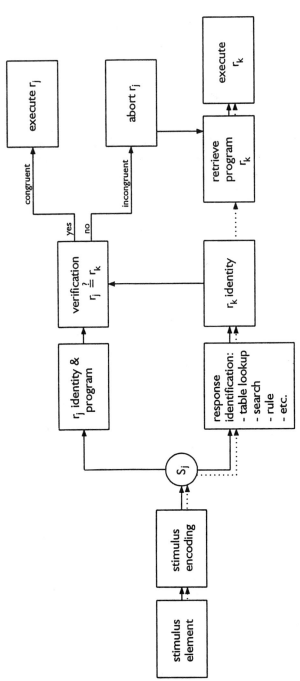

FIG. 4.13. The dimensional overlap model of S–R compatibility. The top branch illustrates automatic activation of the congruent response on the basis of dimensional overlap. The lower branch is concerned with identification of the correct response. From Kornblum, S., Hasbroucq, T., & Osman, A. (1990). Dimensional overlap: Cognitive basis for stimulus-response compatibility. A model and taxonomy. *Psychological Review, 97,* 253–270. Copyright © 1981 by the American Psychological Association. Reprinted with permission.

respond to a digit by adding one to its value. However, full dimensional overlap implies that a highly compatible rule can be defined, which is impossible without dimensional overlap. In this last case, the only way to decide about the correct response is through search of a list of unrelated S–R paired associates. This may easily fail, however. Keep in mind the earlier discussion on the 2 to 3 bit limit on absolute judgment in which a value on some sensory dimension is connected to a digit. This may well be proto-typical for absence of dimensional overlap between stimuli and responses, so it is not surprising that the limit on absolute judgment does not widely differ among sensory dimensions. In the case of two-dimensional stimuli, the second dimension provides an additional number of S–R connections and, therefore, a larger information transmission capacity. Thus, in Pollack's (1953) classical studies, individuals were graphically guided when the task was to assign a number to a tone that varied both in pitch and loudness. The participants first assigned numbers to the dimensions separately, where-upon they were visually guided to a combined number as the final response to the 2-D stimulus. Kornblum et al. (1990) drew a sharp distinction between incompatibility due to absence of dimensional overlap and due to an in-congruent rule with dimensional overlap. In the latter case, knowledge of the rule, however complex, always enables retrieval of the proper response. In the first case, retrieval failures are imminent.

The dimensional overlap model is a more elaborate combination of the dual-route approach as well as the rule-selection approach to response se-lection. The fast route of van Duren and Sanders (1988) refers to the case in which r_k and r_j are known to merge, whereas the slow route has the task of solving the problem of finding r_k. Finding r_k is a matter of rule selection and, perhaps, of profiting from potential salient values that render some conditions more difficult than others.

The model has no problem explaining the basic data on S–R compatibility, such as the pronounced increase of CRT as a function of the number of alternatives in conditions of poor S–R compatibility and the relatively fast CRT when an incompatible S–R connection is repeated (Bertelson, 1963) or relatively frequent (Fitts, Peterson, & Wolfe, 1963). The point is that finding r_k is more cumbersome because there are more alternatives, whereas a particular r_k is likely to be on top of the search list when it has just been handled. The salient values studied by Reeve et al. (1992) further specify properties of dimensions and their overlap. In a more recent test of the model, Kornblum and Ju-Whei Lee (1995) studied four- and six-choice re-actions with hand icons. They used pictures of a hand, with the index finger pointing toward a certain spatial location, or letters as stimuli that were connected to either key-press or verbal responses. It was assumed that hand icons and verbal responses, or letters and key presses, have little dimensional overlap, whereas icons and key presses and letters and verbal responses have. This means that mapping should be highly relevant for the latter but not for the former connections, which was indeed the main finding of the study. In accord with the model, CRT was less strongly affected when, in a condition of nonoverlapping, relevant dimensions, overlapping, irrelevant dimensions were added to the stimuli and responses; participants utilized the S–R congruence of the overlapping irrelevant dimensions.

Eimer (1995) sought to test automatic response code activation (r_j) by measuring LRPs. An imperative stimulus (the letters M or W, presented either to the left or to the right side of the vertical meridian) was preceded by an arrow precue. In one condition, the response—always a left or a right key press—depended on letter identity, whereas, in another condition, it depended on stimulus location. Moreover, participants were instructed to respond only to the imperative stimulus when it appeared on the side indicated by the arrow and to withold response when cue and imperative stimulus location deviated. Precue and location corresponded in 75% of the trials. Eimer reasoned that when participants were instructed to respond to stimulus location, the precue arrow would evoke more controlled preparation of the key-press response than when they were instructed to respond to letter identity. In that case, stimulus location was only relevant for the decision to respond or not to respond. On the other hand, when the arrow precue elicits an automatic spatial r_j, the spatial response code should not depend on strategic considerations and should be equally large with either instruction. This last result was actually obtained. As expected from an automatic process, the LRP was not elicited when the precue consisted of a nonspatial color instead of an arrow (Eimer, Hommel, & Prinz, 1995).

The Simon Effect

Eimer's (1995) study suggested that immediate activation of a compatible response code (r_j) may arise from response-relevant as well as response-irrelevant stimulus features. This has become particularly clear from the work of Simon (1990) and others. In an early study, Simon and Small (1969) used a high (1,000 Hz) or a low (400 Hz) tone to be responded to by pressing, respectively, a left or a right response key. A tone was presented to either the left or the right ear. Ear of presentation was irrelevant, but still, CRT was considerably faster when ear of presentation and side of the correct response coincided. In another study (Simon, 1969), a high or low tone was presented to either the right or the left ear, and participants were instructed to respond to the high tone by moving a lever to the left and to respond to the low tone by moving the lever to the right. Again, CRT was faster when the movement was toward the stimulated ear. Together, these results led to the hypothesis that individuals have an ideomotor tendency to react toward the source of stimulation. This is an example of an orienting reaction.

The Simon effect has been equally obtained with visual stimuli. Thus, an X or an O may be presented either at a central location or in the left or right part of the visual field, whereas responses consist of a left key press to the X and a right key press to the O. Despite the irrelevance of the spatial location, CRT was faster when stimulus and response were at corresponding spatial locations. The essential factor is the spatial location relative to the body and not the spatioanatomical sensory or effector functions. For example, the effect of spatial compatibility did not change when responses were with the hands crossed (Wallace, 1972) or with the index and middle finger of the same hand (H. G. Shulman & McConkie, 1973). The Simon effect (Simon, 1969) did not change either, which implies that hemispheric effects and spatial compatibility are unrelated.

Aside from a very few exceptions (e.g., Stoffels, 1988), the Simon effect has been ascribed to the response selection stage. It is hazardous to assess effects of irrelevant dimensions by means of the AFM because this type of variable is prototypical for asynchronous discrete processing. However, there are other arguments in favor of response selection as locus of the Simon effect. For instance, Hommel (1995) used arrows, pointing either to the left or to the right, that required a spatially corresponding reaction. Briefly, on stimulus presentation, participants received a second stimulus, the color of which indicated whether to continue or to stop the response. The location of the color stimulus was irrelevant but still caused a Simon effect. This result seems to exclude identification of the arrow as locus.

The dimensional overlap model can easily account for the Simon effect. Given the evidence for parallel processing of stimulus features, it is not surprising that an irrelevant spatial dimension is identified and elicits a corresponding spatial response (r_j). There is dimensional overlap between the irrelevant spatial-stimulus dimension and the relevant spatial-response dimension. The point is that the relevant stimulus dimension, for example, the visual stimuli X and K, have no dimensional overlap with the spatial-response dimension. Hence, the correct response (r_k) must be searched for in the list of S–R pairings. CRT is faster when r_j and r_k happen to match and slows down when they do not. The dimensional overlap model can also handle the general finding that the Simon effect vanishes or even reverses in the case of dimensionally overlapping, incompatible S–R pairings. As an example, the stimulus may consist of an arrow that points either to the left or to the right. In the compatible condition, the correct response consists of pressing the key at the right location when the arrow points to the right and pressing the key at the left location when the arrow points to the left. This relation is reversed in the incompatible condition. The arrow may be located centrally or at the left or at the right of the vertical meridian (Fig. 4.14).

The results (e.g., Stoffels, 1988) show a Simon effect in the compatible condition but not in the incompatible one. In the compatible condition, the

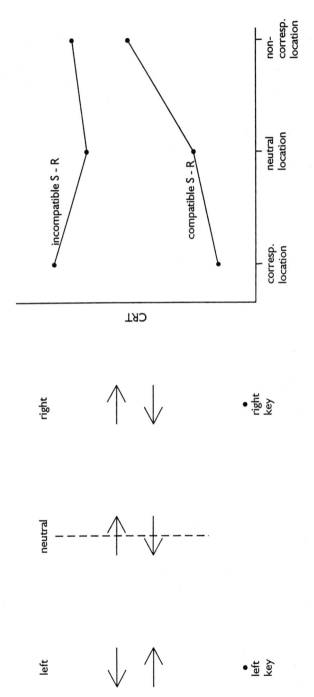

FIG. 4.14. Illustration of the Simon effect. The task is to respond with the key that corresponds to the direction of the arrow (compatible) or corresponding to the opposite direction (incompatible). The location of the arrow may either correspond or not correspond with the location of the response key. The graph shows a typical pattern of results.

dimensional overlap model expects a faster CRT when the two stimulus dimensions elicit the same r_j (the arrow is presented at the right and points to the right, or is presented at the left side and points to the left). However, the stimulus dimensions elicit competing r_js when, for example, the arrow is presented at the right side and points to the left. This delays a comparison of the computed r_k and the correct r_j. This causes CRT to slow down. In the incompatible condition, the two stimulus dimensions may elicit equally conflicting r_js, as in the compatible condition, but due to the incompatible S–R relations, r_k does not match r_j. This leads to abortion of both r_js, irrespective of whether the stimulus dimensions elicited the same or a different r_j. The result is that the Simon effect should disappear. However, the results sometimes show a reversed Simon effect in that CRT is actually faster when direction and location of the arrow diverge and S–R relations are incompatible. A reversed Simon effect may be accounted for by a small adaptation of the dimensional overlap model. The point is that, in the incompatible case, the noncorresponding location indicates the position of the correct response (Hedge & Marsh, 1975). Hence, rather than aborting both r_js, the criterion may be whether r_k merges with r_j of the irrelevant dimension and speeds up CRT.

De Jong, Liang, and Lauber (1994) found qualitatively distinct effects of spatial correspondence of S–R locations (r_j) and the reponse elicited by the transformation rule, that is, compatible versus incompatible (r_k). In their research, they reasoned that the codes, which are elicited by the spatial locations, may be transient in comparison with those computed by the rule. In that case, the Simon effect should be stronger for faster responses than for slower responses in a block of trials because the elicited spatial location code dissipates over time. Indeed, irrelevant, spatially corresponding locations showed a pronounced Simon effect at the lower tail of the CDF that disappeared at the upper tail. Again, spatially noncorresponding locations led to a relatively slow CRT in the case of compatible responses and a relatively fast CRT in the case of incompatible responses, which means that the reverse Simon effect showed up again in the incompatible condition. In a follow-up study, an early, spatially corresponding LRP was found, irrespective of compatibility instruction, which dissipated over time. When the spatially evoked LRP corresponded to the subsequent overt response decision, the later LRP was facilitated to the extent that the early LRP was still active.

These results carry the discussion beyond simply localizing the Simon effect. They entail a more detailed analysis of processes occurring in response selection. A more detailed review of the Simon effect and its relation to the Stroop effect is found in Chen-Hui and Proctor (1995). They concluded that both effects are a function of strength of the association between the irrelevant stimulus dimension and the response to the relevant stimulus dimension, and temporal contiguity between the eventual response activation and the response activation produced by the relevant stimulus dimension. This formulation comes close to that of the dimensional overlap model.

Future Research

One future issue concerns a more detailed listing of the relevant S–R dimensions that should be empirically determined rather than a priori postulated. According to Kornblum et al. (1990), overlap between dimensions might be analyzed by *scaling*, that is, through judgments about how well S–R ensembles correspond for different mappings. The point is that seemingly different stimuli and responses may still have dimensions in common. For example, Kornblum et al. (1990) referred to cross-modality matching in which participants match values from different dimensions. Thus, they may be asked to indicate whether an auditory intensity is felt to match a given visual intensity or to produce a force that is felt to match an auditory intensity. The finding that the participants appear to yield fairly consistent cross-modal matches is suggestive of dimensional overlap. However, the nature of the dimensions and how they play a role in determining S–R compatibility are still largely unknown. Some dimensions, such as spatial location, have been studied more widely, with the advantage that more detailed questions can be raised about spatial properties such as the relative importance of egocentric and external spatial reference points (Umilta & Nicoletti, 1990). Another set of questions on response selection is concerned with further specification of the processing dynamics of the Kornblum (1990) model. It was previously suggested that conflicting stimulus dimensions lead to interfering r_js. Alternatively, dimensions may override each other, differ in salience, or establish a composite r_j as a result of the r_js from different dimensions. Hence, the question is whether r_j is a unitary code and whether it has a constant or a variable quality.

Another class of questions concerns the stability of response codes once they have been selected. The issue may be illustrated by a study from Sanders (1967b), who presented participants with two simultaneous visual stimuli, one from the left and one from the right column of the 2 × 3 matrix of Fig. 4.12. The participants were asked to carry out a single-grouped response to both stimuli. This was no problem when both responses were compatible—the grouped response took even much less time than the sum of two single responses—but it proved to be quite difficult when both responses were incompatible. Does this result mean that different stimuli can elicit their r_js in parallel, which—if confirmed—have simultaneous access to the response system? Again, can r_ks be handled only one at a time, and do two r_ks interfere when they are combined?

Applications. S–R compatibility is undoubtedly the most widely applied choice reaction variable. In fact, the basic research followed rather than preceded the discovery of its applied relevance. Thus, prior to publishing the important basic work (Fitts & Deininger, 1954; Fitts & Seeger, 1953),

Fitts (1951) discussed various, applied compatibility issues. There was, however, a striking difference between Fitts' applied approach and basic approach. In his basic research, he always used *unambiguous stimuli and responses*, in which incompatibility consisted of unnatural S–R connections. In his applied work, Fitts related compatibility primarily to *ambiguous stimuli and responses*. Ambiguous stimuli are multi-interpretable and may evoke different responses. Therefore, it may remain unnoticed whether a response was correct or incorrect.

As already mentioned, absolute judgment refers to conditions in which a sensory code is assessed as relevant or irrelevant or is assigned a specific number. The code may be an auditory call sign from a set of alternative call signs, one of which is relevant to the listener or which may indicate a certain instruction, alarm, or message. In the same way, color coding has often been used for indicating electrical resistance. Absolute judgment was shown to be quite poor and limited to some five tones of different pitch, about five loudnesses, and an about equal number of colors or brightnesses. Absolute judgment of the size of perceived objects only does a little better (about seven alternatives). Thus, absolute discrimination is highly inferior to relative discrimination, in which participants indicate whether two stimuli are the same or different. For instance, some 1,800 tones can be discriminated in relative judgment. The point is that in contrast to absolute judgment, relative judgments have full dimensional overlap. It was mentioned previously that the number of identifiable codes can be increased by adding more orthogonal sensory dimensions. Thus, when a tone differs in pitch and loudness, more alternatives can be discriminated—about eight or nine—which can be further extended by adding more dimensions, maximally, some three or four, which leads to a total of some 36 identifiable alternatives. When dimensions are perfectly correlated, the number of identifiable alternatives does not increase. Although there is some gain in accuracy for the simple reason that when the correct response is not found on one dimension, it may still be found on the other correlated dimension. Redundant dimensions are particularly relevant when identifying degraded stimuli.

The dimensional overlap model can also account for the phenomenon of proximity compatibility. In that case, the issue was that compatibility of a stimulus pattern or object display depended on how well and how uniquely it corresponded to a mental model about what is going on. Depending on how it is framed in the mental model, an ambiguous stimulus may elicit one specific response or more than one response. For instance, a scale reading may either indicate a command or a status. As an example, the display of the relief valve in the Three Mile Island nuclear power plant indicated the issued command—open! close!—rather than whether the valve was actually open or had been closed. During the malfunction in March 1979, the display correctly indicated the command to close the valve. This was interpreted by the operators as evidence that the valve had actually closed, which, due to a technical failure, was not the case. As another example, an instructor may say, "left-wing low" to a trainee, which may either be interpreted as a command to be carried out or as an error to be corrected. The appropriate response to one interpretation is the reverse of the other interpretation (Kantowitz, Triggs, & Barnes, 1990).

In the aforementioned examples, the interpretation of the stimuli was ambiguous, but the stimuli themselves were unambiguous, that is, a scale reading and a verbal command. In other examples, however, stimuli may be ambiguous as well. In the example of Fig. 4.15A, it is unclear where the gates are located. Another example is the horizon display in an aircraft cockpit. Here, the debate has been whether the horizon display or the aircraft should move when the plane is in motion. A moving horizon (Fig. 4.15, Letter b) corresponds with what the pilot actually sees from his outside

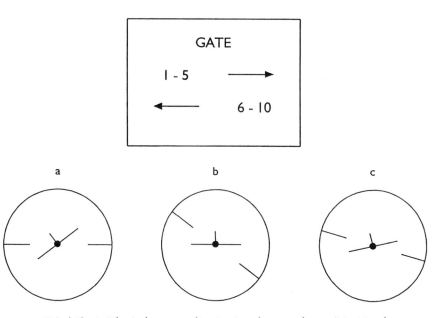

FIG. 4.15. A. What is the correct direction in order to reach gate 4? Reprinted from Kantowitz, B. H., Triggs, T. J., & Barnes, V. E. (1990). Stimulus-response compatibility and human factors. In R. W. Proctor & T. G. Reeve (Eds.). *Stimulus-response compatibility.* Copyright © 1990, with kind permission from Elsevier Science, Ltd., The Boulevard, Langford Lane, Kidlington, 0X5 1GB, UK. B. Displaying the horizon relative to the position of the aircraft: (a) is the true situation and (b) the experienced one. (c) is labeled a frequency-separated display, which turns the horizon for slow and the aircraft for rapid changes. From Wickens, C. D. (1992). *Engineering psychology and human performance.* Copyright © 1992 by HarperCollins Publishers, Inc. Reprinted by permission of Addison-Wesley Educational Publishers, Inc.

view and may seem quite compatible. However, a moving aircraft (Fig. 4.15, Letter a) corresponds to the reality and to the pilot's intention (Roscoe, 1981), so that compatibility with the outside view conflicts with that of the internal mental model. A nice solution is the frequency-separated display (Fig. 4.15, Letter c) in which a rapid turn, which is actually felt, is represented by a turn of the aircraft, whereas a more gradual turn is represented by a turn of the horizon (e.g., Wickens, 1992).

Mental Model and Compatibility

Most cases of compatiblity refer to stereotypic responses that derive from generalized mental models. Among others, this is the case with choosing the null position in a circular display. Clockwise deviations from the 12 o'clock and 9 o'clock positions appear to be corrected faster than deviations from the 6 o'clock and 3 o'clock positions. The reason may be that a combination of a clockwise deviation and a movement in the upper part of the display is experienced as an "increase" requiring compensation. In the 3 and 6 o'clock cases, the two principles conflict and may, therefore, be handled less efficiently (Kantowitz et al., 1990). A similar stereotype is found when locking or opening the trunk of a car. Many people believe that locking requires a clockwise movement of the key. Frequent errors occur when the lock is designed the other way around. With respect to control movements, there is Warrick's (1947) well-known principle that describes the relation between the location of the control knob and the movement direction on a display. The principle holds that one expects a pointer on the display to move in the same direction as the side of the control that is nearest to the display movement. Thus, in Fig. 4.16A, one expects the pointer to go down and in Fig. 4.16B, to go up.

A further illustration is related to a moving window display. According to most people's mental model, an upward movement in a display suggests an increase in value, so that a larger mercury column indicates a higher temperature in a household thermometer. There are problems with realizing this principle in a fixed pointer–moving scale indicator. The problem is illustrated in Fig. 4.17. When the scale in Fig. 4.17a moves down, its value goes up, which conflicts with the stereotype. This may be remedied by having the scale move up (Fig. 4.17b), but now, the low values are at the top, which is again at odds with the stereotype.

Proximity compatibility is harder to realize as the mental model of a situation becomes more primitive, global, or distorted. For instance, the flow diagram of a complex, automatized industrial set of processes is often derived from a technical model, which may not correspond at all with the operator's model. In particular, when incomplete or distorted, a technical representation adds little to extend or correct the mental model. Another instance of poor

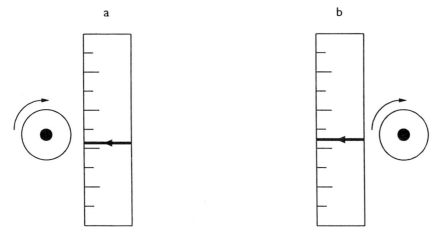

FIG. 4.16. Warrick's (1947) principle: The direction of the pointer is up or down, depending on whether the turn of the knob is "toward" (Fig. 4.16a) or "away" from the display (Fig. 4.16b). From Warrick, M. J. Direction of movement in the use of control knobs to position visual indicators. In P. M. Fitts (Ed.), *Psychological research on equipment design.* Research Report 19, Aviation Psychology Program.

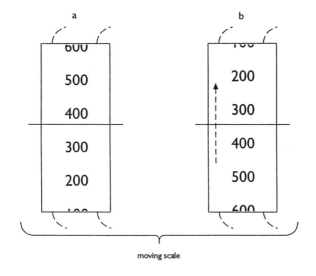

FIG. 4.17. Compatibility problems with moving scale-fixed pointer displays: In (a) the larger values are on top, but the scale moves down when indicating an increase. In (b) the scale moves up but, now, the low values are on top. From Wickens, C. D. (1992). *Engineering psychology and human performance.* Copyright © 1992 by HarperCollins Publishers, Inc. Reprinted by permission of Addison-Wesley Educational Publishers, Inc.

proximity compatibility is an architectual map of a building that is intended as an aid for finding one's way or for showing fire escapes. They are inadequate because they contain many irrelevant details from the perspective of a visitor who has merely a global mental model of the building. Convergence between map position and bodily orientation comes close to situational awareness, which is particularly relevant in orientation in 3-D space. It was mentioned earlier that there are developments in 3-D object displays that add considerably to proximity compatibility. Other instances of proximity compatibility (Wickens & Carswell, 1995) are related to stimulus–stimulus (S–S) compatibility.

Programs for text processing contain many issues that come close to S–R compatibility. The programs require knowledge about how commands correspond to specific keys or combinations of keys on a keyboard. The problem is that a command and its corresponding key combination usually fail to have any dimensional overlap, which means that the S–R relations should be acquired by a painstaking process of paired–associate learning. The result is that the task remains error prone, even when the skill has been acquired. Less practiced operations remain liable to forgetting, so that the operator may simply fail to retrieve an appropriate response at a critical moment. In most programs, the text on the screen does not correspond to what is eventually printed. This is another instance of inferior proximity compatibility. Only a very few programs are based on stereotypical spatial internal models about S–R relations for controlling commands.

Wickens (1992) correctly concluded that dimensional overlap is best between spatial stimuli and manual responses, for example, a pointing response to a spatial location, on the one hand, and between verbal stimuli and vocal responses, for example, reading verbal symbols, on the other hand. There is ample evidence that spatial and verbal representations constitute relatively distinct cognitive categories with little mutual interference but also with little mutual correspondence. Hence, it is now almost commonplace to note that a spatial task, for example, editing a text, is most easily done by spatial mouse-type movements, so that the keyboard can be used for verbal commands about the text itself (Sanders, 1987). This statement may not be valid, though, for highly skilled users with full command of the incompatible key-press instructions on editing.

This should not be taken to imply that the traditional keyboard is optimal for verbal commands. Letters on a keyboard have no meaningful connection to spatial locations; it is a basically incompatible design that can only be mastered and maintained by massive practice. A similar case can be made with respect to shorthand, which equally consists of arbitrary symbols connected to parts of verbal stimuli and a skill that can be rapidly lost without continuous practice. An interesting, alternative keyboard has been proposed by Gopher (1984). Here, an operator handles two keyboards at the same time, one with the left hand and another with the right hand. Both keyboards consist of a 3 * 2 pattern, as shown in Fig. 4.18, with an additional key for the thumb. Each letter of the Hebrew alphabet corresponded to a response chord that consisted of a specific combination of keys so that the shape of that particular letter was mimicked. The results of this study show a considerable saving in the time needed to acquire typing skills. Motor limitations restricted the speed of emitting chording responses, but still, asymptotic performance was quite acceptable in comparison with normal typing speed. In a subsequent paper, Gopher, Karis, and Koenig (1985) successfully extended this research to the Roman alphabet.

A classical example of spatial S–R incompatibility is the traditional arrangement of stove burner controls. Four burners are positioned in a 2 × 2 matrix, whereas the controls are in a horizontal row, which makes poor spatial compatibility. Yet, despite many errors, people usually solve the problem of lighting the stove. The situation is worse when people are faced with undefined display-control relations, as in the examples of Fig. 4.19, which represent displays of a microwave and an oven, whose operations are both completely undefined. Other poignant examples stem from display-control relations of video cameras, video recorders, and television sets. The effect is that the many clever options are never used or must be studied anew at the start of each new attempt to operate the device. Of course, it is all in the manual. However, manuals are often incomprehensible for an average user as well, in particular when the required actions are described in verbal, technical language, which is a basically incompatible way of instruction. One may wonder why many everyday devices are so poorly designed in regard to compatibility. One possible answer is that designers have little understanding of what constitutes a compatible or an incompatible solution (Payne, 1995).

S–S and R–R Compatibility

In his initial papers, Fitts (1951) discussed S–S and Response–Response (R–R) compatibility together with S–R compatibility. R–R compatibility refers to how well simultaneous or successive movements can be combined. As is illustrated in the next section, some movements can be more easily coordinated than others. This implies distinct constraints for the execution of simultaneous and successive control movements (e.g., Heuer, 1990, 1996). A classical illustration of S–S compatibility is found in Small's foreword to the Proctor and Reeve (1990) volume on S–R compatibility. Small describes attempts in the late 1940s to support auditory sonar with a visual display in an attempt to enhance signal detection. One solution was sought in a horizontal light beam, traveling from left to right, whose vertical perturbations were a visual translation of potential targets as well as background noise,

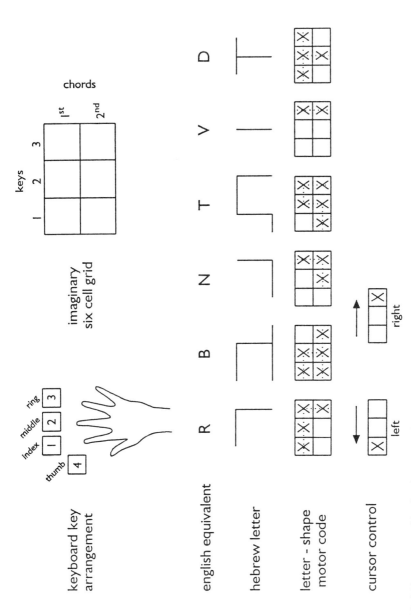

FIG. 4.18. A compatible chording system for typing the Hebrew alphabet. In subsequent studies a similar chording system was developed for the Roman alphabet. Reprinted from Gopher, D., Karis, D., & Koenig, W. (1985). The representation of movement schemas in long-term memory: Lessons from the acquisition of a transcription skill. *Acta Psychologica, 60*, 105–134. Copyright © 1985 with kind permission of Elsevier Science-NL, Sara Burgerhartstraat 25, 1055 KV, Amsterdam, The Netherlands.

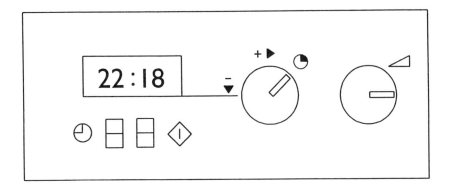

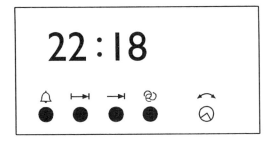

FIG. 4.19. Displays of a microwave (upper panel) and an oven (lower panel). The numbers indicate real time. It is unclear how to operate the function keys.

with a target consisting of a slightly larger vertical perturbation. The results show that the combination of an auditory and a visual display did not lead to a higher detection rate than a single auditory display, which appeared to be due to poor S–S compatibility. An auditory target consists of a change in loudness relative to background noise; hence, a supporting visual display has the most dimensional overlap when it consists of a change in brightness as the compatible visual analogue of loudness.

Another example of S–S compatibility concerns homogeneity among codes. Thus, the constituent elements of a display should be the same, for example, a set of histograms or of pointers, but not a combination of histograms and pointers. It is widely accepted that a set of displays is checked the most easily when the normal setting of all pointers is aligned, for example, all horizontal, and when pointers are grouped according to a common principle (e.g., Fig. 7.14).

According to the dimensional overlap model, S–S compatibility depends on the match between two dimensions, either across or within modalities. As already mentioned, a cross-modality match requires a judgment of, for example, which auditory loudness corresponds to a given visual brightness.

Cross-modality matching has been a popular technique in research on scaling sensory dimensions because it avoids the awkward problem of mapping sensory stimuli to numerals. It was explicitly mentioned by Kornblum et al. (1990) as a promising way of determining dimensional overlap between different stimulus sets, or different response sets.

All of these examples show that compatibility is a major factor in the design of a human–machine interface. The effect of poor compatibility usually can be softened by extended practice so that it may remain unnoticed or underestimated. Yet, even when incompatible display-control relations have been fully mastered and do not seem to affect performance any more, there still remains the problem of higher error rates. The incorrect compatible response (r_j) remains a competitor for the correct incompatible one (r_k). It is likely to come through occasionally, thus, carrying the risk of an accident. In addition, the amount of practice required for mastering incompatible S–R relations is formidable. Mastering typing skills is perhaps the most notorious example that for some mysterious reason, seems to be accepted by almost everybody as "a fact of life."

MOTOR PROGRAMMING

Motor programming refers to more detailed specification of the response code that was established during response selection. As outlined in chapter 3, the specification concerns kinematic parameters such as size, shape, speed, duration, force, and direction (Zelaznik & Franz, 1990). The ensuing code is still a central representation and does not include a detailed set of muscle commands. A common classroom illustration is that, when writing a digit or one's signature, the spatial relations among the elements of the digit or of the signature are hardly affected by the size in which the symbol is written. Again, when a person is skilled in writing with either hand or even with a foot, the handwriting style is relatively unaffected. Despite the fact that completely different muscle groups are involved, letter and word shapes remain much the same.

Schmidt (1988) proposed a distinction between a generalized motor program and motor parameters, the latter of which need further specification. The generalized motor program consists of a combination of invariant motor characteristics, the values of which are assigned by default and need no further specification. The balance between default values and free specification of variables changes as a function of practice. Verwey (1994a) discussed Schmidt's generalized motor program in terms of motor chunks. Chunks are loaded in a motor buffer, from where they are retrieved in convenient parts, ready to be translated into muscular language (Fig. 3.5).

Central motor commands have often been characterized as open loop and automatic, based on three main arguments: Response-produced afferent feedback is too slow for controlling rapid, integrated actions such as in gymnastics. Indeed, visual feedback is known to disrupt rather than to aid skilled, rapid-movement sequences. However, proprioceptive feedback is sufficiently fast to indicate whether an intended action sequence has been properly completed and, when needed, to bring about minor adaptations. Hence, feedback is not irrelevant in skilled motor sequences that cast doubts on the generality of the open-loop assumption (Schmidt, 1988). Execution of preplanned motor commands continue for some time when faced with a countermanding, or stop, signal (Logan, 1995); and a more complex action may take a longer CRT which Henry and Rogers (1960) labeled the complexity effect. These last two arguments are not generally valid either, as evident from results on the stop-signal paradigm and on the complexity effect.

Stop-Signal Paradigm

Here, a new stimulus is presented while executing a response to an earlier imperative one, with the new stimulus instructing to stop all ongoing action. The rationale is to trace whether motor processes are typically ballistic or controlled (Logan & Cowan, 1984; Osman, Kornblum, & Meyer, 1986). The idea is that, once launched, a ballistic process must continue, irrespective of a countermanding command, whereas a controlled process is sensitive to a stop stimulus. Hence, a stop stimulus can only be effective when presented before the start of potential ballistic processes in a choice reaction. More precisely, the effectiveness of a stop stimulus should depend on the processing time required by the stop stimulus to issue the command to abort further processing and the interval between presentation of the imperative stimulus and the stop stimulus (SOA). The longer the SOA, the less the probability that the stop stimulus will stop the response. That means that a response function can be constructed, which, given a stop stimulus, plots the probability of a response as a function of SOA. Thus, CDFs can be constructed for small, medium, and large SOAs in the case of stop trials and for go trials (i.e., trials without a stop stimulus; Fig. 4.20). A comparison between the CDFs for stop trials and go trials is relevant as a control for potential interference between processing the imperative stimulus and the stop stimulus. As SOA is less, CRT in stop trials should be relatively fast. The point is that, when processing happens to develop slowly in a particular trial, the probability of obeying the stop signal increases. Consequently, at a small SOA, slow CRTs should be rare in stop trials. The longer the SOA, the more the CDF should approximate the CDF of go trials.

The research strategy in the stop-stimulus paradigm is to manipulate experimental variables affecting CRT and to determine their effect in the

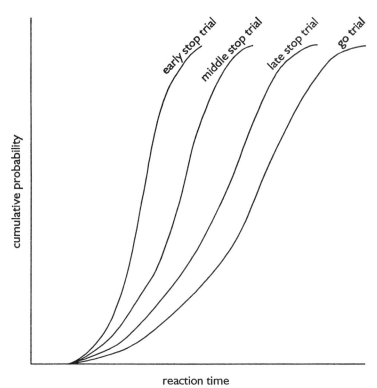

FIG. 4.20. Idealized cumulative distributions for CRT in "stop-signal" trials and in "go" trials. From Osman, A., Kornblum, S., & Meyer, D. (1986). The point of no return in choice reaction time: Controlled and ballistic stages of response preparation. *Journal of Experimental Psychology: Human Perception & Performance, 12,* 243–258. Copyright © 1986 by the American Psychological Association. Reprinted with permission.

case of go trials and stop trials. It is assumed that the time needed for processing and implementing the stop stimulus (S) is almost a constant; this time can be estimated from fully controlled processing conditions in which S is always effective. In that case, the CDF of S can be derived from the response proportions as a function of SOA. At a small SOA, almost all Ss are obeyed, so that there are hardly any responses; no S may be obeyed at a large SOA. Hence, the CDF of S is expressed in SOA. If only ballistic processes are involved, responses will always be carried out, however small the value of SOA. Are there, then, experimental variables that selectively affect a ballistic or a controlled component?

The pertinent research showed that the probability of successful stopping is affected by almost all CRT variables (Logan, 1995): perceptual, central, and motor alike. This was confirmed by psychophysiological data on the LRP, on electromyographic (EMG) responses, and on movement parameters involved in response execution, all of which appeared to have their effect before the point of no return (De Jong et al., 1990). S appears to need some 200 ms, that is, the time to complete a simple reaction, in order to become effective. Analogous to a response signal that indicates to abort processing and to respond rather than to stop, S can be processed in parallel with the imperative stimulus and without noticeable interference with the ongoing choice-reaction processes (Logan, 1995). This is further pursued in the discussion on the psychological refractory period. For the moment, it is evident that there is not much evidence for either ballistic automatic processes in traditional choice-reaction processes or for a dominance of open-loop motor processing.

The Complexity Effect

As previously mentioned, the complexity effect is probably unrelated to motor programming, which stage is supposed to be concerned with specifying kinematic parameters and not with constructing movement sequences. Hence, the complexity effect may reflect sequence construction through loading a movement sequence in its correct order into a motor buffer. The notion of loading information into a buffer—prior to both kinematic parameter specification and initiation of the movement sequence—is widespread and found in the description of sequences as diverse as typing, writing words, pronouncing words, and producing gross-arm movements (Verwey, 1994). As already hinted at in chapter 3, buffer loading may neither occur when a movement sequence is fully unpracticed, in which case a cumbersome element-by-element production is more likely, nor when the sequence is highly practiced. In the latter case, a motor chunk has developed, and it is loaded in the buffer as a single unit, irrespective of its number of constituents. Hence, the complexity effect may be the most pronounced at an intermediate level of practice. In this case, the reaction process includes advance loading of all individual elements of a sequence in their correct order. The longer the sequence, the longer CRT. This view was recently confirmed by Klapp (1995), who studied *a*-reactions in which the stimulus required a sequence of four Morse-type key presses. RT was longer when four key presses were required rather than a single key press, but the effect on RT was most pronounced in early practice. After extensive practice, there remained only a minor effect, perhaps due to retrieving the first element of the sequence from the motor buffer but not due to advance programming and buffer loading (e.g., Klapp, 1981a; Fig. 3.5).

Klapp's (1981a) results are in line with those of Sternberg et al. (1978) and of Canic and Franks (1989). Together, they suggest that loading the response sequence does not occur before the imperative stimulus is presented. This is surprising because an *a*-reaction provides ample opportunity to do so. Verwey (1994) suggested that sequence construction in advance of the imperative stimulus may not occur, in view of rapid decay from the buffer. In contrast to movement sequences, there is growing evidence that kinematic parameter specifications, which supposedly belong to the motor programming stage, occur in advance of the presentation of the imperative stimulus. Thus, Klapp (1995) found no effect of response duration on RT when a response always consisted of the same Morse-type key press, either short (/dit/) or long (/dah/). Advance programming proved equally possible in choice reactions when responses shared a common property or when a response property was precued (e.g., Rosenbaum, 1980).

Advance presetting of kinematic specifications constitutes another major problem for the AFM analysis of motor stages. In the case of choice reactions, advance programming does not occur, but in that case, the problem is how to decide whether effects of motor variables are due to motor programming or to response selection (e.g., Sternberg et al., 1978). Indeed, it is perfectly reasonable to expect an effect on response selection when, for example, one imperative stimulus requires a fast movement and another stimulus a slow movement as response (e.g., Klapp, 1995; Klapp & Erwin, 1976).

As a sequence contains more elements, the probability declines that the whole sequence is loaded in the buffer before the start of the sequence's execution. Instead, the evidence suggests online loading of later elements during execution of earlier ones, which raises yet another problem for the C(RT) analysis of motor processes. Results suggesting online loading of elements come from studies in which different response sequences were connected to different imperative stimuli. The first part of the sequence was always fixed and stimulus independent, with the alternative sequences diverging somewhere in the middle. The effect on CRT was less as the divergence occurred later in the sequence (Rosenbaum, Hindorff, & Munro, 1987), suggesting that participants started executing the sequence and decided how to continue while executing the earlier fixed elements of the sequence. In turn, online loading of later elements slows down the rate of executing earlier response elements. There are various ways in which this has been found to occur. For example, Verwey (1994a, 1994b) found that, in the course of practice, the last element of a sequence of key presses was carried out faster than the earlier ones, suggesting that the final key press was the only one that was not slowed down by online loading. Verwey (1994a) also found that a group of key presses was carried out faster when it was the last group in the response sequence than when it was followed by another group. It is obvious that as more is achieved online, there is less effect on CRT.

Fitts' Law

Other evidence for online programming comes from results suggesting that various parts of an aiming movement are differentially sensitive to withdrawal of visual feedback (e.g., Glencross & Barrett, 1992, for a review). The suggestion is that one can do better without visual feedback during the first part than during the final part of the aiming movement. This is in line with the classical notion that an aiming movement consists of a ballistic open-loop part followed by closed-loop homing in on the target.[5] The time taken by an aiming movement (MT) is described by Fitts' law (Equation 2; Fitts & Peterson, 1964)

$$MT = a + k^2 \log \frac{2A}{W} \qquad (2)$$

in which A refers to the size of the movement and W to the target width. The smaller the W, the more detailed the homing in part of the movement; the longer the A, the larger the ballistic part of the movement. The logarithmic part of the relation was originally seen as support for information theory, that is, movement time in terms of a linear function of uncertainty, but there are alternative accounts. One is by assuming corrective processes when homing in on the target (feedback theory), whereas another alternative assumes a fixed relation among acceleration, distance, and accuracy while programming the movement (e.g., Schmidt, 1987). The idea that homing in occurs during the movement predicts that CRT should be affected by neither A nor W and, indeed, it is usually found that CRT and MT are fairly independent and affected by different sets of variables.

Coordination

Aside from coordination of a movement sequence, coordination of simultaneous movements is of great interest to motor processes; they may be a single-response pattern or constitute a sequence of coordinated movements. One major observation is that movement patterns differ widely in regard to whether they are easy or difficult to execute. Thus, it is hard to draw a circle and a rectangle with different hands at the same time or to carry out a large and a small aiming movement with the same movement speed so that the small one lands earlier than the large one. Instead, the two movements land at the same time so that the speed of the small movement slows down (Keele, 1986). Again, it is hard to tap two rhythms without some harmonic relation between their periods. It is even difficult to monitor one rhythm

---

[5]These conclusions may not be definitive in view of recent results by Spijkers and Spellenberg (1995). They found that aiming accuracy deteriorated more as visual information was withdrawn for a longer period during the movement, irrespective of the segment of withdrawal—that is, during the start, the middle period, or the end—which suggests that the aiming movement is under constant feedback control. A dual process may only occur when the movement exceeds some critical size.

while tapping out another one. When carrying out alternating finger movements with two fingers, certain phases are clearly preferred over others. Although all of these movement patterns are hard, they can be acquired by extended practice. Thus, some people are able to write two sentences at once, one in normal writing with the preferred hand and the other in mirror writing with the nonpreferred hand.

One conclusion is that the two hands tend to be controlled by a single program. Indeed, for a variable such as interval timing, the parameter settings for both hands should be the same or at least have a simple relation, which excludes actions such as drawing two different shapes at the same time. Time coupling refers to the completion of movement elements of two limbs at the same time or at simple intervals and is an essential constraint in movement coordination (e.g., Summers, 1989). In contrast, settings with separate parameter values for distance and direction are easy. It is no problem to move one hand in one direction and the other hand in another direction or to vary movement size and force individually, although it takes an increase in CRT (Heuer, 1990).

The main paradigm for studying movement coordination constraints is through choice reactions by creating conditions in which two simultaneous stimuli require a movement, one with the left hand and the other with the right hand, with equal or different movement characteristics. One question is which parameter values can be set in advance for either of the two hands. Any structural constraint on coordination is bound to affect CRT. Along these lines, Heuer (1990) carried out experiments in which responses consisted of a vertical or a horizontal displacement of a handle. CRT was considerably slower when two responses each had a different movement characteristic, one vertical and one horizontal, than when they had the same movement characteristic. In another study, the handles were operated by different fingers of the two hands—for example, the thumb and the index finger. In this way, the movements could be carried out with the same finger—both thumbs—or with different fingers—one thumb and one index finger—from either hand. This variation did not affect CRT, which led Heuer to conclude that using the same or different fingers did not pose a constraint on coordination.

This last result may seem at odds with evidence on homologous coupling, which refers to a greater efficiency in concurrent movements when using the same rather than different fingers of the two hands. Heuer (1990) proposed that homologous coupling occurs when sequential or simultaneous movements are selected during execution of an earlier movement, but not when fingers can be preset in advance, as in the aforementioned CRT paradigm. Advance programming may be possible in a "slow task" which refers to discrete trials separated by an ample intertrial interval. In a "fast task," trials follow each other in rapid succession, which excludes advance response programming. The moral is that effects on CRT may show up more readily in fast tasks.[6] Another illustration stems from Verwey's (1994a) research on motor chunks. In a slow task, hardly any difference in CRT was found between well-practiced participants who executed a movement sequence as a single chunk and unpracticed participants who handled the movements as separate elements. In contrast, a clear effect between practiced and unpracticed participants showed up in a fast task. In the slow task, the less practiced individuals loaded the sequence in advance of the imperative stimulus. This had the effect that the sequence was carried out almost as equally effective as when a motor chunk had been loaded. This result suggests that retrieval from the buffer was about equally efficient for either group.

Applications. Applications of motor programming and movement execution are manifold, varying from complex skill acquisition to the design of simple controls. As an example, in early practice in car driving, shifting gears and braking consist of separately programmed movements that gradually turn into one motor chunk, which means a considerable saving. The chunk does not only mean that several movements are loaded as a single unit but also that a later group of movements can be loaded while executing the elements of the chunk. The result is a smooth movement flow for practiced sequences. Inadequate motor chunking is among the reasons that less practiced drivers are more accident prone. Similar phenomena are found in other examples of skill acquisition, among which are typing and handwriting.

Various common principles of control design derive from motor programming, including the degree of resistance of a control and proprioceptive feedback about whether a control has been properly operated (M. Sanders & McCormick, 1992). Another major application concerns Fitts' (1964) law on the relation between movement distance and target width. It appears to be widely applicable, that is, in the operation of everything from operating levers and joysticks to mouse and light pens. Fitts' law appears to determine the time needed to move a mouse from one position to another on a computer screen (Card, Moran, & Newell, 1983), which is of obvious interest to back-to-back analysis. The design of controls benefits from results on motor coordination, in particular, when both hands have to be active at the same time. As outlined, there is now adequate knowledge about the types of movements that are relatively easy or hard to combine.

---

[6]Not invariably, though, because movement sequences have proven hard to program in advance. It is obviously relevant to know which variables can and which cannot be prepared in advance of the imperative stimulus. In passing, the suggestion that a fast task excludes advance programming implies an instance of single-channel operation.

MOTOR ADJUSTMENT

Motor adjustment is the final stage in the choice-reaction process that deals with the transition from central to peripheral motor activity. Thus far, it has been mainly concerned with issues regarding preparatory state.

Foreperiod Duration and Preparation

When the foreperiod is constant during a block of trials, C(RT) increases as a somewhat negatively decelerating function of its duration, except at very brief foreperiods (<200 msec), in which case C(RT) increases again (Bertelson, 1967). The effects are comparable for RT and CRT (Sanders, 1980a) although in the case of RT, a fair proportion of catch trials is needed in order to avoid synchronization of stimulus presentation and response (Näätänen & Gaillard, 1974). When varying foreperiods evenly from, for example, 1 to 10 seconds, the hazard function increases to full certainty, and mean RT declines as foreperiod increases. When all foreperiods are long (>10 sec) and clearly discriminable, RT is the fastest at the shortest foreperiod (Bevan, Hardesty, & Avant, 1965). In the case of a constant hazard—the so-called nonaging foreperiod—mean RT has been found to increase slightly at long foreperiods (Näätänen, 1971). The modal pattern of results is shown in Fig. 4.21.

The AFM model considers foreperiod duration[7] as prototypical for motor adjustment. It supposedly affects motor preparation, readiness to respond, or the distance from the motor action limit (Näätänen & Merisalo, 1977). The presumed motor locus is primarily based on evidence about interactions of effects of foreperiod duration with those of instructed muscle tension and response specificity. It was already discussed in chapter 3 that the effect of foreperiod duration is much less when presenting a loud auditory or a tactual imperative stimulus, with the further condition of highly compatible S–R connections. The suggestion was that such stimuli are immediately arousing. This means decreasing the distance from the motor–action limit and enhancing preparatory state. In all other conditions, preparation has to be voluntarily attained and maintained.

It is commonly accepted that attaining preparation takes time and that a high level of motor preparation can only be maintained for a brief period of time (Gottsdanker, 1975). Increasing foreperiod duration means that the estimate of the warning interval becomes less accurate and more variable, so that the moment of high preparation is less in tune with the arrival of the stimulus. For instance, Näätänen, Muranen, and Merisalo (1974) asked participants to press a button when an estimated duration of .25 to 4 sec had elapsed. The estimates were quite accurate at intervals of .25 to 1 sec,

---

[7]Time uncertainty may increase by variable foreperiods within a block or by a longer constant period within a block.

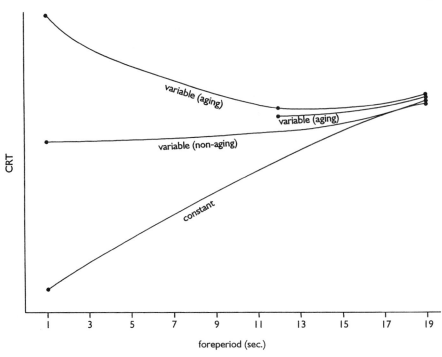

FIG. 4.21. Modal effects of foreperiod on C(RT). Variable foreperiods can have a constant (nonaging) or an increasing probability (aging). In the case of a constant foreperiod, the duration is varied between blocks.

less so at 2 sec, and much less at 4 sec.[8] The difficulty of maintaining a high state of preparation is evident from the finding that RT is already lengthened when an imperative stimulus is 200 msec overdue (Karlin, 1959). The increase of RT at very brief foreperiods is supposed to reflect the time course of preparation that has been found to take some 200 msec.

The analysis of preparatory state by means of variation in foreperiod duration between blocks of trials has the problem that C(RT) is a joint function of cognitive time estimation and actual motor preparation. Hence, C(RT) may merely reflect a more-or-less successful attempt to be ready at the correct moment in time. Gottsdanker (1975) disentangled time estimation and motor preparation by means of the so-called transit-signal technique. With this technique, it is exactly known when but not whether a stimulus may occur. Participants view a disk on which four radius lines are drawn with a 90° separation and which rotates clockwise once every 8 sec. A reference line at the 12 o'clock position marks every 2 sec, a transit of a radius line

---

[8]The extensive literature on time perception and timing (e.g., Kristofferson, 1990) is beyond the scope of this book.

(Fig. 4.22). The imperative stimulus is a 100 msec tone that is always presented at the time of a transit. In a study on attaining preparation the imperative stimulus occurred with a constant low probability (*p*) of .07. However, on 12.5% of the trials, a neon light flashed some time in advance of a transit—the lead time—to inform the participant that the *p* of a tone at the moment of the next transit would be .5 rather than .07. In two control conditions, the neon light was either not used at all or did not convey any information. In another control condition, a tone occurred occasionally at the time of a potential neon flash that was explained to the participants as occasional failures of the equipment.

An informative neon light reduced RT some 80 msec, suggesting that preparation had been successfully manipulated. RT was about equally long when the imperative stimulus was not preceded by the neon light (*p* = .07) and when it was unexpectedly—and, inadvertently, in the eyes of the sub-

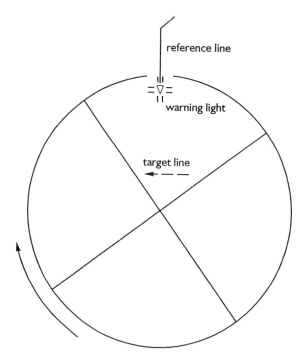

FIG. 4.22. Attaining of preparation. Participants viewed rotating target lines, one of which crossed a reference line every 2 seconds. An auditory imperative stimulus was always presented at a crossing of a target line with the reference line. The probability was .07 but amounted to .5 when a crossing was preceded by an additional visual warning light. From Gottsdanker, R. (1975). The attaining and maintaining of preparation. In P. M. A. Rabbitt & S. Dornic (Eds.). *Attention and performance* (Vol. 5). pp. 33–49. Copyright © 1975 by Academic Press, Inc. Orlando, Fl. Reprinted with kind permission.

jects—presented at the time of the neon flash ($p = 0.0$). This was taken as evidence that preparation had been negligible in the low (.07) probability condition. In order to be effective, the neon light required a 200 msec lead time, which is consistent with estimates on the time course of preparation from studies on the effects of very brief foreperiods (Bertelson, 1967). Sanders (1972) found that once the participants were optimally prepared, CRT slowed down when another warning was presented very briefly before the imperative stimulus (Fig. 4.23). A high state of preparation implies that an overt response is also easily elicited to a stimulus that should not be responded to. Hence, knowing that another warning will be presented briefly in advance of the imperative stimulus is likely to lead to depreparation in order to avoid premature responding.

Aside from attaining preparation, Gottsdanker (1975) also studied maintaining preparation by means of the transit technique. In one study, the disk had two radius lines instead of four. The imperative stimulus had a p of .5 at the time of the first transit of the radius line; if not presented at that time,

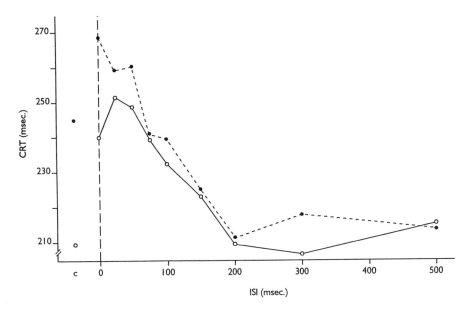

FIG. 4.23. Participants received two warning stimuli before presentation of the imperative stimulus. The first preceded the imperative stimulus either 5 seconds (dashed) or 1 second (solid) and the second between 0 and 500 msec. The single open and filled dots are the controls without a second warning stimulus. The second warning is particularly disadvantageous in the case of the 1 second foreperiod. From Sanders, A. F. (1972). Foreperiod duration and the time course of preparation. *Acta Psychologica, 36,* 60–71. Copyright © 1972 with kind permission of Elsevier Science-NL, Sara Burgerhartstraat 25, 1055 KV, Amsterdam, The Netherlands.

p remained .5 at the time of the second transit, but it could just as well appear midway between the two transits with a smaller *p* of .125. A major variable was the intertransit interval that varied from 200 to 3,200 msec. In control conditions, the potential midway presentation was omitted, and only one transit was used. The results show a fast RT—about 150 msec—for any tone position, either transit or midway, as long as the intertransit interval was less than 600 msec. At a longer intertransit interval, RT remained fast for stimuli presented at a transit position. However, RT rose sharply at the midway position and was about twice as long when the intertransit interval amounted to 3,200 msec. It follows that the state of high preparation was not single peaked but lasted some 600 msec. At longer intervals, participants were prepared to respond at each transit but deprepared between them. Additional studies showed that high preparation may be maintained somewhat longer—a couple of seconds—when a tone has a constantly high *p*, as in the case of a 400 msec interval between successive transits with a constant *p* of .5 at each transit.

Many studies on preparation have used variable foreperiods within a block, with the rationale of excluding the role of time estimation. The reasoning is that when no reliable time estimate can be made, participants are unable to prepare. This should have the effect of a flat RT-foreperiod function. Yet, the modal results show a somewhat longer RT at short foreperiods, which suggests that participants still handle some collective estimate. In view of the relatively low probability thereof, they might be biased against expecting the imperative stimulus at a brief foreperiod. This would predict that the bias disappears when using nonaging foreperiods, that is, foreperiods with a constant hazard function. This distribution, which indeed flattens the RT-foreperiod function (Fig. 4.22), has an emphasis on short foreperiods.

Thus, in the case of aging variable-foreperiods, one might conceive of preparation in terms of a bias against short foreperiods followed by a single preparatory peak when the collective time estimate has become sufficiently high. Yet, this view has problems accounting for the sequential effects that occur in studies on variable foreperiods. RT is considerably longer when a short foreperiod is preceded by a longer one rather than when it is preceded by an equally short one. In contrast, RT is hardly affected, irrespective of whether a long foreperiod is preceded by a short one or by another long one. The sequential effects may be ascribed to repeated preparation (Niemi & Näätänen, 1981), which is supposed to depend on which foreperiod occurred at preceding trials. The idea is that participants are highly prepared at various moments during the foreperiod, with periods of depreparation in between. When the stimulus does not occur during the first preparatory peak, a new peak develops some time later, and so forth. Moment and probability of the first preparatory peak are affected by the foreperiod interval at the previous trial. This hypothesis predicts that sequential effects disappear when there are only a few discriminable foreperiod durations, all of which have a sufficiently large conditional probability. This was tested and confirmed by Gottsdanker (1975). Further support for de- and repreparation came from Loveless and Sanford (1974) who found a repeated CNV wave in the EP before each of a few distinct moments when a stimulus might be presented. In case of insufficient time for repreparation, a single peak may occur, determined by a short-term best guess that has a bias in favor of the average foreperiod (Alegria, 1975).

Los (1996) described the results of the variable foreperiod paradigm as another instance of the effect of block type because blocked (constant intervals) versus mixed (variable intervals) conditions are compared. Earlier in this chapter effects of block type were described in relation to feature extraction, to Grice's (1968) variable criterion model, and to S–R compatibility. The intriguing question is whether issues such as setting a decision criterion, formulating a subjective time estimate, and choosing a processing route are regulated by a central executive or are established bottom up by conditioning or by perseveration of the last event. The latter option is supported by Stoffels' (1996) result that the effect of mixed blocks depends on repetition versus alternation of what occurred during the previous trial. This could suggest bottom-up perseveration of the most recently used route. Los also favored a bottom-up interpretation, which he extended to mixing instructions in the study of S–R compatibility. The issue is discussed again in the section on the role of a potential central executive system (chapter 8).

Related Physiological Phenomena

The CNV wave and the evoked cardiac response (ECR) are important physiological indexes of preparation. The modal ECR shows a heart rate deceleration followed by an acceleration and yet another deceleration (Fig. 4.24) that appears particularly related to motor readiness (van der Molen et al., 1991). The size of the CNV wave and the deceleration of the ECR are correlated with excitation of neurons in cortical motor-related areas, but it would be too hasty to assume a direct causal relation. For example, van der Molen et al. (1991) proposed that the ECR pattern may reflect effort in support of preparation rather than preparation as such.

Aside from the CNV and the ECR, one might well expect an effect of foreperiod duration on the level of motoneurons. EMG activity of the involved muscles does not strongly covary with foreperiod duration, but this may not be decisive because too few motoneurons may fire for covariation to show up. The problem, in particular, is that when the response is a simple button press, an anticipatory response may be triggered when there is too much motoneuron activity. As mentioned, there is more evidence for variation in EMG activity when the response consists of squeezing a dynamome-

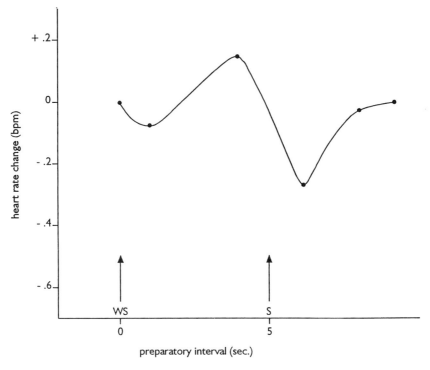

FIG. 4.24. An idealized evoked cardiac response (ECR). WS = warning stimulus; S = imperative stimulus.

ter because an overt anticipatory response is less likely to occur in that case. Yet, a total absence of EMG activity in the involved muscle systems appears to exclude a buildup of preparation (Sanders, 1980a). Therefore, an optimal state of the efferent motor system is certainly a necessary condion for an efficient response. The issue concerns the characteristics of the optimal state, which is not simply a matter of variation in muscle tension.

More subtle changes in motoneuron activity can be traced by evoking proprioceptive reflexes, for example, the Achilles' tendon reflex, at appropriate moments during a foreperiod interval. The reflex should be measured in regard to the limb that is involved, as well as to the one that is not involved, in the response. The point is that the amplitude of the tendon reflex covaries with the number of activated motoneurons. The data typically show an increase in the amplitude of the tendon reflex at the noninvolved limb and not at the involved limb. This suggests selective inhibition rather than activation of the involved limb, perhaps with the aim of freeing the motoneurons of the involved leg from peripheral disturbance. Thus, physiologically, readiness to respond is not simply motoneuron excitation but rather an equilibrium of excitatory and inhibitory impulses (Brunia, 1993).

Applications. Preparatory state is among the highly relevant determinants of CRT. In daily life, it plays a part in all time-critical situations, with responding to the brake lights of a lead car in traffic as a prime example. A reaction to an unexpected danger in a semipaced situation, such as driving, may easily take an additional second, and a poor preparatory state is probably a major cause of chain collisions. The problem is that a continuous, high state of preparation cannot be maintained; therefore, measures should be directed toward avoiding unexpected stimuli. Early warning and alerting signals are relevant in this respect. The alerting signal should not be immediately arousing—for instance, no loud horn signal—in view of ill-considered responses. Another issue is that attaining a high state of preparation is impaired by some stresses, an issue that is discussed in chapter 9.

FINAL COMMENTS

The aim of the chapter was to trace potential processing mechanisms that are characteristic of individual processing stages. In this search, the discussion focused on experimental paradigms, which are probably beyond the scope of the AFM. The problem is that too little is known about the actual bounds of the AFM and its inferred processing stages. One future research task is to determine these bounds in greater detail. As an example, it was noted that most research on perceptual discrimination used line lengths—analog stimuli—whereas most AFM research has used discrete alphanumerics. Do these different materials fit the same stage structure? Similar differences were found in the areas of response selection—in regard to the variety of compatibilities—and of motor programming, that is, aiming, handwriting, movement sequences, and coupled movements. Again, it remains to be seen whether the same stage structure will show up in any case. Research on stage analysis would obviously be fostered when the results from different types of stimuli or various motor demands converge. At the same time, comparisons among effects of different types of stimuli and responses constitute the main avenue toward a more detailed understanding of processing within a stage. A related issue is that this chapter was completely concerned with traditional, discrete choice reactions. Somewhat more complex cases are discussed in the next chapter. Will they still be within the bounds of the AFM? The further extension to complex perceptual–motor skills in chapter 10 is beyond the AFM but is closer to real-life tasks. Back-to-back analysis aims at determining the generalization from simple to more complex settings.

The argument in this chapter was meant as a draft research program rather than a set of established conclusions. Its relevance is defended against theorists who consider stage-like thinking as a dated affair (e.g., Norris, 1990). New modes of theorizing, such as connectionism, may arise but without converging experimental programs, they will remain void of content. From the perspective of real-life tasks, the application sections were still incidental and fragmentary. This is not surprising. Emphasis on basic research means that suggested applications cannot but reflect a variety of spin-offs that may play a part in many different tasks rather than in a narrowly defined set. The applied suggestions may be less fragmentary in the chapters on attention that deal with more complex tasks. Real life is, of course, farther ahead. Whether the gaps can be bridged remains the main point for the final chapter.

CHAPTER FIVE

Reaction Processes: Beyond Traditional Choice–Reaction Time

As mentioned previously, CRT is measured in many areas beyond the traditional choice–reaction paradigm, such as processing complexity and access to the knowledge structure, or access to memory, all of which are beyond the scope of the book. Yet, there are some paradigms beyond traditional CRT that bear directly on stage analysis, namely, target classification, same–different responses, and visual-fixation duration, and they will be the themes of this chapter. The results on target classification and same–different responses do not have much practical spin-off, but they have found wide application in related areas where they are repeatedly met. In contrast, the discussion of visual-fixation duration ends with a large application section.

TARGET CLASSIFICATION

Sternberg's Model

Sternberg's (1969) initial work on the AFM was concerned with CRT in a target-classification task (target–nontarget decision). The consequence was that target classification has always been viewed as intimately related to the AFM. It was studied extensively during the early 1970s but lost some of its popularity in more recent years, presumably because few new insights were added to the discussion. However, it emanated to areas such as automatic versus controlled processing, which are discussed in chapter 8. In the basic paradigm, a set of N stimuli is divided by the experimenter into subsets of targets and nontargets. Prior to a trial, the target set is presented and memorized. Then, a stimulus that has to be categorized as target or nontarget by pressing the appropriate response key is presented.[1] In varied mapping, a new target set is presented on each new trial or, perhaps, after a few trials. Alternatively, the same target set may be used for an extended number of trials, which is called consistent mapping.[2] In his original experiments Sternberg (1969) used varied mapping; the target set consisted of a subset of one to six digits, the actual number of which was varied between blocks of trials, whereas the nontarget set consisted of the remaining digits. The results show a linear increase of CRT as a function of the size of the target set, with a slope of about 40 msec per item.

Sternberg (1969) found additive effects of target set size and target versus nontarget response, both of which were also additive with the effect of stimulus quality. Together, this suggested three processing stages—that is, feature extraction, memory search, and binary decision. Sternberg proposed an exhaustive serial scan during memory search, in which all targets are sequentially compared with the stimulus. A target response is initiated when a match is found; the absence of a match leads to a nontarget response. One might argue that there is no good reason to continue search once a match has been found; search might as well be self-terminating because it stops as soon as a match is there. However, this idea was at odds with the CRT for nontargets. A serial, self-terminating model predicts that the slope of the nontarget responses is twice the size of the slope for responses to targets because, on the average, the absence of a match requires twice as many comparisons as a match. Sternberg (1975) argued that when carrying out a high-speed memory scan, a fast, exhaustive search may be the only option. Stopping scanning when a target is detected may be possible at a slow scanning rate, but not at a fast one.

Memory search in a Sternberg (1969) task deviates from usual search in short-term memory retrieval. For example, one may present participants with a list of digits followed by a probe, indicating a serial position in the list. The participants have the task of retrieving the digit presented at the indicated serial position. In that case, retrieval time is found to increase linearly for the first few serial positions, followed by fast retrieval of the digit presented at the most recent position (Hendrikx, 1984; Sanders & Willemse, 1978). In contrast to Sternberg's 40-msec search rate, the slope amounted to some 150 msec per digit, which is consistent with the estimate of the rate of internal speech and which suggests a covert speech type of retrieval. Participants may have direct access to the first position on the list, followed by

---

[1]The mirror image of this paradigm—that is, present a target followed by a list of simultaneously presented items with the task of finding out whether the list contains a target—is called a visual-search paradigm.

[2]More precisely, it is crucial for varied mapping that a target on trial n may be a nontarget on trial $n + 1$. In consistent mapping, targets can never be nontargets, and vice versa.

forward, covert articulation of the sequence until hitting the probed serial position, whereupon the process terminates by saying the desired digit aloud. The exception is when the last—and, perhaps, the penultimate—digit is probed. These positions also appear to be directly accessible, thus reflecting the recency effect in tests of short-term memory.

The description of target search as an exhaustive serial scan has met various objections. Luce (1986) listed four. First, exhaustive search predicts that for a constant target set, the variance of target and nontarget responses should be about the same, but the data show more variance for target responses. A second objection concerns the effect of the serial position of the matching target. According to the exhaustive model, the serial position in the target list should have no effect because all comparisons are always made.[3] Yet, the last target position usually has a faster CRT. Third, one may introduce a condition in which the same item is repeated in the target list, which, again, should not affect exhaustive search. Yet, CRT to a repeated target appears to be less (Baddeley & Ecob, 1973). Fourth, the way of presenting the target set modulates the rate of search. If all targets are presented in a visual, circular array, the slope appears to be less than when they are presented in a linear array (Gardner, 1973).

The final problem for an exhaustive serial scan concerns the divergent results in varied and in consistent mapping. The slope of the search function disappears altogether after participants have carried out a very large number of trials with consistent mapping, with search becoming about equally fast in the case of a target set of 1 or 4 items (Shiffrin & Schneider, 1977). An exhaustive serial scan can only explain this result by assuming that consistent mapping has the effect of getting an infinite scanning rate. In the same way, CRT is about equally insensitive to the size of the target set when targets and nontargets differ in cognitive category. The size of the target set is irrelevant when targets are always letters and nontargets always digits, or vice versa.

There are three rivals for the exhaustive serial scan, that is, a self-terminating serial scan, an exhaustive parallel scan, and a self-terminating parallel scan. Before presenting a brief outline of these alternatives, it should be noted that in a stochastic form, they are undistinguishable with respect to mean CRT (Townsend & Ashby, 1983). Thus, Fig. 5.1 shows a serial process and a parallel process with equal average intercompletion times. Even if all parallel processed items take the same average time, the average CRT still

---

[3]It is possible to account for a serial-position effect by assuming complex variations on the exhaustive serial model, such as different processing rates before and after processing the target. If a target is processed early in exhaustive search, the speed of processing the remaining elements may increase, so CRT for an early processed target is somewhat less than for a later processed target. Thus, when the last item of the target list is always processed first, a recency effect will arise (Townsend & van Zandt, 1990).

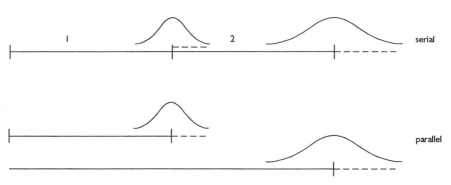

FIG. 5.1. The longer duration of process 2 can be explained by serial (upper) as well as by a parallel (lower) processes.

increases as a function of the number of items. The reason is that the total processing time is determined by the element that happens to take the longest time. The probability that at least one item takes a relatively long time increases as a function of the number of parallel processes.

Self-terminating and exhaustive processes can easily mimic each other as well. As an illustration, the assumption may be that all items, targets and nontargets alike, are scanned in memory. Townsend and Ashby (1983) gave the example in which two items are scanned in memory, with x as a target and y as a nontarget. In the case of (y, y), both items are scanned, with the outcome of a nontarget. When scanning is serial and scanning y takes 100 msec, the total scanning time amounts to 200 msec. In a self-terminating model, (x, y) takes 150 msec—that is, 100 msec if x is scanned first, and 200 msec if y is scanned first—and (x, x) takes 100 msec. An exhaustive model can produce the same results if it is assumed that scanning time for y is 100 msec and for x is 50 msec, that is, when scanning a target takes less time than scanning a nontarget. Admittedly, this is an additional assumption, but the example still shows how vulnerable the various models actually are.

Self-Terminating Serial Search

Theios (1973) also argued that exhaustive search is not necessary for explaining CRT in target classification. Instead, he proposed a so-called push-down stack, in which each item, target as well as nontarget, is taken into account. All items are stored in memory with a proper tag. Presentation of the target set has the effect that the targets push down earlier stored items in a probabilistic way. Therefore, nontargets are more likely to occupy lower positions in the stack. The stimulus elicits a search process through the stack from top to bottom until a match occurs. If an item is repeated in the target set, it receives only one single representation, but it is moved up in the stack. Besides the general effect that targets are responded to faster than nontargets, this model can explain (a) the recency effect—the last presented target is more likely to be on top of the stack; (b) the repeated-element effect, and (c) the effect of circular, visual presentation. In the latter case, storage of the targets does not occur in a fixed order as it does with sequential presentation. A nontarget stimulus also has to find its match, which takes longer than a match with a target because nontargets are usually lower in the stack. Yet, a match with a nontarget means that this item improves its position. The model also accounts for the finding that despite self-terminating processes, CRT to targets and nontargets have about the same slope as a function of set size. When nontargets are more frequent than targets, their position in the stack improves, so nontarget matches should become faster. Indeed, Theios (1973) found that nontarget CRT was faster than target CRT when nontargets were more probable. The model has problems, though, to explain why the effect of target-set size disappears in the case of consistent mapping. The stack is serially searched, which should always take more time because there are more items. One possible escape would be to assume categorical recoding of all items as targets and nontargets, which reduces the stack to two elements. This is imaginable when digits are always targets and letters are always nontargets. Any target would be categorized as a digit and any letter as nontarget, thus eliminating the effect of target-set size. When targets and nontargets are all letters, whereof the targets constitute a consistent subset, the assumption requires gradual emergence of a new categorization principle.

Self-Terminating Parallel Search

The most sophisticated parallel model of target classification is undoubtedly Ratcliff's (1978) stochastic diffusion model, some basics of which were outlined in chapter 2. In brief, on presentation of the imperative stimulus, a parallel search, that is, a buildup of evidence as a continuous random walk, is initiated with respect to whether the stimulus is a target or a nontarget. Search continues until a decision criterion that signals the presence of a target or a nontarget is passed. Processing stops at that point, and a response is carried out. Computer simulations with this model produced the typical linear increase of CRT as well as excellent predictions of the density functions for targets and nontargets with target sets of 3 to 5 items. Effects of serial position and of target repetition are ascribed to a faster buildup of evidence for the last presented target and for a repeated target. The decision criterion (C) and the starting point (Pr) with respect to a response are free parameters that provide additional flexibility and can explain the effect of relative probability of targets and nontargets. The model has no problems, either, with the effect of consistent mapping. As the number of trials with a consistent target and nontarget set increases, the variance in the buildup of evidence decreases. This ultimately leads to a constant value, irrespective of the size of the target set.

SUMMARY AND PROSPECTS

Various, sophisticated variations of high mathematical complexity have been proposed in regard to the preceding types of explanation (e.g., Luce, 1986; Townsend & Ashby, 1983; Townsend & van Zandt, 1990). The general trend is that self-terminating parallel search covers the available empirical evidence the best,[4] even though ingenious, additional amendments to some of the serial models make them fit most data as well. In the absence of further arguments, the models are hard to distinguish on the basis of mean CRT, which is among the reasons that interest in target classification has waned. The paradigm is returned to, however, in the context of automatic versus controlled processing, where it had great impact (chap. 8).

SAME–DIFFERENT JUDGMENTS

In a standard same–different task, two stimuli are presented simultaneously or in rapid succession. The task is to decide whether they are "same" or "different" by pressing the appropriate response key. Sometimes, the stimuli are simple symbols or shapes, whereas on other occasions, they are complex and multidimensional patterns varying simultaneously in shape, color, and size. In still other studies, more-or-less similar letter strings are presented. Most research has used a conjunction instruction, in which full identity is required for a same response, whereas a different response is appropriate otherwise. The alternative is the relatively neglected disjunction instruction, in which a different response is only appropriate when all dimensions are different, but a same response is correct otherwise. In conjunctive studies, most emphasis has been on the fast-same effect and on the criterion effect.

The fast-same effect refers to the phenomenon that, given a conjunction instruction, CRT for a same response is commonly faster than for a different response. This finding excludes self-terminating, serial, or parallel features search that assumes that individuals respond "different" as soon as a difference is detected, and they respond "same" when no difference is detected, which would predict that same responses take more time rather than less. Yet, apart from this failure, a self-terminating search hypothesis correctly

---

[4]It should be noted that this is only valid for alphanumeric stimuli. The rate of search appeared to be slower (90 msec/item) when targets consist of visual angles subtended by a pointer in a dial (Liu, 1996), which might suggest serial search when the stimuli have no well-established, internal template.

predicts the common finding that different responses take longer as there are fewer differences—that is, when the stimuli have more identical dimensions or common attributes. A modal data pattern is depicted in Fig. 5.2.

The fast-same effect is robust and is found in a variety of stimulus conditions. Thus, it occurs equally when stimuli consist of separable or of integral dimensions. It increases as a function of the number of stimulus dimensions, that is, the number of perceptual dimensions or the number of letters in a string—but it disappears when stimuli are hard to identify, as in the case of uninterpretable line patterns (Farell, 1985). The fast-same effect also decreases when different stimuli have a higher probability. Furthermore, many studies report a relatively large proportion of erroneous "different" responses, that is, responding "different" when it should have been "same" (e.g., Krueger, 1978). Krueger and Proctor (1981) concluded that this rules out that the fast-same effect is due to speed–accuracy trade-off, in the sense of a bias toward responding "same." Such a bias should presumably lead to a

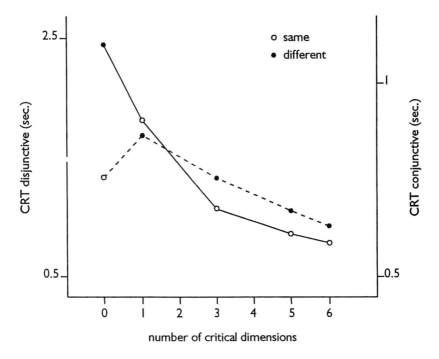

FIG. 5.2. CRT for same–different judgments as a function of the number of critical dimensions. The instruction is conjunctive (dashed) or disjunctive (drawn). From Farell, B. (1985). Same–different judgments: A review of current controversies in perceptual comparisons. *Psychological Bulletin, 98,* 419–456. Copyright © 1985 by the American Psychological Association. Reprinted with permission.

higher proportion of erroneous "same" responses, that is, responding "same" when it should be "different," which is at odds with the data.

With a disjunctive instruction, the fast-same response has no fast-different counterpart (Fig. 5.2). Same responses take longer when the stimuli have less in common, but the different response takes longer than the slowest same response. As a result, the self-terminating feature search hypothesis does well with disjunctive judgments. Another difference between conjunctive and disjunctive judgments is that disjunctive same responses take longer than conjunctive different responses, despite the fact that the same pair of stimuli requires a different response in the conjunctive case and a same response in the disjunctive case (e.g., Farell, 1985).

In the case of multidimensional stimuli, some dimensions may be assigned as relevant and others as irrelevant. For example, the stimulus pair may be a red circle and a red square, in which case the response should be "same" when color is relevant and "different" when shape is relevant. One hypothesis is that both dimensions are serially checked in a random order that predicts that same and different responses should take equally long. The criterion effect refers to the finding that in the presence of deviant, irrelevant dimensions, same responses are actually slower than different responses in the same way that disjunctive same responses are slower than disjunctive different responses.

Encoding Facilitation

This hypothesis ascribes the fast-same effect to repetitive priming. The first stimulus of a pair activates the relevant encoding pathways that are facilitated when the same stimulus is presented again (e.g., Posner, 1978). The view is in line with the finding that the fast-same effect is more pronounced with successive than with simultaneous presentation. Proctor (1981) and coworkers wondered whether, in line with encoding facilitation, the fast-same effect is established while encoding the second stimulus or during the subsequent comparison of the two stimuli. Participants were presented with two successive letters that required either a same–different response (the matching condition) or only a choice reaction to the second stimulus (the priming condition). CRT depended on whether the two letters corresponded physically (a, a), only in name (A, a), or deviated altogether. It was in that order that CRT increased, an effect that was about equally strong in the matching and priming conditions.[5] Proctor concluded that the fast-same effect is due

---

[5]Proctor found no facilitation in the priming condition when the two stimuli were simultaneously presented. Indeed, repetition priming is mainly effective in the case of successive presentation. Similarly, the fast-same effect was much smaller at simultaneous presentation, although it was not fully absent either. To explain the remaining fast-same effect in the case of simultaneous presentation, Proctor suggested that identical stimuli are less deeply processed than different ones (Posner, 1978). Yet, this factor is additional to repetition priming.

to encoding facilitation of the repeated stimulus because, in the priming condition, the two stimuli do not need to be compared. Farell (1985) wondered, though, whether the priming condition might still elicit an implicit stimulus comparison. In the case of successively presented multidimensional stimuli, Proctor suggested that repeating each identical dimension has an individual facilitatory effect and, therefore, enters the comparison process sooner than when dimensions deviate. In this way, fully identical stimuli are responded to more rapidly. Different responses can be relatively fast when many dimensions differ because the response can be given as soon as one mismatch is detected. As a result, different responses are relatively slow when the stimuli differ only in a single dimension.

The encoding–facilitation hypothesis has no problems accounting for the relatively slow "different" responses in the case of the disjunctive instruction because this is the only case without any repetitive priming. It has more problems accounting for the relatively slow, disjunctive "same" responses. Given that each identical dimension is individually facilitated, it should be no problem to detect that some dimensions are identical. The criterion effect raises a similar problem for the encoding–facilitation hypothesis. Another difficulty is that the effect of traditional repetition priming decreases as a function of the interval elapsing between two stimuli (e.g., Posner, 1978), but the fast-same effect does not. Moreover, the fast-same effect is found when one stimulus is "fixed." In that case, a single stimulus is presented and compared with an internal standard (Nickerson, 1967). The result excludes that the fast-same effect is an automatic aftereffect of the first stimulus.

Response Priming

The outcome of the comparisons between the dimensions of the two stimuli may push a response in the direction of either "same" or "different," according to a random walk. Thus, apart from a noise component, identical stimuli would activate only the "same" response, and completely different stimuli only the "different" response. In contrast, different stimuli with some identical dimensions activate both the "same" and the "different" response. The result is response competition that leads to slower "different" responses as more dimensions are identical. Eriksen, O'Hara, and Eriksen (1982) studied the fast-same effect in the flanker paradigm. Two successive stimuli were presented, each consisting of a target that was relevant to the same–different response, and irrelevant flankers that were more-or-less visually similar to the target. The fast-same effect was found to increase as the flankers became more visually similar to the target and among each other. The fast-same effect disappeared in the case of a deviant, irrelevant dimension—the criterion effect—but in various studies, "different" CRT proved to increase as well in the case of a deviant and irrelevant dimension. This poses a problem for response priming that, indeed, expects "same" response times to suffer from a deviant, irrelevant dimension—"same" is less activated—but there is no reason why "different" response times should increase as well (Farell, 1985).

Garner (1988) used hard (e.g., O-C) and easy (L-O) letter discriminations in a stimulus pair and varied color as irrelevant dimension. In accord with the response–competition view, "different" responses were the longest when the two stimuli shared the same irrelevant color. St. James and Eriksen (1991) suggested that the studies reviewed by Farell (1985) might have been insensitive to response competition. They found that in contrast to highly different stimuli, slightly different stimuli produced significantly more lever responses that first went somewhat in the wrong direction before going in the correct direction. This was interpreted as direct evidence for response competition, although the study did not directly address the issue of "different" responses in the case of identical versus different irrelevant dimensions. In addition, a simple response-priming theory faces other problems. Thus, it has difficulties explaining the slow, different responses in the disjunctive condition. The point is that when all dimensions differ, all response activation should go to the different response. Again, without additional provisions, it has problems explaining why, despite the fact that the stimuli are equal, disjunctive, same responses are slower than conjunctive, different responses.

Noisy Operator

Krueger (1978) suggested that the fast-same effect arises during the comparison process that supposedly occurs after encoding the second stimulus. In his view, the comparison consists of a match–mismatch count on all stimulus features. A small number of mismatches may be due to noise that asks for rechecking because neither a same nor a different response will receive sufficient support. The fact that stimuli are basically noisy increases the risk of committing incorrect, different responses—that is, responding "different" when the stimuli are the same—which is indeed the more common error. Because noise may lead to misperceiving same stimuli as different, and not of different stimuli as same, rechecking biases against responding "different." Relatively noise-free stimuli can be directly perceived as "same" without a need for rechecking; therefore, many "same" responses can be fast. Rechecking occurs only in the case of minor mismatches. Hence, "same" and "different" CRT are about equally long when stimuli are either identical or quite different. However, rechecking has the effect that "different" response times increase steeply in the case of small differences.

One potential problem for the noisy-operator theory is that "same" and "different" CRT are about equally affected when stimuli are degraded by adding noise (Nickerson, 1975). One might expect more rechecking as noise increases and, hence, a still more pronounced bias against responding "different," which would imply a larger fast-same effect. The problem may be solved by distinguishing external and internal noise. External noise means mismatches that require rechecking of identical stimuli as well, for the simple reason that they can no longer be perceived as noise free. Hence, both different and same stimuli will be rechecked, which means that CRT increases in either case.

Deviant irrelevant dimensions can also be regarded as external noise. Consequently, more rechecking is needed. The model should, then, explain that the fast-same effect disappears altogether in the case of deviant irrelevant dimensions.[6] Because the noisy operator has its roots in signal-detection theory, one may argue that irrelevant dimensions add so much noise that a change in relative response criteria is brought about. This change would consist of less bias of the criterion against responding "different." The point is that in the presence of irrelevant dimensions, "same" responses are no longer based on completely identical stimuli. This leads to a more balanced criterion toward responding "same" or "different," which has the effect that the fast-same effect vanishes.

Response criteria also determine the results in the case of disjunctive instructions. When stimuli seem completely different, they are rechecked to see whether they still have something in common. This leads to long "different" response times and to relatively faster "same" responses. A real problem for the model is that it seems hard to reconcile a presumed bias against responding "different," with the finding that "same" responses are so much slower in a disjunctive condition than "different" responses in a conjunctive condition (Fig. 5.2). Krueger (1978) proposed that disjunctive discriminations—all dimensions are mismatches (different) versus a single matching dimension (same)—are harder to accomplish than a conjunctive discrimination—all matches (same) versus a single mismatch (different)—but this seems fairly ad hoc.

Dual Processes

Other explanations of the fast-same effect propose a dual process, one for "same" and another one for "different" stimuli. In this view, "same" responses are based on an identity detector. If the identity detector fails, a slower, analytical process is called on for deciding whether stimuli are same or different, which takes longer as the two stimuli differ less (Bamber, 1969). The fast and the slow processes are supposed to proceed in parallel rather than serial because there are variables that only affect the fast-same response

---

[6]It is interesting that same–different judgments are affected by deviant irrelevant dimensions, but categorization is not. It suggests that categorization enables a more analytical process–gating all irrelevant dimensions—than a same–different judgment (Santee & Egeth, 1980).

and not the "different" response. If the two processes were serial, with the identity match preceding the analytical process, any variable affecting the "same" responses should necessarily affect the "different" response as well. As mentioned earlier, Posner (1978) arrived at a similar conclusion about two parallel pathways for physical-identity and name-identity matches. A physical-identity match is based on really identical stimuli and can, therefore, utilize the fast-identity detector, whereas in the case of a name match, the stimuli are not identical in all respects and, therefore, require the more analytical processing route.

The identity detector is supposed to be based on template matching, that is, comparing the two total stimuli, whereas the analytical process relies on comparisons between features. This is consistent with the effect of irrelevant, deviant dimensions that frustrate the identity detector, so the fast-same effect vanishes. The model can easily explain that uncodable stimuli do not show a fast-same effect because they lack a template. The identity detector may fail on occasion; therefore, incorrect different responses are most frequent. Different responses cannot be fast because different stimuli cannot use the identity detector.

However, again, the model has no clear provision for the finding that "same" responses in the disjunctive condition are slower than "different" responses in the conjunctive condition. The slow, analytic process is needed in either case, so there would be no reason why one response is slower than the other. The model also has trouble accounting for the fast-same effect in the case of noise-degraded stimuli. It needs the assumption that the identity detector is insensitive to a limited amount of noise. Again, the template must be resistent to distortions such as changes in visual orientation because the fast-same effect persists in the case of irrelevant, deviant orientations (J. Miller & Bauer, 1981).

Farell (1985) suggested abandoning the traditional distinction between successive encoding and subsequent comparison of the two stimuli. A comparison after encoding the second stimulus might occur only when the stimuli are uncodable. Normally, however, a conjunctive same–different judgment may develop while encoding the second stimulus. In this view, the fast-same effect is due to merging the code of the second stimulus with that of the first one when the stimuli are identical or slightly noisy. In this regard, Farell's view is not far from the identity detector. The conjunctive "different" response is established by default, that is, when the two stimuli fail to merge. Farell proposed a time deadline for detecting identity, which if passed, would automatically lead to a "different" response. When more than one dimension is involved, each individual dimension has its own deadline. The result is that conjunctive "different" CRT decreases as more dimensions differ because passing one deadline suffices for the default diagnosis. This view explains that the conjunctive "different" response is much faster than the disjunctive "same" response. In the disjunctive case, the fast identity detection does not work; hence the disjunctive "different" response cannot occur by default. Instead, the dimensions must be checked on same or different—Farell suggested a serial, self-terminating process—which leads to longer response times, particularly for the disjunctive "different" response. After all, this last case requires checking all dimensions before a response can be carried out.

Stochastic Diffusion

Ratcliff's (1985) stochastic diffusion model can be easily applied to same–different responses (Fig. 5.3). It assumes that a comparison process, which is supposed to follow encoding the second stimulus, delivers at any moment a "goodness-of-match" value, pushing either toward a "same" or a "different" response, as it did for target versus nontarget responses in memory search. It reminds one of the noisy operator in that both models localize the fast-same effect in the comparison process and that both have roots in signal-detection theory. According to the stochastic diffusion model, the fast-same effect is due to a bias toward responding "same."

In support of a response-bias explanation of the fast-same effect, Ratcliff and Hacker (1981) reported a study in which two successively presented four-letter strings were either identical or differed in one to four letters. They found that variation in accuracy instruction—"be cautious with a same-judgment" versus "be cautious with a different-judgment"—affected the size of the fast-same effect as well as the error proportions. The fast-same effect largely vanished when participants were instructed to be cautious to emit a same reaction. From these and other results, as well as from an almost perfect fit of the stochastic diffusion model to the data, they concluded that a bias toward responding "same" suffices to explain the fast-same effect, the error proportions, and the criterion effect.

The common objection to response-bias views is that a bias toward "same" is at odds with the greater frequency of erroneous "different" responses (responding "different" when the stimuli are "same"). This issue was investigated by Ratcliff and Hacker (1981) in simulations of the stochastic diffusion model. They found a small area of parameter settings in which a fast-same response concurred with somewhat more incorrect "different" responses (the dotted lines in Fig. 5.3). The counterintuitive dominance of erroneous-different responses in combination with fast-same responses is accounted for by a combination of a response bias toward "same" in the random walk part and a criterion shift to the right in the signal-detection part of the model (Fig. 5.3). The latter shift means that evidence is more readily diagnosed as "different" than as "same," whereas in the random walk part, it still takes longer to pass the "different" than the "same" borderline. The effect is that

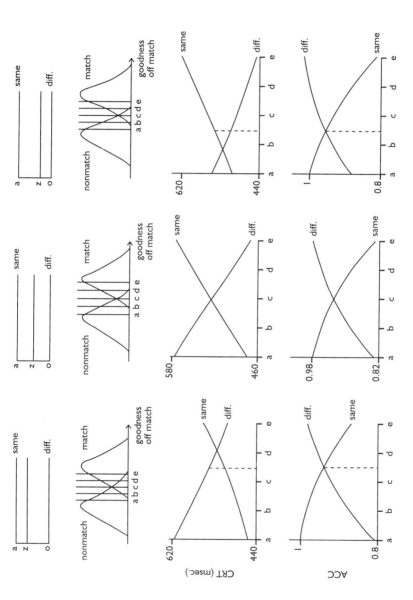

FIG. 5.3. Predictions from Ratcliff's stochastic diffusion model with respect to the speed and accuracy of same–different responses as a function of (a) the direction of the bias (z) toward responding "same" or "different" (top panels), and (b) of the criterion setting (β, a–e) in the SDT analysis (second panels). The lower panels depict predictions on the basis of particular combinations of bias and β. From Ratcliff, R. (1985). Theoretical interpretations of speed and accuracy of positive and negative responses. *Psychological Review, 92*, 212–225. Copyright © 1985 by the American Psychological Association. Reprinted with permission.

despite the response bias, the proportion of erroneous-different responses is larger. The criterion effect always refers to conditions in which an irrelevant dimension blurs the distinction between same and different. As in Krueger's (1978) model this has the effect that the random walk criterion is no longer biased toward deciding "same." The point is that when "same" and "different" are hard to discriminate, a biased setting of the random walk criterion leads to incorrect "same" responses. Moreover, a smaller d' between matches and mismatches dampens the drift rate.

COMMENTS

The same stimuli are used in disjunctive and in conjunctive conditions, so the stochastic diffusion model is faced with the task of explaining the data in disjunctions by changes in criterion as well. The very slow, disjunctive "different" response is easily accounted for. A combination of a random walk bias toward "same" and a signal-detection bias against "different" avoids the error of too easily concluding "different" but makes it difficult to pass the "different" criterion. Given this constraint, it is difficult, however, to account for the much slower, disjunctive "same" response in comparison to the conjunctive "different" response. The model seems to predict relatively fast-"same" responses, although simulation should ultimately decide whether a suitable fit can be found.

It is a problem for dual-process and encoding models that they have no satisfactory account for effects of speed–accuracy trade-off other than as-cribing it to another processing stage. Its initial link to target classification notwithstanding, stage analysis has mainly dealt with traditional choice–reaction processes and, thus far, has little to say about information flow in same–different judgments. It is difficult, therefore, to be more precise about which processing stage might be responsible for a speed–accuracy effect. This does not mean, of course, that a perceptual account of same–different effects is wrong. It only means that further tests, which can separate per-ceptual from decisional aspects in same–different judgments are needed.

The stochastic diffusion model covers a wide range of phenomena on both target classification and perceptual matching. As suggested, it may have problems in accounting for disjunctive conditions. Yet, its main problem may be that it lacks psychological content. So far, the model has been applied to stimulus identification, target classification, and same–different reactions, situations that presumably comprise quite different mental proc-esses. Yet, they are all combined under the general terms of accumulation of evidence and passing a criterion, without any additional argument about potential differences in processes. Moreover, fits of the model are only possible by making explicit assumptions about perceptual and decisional processes. As an example, there is no compelling reason why individuals should typically show a combination of a response-criterion bias toward "same" and a perceptual signal-detection bias toward "different." Again, the reduction of all perceptual factors to a simple goodness-of-fit dimension is unsatisfactory as long as it has not been specified how a perceptual factor affects that dimension. Why, for example, do line length and degrading noise not distort the goodness of fit? (J. Miller & Bauer, 1981). The stochastic diffusion model has little to say about such detailed questions.

FUNCTIONAL VISUAL FIELD

Research on CRT has always strived after the measurement of reaction time uncontaminated by response selection, which would have the advantage that the time-course of perceptual processing can be assessed without worrying about nonperceptual factors. Wundt's d-reaction was meant to achieve this aim but failed due to lack of control and participants completing stimulus identification before responding.

In the following, another candidate for the d-reaction is discussed, namely, the duration of a visual fixation. A visual fixation is always followed by a saccade, so it is possible to create a situation in which the response always consists of the same saccade, whatever the stimulus. For example, following fixation of a stimulus located at the left side of the visual field, the response may consist of a saccade to some location at the right. The question, then, is whether that saccade is triggered by identification of the fixated stimulus. If so, fixation duration would qualify as a measure of perceptual processing uncontaminated by response decision. The idea is not far-fetched. Thus, one important theory on reading is based on the immediacy hypothesis, which states that, indeed, all processing of a stimulus is completed during its fixation (Just & Carpenter, 1980). Their assumption is that even in reading, the saccade to the next word is triggered by identification of the previous word (direct control). The opposite position is that although eye fixations mediate stimulus intake, their duration is basically unrelated to processing information. Thus, fixation duration might be programmed in advance (strategic control). In that case, duration of a visual fixation is, obviously, not a suitable candidate for the d-reaction. The issue has been studied more systematically in the paradigm of the functional visual field together with a number of other questions of interest to processing information.

In the standard version of the paradigm, a participant is seated in front of a semicircular screen. Two stimuli are presented at eye level and at equal distances to the left (stimulus left: SL) and to the right (SR) of the vertical meridian. In most studies, the angular distance between SL and SR amounted to 45°, but on occasion, values ranged from 10° to 100°. At the start of a trial, the participant fixates a fixation light that indicates the position where SL will be presented. A trial starts with a warning tone followed by a standard 1-second foreperiod and by the presentation of SL and SR. The participant inspects SL, shifts the eyes to the position of SR and, finally, carries out a same–different response with respect to SL and SR. Measurement of the horizontal eye movement from SL to SR by a standard electrooculographic technique enables subdivision of the total response time—that is, from presentation of SL to completion of the same–different response—into three parts, namely, TL ("time left," the time elapsing between presentation of SL and the start of the saccade), TM ("time to move," the time taken by the saccade), and TR ("time right," the time from the start of the fixation of SR to the completion of the same–different response) (see Fig. 5.4).

This paradigm raises various issues. One concerns the effects of angular separation between SL and SR and bears, among others, on the question at which angle SL and SR may be perceived jointly as a single stimulus. A second concerns perception and information processing during a saccade. A related question is whether people can start processing immediately on

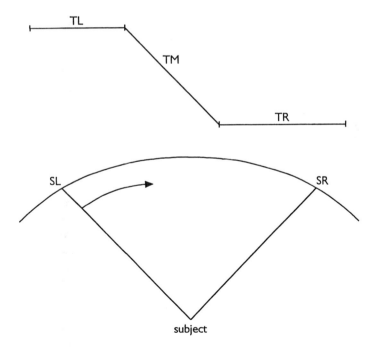

FIG. 5.4. The paradigm of the functional visual field. A left and a right stimulus (SL, SR) subtend a binocular visual angle. SL is always inspected first, followed by a saccade to SR and, finally, by a same–different response. TL (fixation time of SL), TM (movement time), and TR (fixation time of SR until the response) are measured by a standard electrooculographic technique.

fixation of a stimulus. A third issue, which is relevant to the d-reaction, concerns the output achieved at TL. Indeed, regardless of SL, the response to SL is always a saccade to SR. In comparison to the original d-reaction, the paradigm has the advantage that SL must be identified in order to complete the same–different response. Yet, there remains the question whether identification of SL is, indeed, reflected by TL. As argued, there is the serious alternative that much as in deadline notions on CRT, participants exert strategic freedom in deciding when to start a saccade. Moreover, processing SL might continue during the saccade, so it would be inefficient to continue fixation of SL until it has been identified (Russo, 1978). If this were valid, TL would fail as a modern version of the d-reaction. A final set of questions regards integration of information across saccades, which bears on the preceding discussion of the characteristics of a joint response to successive stimuli in a same–different response.

The initial studies were largely concerned with effects of angular separation between SL and SR (Sanders, 1963). Both SL and SR consisted of a vertical column of four or five small dots. The idea was that when SL and SR are in close vicinity, they can be encoded as a single stimulus rather than as two separate stimuli. At a wider separation, this is probably impossible, although some peripheral information may be acquired about SR during fixation of SL. The results suggest qualitative changes in processing SL and SR as a function of angular separation that coincided with the angular separations at which (a) a saccade from SL to SR and (b) a combined eye–head movement from SL to SR was required. When the angular separation was sufficiently small to forego a saccade, the mean time taken by the same–different response was some 100 msec less than when a saccade was needed to shift from SL to SR. In the latter case, mean response time was defined as TL + TR. TM was not taken into account, which reflects the assumption that TM is a "dead" time with respect to processing information. Again, when the angular separation was small enough to forego a head movement from SL and SR, TL + TR was some 80 to 100 msec less than when a head movement was required.

These results led to the distinction of three areas in the functional visual field, that is, the stationary field, the eye field, and the head field. In the stationary field, identification of SR was supposed to rely fully on peripheral viewing, thus defining the area in which both stimuli can be processed as a single unit. In the head field, the same–different response was thought to depend on two independent percepts, one of SL and the other of SR, similar to separate percepts in a successive same–different paradigm. The eye field had a middle position. Here, participants were supposed to obtain a hypothesis about SR during the fixation of SL, the hypothesis of which is verified during TR. Yet, verification is achieved faster than a new percept. This explains why CRT in the eye field is faster than in the head field. In support, it was found that the advantage in the eye field was largely due to a faster TR. TL was also a little longer in the head field than in the eye field, which was ascribed to more time-consuming motor programming of a combined eye–head movement than of a single saccade (Sanders, 1963).

The distinction between the eye field and the head field has proven to be useful in various other tasks. For example, Sanders (1963) presented individuals with a row of eight plus or minus signs that could either be random (e.g., +--+++--) or symmetrical (e.g., +--++--+). Symmetrical rows were recalled far better as long as the the eight signs were displayed within the eye field. This advantage disappeared when displayed in the head field, suggesting that symmetry remains unnoticed when two successive percepts are needed to encode the total composition of the signs. More recent work suggests that the eye field is smaller in the old than in the young (Ball, Beard, Roenker, Miller, & Griggs, 1988) and confirms that the eye field shrinks in the presence of cognitive load (Graves et al., 1993). The consequences for visual search are discussed in chapter 7.

There was no better recall of the signs when the pattern was within the stationary field than when it was in the eye field. At the time, this was ascribed to a failure of recoding the signs into a "single" code. More recently, the notion has emerged that more efficient processing in the stationary field may occur only when the visual features of SL and SR allow a new emerging configuration (Carswell & Wickens, 1990). Indeed, two vertical dot columns (dots–dots) provide an excellent opportunity for a new configuration. If SL and SR contain the same number of dots, they look like a dotted rectangle, whereas the configuration has a "missing" dot when the numbers are unequal. The question is, then, whether processing in the stationary field is also more efficient when SL and SR consist of, for example, the digits 4 and 5 (digit–digit) or a combination of a dot column and a digit. In this last case, a "same" response is required when the digit corresponds to the number of dots. In the digit–digit case, a "same" trial means that the visual patterns of two 4s or two 5s are physically identical, so recoding into a single configuration may be feasible. It seems excluded, though, in the digit–dots or dots–digit conditions because, there, a same–different response depends fully on meaning.

In their experiment (Sanders & Houtmans, 1985b), the aforementioned conditions were studied at angular separations of 10°, 45°, and 100°, all of which are prototypical values for the stationary field, the eye field, and the head field. All four situations showed a similar, shorter CRT at the 45° than at the 100° condition, suggesting that, indeed, the eye field–head field distinction does not depend on the visual features of SL and SR. In contrast, an increased efficiency in the 10° condition was only found in the case of dots–dots. It follows that an advantage in the stationary field is not a general element of the functional visual field but only emerges when SL and SR constitute a new configuration. It is of interest that the new configuration broke down when the angular separation required a saccade, which illustrates the relevance of peripheral vision to object perception. In addition, the study provides a method for determining which properties of a stimulus combination qualify as a new configuration. Visual similarity or mere repetition of identical symbols, as in the digit–digit condition, does not appear to be sufficient for recoding to occur. Instead, recoding into a single unit may only take place if the combination of SL and SR allows perceiving one integral configuration (Garner, 1974).

Encoding During and Following a Saccade

As already mentioned, peripheral hypotheses about SR during the fixation of SL might underly more rapid processing in the eye field than in the head field. Alternatively, the effect could be due to either more opportunity for perceptual processing of SR during a saccade than during a combined eye–head shift or to less efficient encoding of SR after an eye–head shift than after a saccade. The first alternative is unlikely because perception during a saccade appears virtually impossible. This well-established phenomenon is known as *saccadic suppression* (e.g., Matin, 1974). One explanation of saccadic suppression is that the image of outside stimuli has retinal blur during a saccade. The blurred image may be further degraded by visual masking caused by the clear stimuli during the preceding and following fixations. Thus, Campbell and Wurtz (1978) presented a light flash during a saccade that could be reasonably well detected in the dark, whereas detection was poor when clear stimuli were presented during the preceding and following fixations. Other investigators have argued in favor of central inhibition of vision during a saccade, building up before the start and dissipating toward the end (Latour, 1962), as an additional contributor to saccadic suppression.

In the paradigm of the functional visual field, Houtmans and Sanders (1983) separated presentation of SR and SL with a variable SOA. The effect was that SR sometimes appeared during TL, sometimes during TM, and on still other occasions, during TR. The location of SR was indicated by a fixation light that was replaced by SR on presentation. The results in Fig. 5.5 refer to angular separations of 45° (eye field) and 100° (head field) and show that in contrast to the eye field, SOA had no systematic effect on TR in the head field. This result confirmed that in the eye field, information about SR was obtained during TL but not during the saccade.

The data of Fig. 5.5 are also relevant to the question whether, once fixated, SR is encoded faster after a saccade than after a combined eye–head shift. This possibility is not far-fetched because a combined eye–head shift usually ends with a compensatory eye movement, whereas a single saccade does not (Fig. 5.5). The faster eye hits SR first and keeps it fixated while the slower head comes to a stop. The question is, of course, whether proc-

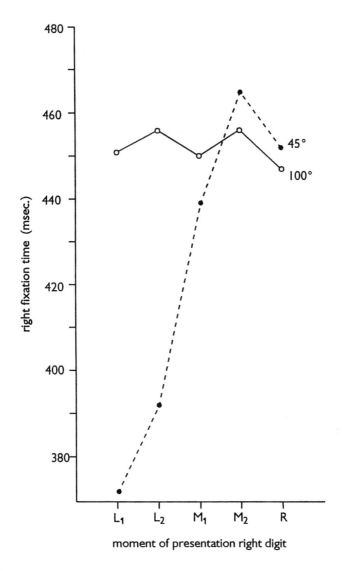

FIG. 5.5. TR as a function of the time at which SR is presented. Visual angles are 45° and 100°. L1 and L2 refer to trials in which SR was presented during fixation of SL (L1 somewhat earlier than L2). M1 and M2 refer to trials in which SR was presented during the saccade (M1 somewhat earlier than M2). R reflects that SR was presented after arrival of the eyes at the location of SR. From Houtmans, M. J. M., & Sanders, A. F. (1983). Is information acquisition during large saccades possible? *Bulletin of the Psychonomic Society, 21*, 127–130. Reprinted by kind permission of Psychonomic Society, Inc.

essing SR is suboptimal during the compensatory eye movement that, in turn, would delay TR. The Houtmans and Sanders (1983) results show that this is not the case. In the head field, TR appeared unrelated to SOA and at a sufficiently long SOA, TR was about equally long in the eye field and in the head field. This suggests that processing TR can start immediately on fixation and is not hampered by the compensatory eye movement. This is in line with psychophysical evidence that vision is not suppressed during a compensatory eye movement (Brooks, Yates, & Coleman, 1980).

The Output of TL and Processing During Saccades

Which output has been achieved at the end of TL? This question was studied by varying the properties of SL and evaluating their effect on TL (Sanders & Houtmans, 1985a). Thus, degradation of SL had about the same effect on TL as on CRT in a traditional choice-reaction condition, which suggests that feature analysis is completed during TL. This was confirmed by two further experiments. In one, the presentation duration of SL was varied (75, 180, and 500 msec), which had no effect on TL. This excludes the possibility that feature analysis of SL during TL occurs only when SL is visible. In another study, participants were forced to leave SL too early. A tone that instructed to start the saccade to SR immediately was presented briefly on presentation of SL. This instruction was hard to obey, but when successful, the results did not favor processing during the saccade. TR was prolonged in succeful trials, suggesting that on those occasions perceptual processing of SL was completed during the fixation of SR. The increase of TR was less for "same" than for "different" responses, which is in line with Farell's (1985) suggestion that a same–different judgment emerges during encoding rather than during a separate comparison process after both stimuli have been encoded.

Sanders and Rath (1991) presented SR very briefly so, again, participants were forced to leave SL early in order not to miss SR. In these studies, participants either anticipated the arrival of SL—thus missing SL!—or fixated SL for about a constant period of time, in which case SR was missed. When under this time pressure, degrading or rotating SL did not affect TL but, instead, TR. Hence, when forced, participants may leave SL on the basis of an early code—the output of the preprocessing stage?—so TL becomes insensitive to stimulus quality and rotation. Thus, when the time pressure was removed by presenting SR somewhat longer, TL increased when SL was degraded or rotated. Moreover, the finding that TR was affected under the preceding time pressure argued against perceptual processing during the saccade. A similar conclusion was reached by Irwin, Carlson-Radvansky, and Andrews (1995), who manipulated stimulus rotation. In some conditions, they presented advance information about the identity and the orientation of the stimulus that, as expected, reduced CRT as a function of the SOA between the advance information and the arrival of the stimulus. In other conditions, SOA was filled with a saccade, in which case the advance information was presented during the first fixation and the stimulus during the second, separated by a 15° or a 45° saccade. In this condition, there was hardly an effect of advance information on CRT, suggesting that processing did not continue during the saccade.

Van Duren (1994) varied the interval, which was either constant or variable (200, 300, 400 msec), between the warning stimulus and SL and found about full covariation of TL and warning interval in all conditions. She also varied stimulus quality within and between blocks and found about the same effects on TL as in a traditional choice reaction. Both results suggest again that the saccade to SR is triggered by the completion of processing SL and not by passing a fixed fixation-deadline (chap. 2).

Together, the picture emerges that a saccade is initiated by the completion of a perceptual code and that perceptual processing does not occur during the saccade.[7] The perceptual code may be the output of the identification stage. The question, then, arises whether this extends to cognitive operations such as target classification and response selection. In studies on this issue, SL was either a predefined target or a nontarget letter. On inspection of SL, the eyes shifted to SR. In some studies, SR indicated how the response keys corresponded to the target and the nontarget at that trial (Boer & van der Weygert, 1988; van Duren, 1993; van Duren & Sanders, 1995). The results of several experiments consistently show that participants did not classify the target during TL except when specifically instructed to do so. The data also show that target classification and other postperceptual operations such as response selection occurred during the saccade. In one study, SL consisted of one out of two stimulus alternatives that corresponded to two response keys in a compatible or incompatible way. SR merely indicated whether the response to SL should be carried out or withheld. The results show no effect of compatibility on either TL or TR, suggesting that the response had been selected during the saccade. This means that the immediacy hypothesis (Just & Carpenter, 1980) is confirmed only for perceptual analysis and not for higher order cognitive operations.[8]

The evidence that the saccade is triggered on completion of the perceptual analysis supports the candidacy of TL as *d*-reaction, thus enabling research on the properties of perception uncontaminated by response choice. One example of such research was already met in the studies on the fate of an

---

[7]The conclusion is fully in line with the results of Sperling et al. (1971), who presented displays in rapid succession with each display in foveal vision, so saccades were not needed. The task was to detect a numeral among letters in one of the displays. This way of presentation enables much faster rates of information processing than when scanning the displays with saccades.

[8]The effect of foreperiod duration on TL is interpreted as a motor effect due to preparation of the saccade. Thus, TL reflects perceptual processing of SL as well as the motor stages involved in initiating the saccade.

unprocessed dimension in regard to discrete or continuous flow of information. Another example is the finding of a lack of effect of relative S–R frequency on TL (F. De Jong & Sanders, 1986), suggesting that relative S–R frequency imbalance has no perceptual locus. The result is in line with CRT studies that failed to find interactions of the effects of relative stimulus frequency and perceptual variables. Thus, there is no evidence for perceptual presetting or preactivating certain dictionary units, which suggests that strategic perceptual control is highly limited. This is also in line with results from Sanders and Rath (1991), who showed that TL is insensitive to variation in SAT. It is also consistent with the finding that the variance of TL is usually small in comparison to that of TR. Most variability in a choice reaction appears to be due to response selection and execution.

Given that TL is a suitable measure of the duration of the perceptual stages, it is possible to apply it to various phenomena, the locus of which has evoked debate, such as Eriksen and Eriksen's (1974) flankers and Navon's (1977) global precedence. In some recent unpublished studies on the flanker effect, TL consisted of a stimulus surrounded by flankers, whereas TR indicated whether the response to TL should be carried out or withheld. The results showed no evidence for any flanker effect, neither on TL nor on TR, suggesting that at least under the conditions of the experiment, the flanker effect is not perceptual and that response competition was sorted out during the saccade.

Integration of Information Across Saccades

In some of the studies by van Duren (1994), SR indicated to withhold or to carry out the response to TL. This is marginal in comparison with other studies in which SR indicated the assignment of the stimuli to the response keys for that particular trial. The difference in processing demands of SR may be essential. The point is that the evidence suggests that a stored code of SL is lost when (a) processing SL has to be interrupted in favor of processing SR, as when SR provides information about how to proceed with SL; and (b) when the processes of SL and SR are unrelated. The consequence of losing the SL code is that it has to be established anew. This conclusion was based on studies in which SL and SR were both presented in the middle of the screen and separated by an SOA rather than by a saccade (van Duren & Sanders, 1995).[9] In that condition, SOA did not prolong CRT when SR had the function of a go–no-go instruction, but it prolonged CRT when it indicated the connection between stimuli and response keys for that particular trial. An SOA may reduce CRT in the case of same–different response with respect to SL and SR because, in that case, processing SR bears immediately on SL (Fig. 5.6).

---

[9]In this case, it is better to denote the stimuli by S1 and S2 than by SL and SR.

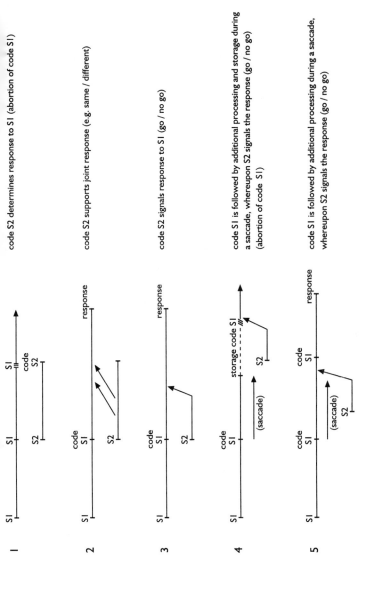

FIG. 5.6. Five possible relations between the codes of SL and SR in determining the response. In all five cases, it is assumed that processing S2 cannot start before a code of S1 has been obtained. In (1) S2 determines the response to S1, a process that leads to abortion of the code of S1 and hence, to a long CRT. In (2) and in (3) S2 either supports a joint response (same, different) or merely indicates to carry out or withhold the response to S1. In those cases the S1 code is undamaged. In (4) and (5), encoding of S1 is followed by a saccade. If the saccade takes longer than some critical duration, the code of S1 has to be stored. A stored code is sensitive to damage from any unrelated S2. When the saccade is completed within the critical period, storage of the S1 code is not needed. In that case the code can survive a simple go-no-go instruction.

The previously mentioned constraint on integration of information from two successive stimuli was already noted by Davis (1967) and suggests that stored codes are of utmost relevance in the integration of information across fixations. This was confirmed by studies of Irwin (1991, 1992). In one experiment, he used a variant of Sperling's (1960) partial report technique. A letter array was presented during one fixation, and a partial-report cue during the next fixation. The rationale was that when integration of information is a matter of fusion of visual information according to spatial coordinates, the partial-report cue might as well be given at the next as at the same fixation as the letter array. However, the results show a pronounced increase of mislocations when the partial-report cue appeared at the next fixation, which argues against spatiotopic visual fusion across saccades and in favor of integrating more abstract representations.

Other objections against spatiotopic fusion across saccades stem from evidence that changes in a visual scene during a saccade may remain fully unnoticed (Rayner & Pollatsek, 1989), with the exception of elements that are focally attended during either fixation. Thus, when in the functional visual field, a "scene" consists of two single stimuli (SL, SR), which stimuli are compared on successive fixations, processing SR proved more efficient when both SL and SR had the same visual features, for example, both intact or both degraded, than when they had different visual features, for example, SL intact and SR degraded, or vice versa (Hansen & Sanders, 1988). Yet, this result does not necessarily imply that all visual features are retained across fixations in order to prime SR. Thus, Los (1994) argued that Hansen and Sanders' results may be due to more abstract route priming.

Integration of information across saccades may benefit from parafoveal information about SR during the fixation of SL. This, indeed, was suggested as the basis of the processing advantage in the eye field. While fixating SL, participants are supposed to obtain a hypothesis about SR, which is retained during the saccade and checked during the fixation of SR. What are the properties of this hypothesis? In one study, Houtmans and Sanders (1984) found that the smaller CRT in the eye field than in the head field was reduced but not fully eliminated when SR was degraded. Therefore, it could no longer be correctly identified during the fixation of SL. Thus, the hypothesis about SR does not seem to consist of semantic information. A further study tested the potential contribution of spatial information (Sanders, 1993b). When peripherally viewed from the location of SL, SR consisted of either a degraded digit, a small red light, a large white dot, or a random dot pattern, with conditions varied across blocks of trials. During the saccade, SR was always replaced by an intact digit. The results show only an eye field advantage when a degraded digit had been peripherally viewed, despite the fact that it could not be identified. The conclusion was that spatial information does not add to the eye field advantage and that it is, so far, unclear which feature actually causes the advantage.

SUMMARY AND PROSPECTS

The functional visual field is a fruitful, simple paradigm in which a variety of performance issues are addressed. One conclusion is that a saccade is triggered when the perceptual stages have been completed and that the structure of these stages remains intact. This is an important generalization in regard to the modularity of processing stages. It also supports the candidacy of TL as a measure of perceptual processing, uncontaminated by response selection. As already pointed out, the paradigm can be used with respect to the question whether a percept has an emergent configuration and with respect to the structure of the visual field.

Applications. The division of the functional visual field into an eye field and a head field has implications for equipment design. The stationary field has less general validity but may be valuable as an index of whether a configuration is perceived as a whole or as separate parts.

One application concerns the angular distance between items on the same line when reading a table. It may be self-evident that the object character of a pair of two items is lost when the items are far apart. The issue is related to the Gestalt principle of proximity and may apply, irrespective of whether the two items constitute a new emergent property. There is actually quite a lot of evidence that spatial proximity of closely related items is essential for efficient inspection. For instance, graphed lines and their labels are more easily identified when positioned next to each other than when the label is in a legend. In the same way, radar blips and their label in synthetic radar should be in close vicinity in order to avoid identification errors (Wickens, 1992).

The main message emerging from the distinction between the eye field and the head field is that the eye field constitutes a unitary scene that allows rapid orientation and reorientation on the basis of peripheral information. In contrast, the head field requires a change of scene and independent, successive percepts that may suffer from overwriting of earlier percepts by later ones. The available evidence suggests that this laboratory result can be widely generalized. For example, Eernst and ter Linden (1967) studied the effects of the size of the visual field in periscope displays in tanks. In one configuration, the tank had two independent periscopes, both of which covered a limited visual angle and could only be viewed one at a time. This led to severe problems in scanning the visual environment and in integrating information from successive percepts, even when the two periscopes were set in a way that they covered adjacent parts of the visual field. The problem was, clearly, that the two periscopes required independent percepts at a visual angle that is normally covered by the eye field. The result was a loss of peripheral information and of efficient orientation to relevant spots in the

visual field. Performance improved considerably by replacing the two periscopes by a single one with a wider angle, although the total visual angle
remained the same in either case.

The distinction between the eye field and the head field suggests that
when aiming at efficient search, a display should not exceed the limits of
the eye field. Two issues may be of interest in this regard. First, the eye
field derives its advantage from hypotheses about what occurs in the periphery. It is well known that as stimulus density increases, peripheral information suffers heavily from lateral inhibition (e.g., Bouma, 1978). Hence,
the eye field-head field distinction applies mainly to the macrostructure of
the visual field, that is, detecting large and rough structures rather than fine
details. Second, the eye field–head field transition does not occur at a fixed
angular separation but depends on cognitive load. The eye field appeared
to widen and shrink as a function of stimulus density and discriminability;
it may reduce to a binocular visual angle of less than 50° when searching
for a little larger target among nontargets and stretch to some 80° to 100°
when detecting single or moving stimuli in an otherwise empty field (Sanders, 1963). Whether a visual task exceeds the limits of the eye field can be
estimated by observing whether a task actually requires head movements.

Another application of the eye field–head field distinction is in transcribing
text. The principle is that head movements should not be needed among
reading the next lines to be typed, checking the lines typed last, and viewing
the keyboard. Efficient reorientation among these task elements is only possible when they are within the eye field. When head movements are needed
to read the next few lines, their location has to be redetermined at each
new inspection. Because the display exceeds the eye field, the correct location cannot be directly derived from peripheral information. Other major
applications are related to car driving. The relevance of a wide and uninterrupted outside view during driving is self-evident (e.g., J. M. Wood &
Troutbeck, 1994). When searching for relevant information from the outside
view, the rear mirror, and the side mirrors, the configuration is optimal when
all three are within the eye field. In most present-day designs, this is not
the case, with the effect being that outside viewing has to be interrupted
when inspecting a side mirror, and *vice versa*. Besides a direct loss in processing efficiency, this may have negative effects on long-term driving. During
a long drive, participants are likely to neglect information from the side
mirrors because continuous reorientation in the head field is demanding
(Sanders, 1963). The advance of computerized equipment in the car may
lead to additional applications of the eye field–head field distinction. Thus,
inspecting an information screen in the car and keeping track of the outside
environment are mutually exclusive when the location of the screen is beyond the eye field. Again, auditory information may diminish the size of the
eye field as well. There is evidence that exceeding the eye field is a relevant
factor in automobile accidents (Graves et al., 1993).

Another application concerns flow diagrams of ongoing processes that should be within the eye field, in particular when information from successive percepts has to be compared or integrated. For example, a complex railway yard should be displayed as a single unit at an angular distance of no more than 45°. In some of the older designs, this was actually the case. When using computer screens, the problem is that a normal screen subtends a fairly limited visual angle. There is, then, choosing between a smaller display of the total yard or dissecting the yard into parts, both displayed on adjacent screens. The first option suffers from a loss of discriminability, whereas the second one has the problem that the eye field is exceeded, with the consequence of independent percepts, instead of related percepts, of the information flow. A third option is to display parts of the yard through separate pages that can only be viewed in succession. This obviously suffers from the same disadvantage, namely, that the information contained in the display has to be processed in successive, independent percepts. The accumulating evidence on failing memory and overwriting codes of earlier by later percepts warns against too simple, computerized versions of displaying information on successive pages. It is almost certain that detailed information is lost at the next percept. This requires considerable rechecking in order to reach a conclusion. The optimal solution may be to project all data on a larger screen, provided that sufficient resolution can be reached.

There is a similar problem when a pedestrian or a driver is about to cross a busy street and looks, in succession, for traffic coming from the left and from the right. From introspection and observation, one inspection does often not suffice to make sure that one may safely cross. This is partly due not only to the fact that information becomes rapidly obsolete but also to the fact that the data from the left and from the right are processed in independent percepts and liable to failures of integration.

In large control rooms used for supervising complex, industrial processes, it is impossible to display all pertinent information within the limits of the eye field. In that case, one may recommend dividing the total set of displays into subsets that are independent in the sense that each subset allows a coherent conclusion. Inspection of successive displays in control rooms may suffer, in particular from overwriting of earlier information by later information. As the basic research suggests, this is liable to happen whenever the response to a particular display depends on the status of the next display. Another example is when information from the next page on a computer screen should be compared with the stored representation of information from the previous page. It remains to be established which level of abstraction is required to avoid failures of memory or overwriting. The finding that a more abstract code, for example, a single classified target, proved to suffer from overwriting suggests that a summary statement on the present page of the information contained in the previous page may be required to warrant efficient supervisory control.

Similarities to Reading

Most of the preceding studies were exclusively concerned with the functional visual field. From a back-to-back perspective, the obvious question is whether the results obtained there extend to findings in areas such as visual search and reading. In reading, acquisition of information from parafoveal vision has been extensively studied by means of fixation-guided text displays (Rayner & Pollatsek, 1989). In a common version of this technique, participants read a text displayed on a computer that also monitors the exact fixation point on a printed line. The computer scrambles the text, except for a window of N characters, to the left and to the right of the fixation point. During each saccade, the window is adapted to the new fixation point (Fig. 5.7). Among others, this technique allows conclusions on the minimal number of characters required for uninterrupted reading. Under standard conditions, this appears to amount to some 15 characters, 5 to the left and 10 to the right of the fixation point.

A variation on the fixation-guided display technique is used to study the role of parafoveal information in integrating information from successive fixations. Here, participants fixate a central point, and on presentation of a letter string in parafoveal vision, they are instructed to carry out a saccade

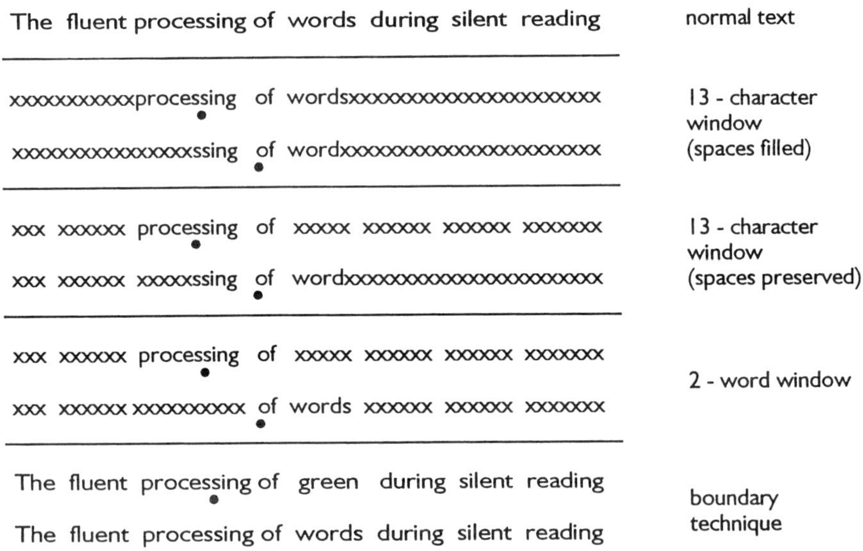

The fluent processing of words during silent reading	normal text
xxxxxxxxxxxprocessing of wordsxxxxxxxxxxxxxxxxxxxxxxxx	13 - character window
xxxxxxxxxxxxxxxssing of wordxxxxxxxxxxxxxxxxxxxxxxxxxx	(spaces filled)
xxx xxxxxx processing of xxxxx xxxxxx xxxxxx xxxxxxx	13 - character window
xxx xxxxxx xxxxxssing of wordxxxxxxxxxxxxxxxxxxxxxxxxxx	(spaces preserved)
xxx xxxxxx processing of xxxxx xxxxxx xxxxxx xxxxxxx	2 - word window
xxx xxxxxx xxxxxxxxxxx of words xxxxxx xxxxxx xxxxxxx	
The fluent processing of green during silent reading	boundary technique
The fluent processing of words during silent reading	

FIG. 5.7. The moving window technique in studies on reading. X's are replaced by letters and vice versa during a saccade. In the case of the "boundary technique" a nonfitting word is replaced by a fitting one during the final saccade. From Rayner, K., & Pollatsek, A. (1989). *The psychology of reading*. Englewood Cliffs: Prentice-Hall. Reproduced with permission of the authors.

to the location of the string. During the saccade, the letter string is replaced by a word that the participants should name on fixation as fast as possible (Rayner, 1978). A general result has been that the efficiency of peripheral preview hardly profited from semantic information. However, a substantial benefit is obtained when the parafoveal and the fixated word had some common initial letters (e.g., *chart* as peripheral preview of *chest*). The benefit was neither due to encoding partial meaning, such as a morpheme, nor to identification of a prefix. In one study, a prefixed word—for example, *re-vive*—proved to benefit as much as a nonprefixed word with the same initial letters, for example, *rescue* (Lima, 1987). The benefit of peripheral viewing also appeared unrelated to integration of visual information across fixations because it did not change when the visual form of the letters was altered during the saccade. Several studies have addressed the possibility that the initial letters receive an articulatory code and that articulatory rather than visual correspondence is decisive for the benefit (e.g., *cite* as preview for *site*—that is, a homophone and visually similar—vs. *cake* as preview for *sake*—that is, no homophone and visually similar). Homophones proved to benefit somewhat but could not explain the full benefit, such as when the initial letters are identical.

The aforementioned conclusions from studies on reading mimic those from the functional visual field in that parafoveal information contributes to information integration and that it is, as yet, unclear in which way. It is easier to falsify than to confirm explanations about how peripheral information facilitates subsequent processing. It is not a matter of a semantic or a perceptual hypothesis about the whole word that argues against "whole word" models of reading through semantic meaning or through analyzing perceptual "envelopes." The first few letters of the parafoveal word appear to be encoded, but the facilitation is not a matter of integrating the visual properties of these letters with the other letters of the word nor of introducing redundancy constraints. It could be that parafoveal knowledge about the first group of letters starts an initial activation of letter and word codes along the lines of Rumelhart and McClelland's (1982) interactive activation model on letter and word recognition, but this remains speculative.

In line with the results on the functional visual field, studies on reading have shown that fixation duration depends on the processing demands of the fixated stimulus. When the physical aspects of a text are randomly varied from fixation to fixation, fixation duration mirrors the demands. Again, the fixation of the previous word lasts longer when the next word is not fixated (Pollatsek, Rayner, & Balota, 1986). Again, a high frequency word is fixated for less time than a low frequency word (Rayner & Duffy, 1986), and fixation duration decreases when a word has been primed or when it can be predicted from the context. There is also evidence that before a saccade is initiated, a word has been identified or, at least, has attained lexical access (McConkie, 1983; O'Regan, 1990).

There are also contradictory results that prevent accepting too simple a picture. First, when parafoveal preview during reading was artificially eliminated, the effect of word frequency on fixation duration vanished. This could suggest that parafoveal information determines the length of the next fixation (Inhoff & Rayner, 1986). Yet, when a low frequency word has a short fixation duration, it is fixated again. Thus, its gaze duration is still longer than that of a high frequency word. Moreover, fixation duration is affected by other complicating factors such as the landing position on the word (Nazir, O'Regan, & Jacobs, 1991; O'Regan & Levi-Schoen, 1987) and the processing demands at earlier fixations. A word has an optimal landing position, that is, somewhat left of the middle, from where it is most rapidly recognized. Again, detecting a typographical error on an earlier fixation affects the duration of later fixations (McConkie, Underwood, Zola, & Wolverton, 1985).

Fixation duration might reflect the time taken by programming the position of the next saccade as well as the processing demands of the presently fixated stimulus (Viviani & Swensson, 1982). In the functional visual field, there is also some evidence for a contribution of motor programming to TL. A combined eye–head movement took somewhat longer than a single saccade (Sanders, 1963), suggesting that a more time-consuming program as a fixation shift is more complex. Again, a small (8°) saccade took somewhat longer than a 45° saccade (van Duren & Sanders, 1995), which may reflect an accuracy component as implied by Viviani and Swensson. Fortunately, motor and perceptual components can be easily disentangled.

The general conclusion may be that despite many similarities of oculomotor behavior in the single saccade paradigm and in reading, there remains the fact that reading is characterized by rapid alternation of fixations and saccades, the dynamics of which put a clear limit on the generalization of the findings on the functional visual field. This conclusion is relevant as well to the issue of direct versus strategic control of saccades in reading and search. The strategic view has a long-standing history and claims that eye-movement guidance in reading is based on a preprogrammed, oculomotor scanning strategy. A saccade is supposed to have a constant length, a fixation, and a constant duration, whereas the variabilities are due to noise and strategic adjustment to processing demands. Yet, the effect of individual words on fixation duration across a sequence of fixations argues against a dominant role of global preprogramming. Again, as in the functional visual field, there are studies on delaying the onset of information intake in reading by presenting a mask (25–300 msec) when the eyes arrive at a new word. This delay is largely compensated by an increase in fixation duration, regardless of whether the delay was fixed or variable in a block of trials (Rayner & Pollatsek, 1981). Yet, this result is complicated by the occurrence of anticipatory saccades—in particular at the longest SOAs—which warns against a fully deterministic conception of direct stimulus control. Thus, the immediacy hypothesis (Just & Carpenter, 1980) has not found general con-firmation.

Mixed models of saccadic control propose a combination of external bottom-up and preprogrammed top-down control. In one version (O'Regan, 1990), the program decides which word to fixate next and where to land, but it is locally determined whether a single fixation of a particular word is sufficient or that another one is required. Thus, Vitu et al. (1995) found that oculomotor behavior is similar when reading normal text or sequences of letter strings constructed by replacing all letters of the text by the letter "z" (e.g., "we are sleepy" becomes "zz zzz zzzzzz"). This suggests that linguistic factors are not all important for saccadic behavior. Still, saccadic shifts differed when reading text or meaningless letter strings. Words in normal text showed a smaller mean fixation duration, had a lower probability of refixation, and a higher probability that a word was skipped. All these factors suggest linguistic effects on the level of the individual word affecting fixation duration, as in the case of the functional visual field.

In another mixed model, Nattkemper and Prinz, (1990) assumed that the next fixation duration is programmed on the basis of information—para-foveal as well as foveal—acquired during the previous fixation. For example, if the previous word leads to a strong prediction about the identity of the next word, a short fixation duration is programmed for that next word. Van Duren (1994) proposed that the programmed duration acts as a deadline rather than as a strict duration. If processing does not exceed the deadline, fixation duration is under stimulus control, whereas a saccade is triggered by the deadline when it is exceeded. There remains the question whether a deadline is set anew at each fixation or remains the same across a sequence of fixations.

SUMMARY

In conclusion, the comparison between results on reading and on the functional visual field show interesting common trends as well as differences, presumably related to the rapid alternation of fixations and saccades in reading. The back-to-back approach suggests further tests by extending the pattern of saccades in the functional visual field. For instance, fixation of SL might be preceded by a saccade or by a series of saccades in order to mimic reading. Again, in reading, one would be interested to know whether there is evidence for the basic finding of the functional visual field that higher order processes may continue during a saccade.

This discussion on reading has been limited to the interplay of fixations and saccades in an attempt to compare the results with those on the functional visual field. Reading will be returned to later when discussing simulation models. It is shown there that models rely heavily on elementary findings about visual scanning. In regard to applications, there are various consequences for layout of verbal displays. An example is the width of a line of text. It should neither be too small nor too large. One may be reminded that some 6 to 10 characters are processed within a single fixation. As the width of a line is smaller, more saccades are devoted to shift lines. Moreover, when recurring to an earlier word, one is obliged sooner to go back to a previous line. This raises a search problem. When width is too large, there may arise the problem of finding the next correct line. Margins are always perceived peripherally and aid in shifting to the next line. Some six to eight fixations of a line of text appear to be optimal.

Eye-movement patterns are also related to comprehension. As a text becomes more difficult, it is desirable to have shorter lines so that less time is spent dwelling on a single line. Economizing on text and improving comprehension by using clear and unambiguous phrases is an important issue in human factors, such as when composing instruction manuals and writing texts. Here, the underlying basic theory concerns higher order cognitive processes that are beyond the scope of the book.

CHAPTER SIX

Introduction to Attention

VARIETIES OF ATTENTION

As mentioned previously, attention used to be exclusively related to information intake, whereas it is now generally recognized that attentional control occurs on all processing levels: perceptual, central, and motor. When faced with overload, attention controls intake of information and guards ongoing processing from distraction (e.g., Broadbent, 1982). Without overload, attention is still involved in selecting and preparing for action. For instance, the effects of foreperiod duration and of relative stimulus frequency (chap. 3) are often discussed in terms of sustained attention (Posner, 1978).[1] Bottom-up as well as top-down factors play a part, in that attention partly derives from exogenous factors such as involuntary capturing and partly from endogenous factors such as voluntary focusing or dividing (Eimer, Nattkemper, Schröger, & Prinz, 1996). Bottom-up processes may be more prominent at the perceptual level, whereas top-down voluntary control may dominate the central and motor levels.

Besides selective processes, strategical issues are of interest (e.g., Sanders & Donk, 1996). Thus, when an individual is performing several tasks at once, attention has to be divided, and the various performances have to be coordinated to prevent chaos (Heuer, 1996). Attention also plays a part as

---

[1]Johnston and Dark (1986) distinguished between attention as "cause" or as "effect" of information processing. Thus, in cases of overload, attention may be instrumental in selecting some and ignoring other stimuli. In contrast, attention has been used to indicate "full emphasis" and, hence, more efficiency in processing. For instance, efficient preparation is an effect and so is alertness in vigilance.

coordinator when planning, selecting, and completing nonroutine actions (Norman & Shallice, 1986). Thus, it is thought to be related to the central executive component of working memory (Baddeley, 1986). Finally, sustained attention is required in vigilance tasks (Koelega, 1996). Is all of this done by a single attentional function or is attention merely a convenient label for a field of research? These themes are preceded by a discussion of some methodological and theoretical pitfalls.

Meaning and relevance of attention may seem self-evident. It is expressed by James' (1890) adage that everyone knows what attention is. Nevertheless, there are severe problems in understanding the concept. Witness, for example, Johnston and Dark's (1986) desperate remarks in their 1986 review in the *Annual Review of Psychology*. The trouble is that one may outline a variety of functions that all seem to be related to attention. At the same time, this variety renders the attention concept elusive. As a result, it often was proposed that the notion of an *attentional function* should be abandoned altogether. The Gestaltists did that (Rubin, 1921) at about the same time, as the early behaviorists (J. B. Watson, 1917). Although attention regained respectability in more recent years, doubts about its status never did disappear.

METHODOLOGICAL ISSUES

What is wrong with attention? The various issues may not only apply to attention but equally well to other mental concepts originating from experience.

Vertus Dormitiva

The first issue concerns what Neumann (1991) called the *vertus dormitiva*. This refers to a situation in which a vaguely defined concept, usually related to some observable phenomenon, is granted theoretical status in order to explain that phenomenon. The label is inspired by Moliere's play *La Maladie Imaginaire*, in which a young physician ascribed the sedative effect of opium to its presumed "sleeping power." However, this is no explanation, since merely some aspect of the observed effects of opium is mentioned. In the same way, attention has been invoked as an ad hoc explanation for a variety of phenomena ranging from binocular rivalry to skill in generating a random sequence. Neumann showed that more recent theoretical views, such as Kahneman's (1973) capacity notion suffer equally from the *vertus dormitiva* error.

At this point, a sharp distinction should be drawn between experimental variables and theoretical constructs. Experimental variables can be described operationally. Thus, foreperiod duration can be measured in seconds, and time on task in minutes or hours. Well-established empirical relations among experimental variables, and a dependent variable such as C(RT), lead to an empirical law that, in turn, may lead to an underlying process model. Behavioral concepts are only allowed at that last stage. Therefore, one should always proceed from empirical laws to behavioral concepts, never the other way around. In other words, loosely defining a concept and then measuring it by way of some task is not allowed. Application of this rule means that in the absence of a satisfactory process model, one should refrain from using behavioral concepts. The argument should be limited to effects of variables and should be concerned with empirical laws.

Unsatisfactory as this may seem, an empirical law is still the first important level of abstraction. The statement "sleep loss affects CRT in this particular task" refers to an isolated effect of a variable (sleep state) on some specific task condition. A stronger statement is "sleep loss increases the effect of stimulus degradation on CRT, in particular when participants work for a prolonged period of time." This statement requires (a) establishing the relation between stimulus quality and CRT, (b) demonstrating that the effect of sleep loss on CRT is more pronounced with degraded stimuli than with intact ones, and (c) showing that a more pronounced effect of sleep loss is particularly evident when participants have worked for some time. Such a set of statements may become an empirical law without any reference to a behavioral construct. In the same way the Gay-Lussac law on the relations among effects of volume, pressure, and temperature of gases does not refer to a physical construct.

Problems are bound to arise when attempting to measure a loosely defined concept. Let us review an example from physics. In the 19th century, attempts were made to measure "ether," a hypothetical substance in outer space that was supposed to mediate perception of stars and planets. The first problem with this proposition is that a phenomenon—the fact that one can see planets and stars—is explained by ether functioning as an ad hoc, mediating substance. The next step is that ether should be measured, but how do we measure something that does not exist? There are similar problems when trying to measure the operation of intuitive concepts such as attention, fatigue, and mental load. Do they exist or do they merely emanate from intuition?

One consequence of using behavioral concepts without sufficient experimental underpinning is that different ad hoc measures, which fail to correlate, are postulated. For example Chapanis (1971) showed that even a seemingly simple concept such as legibility of print fails bitterly when granted theoretical status. Chapanis listed some 30 proposed measures of legibility that show little mutual correlation. Despite intuitive appeal, that is, something is legible to a measurable degree, a theoretical concept of legibility proves problematic and wrong. The point is that the first question should be this: Which processes are involved when reading printed material and to what extent can these processes be generalized to such different reading conditions as a book, an announcement, a subscript, a computer display, or a traffic sign?

Functional Process Models

It is obviously desirable to have measures of well-established behavioral concepts with construct validity. Construct validity means that a concept is based upon a well-developed and predictive functional process model that describes and delineates the mutual relations among the various phenomena involved. A functional process model consists of a number of verifiable statements about hypothetical mechanisms underlying these phenomena, which, together, provide a coherent common description. Such a model need not be the final truth. On the contrary, the prerequisite of a set of verifiable statements implies that a process model can be shown to be incorrect. A process model may have a limited scope, but as long as it is consistent with the data set, it can claim construct validity. Thus, its parameters can be measured. An example is the mercury thermometer derived from the classical atom model that among others, derived from the Gay-Lussac relations of temperature, volume, and pressure. On the basis of that same atom model, a variety of alternative but perfectly correlating measures of temperature can be developed.

Aristotle's views on attention—discussed in Neumann's (1991) excellent historical survey—may illustrate how one might conceive of building a process model. Aristotle suggested that perceptual selection is due to inhibition of weaker sensory impressions by stronger ones. As an alternative, two sensory impressions may not compete but merge, in which case both stimuli are inhibited. The point is that merging leads to a unitary, new percept of the two impressions. As a consequence, they can no longer be perceived separately. This is actually a loss, and, hence, selection serves the function of keeping the two impressions apart. Incorrect and incomplete as Aristotle's view might be, it still fulfills the basic requirements of a process model because it starts from a data set and contains—at least in principle—verifiable statements. Aristotle neither postulated attention as an explanation for perceptual selection nor claimed to offer a complete view or a measure of perceptual selection. Instead, his views represent an attempt to describe what might happen by way of statements that stay close to the data that they address.

The Category Error

As mentioned earlier, a category error is committed when borrowing explanatory concepts from other domains. The error goes back to Descartes' dualism of body and soul. He described bodily phenomena in terms of *res extensa*, which needs a causal explanation. In contrast, mental phenomena belonged to the immaterial *res cogitans*, the phenomena of which should only be classified and described in terms of experience. According to Descartes, involuntary attention is a bodily phenomenon because it occurs automatically through outside stimulation, whereas voluntary attention, as an expression of the Will, belongs to the realm of the soul. Yet, voluntary attention may affect the body, even if only indirectly, via the pineal gland as the point of contact between body and soul. Hence, bodily phenomena may be due to attention. In this way, Descartes opened the door to using attention as a *deus-ex-machina* explanation for bodily phenomena. This was harmful in two ways. First, the "explanations" did not foster understanding. Second, the fact that attention was, at least in part, a matter of *res cogitans* left the feeling that the concept is animistic in some obscure way (Hebb, 1949). Assuming a causal effect of a descriptive mental concept on the presumably mechanistic level of the body is a prototypical category error. It reflects a failure of accomplishing a unitary theoretical description at one and the same level of analysis and allows a mixture of concepts from different levels. To Descartes, these levels were body and soul. A few centuries later, they were physiology and consciousness as parallel realms.

The Homunculus Problem

The presumed animistic connotation of attention leads to the issue of the homunculus. Voluntary attention suggests inner control of behavior, independent from outside stimulation. From there, it is a small step to imagine an inner agent who sorts out those parts of outside stimulation that can be used at any particular moment. The main problem of the homunculus is that nothing is explained by delegating the responsibility for perception and action to it. Yet, as Attneave (1961) argued, this is only the case if we try to make the homunculus do everything. The moment we specify certain processes that occur ouside the homunculus we are merely classifying or partitioning psychological functions. Attneave's view has been instrumental to a more ready acceptance of notions such as a central executive. However, part of the current popularity of parallel distributed models is undoubtedly due to their claim that they can do without an executive controller because control is thought to be distributed throughout the whole system. It remains to be seen whether this claim can be realized. So far, connectionist models of attention still have prominent facilitating and inhibiting control mechanisms in more or less disguise (Detweiler & Schneider, 1991).

Attention As a Unitary Function

A further methodological problem concerns the distinction between attention as a label for an area of scientific inquiry, similar to perception, memory and motor behavior, and attention as a unitary, theoretical construct. Attention has often been viewed as unitary, covering the whole array of phenomena mentioned earlier. However, despite its strong intuitive appeal, it has become increasingly evident that this position is difficult to maintain. The following chapters describe the growing evidence for a variety of attentional processes that although mutually related do not constitute a unitary mechanism. The fact that attention has often been viewed as unitary has its roots in the already mentioned dualistic philosophy. It holds that attention is a unitary expression of the Will and, hence, not in need of any further explanation. In his historical survey, Neumann (1991) pointed out how this view was first expressed by Augustine, who overruled Aristotle's earlier rudimentary process-model type of approach.

Confounding

There remains a final methodological issue, which may well be inherent to the fact that attention is thought to be a control function. Control always implies that something is being controlled, and, hence, it needs simultaneous activity of nonattentional processes. When studying attention, one is concerned with modulation and not with basic properties of processes. The central problem has always been how to properly separate attentional control from the controlled function. An example is how to separate attentional control of perception from perception itself. Confounding has been normal practice as a result of dated theoretical and methodological starting points. For example, Wundt (1896) defined *attention* as an emotional state accompanying apperception; in addition, he viewed an experiment as demonstration rather than as verification of the experimenter's knowledge. Starting from these premises, it proved hard to disentangle attention and perception. In the same way, Titchener (1910) conceived of attention as sensory clearness, one of the attributes of a sensation, to be studied by introspective reports. Theorizing along similar lines, Dallenbach (1920) noticed the danger of confounding attention and perception. He reasoned that the subjective clearness of a stimulus may have a cognitive as well as an attentional component. He proposed, therefore, to study sensory clearness by way of introspective comments on stimuli without any cognitive content, an approach that was abandoned after Titchener died in 1930. It is a striking example of how research can be dictated by preoccupation with theory and method. Yet, the problem of confounding control and controlled function was not limited to the work of the early structuralists. Thus, in the early functionalist literature, it was proposed to consider CRT as a measure of attention. CRT would be less as attention became more intense (McComas, 1922; Wells, Kelly, & Murphy, 1921). It is evident that in this way, attention is confounded with reaction processes.

In the meantime, much has improved. Current experimental paradigms on attention are exclusively concerned with modulation of a function, yet some confounding remains unavoidable. For example, it is still hard to decide whether different results in studies on auditory and visual attention reflect different sensory attentional mechanisms or differences in auditory and visual processing. For instance, auditory processing develops over time, whereas visual processing is more specialized in simultaneous spatial localization, which is not a matter of attention. Thus, provided that the observed differences can be reasonably ascribed to the perceptual processes themselves, a unitary, perceptual mechanism of attention might still underlie control of auditory and visual processing.

A LOOK AHEAD

The major issues in research on attention may be conveniently divided into (a) the presumed loci of selective attention, (b) controlled versus automatic processing and divided attention, (c) attention as a central executive, and (d) sustained attention.

The Locus of Attention

Much debate has centered around the question of whether selective attention occurs early or late. The reasoning is that one has processing limits at some point in the information flow. These limits force making a choice among the available options. According to early selection, the limit occurs early, that is, prior to perceptual identification. Late selection located a bottleneck between perceptual identification and response selection. Either view starts from a stage conception of information flow. Early selection assumes a perceptual filter that decides which information will be admitted to further analysis. Late selection emphasizes expectancy, object perception, and attentional set toward responding. Early and late selection share the assumption that there are initial, preattentional processes without processing limits.

One question evolving from the early–late selection debate concerns the criteria, on the basis of which selection takes place. The criteria themselves cannot have processing limits, for the simple reason that they have the function of guiding selection. According to early selection, the selection criteria are formal and predominantly physical stimulus features such as loudness and pitch in auditory selection and color, orientation, size, or motion in visual selection. In contrast, late selection stresses selection of a response to an identified object. Therefore, the criteria are more motivational and refer to the relevance of the object to performance. Another question concerns the strictness of the bottleneck. How limiting are the selective mechanisms and what are the chances for a breakthrough of the unattended (Broadbent, 1971)? Issues on the locus of selective attention will be discussed in chapter 7.

The preceding questions all arose from studies that required attending to certain categories of stimuli or messages among other competing ones. Instructions prescribed which stimuli were relevant or had priority. The initial research was mainly concerned with auditory messages, but more recently, the main thrust has been on visual selection. In a typical experiment, participants have the task of searching for, or concentrating on, a certain stimulus or a category of stimuli—targets—amidst a number of other stimuli called nontargets, or distractors. It is useful to draw a distinction between studies on visual search within a single glance and those on free search, in which eyes and head are allowed to move freely. Single-glance studies have been primarily concerned with early versus late selection and, more generally, with the analysis of attentional control in conditions of partial report. *Partial report* is a generic term for conditions in which participants report some predefined stimuli from a larger ensemble. The partial report paradigm is closely related to that of covert orienting, in which individuals fixate the eyes on a certain spot and orient on another spot where a target is likely to occur. The obvious question of interest is whether active orienting improves stimulus detection and reduces RT (chap. 7).

Studies on free search also address the issue of which stimulus conditions allow efficient detection, yet their main emphasis is on search strategies and, in particular, on the question of whether visual search is externally or internally controlled. *External control* means that peripheral information obtained during a previous fixation dictates the position of the next fixation. In contrast, visual search may be determined by internalized, statistical properties of the environment—that is, expectancies about what to find and where—which is top-down control in the sense that it is based on internalized knowledge. Another issue in the context of visual search is the role of the functional visual field. Free search is discussed in the final part of chapter 7.

Automatic Processing

Automatic processing was originally coupled to preattentional sensory processes that are supposedly free from capacity limits. However, there is now wide evidence that automatic processing may occur on many levels: perceptual, central, and motor. The information flow usually consists of a combination of automatic and controlled processes. For instance, an automatic process may alert and initiate a controlled process. One question is to what extent automatic processing develops as a function of practice. Is it possible that certain types of behavior become altogether automatic, thus completely bypassing any attentional control? A related question concerns the fate of automatic processes. Are they lost when completed, or can they be retrieved? More generally, what are the properties of automatic processes? These issues are discussed in the first part of chapter 8.

Questions about distraction are, of course, directly related to the efficiency of controlled, focused attention, because the better the focus, the less one is supposed to be liable to distraction. In turn, this relates to how many stimuli or stimulus elements one may focus on simultaneously. Distraction may be due to automatic attention capturing by outside stimuli. This leads to the issue of involuntary versus voluntary attention, which has been studied in the context of the orientation reaction. Whereas most current research on attention is within the information-processing framework, the orientation reaction is one of the few behavioristic legacies with a strong emphasis on physiological components. This is not surprising. Involuntary attention belonged to Decartes' *res extensa*, so it was not suspect in the eyes of the behaviorists.

Divided Attention

The aforementioned research areas are labeled *focused attention* to indicate that the task is to keep relevant and irrelevant stimuli or messages apart. In contrast, divided attention tasks require participants to carry out different tasks at the same time. The labels are somewhat unfortunate because focused and divided attention are also used as theoretical constructs. Thus, divided attention, as a construct, may well play a role in a focused attention task, and vice versa. The two meanings should be carefully distinguished.

Divided attention tasks may be relatively simple, such as when carrying out rapid responses to successive stimuli—testing the so-called psychological refractory period—or more complex, such as testing the simultaneous performance of several real-life tasks. Here, limited-capacity theory has had its widest application. Multiple-task performance, which requires an allocation policy deciding how the scarce resources are divided among tasks (Kahneman, 1973; N. Moray, 1967), is supposed to hit capacity limits. In this way, attention becomes a central executive, controlling the operations of working memory and, eventually, conscious activity. It is relevant that working memory thus conceived is quite different from sensory, short-term memory. Sensory, short-term memory is thought to be preattentional, presumably bound to a specific sensory mechanism and enabling retrieval of temporarily ignored information. Instead, working memory is the operational center in which ongoing activities are controlled. In this last context, attention is still a selective mechanism, concerned with action rather than with incoming messages. The issues will take most of the remainder of chapter 8.

Sustained Attention

The preceding questions are even more compelling in the light of the third main aspect of attention—sustained attention, or concentration. Traditionally, this has been connected to an energetic state underlying the effects of monotony, diurnal rhythm, sleep loss, fatigue, environmental stresses, and psychotropic drugs. Intuitively, intensity of attention is a central component. Is a single, attentional mechanism responsible for perceptual selection, selection of action, and maintenance of alertness? It is surprising to note that energetic aspects play, at best, a minor role in texts on attention, and, if covered, potential relations between intensive and selective attention are not raised. Sustained attention and vigilance are discussed in chapter 9.

The division just discussed does not mean that research on attention has a solid conceptual basis. In fact, there are many problems, some of which emerge from a lack of clear notions about the background of performance limits (e.g., Neumann, 1987). Other problems are due to the fact that attention is sometimes conceptualized as a causal agent, causing and directing selection or sustained effort, whereas, on other occasions, it is used to denote the state of the performer as a whole (Johnston & Dark, 1986). In the pages to come, an attempt is made to avoid these pitfalls by treating attention first and foremost as a field of research.

Focused Attention
and Search

QUESTIONS OF THE 1950S

As outlined in the introduction, the initial questions about selective attention were primarily concerned with detecting auditory stimuli and selective listening to auditory messages. Two auditory paradigms dominated the scene, namely, dichotic listening and shadowing. In both, the question was of how well individuals may process (divide attention) or keep apart (focus attention) simultaneously presented messages. When the individual is focused, one message is attended to, and the other one is ignored. What, then, is the fate of the unattended message? Are there limits in focusing on one and ignoring the other message?

In the original dichotic listening studies (Broadbent, 1958), participants received two brief auditory messages from spatially distinct sources. In some conditions, one message was presented to the left ear and the other to the right ear, whereas in other conditions, the messages were binaurally presented but came from loudspeakers located at separate positions. In still other conditions, the messages were presented binaurally but spoken in a different voice with a different pitch or loudness or, as a control, without any distinctive physical cue at all. The general conclusion of these studies was that selective listening is quite proficient as long as it can be based on a distinctive physical feature such as voice, loudness, or spatial location. Selective listening was less proficient as the loudspeakers subtended a smaller angle and was poor in the absence of any distinctive physical cue. This last condition is more liable to auditory masking (e.g., Hawkins & Presson, 1986), but Broadbent did not consider masking as a relevant factor.

He argued that keeping two different messages apart is almost impossible when their elements are presented in alternation (e.g., *the* my *cat* aunt *sat* is *on* in *the* the *mat* garden), whereas participants have no problem when the elements are presented simultaneously in a different voice or with some other distinctive cue.[1] Two simultaneous messages can even be kept apart when they differ in loudness. As long as both are above threshold, the weaker message is picked up more easily than when the two messages are equally loud, suggesting that masking is not decisive.

The applied questions concerned presentation of simultaneous radio messages, only some of which were relevant to a particular listener. The solution was to have the messages differ in physical quality and to present a call sign in advance that indicated which physical feature is of interest to a specific listener. Spatial location also counts as a physical feature, but its proficiency depends on the angle of separation. The contents of unattended messages are almost completely lost. These recommendations have always served as perfect examples of superb interaction of basic and applied research.

FILTER THEORY

The aforementioned work led to the influential filter theory of selective attention (Broadbent, 1958). According to this theory, a listener has many parallel input channels that correspond to physical dimensions: presentation to left or right ear, sensory modality, voice, loudness, and so on. The processes in the input channels run off preattentive and in parallel. Attentional selection is a matter of tuning in to one channel and understanding what is being said there at the cost of blocking and losing the information from all other channels. Categories of semantic cues about the content of the messages do not qualify as input channels because it is hard to disentangle two simultaneous messages on the basis of their semantic content. Although quite difficult, it is not altogether impossible. Thus, two simultaneous messages can be properly understood as long as one of them contains little information. However, when both messages are nonredundant, only one message can be transmitted at a time (the "cocktail party" effect; Cherry, 1953).

This last point leads to another important element of the filter theory, namely, the common central system (the P-system) to which all channels

---

[1]When elements of two messages are presented in alternation, the forward associative structure of meaningful sentences is broken up, the effect of which is much stronger than that of moderate masking. The associative structure is restored in the presence of a distinctive physical cue such as a different voice. Broadbent did not consider the effect of forward associative structure but stressed only selective listening.

converge. The P-system is limited to processing information rather than stimuli. This explains that two redundant messages can be transmitted at the same time. Another feature of the filter theory is that even in the absence of redundancy, the contents of two brief messages may be retrieved in succession. This conclusion was reached from studies on split span recall in which two lists of three digits each were presented in successive pairs, one set to the left ear (e.g., 3–9–4) and another to the right ear (e.g., 8–3–7). Participants found it almost impossible to reproduce pairwise (i.e., 3–8–9–3–4–7), but they could recall the digits in successive groups that were presented to either ear. Pairwise recall was only possible when presentation was sufficiently slow to allow shifts between the ears. In one study, six digits were presented to one ear and two digits to the other, the two digits coinciding either with the first, the middle, or the last two items of the six-digit list. Participants were instructed to recall the six digits, followed by recall of the two digits. Broadbent (1956) found that recall of the two digits was better when they coincided with the last two than with the first two of the six-digit list. This enabled an estimate of the time the two digits could survive decay, namely about 2 seconds, from a short-term store located before the selective filter (Broadbent, 1956). Similar results were obtained when one list was presented auditorily and the other one visually (split-span recall between modalities).

In all other respects, however, the filter was supposed to operate on an all-or-none basis. Physical cues served as criteria for selection, whereas successful semantic analysis depended on admittance to the P-system. Studies on shadowing, in particular, seemed to provide compelling evidence in favor of filtering. In a shadowing experiment, participants received two continuous streams of auditory information, one stream at each ear, with the task to repeat aloud (shadow) one particular stream. This appeared to be possible but at the cost of an almost complete loss of the information stream at the nonattended ear. Thus, nonattended items were not recognized better than chance in a subsequent recognition test, and a shift in language at the unattended ear remained unnoticed. Yet, as predicted by filter theory, a change in the physical features of the unattended items was immediately noticed. The point is that physical properties bypass the filter and are encoded in parallel (Fig. 7.1).

One may say that preattentive processing is governed bottom up by outside stimulation, and attentive processing top down by internal factors such as instructions, internal representations, and the like. Attentive processing means tuning in to a particular channel and limiting processing to the information input from that channel. Yet, there are instances of breakthrough of the unattended, suggesting that unattended semantic information is not completely blocked. Thus, participants had no problem detecting their own name at the unattended ear (N. Moray, 1959). They also noticed semantic contents at the unattended ear that fit the message at the attended ear. In one study, Treisman (1960) shifted the message in the middle of a trial from the attended to the unattended ear, and vice versa. Participants were instructed to keep shadowing the message presented at the attended ear, an effort that required changing from one message to the other at the moment of the shift between ears. On occasion—some 6% of the trials—participants continued with a few words from the originally shadowed message and, hence, from the message presented at the unattended ear. Other studies showed that shock-associated words, presented at the unattended ear, evoked a galvanic skin response (GSR). In some, but certainly not in all, studies, the GSR for a word presented at the unattended ear proved as large as when that word was presented at the attended ear (e.g., Von Wright, Anderson, & Stenman, 1975). All of this is at odds with the assumption that information arriving at an unattended channel is completely blocked.

In dichotic listening, Gray and Wedderburn (1960) and Yntema and Trask (1963) found that when semantic content alternated between ears, recall was about equally proficient either by ear, by semantic meaning or by semantic category. For example, one may hear "dogs–3–cats" in the left ear, and "7–chase–2" in the other ear, and be equally proficient at recalling "dogs–chase–cats–7–3–2" as at recalling "dogs–3–cats–7–chase–2." In the same way, one may hear "B–3–S" in one ear, and "8–K–1" in the other ear, and recall "B–K–S–8–3–1" or "B–3–S–8–K–1" equally well. This is at odds with filter theory, which holds that especially at a fast presentation rate, shifts between channels are impossible. The problem is that semantic or categorical contents do not qualify as input channel. Analyzing semantic properties is the prerogative of the P-system, yet in line with filter theory, pairwise recall (dogs–7–3–chase–2–cats) was poor.

The notion of shifting between ears in dichotic listening was at the basis of the filter explanation but was challenged by Treisman (1970), who showed that pairwise recall is as difficult with dichotic presentation as with binaural presentation of pairs of digits without any distinctive physical cue. This means that a difference in channel may not be the reason that pairwise recall is virtually impossible. Instead, as already hinted at, the associative forward structure of two simultaneous messages appears to determine recall efficiency. When the forward associative structure is broken down by inserting irrelevant material between items to be recalled, serial recall is uniformly poor. In the case of alternating cognitive or semantic categories—as used by Gray and Wedderburn (1960) and Yntema and Trask (1963)—the forward associative structure is weaker when recalling by ear (dogs–3–cats) than when recalling by category (dogs–chase–cats). Recall appears to be a matter of the relative strength of the temporal associative structure rather than of shifts between ears or categories (Sanders & Schroots, 1968).

These and similar results have been interpreted along two lines that subsequently caused a flurry of research. First, Treisman (1960) maintained the essentials of filter theory in that selection is early because it precedes stimulus identification, is controlled by physical cues, and is needed to protect the P-system from overload. She added that information from unattended channels may be attenuated rather than completely blocked. Thus, some of the unattended items may still reach the P-system (Fig. 7.1). The prerequisite for coming through is that an unattended item has a high probability in the context of a message, and this means a low threshold in the dictionary store. In accord with information theory, the forward associative structure of a meaningful sentence modulates the threshold of forthcoming items. Items such as one's own name always have a low threshold and have a higher probability of breaking through.

Broadbent (1971) incorporated *attenuation* in his revision of the filter theory. Breakthrough of the unattended was ascribed to response set and attentive processing to stimulus set. *Stimulus set* refers to specific physical features serving as selection criteria for processing a particular message. Processing enhances the quality of the information and in this way, stimulus set is coupled to the sensitivity parameter (d') of signal-detection theory. In the spirit of early selection, stimulus set is bottom up, with the exception of the general intention to select only information that has a specific physical feature. Response set, on the other hand, reflects a readiness to identify. It is a response criterion, coupled to the β-parameter and is top-down determined. An item with a low response-threshold comes through more easily, even when the sensory evidence is scant (e.g., Broadbent & Broadbent, 1980). When listening to simultaneous messages, response set may have an effect, but stimulus set remains the primary and most efficient selective principle.

The second interpretation was originally suggested by Deutsch and Deutsch (1963) and has become known as late selection theory. According to this view, all incoming information is automatically encoded—identi-

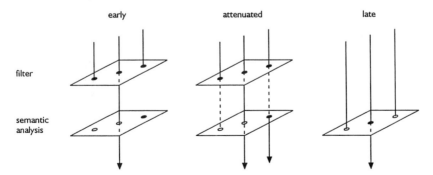

FIG. 7.1. Early selection (Broadbent, 1958), attenuated (Treisman, 1960), and late selection (Deutsch & Deutsch, 1963). An attenuating filter admits a low-threshold unit (black dot) but not a high-threshold unit (open dot) to the central processing system.

fied?—on the basis of parallel analysis of all features, semantic as well as physical (Fig. 7.1). Late selection theory adhered to the limited-capacity notion as global background of selective attention but considered response selection rather than perceptual identification as the locus of the bottleneck and the heart of the P-system. Although all stimuli receive full perceptual analysis, only the most important message is admitted to the response selection system. Importance may be based on a common physical feature, such as when instructed to listen to a specifice voice, but can be determined by a cognitive or semantic category as well. The decision what is most important is top-down determined. Therefore, late-selection theory puts full emphasis on top-down processing.

With respect to studies such as Treisman's (1960), late selection suggests that the instruction, for example, "keep shadowing the left ear," competes for priority with the semantic analysis of the unattended message. This situation leads to occasional continuation of the same message after a shift to the other ear. The massive loss of unattended information in shadowing studies is ascribed to the fact that shadowing requires continuous selection of the stimuli arriving at the attended ear that distorts the semantic codes presented at the unattended stimuli. In dichotic listening studies, there is no immediate response, and hence, variation of semantic content can be a cue that is equally efficient as a physical one.

This led to studies like Treisman and Riley's (1969), in which participants were instructed to stop shadowing after detecting a target at the unattended ear. This was perfectly possible when that target was spoken by a different voice, but difficult when targets were defined by meaning. Early selection has no problems with this result; late selection is compelled to assume that shadowing impairs detection of an unattended target. The finding that a physical cue is easily noticed forces late-selection theory to recognize that some cues are easier or more discriminable than others. In addition, the act of shadowing may interfere more with verbal cues than with physical ones. For a test to be fair, shadowing should be avoided, and the task should be limited to monitoring two simultaneous streams of information in which occasional targets require a response. For instance, all nontargets might be digits, and all targets might be letters; the two streams should be presented either binaurally or one to each ear. In a control condition, individuals should monitor two streams of tones and detect a slight change in intensity or pitch. The slight change is important because physical cues should not be easier to distinguish than semantic ones.

In a summary of selective listening, N. Moray (1975) showed that after sufficient practice, target detection is relatively easy at either ear when there is a nontarget at the other ear. In contrast, target detection is impaired when there is a target at the other ear that receives a covert or overt response. This suggests that selecting a response to a target blocks detection of a simultaneous target at the other ear. Blocking is due to response selection and not to target identification because target detection at one ear is equally impaired at the time a false alarm is emitted to a stimulus at the other ear. This pattern of results proved to be almost the same for tones and semantic targets as, for example, animal names. Shadowing the stimuli at one ear prevents detection of any target at the other ear because shadowing requires continuous response selection of all stimuli at one ear. In line with late selection, Moray concluded that perceptual analysis of either stream of stimuli occurs in parallel. Dichotic presentation or any other distinctive physical cue such as pitch or loudness improves selective listening. The cue provides a common tag to a group of stimuli, but it does not block perceptual analysis of stimuli that belong to the other group.[2]

The preceding results seem to argue against early selection that predicts a difference in the efficiency of detecting semantically versus physically defined targets; and a time-sharing deficit in the case of simultaneous stimuli, irrespective of whether targets or nontargets are presented. Broadbent (1982) countered that when monitoring two simultaneous streams of stimuli, effective time sharing may be possible only when a correct rejection—"this stimulus is not a target"—takes little time. In that case, the other stimulus might still be retrieved from the sensory store to decide whether or not it is a target. As a consequence, early selection predicts a longer CRT for target detection when it is preceded by a correct rejection at the other channel. An effect on detection accuracy will only arise when stimulus analysis takes so much time that retrieval of the other stimulus from the sensory store becomes deficient. This deduction has been actually confirmed by recent research on semantic priming of attended and unattended words. Bentin, Kutas, and Hillyard (1995) presented two simultaneous lists of words, one list to either ear, with the instruction to attend to one ear only. Successive pairs of words from the lists consisted of a prime and a target word that could be semantically related or unrelated. The N400 component of the ERP proved sensitive to target words when semantically primed by the attended but not when semantically primed by the unattended ear. Moreover, the attended words did much better in a subsequent recognition test. In line with early selection, both results suggest that the words from the unattended ear were not semantically encoded. Yet, a further lexical-decision test, with new words and words from the attended and unattended lists, showed slower CRT for new words and about equally fast CRT for attended and unattended words. Hence, in a test of implicit memory, there was evidence

---

[2]This result is relevant from an applied perspective. It suggests that one is capable of monitoring simultaneous messages as long as simultaneous targets do not occur. In the case of simultaneous targets, one is liable to miss one. The problem may be overcome by slowing the rate of presentation. In that case, a target at one channel may be retrieved after a simultaneous target at the other channel has been processed.

for semantic registration of the unattended words. Together, this evidence suggests a passive and inaccessible form of perceptual registration that fits Treisman's (1960) attenuation notion that an unattended word may raise the activation of its corresponding dictionary unit but not enough to permit active operations physiologically or behaviorally.

The aforementioned studies summarize the state of the art in the early 1970s. Subsequent research has developed along three major trends that relate to different features of the filter model, namely, locus of the filter, automatic versus controlled processing, and capacity limits of the P-system. The locus of the filter is the main theme in this chapter. It continues the debate between early and late selection, albeit in the visual rather than in the auditory domain. The reason for the greater interest in the visual domain was that the dominant auditory paradigms, that is, dichotic recall and shadowing, did not differentiate sufficiently between the two major theoretical positions. Moreover, promising visual research paradigms had entered the scene with their main emphasis on the role of attention in spatial localization and orienting. Spatial properties seem less relevant in the auditory domain, particularly equipped as it is for temporal processing (but see Quinlan & Bailey, 1995).

Attention has been invoked as an explanation in more recent studies on processing single streams of auditory information, but they remind one very much of *vertus dormitiva* errors. For example, shifting a single stream of information repeatedly between the ears usually leads to a performance decrement. A perceptual interpretation that repeated shifts may cause a breakdown of the word structure or of the rhythm may be more adequate than assuming recurrent, time consuming attentional shifts between the ears. In fact, research on selective listening had largely disproven the notion of a time consuming shift of attention between the ears (e.g., ten Hoopen, 1996). It is safe to say that most of the issues that have emerged in research on visual selective attention during the last 25 years do not have a well-researched auditory counterpart.

Early Versus Late Selection in Vision

The main paradigm on the locus of visual selective attention consists of visual search for a target among nontargets in an array of stimuli or in an otherwise empty field. The array is sometimes horizontal and sometimes circular, with a fixation point in the middle. In the latter case, the items are presented equally far from the fixation point so that visual acuity and lateral interference are kept constant. On still other occasions, the characters are presented at random positions within a small area of the visual field. Participants either have to report the presence or absence of one or more targets or the position at which a target was detected. They may do so by pressing a response key, in which

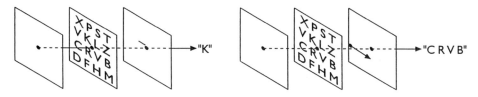

FIG. 7.2. Partial report. In the left part of the figure the bar probes the location of a single letter. In the right part, the arrow probes a complete row.

case CRT is the main measure; alternatively, one may present the array tachistoscopically, followed by a mask, in which case a psychophysical threshold function is measured. For example, in a partial-report task, participants may view a tachistoscopically presented matrix—for example, 4 × 4—of characters and receive a cue at the time of presentation or briefly afterward about which subset to report. The cue may refer to a set of spatial positions, for example, a certain line of the matrix, or to items of the same color or belonging to the same semantic class. A variation is the *bar-probe task*, in which participants recall a single item, the location of which is indicated by a visual cue (e.g., Averbach & Coriell, 1961; Fig. 7.2).

All of the paradigms mentioned have in common the characteristic that participants "search" for a target in a briefly presented display. There is often the implicit assumption of search with a fixated eye to rule out effects of peripheral acuity, eye movements, and visual scanning. However, eye movements are often poorly controlled, so it might be better to say that one is simply not interested in and, therefore, simply ignores potential effects of visual scanning. With regard to the debate between early and late selection, parts of the evidence favor early selection but on closer scrutiny, it is usually ambiguous. Besides, late selection theory has various counterarguments, and early and late selection may well apply to different types of conditions. The next sections deal with covert orienting and visual search in a single glance and conclude with a recent theory that aims at going beyond the early–late dichotomy. Free search and display monitoring are discussed in the final sections.

COVERT ORIENTING

Covert orienting refers to focusing on a specific location in the visual field. The standard technique is to present advance information on the location where a target is likely to appear. The eyes should remain fixated on the central spot so that attentional orienting and visual acuity are not confounded. The general result is that performance, detection accuracy or CRT, improves when the target is presented at the precued location and is at the expense of performance when the target appears at an unexpected location. Covert orienting is distinguished from overt orienting. In the last case, the eyes are actually free to move to the cued location.

An illustrative study on covert orienting stems from Posner, Nissen, and Ogden (1978). Participants saw an arrow at their central fixation point aimed either to the left or to the right to indicate the direction of the most likely target location. Following a 100 ms interval, a single target was presented a few degrees to the left or to the right of the fixation point in an otherwise empty field. In 80% of the trials, the stimulus location corresponded to the direction of the arrow (valid trials), whereas in the remaining trials, the stimulus arrived at the opposite side (invalid trials). The results show a significantly faster RT in the case of valid than of invalid trials. Compared to the condition without advance location information, RT was faster at valid trials and slower at invalid trials. This suggests that individuals are capable of dissociating fixation point and attentional focus. Posner (1980) and colleagues (Posner, Snyder, & Davidson, 1980) ascribed the results to an attentional spotlight that illuminates a limited area of the visual field and can be intentionally moved around.

Spotlights and Zoom Lenses

The spotlight is not very sharp and has a gradient from "light to dark." This means that it is less effective as the distance from its center increases. This should lead to a gradual transition from a somewhat faster to a somewhat slower RT. This was confirmed in a study by Downing and Pinker (1985), who presented an advance cue, consisting of a number from 1 to 10, indicating the most probable (.70) area in which the stimulus might arrive. The results show that RT was slower as the distance from the primed area increased. The gradient proved the steepest in the middle of the visual field, suggesting that the attentional focus is the sharpest around the central fixation point and less in the periphery (G. L. Shulman, Sheehy, & Wilson, 1986; Umilta, Riggio, Dascola, & Rizolatti, 1991). It is evident that in order to find a gradient, the location of the expected stimulus should be clearly defined. Sanders and Reitsma (1982) presented a target, that is, an increase in brightness of a light, either at the central fixation point or at a location 50° to the left; at each new trial, the probability of the location was precued at the central fixation point. As expected, RT was longer in the invalid case in which the cue indicated the far periphery as the most probable location, whereas the target was presented at the central fixation point. However, when the stimulus was presented in the periphery, RT was no faster than it was in a control condition without any advance location information. This suggests that participants tried but did not succeed in focusing on the far periphery.

The spotlight metaphor was supported by evidence that covert orienting cannot be split up among different locations, which seemed to exclude a capacity-sharing view. In a study by C. W. Eriksen and Yeh (1985), participants detected a target that might appear on one of four positions around a central fixation point. An advance cue assigned a probability of .4 to two locations and a probability of .1 to the remaining two locations. The cue was peripherally presented near one of the two .4 locations. A target was detected the fastest at that location, followed by the other .4 location and, finally, at the .1 locations. This means that capacity was not equally shared among the two equally probable .4 locations but that the physically cued location received priority. Similar results were obtained by Posner et al. (1980), who found that RT increased as a function of the angular distance between two possible locations.

Posner's (1980) suggestion of a spotlight beam moving from one location to another predicts an effect of the travel time between two locations. However, the evidence for travel time is contradictory. Even in studies in which RT was found to increase as two possible target locations became wider apart, it is hard to distinguish an effect of travel time from an effect of the gradient of the spotlight (e.g., Kwak, Dagenbach, & Egeth, 1991). Other evidence argues clearly against a spotlight beam. Thus, in a study by Egly and Homa (1984), targets could appear on an imaginary circle, with the diameter as a variable. Advance priming of the size of the diameter facilitated detection at all locations of that diameter. This led the authors to reconsider the possibility of a division of attentional capacity rather than a fixed spotlight (J. F. Juola et al., 1991). An essential difference between this study and those by Eriksen and Yeh (1985) and Posner (1980) may have been whether a specific location was cued in advance. When cuing a specific location, the spotlight may zoom in on that location with a narrow focus and, indeed, travel to another location when the stimulus is not found at the indicated spot. If one does not anticipate one specific location but rather a number of locations, the spotlight may be set more widely to equally illuminate all potential locations. Consequently, a zoom-lens metaphor may be preferred to a spotlight metaphor. In conditions of divided attention, the system may behave as a widely set zoom lens, whereas in focused attention, it may behave as a narrow spotlight.

The zoom-lens metaphor was proposed by Eriksen and Yeh (1985) on the basis of probe studies in which a circular array of alphanumerics was presented briefly. In the center, an arrow-type of probe, presented in advance, together with, or following, the array, cued the probable location of the target. The results show no severe problems in identifying the target when the probe arrived 100 ms or more before the presentation of the array. At a shorter and, in particular, at a negative SOA, performance decreased and confusion increased among items at adjacent locations. C. W. Eriksen and Rohrbaugh (1970) suggested that the probe initiates a time-consuming process of zooming in on the cued location. At shorter and negative SOAs, there is the double problem that the iconic trace is decaying while focusing has not yet been completed. Similar results were obtained by Jonides (1983), who had participants search through circular eight-letter displays for the presence of the target letters *L* or *R*. When the interval between cue and target was sufficiently long, a valid advance cue had the effect that CRT reduced, whereas an invalid cue led to an increase of CRT. Therefore, focusing on the indicated spot appeared to be time consuming.

One implicit assumption of the zoom-lens metaphor is that one should be capable of intentionally adjusting the size of its focus. In one study (LaBerge, 1973), five-letter strings were presented. In the nonfocused condition, individuals decided whether the string was a word or a nonword. In the focused condition, they had to decide whether the middle letter of the string belonged to the first or the second part of the alphabet. In either condition, an occasional trial contained a pattern like +++7+, and the task was to decide whether the pattern contained a 7. In the focused condition, CRT for detecting the 7 depended on the location of the 7, whereas it did not depend on location in the nonfocused condition. This suggests that one may intentionally vary the size of the focus. When the participants are focusing on the middle item, the spot is a minimal size. This is consistent with B. A. Eriksen and C. W. Eriksen's (1974) research on the effect of surrounding flankers on CRT to a central target. The flanker effect was the largest at an angle of .06° and disappeared when the angle exceeded 1°.

Another implicit assumption of the zoom lens is that its effectiveness should decrease as the lens is set more widely. Some support comes from a study by Jonides (1983), who found that with a neutral, unpredictive cue, CRT was slower than with a valid, predictive cue but faster than with an invalid, predictive cue. C. W. Eriksen and St. James (1986) presented a target among seven flankers on an imaginary circle with a 3° diameter. Either a number of adjacent locations or one specific location was primed in advance. The results show faster identification when a single location was primed. It was concluded that the zoom lens is less effective at a wider setting, although the results could also be ascribed to a difference in spatial uncertainty between the conditions. C. W. Eriksen and Webb (1989) cued a set of adjacent locations, or nonadjacent locations, and both had no effect on RT. This result might be taken as evidence against the relation between processing efficiency and the width of the zoom lens. In the adjacent case, one might zoom in on a more limited set of primed locations, something that is not possible when nonadjacent locations are primed. Alternatively, it might mean that the size of the zoom lens can only be crudely varied. Thus, its setting is the same when adjacent or nonadjacent locations are primed.

More recently, Johnson and Yantis (1995) studied a deduction of the zoom-lens model; when the precue is only partially valid, participants adopt a probability-matching strategy of either focusing or widening the zoom lens on the basis of a probability match in regard to precue validity. Their study was similar to that of Eriksen and Yeh (1985) in that one out of four alternative locations was precued. The precue indicated the location of the target (the letter S or Y, which required a choice reaction) with 100% or 50% validity; in this last case, the target letter occurred with equal probability at any of the other three locations. In the neutral condition, the precue was uninformative about the location of the target. At the 50% validity condition, the results failed to show the expected mixture of CRTs from a focused and a widened zoom-lens density function, as estimated from the 100% (focused) and neutral (widened) conditions. In particular, the lower and upper tails of the 50% density function were less than predicted. Johnson and Yantis (1995) found a better fit of an attentional priority model that assumes parallel random walk accumulation of evidence about the target for the four locations, with a bias in sampling rate toward the most expected one. It may be countered that the probability-matching hypothesis follows, at best, indirectly from the zoom-lens model. Yet, the Johnson and Yantis study has been described as an illustration of the more detailed current research issues.

Voluntary Versus Involuntary Orienting

In the initial studies on covert orienting, the precue, that is, an arrow or some other symbolic character, was presented at the central fixation point. This means that participants identified the cue, followed by intentional orienting to the indicated spot. In contrast, automatic orienting might occur irrespective of, or contrary to, intentions when a peripheral cue draws attention to its location. This was studied by Jonides (1981), who had eight potential letter positions on an imaginary circle. The cue could be a centrally presented arrow or a peripheral spot on the location to be attended. The results show that instructions to ignore the peripheral cue could not be obeyed. Moreover, CRT at the cued location was faster, even when the peripheral cue had a low validity. Again, CRT was less affected by a simultaneous, verbal rehearsal task when the cue was peripheral than when it was central. Together, the results support the view that a peripheral cue exerts an automatic effect (Briand & Klein, 1987).

H. J. Müller and Rabbitt (1989) found that even at a 400-ms SOA between cue and target, CRT was faster in the case of the peripheral than of the central cue, suggesting that decoding and intentional orienting is quite time consuming. There may be a slow orienting mechanism for the voluntary case and a fast one for the involuntary one. Müller and Rabbitt studied a condition in which both a central and a peripheral cue were presented with SOA between the two cues as variable. The results show that a later presented peripheral cue interrupted voluntary orienting, as initiated by the central cue. In contrast, a peripheral cue was not interrupted by a central one, suggesting, again, involuntary capturing of attention by the peripheral cue, which overrides a voluntary response.

In line with these results, conditions can be created in which CRT for a stimulus at a cued position is longer than for a stimulus at an uncued position. Thus, Posner and Cohen (1984) presented three rectangular frames, one in the center and two in the periphery of the visual field. A target appeared either in the center frame ($p = .6$) or in one of the peripheral frames ($p = .1$) with 20% catch trials. An unpredictive cue—a brief lighting of one of the peripheral frames—preceded the target, with an SOA varying from 0 to 500 ms. When SOA was less than 150 ms, CRT was faster for a stimulus at the cued location, suggesting unintentional orienting on the cued spot. However, when SOA exceeded 300 ms, CRT was longer for the cued spot than for the central spot and for the uncued, opposite peripheral spot. Apparently, the initial, involuntary orienting was followed by inhibition of the cued spot and by voluntary orienting on the much more probable center spot.

The way of peripheral cuing is not irrelevant. Thus, the cue may be a separate stimulus or an abrupt onset or offset of the target stimulus itself. To study the effect of gradual target stimulus onset, Yantis and Jonides (1984) and Jonides and Yantis (1988) presented distractors and targets by gradually or abruptly omitting elements of continuously present stylistic "8" patterns. The effect was that letters emerged gradually. It is not surprising that without any precue, the time to find a target letter increased linearly with the number of distractors. However, a flat search-function was found when a target letter was presented abruptly in an empty location surrounded by gradually, or more abruptly, emerging letters from stylistic "8" patterns. Again, it was shown in another study that an abruptly presented distractor is processed with priority.

J. Miller (1989) argued that attention is captured by a discontinuity in luminance rather than by onset or offset of the stimulus per se. In support of the luminance hypothesis, Theeuwes (1995) showed that abrupt changes in color, for example, from red to equiluminant green, did not capture attention, but a luminance increment did. In contrast, however, Yantis and Hilstrom (1994) presented a varying number of the previously described stylistic "8" patterns that all turned into letters by abrupt offset of elements. The target letter was signaled by a brief 50-ms brightening of one letter that occurred simultaneously with the offset of the elements. Although brightening the target reduced the slope, the search function did not become flat. In other conditions, the target was signaled by abrupt changes in texture, motion, or stereoscopic depth of the target, manipulations that brought about a flat search-function. Yantis and Hilstrom concluded that the presence of an object is essential to capturing attention. This was underlined by Watson and Humphreys (1995), who showed that onset or offset of an element is equally effective in capturing attention as long as no new object is presented. Thus, in one study, they turned a stylistic "A" into an "H" by omitting the top element and an "H" into an "A" by adding a top element, manipulations that proved equally effective.

One may say that J. Miller's (1989) luminance increment view is more in line with early selection, whereas the object explanation of Yantis and Hilstrom (1994) and Watson and Humphreys (1975) is more consistent with late selection. The point is that in the latter view, capturing of attention is tied to the presence of an object. The assumption is that all objects are identified in parallel, and features such as onset, offset, abrupt changes in depth, motion, and texture are tags that are connected to an object and bias the response selection. Instead, changes in motion, texture, and depth may have been more salient than brief brightening. Once a certain location has been focused, abrupt or gradual presentation appears to have little effect on CRT. Hence, it is really orienting and not processing efficiency of the object that is affected.

These studies on peripheral cuing all involved a wide zoom lens that creates optimal opportunities for automatic orienting. How automatic are the previously mentioned effects when attention is already intentionally focused on a specific spot? Theeuwes (1990) observed that a unique color failed to pop out when a distinct spatial location was focused. On the other hand, H. J. Müller and Rabbitt (1989) presented a 50% valid central cue followed by a peripheral flash after a long (600–1,200 ms) SOA. The target arrived 100 ms after the peripheral flash. The suggestion was that the participants would process the peripheral cue while already being focused elsewhere. The results show that despite focusing by participants, the peripheral cue still captured attention. Similar evidence was obtained in an experiment in which two successive peripheral cues were presented. Once the first peripheral cue had captured attention, its spatial location was voluntarily focused, but this location, in turn, became liable to distraction by the next peripheral cue.

It is doubtful whether participants in the H. J. Müller and Rabbitt (1989) study had really focused because their central cue had a relatively poor validity. When the symbolic cue was perfectly valid, Theeuwes (1991c) found no evidence for distraction due to onset or offset of a peripheral cue. When attention was strictly focused on a single spot, the peripheral cue only had an effect when it was presented in the vicinity of that focused spot. This is in line with the notion that the focused zoom lens has a gradient. Theeuwes concluded that the capturing of attention by a peripheral cue is not completely involuntary because it depends on whether a participant is already voluntarily focusing.[3] Juola, Koshina, and Warner (1995) found that abrupt

---

[3]A further discussion of involuntary attention is found in the chapter on automatic processing.

onset was more powerful than a peripheral arrow in capturing attention. Yet, an abrupt onset could be overridden by a highly valid peripheral arrow. In brief, a central symbolic cue appears to have a voluntary effect, whereas the effects of a peripheral symbolic cue and an abrupt onset are partly involuntary and partly under voluntary control.

Neuropsychological Evidence

Posner and Petersen (1990) formulated a more detailed process model of operations in covert orienting on the basis of neuropsychological evidence. Once a precue has been identified, a sequence of processes is initiated, namely, disengagement from the present focus, movement of attention to the target area and, finally, engagement with the new location. Patients with a lesion in a parietal lobe appeared to have problems with disengagement. They performed a traditional, covert orienting task—that is, on the left or on the right of the fixation point, indicated by an 80% valid central precue. CRT showed that patients oriented normally on the most probable location but had trouble reorienting on the contralateral location in trials with an invalid precue. Moreover, the problem of reorienting arose only when initial orienting on the most probable location had involved activity in the damaged parietal lobe. Once oriented, it appeared difficult to disengage and reorient when the parietal brain area had a lesion.[4]

A different problem arose with midbrain diseases, in particular those involving the colliculus superioris, which is known to control saccadic eye movements. Here, lesions caused a disruption of both covert orienting and saccades.[5] Patients showed neither benefits from a valid cue nor costs from an invalid one, suggesting that orienting simply does not occur when the colliculus is damaged. Interestingly, overt and covert orienting activity appeared to be controlled by the same brain mechanism. Finally, cells of the pulvinar thalamus appeared to fire more frequently when attending a specific location. A lesion in that area may prohibit attentional engagement with a new location because RT was prolonged for any stimulus, cued or uncued, presented at the contralateral side of the lesion.

Covert Orienting and Saccadic Eye Movements

Do saccades and covert orienting depend on similar processes? It is unlikely that they are completely identical because one can shift attention to a new location without necessarily carrying out a saccade to that location. It is

---

[4]The same effect was found when the cued and uncued locations were both in the same half field (Posner & Rafal, 1987). Hence, the effect is not due to shifting from the damaged lobe to the normal functioning one.

[5]Without involvement of the colliculus, saccades are only possible through intentional cortical control.

equally unlikely that they are totally unrelated because the colliculus superioris appears to be involved in either activity. In one study, Nissen, Posner,
and Snyder (1978) instructed participants to prepare the next landing of the
eyes at a specific location. During most trials, preparation was actually followed by a saccade but on occasion, the instruction changed. Instead of
executing the saccade, participants had to carry out a simple reaction to a
stimulus that was presented somewhere in the visual field. Nissen et al.
found that RT for that stimulus was less when it was presented at the intended
landing position. This suggests that preparation entailed a covert attentional
shift. Shepherd, Findlay, and Hockey (1986) also found a close relation
between covert attention and saccades. They manipulated covert orienting
by varying the probability of a peripheral stimulus at a specific, spatial
location. Individuals had the task of responding to the stimulus by a key
press as well as by initiation of a saccade in a direction indicated by a
centrally presented arrow. RT increased when the eyes had to be moved in
the direction opposite to that of the peripheral stimulus spot. Similarly,
Hoffman and Subramaniam (1995) required individuals to make a saccade
to a specific location; at the same time, they should detect a stimulus that
was presented briefly in advance of the start of the saccade. Detection
accuracy was highest when the location of the stimulus and the intended
landing coincided. In another experiment, participants were instructed to
attend to a particular location and to make a saccade to either that location
or to a different one. Stimulus detection was superior at the intended landing
location, irrespective of instructions where to attend. The conclusion was
that covert orienting on a spot cannot be maintained when individuals are
moving the eyes in another direction.

The reverse question is whether covert attending elicits a saccade. Shepherd
et al. (1986) addressed this question by studying the latency of a saccade when
a peripheral stimulus was presented briefly before the start of the saccade. If
the stimulus was presented at the intended landing spot of the eyes, saccadic
latency was reduced, whereas it was increased when it was presented at the
opposite side of the intended direction of the saccade. Fisher and Breitmeyer
(1987) studied the effect of a temporal interval between presentation of a
central fixation light and a peripheral light; this variation was meant to elicit a
saccade to that peripheral spot. In one condition, the central fixation light
vanished before the saccade had been initiated, and in two other conditions,
the central light remained on throughout a trial. In one of these last conditions,
participants were instructed to ignore the central light, whereas in the other
one, they were asked to focus on the central light until reacting to the
peripheral one. The latency of the saccade was longer in the last condition
than in the former two, suggesting, along the lines of Posner and Petersen
(1990), that focusing on a new position leads to more problems when one has
to disengage from an earlier fixated location.

Orienting and the Early–Late Debate

The early–late issue was raised briefly in the discussion on the effect of abrupt stimulus onset. More generally, the discussion followed Broadbent's (1971) broad distinction between stimulus set (early selection, d') and response set (late selection, β), with the general trend suggesting an effect on d' rather than on β. This has been viewed as favoring early selection in that focusing or widening the zoom lens determines the size of the spatial area from where visual information is admitted to central processing. Thus, Bashinsky and Bacharach (1980) presented a near-threshold stimulus at some location in the right or left visual half field. Participants decided whether a stimulus had been presented and if so, they indicated its location in one of the half fields. One of the half fields was precued by an arrow or by a neutral cue. The arrow enhanced detection (d') for the indicated half field without a loss of d' for the other half field, whereas false alarms were hardly affected. In contrast, localization of a detected stimulus was superior in the attended half field and impaired in the unattended half field. Thus, the zoom lens may be wide open in the neutral condition and somewhat focused in the arrow condition. One cannot focus too narrowly, though, because the stimulus might still occur at various locations within the precued half field. The finding that under these conditions, localization suffers at the unattended side, but detection does not, suggests that localization rather than detection profits from attentional focusing.[6]

Downing (1988) found that precuing by a central arrow improved d'. In his study, a target was presented among 12 distractors. A similar result was also found by Müller and Humphreys (1991), who, the effect on d' notwithstanding, still argued in favor of late selection. Similar to Watson and Humphreys (1995), they proposed that an identified object at a precued location receives priority in entering the response selection stage. However, late selection faces the problem that demands on covert orienting do not appear to interfere with simultaneously selecting a response to another stimulus. If covert orienting reflected response selection, interference with selecting another response would be expected (Pashler, 1991).

It is relevant in this regard to draw a distinction between multielement displays (MED), as used by Downing (1988), and single element (SED) displays, as used by Bashinsky and Bacharach (1980). The effect of a precue on d' appears to be more robust in MED than in SED, in particular when tested psychophysically. Shiu and Pashler (1994) found that precuing affected identification of a stimulus in SED but only when the display included some form of spatial uncertainty. Thus, identification of a single element did not suffer from invalid precuing when masked by a single mask at its specific

---

[6]The study had fairly long exposition times so that an effect of eye movements cannot be excluded.

location, but it did suffer when multiple masks were presented at different spatial locations. Multiple masks also led to location errors in the case of an invalid precue. A positive effect of exact specification of the spatial location where a target has been presented was also found by van der Heijden et al. (1992). Shiu and Pashler proposed that introducing spatial uncertainty in SED has the effect that noise from irrelevant locations blurs the target. Blurring would be the standard problem in MED displays. There, a precise mapping of location and target stimulus is obviously essential to preventing errors. This explains that precuing is more beneficial in MED. Shiu and Pashler concluded that the effect of focusing the zoom lens might not be to enhance efficiency of detecting the focused stimulus, as early-selection theory would hold, but to suppress noise from irrelevant locations. This interpretation is very much in line with van der Heijden's (1992) post-categorical filter theory and Prinz' (1987) theory about the role of background stimuli in free search. It differs from H. J. Müller and Humphrey's (1991) late selection view in that the notion of noise suppression does not imply that the response selection stage is involved. Finally, the Shiu and Pashler results illustrate that an increase in d' merely means an improved signal-to-noise ratio and not necessarily an enhanced illumination of the target.

Negative Priming

Suppression of distractors is sometimes referred to as *negative priming* (Tipper, 1985). Participants are required to select a target while ignoring a simultaneously presented distractor of the same class. On a critical trial, the target was an item that had been a distractor on the preceding trial. CRT was delayed in a critical trial. This delay suggests distractor suppression at the previous trial. Recent evidence suggests that suppression is not concerned only with the identity but also with the location that a distractor occupied in the visual field, a finding that relates negative priming to covert orienting. For example, Tipper, Brehaut, and Driver (1990) presented participants with a display that contained four position markers indicating four locations, two of which could be occupied by either a target (@) or a distractor symbol (+). The participants indicated the location of the target by pressing a corresponding response key. Then another display was presented that only contained a target. Again, the participants responded by pressing the key corresponding to the location of the target. CRT proved slower when the target appeared in the location that had been previously occupied by the distractor than when the target appeared in a previously unoccupied location. This finding was interpreted as evidence for suppression of distractor locations. As an alternative, Park and Kanwisher (1994) argued that the slower CRT might be due to a change in pattern between the two successive displays. First, they found that CRT slowed down also when the first display did not contain a target, so distractor suppression was not due to target selection. Second, Park and Kanwisher had target and distractor change roles between the successive displays. Hence, the target could occupy the same location on the two successive displays but could differ in pattern. CRT still slowed down in that condition, the interpretation being that in this case, negative priming is not due to distractor suppression but to a difference in target identity on two locations inspected in rapid succession. Milliken, Tipper, and Weaver (1994) suggested that both processes (distractor suppression and changes in target identity) may play a role and may together be aspects of a schema that optimizes search efficiency. As is noted further on in this book, schemalike arguments are more prominent in the literature on multiple-fixation search.

Inhibition of Return

Inhibition of return refers to relatively inefficient orienting to a visual stimulus, presented at the previously attended location, even though attention shifted to a new location a moment ago (Posner, Rafal, Choate, & Vaughan, 1985). The phenomenon has been found in conditions of stimulus detection, of key-press responses and of saccadic latency when moving the eyes back to the previously attended spot (Posner et al.). In a standard task, three horizontally aligned boxes are presented, the middle of which is fixated. Then, one of the peripheral boxes is cued by a flicker; after a brief interval, this is followed by a flicker of the middle box. This has the effect that attention is drawn back to the middle box. Once attention has been drawn back, a peripherally presented stimulus appears to get a slower response when presented in the initially cued peripheral box than in the uncued one (Rafal, Calabresi, Brennan, & Sciolto, 1989). In the same way, a saccade is initiated more slowly to the initially cued peripheral location (e.g., Abrams & Dobkin, 1994). It is interesting that inhibition of return was much less, when the peripheral location was cued by a central arrow rather than by a peripheral cue. Hence, Abram and Dobkin suggested two factors affecting inhibition of return, that is, involuntary sensory elicitation of a location by a peripheral precue and oculomotor inhibition. Moreover, they found that the sensory effect was bound to the object rather than to its spatial location. In the critical study, the precue indicated an object positioned at some location, for example, up or down in the vertical plane. Briefly before presentation of the imperative stimulus indicating where to direct the saccade, the object rotated 90° to the horizontal plane. Inhibition of return, that is, longer saccadic latency, was found to be connected to the new location and not to the original location of the object. The oculomotor component of the effect seemed bound to spatial location and not to the object. This is consistent with the idea that oculomotor activity is controlled by the subcortical colliculus superioris that is not engaged in object recognition.

The suggestion that inhibition of return comprises a spatial as well as an object component was confirmed by Tipper et al. (1991, 1994). For instance, the object component only plays a part when it actually can be seen at the time of precuing. On the other hand, inhibition of the spatial component occurs in the absence of any object feature. Tipper et al. (1994) also found that the spatial and object components occurred in parallel. When the object was moved away to a new position, inhibition of return was found for the new position as well as for the original location. It is evident that the evidence for object-based inhibition of return poses problems for any simple early-selection theory. The parallel operation of object and location is most easily accounted for by van der Heijden's (1992) postcategorical filtering model.

ERP and Covert Orienting

In most ERP studies on covert orienting, participants are instructed to attend to the same position throughout a block of trials. A series of standard stimuli is presented on both the attended and the contralateral, unattended spot. An overt response is only required to an occasional target on the attended location. Covert search for targets at the attended spot appears to have two major ERP effects. First, it increases the amplitude of the early P1 and N1 components to stimuli at an attended spot (Fig. 7.3), and second, it causes a general processing or selection negativity (a larger N2 and a smaller P2). The effects on the early components are thought to reflect spatial localization, whereas nonspatial detection criteria such as color or size play parts in the processing negativity (Mulder, Wijers, Brookhuis, Smid, & Mulder, 1994; Näätänen, 1992; Wijers, Lamain, Slopsema, Mulder, & Mulder, 1989). Mangun and Hillyard (1990) found an enhanced P1 when, as in Posner's (1980) initial work, the location to attend was precued by a central arrow. As in Fig. 7.3, they found little evidence for any extended ERP to stimuli at the unattended location. In line with early selection, they concluded that processing information at the unattended location is largely blocked.

It would be hazardous to generalize the ERP results too hastily. Thus, Eimer (1994) noted correctly that participants always respond in behavioral studies, irrespective of whether the stimulus is presented at the attended or unattended side or location. In contrast, participants react in ERP studies only when a target appears at the attended side. Eimer suggested that in ERP studies, participants may have had a stronger focus on the attended spot than in behavioral studies. As a test, he precued the location at which an *M*, *N*, or *W* would be presented by way of a 75%-valid central arrow. The *M* was presented in 75% of the trials and did not require an overt response; the *N* and *W* occurred equally often and required a response but only when presented at the attended location. Under these conditions, Eimer observed an enhanced P1 and N1, as shown in Fig. 7.3. In another condition, Eimer instructed the participants to react also to the N or W when presented at the unattended side. The result was that the

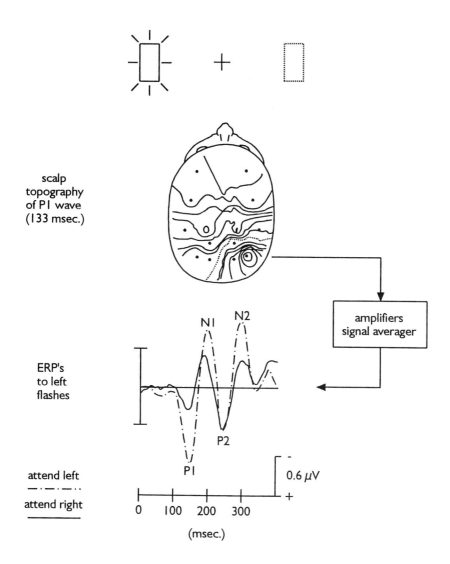

scalp
topography
of P1 wave
(133 msec.)

ERP's
to left
flashes

N1　N2

amplifiers
signal averager

P2

attend left
—·—·—··

P1

0.6 μV

attend right

0   100   200   300

(msec.)

FIG. 7.3. ERP to flashes presented at the left part of the visual field when subjects are instructed to attend to the left (dashed) or to the right (drawn) part, while keeping a + fixated. The effects are predominantly occipital and parietal in the right hemisphere. From Mangun, G. R., & Hillyard, S. A. Electrophysio-right hemisphere. Also from Mangun, G. R., & Hillyard, S. A. Electrophysiological studies of visual selective attention in humans. In A. Scheibel & A. Wechsler (Eds.), *The neurobiological foundations of higher cognitive functions.* New York: Guilford. Reproduced by permission of the publisher.

effects on P1 and N1 disappeared. Yet, he found the usual RT advantage to the attended side, illustrating that a behavioral effect of covert orienting can occur in the absence of an early ERP effect.

LATE SELECTION

The Category Effect

As mentioned previously, CRT and accuracy are usually independent of the number of distracting items in a display when target and nontargets have a distinctive physical feature such as color, size, orientation, motion, and so on. Yet, a flat search-function is sometimes found when the distinction between target and nontargets is categorical, such as when searching for a digit target among letter nontargets (Fig. 7.4). In the case of a flat search-function, the target is said to "pop out," which according to early selection, means that target detection has occurred preattentively and in parallel (e.g., H. E. Egeth, Jonides, & Wall, 1972). In the absence of pop-out, CRT increases linearly as a function of the number of distractors in the display with a 2:1 ratio of the slopes for trials in which a target is absent (no–response) or present (yes–response). Early-selection theory suggests a self-terminating serial search as the typical attentive search process. Stimuli are successively analyzed until a target either is found or reported absent. The theory suggests a dichotomy between conditions that do or do not permit pop-out.

In contrast, late selection considers the differences in the slope of the search function as a continuum, reflecting the relative difficulty of response selection.[7] Late-selection theory has argued that pop-out on the basis of a categorical distinction is at odds with early selection. It should be noted that although digits may indeed pop out among letters—the category effect—pop-out can be easily spoiled. For instance, Francolini and H. E. Egeth (1979) presented red- and black-colored items and instructed participants to search for a red-colored digit among letters. In this case, the digit failed to pop out; only the red items popped out from the black ones.[8]

In one set of studies, Shiffrin (1975) presented four letters either simultaneously or in rapid succession, with known order of the successive spatial

---

[7]Van der Heijden (1992) argued against the usual strong connection between serial processing and early selection and parallel processing and late selection, the confounding of which he holds responsible for the many contradictory results in the field. In his model, parallel processing does not exclude early selection and may not always be typical for late selection. For instance, Broadbent's (1971) response set is an example of late selection without parallel processing. This objection should be kept in mind when reading the following sections.

[8]This finding is consistent with the view that only the largest difference among features pops out. A late selection theory would maintain that only the most discriminable difference gains access to the response selection system.

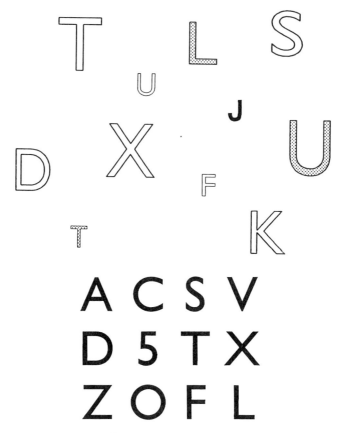

FIG. 7.4. The pop-out effect due to a deviant physical feature (the J), and to a categorical difference (a digit among letters). From Wickens, C. D. (1992). *Engineering psychology and human performance.* Copyright © 1992 by HarperCollins Publishers, Inc. Reprinted by permission of Addison-Wesley Educational Publishers, Inc.

positions where a letter was presented. He also took care that saccades could not occur. The task was to detect the presence or absence of a predefined target letter among the four presented ones. The presentation time of the four letters in the simultaneous condition was equal to that of a single letter in the successive condition. This means that participants had much more time for processing in the successive condition, yet detection accuracy was about equal in either case.[9] This suggests that the four simultaneous

---

[9]Similar results have been obtained with auditory, tactile, and mixed modality presentations. It should be kept in mind that evidence for parallel processing is only found in the case of well-learned categorical differences between targets and nontargets. The role of practice in establishing a new internal category is discussed in the context of studies on automatic processing (chap. 8).

letters could be processed in parallel. Duncan (1980) found that when an array contained *two* targets, both requiring separate detection, successive presentation was superior to simultaneous presentation. In this study, participants were asked to decide whether (a) an array contained a single target or no target or (b) whether the array comprised one or two targets. In this latter condition, successive presentation was much easier; in the first condition, simultaneous or successive presentation had little effect on detection accuracy. Thus, analogous to auditory monitoring of two messages, the decisive factor appeared to be the number of simultaneous targets that needed independent detection. Duncan considered his results as support for late selection. He suggested that all items from an array are simultaneously encoded not only with regard to form, color, and size but also with regard to semantics. Yet, this does not permit either conscious detection or retention which are bound to the actual outcome of response selection.

Late selection seems to be at odds with the mainstream of studies on covert orienting as well as with those on partial-report tasks and on bar-probe tasks. The typical outcome of these paradigms is that partial report is better than whole report but only when the cue for partial report is a simple physical dimension, for example, indicating a location or a common color, and not when the cue is an alphanumeric class that asks, for example, to report all digits among letters (Sperling, 1960; Von Wright, 1970). Such results have been considered as strong evidence in favor of early selection. There would be parallel processing of all items on the feature level, leading to precategorical visual, or iconic, storage. In turn, iconic storage would be followed by selection on the basis of a common physical feature such as a cued row. Only the selected items are supposed to be admitted to the P-system and are fully identified. In contrast, the nonselected items are subject to rapid decay. The main difference between the visual and auditory sensory stores concerns the length of time the items are available; the estimate for the auditory system amounts to 1 to 2 sec, whereas the visual icon does not appear to last longer than 250 ms.

As already mentioned, late selection proponents acknowledge that physical cues are easier and more discriminable than semantic cues, but they consider this to be a relative rather than an essential difference. In support of this view, Duncan (1983) found evidence for partial-report superiority when digits and letters were presented at random positions in a circular array, and participants had the task of only reporting the digits. Indeed, there is now wide evidence that partial-report studies do not allow a simple explanation in terms of a two-stage storage model in which items are either lost or read from iconic storage.

In contrast to Duncan (1983), Kahneman and Treisman (1984) defended the early-selection view that physical and semantic criteria for report are basically different. They noted that a semantic criterion always implies object identification, for example, "house," whereas a physical criterion does not.

For example, detecting the "red" of a red object means that participants are aware of something red in the visual field, but identification of the red object or event is not needed. This contrast underlies the difference between stimulus set (filtering) and response set, the first representing an orientation toward detecting a common physical feature and the second a selective set toward identifying a certain object. The early-selection view has been further elaborated in the feature-integration theory that, again, stresses the unique role of spatial localization of objects in the visual field.

As mentioned, proponents of late selection put heavy emphasis on the category effect. This emphasis implies that all items are semantically identified in parallel and that the target is distinguished from other stimuli through a category code in the same way as a red target is distinguished from blue distractors. There remain three main problems, though. First, there is the question why a target digit does not pop out when the nontargets are also digits (Jonides & Gleitman, 1976).[10] Deutsch (1977) proposed that because links in memory within categories are much stronger than between categories (Sanders & Schroots, 1969), response selection is hampered when searching for a digit among other digits. This is a typical late-selection argument that puts full emphasis on response set and top-down processing. Second, there is evidence that the category effect may ultimately rely on common physical features because it was found to vanish when all letters had the same physical features, that is, stylistic symbols (Krueger, 1984). Finally, Theeuwes (1991b) presented two target letters among digits; participants had to decide whether the two target letters were the same or different. In this case, CRT increased linearly as a function of the number of distractors (digits), which argues against the late-selection view that all items have been identified prior to selection and are available for further analysis.

FEATURE INTEGRATION THEORY (FIT)

The most important elaboration of the early-selection view to visual selective attention is undoubtedly Treisman's FIT. The initial formulation (Treisman & Gelade, 1980) was revised on a number of occasions (Treisman, 1993; Treisman & Gormican, 1988; Treisman & Sato, 1990); therefore, FIT is summarized in chronological order and complemented with suggestions from other researchers.

---

[10]In fact there is evidence that a flat-search function develops after highly intensive consistent practice with a fixed set of letter targets among other letter nontargets, which has been viewed as support for late selection (Shiffrin & Schneider, 1977). Yet, it is not impossible that individuals learn a common feature-like code (Hoffman, 1986). In addition, the stimuli in the Shiffrin and Schneider studies comprised a small visual angle that may have precluded separate spatial processing of the stimuli.

The starting point of FIT is the traditional two-stage view on visual se-lective attention. In the preattentive stage, stimulus features are encoded in parallel by way of a set of maps that register features such as color, size, tiltedness, stereoscopic depth, and motion for all stimuli. In the original version, there was a separate map for each feature. Thus, each color had its own map, with the total set of maps defining the color dimension. En-coding features was supposed to occur in parallel across the visual field for all stimuli, and this occurrence would lead to rough parsing, figure–back-ground separation, and texture segregation by way of areas with the same features. It does not lead to spatial localization or identification of a particular item. This is in line with the early-selection view that parallel analysis is limited to physical features.

In addition to the feature maps, FIT assumed a master map of spatial locations that indicates which features are present at each particular spot in the display. The set of features that are present on the selected location of the master map are integrated. This integration leads to recognition as well as localization of the item (Fig. 7.5). Feature integration always implies conjunction of features, which is characteristic of the second stage of attentive processing. The attended area on the master map depends on the width of the attentional spotlight (Treisman & Gormican, 1988). It is clear from Fig. 7.5 that when a particular location on the master map is consulted, there is, initially, a unitary raw representation, the features of which are analyzed and integrated into an identified object (Treisman, 1988). The proposed integration procedure gave FIT its name. As an alternative view, information from irrelevant locations may be attenuated so that the features of the at-tended spot can be processed with minimal cross-talk from competing, ad-jacent items. This could produce adequate conjunctions without assuming a separate feature-binding procedure (Mozer, 1991). In either case, attentive search always implies precise item or object localization.

In the original version of FIT, pop-out was a result of unique, preattentive activity in a particular feature map—for example, a single red item—in comparison to the other feature maps—for example, all green items. An item that pops out is detected but not localized at the preattentive level. It has the advantage, however, that preattentive pop-out directs attention to the location of the unique item. This, in turn, leads to rapid attentive iden-tification of the object. The result is a flat-search function, namely, a constant search time for a pop-out item, independent of the number of other items on the display. If a display does not contain a target, CRT may increase somewhat as a function of the number of items. Although the absence of pop-out is also rapidly detected—for example, only the green map is acti-vated—there may be a time-consuming, additional check.

Another consequence is that pop-out can never occur when target de-tection requires a conjunction of features. Thus, a single red item among

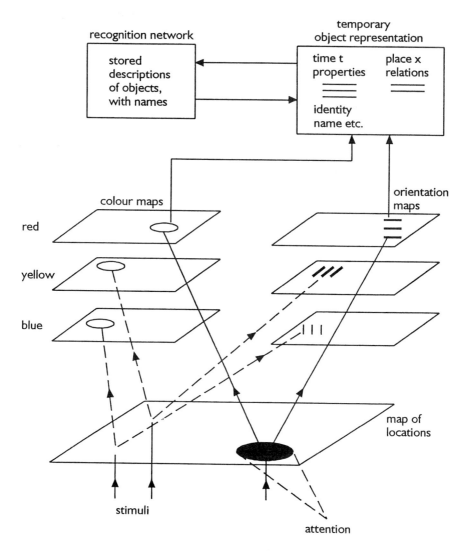

FIG. 7.5. Feature integration theory. Stimuli are analyzed in terms of features. Only the features of a stimulus at an attended spot are integrated, and this leads to recognition of an object at a specific spatial location. From Treisman, A. M. (1988). Features and objects: The fourteenth Bartlett memorial lecture. *Quarterly Journal of Experimental Psychology, 40*, 201–237. Reprinted by permission of Psychology Press. Permission was kindly granted by the Experimental Psychology Society.

blue items pops out, but a single red X between red Os and green Xs does not (Treisman & Gelade, 1980). In the latter case, a target consists of the conjunction of a shape and a color that are both constituents of the other items as well. The inference "this is a red X" can be only the result of integration of color and shape and, hence, of attentive processing. The result is a slow serial search of the display until a target is found or reported absent. A recent illustration of the role of attention in perceiving feature conjunctions stems from Modigliani, Wright, and Loverock (1996), who presented a sequence of single stimuli consisting of color–texture conjunctions. One group was instructed to count the frequency of a certain feature (incidental instruction), whereas another group was instructed to encode the total items in order to enable subsequent recognition (deliberate instruction). The results of the recognition test show that the incidental instruction had a strong negative effect on recognizing feature conjunctions. Similarly, Wright, Katz, and Hughes (1993) found little evidence for recognizing features such as location of small gaps and of inattended complex figures that were interleaved with an attended complex figure, emphasizing again the role of attention in encoding.

Interestingly, Treisman and Gelade (1980) obtained similar results for conjunctions of color and shape and for local features of letters. Thus, search for an R among Ps and Bs was easier than search for an R among Ps and Qs. It was concluded that in the former case, the R has a unique feature, namely, the diagonal line, which can serve as a primitive for preattentive detection.[11] The analysis of letters into features is also suggested by the occasional occurrence of illusory conjunctions, which are incorrect combinations of briefly presented features. Illusory conjunctions are most readily demonstrated by way of incorrect combinations of colors and shapes, but they are also observed in the case of letter features. For example, if Os and Rs are simultaneously presented, an O might be identified as a Q. In that case, the diagonal line of the R is integrated with the O in the feature integration process (Treisman & Schmidt, 1982).[12]

The activation of a feature map depends on the discriminability among the features of the same category. Thus, when targets and nontargets consist

---

[11]This view suggests that pop-out of digits among letters, and vice versa, is not a matter of semantic analysis but of feature analysis. Thus, FIT argues against the late-selection assumption that all items are identified.

[12]The initial interpretation was that illusory conjunctions demonstrate "free floating" features that have not yet been conjoined and localized. However, illusory conjunctions occur more frequently when features are spatially closer than when they are farther apart, which suggests an effect of position. Second, Donk (1995b) recently found that the occurrence of illusory conjunctions depends on the speed of processing individual features such as color and orientation, which, in turn, depends on their relative discriminability. An illusory conjunction has a higher probability of occurrence when a critical dimension has been incompletely processed.

FIG. 7.6. An illustration of the effect of a unique feature and of the unique absence of a feature on pop-out. From Wickens, C. D. (1992). *Engineering psychology and human performance.* Copyright © 1992 by HarperCollins Publishers, Inc. Reprinted by permission of Addison-Wesley Educational Publishers, Inc.

of different line lengths, the target pops out more readily as target and distractors are more distinct. The fact that only unique activity in a feature map elicits pop-out predicts that a unique presence of a feature pops out, whereas a unique absence of that feature does not (Fig. 7.6). The point is that the vertical feature map in Fig. 7.6 is strongly activated, irrespective of whether all, or all but one, circles contain a vertical line.

Properties of Features: Detecting the Largest Difference

Sagi and Julesz (1985) presented one to four horizontal or vertical line segments as targets embedded in a background of diagonals that all had the same orientation. The task consisted of a same–different reaction with respect to whether the targets had the same orientation or a different one. The results show that this could not be achieved by pop-out and required serial search of the targets. This is an ambiguous result. On the one hand, it might be considered as evidence that attending to spatial location is a prerequisite for identifying each individual target. Thus, one may detect a difference between targets and nontargets preattentively without getting information about whether the targets are aligned. On the other hand, from the perspective of FIT, one may doubt whether spatial localization of individual targets is really needed. Why is alignment among targets not inferred preattentively from activation of their respective feature maps?

One suggestion is that there are preattentive dimension maps as a summary for all elements of a category (Cave & Wolfe, 1990; Wolfe, 1994), and these maps should be distinguished from feature maps for individual colors such as green, red, and so on (Treisman, 1988). The dimension maps belong to the Guided-Search model of visual search. They record differences in the activation of individual feature maps (Cave & Wolfe). A single red item among many green items pops out because the activation of the green feature map is high and that of red is low, which means that a large difference is entered in the color dimension map. On the other hand, when a display consists of 15 items made up of 5 different and equally frequent colors, there is no pop-out of any particular color because there are no differences among the activation levels of the 5 feature maps. Among others, effects of discriminability are better accounted for in this way. Differences among less discriminable colors contribute less to the color dimension map than differences among highly discriminable colors.

In the same way, a single moving advertisement pops out from a stationary background, but the same moving advertisement does not pop out in the presence of many other moving advertisements. Yet, one fast-moving advertisement among many other slower moving ones pops out again. Theeuwes (1991c) proposed that the item associated with the *largest* difference in features pops out. He found that when searching for a unique color (green among red), a unique form (square among circle) did not interfere with finding the color. On the other hand, the color appeared to interfere when searching for a unique form. This result reversed when the difference in color was reduced (yellow among orange). In that case, search for a unique form was not hampered by the color differences, whereas search for the unique color was now hindered by the presence of the unique form. The Sagi and Julesz (1985) results are easily explained by Theeuwes' proposal. A single divergent line has the effect of a large difference in activation of the feature maps and, hence, on the orientation dimension. Adding three or four additional divergent lines leads to less difference, and this means less pop-out. Moreover, there is little or no difference in activation between the horizontal and vertical feature maps, which renders a preattentive judgment about alignment of the targets impossible.

Properties of Features: Bottom-Up Versus Top-Down Control

If activation of the feature maps is preattentive, it should be automatically established and, therefore, beyond strategic control (bottom up). This implies that advance knowledge about a deviant stimulus should not affect pop-out of the most salient deviation. The evidence on this issue is variable, however. When individuals knew that the deviant at a particular trial would be a specific color among potential other colors, advance information did not significantly affect CRT. However, preknowledge had a positive effect when the deviant would be a color among potential deviants from other dimensions. For example, the target could be a blue vertical bar among green vertical bars, a horizontal bar among vertical ones, or a longer bar among shorter ones. In this case, advance knowledge about which target dimension would deviate in a particular trial speeded up CRT (Treisman, 1988). She concluded that preknowledge about the deviant target dimension enabled the participants to suppress the activity of the feature maps of the other categories, which is a top-down activity and, hence, at odds with full automaticity of preattentive processing (Treisman & Sato, 1990).

Yet, the evidence about the effects of advance knowledge is not unequivocal. For instance, Pashler (1988) found no effect of preknowledge when the target could be either an O among dashes (/)or a specific color (a red dash among green dashes). Again, Theeuwes (1991b) found that information of an irrelevant dimension could not be ignored on purpose. He presented five, seven, or nine colored stimuli (circles or triangles) in a circular arrangement. All stimuli contained a tilted line except the target, which was horizontal or vertical. The task was to determine whether the line embedded in the target stimulus was horizontal or vertical. The target always had a unique form or color. The control condition had only one unique stimulus, whereas the experimental condition had two unique stimuli—one in form and another one in color. One dimension, that is, color or form, was instructed to be relevant, and the other to be irrelevant. The results (Fig. 7.7) showed flat search-functions that indicated parallel search among the stimuli on the display. At the same time, the irrelevant dimension interfered by raising overall CRT, with the amount of increase depending on the relative discriminability within a perceptual dimension. Thus, preknowledge about the relevant dimension did not eliminate interference from an irrelevant dimension. Therefore, Theeuwes extended his proposal that only the dimension with the largest difference pops out. The suggestion is that if the dimension with the largest difference is irrelevant to the target, it will be rejected, whereupon the dimension with the one but highest difference pops out. The rejection is under attentional control—the pop-out leads to attentive analysis—and takes time, but the remaining processes are bottom up.

This is not the full story, though. In the studies discussed so far, the unique stimulus always provided a 100% valid indication that it contained the target. In another experiment (Theeuwes, 1990), the stimulus, unique either in form or in color, and the position of the target were uncorrelated. In other words, the target had an equal probability of appearing in the unique stimulus or in one of the other nonunique stimuli. Under these circumstances, the unique stimulus did not receive a priority treatment, and so did not automatically attract attention. Instead, target search was slow and presumably serial. This result is consistent with the evidence on covert orienting that suggests that individuals have the ability of strategically controlling the focus of the zoom lens. If they know that the target is always embedded in the unique item, the lens is widely set—a divided-attention set—to detect any pop-out. In the same way, a wide zoom lens is required for texture segregation and for global alignment of shapes (Fig. 7.4). On the other hand, the zoom lens is focused—a focused-attention set—on one stimulus at a time when the target may be embedded in any element. In

form   color

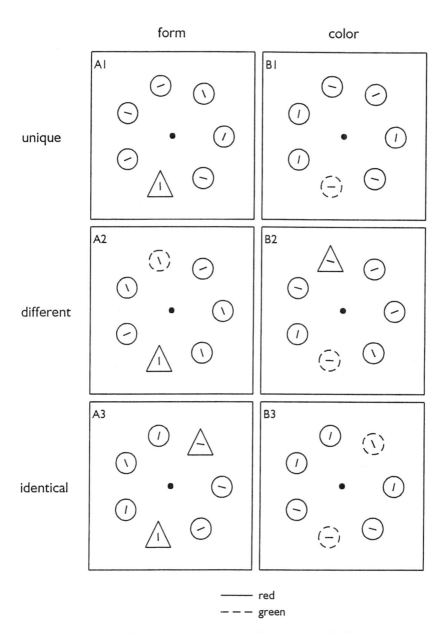

FIG. 7.7.A. Displays from Theeuwes (1992). The task was to decide whether the line embedded in the target was horizontal or vertical. In the non-distractor condition, the target had a unique form or color (top panel). The different-distractor condition had two unique targets, one in form and the other in color (middle panel). The identical-distractor condition had two targets, either unique in form or unique in color. From Theeuwes, J. (1992). Perceptual selectivity for color and form. *Perception & Psychophysics, 51,* 599–606. Reprinted by permission of Psychonomic Society, Inc.

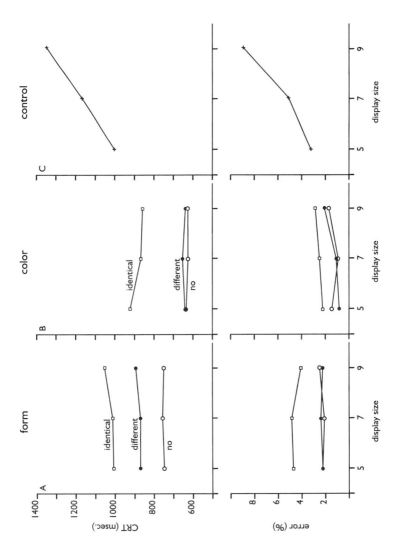

FIG. 7.7.B. Data from Theeuwes (1992). The form-distractor has no effect when the color is relevant, whereas the color distractor has an effect when the form is relevant. However, the effects are independent of display size.

that case, pop-out vanishes because the unique item is outside the scope of the zoom lens.[13] The prime role of spatial focusing has been confirmed by ERP studies that show little effect of a relevant color at an unattended location in comparison with an attended location (e.g., Wijers et al., 1989).[14]

The setting of the zoom lens is a clear example of attentional control and strategy. Theeuwes (1993) defended the view that once the lens has been set, the operation of the feature maps is completely bottom up. In contrast to Treisman and Sato (1990) and Cave and Wolfe (1990), Theeuwes did not assume that individuals strategically manipulate a feature map or a dimension map. According to the best traditions of early selection, he suggested that top-down control cannot access preattentive structures—it may only modulate admittance to subsequent central processing. The issue seems unsettled, though, because there is other evidence suggesting that individuals may selectively search subsets of features and ignore other features (Kaptein et al., 1995; H. J. Müller et al., 1995). In particular, results on parallel conjunction search are hard to explain without assuming top-down control activity. It could be that Theeuwes' proposal is relevant to search for, and interference from, single features but not to conjunction search.

Albeit for different reasons, Treisman (1993) also contrasted conditions of divided and focused attention with respect to selection of visual information. This was inspired by an observation from Enns (1990) that light–shade combinations of 3-D figures pop out, but they do not pop out when the same combinations belong to 2-D figures (Fig. 7.8). Thus, the 2-D pictures seem to require attentive search (conjunction of features), but the 3-D pictures do not. Treisman proposed a divided-attention set when viewing a 3-D scene that would allow "assessment of global features, like illumination, surface orientation or optic flow" (p. 14). Normally, the illumination is on the top and, hence, a deviation can be spotted. Such a structure is absent in 2-D pictures and, consequently, individuals resort to focused search. Like Theeu-

---

[13]This result may seem at odds with those on pop-out in the case of automatic processing of well-learned target sets (Schneider & Shiffrin, 1977). In these studies, a relevant target could only appear on the two diagonal positions of an imaginary square, and an irrelevant distracting target might arrive on the other diagonal. The fact that more than one position was relevant may preclude focusing of the zoom lens, and, therefore, induce interference from items from the irrelevant diagonal. The relevance of focusing with regard to interference from other letters has also been demonstrated by Yantis and Johnston (1990), who found little evidence for interference in the case of strong focusing. This result is fully in line with Theeuwes (1993). Thus, focusing appears to be a potent intervening variable in the discussion on early versus late selection.

[14]When the relevant and irrelevant locations are in close vicinity, the priority of location over color selection in the ERP tends to disappear, which is consistent with the notion that the spotlight has a gradient (Hillyard & Münte, 1984). It is obvious that one also expects a different picture in divided-attention conditions. Indeed, processing negativity starts at about 150 ms after stimulus presentation. In addition, physical cues such as color, size, and orientation have a pronounced effect on N2 (Wijers et al., 1989).

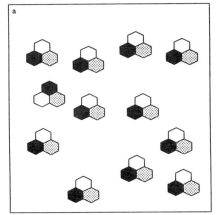
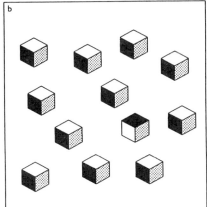

FIG. 7.8.   In Fig. 7.8B the shading of the top pops out while pop-out is absent
for patterns of matched complexity that cannot be interpreted as 3-D (Fig.
7.8A). From Enns, J. T., & Rensink, R. A. (1992). A model for the rapid interpretation of line drawings in early vision. In D. Brogan, A. Gale, & K. Carr
(Eds.), *Visual search, Volume 2: Proceedings of the second international
conference on visual search*. Copyright © 1992 by Taylor & Francis, London.
Reproduced with permission of the publisher.

wes (1993), Treisman noticed that one cannot focus attention and, at the
same time, benefit from the advantages of divided attention. For instance,
texture segregation disappeared when focusing on a single element.

What Are Features?

In the initial FIT, it was implicitly assumed that any color, orientation, or
other element belonging to any feature dimension had its own map. The
finding that quantitative differences among features within a dimension affect
the extent and occurrence of pop-out (e.g., Theeuwes, 1991c) cast doubt
on this assumption. Recently, Treisman (1993) suggested that a dimension
may have only a limited number of feature maps. Specific dimension values
may be composed of ratios of values on feature maps. For example, a
combination of a value on the red and green feature maps may render
yellow; similarly, a combination of values on the horizontal and vertical
maps may render a tilted line. In the same way, Wolfe (1994) suggested
that top-down activity is limited to a few broadly tuned channels.

Thus, yellow may have no map of its own but consist of a composite of
adjacent colors; similarly, a tilted line would be a composite of the vertical
and horizontal maps. The prediction is an asymmetry in pop-out between
targets and distractors from both a unique and a composite dimension. In
the same way, a tilted line should pop out from a background of vertical
lines, whereas a single vertical line should not pop out from a background

of tilted lines. The point is that a single tilted line benefits from the unique activation of the horizontal map (Treisman & Gormican, 1988). No pop-out should be found when a target is tilted among nontargets with a different tilt, or when a target has a color from a composite of feature maps among nontargets with a color from a composite of different color maps. Another issue relating to features is what actually makes up a perceptual dimension. Treisman proposed a distinction between surface features such as brightness, color, texture, motion, and depth and shape features such as orientation.

Conjunctions of Features

As mentioned, the initial FIT proposed slow, serial, self-terminating—that is attentive—search when a target consists of a conjunction of features. Treisman and Gelade (1980) assumed a random serial search among items with approximately equal search rates as long as the stimuli have an equal speed of feature integration. The problem with this view is that the rate of conjunction search varies widely. Among others, the actual rate appears to depend on the stimulus density of the display. Search is usually slower as stimulus density is higher (A. Cohen & Ivry, 1991). Pashler (1987) suggested that a low stimulus-density may permit joint processing of several items by a wider zoom lens setting that would speed up average search rate. Zacks and Zacks (1993) found a higher search rate with a psychophysical forced-choice procedure—Which one of two successively presented displays contained a target?—than with measurement of CRT. It could be that a psychophysical procedure promotes a wide setting of the zoom lens in an attempt to acquire as much information as possible during the brief presentation period.

However, when display density is properly controlled, there remain considerable variations in the search rate of conjunction targets. For instance, A. Cohen (1993) found a slow search for a blue *O* among yellow *O*s and blue *X*s, whereas search was much faster for a yellow *O*, a yellow *X*, and a blue *X* among comparable distractors. Why is search for a blue *O* relatively slow? One may try to account for the asymmetry in terms of single- or composite-feature maps, as outlined previously. If yellow comes from a composite map, it may pop out more easily than the single-mapped blue. In the same way, the *X* may come from a composite map and pop out more easily than a single-mapped *O*. Hence, the blue–*O* combination would be particularly hard to find. Yet, this interpretation remains ad hoc as long as there is no commonly agreed list of single maps.

The Guided-Search model (Wolfe, 1994; Wolfe, Cave, & Franzel, 1989) proposes a serial search that is not random but guided by the joint information from all dimension maps that contribute to the display. Thus, when a target requires a conjunction of a red color and a horizontal orientation, the preattentive color maps may signal "red" as the relatively largest color difference on the color dimension map, whereas the orientation maps may signal "horizontal" as the largest difference on the orientation dimension map. The fact that the participants know the constituent features of the target adds to the relative activation of the particular feature maps—"red" and "horizontal" in the preceding example—and hence to the recorded differences among features on the corresponding dimension maps. Thus, even if there are no clear bottom-up differences in activation of the feature maps, top-down activation of those features that make up the target may lead to a recorded difference in activation. The model assumes that the largest differences in activation on all dimensions are summed up in a joint activation map. Attention is directed first to the item with the highest value on the joint activation map, followed by the next highest, and so on, in decreasing order. In this way, a conjunction target is found more rapidly than when search is random. Among others, this assumption may cover findings like Duncan's (1989) that parallel search remained possible even when the distractor colors were quite heterogeneous, a result that is clearly at odds with the earlier versions of FIT. The problem with the assumption of top-down intervention is that the presumed asymmetry in search rate requires ad hoc postulates about how activations on the joint activation map are established.

There are cases of conjunction search that have a flat search-function. In other words, the searched item pops out as if it came from a single-feature map. One instance stems from H. E. Egeth, Virzi, and Garbart (1984), who had participants search for a red *O* among red *N*s and black *O*s. The number of nontargets amounted to 4, 14, or 24. When there were only a couple of red letters, for example, two red *N*s and one red *O*, participants were capable of ignoring the black items and limiting serial search to the red items. A similar result was obtained by Noble and Sanders (1980). The original FIT can still handle this result in terms of a difference in activation between the red- and black-feature maps. The few reds pop out, followed by selective serial search among the red stimuli. However Kaptein, Theeuwes, and van der Heijden (1995) found that when properly controlling for differences in salience, participants could still intentionally limit search to a subset with a specific feature such as a specific color. Hence, rapid selective search of an item is not the exclusive prerogative of bottom-up pop-out of a single feature. In addition, there is some top-down control through segregation of target-relevant from target-irrelevant features.

There are other cases of rapid detection of conjunction targets that all have in common the characteristic that items are made up of highly discriminable dimensions such as color and motion, or color and stereoscopic depth. Another example concerns red and green colors and horizontal and vertical bars. When searching for a single, red, vertical bar among red, horizontal bars and green, vertical bars, with about equal frequency of colors and orientations, the red, vertical bar appears to be detected rapidly, the requirement of conjunction notwithstanding. Treisman and Sato (1990) and Treisman (1993) suggested top-down intervention on the preattentive level by way of selective inhibition of links from the feature maps to the master map of locations (Fig. 7.5). For instance, if one inhibits the connection between the horizontal feature map and the master map of locations, the effect is that the horizontal–vertical variation ceases to play a part, thereby reducing the task to detection of a single feature, namely, a red vertical among green verticals.

This leads to the recurrent problem of how to avoid notions that can explain any result, fast or slow search alike, by top-down intervention. The inhibition proposal should define constraints that specify whether a feature map may or may not be inhibited. Treisman (1993) suggested that inhibition is only possible when each stimulus, target as well as nontarget, activates a single-feature map—red, green, horizontal, vertical, and so on—and not when composites of two maps are activated. Thus, inhibition is less efficient as more feature maps are involved. The main difference between the already discussed guided-search notion and the revised FIT is that guided search assumes a top-down increase in activation of a dimension, whereas the revised FIT suggests top-down inhibition of a dimension.

Still another example of fast search concerns the case of letter conjunctions, for example, an L among nontarget Ts or an inverted T among upright Ts (Humphreys, Quinlan, & Riddoch, 1989). It has also been found that the search function for a single feature (an upright T among tilted Ts) is about the same as for the conjunction in the case of an upright T among Ls. The slope of the search function increases as the nontargets are more heterogeneous, for example, an upright T as target among rotated Ts, some of which are rotated 180° and others 270° (Duncan & Humphreys, 1989; Fig. 7.9, upper). A conjunction such as an L, is also more easily detected among homogeneous than among other heterogeneous conjunctions (Fig. 7.9, lower). To solve this problem, Treisman (1993) raised the possibility that well-known shapes, such as letters, might have their own feature map, but she recognized that this possibility is ad hoc.

ATTENTIONAL ENGAGEMENT

These last types of results led Duncan and Humphreys (1989) to reject FIT altogether and to interpret the data on visual search along the lines of late selection through similarity among targets and nontargets. The slope of the search function is supposed to increase as targets and nontargets become more similar and also as nontargets have less mutual similarity. For example,

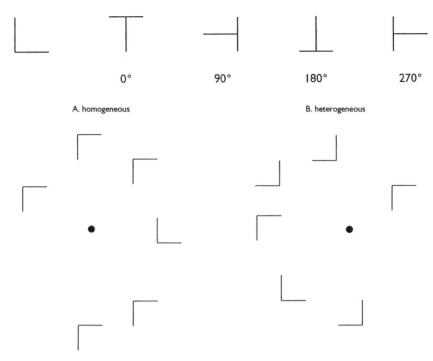

0°   90°   180°   270°

A. homogeneous   B. heterogeneous

FIG. 7.9. Upper: Detection of a *T* depends on the rotation of distracting *T*s. Lower: An *L* is detected more easily among (A) homogeneous than among (B) heterogeneous conjunctions. From Duncan, J., & Humphreys, G. W. (1989). Visual search and stimulus similarity. *Psychological Review, 96,* 433–458. Copyright © 1989 by the American Psychological Association. Reprinted with permission.

a red target pops out less well when the nontargets are homogeneously orange than when they are homogeneously green. Again, a red target pops out less well when the nontargets are heterogeneous, for example, consist of different colors. More generally, Duncan and Humphreys rejected the dichotomy between flat and linearly increasing search-functions that constitutes the typical early-selection distinction between preattentive and attentive processing.

In their view, the first stage of processing is a perceptual description that consists of a hierarchically structured parallel representation in short-term memory of all inputs across the visual field. A representation is structured under Gestalt principles in that units consist of parts that belong together. It is hierarchical because larger units may be made up of smaller units. The second stage concerns *short-term memory processing,* which has a limited capacity. The weight of a representation decides whether it is further processed. The weight depends on the extent to which a perceptual unit matches or is similar to the internal representation of the target. A match is usually easy when a target has a single, specific feature, for example a color, but the match of a single feature may be difficult when the feature is a complex shape. Dissimilar targets and nontargets always lead to an easy match, so a strong weight can be rapidly assigned, which results in fast detection. The match with the internal representation is harder as targets and nontargets become more similar. Thus, it takes a longer average time for that target to be processed in short-term memory. Similarity varies along a continuum, and in contrast to FIT and the Guided-Search model, there is no dichotomy between parallel feature search and serial conjunction search. Usually, though, conjunction targets will be more similar to the nontargets for the simple reason that some features of the nontargets also match the internal representation of the target. An important, further element of the theory is that a low weight of a representation extends to the whole hierarchical group to which that representation belongs, thus allowing rapid rejection of whole groups of nontargets. As nontargets become more heterogeneous, they are less hierarchically structured. Hence, they are less rapidly rejected, causing delays in target detection.

A major difference between FIT and Guided Search and similarity theory—better called attentional engagement theory (AET; Duncan & Humphreys, 1992)—concerns the relative emphasis on top-down control and on the role of spatial localization in visual selection. FIT and Guided Search acknowledge top-down activity on the preattentive level in the sense of inhibition or activation of feature or dimension maps. Yet, in line with the tradition of early selection, the role of top-down activity is supposed to be limited in the same way as the role of response set was limited in Broadbent's (1971) formulation. In contrast, the AET model proposes that target detection depends on matching all stimuli to their internal representations, which is primarily a top-down activity. An exception is the effect of the degree of similarity among nontargets that determines the relative weight of their representations in a bottom-up fashion. A second major difference is that FIT distinguishes sharply between spatial localization and identification—the "where" and the "what." Without localization, there is no visual identification. In the AET view, the full emphasis is on object selection, that is, response set, in which spatial localization has no special position. Third, FIT assumes serial attentional search for conjunctions as distinct from parallel preattentive search, whereas AET assumes parallel encoding of all stimuli, although with pronounced differences in encoding rate that depend on similarity. One problem for serial search comes from a study in which the participants decided whether a display contained two identical targets or contained at least one target. The results show that the slope of the target-absent CRT as a function of display density was steeper when the task required detection of both targets than one target. This would not be predicted by FIT because when targets are absent, the display should be exhaustively searched in either condition. When all items are processed in parallel, it is less time consuming to decide that there is at least one target than two identical targets, which is directly reflected in the slope of the target-absent function (H. J. Müller, Humphreys, & Donnelly, 1994).

The principles of AET have been cast into the so called *search via recursive rejection* (SERR) connectionist model by Humphreys and Müller (1993). SERR starts off with activation of simple features such as color and orientation, the results of which are fed into combined-feature units. These more complex units are organized in separate topographic maps to enable parallel encoding. Object recognition occurs by matching encoded objects to internal templates.

As a general account, AET may be untenable, though. For example, Sperling, Wurst, and Lu (1993) showed that when all visual information is presented in very rapid succession on the same spot, filtering on the basis of physical or semantic cues is difficult or impossible. Hence, a major role of stimulus features seems to consist of guiding attention to a specific spot. From a neurophysiological perspective, there is also considerable evidence that localization (where) and identification (what) are relatively autonomous systems. Stimulus features such as color, pattern, and shape are processed in the ventral stream of occipitotemporal visual areas, whereas spatial relationships are represented in the dorsal stream of the occipitoparietal area (Allport, 1993). One may also be reminded of the ERP evidence that attending a specific location is reflected by enhanced P1 and N1 amplitudes in the ERP, whereas the stimulus features of the attended spot are reflected by the later selection negativity. Annlo-Vento and Hillyard (1996) found that reacting to motion at the attended spot is also reflected by selection negativity, despite the fact that motion, like spatial location, has a dorsal occipitoparietal localization in the brain. Hence, attending to spatial location rather than a location-bound visual feature appears to enhance the early components.

Another clear illustration of the special position of spatial information stems from some of the work of Theeuwes (1989), who asked participants to carry out a choice reaction to a horizontal or vertical line element, surrounded by a circle or by a diamond-shaped frame, and presented either 6° to the left or to the right of the fixation point, amidst other line segment distractors (Fig. 7.10). In one set of conditions, the left or right spatial location of the frame was cued in advance by a bar. In another set of conditions, the type of frame was probed (diamond or circle) but without indication about whether it would appear to the left or to the right. The results (Fig. 7.10) showed that cuing spatial location was effective in that CRT was faster when the cue was valid and slower when it was invalid. Apparently, one can direct attention to a certain spatial location, which is in accord with the literature on covert attention. In contrast, cuing form did not affect CRT. The precue did not lead to faster responding, a situation that suggests that advance "setting" of the form, that is, diamond or circle, does not speed up identification.

This result does not exclude instances of object selection, that is, response set, as an attentional activity that is additional to identification through feature integration. Thus, Rensink and Enns (1995) found that search for Müller–Lyer stimuli (Fig. 7.11) is based on the complete configuration of the stimulus rather than on conjunction of line segments. In their basic study, the target was distinguished from the distractors by wing type. Three main conditions were studied. In one (Fig. 7.11A), the inner segments were equally long, but due to the position of the wing, the target seemed longer than the distractors. In the second condition (Fig. 7.11B), target and distractors seemed equally long. In the third condition (Fig. 7.11C), the target seemed, and was, actually shorter than the distractors.

Note that if the wing served as a separate feature (junction based), flat search-functions should be observed in all conditions because wing type would be the only relevant aspect. In the case of integration of separate components (segment based), the configuration should be established faster as more components differ. Hence, search in Condition A should be slow, but it should be faster in Conditions B and C. If search is based on the total

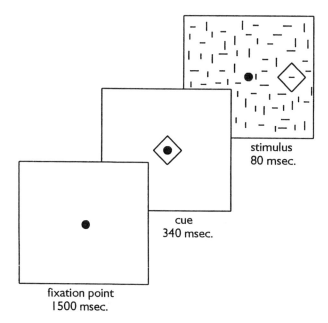

FIG. 7.10. Experimental set-up of Theeuwes (1989). In this condition, the probe indicated that the target will be surrounded by a diamond and not by a circle, but the probe did not inform the subject about the spatial location of the target. Figure continued on next page.

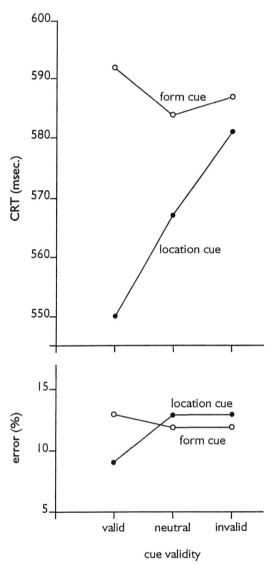

FIG. 7.10. (*Continued*). Results of Theeuwes, J. (1989). Effects of location and form cueing on the allocation of attention in the visual field. *Acta Psychologica, 72*, 177–192. Copyright © 1989 with kind permission of Elsevier Science-NL, Sara Burgerhartstraat 25, 1055 KV, Amsterdam, The Netherlands.

configuration (assembly based)—for example, its apparent length—Condition B should be the hardest because the total lengths of the stimuli seem the same, and A and C should be faster because their lengths seem to differ. The results supported this last view. Search was the slowest in the seemingly equal length condition (Fig. 7.11B) and much faster in the other two conditions. A flat search-function was never found.

Treisman (1993) accepted the possibility that search may also be mediated by object files projecting on the master map of locations, a situation that comes

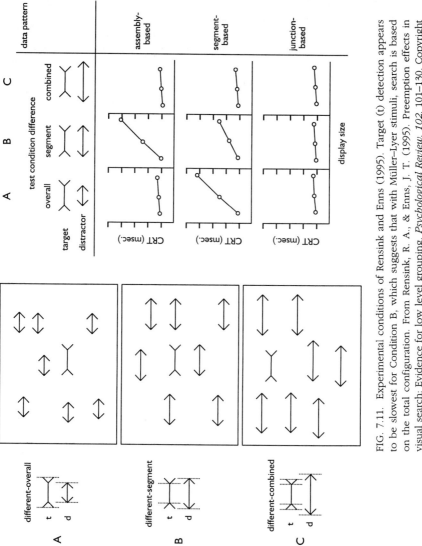

FIG. 7.11. Experimental conditions of Rensink and Enns (1995). Target (t) detection appears to be slowest for Condition B, which suggests that with Müller–Lyer stimuli, search is based on the total configuration. From Rensink, R. A., & Enns, J. T. (1995). Preemption effects in visual search: Evidence for low level grouping. *Psychological Review, 102,* 101–130. Copyright © 1995 by the American Psychological Association. Reprinted with permission.

close to Duncan and Humphreys' (1992) internal representations. Object files "are the structures that individuate *objects* and maintain their identity through change and motion" (p. 24, italics added). Thus, an object file of a *T* might be used to detect a single *T* among inverted *T*s. This means that in that case, configuration, not feature integration, is decisive for localizing the target. If a configuration allows object selection, search is more efficient than through the painstaking process of feature integration. Yet, as has always been recognized, searching for a match by way of an object file can never be as effective as localizing a single feature such as a unique color. In this latter case, the search function is really independent of the number of nontargets. In the case of object selection, detection may be fairly rapid but breaks down when the number of nontargets exceeds a critical limit of, for example, 8 to 10 items (see also the discussion on automatic processing in chap. 8).

In conclusion, FIT faces the problem that search sometimes appears to depend on the total configuration of a display. One striking instance stems from a study by Driver, MacLeod, and Dienes (1992), in which participants searched for an *X* oscillating along the "top left to bottom right" diagonal among *O*s oscillating along the same diagonal and *X*s oscillating along the "top right to bottom left" diagonal of the display. Search was rapid when both diagonal sets were oscillating in phase. Search was still efficient when one set was out of phase, but it became very difficult when elements of either set were out of phase. In other words, it was essential for rapid search of the *X* that the oscillations constituted a systematic pattern or a structured Gestalt as background for segregating the two diagonals. The point is that FIT mainly addresses individual spatial elements rather than the total structure.

It is interesting that the discussion between proponents of integration of features versus immediately given Gestalts can be traced back to the 1920s when G. E. Müller (1923) defended feature integration and Köhler (1925) Gestalt. A difference between this classical discussion and the present one is that the issue seems no longer either–or. There are clear instances when identification is guided by simple features, in particular, when there are many scattered simultaneous stimuli and distinctive features (Treisman, 1993). There are other instances in which the total configuration is decisive. A major future task is to specify the conditions under which either processing mode dominates. It is evident that the really relevant dimensions in this respect have not yet been uncovered. Moreover, most studies on search have used artificial stimulus-displays with scattered separate objects. Hence, the part of total configurations and, in particular of meaningful structures, may have been underestimated when searching landscape-type displays. In the next section, a theory on visual selective attention is discussed in which object and configuration on the one hand and spatial localization on the other hand receive about equal weight, and may well be the first serious attempt of going beyond the early–late selection debate.

POSTCATEGORICAL FILTERING

Early Versus Late Selection in Partial Report and Bar-Probe Tasks

It was briefly mentioned that the early studies on partial report found physical cues to be the most effective for target detection, whereas categorical and semantic cues were ineffective. Yet, some later studies showed a beneficial effect of categorical cuing as well. In order to be beneficial, a categorical cue needs to be presented in advance of the display, and the instruction about the class of items to report should remain the same throughout a block of trials (van der Heijden, 1992). These prerequisites remind one of the role of consistent mapping in the development of automatic processing (chap. 8). In line with the Broadbent–Treisman views on early selection, consistent mapping creates optimal conditions for response set. Categorical cues may enable full encoding of attenuated stimuli, yet the effect of physical cues is more general and more effective.

The results on the nature of errors in bar-probe tasks are harder to handle for early-selection theory. The point is that bar-probe tasks show location errors, that is, participants tend to report letters that occupy a location in the vicinity of the bar probe. Location errors appear to increase as the bar probe arrives later (e.g., Mewhort, Campbell, Marchetti, & Campbell, 1981; van der Heijden, 1992, for a review) and are less frequent as the distance from the correct location increases. Thus, errors appear not to be due to reading failures from a decaying preattentive trace. Instead, misalignment of the probe leads to more and more inaccurate localization.

This has been considered as favoring late selection in bar-probe tasks. All stimuli might be transferred to a visuospatial buffer that stores identified characters together with their spatial positions. Retrieval of a probed item occurs on the basis of localizing that item in the postcategorical buffer (Mewhort, Butler, Feldman-Stuart, & Tramer, 1988).[15] This view assumes that all spatial locations are transferred from a raw feature buffer to a more abstract character buffer. The consequence is that late selection occurs on the basis of an early-selection criterion—that is, spatial position. And that is odd.

Van der Heijden (1992) rightly wondered whether the evidence on location errors really requires postcategorical storage or whether probe misalignment may occur at an earlier, precategorical level. More recent studies by Mewhort, Johns, and Coble (1991) may support this last option. CRT in a bar-probe task is prolonged when the letters are degraded. This increase in

---

[15]Mewhort et al. also assumed a rapidly decaying precategorical feature buffer that is relevant to phenomena of visual persistence but not to retrieving information in a bar-probe task. All information is supposed to enter the character buffer, albeit in a more abstract form in which physical properties are no longer represented.

CRT is found irrespective of whether the letters are flashed twice, first without and then with the bar probe, or the bar probe is presented in advance of the letter array. The first condition in particular raises a problem. Parallel identification of the letters may be delayed by degradation, but because identification can occur before presentation of the bar probe, degradation should either not affect CRT at all or, at least, less than in the second condition where the full degradation effect should be found.

The idea that early selection might still underly errors in a bar-probe task also comes from some work of van der Heijden et al. (1987), who used a circular display rather than the traditional horizontal one. A circular display has the advantage of keeping the effects of peripheral vision and lateral inhibition constant. Van der Heijden et al. argued that rapid decay of symbols from a precategorical store would have the effect that misidentification of letters, that is, mentioning a physically similar symbol, occurs mainly when the symbols have partially decayed. The reasoning is that the probability of a misidentification should be less when the trace is still fully intact and should be less again when the trace has fully decayed. While the trace is decaying, the distinctive features of similar letters will tend to vanish, and this would cause misidentification. The results of van der Heijden et al. were in keeping with this reasoning.

Van der Heijden's (1992) Postcategorical Filtering

There remains, of course, the problem for early selection of how to explain the phenomenon of location errors or misalignment of the bar probe. In the context of a more general model on selective attention in vision, van der Heijden (1992) proposed that all items from an input module that contains raw data about the combinations of identity and location are forwarded independently and in parallel to both an identity module and a location module. These two systems should somehow come together because identification of visual stimuli usually requires localization. It is assumed, therefore, that selected locations are fed back from the location module to the input module from where it can contact the corresponding information in the identity module (Fig. 7.12). For instance, in covert attending to a single item, the location module registers that there is a stimulus at some location in an otherwise empty field. This triggers the feedback loop for that location to establish contact with the identity module. Advance cuing of a location means that feedback from that location receives priority. Location errors may be due to imprecision of location feedback. Therefore, the incorrect element in the input module is activated. Again, the location module has a limited spatial resolution that accounts for the gradients found in covert attention. Information in the input module decays over time. This decay renders location feedback less effective as SOA between stimulus presentation and bar probe increases. Finally, feedback about a specific location facilitates identification

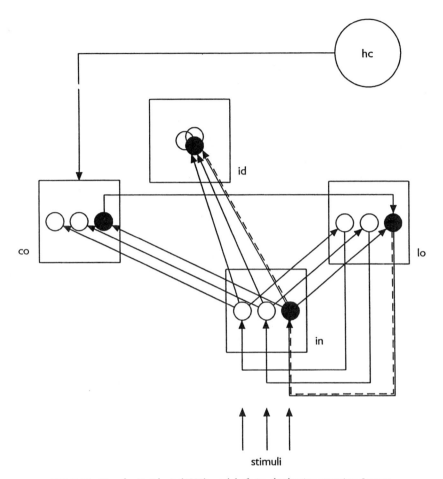

FIG. 7.12. Van der Heijden's (1992) model of visual selective attention. Incoming stimuli [in] are analyzed by way of feature modules like color [co] and location [lo], but they also activate entries in an identity module [id]. A unique feature [black circle] feeds back to the location module which, in turn, feeds back to the input module [in] and from there to the identity module. In this way one of the stimuli in the identity module is selected for action-directed processing. Although this is much less efficient, search may also be guided by "higher centers" [hc]. From van der Heijden, A. H. C. (1992). *Selective attention in vision*. London: Routledge. Reproduced with permission from the publisher.

but may turn into inhibition when the SOA between cue and display exceeds a critical value. In line with evidence on habituation, a sensory deviation triggers feedback from the location module with the most ease.

When limited to the previously mentioned modules, the model cannot account for effects of symbolic cues or verbal instructions about where to expect a stimulus or about which stimulus to reproduce. Hence, the location module can also be voluntarily activated by higher centers. These higher centers play a role as well in having individuals obey instructions about responding to a specific color, orientation, form, or any other physical attribute. In this way, they enable selective search of a specific color. Like Treisman (1988; see Fig. 5), van der Heijden (1992) assumed spatial maps for physical attributes that activate the corresponding spot in the location module. Because physical attributes enable rapid search, a direct link is assumed between the attribute maps and the location module. In contrast, activation of a location by a higher center takes much more time to develop. The point is that the higher centers have the time-consuming task of decoding the instruction and of transforming it into a location code. In category search, the higher centers may be alerted by the identity module. Therefore, selection takes the full localization loop, which is possible but not very efficient. Thus, a semantic category can only be used as a criterion for selecting a target in a circular array of stimuli when the instruction about the category is given sufficiently long before presenting the display.

The implication of parallel recording in the identity mode of all stimuli arriving at the input mode is that there is no basic capacity limit to perceptual processing. However, there is the constraint that without localization, information from the identity module cannot be used for action. Here, van der Heijden (1992) follows the lead of Allport (1987) and of Neumann (1987), who ascribed limited capacity to restrictions in carrying out simultaneous actions rather than to limits in perceptual processing. "Behavioral chaos would result from an attempt to simultaneously perform all possible actions for which sufficient causes exist" (Neumann, p. 374).

This leads to a basic difference between the model of Treisman (1988, 1993) (and of many other models on attention) and van der Heijden's (1992). Feature integration theory is concerned with the role of attention in object identification, that is, attention is gluing the features of an object. In line with the best traditions of early selection, identification cannot occur without attention because perception is capacity limited. In contrast, van der Heijden assumed unlimited perceptual processing capacity in that everything reaches the identity module, but one has a limited potential for action. This limit, which sounds like late selection, requires selection among the items in the identity module. Yet, selecting an item from the identity module can only occur through localization, which is a basic tenet of early selection. In this way, the notion of unlimited capacity is tied to early selection.

The two theories converge in many other respects. They both emphasize the roles of spatial localization and feature maps in directing attention. Van der Heijden's (1992) theory is also compatible with Theeuwes' (1993) and Wolfe's (1994) assumption that the location corresponding to the largest feature difference is automatically activated and that the width of the range of activated locations can be controlled to some extent. Van der Heijden expressed doubts about spotlight and zoom lens notions because it is usually not specified, in particular not when the situation is under top-down control, who directs the spotlight or who sets the zoom lens. He argued that this opens the back door to a homunculus conception. It should be noted that assigning a role to higher centers in operating the location module does not solve this problem either.

Phaf, van der Heijden, and Hudson (1990) presented a neural network model of van der Heijden's (1992) views. It has three layers concerned with input, attribute analysis, and output. The input layer consists of a set of modules, each of which contains a combination of attributes, for example, location and color, and form and color, or a word-attribute combination such as word and location. The separate features are analyzed on the attribute level; then ultimate values about location, form, and color are transmitted to the output level. Words are directly transmitted to the output level, but the location of a word has to be determined at the attribute level before it can be used (Fig. 7.13). This is in line with van der Heijden's notion that localization and

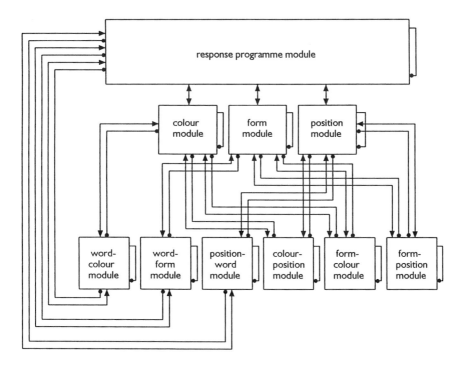

FIG. 7.13. A neural network representation of van der Heijden's (1992) model. From Phaf, R. H., van der Heijden, A. H. C., & Hudson, P. T. W. (1990). SLAM: A connectionist model for attention in visual tasks. *Cognitive Psychology, 22,* 273–341. Copyright © 1990 by Academic Press, Inc., Orlando, Fl. Reprinted with permission.

identification are strictly separate. The output and attribute layers correspond to the identification, location, and feature modules of Fig. 7.12.

EVOKED POTENTIALS AND THE EARLY–LATE DEBATE

ERP measures have the advantage in research on selective attention that they are evoked irrespective of an overt or covert behavioral response. This is particularly relevant with respect to the question about the level on which unattended stimuli are analyzed (but see Eimer, 1995). It is not surprising that ERPs are modality specific because properties of stimulus processing and attention are jointly measured. Hence, ERP data on auditory and visual attention are discussed separately.

Auditory Selective Attention

The original finding was that selective attention enhances the N1 component. Subsequent studies showed that this is likely to be part of a more general negative shift of the ERP (processing negativity) that extends well beyond the N1 (Näätänen, Gaillard, & Mäntysalo, 1978).[16] Yet, an earlier part of the negative shift has been distinguished from a later one on the basis of scalp location. The early part is thought to be related to selection of the attended channel, whereas the later part could reflect further processing of attended stimuli. Processing negativity has been observed for various channels such as pitch, location, and intensity, with its onset time depending on the discriminability of the channels. Moreover, as channels are less discriminable, stimuli at unattended channels show more processing negativity. This suggests that it is harder to establish intentional selection of one channel.

All stimuli, targets as well as nontargets, arriving at the attended channel show about equal early processing negativity. In addition, a target at the attended channel brings about additional effects on N2, P3, and a subsequent negative shift labeled mismatch negativity (Näätänen, 1982). The effects on N1 and on P3 are usually discussed in terms of early-stimulus selection (N1) and late-response selection (P3), respectively. Targets arriving at an unattended channel usually show no effect on P3, and this seems at odds with late selection as well as with an occasionally successful response set to an attenuated trace.

Mismatch negativity has also been considered as a correlate of response set. Yet, it is mainly observed in the case of occasional auditory stimuli that deviate in pitch or loudness from a usually occurring standard stimulus.

---

[16]It has been a matter of debate whether the N1 might be affected as well (e.g., Näätänen, 1992). The issue is relevant in view of the extent to which selective attention brings about an exogenous or an endogenous modulation.

Mismatch negativity occurs both at the attended and the unattended channel, thus overruling the instructions on which channel to attend. However, mismatch negativity is primarily found in the case of occasional deviations in *physical* characteristics, which is at odds with a description in terms of response set. After all, response set has been always related to semantic properties of stimuli.

Näätänen (1982, 1990) proposed an attentional trace theory that assumes a parallel sensory analysis for all stimuli, both task related and unrelated. Task-unrelated stimuli are only subjected to a bottom-up feature analysis, leading to a representation or trace in a sensory memory that is enhanced when a stimulus is repeated. Another aspect of recording task-unrelated stimuli is a transient detection system that is sensitive not only to change, for example, onset and offset of a stimulus, but also to a sudden change in the features of an established representation. If the transient system exceeds a threshold, a stimulus is detected and centrally processed. In this way, the transient system reflects involuntary attention.

The analysis of task-related stimuli comprises a voluntary, maintained trace of the characteristics of the attended channel, such as a specific spatial location or a certain pitch. The trace of the channel, labeled the attentional trace, is matched with the bottom-up stimulus traces to detect whether a stimulus has been presented to the attended channel. A match between the attentional trace and the bottom-up representation gives an impulse to the transient system. Thus, the detection threshold is exceeded. However, the transient system is inhibited by a mismatch. As suggested, a sudden salient change in features is also detected at an unattended channel.

The attentional trace theory resembles early selection because the comparison between the attentional traces and the bottom-up traces occurs on the basis of early physical features. On the other hand, the bottom-up traces proceed independently of the attentional trace. In this way, the theory resembles van der Heijden's (1992) model in which identification and localization also develop in parallel. A major difference is that spatial localization has no special status in the attentional trace theory. Yet, the ERP data on visual selective attention show clear evidence for a special status of spatial localization.

Visual Selective Attention

Visual and auditory selective attention share the phenomenon of processing negativity and the effect on P3. They diverge in that there are qualitatively different EP effects for spatial location and nonspatial stimulus attributes, whereas qualitatively similar EP effects have been found for the various auditory attributes. The main evidence in the visual domain is based upon studies on orienting. As a brief summary of that discussion, intentional spatial orienting has early effects on P1 and N1 and causes processing negativity at 150 ms or more after stimulus onset, which is much later than in the auditory domain. In contrast to spatial localization, other visual cues such as color and size show only late-processing negativity, suggesting again that they reflect postperceptual processing.

APPLICATIONS

The principles of focused attention are particularly relevant to search for information on displays. The issue is how to display data to promote rapid detection of a desired item among a variety of other items. One wants to present as many data as possible on a page that counteracts rapid detection of individual items. The principles of pop-out and texture segregation are obviously of interest. Highlighting a target has the effect of immediately directing attention to its location. A unique difference in color, motion, or depth is the most effective, followed by a difference in size, type of print, form and, finally, cognitive category.[17] A semantic difference between targets and distractors is usually ineffective. As a general principle, unidimensional differences should be used between features of targets and nontargets, and one should usually avoid targets that are conjunctions.

Positive effects of highlighting a single target abound, its benefits increasing with the number of distractors. One should take care that the distinctive feature has high validity (Fisher & Tan, 1989). If the distinctive feature is also part of a nontarget, attention drawn to a highlighted nontarget slows down detection of the target. Yet, target search is still relatively fast when the frequency of occurrence of the distinctive feature is low and when the target is always characterized by the distinctive feature (Noble & Sanders, 1980). In that case, search can be restricted to the small subset of stimuli that contains the distinctive feature, and irrespective of their number, the other items on the screen can be ignored. Thus, one may safely have a small group of red items, among which are targets and nontargets, and many black items that are all nontargets. It is essential that a black target cannot occur. If that occurs, it is either detected very slowly or participants may carry out a strictly serial analysis of the items. This means that pop-out is ignored and that single items are successively focused (Theeuwes, 1991c).

It follows directly from the results on focused attention that the number of colors on a display should be limited. The more colors that are used, for

---

[17]Intuitively, one might suspect that blinking a target and reverse video—that is, a single-white-on-black item amidst black-on-white items—are equally effective as a difference in color. Yet, this is not the case. Blinking delays target identification due to impoverished perceptual stimulus quality, whereas reverse video suffers from lateral inhibition in the periphery. These factors partially offset the benefit of pop-out (Fisher & Tan, 1989).

example, for indicating different stimulus categories, the less effective an individual color pops out because the differences in activation among the feature modules vanish. One instance in which pop-out proved to vanish was a prototype of a color sonar display in which the relative strength of an echo was indicated by a certain color. The presence of many colors on the screen and the additional fact that noise elements might have a strong echo as well had the effect that there was hardly any pop-out of an echo. As mentioned, similar problems have been found with motion in public advertising: One moving object has a high attention value, but there is little pop-out when there are many moving objects. Another instance of pop-out concerns alignment of optimal settings of dials (Fig. 7.14, upper). The principle is that a single deviation from a general state is rapidly detected.

Another major application is concerned with using unique features for different categories of information on a screen. The relevance of such distinctive features is demonstrated in Fig. 7.14, lower: Tilted and upright *T*s do much better in texture segregation than tilted *T*s and *L*s do. The reason is that "tilted" and "upright" are detected by separate analyzers, so texture segregation is achieved preattentively on the basis of the activated areas of feature maps. Therefore, *T*s and *L*s are conjunctions of the same features and cannot serve as segregators. In contrast, when attention is focused, a *T* and an *L* are better discriminated than an upright and a tilted *T*. The point is that when focusing, one proceeds immediately from feature analysis to conjunctive object identification. Various other illustrations of the same principles are found in Wickens (1992).

In accordance with Gestalt laws, different feature types should be grouped at distinct parts of the screen (Fig. 7.15); there are clear limits, however, to the number of groups that can be efficiently distinguished. The more groups, the more salient the distinctive features should be. When subdividing groups, one has to use a different feature for each subdivision. This feature should be less salient than the feature used for distinguishing the main groups.

SELECTIVE SET

With respect to focused attention, Kahneman and Treisman (1984) drew a sharp distinction between conditions of selective set and of overload. In the case of selective set, there is only one relevant spatial location or, at best, a small region in which imperative stimuli may appear. The complexity of the potential stimuli is relevant with respect to the width of the region. The more processing load, the less evidence for interfering semantic distractors, or as processing load is heavier, the zoom lens is set more narrowly (N. Lavie, 1995). In selective set, all stimulus features are encoded in parallel

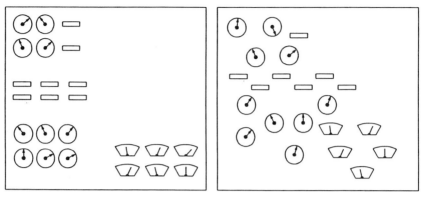

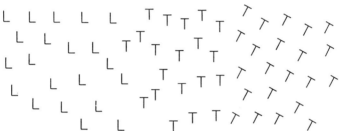

FIG. 7.14. A. Optimal grouping of dials. B. Texture segregation in divided and in focused attention. In divided attention, upright and tilted *T*s are better segregated than *T*s and *L*s. In focused attention, *T* and *L* are distinguished more easily than an upright and a tilted *T*. Adapted from Wickens, C. D. (1992). *Engineering psychology and human performance.* Copyright © 1992 by HarperCollins Publishers, Inc. Reprinted by permission of Addison-Wesley Educational Publishers, Inc.

and affect processing; they cannot be gated at an early stage but instead, they compete, as was already seen in the Eriksen flanker paradigm.

The most widely researched example of competition among features is the Stroop task (MacLeod, 1991; Stroop, 1935). A stimulus consists of a color word (e.g., RED) printed in either a different (incongruent) or the same (congruent) color, with a neutral word-control condition (e.g., BEAR). Participants have the task of naming the color in which the presented word is printed. In comparison to the neutral condition, CRT in the incongruent condition is slower, but it is slightly faster in the congruent

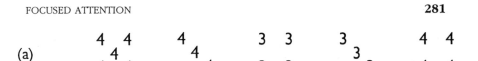

(a)

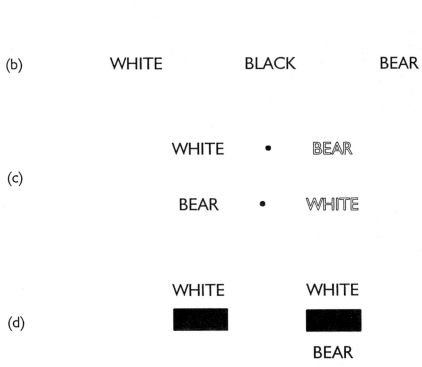

(b)

WHITE   BLACK   BEAR

(c)

WHITE   •   BEAR

BEAR   •   WHITE

(d)

WHITE   WHITE

BEAR

FIG. 7.15.   Two different versions of Stroop stimuli (a, b). Fig. 7.15C illustrates
the Kahneman and Henick (1981) effect. It is harder to name the color (black)
if it says "white" than if it says "bear." Fig. 7.15D illustrates the Kahneman and
Chajczyk (1983) dilution effect. Naming the colored bar (black) is harder when
the word "white" is on top of the bar than when an additional neutral word is
below the bar.

condition.[18] Some properties of the Stroop task are discussed in the next
few pages. For the moment, it is relevant to note that competition diminishes
strongly or even disappears when a color-word and an incongruent colored
bar are presented at separate locations. This was found by Kahneman and
Henik (1981), who presented two words, one at the left side and one at the
right side of the visual fixation point. One word was printed in black, and
the other in colored ink; participants had the task of reporting the color.

[18]There are many variations on this theme: For example, locations versus location words
(e.g., top, bottom) and numerosity versus numerals, which all show a similar type of effect.
Eriksen flanker studies also belong to this class.

This was much harder when the word and the color of the same word were incongruent than when the incongruent word was printed in black on the other side of the fixation point (Fig. 7.15c). This is consistent with early selection, which holds that the location of the color catches attention first, when the zoom lens focuses on that location. The information at that location, including the word, is processed, whereas semantic information from the other location is blocked and does not compete. A late-selection view, on the other hand, assumes identification of *both* items, irrespective of their location. Hence, an incongruent word at the other side of the fixation point should show an equally large Stroop effect.

Van der Heijden et al. (1984) carried out almost the same study, with the difference being that the most difficult case, that is, the integrated incongruent color-word, was omitted. In that case, a small (37 ms) interference effect appeared when the incongruent word and the ink color were at different sides of the fixation point. This fits van der Heijden's (1992) view that all information reaches the identity module in parallel. The discussion, then, boils down to the width of the zoom lens or, in van der Heijden's terms, to the width of the spot from which location information reaches the identity module and enables responding to the identified contents at that spot. Still, van der Heijden maintained and observed that even when an incongruent word is outside the focused spot, it might interfere somewhat. After all, the nonlocated information is supposed to be recorded in the identity module.

Whatever the more detailed interpretation, it is evident that once Stroop-like stimuli are within the attentional focus, their attributes are poorly filtered. For instance, Kahneman and Chajczyk (1983) presented a colored bar at the central fixation point and a single word either above or below the bar (Fig. 7.15D). The task was to name the color of the bar. If the word was an incongruent color word, CRT was longer; if word and color were congruent, CRT was less in comparison with the control condition where a neutral word was presented. Apparently, the participants could not prevent reading the word.

In another condition of the same study, two words were presented, one above and one below the colored bar. If one word was neutral and the other incongruent with the colored bar, the delay of CRT was less pronounced than in the case of a single word or of two incongruent words. It seems that both words were read and that the neutral word weakened the effect of the incongruent one (the dilution effect). The fact that word and color are both encoded is also evident from the work of Simon and Berbaum (1988) who presented a Stroop stimulus that was followed after 2.5 seconds by a probe containing only one of the two attributes (i.e., a color word or an ink color). Participants carried out a same–different response on the basis of instruction about which attribute to take into account. The results show that in all comparisons, the same–different responses were faster when the relevant and irrelevant attributes of the Stroop stimulus were congruent than when they were incongruent. The Stroop stimulus and probe were separated by 2.5 secs, which suggests that both word and ink color had been firmly encoded and stored and that they interfered with the probe at the time of retrieval. It is of interest that incongruence did not affect the same–different response when the participants knew in advance which attribute would be relevant. Hence, it appears possible to filter out an irrelevant attribute during the interval (Simon & Baker, 1995).

Stroop Interference

A basic feature of the Stroop task is the asymmetric interference pattern, that is, naming the ink color is more affected by an incongruent color-word than naming the color word by an incongruent ink color. One popular explanation of this asymmetry has been in terms of independent parallel encoding of stimulus attributes (Posner, 1978). One pathway processes the ink color and another the color word, and one of the two wins the race. A model is shown in Fig. 7.16. The word *blue* acquires a name code and the ink color gets a physical code, that is, the impression of black, along separate pathways. The name code (blue) is accomplished faster than the subsequent verbal label (black) of the physical impression.[19] The point is that the word *blue* is read directly, whereas the name of the ink color (black) requires the extra translation from physical impression to verbal code. The consequence is that when the response consists of vocal naming, the name code of the word (blue) is completed earlier and is first to activate the response system. This results in a rapid response when, indeed, the instruction requires naming the word. In contrast, in the case of naming the ink color, the ready-made name code of the word competes with the slower, established name code of the ink color.

The race model predicts a reversal of the Stroop effect when the response consists of color matching. In this case, participants are instructed to press a colored key that corresponds to the color of the ink. Here, one can rely on the physical code of the color, which is more readily available than the color impression of a word.[20] The original Stroop effect should reoccur when the response keys have verbal color-name labels. In fact, this pattern of results has been obtained (e.g., Virzi & Egeth, 1985). One may wonder why

---

[19]This may seem at odds with the result that physical identity matching (A, A) of letters is faster than name identity matching (A, a). The difference is that in the Stroop task the physical code is concerned with a physical impression of the word color and not with a physical letter shape.

[20]This model, like many other Stroop models, fails to specify how, during response selection, participants "know" what is the correct response.

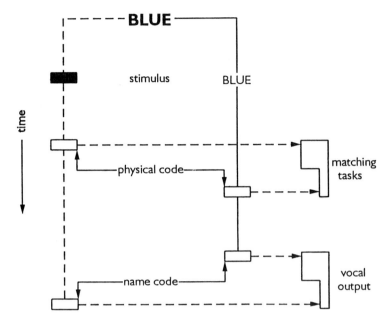

FIG. 7.16. Posner's (1978) race model of the Stroop effect. From Posner, M. I. (1978). *Chronometric explorations of mind.* Copyright © by Lawrence Erlbaum Associates, Hillsdale, NJ. Reproduced with kind permission of the publisher.

a neutral word hardly interferes. After all, its word code should be completed earlier than the name code of the ink color as well. The common interpretation is that color names have strong, mutual, semantic connections. Consequently, the activation of a "wrong" color name inhibits the selection of the correct one. It is evident that the race model ascribes the Stroop effect to response selection. Perceptual encoding is automatic, occurs in parallel, and cannot be intentionally avoided.

The ink color may be preexposed to give it a lead. In that case, the race model predicts a reversed Stroop effect because in that case the ink-color code should be completed earlier. The data show that SOA has a slowing effect on CRT when the irrelevant attribute is presented before the relevant one—that is, more interference—and a speeding effect when the relevant attribute precedes the irrelevant one—that is, less interference. Yet, the Stroop effect does not reverse (Glaser & Glaser, 1982). Again, the effect of SOA appears to occur mainly in conditions where responses are not optimally compatible, such as a verbal response to an ink color or a press of a colored response key to a color word. SOA has much less effect when the task requires naming a color word and pressing a colored key as response to the ink color. Thus, the results on SOA clearly argue against an explanation of the Stroop effect in terms of mere differences in processing duration (e.g., MacLeod, 1991; Sugg & McDonald, 1994).[21]

A current alternative explanation simply stresses translation of stimulus attributes into response categories. Naming a color-word needs no translation, whereas naming an ink color does; verbal responding to numerosity, for example, a certain number of dots, needs translation, whereas naming a numeral does not. When naming an ink color the translated name code of the color and the untranslated code of the color-word converge. This creates the conflict in which a translated code is at a disadvantage. In fact, this view can be easily accommodated by the overlapping dimensions model of S–R compatibility (Kornblum et al., 1990; chap. 4). It remains an essential feature of translation models that ink colors and color-words are analyzed by different perceptual systems (Virzi & H. E. Egeth, 1985). Each system has its privileged and highly compatible pathway to a response, and the pathways suffer little inhibition from each other. Hence, the untranslated word code is the strongest and wins from the translated ink–word code. When a translated code is given a lead, the best that one may achieve is elimination of interference. In contrast to translated codes, untranslated codes occur automatically.

A major difference between this automaticity view and the race model is that degree of learning, rather than speed of processing, is decisive. A fast, less well-learned process may interfere with a slow, well-learned process. Consequently, interference is supposed to arise in the course of processing and not just at the response selection stage (MacLeod, 1991).

Intentions

The automaticity view has a problem accounting for the finding that interference is less when the ink color and the word are separately presented. It also has difficulties explaining the dilution effect. It was argued previously that untranslated features of Stroop stimuli may only be processed automatically and in parallel when the stimuli are within the attentional focus. Setting the zoom lens is intentional, which is an important constraint on automatic processing in the Stroop task. A second constraint is that despite a delay in CRT, individuals can actually solve the conflict and carry out the instructed response. They can select the intended action from among the conflicting

---

[21]In fact, Sugg and McDonald found some effect of advance presentation of an incongruent color-word on pressing a colored key in response to the ink color. There was no effect of an advance ink color on pressing a word-labeled key in response to the color-word. A processing duration model has obvious problems explaining this asymmetry. It suggests that preexposing an irrelevant ink color has a different effect than preexposing an irrelevant color-word. Translation models should acknowledge a greater resistance against interference when processing words.

response tendencies. How are intentions realized and how do they interact with the suggested automatic processes?

Van der Heijden (1992) correctly noted that this point is not often raised. It is a relevant additional component in his postcategorical filtering model and describes the interplay between intentions on the one hand and automatic or controlled aspects of computation on the other. Van der Heijden argued that a theory of selective attention requires much more than perceptual selection. Thus, intentions prescribe which properties of an object are relevant to action and which should be ignored. Here, the discussion is limited to how intentions enable obeying a simple instruction such as reporting the ink color and not the color-word in a Stroop test.[22] Perceptual selection of an object is accomplished by highlighting a particular spatial location in the location module that is, then, fed back to the input module, that is, the input layer of the neural network model. Selecting a particular feature of a stimulus is done by highlighting the corresponding attribute module in the neural network which, in turn, biases the response layer toward responding to that attribute. This bias enables dominance of that attribute over competing ones.[23] Thus, in the Stroop task, the response layer receives information about two color-words—that is, of the word and of the ink color—and the bias enables a victory for the instructed one. Note that it is the strength of the connections rather than their processing speed that is decisive in a connectionist view. Thus, in the dilution effect, the neutral word induces a reduction in the strength of the color-word representation, and, hence, in the strength of the input of the color word to the response layer.

Most Stroop models have the common feature that focused object attributes are supposed to be processed independently and in parallel. When a race model is rejected, one may wonder how, in the Stroop task, parallel processing may account for the asymmetry that congruent attributes are hardly facilitated, but incongruent attributes suffer greatly from interference. Jacoby (1991) proposed the so called process dissociation procedure that estimates the probability that an individual will name the ink color of a congruent stimulus within a response deadline, that is,

$$P(correct \mid congruent) = P(word) + P(color) - P(word * color)$$
$$= P(word) + P(color) \{1 - P(word)\}$$

in which P(word) and P(color) are the probabilities that the word or color code controls the response. The equation is based on the fact that a code of either the ink color or the word suffices. In the same way:

---

[22]The role of intentions in controlling dual-task performance is discussed in chapter 8.

[23]Intentional manipulation of feature modules is consistent with Treisman's (1988) revised feature integration theory in which an attribute module can be intentionally facilitated or inhibited.

$$P(\text{correct} \mid \text{incongruent}) = P(\text{color}) \{1 - P(\text{word})\}$$

so that P(color) and P(word) can be estimated from the proportion of correct responses in a psychophysical setting. The point is that facilitation will be less than interference when P(color) > .50. Lindsay and Jacoby (1994) argued that it is fair that when participants are instructed to name the ink color, P(color) is considerably more than .50. Lindsay and Jacoby also found that degradation of the ink color meant that facilitation and interference effects on CRT became symmetrical. In an accompanying psychophysical study, they found that degrading the ink color reduced P(color) but did not affect P(word). In the same way, degrading the word selectively affected P(word) suggesting that the codes for word and color develop in parallel and do not interact.[24]

May perceptual properties of a focused object be ignored or intentionally selected? So far, the evidence seems to indicate that this is impossible. Once attended to, all properties of an object are automatically processed up until identification. Yet, the focus of spatial attention may affect perceptual organization. A well-known example is the Necker cube, the organization of which appears to depend on the fixated spot as well as the direction of covert orienting (Peterson & Gibson, 1991). It could be that focusing is especially relevant to perceptual structure when an object is so large and complex that it cannot be covered by focusing on a single spot.

Applications. One important application is concerned with the so-called head-up display in which two displays are superimposed. For example, when driving a car, one may superimpose a view of the speedometer on the view of the road. If one were unable to ignore properties of an attended area, the head-up display of the speedometer should be processed in parallel with the outside view. Hence, as long as one is capable of avoiding Stroop-type interference and confusion, a head-up display might be more efficient than the traditional situation in which the speedometer and the outside view are spatially separated. There is evidence, however, that when inspecting superimposed displays, an individual may focus on one and ignore the other rather than process both displays in parallel (e.g., Larish & Wickens, 1991). The difference in depth between the outside view and the superimposed display may function as a spatially distinctive cue that allows a different focus (Andersen & Kramer, 1993). So far, these mechanisms are still little understood.

---

[24]The authors make the point that their technique avoids the problem of the neutral baseline for inferring facilitation and interference. With regard to the effects of degrading the ink color or the word, one should conclude that degradation increases the amount of translation involved in achieving the code and weakens the strength of that code in the competition for control.

SUMMARY

During the last decades, research in the area of focused attention and search has progressed considerably. Despite the shift from auditory to visual attention, the issue of early–late selection has been relevant ever since the formulation of Broadbent's (1958) filter theory. In addition, there is the useful distinction between perceptual overload, for example, two auditory streams of information detecting a visual stimulus from among many distractors, and selective set. The latter case shows abundant evidence for parallel identification of stimulus attributes and for object processing. Yet, spatial localization is not a problem in studies on selective set. The more perceptual overload, the more evidence for the power of early selection on the basis of physical attributes.

An important advance is the insight that spatial localization has a prime role in guiding visual selective attention. Most researchers maintain that its role is unique, and all agree that it is the most effective cue in search. Much research has centered on FIT, which was the main theoretical framework during the 1980s. It has become clear, however, that it is untenable to entertain a notion of attention as the glue among features in object identification. A promising alternative is to assume parallel identification and subsequent tagging of the spatial position of stimuli to allow action-directed processing. This approach also has the virtue that it goes beyond the traditional notion of limited perceptual capacity as the main reason for selective attention. The increasing interest in the role of attention in coordinating and selecting action means an important extension of the initial, almost exclusive, emphasis on perceptual selection.

Another advance is the notion of spatial focus, which may be set more or less widely. This ability means that a narrower or somewhat wider visual area is covered. As the focus becomes narrower, there is more evidence for early selection or for exclusion of information from nonfocused spots. When widely set, physical features as well as objects may be detected, provided they are sufficiently salient in the display. This was also the case in selective listening. Yet, object selection, as stressed by late-selection theory, is almost invariably poorer than feature selection. In fact, this has been recognized ever since the extension of filter theory with attenuation and response set in the early 1970s (Broadbent, 1971).

Future research issues include tests of van der Heijden's (1992) views on identification and, in particular, a more detailed specification of the nature of the contents of his identification module: form, object, or meaning? Is the identification module a *tabula rasa* when the stimuli are presented? What are the relations between the stimulus code in the identification module and object selection, the role of which has evoked so much debate in recent years? Is it, aside from incidental breakthroughs, possible to initiate action without getting feedback from the location module? Future research will almost certainly deal with less constrained conditions to check the validity of the theoretical notions beyond the domain of a single glance. One obvious extension concerns conditions of multiple free scanning.

MULTI-FIXATION SEARCH AND SCANNING

Structural Versus Strategical Constraints

Multi-fixation target search is characterized by frequent alternations between fixations and saccades. The question is what governs search, or, in other words, what determines the position of each new fixation? From a back-to-back perspective, it is of obvious interest to know whether results obtained in covert search generalize to free search. Constraints in search can be described on three levels: sensory, anatomical, and information-processing. Sensory constraints refer to limits of peripheral vision, such as arising from receptive fields, masking and lateral inhibition (Geissler & Chou, 1995); anatomical constraints refer to bodily limits and include the size of a saccade, while information-processing constraints refer to attentional limits.

Sensory Constraints

Visual search is limited by low-level sensory factors, including intensity, color, and, perhaps in particular, retinal eccentricity. In an attempt to assess the effect of such factors on search, Engel (1976) distinguished *conspicuity* and *visibility*. A conspicuous stimulus is detected without prior knowledge about its location, and visibility refers to detection with preknowledge about the target location. The visibility area is obviously larger and presumably reflects the sole effect of sensory factors on search, whereas the conspicuity area includes an additional, higher level attentional component. The visual lobe, or conspicuity area, represents the psychophysical area around the fixation point within which a target can be detected in a single fixation with some fixed probability. Recently, Geissler and Chou (1995) argued that search time can be largely predicted by low-level sensory psychophysics, in particular those relating to eccentricity. They measured the visibility area in order to obtain an estimate of visual discrimination uncontaminated by covert attention. Their basic psychophysical measure was a so-called *discrimination window*. It consisted of a 3-D plot of detection accuracy, under various target–background conditions, that was a joint function of presentation time and target eccentricity. The results of this measure were used as a predictor for the speed of multi-fixation search with an unknown target position.

In a similar vein, Donk (1995b) argued that eccentricity is of primary interest in search. She had participants search for either a target with one unique feature or for a target defined by the absence of a feature. Her main interest was the relative size of the visual lobe in each case. Not surprisingly, the lobe was smaller when a feature was absent than when it was present. However, within the limits of the respective lobes, the processes involved in searching for presence or absence of a feature did not differ. This argues against qualitatively different processes, as are assumed, among others, by all versions of FIT. When searching for the absence of a feature, more frequent saccades compensated for the deficient peripheral information. It is striking that the effect of eccentricity on target detection, which has been a main concern in research on visibility and conspicuity, has been neglected in single-glance studies.

Geissler and Chou (1995) proposed an algorithm for overt search that comes close to Engel's (1976), who measured conspicuity rather than visibility, but that may not be essential. Engel proposed that overt search proceeds by systematically shifting the lobe to a new area in the visual field. This continues until the target is within its limits, which means that the target has a certain probability of being detected. A detection evokes a rapid saccade that is meant to fixate the target.

A correspondence between the lobe and overt search is not self-evident. First, due to lack of rationale about the borderlines of the lobe, there is no unanimity on the desired detection probabilities. Sometimes, a hard-shelled and a soft-shelled lobe are distinguished, the hard-shelled one with a 50%-detection probability and the soft-shelled lobe with much less than that. The 50%-detection contour is sometimes considered as the edge of the conspicuity area because of the assumption that a target occurring inside that contour will usually be detected. Measurement of the visual lobe differs in (a) demands on target detection, for example, simple detection versus spatial localization of the target, and (b) the nature of the target and its background. The size of the lobe as well as the visibility area depend on variables such as display density[25] and target–nontarget similarity. However, these variables may also affect the shape of the lobe. The variety of lobe measures frustrates their adequate comparison. Some studies found a regular, elliptic lobe with wider horizontal than vertical extension, analogous to what is found in perimeter studies of peripheral acuity. In other studies, the shape of the lobe proved to be irregular and barely elliptic (Sanders & Donk, 1996).

Despite these difficulties, estimates of the lobe or the discrimination window appear to be valid predictors of search performance. It has been found repeatedly that the lobe area is inversely proportional to search time, although the correlations are not as impressive as one would expect and less

---

[25]Display density refers to number and properties of the nontarget stimuli.

than those reported by Geissler and Chou (1995; e.g., Courtney & Chan, 1986). One reason for a lack of correlation might be the tachistoscopic measurement of the lobe. R. M. Klein and Farrell (1989) argued that brief exposure may enable information accrual from a decaying icon. This is probably impossible in overt search. It might be preferable, therefore, to estimate the size of the lobe directly from overt search rather than from tachistoscopic measures.[26] N. H. Mackworth (1976) attempted direct measurement of the lobe by presenting participants with displays consisting of a matrix of small circles. The vertical separation between the rows was a major experimental variable. The participant's task was to search for a small square among the circles by scanning the rows from left to right without stopping or looking back. Mackworth reasoned that the smallest vertical distance between two rows where the participants interrupted horizontal search and jumped directly to a target on the next row might serve as an estimate of the vertical width of the lobe. In the same way, the horizontal width of the lobe may be estimated by having the participants carry out a vertical scan of the columns of a matrix and determine the minimal width between columns at which the eyes interrupt the vertical scan and fixate a target on the next column. The results suggested that the horizontal as well as the vertical distance between the circles affected scanning.

A similar method was proposed by Prinz and colleagues (e.g., Nattkemper & Prinz, 1990). Participants were instructed to scan a list of letters row by row, as in reading, in order to detect a single target as fast as possible. One variable was the vertical distance between every two rows. Eye movements were measured to determine the vertical detection distance, that is, the distance between successive rows before a target was detected in the next row while scanning the previous one. Another approach was taken by Widdell (1983). His reasoning was that during a successful fixation, the target is detected in the periphery. The final saccade directs the eyes to the target, thus concluding search. Widdell measured the distribution of the size of the final saccades, and this led to an estimate of the lobe. Promising as these dynamic techniques are, their relation with tachistoscopic measures and search times still has to be established.

Anatomical Constraints

Anatomical constraints are related to the structure of the functional visual field (chap. 5). Briefly, hypotheses are supposed to be obtained about all stimuli in the eye field. This information enables rapid reorientation from one to another stimulus and guarantees a schematic representation of all

---

[26]If this conclusion were valid, it would cast some doubt on generalization of results from search, with a fixated eye, to the dynamics of free search.

the contents of the eye field. Hence, search occurs in the context of a constant background schema or scene. Information acquisition from successive fixations is not a matter of independent percepts because processing is supposed to consist of verifying hypotheses and fixations take place within a constant background schema. In contrast, there are no hypotheses about stimuli in the head field, a head movement bringing about a new scene. Thus, in the head field, successive fixations represent independent percepts.[27] The transition from the eye field to the head field is not constant. In the case of two clearly visible, large-size stimuli in an otherwise empty field, the eye field covered a wide area of some 80° (binocular), but that is probably close to the upper limit. The eye field is smaller as a stimulus configuration becomes more complex.

The earlier discussed studies (chap. 5) on the functional visual field were not concerned with search, so one may doubt whether the results can be generalized to multi-fixation search. However, Sanders (1963) carried out a search experiment in which six columns of dots were presented in a horizontal row (Fig. 7.17). All but one contained four dots, and one had five dots. The task was to identify the location of the five-dots column and to press the corresponding response key. Immediately thereafter, a new display was presented. The main independent variable was the binocular visual angle subtended by the six columns. The data were analyzed as a function of the visual angle subtending the five-dots column between successive trials. For example, the angle was 0° when the five-dots column had the same location in two successive trials. The angle could maximally cover the full six-columns display when, on successive trials, the column with five dots occupied the first and sixth location, or vice versa.

When the full binocular visual angle was within the eye field, a perfectly linear relation was found between visual angle and CRT. The one exception that can be duly ascribed to a repetition effect was when successive five-dots columns were at the same location. The slope of the function of Fig. 7.17 reflects the time needed to shift the eyes directly from the previous five-dots location to the next, suggesting that the new location is spotted without delay. When the total visual angle exceeded the eye field, CRT was found to have a larger intercept for visual angles over 35°. The additional time may be due to the new percept needed in order to spot the next five-dots location. There was hardly any difference between performance in the eye field and the head field when the visual angle, covered by successive trials, was less than 35°. This suggests that in the head field, utilization of hypotheses is limited to a fairly small area. Thus, it is of interest that the visual angle where a next target is directly spotted depends on the angle that is covered by the full display. For

---

[27]There remains a cognitive schema of the environment that may bias the percept (e.g., Poulton, 1950).

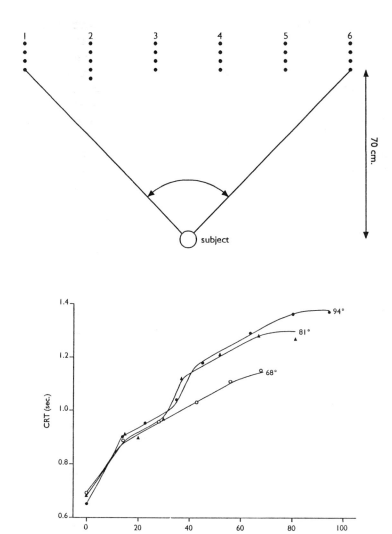

FIG. 7.17. Experimental display and data from Sanders' (1963) study on visual search as a function of display angle. The task was to locate the five-dots stimulus and to press the corresponding response key in a continuous self-paced reaction task. The total display subtended 94°, 81°, or 68° Mean CRT is plotted as a function of visual angle subtended by the location of successive targets.

example, at 68°, the target was directly spotted when the full display was within the eye field, but not when it was in the head field.

Is there a relation between these results and those on the visual lobe? Sanders (1970a) distinguished between the microstructure and the macrostructure of the visual field. The microstructure is the domain of the visual lobe; it is characterized by local detail and a high stimulus-density, both of which imply that conspicuity is restricted by lateral inhibition. Although searching the microstructure of a display is usually within the eye field, lateral inhibition prohibits hypotheses. They are only obtained in the macrostructure, which refers to rough characteristics of the visual scene, which do not suffer from lateral inhibition. Thus conceived, the eye field can be considered as the limiting case of the visual lobe. In the microstructure of the eye field, the only advantage might be the constancy of the scene. This has never been studied in detail but there is ample evidence from other sources, that a constant background is relevant to efficient search.

Information-Processing Constraints

These may conveniently start with Neisser's (1963) well-known continuous visual-search task in which participants searched a matrix of letters (Fig. 7.18) in order to detect a target letter that occurs at one, and only one, location in the matrix. The participants were instructed to scan the rows of letters from left to right and from top to bottom to eliminate individual differences in search strategy. Search time was plotted as a function of the position of the target in the matrix. The result was a perfect linear function with a search rate of 3 to 10 letters per sec, the actual rate depending on the similarity between the features of the target and the nontarget letters. The rate was slower as features became more similar. Neisser also presented a target letter in all rows but one, in which case the participants had to detect the row where the target letter was absent. Search for letter absence proved to be much slower than for letter presence, which reminds of Treisman and Gormican's (1988) findings about search for the presence or absence of a feature.

Neisser's (1963) results show that letters are not completely identified during search. In such a case, the absence of a target in a row should be detected faster than its presence because, when searching for the absence, one may proceed to the next row as soon as the target has been spotted. In contrast, all rows should be completely searched when looking for the presence of a single target. In line with early selection, Neisser suggested a fast and parallel preattentive feature analysis of the letters in a row. A letter is only subjected to further analysis when feature analysis suggests that it might be the target. Identification of a letter requires a time-consuming focus on its location. The nature of nontarget letters is of interest because feature testing becomes more detailed as target and nontarget letters resemble each other.

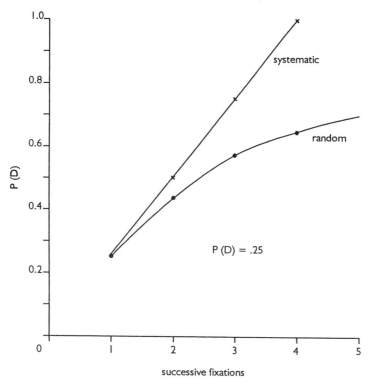

FIG. 7.18. The prediction about the cumulative probability of target detection of random and of systematic search models. The probability of detection at each fixation equals .25.

It is of interest that the foregoing results apply, in particular to verbal stimuli. Thus, Liu (1996) presented participants with eight dials located on an imaginary square. Each dial contained a pointer emanating from the center and subtending 1 out of 16 equally spaced angles (0°, 22.5°, 45°, etc.). The participants had to detect a critical angle that was either present on one of the dials (target present) or not (target absent). As in Neisser's (1963) study the instruction was to scan the dials in a strict order, always starting with the same dial. The size of the memory set of critical angles was varied from 1 to 4 among conditions, with a different set being presented in advance of each new trial. Similar to Neisser, Liu found a linear increase in search time as a function of the location of the dial that contained a critical angle. However, search rate was much slower (815 msec/item) than in Neisser's studies, suggesting that the pointer angle of each dial was completely identified. The effect of a larger memory set of critical angles was more pronounced as search in a trial took more time, suggesting that the participants had problems with keeping the memory set active during search.

This was confirmed in a second study that showed that the increase in search time disappeared when the set of critical angles was the same throughout the session. Still, with a consistent memory set, the rate of memory search remained slower for angles than for letters (Schneider & Shiffrin, 1977; Sternberg, 1969). Together, Liu's data suggest that nonverbal stimuli need much deeper processing than verbal stimuli; visual angles may have fewer well-established internal codes to rely on.

There is a clear analogy between Neisser's (1963) two-process view and Treisman's (1988) FIT. This is underlined by Williams (1967), who measured scan paths on large displays that contained two-digit numbers differing in color, shape, or size. The target number had a unique feature. A major finding was that numbers with the same color as the target were more frequently fixated, whereas shape proved much less distinctive. This is consistent with research showing that color is a more potent critical feature and that size occupies a middle position. In the same way, Willows and McKinnon (1973) found that when presenting alternating lines of text with a different color, participants could easily limit reading to lines with the same color without being distracted by lines in the other color. Further support for the two-process theory comes from the results of Gould and Dill (1969) that targets are fixated longer than nontargets and that nontargets that resemble targets are fixated longer than dissimilar nontargets.

Despite this impressive support, the two-process model has not remained undebated. As in search within a single glance, the discussion has centered around the nature of the features needed for separating targets from nontargets. In turn, this concerns the question of how extensively a stimulus is encoded during search, which is a return to the early–late selection debate. For instance, Rabbitt (1967) found that search for a straight-lined target letter slowed down when changing the set of nontarget letters, despite the fact that nontarget letters, old as well as new, always consisted of straight-lined letters. This finding suggests that participants benefited from learning common properties of the nontarget letters and stresses the relevance of the structure of the background. More importantly, the learned common properties of the nontargets in Rabbitt's study were almost certainly not only physical.[28] Learning to recognize properties of targets and nontargets is at odds with the basic tenet of early selection. In the discussion of the Stroop task, it was argued that results suggesting late selection may be due to a lack of attentional focus. Response set dominates without a narrow focus, and because it is object based, response set can account more readily for learning a common, nonphysical set of properties. In general, there is less evidence for response set in multi-fixation search than in covert search, but

---

[28]The observation that a common set of properties may be learned reminds also of the work of Shiffrin and Schneider (1977) on automatic and controlled processing (chap. 8).

it is certainly not absent. To reconcile the gap between early and late selection in overt visual search, Prinz (1987a) proposed a view that reminds of van der Heijden's (1992) postcategorical filtering. He suggested that selection may proceed simultaneously at a sensory, preattentive, and global level corresponding to van der Heijden's localization module and at a semantic, attentive, and local level that reminds of van der Heijden's identification module.

Target Versus Background Control of Search

Most models on selective attention and visual search assume that participants have some internal template or feature list of the target that is compared with incoming information until a reasonable fit has been established. However, there is growing evidence that participants have an internal model of the nontarget background as well to check whether the background contains deviations. This is in line with research on the orientation reaction that suggests that people have an internal model of the complete perceptual context and can detect deviations from that context. The principal findings on multi-fixation visual search are consistent with background control. Thus, the presence of one target somewhere in the list implies search for a deviation from the normal context. When there are several instances of the target in the display, search is slower. This is much the same as when, in a Neisser task, the task is to detect the absence of a target in one row. Again, a deviation is noted more rapidly as the features of a single target differ more strongly from those of the background.

Prinz (1987a) reviewed various lines of evidence for background control. First, there is the phenomenon of the pseudotarget that refers to the observation that in a Neisser (1963) type of task, the participants show a relatively long fixation time on new nontargets, that is, nontargets that had not yet appeared in the letter matrix (Prinz, Tweer, & Feige, 1974). There is the potential artifact that a new nontarget shares more features with the target, but that was carefully controlled in this study. The second result concerns the effect of nontarget, sequential redundancy. Search appears to be faster as nontargets have more sequential redundancy, suggesting that the relations among nontargets are relevant (Nattkemper & Prinz, 1984). Again, participants gradually learn when nontargets are clustered, an activity that allows rapid rejection of a whole cluster. Scan paths are more fixed when a background is familiar and are more variable when a background is unfamiliar (Rabbitt, 1981). Background control is also much more relevant when searching in a coherent, meaningful scene rather than in a homogeneous or a scrambled, meaningless background (Biederman, 1972). A coherent scene may correspond better to an internal schema of knowledge of the world. This does not mean, however, that a target is more easily found in a coherent scene. For instance, there is clear evidence from Gestalt psychology that target detection is difficult when the target is hidden in a well-structured background (e.g., Metzger, 1954). A recent example stems from Moraglia et al. (1989), who had participants search for a horizontal line segment in displays containing a varying number of other line segments that differed in orientation from the target as well as from each other. Target detection took more time when the line segments were positioned randomly than when they were arranged in concentric circles. Thus, background organization may direct an observer's path toward or away from the target. The sweepline on radar displays is an application of this principle. As long as participants follow the sweep, they will cover the whole display (Teichner & Mocharnuk, 1979).

Briefly, the results on background organization show that search benefits from nontarget redundancy and that search is guided by known environmental nontarget structures. The first aspect fits traditional early-selection theory that has always maintained that structure reduces perceptual load (Broadbent, 1958). In terms of FIT, an unstructured background is likely to decrease the difference in activation among the various feature modules, thus suppressing potential pop-out. The second aspect is harder to account for by early selection. It seems more in line with the view that conspicuity of a target depends on whether that target fits or disrupts a whole stimulus configuration, that is, a configuration that has been fully analyzed before selection occurs. This is along the lines of late selection (e.g., Humphreys, Riddoch, & Quinlan, 1985; Humphreys, Quinlan, & Riddoch, 1989; see also Smets & Stappers, 1990) and van der Heijden's (1992) postcategorical filtering.

VISUAL SCANNING STRATEGIES DURING SEARCH

Search Strategies

The previous section was concerned with structured search. Participants searched a stimulus array in a strict order so that the mode of visual scanning was completely prescribed. In contrast, unstructured search means that visual stimuli are scattered randomly on the display and that individuals do not follow any scanning sequence. In such a case, eye movements may be conceived of as a stochastic process that consists of sampling portions of the display at each fixation (Monk, 1984). This stochastic process can be modeled as random or systematic. Random search means that the probability of detecting a target remains constant over successive fixations and that a fixation point does not depend on the location of previous fixations. The implication is that the location of the next fixation is not determined by peripheral information from the present fixation, by the general history of previous fixations, or by any preconceived, top-down plan. There is no memory for locations that have already been fixated and in addition, a next fixation is not determined by anything of interest in the periphery.[29] It follows from random search that the detection probability is constant, so the CDF of successful search times is a negatively accelerated exponential function. The point is that when the probability of detecting the target at the first fixation equals P, it equals $(1 - P) \times P$ at the second fixation, $(1 - P) \times (1 - P) \times P$ at the third fixation, and so on, detection rate declines exponentially.

In contrast, systematic search assumes perfect memory. Therefore, a spot is never inspected twice. It is usually assumed that individuals scan the display according to a preconceived plan, for example, from left to right or from top to bottom. When the plan is perfect, the target is always found and search time cannot exceed a certain maximal value. Each new fixation adds a constant to the probability of detection, resulting in a linear CDF of search times (Engel, 1976), with the slope of the distribution depending on the size of the visual lobe (Fig. 7.19).

The CDF of search times is usually exponential. This suggests that the random model is the best predictor of multiple search (e.g., Drury, 1990). Yet, a random model is probably too simple. First, the CDFs are usually somewhat between the predictions of the two models, and they favor systematic search at the lower tail and random search at the upper tail of the distribution (Morawski, Drury, & Karwan, 1980). Second, the systematic search model is an extreme statement in that it excludes the possibility of overlooking parts of the display and looking without seeing, which refers to the fact that fixation does not always lead to detection (N. H. Mackworth, Kaplan, & Metlay, 1964). When these elements are added to the systematic search model, the prediction remains a linear search function, but some targets are not detected during the first round, thus requiring a second round of search. The result is that the CDF becomes exponential at the higher end, and this is consistent with the actual findings.

It may seem natural to test search models by scan-path analysis, but scan paths of homogeneous fields are often unsystematic and highly variable. The few general results include the so-called edge effect, namely, that participants ignore the edges of a display and favor the center; and a trend toward searching from left to right and from top to bottom (Yarbus, 1967). These trends are far from general, though; scan paths of homogeneous fields show frequent repetitions and seemingly random saccades, all of which

---

[29]An exception is the final saccade toward a target; however, this may not be part of the search process. A random search model may recognize the effect of peripheral information on the size of the lobe and, hence, on the size of the saccade to a new spot. The random model has only been entertained for free multi-fixation search and not for reading or scanning lines, in which cases there is ample evidence that the next fixation point depends on peripheral information from the previous one.

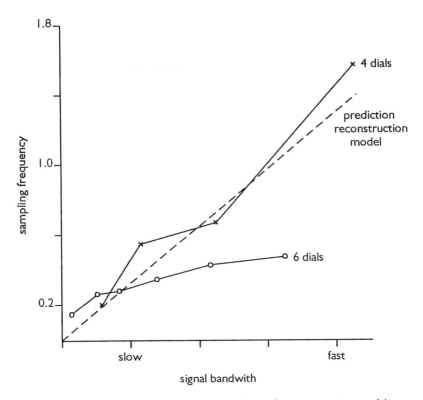

FIG. 7.19. The prediction of Senders' (1983) stimulus reconstruction model and the actual sampling frequency of the instruments. In the case of six dials, low bandwidth dials are oversampled, and high bandwidth dials are undersampled. From Senders, J. W. (1983). *Visual sampling processes.* Copyright © 1983 by Lawrence Erlbaum Associates, Hillsdale, N.J. Reproduced with kind permission of the publisher.

seem to argue against systematic search. At best, search may be guided by rough, preconceived principles that are easily interrupted by peripheral cues and are supplemented by a pronounced, random component.

Random and systematic scanning are normative models. Stark and Ellis (1981) argued that saccades and fixation positions are controlled by cognitive, internal schemata about the perceptual environment that are matched with actual sensory information. Homogeneous fields have no underlying cognitive schema, so one is forced to use some primitive search strategy, as outlined previously. The situation is different when inspecting a meaningful display such as a picture or a landscape for which cognitive schemata are available. In that situation, a region is fixated more frequently to the extent that it is judged to be more informative (N. H. Mackworth & Morandi, 1967). In fact, the effect of familiarity of the display on the scan path is another illustration of the relevance of cognitive schemata in search (Rabbitt, 1981). In one study, participants received advance information about the theme of a picture. Following presentation, unexpected objects were fixated longer than expected ones (Antes & Penland, 1981), suggesting that abstract, verbal advance information may generate a concrete set of objects as a basis for scanning. Expectations are also relevant to the size of a saccade. Thus, Jacobs (1987) had participants search for a potential target (C, c, or k) in lines of xs. Jacobs analyzed the lines where no target occurred and found that saccade size depended on the size of the expected visibility limit, that is, on the expected size of the lobe for a particular target. In line with Engel (1976), Jacobs (1987) suggested that participants decide about the presence or absence of a target during each fixation, ending with a saccade to the location of the target or with a saccade outside the lobe to enable an efficient next fixation.

Optimal Scanning and Monitoring

The most elaborate theoretical analysis of cognitive search components stems from monitoring multiple instruments. The general tenet of this research is that participants internalize the statistical properties of the instrument dynamics in order to determine the optimal fixation rate of each instrument. The task is usually to detect a drift from some predefined optimum or to detect when a pointer enters the danger zone. Applied examples are found in a cockpit and a control room, where, in both situations, a human operator has to trace significant deviations from a normal pointer value. Early work in this area was based on scan-path analysis of instrument fixations and on relative frequencies and fixation durations during an actual or a simulated flight. This research (Fitts, Jones, & Milton, 1950) resulted in recommendations about the arrangement of instruments to enable efficient control. These recommendations included frequency of use, that is, the most frequently inspected instruments should be at a central location in the visual field; sequence of use, that is, instruments that are fixated in succession should have adjacent positions; and importance, that is, important instruments should also have a central location, even when they are not often fixated.

More recent research has been concerned with normative-theoretical scanning models based on some principle of achieving optimal performance. All models share the view that optimal scanning depends on the display dynamics. Practice leads to a cognitive schema about display dynamics that dictate where to fixate at any particular instant. The dynamics are concerned with the present state of a variable (factor a), its rate of change (factor b), and the probability of a change in sign (factor c). For example, when inspected, a pointer on a circular display has a certain value, a certain rate of change (slow–rapid), and a certain probability of reversing its direction.

There is no need for a new inspection when the value of the pointer is away from the danger zone, especially when it is known to change slowly and to have a high reversal probability.

One early model was based on information theory (Senders, 1983). It stated that an operator aims at continuous reconstruction of the values of all instruments. To achieve this aim, a display should be periodically inspected, depending on the generated amount of information per unit time in terms of rates of change and of probability of reversal (factors b and c). Senders carried out studies on controlling four or six instruments during a simulated flight. The model had a reasonable fit at four instruments, but predictions and results deviated when monitoring six instruments. Slowly changing instruments (slow displays) were fixated too often at the cost of rapidly changing ones (fast displays).[30] Senders proposed that information from a slow display might be sensitive to short-term forgetting, so a fresh status report is needed. Alternatively, a fast display may be overloading, so there is not enough time for achieving reconstruction. Overload is more likely as more displays are controlled. Indeed, deviation from prediction was most pronounced in the case of six displays.

The reconstruction model was succeeded by decision-based conditional sampling models that were most popular during the 1960s. They suggested that participants only fixate an instrument when the perceived risk of missing a critical signal exceeds a criterion value. This means that in addition to rate of change and probability of reversal, an observer fixates an instrument more often as a reading gets closer to the critical zone (factor a). In the case of a safe reading, a next reading can be postponed until that earlier reading is dated. An advantage of the conditional sampling model is that it is intuitively more plausible. In the reconstruction model, a participant has the passive role of a mechanical information transmitter. In the conditional model, participants operate a decision criterion, which means that they behave on the basis of both motivational and cognitive variables. It is interesting that the models nicely reflect the dominant theoretical trends of their time.

Senders (1983) reviewed several variants of the conditional sampling model that are primarily concerned with the way of setting the risk criterion. In one model, participants only fixate an instrument when the probability of entering the critical zone is maximal. This means that the aim is not to detect the moment that the critical zone is entered but only whether a reading has actually entered. In another version, the acceptable risk depends on the distance of a reading from the danger zone, becoming less as this distance becomes smaller. The variants obviously affect the predicted frequency of fixation. Thus, an instrument is fixated less frequently when par-

---

[30]Another problem is that periodic sampling needed for reconstructing the signal cannot explain the considerable variance of fixation intervals.

ticipants accept the possibility that a reading may have actually entered the critical zone.

The main problem of the conditional sampling models is that they predict a steep increase in fixation frequency as a display changes more rapidly, much steeper than is actually observed. The conditional sampling models also assume that participants keep track of the state of the various displays in parallel. In contrast, Carbonell (1966) proposed a queuing model in which displays line up with the most urgent one—in terms of conditional error probability—first in line. Yet, this variant cannot cope either with the divergence between predicted and observed fixation frequencies.

There are more models along the same line (e.g., Stein & Wewerinke, 1983) that all depend on (a) the rate a display generates uncertainty (fast–slow), (b) the permissible error, (c) the limits that should not be exceeded, (d) the probability of a critical error on one display while attending another one, and (e) the payoffs associated with a missed critical reading and the costs of a reading. As mentioned, the main problem for the normative models is that their predictions strongly deviate from the data. One might argue that in principle, the optimal models provide the correct description of search for deviations but that the human operator is imperfect, due to forgetfulness, an incomplete cognitive schema of the dynamics of the displays, and failures in making the correct calculations. Thus, experienced pilots should behave according to the model, but thus far, empirical support is scant.

The drastic alternative is that human search is not primarily based on the statistical prescriptions contained in the optimal models. For example, van Delft (1987) argued that humans might simply search instruments in a fixed sequence, although perhaps somewhat modulated by rate of change and reversals. In support, van Delft found that the frequency of observing a particular display depended on whether the values of the other displays were changing relatively slowly or fast. Thus, a display was fixated more frequently when it was the slowest rather than when it was the fastest one of the set. This is at odds with the assumption of most normative models that the statistical properties of the displays are traced independently.

Donk (1994a) had individuals monitor four or six displays, and then she measured (a) mean fixation frequency of each display, (b) intervals between successive readings of a display, (c) fixation transitions between displays, and (d) dependence of the next reading of a display on the value at its previous reading. Her results suggest that the search strategy was not the same for all displays. Fast displays always required a high inspection rate, so the participants did not bother about conditional probabilities but adopted a strategy of a fixed reading sequence. The net effect was undersampling with regard to the prediction of a standard conditional-sampling model. Evidence for conditional sampling was only found for slower displays, which were only occasionally inspected. Here, the moment of inspection depended on the value of the previous reading and on the rate of change (Donk, 1994b; Donk & Hagemeister, 1994). Donk (1994a) also found that irrespective of the display dynamics, horizontal saccades were more frequent than diagonal saccades for displays that were arranged in a 3 * 2 or a 2 * 2 matrix. A contribution of spatial configuration may not be surprising because it is consistent with reading habits. Yet, it is outside the realm of the normative models, completely based as they are on the cognitive schemata of the statistical display dynamics.

Applications. Research on visual scanning has an applied origin regarding the strategies that operators use in controlling the state of a number of signal sources. Thus, the previously discussed tasks were all concerned with detection of critical events while supervising complex processes. One applied interest concerns principles on the relative location of displays, so the probability of detecting the most essential deviations first is increased. When designing a configuration of displays, it is relevant to know that fixations do not only depend on the statistical properties of the displays but also on the perceptual structure of the configuration. When all displays require frequent inspection, their perceptual configuration probably determines the search strategy. One perceptual variable affecting the efficiency of search is the visual angle, which subtends all displays together. This angle should preferably not exceed the eye field.

These rules apply in particular when the number of displays is not too large. In the case of many displays, there will be simply insufficient search time. One solution is to use summary displays that indicate the relative priority of certain subsets. For example, when supervising a multitude of displays, as in a nuclear power plant, one may register deviations on a summary display. When a process fails, there are usually a variety of deviations that together define the nature of the failure. Hence, one would like to have a summary statement about which particular readings deviate. Diagnostic displays are an alternative option.

It has become abundantly clear that pop-out is not an absolute property of a stimulus but depends on the background in which it is embedded. In a similar way, the size of the visual lobe depends on the total context. The correlation between pop-out and the size of the visual lobe can be used to construct a conspicuity tester that estimates conspicuity of a stimulus in its specific context by measuring the eccentricity at which that stimulus can still be detected (Kooi & Valeton, 1997; Wertheim, 1989). This can be used to measure conspicuity in a variety of conditions such as camouflage, road signs, and products on display in a supermarket.

One basic tenet of this chapter was the extent to which search is controlled by exogenous, feature-determined factors (stimulus set) or by top-down, object-determined factors (response set). As noted, a target, that is, a particular letter, was often embedded in homogeneous noise from other letters. The consequence has been a neglect of more common, natural perceptual scenes. Still, the evidence on background control of search stresses the relevance of the particular environment in which search takes place. This raises the question how far results from searching homogeneous fields can be generalized to more real-life scenes (e.g., Stark & Ellis, 1981).

Visual search is of obvious interest to driving. The relevance of conspicuity is self-evident. In fact, visual search while driving may be particularly guided by top-down, controlled schemata of the environment, that is, by knowledge of the world and by expectations about what will occur. It may be mainly a matter of checking whether conditions still comply with expectation. Expectations are summarized in protypical schemata of scenes that indicate the properties and mutual relations among objects (e.g., Biederman, Mezzanotte, & Rabinowitz, 1982). Thus, a prototypical scene for an intersection of two provincial roads may consist of traffic lights and special marking of the lanes for through and turning traffic. The activation of a scene, then, induces expectations about what will be seen. It is relevant to know whether features of human, internal models correspond to those intended by the designer of the road scenes. One illustrative example of the relevance of internal models in search stems from a study by Theeuwes and Hagenzieker (1993). They presented individuals with pictures of roads taken from the inside of a car. The instruction was to search for specific traffic signs. They found that search times depended on whether a sign was at an expected spot.[31] Improper expectations caused incorrect interpretations that could lead to accidents. Focusing attention on expected spots during the analysis of well-known scenes appeared to inhibit automatic attraction of attention by conspicuous objects elsewhere (Theeuwes, 1993). This is along the lines of the basic evidence. Future research should continue to be concerned with generalization of the basic results to real-life scenes, which is another instance of the back-to-back approach.

SUMMARY

Visual scanning has various themes in common with selective attention in a single glance. Examples include the similarity between the views of Neisser (1963) and Treisman (1988) and, more recently, between those of Prinz (1987) and of van der Heijden (1992). However, aside from the convergences, there are various issues that do not yet have a counterpart. Examples

---

[31]The role of the internal model is also nicely illustrated by the finding that experts on X rays search for indications at expected spots, but a novice tends to scan the whole picture (Kundul & La Follette, 1972).

are inhibition of return and the relative importance of object versus location in search. The main difference may be that multi-fixation studies have more emphasis on the properties of internal schemata of the environment in guiding search. Schemata consist of internalized perceptual structures, statistical properties of process dynamics, and of strategical intentions, but whatever their specific nature, they are invariably top down. This contrasts with the relative emphasis on bottom-up processing in the earlier sections of this chapter. The difference may be due to the fact that scanning paradigms raise questions beyond those in which items are detected in a single glance. In other words, bottom-up processing has dominated visual selection in a single glance, whereas top-down processing dominates scanning. Top-down processing is clearly acknowledged in van der Heijden's postcategorical filter model that may be the best present heuristic for bridging the gap between single- and multi-fixation paradigms.

The literature appears to be more consistent with a stage approach than with a capacity approach. A capacity notion was only met in the area on covert orienting; there reference was made to the "capacity" of the zoom lens. It is evident that this capacity concept deviates from the processing limits as implied in Broadbent's (1958) P-system; this illustrates how easily the capacity concept can be granted different meanings without a clear awareness of the change. Moreover, there are now serious doubts about the earlier adage that focused attention presupposes capacity limits. In contrast, the notion of information flow along stages was implicit in most of the reviewed work on focused attention and search. As an example, action—response selection and execution—can only start when localization in the identification module has been achieved.

Automaticity and
Divided Attention

The wide setting of the zoom lens and the breakthrough of the unattended are instances of divided attention in the sense of distraction from focusing. In this chapter, the perspective shifts from distraction to performance of more than one task at once, which is related to the issue of mental workload. Here, the notion of a human being as a limited-capacity processor has its deepest roots. Hence, the question is how well the capacity concept does in its homeland. Besides limited-capacity theory, the notion of a central executive controller is considered. How freely may capacity be distributed among different tasks? Limited capacity and central executive notions are confronted with more recent connectionist-inspired approaches that have "interference" as their password and claim to do without a central executive.

How much capacity is consumed by a particular task? The usual answer is that this depends on practice and automation. Because the issue of automaticity pervades theorizing on dual-task performance, the chapter starts with a summary on automaticity and the orienting reaction, both of which are strongly related. This is followed by a review on dual-task performance proper. The final part of the chapter addresses a widely studied microcase of dual-task performance, namely, the psychological refractory period (PRP). It is a microcase because the dual task is limited to two independent discrete responses to two stimuli that are presented in rapid succession. The PRP paradigm has a special status because the findings there deviate considerably from those obtained when performing a more complex dual task that directly bears on the issue of generalization from the simple to the more complex.

AUTOMATIC VERSUS CONTROLLED PROCESSING

Automatic processing plays an important part in a wide variety of experimental situations. It was already met or implied in preattentional processing of features, letter recognition, covert attending, response selection with highly compatible S–R connections, repetition effects, the Stroop effect, and motor chunks. The automaticity concept also features prominently in capacity models and in more recent interference theories of dual-task performance. All the evidence shares the element of performance after a great deal of practice. It was already suggested that processing stages can be effectively bypassed via direct shortcut-type of connections and via integrated structures, or chunks. Despite variations in phrasing, this is the recurrent theme in all views on dual tasks. In the present section, general principles of automatic processing are scrutinized, and some specific paradigms on automatic processing are discussed with the aim of arriving at a more coherent coverage.

The Need for Attention

A common metaphor of the organization of behavior is a hierarchically, or perhaps hetrarchically, organized company in which a top level decides about general policy issues and develops general plans. The details of this are elaborated by successively lower levels, while most of the actual work is carried out by still lower levels (Pew, 1984). Each level has its own responsibilities and desired skills. Applied to human behavior, one may assume a higher order, planning and organizing level that, in terms of Rasmussen's (1986) classification, is predominantly knowledge based. The plans are elaborated in greater detail and carried out by way of a variety of rule-based and skill-based actions that are usually less conscious and may automatically run off, although the higher levels still exert some control. Thus, a higher level is kept roughly informed about what lower levels accomplish, in particular when something goes wrong, despite the fact that a higher level is usually not well equipped to take over the role of a lower level. For example, walking is usually not under high-level control, but when stumbling, the higher level is informed but cannot do much more than watch the attempts of lower levels to regain equilibrium. Kinesthetic and proprioceptive feedback inform the lower level about the relative error in bodily position and about the degree of success of the corrective actions. Still, the information to the higher level is relevant because, when actually falling down, the higher level may initiate procedures that minimize damage.

　　Greater automaticity of the lower levels is a result of extended practice. The result is that automatic actions are fast and less dependent on higher order feedback.[1] Yet, they are also less flexible because they are standardized and operate on default parameter values that limit them to a more narrow range of variation. In contrast, controlled actions are slower and more dependent on feedback but have the advantage of greater flexibility. The relatively slowness is among the reasons that they cannot perform the actions of the lower centers with equal efficiency. Cooperation of the various levels is obviously mandatory. Thus, the act of walking may be largely a matter of automatized lower level control, but parameters such as direction and speed are prescribed by higher level planning.

Three characteristics are usually connected to fully automatic processes. First, they occur involuntarily and without intention, which brings about the aforementioned lack of flexibility. Second, they do not load the processor, so they can be carried out in parallel with other activities that reflect their speed and efficiency. Finally, they lack conscious awareness. In contrast, controlled processes are voluntary, planned, and prepared; they load the processing system, so they are carried out serially; and, finally, one is usually aware of controlled processing. This may create the impression that automatic and controlled activities can be easily distinguished, but this is not the case. First, a process may show only one or two of the three mentioned automatic features. Second, automaticity often develops gradually, so a strict dichotomy between controlled and automatic is uncommon. Third, automatic and controlled processing are strongly intertwined. For instance, a controlled activity may be automatically elicited, in which case the automatic activity precedes the controlled one. In this way, an automatic process may indirectly cause interference (i.e., load the system) due to the subsequent controlled activity (Neumann, 1984). An example is the Stroop effect, in which presumably automatic word recognition elicits a subsequent response conflict. The reverse is that automatic capturing of a stimulus depends on whether one is intentionally focused on some other spot. When focused, automatic capturing occurs less easily than when the zoom lens is set widely. Thus, intentions may either inhibit or facilitate automatic processing. A somewhat trivial example of inhibiting an automatic process is to carry out a saccade away from a spot where an expected stimulus is actually presented. A less

---

[1]This should not be taken to imply that feedback plays no role at the lower automatic levels. First, feedback is essential as information about the quality of the actions. For example, proprioceptive feedback from the keys is essential for an experienced typist as confirmation that they have been actually pressed. Unexpected or unusual feedback from a key is immediately reported to a higher level, which, in turn, has the effect that performance is disturbed or even stopped (e.g., Shaffer, 1978). Second, internal feedback loops allow fast error correction within the limits of the range of variation that the level permits. Fast corrections also imply that efficient care is taken of small deviations from an optimal course in motor behavior. In this sense, automatic actions are flexible but within strict limits.

trivial example comes from studies on the eye blink reflex in response to sudden auditory stimuli. The eye blink response is a perfect example of an automatic process, yet visual focusing of attention weakens the strength of the eye blink response to an auditory stimulus, even with infants as participants (Anthony & Graham, 1983).

In view of such restrictions, Kahneman and Treisman (1984) distinguished strong and partial automaticity. Strong automatic processes are unaffected by intentionally focused attention, whereas, in contrast, intentional focusing inhibits or facilitates partial automatic processing. Evidence on the facilitating effect of focusing attention abounds in the literature on covert orienting. Another example concerns the dilution phenomenon (Kahneman & Chajczyk, 1983), in which the negative effect of a conflicting color word on naming the color of an adjacent colored bar was weakened by the presence of an additional neutral word. The fact that a neutral word and a conflicting word interfere suggests that their processes are not fully independent. In turn, this is at odds with strong automaticity.

Automatic processing may develop at any processing stage, but one should not assign the label of automaticity to any particular stage. For some time, it was believed that processes of stimulus preprocessing and feature extraction occur in parallel and against intention (*preattentional automatic processes*). Indeed, it may be safe to say that automaticity is more pronounced in perceptual processing than in response selection and action. This does not mean, however, that perceptual processing is always automatic. Thus, effects of dual tasks and of practice are found when stimuli are degraded, interrupted by a mask, or, more generally, when viewing conditions are hard or unfamiliar (Comstock, 1973). The point is that most research has been carried out with highly familiar perceptual stimuli. This may create the impression that perceptual processing is automatic and may lead to underestimation of perceptual learning. Main tasks for future research concern delineation of the conditions in which automatic processing prevails, acquisition of automaticity, and intertwining between automatic and controlled processes.

Costs–Benefits Analysis

Posner and Snyder (1975) argued that one cannot decide intuitively whether an activity such as a choice reaction or components of an activity are automatic or controlled. They proposed a costs–benefits analysis to decide whether a process is controlled or automatic. The rationale was that, when a particular activity is controlled, it is prepared or completed at the cost of inhibiting other potential activities. This is in line with the notion that attention-demanding actions require capacity and, hence, tend to exclude each other.[2] Thus, when

---

[2]Capacity theory only expects costs of attending a controlled action when the demands of that action exceed total capacity. The finding that a simple preparatory set invokes costs actually poses a problem for capacity theory and is more in line with interference.

preparing a specific reaction, for example, on the basis of a precue or preknowledge, the prepared reaction is carried out faster, at the cost of a slower reaction when an unexpected alternative is presented. Examples of costs are met in the effects of relative stimulus frequency and time uncertainty on CRT. If a particular stimulus is expected or arrives at an expected moment, CRT is relatively fast, at the cost of a slower CRT to unexpected stimuli or to stimuli occurring at an unexpected moment. Another example concerns the costs for nonattended locations and the benefits for an attended one, as observed in covert orienting. Even when attention is involuntarily captured by a position in space, suggesting automaticity, subsequent covert orienting still appears to invoke costs as well as benefits (Posner, 1978). This is an interesting example of intertwined automatic and controlled processes.

An automatic process profits from a valid precue. However, in contrast to a controlled process, an automatic process invokes no costs when the precue is invalid so that a nonanticipated action is required. The reason is that in the case of automatic processing, a precue activates its corresponding code, thus facilitating the activity corresponding to that code, without affecting the state of other codes. The point is that automatic activation of a code by a precue is supposed to be a matter of passive pathway activation. In contrast, controlled activation of a code is accompanied by inhibition of other potential codes. As an example, Posner and Snyder (1975) reported a study in which pairs of letters (e.g., AA; AB) were presented in a same–different task. A letter pair was preceded by a prime that matched or mismatched the forthcoming letter pair. The prime had either a high or a low validity. A high-validity prime had a .80 probability of being valid (e.g., A – AA; B – BB), whereas the probability of a low-validity prime was .20.[3] When the prime had low validity, the results showed benefits in the case of a match but no costs of a mismatch. In other words, when prime and letter pair happened to match, CRT was less than in the neutral control condition.[4] When they mismatched, that is, the majority of the same responses, CRT was about as equally long as in the neutral control condition (Fig. 8.1). Thus, the results suggest facilitation in responding to an AA pair when preceded by an A prime, without causing an inhibition when the AA pair is preceded by a B prime.

However, when the prime had high validity and was therefore predictive, benefits without costs were only found at a small interval (SOA) between the prime and the letter pair. Costs arose when SOA exceeded 300 ms, an interval that is about equal to the time to complete preparation (Fig. 8.1). This result suggests rapid automatic activation of the primed letter, causing

---

[3]In that condition, the probability of a mismatch between prime and letter pair (A – BB; B – AA) was .8; the present discussion is limited to the subset of "same" responses: AA, BB.

[4]In the neutral control condition, the prime was a noninformative "+" sign serving merely as a warning stimulus.

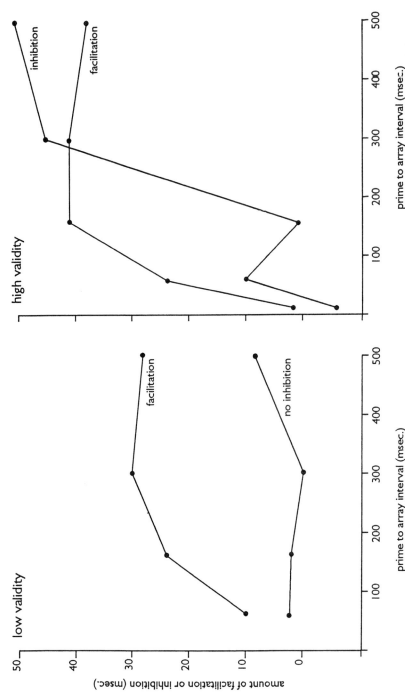

FIG. 8.1. Facilitation and inhibition as a function of the interval between prime letter and letter pair in a same–different task. In the left panel the prime letter had low (.2) validity, whereas it had high validity (.8) in the right panel. A low-validity prime facilitated in the case of a match and did not inhibit in the case of a mismatch. A high-validity prime facilitated and inhibited, but inhibition developed more slowly. From Posner, M. I. (1978). *Chronometric explorations of mind.* Copyright © 1978 by Lawrence Erlbaum Associates, Hillsdale, N.J. Reproduced with kind permission of the publisher.

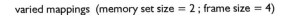

varied mappings (memory set size = 2 ; frame size = 4)

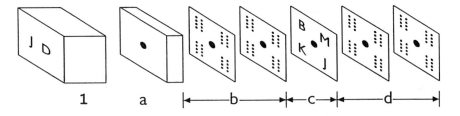

consistent mappings (memory set size = 4 ; frame size = 2)

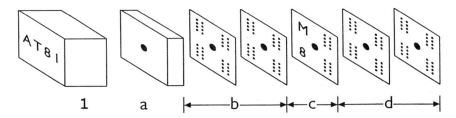

FIG. 8.2. An example of two positive trials in combined memory and visual search. In the example of varied mapping, the target set is {J;D} and it is {A;T; 8; I} in the example of consistent mapping. From Schneider, W., & Shiffrin, R. M. (1977). Controlled and automatic human information processing: Detection, search and attention. *Psychological Review, 84,* 1–66. Copyright © 1977 by the American Psychological Association. Reprinted with permission.

immediate benefits without costs, followed by gradually emerging controlled preparation of the primed letter pair.

Interesting as these results are, costs–benefits analysis has problems as well. One is that when a precue may be invalid, one cannot be sure that participants will fully prepare processing the primed stimulus. If preparation fails, even occasionally, both benefits and costs are underestimated. It may be countered, though, that when the probability of a valid precue exceeds .80, participants tend to respond about as equally fast as when they are completely certain (de Klerk & Oppe, 1970). A second potential problem was raised by Jonides and Mack (1984) and concerns the difference between precues in neutral trials and in experimental ones. Thus, in the various studies of Posner and associates (Posner, 1978) the neutral precue may be noted with a plus sign, and the informative precue with a letter when priming the subsequent letter pair, or it may be noted with an arrow when priming a spatial position. It is clear that neutral and experimental precues should have the same effect on controlled preparation. The point is that if precues differed in their general alerting properties, there is no valid baseline for estimating costs and benefits. Jonides and Mack found that the aforementioned prerequisite is not always met. Yet, their proposal to omit neutral trials would imply that it becomes impossible to assess automaticity. It is perhaps better, therefore, to follow van der Heijden's (1992) suggestion to choose the neutral and experimental cues with care and to check for potential differences in alerting before carrying out a costs–benefits study.

Automaticity in Visual-Memory Search

The distinction between automatic and controlled processing received a strong impulse from the work of Shiffrin and Schneider (1977). The modal form of their influential research paradigm consists of a combination of a Sternberg target-classification task and a visual-search task. One to four stimuli, usually alphanumerics, make up the frame size (D); the task is to decide whether a frame contains an item from a previously instructed target or memory set (M), which is also varied between one and four items. CRT is the dependent variable. In other conditions, a number of frames are flashed briefly and in rapid succession, and participants judge whether one of the frames contained a target. Here, accuracy is the dependent variable (Schneider & Shiffrin, 1977; Shiffrin & Schneider, 1977). A major independent variable was consistent (CM) versus varied (VM) mapping. When the target set was varied between trials (VM), the the slope for a "no" response was about twice the slope for a "yes" response (Fig. 8.3), which is in line with serial self-terminating search of D and M. One item from M is selected and successively compared with anyone of the displayed stimuli; this is repeated with the next M item until a target is found or reported absent.

The results are quite different in the case of consistent mapping (CM), a condition that has the same target set during all trials. The common finding in CM is that a flat search-function develops after prolonged practice. In the original studies, Schneider and Shiffrin (1977) used digits as targets and letters as nontargets throughout all experimental trials in their CM condition. Hence, a target (a digit) could never be a nontarget, and a nontarget (a letter) could never be a target. In the VM condition, both targets and non-targets consisted of letters, and a new target set was defined at each trial. In later studies, Schneider and Shiffrin deconfounded the effects of CM processing and alphanumerical category. In their CM condition, a special group of letters was defined as target set throughout all trials so again, targets could never be nontargets, and vice versa. In early practice, CRT hardly differed in CM and VM, but after some 20,000 trials, CM showed an almost flat search-function. This suggested that the group of target letters had acquired category status, distinct from the nontarget letters. As said, in other studies, a succession of frames was briefly presented with accuracy as a dependent variable. The results agreed with those of the CRT studies in that VM needed a much longer presentation time than CM in order to achieve

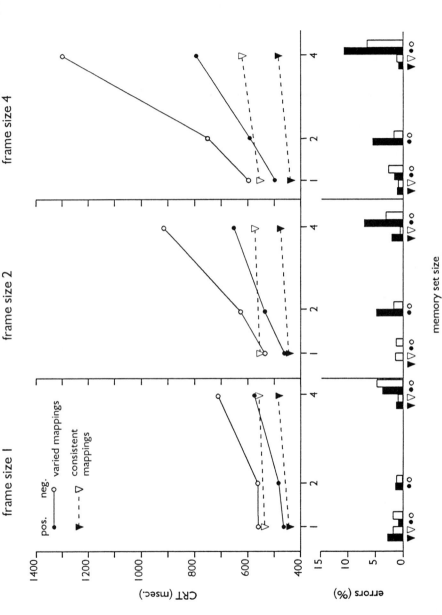

FIG. 8.3. CRT as a function of target-set size, frame size, and type of mapping. From Schneider, W., & Shiffrin, R. M. (1977). Controlled and automatic human information processing: Detection, search and attention. *Psychological Review, 84,* 1–66. Copyright © 1977 by the American Psychological Association. Reprinted with permission.

315

50% accuracy. Schneider and Shiffrin proposed parallel search in the case of CM as a qualitatively distinct automatic processing mode in comparison to a serial, self-terminating controlled processing mode in the case of VM.

One question is, "what do participants actually learn in the case of CM?" From the perspective of late selection, targets and nontargets might become more discriminable. Eventually, the items from the consistent target set would become a separate category, distinct from the nontargets. Alternatively, an automatic-processing mode might imply that learning leads to bypassing a bottleneck and to eliciting an automatic-attending response.

Automatic processes are supposed to occur irrespective of intentions and it should not be easy therefore to turn off an automatic-attending response. This was tested in a condition in which, after extended CM practice, participants were suddenly given a new target set in which a previous target could now occur as nontarget. If automatic, the original target should still elicit an automatic but now invalid detection. Shiffrin and Schneider (1977) trained participants to detect consonants from one half of the alphabet among nontargets from the other half of the alphabet. After some 2,000 trials, targets and nontargets were reversed. This had the effect of reducing detection accuracy below the level at the start of original learning (Fig. 8.4). This result is expected because a former target still elicits an automatic-attending response that is checked first and rejected as a distractor, followed by serial search for a potential new target. The fact that a distractor receives priority explains that detection accuracy could not even attain the initial level of detection accuracy. In early practice, serial search is supposed to start at some random point in the frame.

In summary, the flat CM search-function can be explained by a combination of acquired categorization of the target set and automatic target detection. Another indication for a qualitative difference between automatic and controlled processing was the ability to intentionally focus on specific items in a frame which proved to be quite possible in VM search. In one study (Shiffrin & Schneider, 1977), participants were told that, "D would be four," but that only stimuli appearing at one specific diagonal were relevant. A comparison with a D = 2 condition showed that detection accuracy was about equal in either case. However, it was superior to that in a D = 4 control condition in which a target could occur at any of the four positions. Focusing was impossible when the ignored diagonal contained a stimulus that had belonged to an earlier CM set. This is additional evidence that automatic detection of such stimuli occurs unintentionally.[5,6] It is of interest

---

[5]This result seems at odds with the notion that automatic processes do not consume capacity or do not interfere with other processes that demand capacity at the same time. The suggestion is, indeed, that the automatic-attention response is not interfering, but that controlled processes, following and elicited by automatic attending, cause interference.

[6]It could well be that the instruction to focus on one diagonal and to complete the reaction is a prerequisite for unintentional processing at the nonattended diagonal.

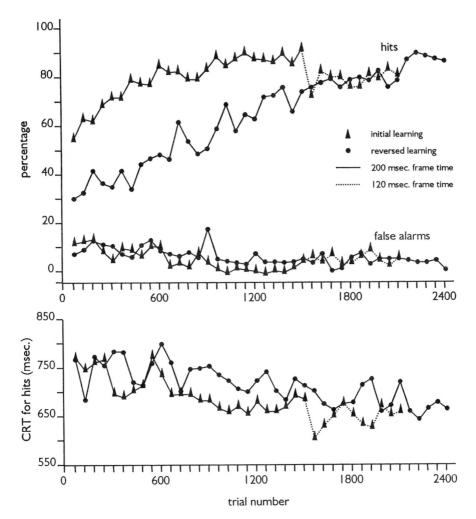

FIG. 8.4. Proportions of hits and false alarms in initial learning and following a reversal in target set. Note that the level of initial learning is not attained after the reversal. From Schneider, W., & Shiffrin, R. M. (1977). Controlled and automatic human information processing: Perceptual learning, automatic attending and a general theory. *Psychological Review, 84*, 127–190. Copyright © 1977 by the American Psychological Association. Reprinted with permission.

that once acquired, the efficiency of CM processing remains intact after a prolonged period of nonuse, even up to 9 years (Cooke, Durso, & Schvaneveldt, 1994).

In still another study (Schneider & Fisk, 1982), participants had VM search (detecting a particular digit among other digits) on one diagonal and CM search (detecting a letter among digits) on the other diagonal, with accuracy as measure. In the single-task control conditions, they had either VM or CM search on one diagonal only. The results show that a VM task and a CM task could be carried out together without any noticeable loss in detection accuracy. Detection accuracy suffered heavily when having VM on both diagonals, which follows naturally from the effect of increasing D on VM search. Schneider and Fisk concluded that task load is not affected when automatic processes are added to controlled processes. In other studies, Fisk and Schneider (1983) found that CM search could well be combined with a notoriously demanding second task such as digit-span recall or word categorization. Again, this is expected from an automatic process. It has already been mentioned that automatic attending may be followed by controlled processing when selecting and executing a response. This appeared to be the case when two stimuli, one VM and one CM, both required an overt response at the same trial. This led to considerable interference that reminds one of simultaneous response decisions in auditory-target detection (Treisman & Riley, 1969).

From the perspective of the early- versus late-selection debate, it is relevant whether automatic processing of letters among digits and the development of automatic processing of a CM-letter subset can be conceived of as acquiring a group of common letter-like physical features (early selection) or reflecting a semantic effect (late selection). Results from Schneider and Fisk (1984) suggest the latter option because automatic detection of well-practiced words was found to extend to new exemplars of the same category, for example, animal names. The fact that transfer was found on the word-category level seemed to imply detection on the basis of semantics. However, the study appears to suffer from methodological problems that render the conclusion dubious (Pashler & Baylis, 1991). Pashler and Baylis found transfer of practiced letters or digits to new exemplars, but their study was a straight CRT study and not concerned with selective attention. Thus, as yet, the issue seems undecided.

There also remains the problem that the previously mentioned results have been usually obtained in a setting in which all stimuli are presented within a small spatial region and under divided-attention conditions. Hence, early selection may not have been the primary selective mechanism. Recently, Logan and Etherton (1994) studied automatization with respect to co-occurrence of stimuli. Their participants were presented with word pairs and had the task of detecting a target that was defined as a word that belonged to a certain word category. Throughout the study, targets belonged to the same category, so mapping was consistent. In addition, though, word pairs could vary or remain consistent, with this last condition leading to co-occurrence of words. The study was done with (a) focused attention, in which participants were precued about the position of a potential target word, (b) divided attention, in which either word of a pair could be a target, and (c) in dual-task conditions, in which participants had to carry out a separate response to either word that was a target. In a subsequent transfer of training condition, the results show learning of co-occurrent words in the divided attention and the dual-task conditions but not in the focused-attention condition. This suggests that the participants could filter out the noncued word by focused-attention—it was not stored in memory—whereas both words of the word pair were stored in the other two conditions. More importantly, co-occurrence was also stored despite the fact that nothing in the instructions required encoding of co-occurrence. Logan and Etherton reasoned that co-occurrence was not learned by controlled processing but was an automatic by-product of target search.

Evoked Potentials and Consistent Mapping

Various studies have addressed the issue of automatic processing in CM from the perspective of evoked potentials and, in particular, of the P3 amplitude. This wave is sometimes viewed as a reflection of controlled processing that predicts that P3 should diminish or even vanish altogether in the case of CM. The results show little support for this deduction, however, because, usually, P3 amplitude is about equally large for VM and CM (van Dellen et al., 1985). Yet, variation in M or D had little effect on the P3 amplitude in the case of CM. In the case of VM, P3 amplitude became less as M or D increased, and, in particular, when participants performed a second perceptual–motor task at the same time (Strayer & Kramer, 1990). The suggestion is that P3 amplitude diminished in a dual-task condition because less capacity could be allocated to the search task. Analogous to what has been found in CRT, P3 latency appeared to increase in VM, whereas it remained about the same in CM, irrespective of the size of M. Again, the effect of target probability on P3 amplitude vanished in CM but remained clearly present in VM. In summary, there is evidence that VM affects both the latency and amplitude of P3, yet the fact that P3 does not vanish in CM suggests that it does not have a simple relation to processing efficiency in visual-memory search.[7]

Applications. The evidence on automatic (CM) versus controlled (VM) processing in visual-memory search is illustrative for the large differences in performance between novices and experts. The data have been applied to training in command and control situations as well as to training in the traditional classroom. The idea is that a real-life task should have as many consistent components as possible. They are automatized, are readily available, and become insensitive to distraction, fatigue, and environmental

---

[7]Some may maintain that the evidence shows that P3 amplitude and automatic versus controlled processing in visual-memory search are unrelated. Others may hold that the lack of effect on P3 amplitude shows that the dichotomy between automatic and controlled is false.

stresses. Variable components of the same task gain much less from practice because they benefit only from general learning, that is, familiarization with the display and general aspects of the task setting. Hence, the proverb, "Practice makes perfect," only holds for consistent task components and is, therefore, not generally valid. Another relevant property of consistent components is that they appear to be more resistant to forgetting (Fisk & Hodge, 1992). Thus, it is a useful heuristic in system design to develop consistent categories and units that can acquire the status of automaticity. Display codes in air-traffic control is a prime example in which consistency of codes and categories is absolutely essential (Schneider, Vidulich, & Yeh, 1982).

It is of interest that there is a third avenue between VM and CM. Thus, in the first group of trials, elements of a certain category, for example, clothing, might be targets, and elements of another category, for example, furniture, may be distractors. In the second group of trials, animals may be targets and body parts may be distractors. In a third group of trials, furniture may be targets and clothing may be distractors. Thus, targets can become distractors, and vice versa, but once the elements of a category qualify as targets or distractors, all its elements qualify. The CRT of this condition are between CM and VM, provided that the elements of a category retain their status as target for at least 10 trials (Rogers, Lee, & Fisk, 1995). Although theoretically unclear, this third avenue has applied relevance because there are many real-life situations in which whole categories may change status as targets and distractors.

Another application regards training in symbol classification. Consistent task components appear to benefit most from part-task training. Hence, consistent components should be designed and trained separately (Fisk, Ackerman, & Schneider, 1987). It is relevant that CM does not only apply to individual stimuli but also to the conceptual level of a well-established category (Kramer, Strayer, & Buckley, 1990). The main advantage of automatizing a category is that it extends to new exemplars of that category, that is, exemplars that have not been met yet. If there is CM on the level of an individual stimulus (i.e., certain symbols are always targets), but inconsistency on the categorical level (i.e., not all exemplars of that category are targets), participants still develop automatic processing for the consistent examplars. The main problem in the case of inconsistent elements of a category is that there is no transfer to new category members (Fisk & Jones, 1992). The finding that automatic processing generalizes from individual stimuli to categories is, obviously, a relevant step with regard to generalization from simple to more complex conditions.

THEORIES ON AUTOMATIC PROCESSING

It has often been assumed that controlled and automatic activity are two qualitatively distinct processing modes. Among others, this position was held by Posner and Snyder (1975), Shiffrin and Schneider (1977), and Logan

(1988). Other researchers have tended to consider controlled and automatic processing as extremes of a continuum (Kahneman & Henik, 1981; Neumann, 1984). As a broad summary statement, there is consensus that automatic processing relies on well-established, direct relations between input and output, whereas controlled processing requires intervening computational activity to establish or activate the desired relation.

Neumann's Theory

Neumann (1984) argued that an action can only be carried out when its parameters are fully specified. For instance, naming the color of an incongruent color-word (the Stroop task) requires specification of the displayed stimulus, the production of the color rather than the word, the name of the color, and how to carry out the correct response. The necessary specifications come from three sources: input information, stored procedures for carrying out actions,[8] and a special attentional mechanism that, in the absence of a specific skill, can link input information to a stored action procedure. In the case of underspecification, the input information is not properly linked to the desired response, such as when an incompatible response is required, for example, saying "red" to the word *green*. In that case, the attentional mechanism provides the extra parameter specification so that the action of saying "red" can be carried out, although at the cost of extra time. Overspecification is another case in which the attentional mechanism plays a role. In this case, there are various simultaneous inputs that all have their skilled links to their specific responses, but the attentional mechanism has to specify which response has priority. This may be accomplished by, for example, spatial focusing or by attending to information presented to one ear.

Neumann (1984) called a process automatic when all parameters are optimally specified; therefore, it does not suffer from either under- or overspecification. In that case, specification may occur by default. This means that the attentional mechanism is not needed to complete the action. It is obvious that perfect specification is the result of long-term learning. Once the skills have been acquired, automatized actions can be completed in parallel and can occur in spite of intention. It should be noted, though, that there usually remains some effect of attention in the sense of a general intention for action. For example, reacting to a Stroop stimulus requires intentional attending to the spot where the stimulus will be presented. How-

---

[8]Neumann (1984) referred to these procedures as skills. A *skill* implies integration between input information and its correct corresponding action, such as in saying "green" to perceiving the word "green." Examples of the action part of a skill are a motor program that enables someone to say "green," and a program for the production of integrated spatiotemporal sequences of finger movements in typing. Note that this usage of the word skill deviates from the everyday meaning in which it refers to highly practiced tasks such as skilled piano playing.

ever, there are other instances of automatized actions that do not require
intentionality. Thus, a stimulus may well elicit an orienting response while
a person intentionally focuses on another task or on another spatial location.
Neumann has applied his automaticity concept to dual-task performance.

Detweiler and Schneider's Theory

This model is discussed in greater detail in the section on dual-task performance. Here, only the automatic-processing component is highlighted. It
resembles Neumann's in that it also starts from specialized elementary processing units, such as a sensory input unit, a semantic unit, and a motor unit.
Automatic processing is the result of strong, specific associative connections
between corresponding elementary units and the establishment of priorities
through which a unit knows how urgently its message should be transmitted.

In the case of controlled processing, for example, VM in visual-memory
search, the associations between corresponding elementary units are weak
or absent and should, therefore, be intentionally established. Memory modules on a hierarchically higher level contain and maintain active message
vectors in order to keep the instructed target set available. Moreover, there
is a provision for determining whether the message vectors of the visual
input and the memory module match. This is done by a comparison module
that receives its information from both the input and memory modules.
Finally, then, the appropriate response (which key to press) has to be determined on the basis of the outcome of the comparison module. All these
processes are repeated for each new visual input, whereas competing activations of other modules must be actively inhibited (Fig. 8.5, phase 1).

The previous description of controlled processing characterizes initial
learning. Detweiler and Schneider (1991) distinguished five phases in the
transition from controlled to automatic processing.[9] In the second phase,
the memory module is supported by a context store that contains instructions
about which stimuli are targets and nontargets; they become more active as
practice proceeds. The context store allows faster, serial comparison-proc-
esses and, moreover, it refreshes the decaying contents of the memory
module. Thus, besides allowing a more rapid decision, the context store
renders processing less vulnerable. In phase 3, the memory comparisons
are still serial, but they proceed faster because multiple associations develop
between the memory module and the context store, on the one hand, and
the elementary target–no target output modules on the other hand. The role
of direct input from the memory module becomes marginal in this phase,
with the comparisons being mainly based on stable context storage of the

---

[9]The very fact of transitions from controlled to automatic processing implies the hypothesis
that automatic processing can only develop from originally controlled processing.

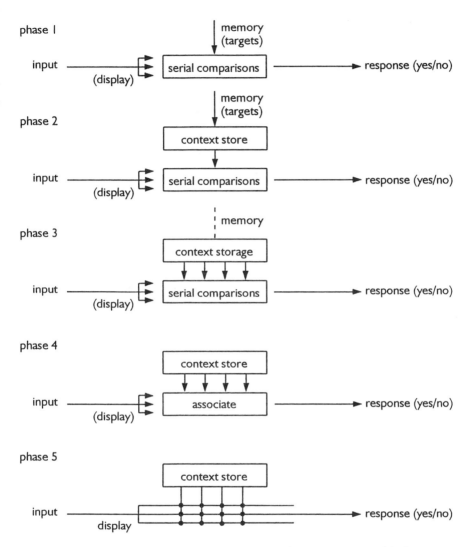

FIG. 8.5. Five phases toward automatization in the connectionist model of Detweiler and Schneider (1991). Note that the controlled phases (1–3) have serial comparisons between targets and input. In the final phases there are direct and, finally, parallel associations between input and output (4–5). From Detweiler, M., & Schneider, W. (1991). Modelling the acquisition of dual task skill in a connectionist/control architecture. In D. L. Damos (Ed.), *Multiple task performance*. Copyright © by Taylor & Francis, Washington. Reproduced with permission from the publisher.

target set. In phase 4, a shortcut is established between input and output modules; therefore, serial memory comparison is no longer required; hence, it is the first automatic stage. Yet, the input–output connections are still subject to central control. This disappears in the final automatic stage when all comparisons run off in parallel (Fig. 8.5).

Logan's Theory

The notions of Neumann (1984) and Detweiler and Schneider (1991) are based on rules and the strength of associative connections. In contrast, Logan (1988) proposed that automatic processing is based on multiple representations. Each reaction leaves a trace (an instance) that is stored as a separate representation. Practice has the effect of creating more instances. It is of obvious interest that instances of the same event are virtually identical. A response is said to be automatic when it comes from direct access retrieval of past solutions from memory or, in other words, when one of the stored instances is reactivated. In contrast to Detweiler and Schneider (1991), this view does not assume that automatic processing is necessarily preceded by controlled processing because instances are established by bottom-up storage in memory. The finding that incidentally learned co-occurrence of words in a word pair acquires the property of automatic processing is thought to support instance theory (Logan & Etherton, 1994).

The probability of reactivating an instance depends, of course, on their number. As long as the response is not based on direct retrieval of an instance, the correct solution can only be found by applying an instruction-based rule. In line with Neumann (1984), Logan (1988) assumed controlled processing implies that the instructed rule specifies the parameters needed for a response to occur. At an intermediate stage of practice, an instance may be reactivated at some trials, whereas the rule is needed at the remaining trials. Logan suggested a race between the time needed for direct retrieval and application of the rule. Some investigators connect open-loop control—a concept borrowed from motor behavior—to direct instance-based retrieval and closed-loop control to instruction-based rule.[10] Determining the appropriate rule is accompanied by feedback-based checks on correctness. In contrast, direct access through instances is supposed to proceed open loop, so errors have a higher probability of remaining undetected (Underwood, 1982).[11]

---

[10]It should be stressed that a reference to open-loop control does not mean that automatic processing has no lower level feedback and feedforward, enabling rapid small error corrections. It only refers to feedback to, and dependence on, higher levels of control.

[11]In direct instance-based processing, error detection only occurs after the fact. In contrast, a tendency toward an error might be more easily prevented when the response is governed by a rule.

It is of interest that the assumptions on instances and on the contrast between open-loop and closed-loop processing imply a dichotomy between automatic and controlled processing, namely, direct retrieval of an instance versus reinstatement of a rule. The main difference between instance and associative strength theory is that the former suggests a mixture of automatic and controlled trials at an intermediate stage of practice, whereas the latter predicts a gradual transition. A mixture notion predicts an exponentially shaped learning curve, but in all fairness, so do all theories on skill acquisition. In addition, though, instance theory suggests a race between automatic and controlled processes, which results in a clear prediction about a bimodal distribution of response times during acquisition. A strength notion may assume variability in strength that would also lead to more automatic processing at some trials and more controlled processing at other trials. Yet, this would not normally have the effect of a bimodal distribution of response times.

INVOLUNTARY ATTENTION
AND THE ORIENTING REFLEX (OR)

The distinction between voluntary and involuntary attention is classic (e.g., James, 1890) and is usually related to intentional, top-down activity versus unintentional, bottom-up activity. Thus, involuntary attention is assumed to be externally determined and automatically elicited, such as a sudden loud noise that captures attention without any actual intention. It is an abrupt change in the structure of external events and belongs to Berlyne's (1960) collative stimulus variables, namely, intensity, quality, and novelty. Pop-out is also a deviation of a single element from a dominant structure and, therefore, belongs to the same category. Another instance of involuntary attention was met in the discussion on mismatch negativity of the evoked potential in conditions of selective attention. The issue was also at stake when an abrupt visual onset of a peripheral stimulus appeared to capture attention in covert orienting. However, the fact that involuntary capturing of attention also depends on the extent of intentional focusing on a specific spot suggests that the external event may not be completely decisive.

In line with Neumann's (1984) argument, attentional, as well as motivational, factors appear to facilitate or inhibit involuntary capturing. In addition, there are cases of involuntary attending that are unrelated to the collative variables; they are not simply bottom-up either. The contribution of motivation may be illustrated by the observation that a crying baby has a greater attention value for a parent. Moreover, involuntary attention is not only triggered by an abrupt sensory deviation, as in the case of spatial pop-out or of an unexpected sound, but also by a deviation from an expected sequence of events. Again, consistent mapping, resulting from long-term practice, elicited automatic capturing. These latter cases are not concerned with a deviating external stimulus but with a deviation from an internal model about the current events (Sokolov, 1963). The concept of an internal model of the environment has been central in theorizing on the OR.

The OR is often defined as the complex of behavioral and physiological reactions to a change in stimulus situation. The most relevant physiological characteristics of the OR are blocking of the alpha rhythm in the EEG, decrease in skin resistance, vasodilation of the blood vessels in the head, HR deceleration, increase in pupil diameter, a delay in breathing, and an increase in pulse frequency (Näätänen, 1992). Ongoing activity is terminated (behavioral inhibition), and there is orientation toward the eliciting stimulus (i.e., looking and pricking). The whole organism gets into a state of attentive readiness to cope with the change. In short, it is the classical arousal response, which is discussed elsewhere in greater detail. The OR is usually the strongest in the case of a single deviating stimulus and habituates when the same deviation is repeated. An example is the diminishing response of a cat to a repeated auditory stimulus such as clapping the hands with a regular interval.

Behavioral inhibition is one of the three emotion systems proposed by Gray (1987). Apart from OR conditions, behavioral inhibition is observed when a conditioned stimulus for punishment is presented. It also seems to be at the basis of anxiety. It may sound paradoxical that, inhibition of behavior nothwithstanding, the OR contains all features associated with high arousal—a dissociation that suggests that the OR is not governed by a single energetic system. Gray's other emotion systems are approach, when presented with a conditioned reward stimulus, and fight or flight, when faced with an unconditioned punishment stimulus. In this last case, behavior is not inhibited. Instead, the stimulus merely elicits direct action. The present discussion is limited to the OR.

There is abundant evidence that an OR is elicited by a change in stimulus configuration, physical as well as semantic. Thus, it is elicited by a decrease, as well as by an increase, in stimulus intensity, with the strength of the OR depending on the degree of change. Again, a combination of a loud and soft burst of noise habituates when repeatedly presented but dishabituates when, unexpectedly, only the loud noise is presented (Sokolov, 1975). In a study by Badia and Defran (1970), a tone and a light were presented 15 times in alternation. Omitting the light on the sixteenth presentation led to an OR. An even more convincing case is the classical result of Unger (1964), who presented a sequence of letters in their usual alphabethic order (A-B-C-D, etc.). The regular sequence was suddenly interrupted (e.g., L-M-N-O-*B*), whereon the unexpected letter elicited an OR. Deviation from a standard numerical sequence (12345677 or 12345689) had a similar effect (Unger, 1964; Velden, 1978).

Sokolov (1963) proposed the neural internal model as the major explanatory construct for the OR. Collative variables, such as intensity and color as well as interval duration and sequence structure, are stored as a neural model of the perceptual environment. The neural model develops as a function of repeated stimulation and blocks the input to the reticular formation in the brain, which, in turn, inhibits the OR. A deviating stimulus is not absorbed by the neural model so that blocking of the reticular formation is lifted. The result is an OR that is more pronounced as the deviation becomes more outspoken.[12] The effect on the reticular formation is supposed to occur bottom up when the deviation consists of a physical stimulus property. In the case of a cognitive deviation (e.g., the interruption of the alphanumeric sequence), the effect on the reticular formation is indirect via corticoreticular efferent pathways. In research on C(RT), a stimulus beyond a critical sensory intensity was said to be immediately arousing and led to bottom-up elicitation of preparatory state, which obviously reminds of an OR of the first type. The moral is that ORs share the property that a change is noticed and taken into account; they differ in the extent to which an overt action is elicited or prepared.

The explanation of the OR in terms of deviation from a neural model has not remained undebated. For example, Bernstein (1969, 1981) argued that an OR is only elicited when a deviation is relevant to behavior. This means that rather than a deviation as such, cortical evaluation of its relevance is decisive for the OR to occur. A repeated relevant stimulus does not habituate either, which is at odds with the simple bottom-up explanation suggested by the neural model. A new stimulus is usually perceived as relevant as well, so that contributions of newness and relevance are not easy to disentangle.

Mismatch Negativity and the OR

Early psychophysiological studies on the OR relied largely on the slow electrodermal response. In contrast, more recent studies have primarily used ERPs with the oddball study as the most popular paradigm. An *oddball study* consists of a sequence of identical stimuli (the standards) with incidental deviations in intensity, duration, spatial location, interstimulus interval, or frequency. The major result is that a deviant stimulus elicits a strong P3 (Donchin, 1981). This led to the conclusion that the P3 reflects stimulus evaluation. In the passive variant of the oddball paradigm, stimuli are completely irrelevant. For instance, participants may carry out a reading task, or they may be instructed to detect target tones among distractors presented

---

[12]The theory has been elaborated in greater physiological detail (e.g., Sokolov, 1975). The same can be said with respect to accounts on the OR in terms of behavioral inhibition (Gray, 1987). They are beyond the scope of this book.

to the right ear, whereas the oddball stimuli are presented to the left ear. In that case, a deviant stimulus elicits mismatch negativity (MMN), which was already referred to in the discussion of early versus late selection. It was mentioned there that the MMN starts at about the same time as the N2 and consists of a further negative shift of the ERP. It is interesting and in line with early selection of physical features, that at least in the passive oddball task, the MMN is only elicited by physical deviants and not by cognitive ones (Näätänen, 1992). An MMN tends to be followed by a more pronounced P3, although, again, less clearly in a passive oddball task. Hence, the P3 might reflect controlled activity following an involuntary attention switch to the deviant. The fact that P3 shows little effect in the passive oddball task is consistent with the view that an unattended deviant may be registered but is not subjected to further analysis. Along the lines proposed by Sokolov, Näätänen (1990) suggested that the MMN reflects a direct neuronal mismatch due to newness and is unrelated to relevance. The argument is that MMN occurs regardless of the relevance of the sensory channel where the stimuli are presented. There remains the possibility, though, that on arrival at the unattended channel, a deviant stimulus is still registered as potentially relevant; consequently, a significance theory is not completely ruled out.

It should be noted that the MMN is mainly found with auditory stimuli and hardly with visual stimuli. This may be seen as a problem for the suggestion that the MMN reflects an OR, but on the other hand, the result may merely reflect that auditory stimuli capture attention more readily. Thus, the MMN may be more pronounced as more divergent visual standards and deviants are used. Again, tactile stimuli capture attention more easily than auditory stimuli do; therefore, MMN should be the most pronounced in a tactile oddball study. These differences between sensory modalities in regard to the MMN suggest that next to behavioral relevance, the type of sensory stimulation affects the OR as well.

The amplitude of the P3 appears to depend on the OR as well but as argued, this may reflect voluntary processing following the OR rather than the OR itself. In line with this view, the effects on P3 amplitude are the most evident in an active oddball study in which deviant stimuli have to be analyzed and further processed. On the other hand, a larger P3 occurs equally in the case of irrelevant deviants that can be achieved by varying the standard. However, as would be expected from an OR, the effect of variations in the standard disappears as practice proceeds. In terms of Soko-lov's (1975) theory, an extended neural model is established; this now also accounts for variations in the standard that an OR is no longer elicited (Rösler, Hasselmann, & Sojka, 1987).

The P3 amplitude is also affected by cognitive deviants, targets as well as nontargets (Nasman & Rosenfeld, 1990). Similarly, Besson and Macar (1987) found that P3 amplitude was sensitive to a deviant stimulus consisting of a change in the gradient of the size of a geometrical pattern, a change in the gradient of the frequency of a tone, and a change in the tune of a well-known melody. In contrast, an N400 was found when the deviant consisted of a word that did not fit into a sentence (e.g., He ate from the computer). Thus, deviations from a semantic sequence differed from deviations from a perceptual event structure. It is worthwile to note that all these effects were only found on P3 and not on MMN. This suggests that they are, indeed, due to subsequent processing and not to capturing involuntary attention.

Applications

The OR and involuntary capturing of attention have positive as well as negative performance effects. A positive effect is that a sudden relevant alarm interrupts ongoing activities and redirects attention in order to cope with a potential danger. As shown, attention is captured more easily by an auditory alarm than by a visual one. The negative effect concerns distraction by irrelevant deviants, and, indeed, most applications are concerned with attempts to prevent distraction. Interruption of ongoing activity is particularly disruptive when contents of working memory are affected. For example, the classic work of Woodhead (1964) showed convincing effects of brief bursts of noise on arithmetic calculations. Subsequent work has shown equally pronounced effects of unexpected noise bursts on active short-term retention (Salame & Wittersheim, 1978). They habituate rapidly, though, suggesting that the effect is caused by the unexpected change rather than by the noise as such. In line with many other findings, noise does not habituate when a deviant stimulus is experienced as relevant, as in the case of aircraft noise in a classroom.

The moral is that one should be careful with auditory alarms, which should only be used to indicate real emergencies. Other deviant stimuli should be avoided because they are merely distracting. Examples are aircraft noise, an intruding conversation, and even sound produced by walking. Blowing a horn in traffic is indispensable as an alarm, but it is also disruptive and leads to ill-considered reactions. Another instance of a negative effect of an alarm, although unrelated to the OR, is that of a fire department that may have a 100dBA alarm that continues for a minute, thus disrupting any verbal communication during that period.

Comments

Automaticity plays a part in a variety of mental processes, among which are motor chunks, feature analysis, covert attending, and S–R compatibility. This discussion centered on three paradigms (i.e., costs–benefits, visual-memory search, and automatic-attention capturing) in order to delineate common features of automatic processing and to illustrate intertwining of automatic and controlled processing. Indeed, one may safely say that hardly any human action is completely automatic in the sense of unintentional, that is, without awareness and free of capacity limits. On the other hand, it was confirmed that extended, consistent practice considerably simplifies information-processing in the sense of more direct connections between stimuli and responses and less involvement from higher control levels in the behavioral hierarchy. It may be objected that the discussion did not address automatic processing in complex skills such as typing or reading. This is postponed to chapter 10. At that time, the back-to-back question is raised to what extent the analysis of complex skills benefits from the presented evidence.

The emphasis was on information flow through stages of processing rather than on capacity limits. In the literature on automaticity, there is actually little reference to the capacity concept apart from the fairly trivial observation that capacity demands are fewer as behavior becomes more automatic. This may be a primitive way of saying that less complex processing structures are involved. Reference to processing structures leads to much more detailed questions than the simple notion of capacity demands. The issue appears again after the discussion of the literature on dual tasks that as said, has been the traditional stronghold of capacity theory.

DIVIDED ATTENTION IN DUAL TASKS

The Capacity Concept

The capacity concept has been so pervasive in research on dual tasks that it is useful to introduce some broad distinctions. First, all that follows is concerned with resource volume, in which the only strategical element is concerned with how to distribute the available resources among tasks without changing the nature of the processes involved. There are three competing capacity models that differ in the way capacity may be allocated (Sanders, 1979). According to Processor A, capacity is a single pool that can be freely allocated to various internal processes and concurrent activities at any particular moment in time (Moray, 1967). The amount of capacity that is devoted to a task is determined by its actual demands. In the case of simultaneous tasks, two activities can be perfectly shared as long as the total capacity limits are not exceeded. Each task has its own program and database. In addition, there is a capacity-consuming coordination program, sometimes labeled *central executive*. In the case of Processor A, it makes perfect sense to speak about capacity devoted to two activities at the same distinct moment in time or, in other words, about parallel performances, in the strictest sense of the word. Although a digital computer operates serially, the time constant of the processor is sufficiently small to forego this property for all practical purposes. Finally, the capacity of the processor is limited, as was the capacity of the computers of the 1960s.

Strictly speaking, Processor B is not a capacity model because it deals with time segments only. The capacity needed for a particular activity is expressed by the time taken by that activity, which, in turn, depends on its demands or complexity. As long as an activity continues, there is no room for any other activity. Thus, allocating capacity equals allocating time, and there is no parallel processing of different activities. The only way in which simultaneous tasks can be carried out together is through allocating time segments of some reasonable duration to either task. Processor B is a single-channel processor that has not played a major role in accounts on dual-task performance but has prominently featured in theories on the psychological refractory period, the prototype of a miniature dual task. In accounts on more complex dual tasks, a Processor A has often been implicitly assumed.

The single, undifferentiated pool of Processor A is fully in line with the original transmission channel of information theory. Alternatively, Processor C assumes distinct resources for different types of internal processing that are not exchangeable. The main consequence of Processor C is that even when demands are high, certain resources remain unused because they simply do not fit. In that case, the question arises as to which internal processes have their own capacity. In principle, the individual capacities of a Processor C can either function as a Processor A or a Processor B, or some could be like A and others like B. Processor C was popular in the multiple-resource account on divided attention. In the following, the emphasis is on Processor A and C models. Processor B is reintroduced in the section on the psychological refractory period.

More recent theoretical views have challenged the basic tenet that capacity is limited and aimed at an alternative conceptual description (Detweiler & Schneider, 1991; Navon, 1984, 1989; Neumann, 1987). It is interesting that the main defenders of the capacity view (Gopher, 1986, 1992; Wickens, 1991) have a strong interest in applications for which the resource concept has some heuristic value, in particular with respect to the measurement of mental load. The new conceptual description leans on activation and inhibition patterns of internal codes at various levels of processing that may interfere when different tasks compete for the same patterns and routes of the information flow.

Single Capacity Models

Three main Processor A models can be distinguished on the basis of their leading metaphors, namely, (a) capacity of a digital computer, (b) energetic capacity, and (c) economical resources.

The Digital Computer. Here, different tasks may be time shared within capacity limits. The total available capacity can be freely shared, but a part of the capacity is consumed by coordination. The P-system in Broadbent (1958) was a fixed-capacity communication channel. Moray's (1967) digital computer metaphor also had a fixed capacity, but in contrast to a communication channel, it could save capacity by more efficient programming, which provides a basis for effects of practice and learning. Yet, this provision in Moray's model abolished the original hope of establishing absolute human capacity limits in terms of bits of information transmission. From the perspective of the computer metaphor, the amount of capacity cannot be determined from performance measures. Moray's model is prototypical for Processor A because capacity is aspecific and accommodates any kind of mental process. This is evident from later formulations, for example, resources are "such things as processing effort, the various forms of memory capacity and communication channels" (Norman & Bobrow, 1975, p. 45), or "acquired information about the structure of particular tasks and about the external world which are used by the subject in order to actively control their perceptual selectivity and their choice of responses" (Rabbitt, 1979, p. 129).

Energetic Capacity. Kahneman (1973) considered attention, capacity, and effort as synonyms. His views were similar to those of Moray (1967) in regard to the idea that there is a single undifferentiated volume of capacity that can be split among tasks and that participants have some freedom in dividing the available means. The main difference is that Kahneman viewed the issues from an energetic perspective. Capacity allocation is mobilization of mental energy that enables the operation of computational-processing mechanisms. The nature of the relations between capacity and computational processes was not stressed by Kahneman. Indeed, this would not be in line with a processor A.

Yet, Kahneman (1973) made a distinction between performance limits due to capacity and structural interference, which referred to anatomical and physiological limits on input and output. One cannot see two things at the same time when stimuli are masked or too far apart in the visual field. It is equally impossible to carry out two responses with the same effector at the same time. Trivial as these constraints are, they still impose drastic limits on human performance,[13] irrespective of processing capacity. With respect to dividing capacity among tasks, Kahneman assumed an allocation policy that depends on momentary intentions, the evaluation of the demands, and utilities.

Kahneman's (1973) model has some additional relevant features. First, capacity is never fully utilized by a task or by a set of tasks. There is always

---

[13]Recently, Meyer et al. (1995) ascribed all performance limits to structural interference.

some spare capacity left to monitor the environment in order to enable detection of relevant new stimuli. Second, the amount of capacity is not fixed but depends on arousal. There is more capacity in a state of high arousal than in a state of of low arousal, although, in line with the inverted-U model, too high a level of arousal may bring about a negative effect on performance. Thus, arousal and capacity covary to some extent but are not identical. After all, there are factors affecting arousal—a high level of stimulation, muscular strain, anger, and anxiety—which are, at best, indirectly related to the amount of available capacity. The most direct relation may be that high-task demands tend to raise the level of arousal that increases capacity through positive feedback. Third, the difficulty of a task is defined in terms of capacity consumption; a more difficult task simply has more demands. The meaning of difficulty was barely specified by Kahneman. The aforementioned assumptions led to a relation between performance and capacity consumption, as shown in Fig. 8.6.

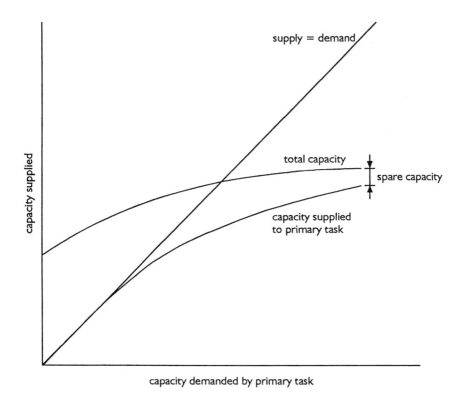

FIG. 8.6. Capacity demand and supply in Kahneman's (1973) model. From Kahneman, D. (1973). *Attention and effort.* Copyright © 1973 by Prentice-Hall, Inc., Upper Saddle River, NJ. Reproduced with permission from the publisher.

A consequence of this view is that behavioral measures are inadequate for analyzing capacity allocation because one does not know the amount of spare capacity or how much capacity is available at any particular moment. Instead, Kahneman (1973) proposed that capacity consumption should be estimated by physiological indexes, and he favored pupil dilatation as the most promising one. Thus, pupil dilatation increased as a larger number of auditorily presented alphanumerics had to be rehearsed. Pupil dilatation has the serious problem that due to its sensitivity to light, it is unsuitable as a measure of capacity consumption in most visual conditions. Thus, despite the fact that various results have confirmed the idea that pupil size covaries with processing demands (Beatty, 1982), this restriction has probably prohibited a thorough follow-up of Kahneman's proposal. Still, the development of performance-independent physiological measures of capacity allocation has remained a prime research issue, in particular in the area of mental load.

Economical Resources.   The final Processor A-type capacity model derived from an economical metaphor in which capacity is a matter of a fixed amount of scarce resources that are distributed over tasks according to a priority prescribed by the relative utility of the tasks. An important development was Norman and Bobrow's (1975) notion of the performance-resource function (PRF) that describes the relation between performance and resource investment. A PRF has two portions, respectively labeled *resource limited* and *data limited*. In the *resource-limited* portion, performance improves as more resources are allocated. This continues until an asymptote is reached. The *data-limited* portion of the PRF starts when the asymptote is reached. It is concerned with the area in which performance does not further improve when more resources are allocated (Fig. 8.7).

The data-limited portion of the function reflects the wisdom that in many tasks, one gains little by trying harder. Performance may be limited because one cannot do better than perfect. For example, it takes some resources to retain a three-digit number for 5 minutes, but performance cannot be improved by investing more resources than are actually needed to rehearse the three digits. Other tasks (i.e., reading words in an unknown language) cannot be performed at all, irrespective of how many resources are invested. There are other tasks, though, in which performance improves by investing more resources. They have in common that performance is suboptimal. As an example, pressure to do better has an effect on performance in vigilance tasks. Instructions to do better also increase the rate of solving self-paced sequences of simple arithmetic problems (Yeh & Wickens, 1988). This evidence nothwithstanding, it is usually not feasible to obtain empirical PRFs by varying instructions about resource investment. The problem is that participants cannot easily be instructed to perform suboptimally.

The differences among the A models are nicely illustrated by the way the notion of task difficulty is viewed. In the economical model, task difficulty

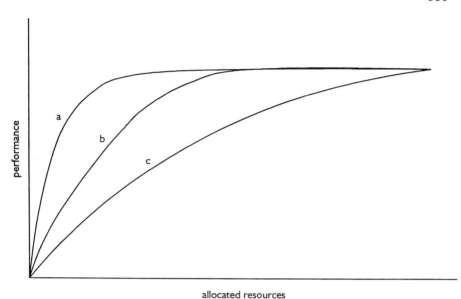

FIG. 8.7. A performance-resource function plots performance as a function of allocated resources. In an easy task (a), data limits are reached much sooner than in the more difficult tasks (b, c). Difficulty is defined as marginal efficiency of a resource.

is defined as the marginal efficiency of resources or, in other words, as the slope of the resource-limited part of the PRF. In an easy task, one gets more performance for a single resource than in a difficult task. This means that an easy task benefits considerably when a few extra resources are allocated (Fig. 8.7A), whereas a difficult task benefits much less (Fig. 8.7B & Fig. 8.7C). In contrast, a reduction in resources, when proportionally divided between two tasks, should have a larger negative effect on the easier task. This has actually been the common finding (Navon & Gopher, 1979).

There is an essential difference between this position and the one in which difficulty is defined in terms of resource demands (Kahneman, 1973). Here, a difficult task consumes more capacity, thus leaving less spare capacity for a second one. The result is a waterglass model. A difficult task fills most of the glass, leaving only a little space for another, easier task. If capacity is reduced, that is, if the glass gets smaller and if the reduction is proportionally divided between both tasks, then the difficult task suffers more because that task fills most of the glass.

The difference between the models is that the economical view assumes that participants always aim at maximal resource investment. Irrespective of whether a task is easy or difficult, participants always spend all resources. The difference between a difficult task and an easy one is simply that participants perform more units on the easy task than on the difficult one, but total resource investment is the same in either case. For example, more reactions are completed per unit time in a two-choice than in a five-choice self-paced serial-reaction task, but all available resources are invested in either task.

It is common to plot dual-task performance on a Performance Operating Characteristic (POC) that describes the exchange relation between two performances. Some possibilities are described in Fig. 8.8. Figure 8.8A is a 45° linear exchange relation in which case both tasks are equally hard to do. Deviations from 45° (Figs. 8.8B and 8.8C) mean that Task A and Task B differ in difficulty. Indeed, reallocation of a few resources from the harder to the easier task is more benificial to the easier task because there, resources have a larger marginal efficiency. In all three cases, there is full resource utilization, whatever the performance combination. This is evident from the fact that Task A suffers when a few resources are reallocated to Task B, and vice versa. Again, if fewer resources would be available and if this reduction would be proportionally divided between the two tasks, the easy task would suffer more.

The key question is, of course, whether the two tasks can utilize all available resources. This may not be the case when they are highly data-

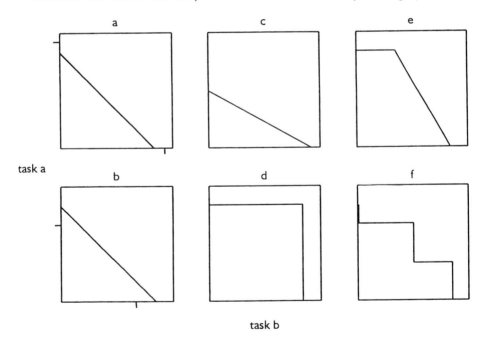

FIG. 8.8. Examples of performance-operating-characteristics (POC), depicting potential performance trade-offs between two tasks. Figs. 8a, 8b, and 8c show examples of linear trade-off. Fig. 8d illustrates that both tasks can be combined without any performance loss on either one, whereas Fig. 8e shows initial time-sharing followed by a linear trade-off. Finally, Fig. 8f shows the case in which trade-off is not gradual, but occurs in a few rough steps.

limited; thus, the glass cannot be filled to capacity. As a consequence, the waterglass model applies. However, the economical view holds that dual-task performance should not be studied and, actually, cannot be theoretically tested under data-limited conditions.

Figure 8.8D pictures the case in which both tasks are perfectly time shared. Due to data limits, they cannot consume all available resources, not even when carried out together. For example, Task A might consist of incidental dial-reading and Task B incidental, mental calculations. In Fig. 8.8E, maximal performance on Task A does not consume all available resources either; this enables some performance on Task B without affecting performance on Task A, followed by a linear exchange relation between the two tasks.[14] Figure 8.8F describes the situation in which switching resources from Task A to B occurs in a few discrete steps. Finally, Figs. 8.8A and 8.8B introduce the concepts of concurrence costs and benefits. The indexes on the abscissa and the ordinate indicate performance in Task A or Task B when performed singly. The fact that one is faced with two tasks may take already some resources for coordination (concurrence costs; Fig. 8.8A), even if all emphasis is on Task A and none on Task B. Alternatively, performing Task A may benefit from a combination with Task B due to task integration or to common timing of actions.[15] Thus, parameters of Task B may be beneficial to performance on Task A, even when all resources are devoted to Task A (concurrence benefits; Fig. 8.8B).

Problems for Single-Resource Models

A number of experiments have shown that a single-capacity view is too simple. First, there are various reports suggesting that after extended practice, complex tasks, such as piano playing or typing, on the one hand, and shadowing, on the other hand, can be time shared without considerable loss of efficiency in either one (Allport et al., 1972; Rollins & Hendricks, 1980; Shaffer, 1975). Yet, this is only found when participants are highly proficient in piano playing or typing. It can be argued, therefore, that the actions have become automatized; thus, resource demands are reduced to a level on which additional shadowing is possible. In another study, split–

---

[14]This is, in fact, most consistent with a type A processor. Task A has data limits, so there remains spare capacity. Performing Task B can concur with Task A until all resources are used. Adding more demands on Task B, then, leads to a reduction in performance on Task A. The question whether Tasks A and B are really processed in parallel may be studied by considering whether Task A uses all available time.

[15]Concurrence benefits are a violation of the notion of task invariance and, therefore, a test of that assumption. For instance, Helmuth and Ivry (1996) found, in a study on repetitive tapping, that within-hand variability was reduced when tapping with both hands in comparison to tapping with one hand. The authors proposed separate timing mechanisms for each hand, the output of which is integrated prior to executing a tap.

span recall between modalities (an auditory and a visual group of digits) proved superior to split–span recall within a modality (both groups auditory or visual).[16] Again, detecting a specific letter combination within a word, presented in either one of two simultaneously presented lists (divided attention)—for example, "end" in Brenda, lender, endear, pretend—was better when monitoring one auditory list and one visual list than when both lists were auditory or visual (Treisman & Davies, 1973). When participants were instructed to focus on one list, performance proved much less dependent on the modality of the other list. More generally, instructions to focus led to better performance than did instructions to divide attention. Thus, presenting an auditory and a visual list did not eliminate all limits on processing. Together, the data suggest separate input analyzers for the auditory and the visual modalities that, then, converge with a common central system.

Problems for a single-resource model also arose from what Wickens (1992) called *structural alterations*, which refer to changes in the structure of a task while keeping its difficulty constant. For instance, one may carry out a manual-tracking task in combination with a choice-reaction task and find that simultaneous performance interferes more when the choice reactions are carried out manually than vocally (Vidulich, 1988; Wickens, 1980). The same effect had been noticed by Trumbo and Milone (1971), who found better vocal recall than written recall of digits when performed in combination with manual tracking. One may ascribe this difference to structural interference, albeit conceived in quite a wider sense than originally implied by Kahneman. Still, manual tracking with one hand may be hard to combine with discrete responding with the other hand, so the preceding results may not reflect a capacity limit. In other studies, the difficulty of a task was manipulated, which, surprisingly at first sight, did not always affect performance in the second task. In a classical study by North (1977), participants responded to digits whose difficulty was varied by changing S–R compatibility. The effect of compatibility variation was quite pronounced when the second task consisted of canceling certain critical digits. Digit canceling was done more poorly when the CRT task was incompatible. However, the compatibility manipulation had no effect when manual tracking was the second task (difficulty insensitivity).

---

[16]This may seem at odds with earlier findings (Broadbent, 1958) that suggested that performance in split–span recall was about equally good, irrespective of splitting between or within modalities. It may be noted that first, all studies agree that pair-wise recall is always deficient, irrespective of whether the span is split between or within modalities. Second, in the earlier studies the comparisons of channel-wise recall between and within modalities were across experiments, whereas Treisman and Davies compared split–span recall between and within modalities in a single experiment. Finally, Treisman and Davies (1973) observed that split–span recall between modalities also benefited when their output modes differed (written visual recall and vocal auditory recall). The older studies had always used the same output mode for both groups of items.

Navon and Gopher (1979) and Heuer (1985) argued that a valid test of a single-resource theory requires four tasks (A, B, C, D). If Task A interferes more with Task C than with Task D, then Task B should also interfere more with Task C than with Task D. One of the earliest results that violated this test stemmed from Brooks (1968), who found that a task requiring spatial working memory (Task A) was performed better in combination with a verbal processing task (Task C), whereas a task requiring verbal working memory (Task B) could be performed better in combination with a spatial processing task (Task D). Again, Wickens and Sandry (1982) had participants perform a memory-search task with either verbal (Task A) or spatial stimuli (Task B), a manual-tracking task (Task C) and a memory task for abstract words (Task D). Verbal memory search (A) was more easily combined with manual tracking (C) than with recalling abstract words (D). Yet, spatial memory search was performed better in combination with recalling abstract words (D) than with tracking (C). Various other examples of studies that also violate the four-tasks principle are discussed by Wickens (1992).

Another test of the single-capacity view was proposed by Navon and Gopher (1979). It is based on the fact that the PRF of an easier task has a steeper slope than the PRF of a harder task (Fig. 8.7). The implication is that when either an easier or a more difficult task is combined with a third task (Fig. 8.9A), the slope of the easier task in the POC should be steeper than the slope of the harder task, provided that no data limits are hit in either task. When the first two tasks tap different resources, a difference in slope cannot be predicted. For example, the easier task may not share many resources with the third task and, therefore, may suffer little in the dual-task condition. The harder task may have more in common with the third task and, therefore, may suffer more from time sharing than the easy task. This reasoning reminds of the AFM logic for CRTs, which is also based on patterns of mutual relations among task conditions. An interaction in the POC would suggest that both tasks tap a common resource, whereas additive effects would imply that different resources are tapped. The analogy can be seen as a nice example of back-to-back convergence between the stage- and the multiple-resource approach (Gopher & Sanders, 1984).[17]

The preceding test was applied by Gopher, Brickner, and Navon (1982). They combined manual pursuit tracking with serial reactions in which a chord of two responses was produced to a stimulus letter. The difficulty of the serial-reaction task was varied. In the easy condition, four compatible letter–

---

[17]The AFM uses physical time units; thus, additivity and interactions are directly interpretable. Resource theory has the complication that any performance measure may be used, so scale transformations are permitted. Hence, one has to justify unit and scale of measurement before additivities and interactions can be properly interpreted (Gopher & Sanders, 1984). The consequence is that "stage analysis" by measuring POCs is troublesome and may be only worthwhile in the case of well-argued advance hypotheses about separate resources.

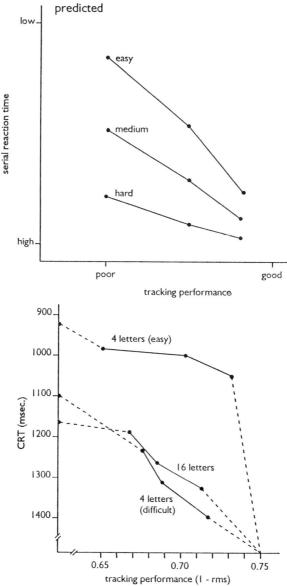

FIG. 8.9. A. The upper part illustrates the prediction of a unidimensional resource model that in the case of a combination of a serial-reaction and a tracking task, the effects of the demands on the serial-reaction task, and performance trade-off should interact. B. The lower part shows that this prediction was not confirmed. In fact, the easy serial-reaction task could be almost time shared with tracking, whereas the harder versions showed a linear trade-off. From Gopher, D., Brickner, M., & Navon, D. (1982). Different difficulty manipulations interact differently with task emphasis: Evidence for multiple resources. *Journal of Experimental Psychology: Human Perception & Performance, 8,* 146–157. Copyright © 1982 by the American Psychological Association. Reprinted with permission.

chord combinations were used; another harder condition had four incompatible letter–chord combinations; and a final condition had 16 letter–chord combinations with some compatible and incompatible chords. In order to obtain a POC, the relative priority of manual tracking and serial responding was varied. The results show that compatible serial responding suffered little when tracking had more priority, whereas there was an about equal steeper slope for the other two conditions (Fig. 8.9B). This is at odds with a single-resource model that, as previously argued, predicts a steeper slope for the easy task.

Multiple Resources

Multiple resources were first proposed around 1980 (Navon & Gopher, 1979; Sanders, 1979; Wickens, 1980, 1984) and were readily accepted to meet the growing problems for the Processor A. Before discussing some of the pertinent results, it is relevant to consider a few properties of a Processor C. First, it usually has much spare capacity, namely, whenever a task cannot utilize certain categories of resources. This has consequences for behavioral measures of perceptual–motor load, which will be discussed later in this chapter. Second, a Processor C creates a considerable problem for the notion of task difficulty because a simple definition in terms of resource demands or marginal efficiency of a resource no longer applies. One task may considerably load on particular resource pool but only use very little of the other pools. Another task may require all resource pools but without imposing a heavy load on any of them. Which task is harder? A multiple-regression analysis is needed, with appropriate weights for each resource pool.

One may indeed try to solve the problem by some weighing function, but this will probably turn out to be quite complex when one wants to comply with intuitive notions about difficulty. For instance, a task is usually considered to be hard when it cannot be successfully completed. This is the case when one resource type is overloaded while the other resource categories may be fully unused. Should this task be considered as more difficult than a task in which all resources are mildly loaded? Are there easy tasks that are still hard to do? Or is it better to abandon the difficulty notion altogether as scientifically unsound?

Multiple resources also cause problems for a single-attention mechanism. The single-capacity view could simply define attention in terms of resource allocation. Other problems concern assessment of the various resources and the danger that their number proliferates. There is an analogy with research on intelligence, which started out with one general factor and ended with a range of specific factors (Heuer, 1985), although, more recently, the swing seems to be on its way back. One might be led on in the hope that the number of resources are limited to a few main dimensions. Wickens (1984) proposed a 3-D structure consisting of processing mechanisms, codes of input, and modalities of input as elementary resource categories.

The processing mechanism dimension is thought to consist of two resources, one relating to perceptual–cognitive and the other to response processes. This suggestion reminds of the energetical resources, one controlling perceptual and the other response processes in Sanders' cognitive-energetic model. There are actually various studies that suggest two tasks can be combined best when one has primarily perceptual, and the other primarily response, characteristics. In one study, Kalsbeek (1967) found heavy interference between a paced, auditory binary-choice task and various perceptual–motor tasks, including handwriting and maze drawing. However, there was little interference between the binary-choice task and solving Raven matrices—a visual pattern-discrimination test in which loading the response system is hardly loaded. In the same way, Michon (1966) found interference between generating a regular interval through manual or foot tapping and a range of perceptual–motor tasks. However, Brown (1978) noted that tapping interfered much less when the second-task demands were primarily perceptual. Shingledecker et al. (quoted in O'Donnell & Eggemeier, 1986) studied the issue more systematically and combined tapping with more or less demanding tracking, Sternberg target classification, and display monitoring. The results show that tapping was more irregular as the demands on tracking increased but not when the demands on target classification or display monitoring increased (e.g., Donk & Sanders, 1989). Several similar findings were discussed by Wickens (1991, 1992) and by O'Donnell and Eggemeyer (1986).

The *codes of processing* dimension refers to violations of the single-resource notion when combining spatial and verbal tasks. Indeed, there is considerable evidence that verbal and spatial processes differ along all levels of information flow, perceptual, central as well as motor. The evidence on the perceptual level was already met in the context of focused attention and visual search. The body of research on the close association between the spatial–verbal dimension and the cerebral hemispheres—the left hemisphere specialized in verbal–discrete processing and the right hemisphere in spatial–analog processing—is only mentioned in passing (e.g., Polson & Friedman, 1988). On the behavioral level, there is a wealth of evidence from research on working memory. In one study, Sanders and Schroots (1969) found that when measured singly, the memory span for spatial positions and for alphanumerics amounted to, respectively, some four and seven items. In combination (i.e., a list of digits followed by a list of spatial positions for subsequent serial recall), the span amounted to about 10 items, suggesting that the two lists are stored fairly independently. Subsequent evidence on the nature of verbal and spatial codes has resulted in the notion of a phonological rehearsal loop and a visuospatial sketchpad as distinct, short-term memory systems (Baddeley, 1986, 1996).

On the response level, the main distinction is between vocal and manual responses. There is much evidence that a combination of two tasks that both require manual responses is harder than when one task requires a manual response and the other a vocal one. The evidence stems in particular from continuous tracking or serial responding by key pressing as the primary task and discrete manual or vocal responses to probe stimuli as the second task.

Visual versus auditory input was thought to reflect separate input modality resources (Wickens, 1984) in order to explain results such as Treisman and Davies' (1973) that sharing an auditory and a visual message is easier than sharing two auditory or two visual messages. However, more recently, Wickens (1991) reconsidered his position. Although performance in cross-modal dual tasks is often superior to that in intramodal dual tasks, it is hard to exclude a potential contribution of structural interference due to auditory masking in the case of simultaneous, auditory messages and to peripheral acuity in the case of simultaneous, visual messages. When structural interference was properly controlled, there was even evidence that a continuous visual task—for example, tracking—was interrupted more by an additional auditory than by an additional visual stimulus, either of which required a discrete choice response (Wickens & Liu, 1988). The auditory stimulus may have induced a shift on the POC in its favor and at the cost of tracking rather than produced a processing benefit due to better cross-modal processing efficiency.

The multiple-resource view has the merit of capturing an important aspect of dual-task performance, namely, that there are various processing dimensions that function fairly independently. Thus, most examples of almost perfect time sharing (Allport et al., 1972; Shaffer, 1975) concerned tasks that differed on all three of Wickens' dimensions. Piano playing proceeds from a visual input to an analogue central representation to a manual sequence of responses, whereas shadowing consists of an auditory input, a verbal code, and a vocal output. The differences between the dimensions were less in the case of Shaffer's secretary, who was capable of time sharing typing and shadowing without a noticeable loss in either task. The inputs and outputs differed, but at least intuitively, both typing and shadowing seem to appeal to verbal processing resources. It is not excluded, though, that in expert typing, visual letter features are directly translated into motor commands. Thus, the typing speed of experts precludes that each word is internally vocalized before being passed on to the motor system. It is relevant to note that Shaffer's participants were extremely proficient in their primary task, namely, piano playing and typing,[18] which might have led to data limits and, therefore, to less resource utilization.

---

[18]It is not easy to replicate Shaffer's findings. I once tried it with a highly proficient department secretary but failed to find perfect time sharing. Where have all the perfect secretaries gone?

Perfect time sharing is not very common, and if observed, requires a high level of practice. For example, Donk and Sanders (1989) had participants share tapping a regular interval and counting the number of targets in a visual target-search task. In the latter, a sequence of frames was presented, with a D of four and an M of two items (Shiffrin & Schneider, 1977). The demands on counting were manipulated by varying the presentation rate of the frames between one and two per second. A sequence of frames was presented for a minute, whereon the number of detected targets was reported. The rationale was to create a situation in which one task—tapping—had no perceptual input, an analogue central representation, and a manual overt motor-output. In contrast, counting had a visual input, a verbal central representation, and no overt motor-output, thus, creating ideal conditions for perfect time sharing via multiple resources. The instructions emphasized counting, and indeed, counting performance was about equally well in the dual and the single tasks. In line with the findings on difficulty insensitivity, tapping performance was not affected by the demands on counting targets. Yet, tapping was much more regular in the single task than in the dual task. This argues against perfect time sharing, which might be expected when multiple resources are involved.

Again, in the case of strictly independent, discrete serial reactions, there is little evidence for better time sharing when the input or output modalities are the same or different. Thus, Gladstones, Regan, and Lee (1989) had participants perform two paced, serial-reaction tasks, singly and in combination, and found no indication for better shared performance when the stimuli of one task were visual and of the other task auditory in comparison with visual stimuli in both tasks. Performance did not profit from a difference in effectors, that is, when one task had a vocal and the other a manual response in comparison with two manual responses.

A related problem concerns the so-called visual dominance effect. In a classical study, Colavita (1971) required participants to respond as fast as possible to either a light (with one hand) or to a tone (with the other hand). On incidental occasions, the stimuli were presented simultaneously, whereon participants tended to respond to the light only. Klein and Posner (1974) obtained a similar result when visual and tactual stimuli were occasionally presented together. Again, when the stimuli consisted of a combination of a light and a displacement of a limb, CRT to the displacement stimulus was slower than when the displacement stimulus was presented alone. Posner, Nissen, and Klein (1976) argued that visual dominance implies that attention is primarily focused on visual stimulation at the cost of information from other sensory sources. Yet, this suggestion is incompatible with the notion of different resources for visual and auditory information that predicts information from both modalities can be processed in parallel. From a multiple-resource perspective, one should expect that when a visual and an auditory stimulus are presented together, participants cannot escape from carrying out both responses at the same time.[19]

Neumann (1987) suggested that two responses may be particularly hard to time share when they reflect independent actions. The prototypical example is the psychological refractory period (PRP), which is discussed in the next section. In contrast, well-practiced, complex tasks do not consist of independent stimuli and responses but of integrated and mutually related sequences summarized in chunks and groups of actions initiated by a single command. New sequences of stimuli can be encoded, and selections can be made while a previous string of reactions is still being executed. This may provide skilled performance its continuous and flexible appearance. In other words, practice may have the effect that response sequencing in skills such as typing and piano playing becomes largely a matter of the motor stages rather than of response selection. Response selection is freed for other activities, and performance limits are more closely tied to the effector systems. These views are fully in line with the results from Verwey's laboratory studies.

Attention Control and Practice

The preceding results have sometimes been taken as suggesting an additional central general purpose or control resource responsible for scheduling and selecting resources, much in the sense of N. Moray's (1967) coordinating program, Keele's common timing mechanism for perception and action (e.g., Keele, Pokorny, Corcos, & Ivry, 1985) and Baddeley's (1996) executive controller. This resource may have a Processor B type of bottleneck in that it is easily overloaded. Thus, when performances in a dual task are resource limited—so that there are heavy demands on resource scheduling—a performance loss may be due to deficient scheduling rather than to specific resource limits. If one or both tasks have data limits, scheduling is easier, so perfect time sharing should become more possible. Scheduling is often seen as a matter of attention control, which implies a strategical principle or an allocation policy (Kahneman, 1973). Relevant issues for research on attention control are (a) the extent to which a person is aware of how resources are allocated to different tasks, (b) how successful one is in controlling relative allocation, (c) the refinement of changes in allocating resources, (d) the costs and benefits of alternative strategies, and (e) the trainability of attention control (Gopher, 1992).

There are various examples of successful strategic control. It was argued earlier in chapter 7 that one is capable of voluntarily setting the zoom lens. In

---

[19]Visual dominance is mainly found in case of reactions to stimuli from a regular stream of visual and auditory information so that they may have been habituated. Thus, the effect should not be confused with orienting to incidentally occurring stimuli.

divided attention, changes in priority between two tasks lead to graded shifts along the POC (e.g., Gopher et al., 1982). Moreover, one may shift priority from one task to another, although this is not always perfect or easy. For instance, more refined variations in priority among tasks cannot be achieved simply by instruction. They need augmented feedback[20] about the desired relative emphasis. Again, a low-priority task requires a minimal level of control in order to achieve anything at all. Below that minimal level, performance drops to zero. The notion of an executive controller repeatedly recurs and is considered in more detail in a subsequent section in this chapter.

As evident from the findings on perfect time sharing, practice has highly pronounced effects on dual-task performance. In single-resource theory, this has been simply interpreted in terms of reduced capacity demands following automatization. However, there is evidence that the pattern of demands changes as a function of practice as well (Fleishman & Hempel, 1955; Heuer, 1984). Some demands decrease, whereas others may increase (Logie, Baddeley, Mane, Donchin, & Sheptak, 1989). Thus, a verbal component often plays a role in early practice of a perceptual–motor task but vanishes almost completely in later practice. Instead, a motor–speed component gains significance. This affects the pattern of dual-task interference rather than simply diminishes capacity demands. In fact, some combinations of dual tasks may actually suffer from practice, namely, those that, when practiced, appeal more to the same resources. In general, though, the changing pattern of abilities as a function of practice supports the earlier argument that automatic processing is a matter of less involvement of higher cognitive levels and more integrated activities of lower levels. As concluded from the studies on the AFM, critical and time-consuming stages are bypassed.

The aforementioned results still fit a multiple-resource theory. However, attention control itself profits from practice as well. For example, practicing two single tasks until full proficiency—thus, strongly diminishing their resource demands—does not mean that they can be easily carried out together. Schneider and Fisk (1984) had participants perform three types of single tasks, namely, searching for particular digits, and detecting targets for CM and VM word categories. After extensive practice in the single tasks, digit search and word-category detection, either in a CM or a VM setting, were carried out concurrently. This had the effect of a heavy performance loss in either case. The combination of digit search and CM word-category search benefited from additonal dual-task practice, whereas digit search and the VM word-category task did not. Indeed, this result suggests the relevance of automatic processing as well as of specific dual-task practice. Again, Venturino (1991) found a dramatic performance decrement when, after in-

---

[20]There should be continuously displayed measures of both performances, showing the relative trade-off.

tensive practice on single tasks, participants performed a dual task, irrespective of whether the codes of the two tasks came from the same—for example, verbal–verbal—or from different resources—for example, verbal–spatial. Yet, in line with the results on multiple resources, dual tasks with codes from different resources profited more from continued dual-task practice. Finally, Detweiler and Lundy (1995) found a decrement when shifting from single- to dual-task performance in the case of two CM tasks, which argues directly against a simple resource notion. The applied consequence is that when a job consists of dual-task performance, single-task training has its limits. One should start practicing the dual task fairly soon. This is not to say that part-task training is useless. As mentioned earlier, CM parts of a complex task benefit from training in isolation. There is merely the warning that a total task is more than the sum of its parts.

The moral is that scheduling and coordinating task elements is a skill that develops over time and adds to proficient dual-task performance as well as to the impressive effects of practice (Hirst, Spelke, Reaves, Caharack, & Neisser, 1980; Neisser, 1976).[21] The role of practice on scheduling has also been illustrated by Gopher (1992), who found that when practicing a combination of tracking and letter typing, participants did better when the relative priority between the two tasks was varied across trials than when it was kept constant. Again, training on a complex video game (i.e., Space Fortress) had more effect when the instructed priority of the components of the game was varied across trials than when priority was kept constant (Gopher et al., 1989). Both results not only suggest the relevance of practicing dual-task performance as such, but also of practicing flexibility in attention control through variations in the allocation of different amounts of resources to different tasks. Can it be concluded, then, that there are stable, individual differences in attention control? This question is returned to later in this chapter.

As suggested, one of the functions of the general resource might be coordination of the different tasks and timing of their properties (e.g., Keele et al., 1985). Indeed, there is ample evidence that performance benefits from activating common processing routines and timing mechanisms. For instance, performance of two tracking tasks is better when their temporal dynamics are the same than when they deviate (e.g., Fracker & Wickens, 1989). In the same way, two rhythmic activities can be more easily time shared when their rhythms are the same or have, at least, some simple relation, whereas it is much harder when the rhythms differ in a complex way (e.g., Klapp, 1981).

---

[21]It should be added that Hirst et al. (1980) largely ignored potential automatization of individual tasks in successful dual-task performance. Moreover, there may also be automatization in scheduling and coordinating elementary operations of either task. Resource theories do not offer anything about how automatization may develop or about how processing may change over time.

Still, the preceding instances might reflect more efficient resource utilization within a specific motor resource and not coordination among different resources. The problem is that the available options for coordination and common timing are not always utilized. For example, Donk and Sanders (1989) varied the presentation rate of the frames in their study on simultaneous search and tapping discussed earlier. In the fast condition, the average presentation rate of the frames was the same as the instructed tapping rate (two per second); in the slow condition, the average presentation rate was half the tapping rate (one per second); and in the third condition, the rate of presentation was between the fast and the slow ones. Moreover, the presentation rates of the frames were either constant or somewhat variable. The reasoning was that tapping regularity should benefit from a constant fast rate because this would allow synchronizing a tap with the arrival of a frame. In contrast, an intermediate variable presentation rate of the frames did not allow any synchronization at all. Yet, the results failed to show any effect of variations in presentation rate on the regularity or the average interval of tapping, which suggests that no common timing had been achieved.[22] This may be due to the fact that the tasks had very little in common. Visual search and tapping were used in order to eliminate any overlap between the two tasks. They are a typical example, therefore, of what Sperling (1984) coined concurrent tasks.

Sperling (1984) distinguished *concurrent tasks*—that is, tasks without common stimuli and responses—from *compound tasks*, in which the stimuli and responses are inherently interactive and competing. What is done in one task must affect performance in the other; therefore, outcome conflict and interference among tasks should be much more pronounced. This distinction is not far from a reformulation of multiple-resource theory. It should be noted that terms such as *interference* and *output conflict* suggest negative effects, but positive effects are not excluded, provided that the two tasks have a common inherent structure from which their performances benefit. Practice often has the effect that originally multiple tasks integrate into a single one (e.g., Korteling, 1994). Integration is obviously related to automatization, although on a more complex level than in the earlier discussions on automaticity.

Outcome Conflict and Interference

During the 1980s, the heuristic value of resource models came under considerable attack (Navon, 1984, 1985; Neumann, 1987). One criticism con-

---

[22]Similarly, Detweiler and Lundy (1995) hardly found any effect of synchronous or asynchronous presentation of verbal and spatial displays in a dual-CM detection task. Participants who practiced with synchronous displays showed no decrement when transferred to the asynchronous condition.

cerned the notion of limited capacity itself that was fostered by the enormous capacity of the brain—and of the new generation of computers. Broadbent (1971) suggested, "If the presence or absence of all possible patterns from all the sense-organs is being analysed simultaneously, the number of possible combinations is very large" (p. 147). Neumann (1987) argued that this statement is debatable because it is unlikely that irrespective of focusing or dividing attention, participants attempt analyzing all possible combinations. Second, there is the critique that capacity theory never provided any detailed process model on performance limits. It simply stated that capacity is limited. Performance limits were ascribed to presumed capacity limits which is a *vertus dormitiva* as long as it is not specified how and why capacity is limited. Indeed, perhaps most importantly, the metaphor of the limited-capacity computer is no longer current, replaced as this device is by the new generation of parallel processors with virtually unlimited capacity.

A third criticism is that, "On the one hand interference is usually much more specific than predicted on the basis of a limited amount of resources, and on the other hand there is quite unspecific interference that seems not to depend on any specific resource" (Neumann, 1987, p. 365). As a case of specific interference, there appears to be more cross-talk between two simultaneous arithmetic tasks than between a spelling task and an arithmetic task, despite the fact that all three tasks are supposed to use the same verbal resource (Hirst & Kalmar, 1987). In contrast, irrespective of the nature of the stimuli, there is almost always heavy interference in the case of the PRP. As recently confirmed by Gladstones et al. (1989) for the condition of two simultaneous, serial-reaction tasks, the results on the PRP show that CRT is invariably delayed, irrespective of input or output modality or of the level of practice. There are other instances as well in which performance benefits little from practice, as in the case of target classification with VM. As a fourth critique of the capacity concept, nothing is gained by postulating a new resource for each new case in which time sharing is found. As an alternative, therefore, dual-task limits tend to be ascribed to interference, for example, confusion and cross-talk among competing processes.

Wickens (1991) also acknowledged the occurrence of interference beyond resources, which he considered to be particularly relevant when two tasks are similar and, thus, require the same type of resources. There may be *cooperation*—conceived of as a single, more complex action plan for both tasks—or *confusion*, which refers to problems in establishing correct connections between inputs and outputs. Thus, when performing two simultaneous spelling tasks or two simultaneous mental arithmetic tasks, there are problems of separating elements of the two individual tasks. This makes it hard to avoid cross-talk or outcome conflict (Hirst & Kalmar, 1987; Neisser, 1976). This has led to the formulation of alternative theory, away from limited capacity and toward analyzing demands on mental functions and processes in a common abstract space. As task demands are closer in that space, their processes are more likely to interfere.

Allport (1980b) and Kinsbourne and Hicks (1978) were among the first more recent investigators to defend an interference account of performance limits. In their view, dual-task interference is due to competition for the same type of codes during the information flow. Individual codes activated by either of two tasks may be confused on various levels. Moreover, there is potential confusion when combining inputs with their appropriate outputs. In this case, the S–R rules appropriate for one task may intrude into the other task and vice versa. For example, Shafffer (1975) reported that his secretary occasionally typed words that should have been shadowed and shadowed words that should have been typed. These examples concern confusion. Alternatively, codes may be overruled or merge. In a dual task consisting of manual tracking and discrete choice reactions, tracking proficiency impaired briefly before a choice reaction (Netick & Klapp, 1994), which result was ascribed to outcome conflict in motor programming and preparation. In the motor domain, there are examples of merging through coupling simultaneous movements. In the perceptual domain, stimuli of either task are liable to be missed when they are not separately processed. A failure to do so may be due to sensory masking or to integration of stimuli into a single perceptual unit—a new common Gestalt.

Confusion among input and output codes was also found in a study by Navon and Miller (1987), in which two words were simultaneously presented, one on the left and one on the right, each with a different instruction with respect to classification. For example, the word on the left should be classified in terms of whether it was the name of a city (yes–no), whereas the word on the right had to be classified in terms of whether it was a person's name. CRT increased when the words on the left and on the right were identical—for example, Washington, which is a city as well as a person's name. The effect on CRT was still more pronounced when the same word— for example, New York—required a "yes" (left) and a "no" (right) response. According to Navon and Miller, these results argue against a capacity explanation. The resource demands of one task—for example, city naming— should not be affected by the type of information in the other task—that is, person naming. Instead, the results indicate cross-talk between competing S–R connections.

Neumann (1987) suggested two major reasons for the occurrence of performance limits. They are both concerned with controlling action, namely, effector recruitment and parameter specification. Effector recruitment refers to selecting "which skills are allowed to recruit which effectors at a given moment in time" (p. 376); thus, performance limits are due to organization and coordination of action. The main role of effector recruitment is inhibiting and aborting competing response tendencies in favor of the selected one.

In this way, effector recruitment may lead to a bottleneck in response selection.[23]

As mentioned in chapter 4, parameter specification refers to getting the proper parameter values for completing an intended action. Practice has the effect that parameters acquire *default values*, which means that they are fixed within certain limits and become part of a hierarchically organized automatic action plan. Default values imply utilization of direct standard connections between input and output. This merely reiterates the earlier discussions on automaticity. Catching a ball is an example. Experienced catchers use default values and do not need to actively specify the parameters of any individual movement involved in catching. However, when less practiced, specification has to take place before an action can be initiated. In the same way, when an individual is inexperienced in typing, each movement to a specific key should be separately specified. Parameter specification is always concerned with selecting appropriate objects—words, stimuli, keys—among many available ones. As argued, parameter specification at the time of an action prohibits other actions to occur at the same time.

In summary, the general tenet of Neumann's (1987) paper is that selective attention is not a matter of capacity limitations of a processor that forces participants to choose among potential alternatives. Instead, selection is needed to guarantee consistent response selection and action among the many distracting options. It is a typical late-selection view with the exception of the *interrupt mode*, which has the function of signaling that something important happened in the environment.

A similar approach was proposed by Navon (1989) who suggested an anarchic intelligence system as a new metaphor for attention. In this view, the mental machinery is supposed to consist of many highly specialized autonomous modules. There are no problems as long as the pursued goals are known, which modules are involved in accomplishing them, and in which way the modules contribute to the solution. In other words, all is well as long as established direct connections are utilized, which, again, bear on the automaticity issue. However, sometimes, goals may require new ways of cooperation, organized through communication among the modules. Attention refers to these communication processes; in other words, it is a provision to prevent chaos. One option is attenuating the modules that do not take part in solving the goal (selective decoupling). Attention is more

---

[23]Neumann's (1987) view includes an interrupt mode while completing an action. The interrupt is called on by an OR and accounts for early selection. Effector recruitment may become more sophisticated by action planning, which allows more complex ways of recruiting and of programming several, initially separate, actions into a single new unitary action. This may explain perfect time sharing of difficult tasks. Complex action planning is only slowly acquired by very extended practice. Yet a simple response, as needed in the PRP, remains a unitary action. Simple as it may be, it still excludes other actions.

urgently needed as irrelevant modules become more active and, hence, require stronger attenuation. Active modules produce outputs that are collected in hierarchically supraordinate structures. Some modules—either relevant or irrelevant to the pursued goals—may have outputs that are incompatible with those of other modules. This leads to competition and outcome conflict and, hence, to a delay in reaching the goal. Controlling modules is particularly hazardous when performing relatively unpracticed dual tasks because either one requires a good deal of active communication among the modules. As an example of failing communication between modules, Shaffer (1975) gave his secretary simultaneous visual and auditory semantic inputs and had her time share typing and shadowing. It proved much harder to shadow the visually presented words and to type the auditorily presented words than the other way around. Apparently, the best established cooperation is between visual words and typing and between auditory words and shadowing. Practice has the effect of eliminating the need for cooperation and communication among the modules because the relevant modules have become an integrated team for achieving that specific goal.

The preceding views on interference are not far from the connectionist model proposed by Detweiler and Schneider (1991). It consists of three main levels, that is, a microlevel, a macrolevel, and a system level. The microlevel (Fig. 8.10) is concerned with individual codes. A message vector representing an outside event and made up of a vector of activation values enters an elementary module that consists of a layer of input (I) and output (O) units, as well as local control structures. The message vector maps on the input units by way of a matrix of weights that translates the message vector into an input vector. In turn, the input vector projects on the output units by another matrix of weights. In addition, an elementary module has a gain (G) and a feedback (F) unit as local control structures. Both may exert an inhibitory effect by weighing the strength of the output vector to the next module, thus moderating the activity of the output vector. The control structures are driven by so-called report units that receive their input from a summary statement about the input–output matrix of weights. One report unit is called the activity report (A); it reports whether and how active a vector is in the module. In addition, it excites an inhibitory unit that regulates feedback to the module. If the activity level of a vector is too high, activation of the input layer is inhibited to prevent overactivity of the module. The other control structure (P) is called a priority report, which indicates the relevance of the message in achieving the task. The reports on activity—bottom-up from the local unit itself—and on priority—top-down from the system level—are transferred to the local control structure. The report units excite an inhibitory unit (1), which activates another inhibitory unit (2), which, in turn, activates the inhibitory unit that regulates the gain. A strong activation of (1) means a strong inhibition of (2), which, in turn, leads

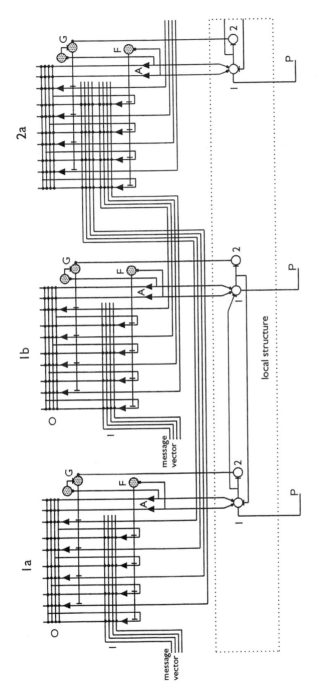

FIG. 8.10. An illustration of the microlevel of Detweiler and Schneider's (1991) connectionist model of information-processing. Modules 1a and 1b receive a message vector that competes for admittance to Module 2a. Input and output units are represented by black triangles. From Detweiler, M., & Schneider, W. (1991). Modelling the acquisition of dual task skill in a connectionist/control architecture. In D. L. Damos (Ed.), *Multiple task performance*. Copyright © 1991 by Taylor & Francis, Washington. Reproduced with permission of the publisher.

to less activation of the inhibitory gain unit. The net effect is little inhibition of the output vector. Unit (1) also inhibits the corresponding units (1) of other modules on the same level.

In this way, the local control structure determines which message vector on a particular level of processing may transmit its output vector to a module on the next level. One of the modules wins by the principle of winner takes all, but the activation of unit (1) declines rapidly over time. This offers an opportunity to the next most active and high-priority module to take over. This leads to a sequence of modules transmitting their output vectors to the next level.[24]

The *macrolevel* consists of sets of modules and their mutual connections, both of which are organized in levels and in regions of processing. The levels are analogous to stages of information processing—the lower part of Fig. 8.11—whereas the regions are concerned with the nature of the operations within stages, for example, semantic, spatial, auditory, and visual. Each region has its own set of levels. For example, the visual region may consist of sensory registration, feature extraction, and visual-form identification. The *system level*, finally, is concerned with relations among regions. The innermost level of a region—for example, word form at the visual level—communicates with other regions by sending vector messages. Modules belonging to different regions communicate with each other as well, thus creating a variety of associations and activities in parallel with the original sensory message and its response. Yet, the potential for parallel processing does not imply that there is always a successful outcome. The point is that the various message vectors that enter a module are combined, and this easily creates a problem of how to decipher individual messages.

In the Detweiler and Schneider (1991) model, a central control structure[25] regulates the interplay among the regional modules so as to prevent chaos. The central control structure acts in the same way as the local control structures but on the scale of a region rather than of an individual module. Thus, it receives an activity report about a region as a whole; it is composed of the reports of the elementary modules. Central control is responsible for selecting and switching among adequate regions at appropriate moments in time as well as for inhibiting message vectors in regions that are irrelevant to a task. The more a certain set of actions or reactions has been practiced, the stronger their message vectors in the elementary modules and their outputs to specific

---

[24]Aside from local control, there is also potential central control that directly affects gain and feedback and, hence, the activity and priority level of a module.

[25]The concept of a central control structure meets the homunculus objection. As noted on various occasions, connectionist types of models claim that control is distributed throughout the system so that they can do without any central executive function. It remains to be seen whether this claim can actually be achieved, but it is certainly not realized in the Detweiler and Schneider model. The issue of the executive controller will be returned to later in this chapter.

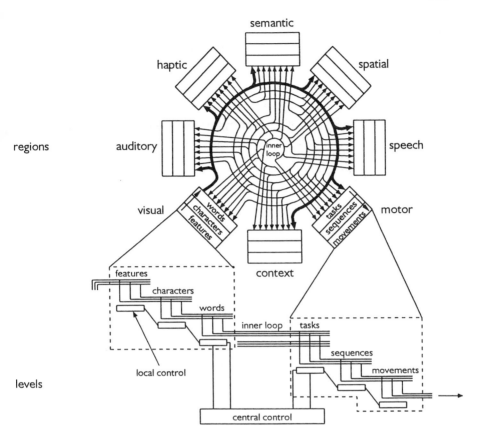

FIG. 8.11. Illustration of the macrolevel and system level of Detweiler and Schneider's (1991) model. In the example, the input levels of processing are concerned with reading a word. The inner loop defines the relation between input and output levels as defined by instructions. From Detweiler, M., and Schneider, W. (1991). Modelling the acquisition of dual task skill in a connectionist/control architecture. In D. L. Damos (Ed.), *Multiple task performance.* Copyright © 1991 by Taylor & Francis, Washington. Reproduced with permission of the publisher.

modules on the next level. Again, the more practiced, the stronger the inhibition of complete regions and their modules on levels that are irrelevant to the pursued response (Fig. 8.11).

The result is automatic processing. In this model, this means that the central control structure is no longer involved. Instead, the appropriate modules elicit each other in a fixed sequence and take care of inhibiting competing activity. In contrast, *controlled processing* requires considerable involvement of the central control structure in regulating communication among various regions. Although automatic processing has the effect of reducing the total activity of the system, the model does not predict that automaticity excludes interference in dual-task performance, as was implied by a simple capacity model. As discussed, automatic processes may elicit an automatic attention response or an OR that interferes by way of distraction.

When performing a dual task, the model specifies various coordinating activities that are all on the level of the central control structure. Appropriate regions are addressed at particular instances. In addition, the central structure decides which regions belong together. For example, a key-press reaction in a visual target-classification task requires the visual, memory, and motor regions, whereas a vocal response in a tone detection task requires the auditory and speech regions. One task of the central control structure is to prevent cross-talk—for example, emitting a vocal response in case of target classification and a manual response to a tone—by activating or inhibiting regions at appropriate moments via the priority reports. Confusions may arise when two tasks use the same regions, in which case message vectors of either task may address the same modules within a region. In line with the connectionist approach, different vectors merge; thus, the original messages have to be deciphered. This problem—and in particular, the issue of how to prevent the same modules being addressed—may be solved by the local control levels, but if they fail, the problem is transferred to the central control structure. The central structure has also the task of deciding which operation to omit at which moment when the system gets overloaded. Moreover, it plays a role in calling upon noncompeting structures in dual tasks. In a multiple-resource model, this could only be achieved by an appeal to different resource types. In the connectionist model, this is not necessarily beneficial because going from one region to another—that is, a shift in resource—usually means that the central control structure carries out a time-consuming switching operation. If, as in the case of controlled processing, the individual tasks already require such switches, additional switching operations may be more detrimental than when both tasks stay within the same regions.

Comments

It has become evident that present-day theorizing on dual-task performance and divided attention is rapidly moving away from the limited-capacity processor. Processor A falls short in view of the wide evidence that an undifferentiated pool of resources used by any type of task cannot capture the diversity of patterns of dual-task performance. This comes on top of the problem that Processor A is void of architecture and that it does not fit a current metaphor. Processor C has somewhat more architecture because resource categories reflect at least some main cognitive and perceptual–motor dimensions. There was even evidence for convergence between multiple resources and stage analysis. Yet, both describe dimensions rather than process mechanisms within dimensions. There is also the legitimate objection that the dimensions are nothing but a loose set of faculties without any coherence. A similar problem is met in the factor analytic abilities approach in chapter 10 that can be considered as an extreme case of multiple resources. Within the dual-task paradigm, there are additional objections to multiple resources in regard to the nature of the general resource needed for explaining dual-task decrements when two tasks tap completely different resources and factors beyond resources, such as cooperation and confusion, in order to explain variations in dual-task effects when both tasks need the same resources.

Current theorizing favors notions, such as "disambiguation between competing options," "cooperation between appropriate regions," and "deciphering merged messages," in order to avoid confusion and anarchy in action. The accounts of Neumann and Navon and the connectionist model of Detweiler and Schneider all converged in this direction. This is a highly interesting development that is, as yet, far from complete and, therefore, still hard to evaluate. The interference notions are more in line with a stage approach than with a resource approach because they suggest specific rather than general sources of interference during the information flow. A potential problem for the interference models may be a lack of predictive power about when and where to expect a dual-task decrement. So far, the theories have been insufficiently specific about their constraints and too occupied with attempts to describe existing data beyond limited capacity. Although the connectionist simulations are quantitative, their detailed predictions depend on how their parameters are set. This means that they are still very much open to post hoc adaptation. Consequently, more specific and detailed constraints on parameter values are needed to render the interference models testable.

With regard to future reseach, it would be worthwhile to consider patterns of interference as a function of the processing stage where such a pattern is supposed to arise. Stage analysis suggests that patterns of interference among tasks are bound to individual stages, examples of which were already met in the discussion on combining different types of action with regard to motor programming (Heuer, 1990, 1996). Again, motor preparation seems selective. This may imply constraints on completing different actions at the same time. Response selection has its limits as well, and they are illustrated in the discussion of the enormous interference when grouping incompatible responses.

These examples are incidental; future research should aim at a more systematic description of patterns of outcome conflicts among tasks and, hence, of dual-task limits, as rooted in stage analysis. Recent results by Tsang, Shaner, and Vidulich (1995) underscore the issue. They compared the limited-capacity and outcome-conflict views in a dual task consisting of manual pursuit tracking and of Sternberg's target classification with a discrete key press as response. A capacity-allocation view allows graded performance shifts when changing the priority of either task, but this is not basically inconsistent with a notion of outcome-conflict management either. However, the authors suggested that knowing the exact moment of arrival of the classification stimulus should provide an opportunity for avoiding outcome conflict by switching rapidly between the two tasks, whereas a change in capacity allocation is not supposed to occur that fast. Moreover, they argued that in contrast to general capacity, the notion of outcome conflict suggests that performance decrements are strictly bound to moments when a conflict arises.

Their mean performance data show the usual, moderate performance decrement when combining a spatial tracking and a verbal classification task. This mild decrement is presumably due to the fact that the tasks share visual inputs and manual outputs. The results also show the expected graded performance shifts when priority changed in favor of either tracking or classification. A moment-by-moment analysis of tracking proficiency at the time a classification response was carried out confirmed Netick and Klapp's result (1994) that tracking error increased during the classification response. In addition, however, Tsang et al. (1995) found that the largest tracking error occurred about a second after completion of the discrete response. This result was interpreted as favoring the capacity view rather than outcome conflict. Yet, it is obviously not excluded that when manual control is degraded at the moment of the conflict, its effects appear somewhat later. Moreover, restoring control over tracking may take some time. Tracking error was less when the time of arrival of the classification stimulus was predictable but only when either one of the two tasks had priority and not when they had equal priority. This was also interpreted as more in line with capacity theory because outcome conflict should not be affected by task priority. This may be a dubious deduction, though, but it still underlines the need of more precise specifications of the conditions under which outcome conflict is supposed to arise.

There are analogies as well as differences between interference theory and multiple-resources theory. Thus, Kinsbourne and Hicks' (1978) regions in cerebral space are not too far from Wickens' multiple resources, and their general control system reminds of the aspecific coordinating resource. The main advantage of the interference theory is that it demands more detailed specification of processes, whereas, as said, multiple resources have the flavor of a set of detached faculties. Such a set may suffice, though, as a coarse summary of experimental results suitable for recommending applications. This is probably the reason that resource notions are still quite popular in the areas of workload and taxonomic analysis of tasks. Finally, there is the issue that all resource theories bear heavily on a coordinator or central executive with the repeatedly observed danger of assuming a completely responsible homunculus. Thus the time has come to scrutinize the central executive in somewhat more detail.[26]

The Central Executive

Irrespective of the specific theoretical framework, the central executive has been assigned various powers with respect to performance strategies that are particularly relevant to controlled processing. More specifically, the central executive was engaged in the preceding discussion with (a) allocating resources, (b) coordinating actions, (c) determining priorities among tasks, (d) resolving interference in order to prevent chaos. Moreover, a central control system was or will be met when (e) monitoring optimal performance through investing effort, (f) setting the zoom lens in visual attention, and (g) deciding which spatial area should be focused.

Because the controller is primarily relevant to controlled processing, it is common to distinguish an executive and a lower level of control. Following Norman and Shallice (1986; see also Shallice & Burgess, 1993), the lower level operates on the basis of contention scheduling. When different, well-learned operations compete for action, the potential conflict is resolved by mutual inhibition of either one. The strongest option wins, thus avoiding a real conflict. It is easy to see that contention scheduling again comes close to habitual automatic processing. In contrast, Norman and Shallice's higher supervisory attention system (SAS) is supposed to intervene by selectively enhancing some and inhibiting other operations in the same way as the priority reports in Detweiler and Schneider's (1991) model (e.g., Navon, 1989). Thus, SAS is paramount in Logan's stopping task in which a stop stimulus signals that any ongoing operation should be immediately stopped. A weaker option may receive additional activation. This has the effect that it beats a stronger one. In this way, a strong, habitual response can be overcome when, as in a Stroop task, that habitual response is inadequate. The SAS system is supposed to be unitary and limited in capacity, thus, reminding of the general resource in the multiple-resource approach.

SAS is particularly active in the case of knowledge-based activity. The evidence in favor of qualitatively different control systems for knowledge-based and for routine cognitive activities stems mainly from neuropsychology and from research on short-term memory (STM). Patients with lesions of the prefrontal cortex—corresponding to Posner's anterior cingulate gyrus structure—appear to have problems in situations that involve planning (e.g., scheduling actions in dual tasks), troubleshooting, and overcoming habitual responses, as in the Stroop task (Norman & Shallice, 1986).[27] Such patients are

---

[26]A central executive may be implausible from a biological perspective. Yet, this argument is not decisive when levels of scientific enquiry are thought to be autonomous.

[27]Recently, Gehring and Knight (in preparation) found that patients with prefrontal cortical lesions showed impaired focusing of attention in a visual selective-attention task with noncorresponding distractors.

also distractable and unorganized. On the other hand, they experience no special problems completing a habitual sentence-completion task (Shallice & Burgess, 1993).

Multiple-task performance usually places a heavy load on short-term retention with respect to keeping apart the momentary demands of the tasks, temporarily storing information about one task while dealing with the other one, and actively rehearsing material that is sensitive to rapid forgetting.[28] As mentioned, Baddeley and Hitch (1974) proposed two STM systems, namely, a visuospatial sketchpad and a phonological rehearsal loop which are active when processing, respectively, spatial and verbal data. The two systems reflect the common result that visuospatial and verbal material do not strongly interfere. Among others, this was found in studies on memory span (e.g., Sanders & Schroots, 1969). In addition, Baddeley and Hitch postulated a supervisory attentional-control mechanism for coordinating the visual and phonological system and for guaranteeing optimal processing in view of the vulnerability and capacity limitations of working memory. There are various experimental techniques that aim at selectively addressing one of these three systems. Thus, participants may produce the word *the* at a rate of one per second (interferes with the articulatory loop), tap key-pad patterns at a one per second rate (interferes with the sketchpad), or generate random letters from the alphabet (interferes with the executive controller).

When generating a random sequence, the central control system has the task of interrupting the tendency to produce habitual, nonrandom sequences. For instance, Baddeley (1966) found that sequential redundancy increased as participants produced letters at a higher rate. A higher rate leads to more habitual responses simply because the central executive needs time for rejecting a habitual response in favor of a more random one. Generating a random sequence never gets automatized and continues to load the central executive, which explains why this task has been popular as a secondary task in the measurement of mental load.

Generating a random sequence may be nonverbal through random key presses. Baddeley (1996) reported that nonverbal, random-sequence generation could be combined with articulatory suppression of the phonological loop—counting aloud from one to six—but not with a verbal fluency task that required participants to generate as many items as possible from a specific category. He argued that rapid retrieval from long-term memory is another expression of central control, albeit different from the one met in the control of dual-task performance. Thus, some patient groups with damage of the frontal lobe do not show a decrement in verbal fluency, but they do in dual-task performance (Baddeley).

---

[28]A striking instance of the need for attentional control in a memory-span task is the highly disruptive effect of a distracting stimulus, such as a sudden ring of a telephone. A memory-span task cannot be properly carried out without continuous attention (Sanders, 1975b).

Indeed, separating streams of information from two tasks has been traditionally considered as another major function of the central executive, with an emphasis on coordinating information contained in the two STM systems. Baddeley (1993) discussed some evidence on dual-task performance in which a tracking task was carried out together with an STM task that either loaded the articulatory loop (digit span) or the visual sketchpad—CRT. Alzheimer's disease (AD) patients suffered disproportionally from such combinations and showed similar, excessive problems when required to keep track of several things at once. For instance, they performed very poorly when asked to monitor the actual values of a number of changing numerical-information sources. Special precautions were taken to avoid confounding dual-task performance with potential poor functioning of the visual and verbal systems themselves. This was done by adapting the level of difficulty of the memory span, CRT, and the tracking task to the point that all groups of participants were performing equally well when a task was carried out singly. Hence, the results suggest that the problem of AD patients consisted of coordinating and controlling multiple tasks. In other words, they appeared to suffer from malfunctioning central control.

However, Allport, Styles, and Hsien (1994) recently issued a warning against putting too much emphasis on the central executive on the basis of studies on shifting task set. The basic manipulation was that task instructions continually changed. For instance, participants might have the task of either incrementing or decrementing a two-digit number by threes as fast as possible. In control conditions, one instruction (i.e., incrementing or decrementing) remained the same for a whole session, whereas the instruction changed repeatedly in the experimental conditions. In one study, Allport et al. presented a display with one to nine instances (G) of the same digit (V), for example, all threes (Fig. 8.12). In one control condition, participants determined whether G was odd or even, while in a second control condition, they decided whether G contained more or fewer than five items. In two other control conditions, the same tasks concerned V (odd vs. even; larger or smaller than five). In still other conditions, participants alternated instructions between trials with respect to G (in trial n odd/even; in trial $n+1$ more or less than five items) and V (odd/even; more or less than five). In a final set, participants alternated two dimensions, that is, in regard to G and V as well as to odd/even and more or less than five. For example, on trial n they decided whether G exceeded five items, whereas on trial $n+1$, they decided whether V was odd or even. The results show that changing a task set had a large effect on CRT, which proved unaffected by the processing demands of the tesk. Thus, G was more time consuming than V, reflecting a Stroop-like effect, and the odd/even judgment took more time than the judgment on "larger or smaller than five," but this did not affect the time taken by shifting a task set. In other words, the fact that a shift was carried out and not the difficulty of the shift was decisive,

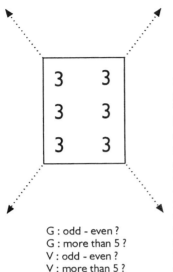

FIG. 8.12. An example of a display in Allport's task-switching studies: The tasks are odd/even and number judgments with respect to the number (G) or the value (V) of a set of digits. From Allport, A. (1993). Attention and control: Have we been asking the wrong questions? A critical review of twenty-five years. In D. E. Meyer & S. Kornblum (Eds.), *Attention & Performance* (Vol. 14). Copyright © 1993 by the MIT Press, 55 Hayward Street, Cambridge, Mass. Reprinted with permission.

a phenomenon that was confirmed in further studies with more pronounced differences in task difficulty.

Allport et al. (1994) argued that this result raises severe problems for a unitary, capacity-limited SAS system that predicts that shifting a task set should take longer as a switch involves more dimensions or when stronger habitual responses have to be overcome. Moreover, the costs of shifting a task set were hardly affected by the intertrial R–S interval, a finding that argues against the hypothesis that the central executive may voluntarily switch task set between two successive trials. In that case, the time taken by a switch should disappear as the R–S interval was larger. Instead, disengagement from an earlier task set awaited the arrival of the new stimulus. The response tendency, induced by the previous stimulus, could only be overcome when processing the new stimulus (task-set inertia). In line with this evidence, switching was less of a problem when the stimulus constrained the response. Thus, one may have to switch on alternate trials between a Stroop task (naming the ink color of a word) and a D task as outlined earlier. The fact that a color-word, rather than a number of digits, is presented facilitates the switch because the stimulus excludes certain response categories. Furthermore, the results of Allport et al. showed evidence for proactive interference in that earlier experience in an I task hampered the subsequent instruction to name digits. Thus, the bulk of the evidence stresses habitual contention scheduling rather than executive reconfiguration.

In the same way, Rogers and Monsell (1995) presented participants with digit-letter combinations (e.g., G7). The responses were carried out by the left (LI) or right (RI) index finger. The task was to decide whether the digit was odd (RI) or even (LI) or whether the letter was a consonant (LI) or a vowel (RI). Every two trials, the task set alternated from responding to the digit to responding to the letter, or vice versa. As control condition, a neutral symbol was combined with the letter (e.g., G#) or with the digit (? 7), with the neutral symbol never requiring a response. In one set of conditions, the R–S interval between successive presentations amounted to 150 msec, which always led to considerable switching costs, although somewhat more when competing stimuli and responses were involved (Fig. 8.13). Contrary to Allport et al. (1994), switching costs were less, although they did not vanish altogether, when the R–S interval amounted to 600 msec or more and was kept constant within a block. This was interpreted as a contribution of an executive control system moderating the habitual effects.

The main conclusion of the discussion may be that, indeed, one should be careful in assigning too much power to the central executive. First, there might well be a hierarchy of executive controllers, as was actually implicit in Detweiler and Schneider's (1991) local and central control structures. Second, the operations of the central executive may depend more on the ongoing operations of the controlled functions than originally envisaged. Much more research should be devoted to this important topic.

Individual Differences and the Central Executive

Individual differences in attention or concentration have been often related to the relative efficiency of the executive controller. For instance, an everyday problem concerns distractability of pupils in classrooms, which suggests, at least from the teacher's point of view, suboptimal functioning of the executive system in proper scheduling of relevant actions and in investing effort. In the classic factor analytic studies by Wittenborn (1943), the attention factor loaded on tasks that demanded flexibility. As a prototypical example, three digits were successively presented, and participants were instructed to write a plus sign when the first digit was the largest and the second the smallest digit, or when the three digits had an ascending order, whereas no response was to be given to any other combination. Stankov (1983, 1988) suggested that such tests appeal to a skill of flexibility in controlling two different conditions at the same time—that is, deciding at the same time about size and order of the digits— which comes close to Baddeley's notion of executive control in working memory. Aside from flexibility, there are factor analytic studies suggesting that planning may be a separate component of executive control.[29] In Fleishman's mental abilities catalog (Fleishman & Quaintance, 1984), flexibility is called

---

[29]Another type of traditional attention test emphasizes processing speed. Indeed, individual differences in processing speed (CRT, RT) are highly reliable. Some individuals react consistently faster than others, but this appears unrelated to the varieties of attention as discussed in this book. For instance, maintaining processing speed appears to be a much less reliable individual characteristic. Neither do speed tests significantly correlate with flexibility tests (P. F. de Jong, 1991).

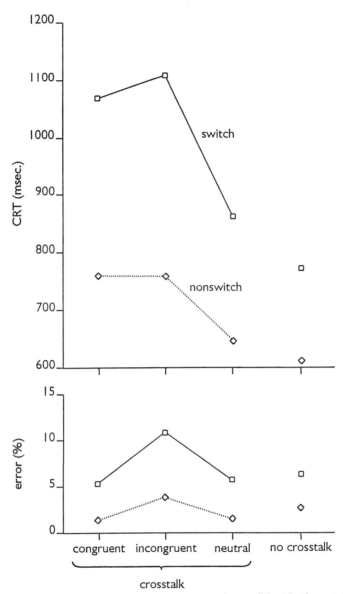

FIG. 8.13. Results of Experiment 1 by Rogers and Monsell (1995). The *switch* data refer to trials on which task set had just switched; the next trial, then, was always a *nonswitch*, followed again by a *switch*. *Congruent* and *incongruent* mean that the presented letter and digit were associated with the same response (congruent) or with different responses (incongruent). *Neutral* means that a stimulus pair consisted of a letter (or digit) and a neutral symbol. A block of trials was characterized as *cross-talk* when congruent, incongruent, and neutral trials were mixed. In non-cross-talk conditions, a letter (or digit) was always accompanied by a neutral symbol. From Rogers, R. D., & Monsell, S. (1995). Costs of a predictable switch between simple cognitive tasks. *Journal of Experimental Psychology: General, 124*, 207–231. Copyright © 1995 by the American Psychological Association. Reprinted with permission.

time sharing, which reflects the ability to shift back and forth between various sources of information and is supposed to be a central aspect of divided attention. Moreover, the ability labeled *selective attention* refers to concentrating on a boring task and is related, therefore, to individual differences in vigilance. Finally, Fleishman found an *auditory attention ability* which is used when focusing on a single auditory information source among other distracting and irrelevant auditory stimuli.[30] Finally, Fleishman failed to find evidence for planning as a separate attentional ability.

P. F. de Jong (1991) developed and examined various tests on flexibility and planning. Thus, the star-counting test was meant to assess flexibility. In this test, participants receive a number and a matrix consisting of stars, occasional blanks, and plus or minus signs (Fig. 8.14). The task is to count the stars and add the number of stars to the initially received number until a minus sign is hit, which indicates that the next group of stars should be subtracted. Hitting a subsequent plus sign indicates to shift from subtraction to addition, and so forth, until the end of the matrix. The final outcome should be entered on the dotted line.

In the example of Fig. 8.14, the initial number is 15 and the suboutcomes are 24, 20, 27, 22, 30, 26, and the final outcome amounts to 29. There is an obvious similarity between this task and those on shifting a task set in the experiments of Allport et al. (1994). Another test of de Jong (1991) was the arithmetic puzzle test meant to study planning. Here, an item consisted of a number of digits and operators, the combination of which produced the correct answer (Fig. 8.14). In the first example, the operator should start off with a minus sign and proceed with a plus sign, whereas in the second example, the first and last operators are plus signs, and the middle one is a minus sign. The task is to indicate the position where a minus sign is appropriate. In both the star counting and the arithmetic puzzle tests, the score is the number of correct solutions. Speed is irrelevant.

Among others, de Jong (1991) found that the preceding two tests correlated and loaded heavily on the factor of working memory with a traditional memory-span task as prototypical test. In this way, a relation between attention tests and working memory had been established, but again, there was no evidence for separate planning and flexibility components of the central executive. There was little relation between the scores on star counting and arithmetic puzzles on the one hand and scores on traditional processing speed tests of attention—letter or pattern cancellation—on the other hand. However, there was a significant correlation with processing speed in a Stroop task. This result underscores the set of functions that have been commonly ascribed to the executive system, namely, flexibility in a task set, inhibiting habitual responses, and close relation to working memory. Either

---

[30]It is unclear why the ability of focused attention should be limited to auditory stimulation. This may be due to the limited number of factor analytic studies on attentional abilities.

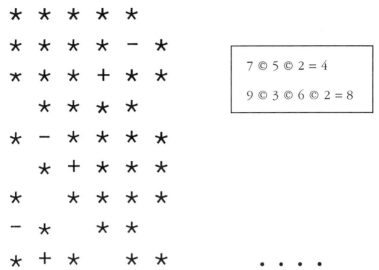

FIG. 8.14. An example of an item of the counting test of P. F. de Jong (1991). The task is to add (+) or subtract (−) the number of stars, according to the most recent instruction, and to enter the final outcome on the dotted line. Two examples of the mathematical puzzle test are shown at the right side. From de Jong, P. F. (1991). *Het meten van aandacht* [The measurement of attention]. Doctoral dissertation. Amsterdam: Free University. See also de Jong, P. F., & Das-Smaal, E. (1990). The star counting test: An attention test for children. *Personality and Individual Differences, 11,* 597–604. Copyright © 1990 and reproduced with kind permission from Elsevier Science, Ltd., The Boulevard, Langford Lane, Kidlington, 0X5 1GB, UK.

test had arithmetic demands, and it was not surprising, therefore, to find a correlation with traditional measures of intelligence. It is relevant, though, that the star counting and arithmetic puzzle tasks also correlated with judgments of teachers about attentional deficits that were assessed by a questionnaire. In other words, a task requiring repeated shifts in a task set can be used as a predictor of concentration in the classroom. This is an interesting applied spin-off of the concept of executive control. As a general conclusion, the work on individual differences bears on the central executive and is consistent with intuitions about concentration as an individual characteristic. However, theoretically, the work has failed to distinguish among some of the hypothetical features of the controller, such as flexibility and planning. Moreover, the problem of separating processes of working memory from their executive control has not been solved.

PERCEPTUAL–MOTOR LOAD

Applications of dual-task performance bear first and foremost on questions about work load, a concept that nicely fits the aspecific limited-capacity model. The more capacity is consumed the more a task is loading, and the less spare capacity is left. According to Gopher and Donchin (1986), "Mental work load may be viewed as the difference between the capacities of the information processing system that are required for task performance to satisfy expectations and the capacity available at any given time" (pp. 41–43). This view has been echoed in all proposals on the measurement of workload, namely, timeline analysis, primary task measures, the subsidiary task, physiological measures, and subjective estimates. More extensive treatments are found in the reviews by O'Donnell and Eggemeier (1986), Gopher and Donchin (1986), and Wickens (1992).

Timeline Analysis

Timeline analysis can be used as an empirical workload estimate in an existing task or as analytical tool in system design. One simply records the periods when an operator is busy with a task or with one of its components. This technique stems originally from time-and-motion study in which the times that were needed to complete elementary task operations with the aim of determining the rate of pace of a conveyor belt were measured (Siegel & Wolf, 1969). Time-and-motion study used to be mainly concerned with observable motor activities but more recent applications have included estimates of the times taken by unobservable activities. Moreover, timeline analysis has become increasingly popular as a tool for estimating work load in the design phase of a system, in which case the analysis is based upon a detailed description of the designed task components and upon a PERT network of their interrelations.

Another major assumption of timeline analysis is that operators cannot carry out more than one operation at a time, although more recent applications allow for some parallel processing in order to mimic the results on multiple resources (e.g., Laughery, 1989; Parks & Boucek, 1989). Yet, temporal overlap of task components usually creates queuing that, then, inevitably leads to overload. If components overlap and cannot be processed in parallel or benefit from slack, there is a predefined priority about their order of completion; in addition, there are estimates about the duration that a component may survive a processing delay. Overload means that the probability of losing components reaches an unacceptable level. This has the consequence that the design should be adapted. Recent examples of programs that allow user-defined sequences of task components and incorporate assumptions from multiple resources are MicroSAINT (e.g., Laughery, 1989) and WINDEX (North & Riley, 1989).

Timeline analysis has the problem that aspects of cooperation and confusion are not taken care of. The techniques are insufficiently sensitive to subtle but serious instances of interference that may lead to underestimating actual workload. On the other hand, workload may be overestimated when simply starting from a single-channel queuing principle. Sometimes actions may occur in parallel.

Primary Task Measures

Primary task measures attempt to avoid some of these theoretical problems by merely estimating workload from performance itself by noting potential error sources. This has been a popular approach in applications of control theory to tracking and to supervisory control. For instance, one might establish a gain function in the frequency domain and compare error corrections, as required by the task relative to performance limits of the operator. Once a valid gain function has been established, the control model can serve as an analytical tool for determining workload in the design phase of a system, although one has to be confident that the same gain function indeed applies to the new task.

Primary task measures such as CRT and accuracy have been used to assess load among task conditions. Such measures appear particularly useful when one configuration appears to take more time or to produce more errors than another one, despite the fact that both configurations are meant to accomplish the same mission. Yet, primary task measures may be insensitive when a ceiling or a floor is hit. Thus, performances may be perfect in all conditions but still vary in workload. For example, a task may consist of various components that are completed along the lines of a PERT network; some components may produce a varying amount of slack that does not show up in the performance measure but still affects workload.

Another primary task measure is by way of *testing the limits*. In this technique, the demands of a task are forced up to the point that operators can no longer avoid errors. One needs a valid dynamic simulator to test the limits. One example was taken from air-traffic control (ATC) and concerned establishing the upper capacity limit of a particular ATC system, with the aim of determining the capacity of the airport as well as fair demands on trainees. The demands on ATC, in terms of the number of aircraft to be handled, were increased in the simulator up to the level at which experienced operators could not avoid errors such as planes flying too closely or exceeding the bounds of the airway. The relation between the number of controlled aircraft and error proportion was determined. This allowed an estimate of the maximally permissible load and, from there, an estimate of the load under normal operating conditions. An advantage of testing the limits is that it is not theoretically vulnerable because it only addresses the performance limits in a specific task. The disadvantages of the method are that one needs a valid simulator and that performance measures may be crude. Prior to committing errors, an operator might omit safeguards needed for a safe traffic flow, which, if left out, do not immediately show up in errors. In turn, this would lead to overestimating the capacity of the system.

The Subsidiary Task

The subsidiary task approach to workload has relied heavily on the single-aspecific resource view in that secondary task performance is assumed to be inversely related to primary task demands (e.g., Knowles, 1963). In the version most widely used, participants are instructed to aim at optimal performance on the primary Task 1 and to limit secondary Task 2 performance to potential spare capacity. In terms of a POC, this should ideally lead to the situation as depicted in Fig. 8.15, left panel. In another version, the secondary Task 2 receives whatever resources it needs, with the aim of determining the effect of perfect secondary task performance on the primary task (Fig. 8.15, right panel).

A wide variety of secondary tasks has been studied over the years (O'Donnell & Eggemeier, 1986), among which are included regular interval production, CRT, tracking, target classification, random number generation, mental arithmetic, and short-term memory load. However, the secondary task technique faces various serious problems: (a) POC analysis shows that a primary task may be negatively affected by the second task, which raises doubts about its reliability as an index of load; (b) the evidence for multiple resources suggests that secondary tasks may be differentially sensitive to the nature of the demands, as was illustrated previously; (c) practice is prone to improve secondary task performance that, in turn, may lead to the incorrect conclusion that the primary task is not so loading after all; (d) practice

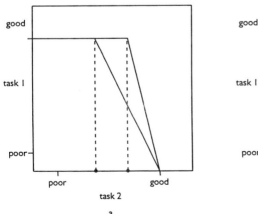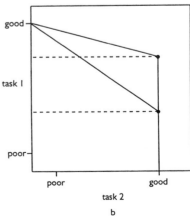

FIG. 8.15. Estimates of mental load in dual tasks by way of instructions to avoid a performance decrement in Task 1 (a) or in Task 2 (b).

may lead to more effective dual-task performance, which clouds the issue; (e) there is the unwarranted assumption that total capacity is constant.

The evidence on multiple resource is perhaps the most damaging for the secondary task technique. For instance, interval production (Michon, 1966) has been found to suffer the most when coupled with tasks with a predominant motor element, whereas generating random letter combinations (Baddeley, 1966) differentiates the best in the case of a cognitive task. Other objections may be less compelling. Care has usually been taken that the secondary task needs little practice and that there are safeguards against degrading the primary task. For example, interval production is rapidly mastered and can be easily interrupted. The fact that performance on a particular secondary task is related to the demands of at least a subset of primary tasks suggests that the basic idea of the secondary task technique need not be abandoned yet. Thus, Zeitlin (1995) found that delayed digit recall[31] was a sensitive measure of transient changes in workload during driving. The problem is, of course, which task to use under which conditions.

To meet the issue of multiple resources, a battery of secondary tasks may be used, each of which taps a different resource. In this way, the pattern of secondary task performances would indicate which resources a primary task actually needs. Various batteries have been launched to estimate work load and to assess individual differences. One is the Criterion Task Set (CTS) (Shingledecker, 1984) that comprises nine tests, among which are included Sternberg's target classification, Michon's interval production, mental arithmetic, spatial identity matching, tracking, linguistic identity matching, and grammatical reasoning. The tests were selected with Wickens' (1984) multiple resource scheme in mind. Another battery is the *Taskomat* (Boer & Jorna, 1987), which contains variations of choice-reaction variables, most of which are derived from stage analysis, that is, stimulus quality, S–R compatibility, time uncertainty, visual-memory search along the lines of Shiffrin and Schneider (1977), Eriksen's response conflict, pursuit tracking, and dichotic listening. Thus far, however, the main benefit seems that norms are being established with respect to these well-researched performance paradigms. There is not yet systematic evidence that the tests of the CTS and the Taskomat tap different resources and make up an appropriate workload profile.[32]

An illustration of the problem is provided by the aforementioned field study of Zeitlin (1995) on secondary task performance during driving. Delayed recall of digits clearly differentiated and correlated .80 with subjective

---

[31]Delayed digit recall refers to a task in which participants receive a continuous stream of digits and, upon presentation of a tone, are asked to recall the digit that was presented a couple of instances back. This requires a continuous update of the last few presented items (Mackworth, 1959).

[32]A third battery (BAT) has the purpose of a pilot selection test and is briefly considered in the discussion of individual differences.

estimates, whereas Baddeley's random-digit generation was insensitive to the variation in driving conditions. The problem is that either task is thought to be related to the operations of the executive controller, which is thought to play a crucial role in handling peak load during driving. The issue appears far from settled.

Physiological Measures

Kahneman's (1973) view that capacity limits vary as a function of energetic state cast doubt on the validity of behavioral measures of workload. Data on testing the limits or on the quality of a secondary task might vary too widely to be reliable. In that case, measures of a participant's physiological state might provide a better index of invested capacity and a better indication of current capacity limits. Kahneman proposed pupil dilatation on the basis of evidence that pupil diameter increased with demands in cognitive tasks, such as rehearsing items for subsequent serial recall and mental arithmetic. These results were supported by subsequent research (Beatty, 1982) but nevertheless, pupil dilatation has never become popular. One reason is that pupil-size measures are complex and restrain head movements. Another reason is that the normal function of the pupil reflex, namely, regulation of the amount of light reaching the visual system, prohibits a reliable use as load index when inputs are visual.

Cardiac measures of mental load were first systematically studied by Kalsbeek (1967), who found that the variability of the heartbeat interval, observed in a state of relaxation, decreased when participants carried out a paced, two-choice reaction task, and more so as the rate of pacing increased. Elaborating on this research, Mulder (1980) subjected heartbeat intervals to frequency analysis and found evidence for three peaks, namely, a .25 Hz peak connected to respiration, a 0.1 Hz peak reflecting slow adaptations in blood pressure, and a 0.03 Hz peak related to temperature regulation. Variations in cognitive-task demands, among others, on M in target classification, selectively suppressed the 0.1 Hz peak. Subsequent research on the prospects of cardiac measures as an index of workload has had variable success, with more consistent results in the laboratory than in the field. The 0.1 Hz peak is usually found to decrease when changing from rest to task, but there is scant evidence that suppression of the 0.1 Hz peak covaries with variations in load within a task (Jorna, 1992). One problem may be that an OR, elicited by an unexpected stimulus, increases heart rate as well as heart-rate variability. Again, heart rate appears to increase at the start of a new experimental session (e.g., Riemersma et al., 1977). The consequence is that stimulus properties and workload are confounded in the estimates of heart-rate frequency and variability. The most promising and established application of cardiac measures may be to conditions of underload and monotony. They are excellent indicators of sleepiness and loss of vigilance (O' Hanlon, 1971).

A final physiological estimate of workload stems from ERPs. The original application concerned the amplitude of the P3 that was elicited by a secondary task. This P3 could serve as an indirect measure of controlled processing required for a primary task. For example, a primary task may consist of pursuit tracking and a secondary task of a sequence of tones that all have the same frequency except for a few incidental deviant ones (the oddball paradigm). The task is to count the few deviants that have surprise value and, therefore, elicit a P3 with a large amplitude, at least when the oddball task is carried out singly. P3 amplitude appeared to be much less when both tasks were carried out together (Israel, Wickens, & Donchin, 1980), suggesting that the capacity required for tracking diminished the capacity allocated to the oddball task, which, in turn, is reflected by a smaller P3. It is of interest that variation in demands on compensatory tracking failed to affect P3 amplitude, whereas variations in demands on visual monitoring did (Israel, Chesney, Wickens, & Donchin, 1980). This is in line with the suggestion that P3 amplitude reflects only perceptual and central resource allocation.

Strayer and Kramer (1990) had participants perform a target-classification task together with a running-memory task.[33] They varied relative task priority and found covariation of the performance measures and the P3 amplitudes. Again, Humphrey and Kramer (1994) used gauge monitoring and an arithmetic task, both singly and in combination. In the gauge-monitoring task, the cursor positions of six moving gauges were monitored in order to detect whether a cursor had entered a critical zone. The current locations of the cursors were invisible, but the location of each cursor could be disclosed by an observing response. ERP measures were time locked to the observing responses and divided into ERPs to critical and noncritical cursor locations. The center of each gauge served as a display area for the operator and operand digits of the arithmetic task. The demands on either task were varied. The results show that P3 discriminated between single- and dual-task conditions in regard to monitoring and mental arithmetic, and between critical and noncritical cursor locations. However, P3 amplitude did not differ between the harder and easier versions of either task, neither in the single- nor in dual-task setting. This was interpreted as evidence that P3 only reflects perceptual-task demands. In another study, P3 was elicited by a task-relevant stimulus that was embedded in a tracking task. In that case, P3 amplitude increased as the demands on tracking increased. This result was regarded by Donchin, Kramer, and Wickens (1986) as "particularly encouraging to

---

[33]In a running-memory task, a sequence of items is presented. The sequence unexpectedly stops, followed by recall or recognition of as many of the last presented items.

the utility of the ERP as a measure of workload in extralaboratory environments" (p. 716).

Along the same lines, Kramer, Sirevag, and Braune (1987) had participants carry out instrument flight-rule missions in a simulator, and they manipulated workload by varying turbulence. P3 amplitudes, elicited by deviant oddball stimuli, discriminated among levels of workload in the flight task (Kramer & Spinks, 1991). Yet, other flight simulation studies had less success, which might be due to a lack of control whether the task manipulations were, indeed, concerned with perceptual and central resources. However, in a recent experiment, Fowler (1994) used simulated aircraft landing and varied turbulence and degree of hypoxia. Surprisingly, this research showed a covariation of both workload and hypoxia stress with P3 latency rather than with P3 amplitude. Hence, the results on P3 are not fully consistent in more complex task conditions.

There is also the embarrassing result that P3 amplitude is equally large when a task permits automatic processing or requires controlled processing (Strayer & Kramer, 1990). Thus, stimuli in a CM target-classification task showed an invariably large P3 that was insensitive to dual-task demands. It has been suggested that automatic processing elicits an automatic-attention response that elicits controlled processing, which, then, determines the amplitude of P3. Yet, this interpretation is at odds with the original view that P3 amplitude directly reflects the degree of controlled processing. As an alternative, P3 may merely reflect target detection that occurs automatically in automatic processing and that depends on resource allocation in controlled processing. This would, obviously, limit the value of P3 as an index of mental load. Another problem with the application of ERP concerns measurement, which is technically cumbersome in real-life tasks, whereas no norms are available on what should be expected in regard to P3 amplitude.

Subjective Measures

Until the early 1980s, subjective measures of workload were considered as suspect due to the fact that it proved hard to compare subjective judgments across tasks. For example, how would one compare the load imposed by translating a text from Latin with the load of driving a car (Sanders, 1979)? Or, perhaps intuitively less absurd, how would one compare the load imposed by flying a jet with the load imposed by flying a helicopter? Still, such questions were raised, and subjective estimates were formulated, with salary scales in mind. One of the problems was, of course, that the judges were usually inexperienced in at least some of the tasks. More recently, new procedures have been developed, though, with the more limited aim of detetecting variations in load within a task. For instance, what are the loading factors when driving a bus or flying a helicopter? The more recent procedures are based on psychometric techniques, have a multidimensional perspective, and are validated by comparing subjective estimates with performance measures (O'Donnell & Eggemeier, 1986). In some cases, participants issue estimates about workload on different dimensions, the values of which are combined into a single composite score. As an example, the SWAT technique requires participants to produce estimates by saying "0," "1," or "2" with respect to experienced "time load," "mental effort," and "stress" at various moments during a task. Thus, a pilot may say "1, 1, 2" at some specific moment during a flight to indicate a moderate level of time load and effort and a high level of stress. An ultimate load estimate is obtained by conjoint measurement of the mutual relations among these three dimensions for each individual participant. SWAT has been widely investigated and appears sensitive to momentary variations in demands. The method can be used to determine the effect of changes in design intended to reduce load.

There remains the issue that subjective estimates and performance measures of work load do not always covary. Thus, Yeh and Wickens (1988) found conditions of perfect performance and varying subjective estimates, and vice versa. For instance, a small increase in the load of an otherwise little demanding task appears in subjective estimates, but not in performance. On the other hand, variations in load at a level of near full resource investment are well reflected in performance, but not in subjective estimates. The point is that beyond a certain level of demands, subjective estimates appear to reach a ceiling. Again, performance has been found to gain from adding extra resources, for example, by giving monetary rewards when performance improves, but this has the effect that subjective estimates of work load increase. Yeh and Wickens also found that subjective load estimates are higher when two tasks are time shared than when a single task is carried out, given that the total time expenditure is the same in either case. The examples show that particularly in the case of high or low demands, subjective estimates and performance measures may dissociate. In addition, given the same level of performance, the estimates widely vary among participants. Thus, subjective measures cannot be simply compared across participants and do not lead to a general norm. Yet, subjective measures have proven quite useful to trace variations in load and to detect peaks within tasks such as driving and flying.

Comments

Theory and measurement of workload have progressed considerably during the last few decades. Due to the multidimensionality of human information-processing, a second task measure of spare capacity is often dubious and, sometimes, bluntly wrong. The method of testing the limits is attractive because it marks the point at which operators can no longer cope with task demands, irrespective of how the demands are composed. Yet, the method requires a validated simulator. In many cases, timeline analysis and subjective estimates provide a fair approximation to the question of whether task demands are within human-performance limits. Measurement of the physiological state remains of interest, in particular in relation to stress and its aftereffects, but, in the short term, it may not become operational as a measure of workload. Thus, subjective estimates, timeline analysis, and the primary task measure of testing the limits are among the most effective approaches. Analytic measures such as timeline analysis are most often applied when a system is still under design. It is a major tool for deciding which functions should be allocated to machines and human operators and which combination of tasks may be given to a single operator.

THE PSYCHOLOGICAL REFRACTORY PERIOD (PRP)

Basic Findings and Models

At this point, the discussion shifts to the PRP, the microcase of a dual task. As already mentioned, the PRP paradigm requires independent reactions to stimuli that are presented in rapid succession. It also has properties that clearly deviate from the main findings on dual tasks. For example, the PRP is the major case in which Processor B has been seriously considered. It will be remembered that Processor B is a single channel that blocks processing the next stimulus as long as it is busy processing the previous one. Moreover, as already referred to, C(RT) in the PRP hardly gains from practice, or in other words, it shows little evidence for a development of automatic processing.

In a typical PRP study, two stimuli are presented in rapid succession. Both require an independent response so that the second stimulus (S2) arrives during the response to the first one (S1). The amount of overlap is manipulated by a variation of the interstimulus interval (ISI), and the main measure of interest is C(RT) to S2 as a function of ISI. When the two responses are carried out independently and in strict succession, C(RT)1 takes about equally long in the PRP condition and in the control condition in which S1 is presented alone. Processor B predicts that the reaction process to S2 can only start after C(RT)1 has been completed. Hence, C(RT)2 should decrease as a linear function of ISI until ISI equals C(RT)1, whereon C(RT)2 should level off to the value of C(RT) when S2 is presented alone (Fig. 8.16).

The earlier research was summarized by Welford (1967, 1980). The data appear roughly in line with the single-channel view, although the delay of C(RT)2 is usually somewhat less at a small ISI and tends to persist when ISI equals or exceeds C(RT)1. Most initial studies used simple reactions with temporal variation of ISI (e.g., Davis, 1959), which led to the alternative

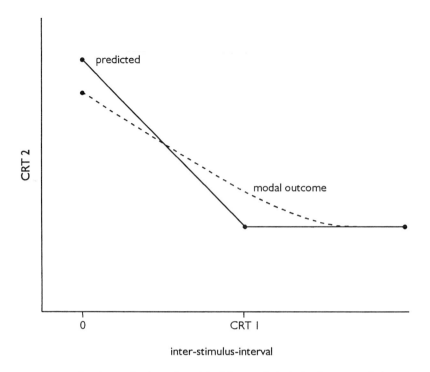

FIG. 8.16. The single-channel model of the psychological refractory period and the modal outcome. Usually, the increase in CRT2 is less than predicted at a small ISI and too much at a larger ISI.

hypothesis that the delay of RT2 is due to a difference in expectancy about the time of arrival of S1 and S2. Participants are certain about the moment that S1 is presented, but due to the variation of ISI, they are uncertain about S2, which could lead to a somewhat longer RT2, even when S1 and S2 can be processed in parallel. This was the main reason that most later studies used choice reactions with a constant ISI within a block of trials. However, in that case, CRT2 showed about the same type of delay, the size of which depended on the demands on S1. For example, Karlin and Kestenbaum (1968) varied the number of alternatives of S1 (visually presented digits) from two to five possibilities, with each digit requiring a key-press response .with a different finger of the same hand. S2 consisted of one out of two tones and was presented after an ISI that varied between 90 and 1,090 msec. The results show that CRT2 was more delayed as the number of alternative digits in S1 increased although, again, the slope of the ISI–CRT2 function was less than one. Along the same line, the delay of CRT2 was more pronounced when S1 required an incompatible rather than a compatible response. In contrast, the effect of a fixed or variable ISI on CRT2 proved to be marginal (Bertelson, 1967a).

Welford (1967, 1980) argued that the ISI–CRT2 function is affected by the variability of the duration of the reaction processes. Therefore, it may be better to plot interresponse intervals (IRI) rather than ISI. In addition, he suggested that the delay of CRT2 that remains after the completion of CRT1 could be due to feedback of the response to S1, which could extend the blockade on processing S2. An effect of response feedback was likely in some of the early studies that used a step change in pursuit tracking as S1 and S2. The tracking response to S1 might be fed back and, thus, cause an additional delay. However, additional delays were found as well in the case of key-press responses, even when S1 had a *covert response*—a condition in which S1 required a *c*-reaction. Separate analysis of those trials that required either an overt or a covert response showed a longer delay of CRT2 for overt than for covert reactions to S1. However, in both cases, the delay of CRT2 was found to persist, which is at odds with a presumed effect of response feedback (Sanders & Keuss, 1969).

Preparation Theory

As an alternative, the persistence of the delay of CRT2 might be due to a difference in preparatory state of the responses to S1 and S2. This has been labeled a weak expectancy hypothesis. The idea is that participants are fully prepared to respond to S1, whereas attaining preparation for S2 can only start after CRT1 has been carried out. It is evident that this view reflects another instance of single-channel processing because it assumes that preparation is limited to a single response. Attainment of preparation is completed within about 200 msec. Thus, the effect on CRT2 may persist for some 200 msec after the response to S1 has been completed.

The reverse is that anticipating the arrival of S2 may affect processing S1. Thus, Noble, Sanders, Trumbo, et al. (1981) found that occasional presentation of a fully irrelevant stimulus after S1[34] increased C(RT) some 30 msec, even when the two stimuli were separated in time by more than a second. This could imply suboptimal preparation of the response to S1. Yet, the 30 msec delay proved highly resistant to variations in processing demands of S1. This argues against a particular processing stage as locus of the effect. The point is that when the 30 msec delay of CRT1 is due to deficient motor preparation of the response to S1, the size of the delay should depend on the uncertainty about the time of arrival of S1. According to the AFM analysis (Sanders, 1990), high time uncertainty has the effect that the response to S1 can hardly be prepared. Thus, the 30 msec delay should vanish. Yet, the effect of potential presentation of S2 amounted to 30 msec, irrespective of

---

[34]The second stimulus did not require any processing and was presented on only 10% of the trials.

the foreperiod duration preceding S1, which excluded the motor adjustment stage as locus. It is, of course, not excluded that the delay is localized elsewhere in the information flow, but Noble et al. (1981) failed to find an interaction with any other variable affecting C(RT), neither perceptual nor central nor motor. In other words, the delay of C(RT)1 was an added constant that occurs when anticipating a second potential stimulus—even a fully irrelevant one—in fairly close temporal vicinity of S1. The nature of the effect is, as yet, unclear.

Koch (1993) argued that in all traditional PRP studies, the order of the responses is known. This means that S1 and S2 have a different status. Aside from possible differences between S1 and S2 and their corresponding responses, there is the fact that S2 always arrives after S1. Thus, the arrival of S1 provides information about S2 in that it may appear from now on. Processing this information and, hence, reducing the uncertainty about S2 supposedly takes time and might delay CRT2, in particular, at a very short ISI.

Koch (1993) described stimulus processing in the PRP as accumulation of evidence for S1 and S2, with accumulation rate, initial level of activation, and criterion setting as parameters. In a traditional PRP study, the accumulators for the S1 alternatives have advance activation and a strict criterion setting because the instructions demand fast responding to S1. Participants can safely preactivate the S1 accumulators because they know that S1 will be presented first. Once S1 has arrived, the accumulators of the S2 alternatives can be preactivated. This is referred to as *set*.[35] When S2 has more alternatives, the set is less productive because more S2 accumulators are involved.

As the uncertainty about ISI is less, the criterion of the S2 accumulators can be set more sharply. This is referred to as "preparation." CRT2 is determined by a combination of preactivation and criterion setting. Koch (1993) assumed single-channel processing with respect to the preactivation of the accumulators and to the criterion setting in the sense that one cannot be set and prepared for S1 and S2[36] at the same time. In one version, Koch also considered a single channel during processing S1. Preparation of and set toward S2 might only start upon completion of the response to S1. In another version, preparation and set toward S2 were assumed to start upon arrival of S1 and, hence, to occur in parallel with processing S1.

It follows from this last version that the PRP effect should disappear when participants are equally unprepared and set for S1 and S2. This was attempted

---

[35]It is evident that *set* does not refer to motor preparation in the sense of the AFM. Instead, preactivation is a perceptual effect in the tradition of the single-process models.

[36]One may not obey the instruction to respond to S1 as fast as possible by preactivating the S2 accumulators in advance of the arrival of S1. In this respect, the theory resembles Kahneman's capacity-sharing theory. In this way, it has no problem explaining the results of Noble et al. (1981). The potential presentation of another stimulus lowers the preactivation of the S1 accumulators.

by making the order of S1 and S2 unknown. Two groups of stimuli and responses were defined, but it was unknown from which group the first stimulus would come. Yet, once the first stimulus had been presented, the second stimulus always came from the other group. Koch (1993) found that the PRP effect largely disappeared provided that both reactions were highly compatible. In that case, the response to S2 did not take noticeably longer than the response to S1. The PRP effect disappeared altogether when potential response conflict between the responses to S1 and S2 was eliminated by having one manual and one vocal response rather than two manual ones.[37]

Koch's (1993) study is reminiscent of the work of Elithorn and Lawrence (1955), who argued in favor of a similar expectancy hypothesis. However, the problem with their variant on the PRP paradigm is that it is hard to define a baseline for the CRT2 delay. CRT1 cannot serve as baseline because S1 has a larger number of alternatives than S2. Indeed, a basic feature of Koch's paradigm is that presentation of S1 diminishes the alternatives of S2. Fewer alternatives mean a faster CRT2, so a delay of CRT2 may be easily obscured. It would be worthwhile to study an unknown order of S1 and S2 without a reduction in the number of alternatives of S2. This may be realized by using the same S–R sets for S1 and S2. S–R repetitions should be avoided because, in particular at a small ISI,[38] a rapid sequence of identical responses is hard to achieve.

The slope of RT2 as a function of ISI may be compared with the case of a known and an unknown order of S1 and S2. Indeed, the available evidence suggests that the slope is larger when the order is known. This lends support to a contribution to the delay of preparation, as defined by Koch (1993). The question is whether it is sufficient as a full explanation. As suggested in footnote 37, this may only be so in highly compatible conditions and not when the response selection mechanism is more involved in the information flow.

Grouping

Welford (1967) suggested grouping S1 and S2 as a potential explanation for the incomplete delay at small ISIs (Fig. 8.16). Grouping was also invoked

---

[37]Pashler (personal communication, June 1996) compared a control condition (S1–R1 only) with two experimental conditions. In the first, one stimulus was presented from either the set of S1 or S2—participants were unaware of which set—followed by one response. In the second, two stimuli were presented, one from the set of S1 and the other from the set of S2, in an unknown order. In the case of high S–R compatibility, the CRTs were about equal in both experimental conditions and longer than in the control condition, which suggests that preparation was the major cause of the delay. However, if compatibility was somewhat less, the dual response took considerably longer than the single one—supporting a response selection bottleneck. These results suggest that preparation is only a dominant factor when response selection is marginally involved.

[38]See a similar argument in the discussion of the typing skill.

to explain the observation that on occasion, participants did not respond at all when, in a pursuit-tracking task, S1 and S2 consisted of two rapid successive steps of a horizontally moving point—first up and then down, or vice versa. Thus, S2 cancelled S1.[39] Welford assumed that at a very small ISI, the downward step of the track had been perceived before the response to the upward step had been initiated. Thus, the failure to respond was taken to indicate that the two stimuli had been processed as a single group.

Sanders (1964) studied grouping more systematically. S1 and S2 both consisted of one out of two alternatives from separate groups of visual stimuli. Responses to S1 and S2 were carried out with two fingers of the left and the right hand, respectively. In some blocks of trials, participants were instructed "to collect all perceptual information before emitting any response," whereas in other blocks, they were admonished "to handle stimuli and responses in strict succession." The results show that at a small ISI (less than 50 msec), the instruction to "group" led to a much faster total response time.

In a subsequent study, Sanders and Keuss (1969) presented participants with a train of one to four stimuli in rapid succession. They saw a matrix of 4 × 2 lights and four response keys, with one key below each column of the matrix. When a trial consisted of a train of four stimuli, one out of the two lights from the column the most to the left flashed first, followed by one from the next one, from the third, and, finally, from the fourth column. When a trial had only two stimuli, the train stopped at the second column from the left, and so on. The instruction was to press the response key below a column when the upper light flashed and to refrain from responding when the lower light flashed. For example, all four keys had to be pressed when all four upper lights flashed, whereas no key was pressed at all when all four lower lights flashed. In one group of conditions, participants were instructed to "group," that is, to emit one combined response after having seen the complete train of flashes; in another condition, participants had to respond in strict serial succession from left to right. The results show again that grouping was much more efficient when ISI was small, with the relative efficiency of grouping increasing as a function of the number of overt responses. One finding was that the time to carry out a grouped chord of four overt responses took about as long as when the four lights required only

---

[39]The original tracking studies suffered from the problem that both responses were carried out with the same hand with which a joystick was handled. This introduces a trivial delay because one can obviously not use the same limb for different purposes at the same time. It is a typical example of Kahneman's (1973) structural interference. Later studies used different fingers for key-press responses as successive reactions. In this case, one may—apart from deciding which responses to emit—still have a problem determining the order of responding. Studies in which participants emit successive responses with full certainty about the responses and their order, show interresponse intervals of 100 msec at the most. Moreover, such responses may be emitted as one grouped response. Thus, although deciding about the correct order may contribute to the PRP, it is certainly not the full story.

a single overt response[40] (Fig. 8.17). In contrast, each new overt response took an additional 100 msec when responses were carried out in succession. Hence, the difference in efficiency between grouping and serial responding could be fully ascribed to the number of overt responses, suggesting that a decision to initiate a response is blocked while carrying out the previous overt response (Kantowitz, 1974; Keele, 1973).[41] It is interesting that CRT for grouping and successive responding did not noticeably differ when only the stimulus farthest to the right required an overt response (Fig. 8.17). The time to carry out that single response increased linearly as a function of the number of presented stimuli. These results suggest that the instruction to group or to respond in succession did not affect the time required for a covert response. With either instruction covert responding can be explained by a time-consuming, single-channel decision not to respond. Consequently, the results are troublesome for a theory that places primary emphasis on motor preparation, whereas they are consistent with single-channel processing during controlled processing.

In the preceding studies, it was no problem integrating the multiple, overt key-press responses into a single grouped one. This was different in another experiment on the relative efficiency of grouping and successive responding (Sanders, 1967a). Here, participants saw a matrix of 2 × 3 lights flanked at both sides by three response keys (Fig. 8.18). Two lights were presented simultaneously or in rapid succession, the first one from the left column and the second one from the right column. S–R relations could be compatible or incompatible, that is, the responses corresponded or did not correspond spatially to the lights.

Grouping the two responses was again found to be highly efficient in the case of compatible S–R relations, but it proved highly inefficient when S–R connections were incompatible (Fig. 8.18). Two grouped, incompatible responses took much more time than two successive, incompatible responses. Thus, aborting a compatible code in favor of an incompatible one (Kornblum et al., 1990) may have a limited effect on CRT as long as that incompatible response can be immediately carried out. However, if that incompatible response must wait abortion of a second compatible code in favor of a second incompatible one, the aborted and actual responses appear to interfere. This interpretation is consistent with unpublished data from the author that shows grouping one incompatible and one compatible response can be efficiently completed. The same goes for the case in which two incompatible responses were repetitions of the same instance—that is, had the same relative spatial locations (Fig. 8.18).

---

[40]This occurred when three of the four responses were covert.

[41]One may suggest a strategy of programming a minimal spacing between successive responses as an alternative to blocking of processing. Yet, in that case, one may expect a more efficient strategy as a function of practice. In the Sanders and Keuss (1969) study, participants were practiced for a very extended period of time without any significant change in the general pattern of results.

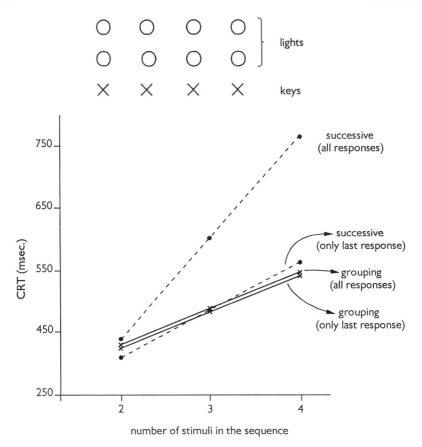

FIG. 8.17. A schematic representation of the experimental setup of Sanders and Keuss (1969). Participants received a train of 1–4 lights (O) presented from left to right and one light per column in a 4 * 2 matrix. They only responded when a light was presented in the upper row by pressing its corresponding key (X). The results concern the conditions in which either all responses or only the last response were required, with the instruction "to group" or "to respond successively from left to right." Adapted from Sanders, A. F., & Keuss, P. J. G. (1969). Grouping and refractoriness in multiple selective responses. *Acta Psychologica, 30,* 177–194. Copyright © 1969 with kind permission of Elsevier Science-NL, Sara Burgerhartstraat 25, 1055 KV, Amsterdam, The Netherlands.

Other Alternatives to the Single Channel

These last results may suggest a role of response conflict when carrying out simultaneous or successive responses. Response conflict occurs when carrying out rapid successive responses with the same or with similar limbs. This is reminiscent of Kahneman's (1973) peripheral structural interference.

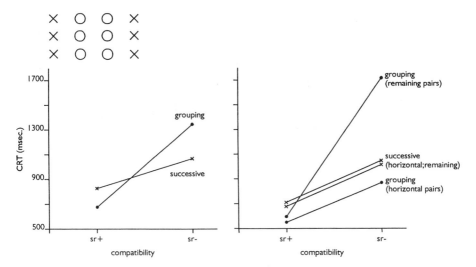

FIG. 8.18. A schematic representation of the experimental set-up of Sanders (1967). A stimulus consisted of one light from the left and one from the right column. The responses consisted of pressing the spatially corresponding keys (compatible) or noncorresponding keys (incompatible) with the instruction "to group" or "to respond successively." The results show a very clear interaction with S–R compatibility. Adapted from Sanders, A. F. (1967). The effect of compatibility on grouping successively presented signals. *Acta Psychologica, 26*, 373–382. Copyright © 1967 with kind permission of Elsevier Science-NL, Sara Burgerhartstraat 25, 1055 KV, Amsterdam, The Netherlands.

In fact, a response-conflict theory has been proposed as a general explanation of the PRP that comes close to the suggestion that the single-channel bottleneck is mainly localized at response initiation and execution (Kantowitz, 1974; Keele, 1973). The main point of response-conflict theory is that the delay of CRT2 is only half the story because the requirement to carry out a second reaction affects CRT1 as well. The joint demands on S1 and S2, together with the nature of the responses, determine the degree of response conflict. Thus, there is less conflict as responses are more widely spaced in time. This accounts for the effect of ISI. Again, response-conflict theory expects less conflict—in particular at small ISIs—when the responses to S1 and S2 consist of movements in the same direction than when they are into opposite directions (Gottsdanker & Way, 1966). The effects of a potential second stimulus on CRT1, as in the work of Noble et al. (1981), may be viewed as further evidence for response conflict. However, in that study, the second stimulus did not require a response; it was even irrelevant and can, therefore, hardly have evoked response conflict.

Greenwald and Shulman (1973) found the PRP effect to disappear in the case of two ideomotor compatible sets of S–R relations. One set consisted of movements to the location of a visually presented stimulus and the other set of vocal naming of auditorily presented letters. Response-conflict theory holds that conflict will be eliminated when responses come from qualitatively different sets such as movements and vocal responses. However, Greenwald and Shulman also found that the PRP was not eliminated in the case of incompatible, qualitatively different responses. This finding may be analogous to the effect of compatibility on the PRP delay in Koch's experiments and to the effect of compatibility on the efficiency of grouping.

Similar results were obtained by Pashler, Carrier, and Hoffman (1993), who found no delay of CRT2 when S1 consisted of either a high or a low tone, requiring a manual choice reaction, and S2 was a peripheral light requiring a saccadic eye movement toward its location. A delay was found, though, when S2 was a colored, centrally presented visual stimulus that indicated the direction of the saccade. In the same way, a reaction to a stimulus indicating to stop further processing (the stop signal paradigm) occurred in parallel with the ongoing reaction process except when the stop signal not only instructed aborting the reaction, but also required a response of its own. Single-channel theory can explain these results by assuming that the single channel has its prime site in response selection. When one or both responses do not need the response selection mechanism, the single channel is bypassed. Most data on grouping are at odds with response-conflict theory as well because a grouped response is only more efficient than two successive responses when the S–R relations are compatible. Response-conflict theory predicts that there should always more response conflict in grouping. However, the response decisions rather than the responses per se appear to elicit conflict.

An increase in demands on S2 tends to prolong CRT1 (Kantowitz, 1974). This is usually not accounted for by single-channel theory, and it may be avoided by stringent instructions to put all emphasis on CRT1. Effects of S2 on CRT 1 are a prime issue in response-conflict theory that assumes that response conflict increases as a function of the total demands on processing S1 and S2. Yet, not any demand on S2—such as stimulus degradation—is response determined, but it may still affect CRT1. Response-conflict theory should specify, therefore, the conditions under which a conflict is supposed to occur. It is possible that response conflict contributes to the delay in the case of similar responses and marginal demands on response selection. An example may be motor interference such as that found by Koch. Other evidence in favor of a contribution of response conflict stems from the study on multiple c-reactions by Sanders and Keuss (1969). They found that both in grouping and successive responding, some combinations of overt and covert responses were carried out faster than others. However, this effect largely vanished as a function of practice, whereas the PRP effect, as such, did not diminish either in this study nor in most other research (Pashler, 1994). This is in clear contradiction with the basic tenet of response-conflict theory.

The effects of S2 on CRT1 have also been viewed as support for capacity sharing (Kahneman, 1973). The relative duration of CRT1 and CRT2 might be merely a matter of how capacity is divided between processing S1 and S2. If all capacity is devoted to S1, the system may act like a single channel because no capacity is left for S2. However, the capacity view faces severe problems. First, it cannot explain without additional assumptions[42] why grouping is more efficient than successive responding. The point is that if only the total demands are relevant, the general efficiency should not be affected by way of dividing capacity. Another major problem for the capacity theory is that it cannot explain why there is any delay at all. Would capacity be so severely limited that time sharing two choice reactions is impossible? Again, capacity theory would expect that as in more complex dual tasks, practice leads to better time sharing. Yet, the PRP delay is highly resistent to practice (Gottsdanker & Stelmach, 1971; Sanders & Keuss, 1969). As mentioned earlier, the only condition in which the PRP may be eliminated is a combination of ideomotor compatible responses and different effectors. What is special about the PRP? Is the effect fully due to structural interference? Indeed, this would position it beyond the capacity discussion. Where, then, does structural interference end and capacity start? How does structural interference account for the effects of variations in perceptual and response demands on the size of the delay?[43]

AFM and Refractoriness

The popularity of capacity theories during the 1970s and 1980s had the effect that interest in research on the PRP declined. The point was that it does not make sense to study relations between response times to successive stimuli when it is all a matter of how capacity happens to be divided. It is not surprising, therefore, that Kantowitz' (1974) review has been a timely survey of the literature up till now. From the perspective of Processor B, the PRP paradigm makes sense because it is the prime paradigm for studying potential bottlenecks in the information flow. In recent years the notion of a central single-channel bottleneck was revived by Pashler and associates, who applied processing-stage notions to establishing potential loci of a bottleneck.

---

[42]One provision concerns structural interference that may be extended to interference from using related effectors—for example, two fingers from the same hand or the same finger from different hands. Yet, the concept loses explanatory power as its meaning is widened.

[43]Recently, Pashler (1994) reported a PRP experiment that put equal emphasis on responding to S1 and S2. In six participants, this led to consistent grouping of responses. In 17 other participants, it led to a bimodal distribution and a negative correlation of RT1 and RT2, reflecting that either RT1 or RT2 was first completed on a particular trial. Capacity sharing would always predict grouping, whereas a bottleneck account can cover grouping but is more akin with successive handling of S1 and S2, whichever is done first.

In accord with the results on the AFM, a first group of stages is concerned with perceptual encoding, followed by a response selection stage and finally by a group concerned with response organization and execution. These three groups are supposed to play a part in each single reaction, whereas across reactions, any stage may be active in parallel with any other stage. Thus, encoding of S2 may occur in parallel with response selection or execution of S1, and response selection of S2 may occur in parallel with response execution of S1. The question is whether a stage can be busy handling S1 and S2 at the same time. This depends on whether that stage is part of a processing bottleneck.

Along these lines, Pashler (1984, 1991, 1993, 1994) proposed the logic as shown in Fig. 8.19. Suppose CRT1 is carried out without suffering from interference from any operation on S2; this means that CRT 1 consists of the simple sum of the aforementioned three groups of processing stages. Moreover, suppose that perceptual processes of S1 and S2 can occur in parallel, whereas response selection cannot. Thus, after encoding of S2, response selection of S2 has to await completion of response selection of S1. The consequence would be that as ISI (or its synonym SOA) is less, there is a larger interval between completion of perceptual encoding of S2 and completion of response selection of S1. In other words, S2 has slack between the completion of encoding and the start of response selection. Consequently, the encoding demands on S2 can be increased without affecting CRT2 because the additional demands on S2 merely consume part

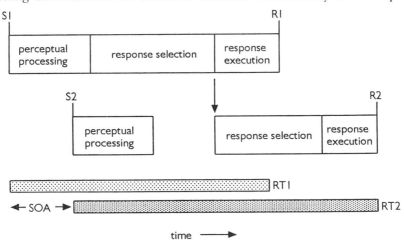

FIG. 8.19. Pashler's response-selection queuing account of the psychological refractory period. Perceptual processing of S2 may be prolonged without causing an additional delay in responding. From Pashler, H. (1993). Dual-task interference and elementary mental mechanisms. In D. Meyer & S. Kornblum (Eds.), *Attention & Performance, 14.* Copyright © by the MIT Press, 55 Hayward Street, Cambridge, Mass. Reprinted with permission.

of the slack. The situation changes at a longer ISI, in which case perceptual processing of S2 is still in progress at the moment that response selection of S1 has finished. In that case, slack plays no role because response selection of S2 may start immediately when it has been encoded. The result is an underadditive interaction of the effects of a perceptual variable in conditions of single and dual reactions. In contrast, factors affecting response selection would never create slack, and consequently, the effects of these factors would be additive in the single- and dual-task conditions.

Pashler and colleagues (e.g., Pashler, 1994a) examined a wide range of S2 variables on the occurrence of slack. Their results suggest that perceptual processing of S1 and S2 occurs in parallel at least as long as the perceptual processing demands are not too heavy. For example, variation of the visual intensity of S2 had less effect on CRT2 in the dual condition than in the single one, whereas the effect of intensity in the dual condition increased with ISI. Converging evidence for the occurrence of slack in the case of stimulus identification came from studies in which S2 was presented tachistoscopically, with detection accuracy as measure. Detection accuracy proved unimpaired when S2 was presented during the response to S1. In contrast, variables such as stimulus repetition and S–R compatibility of S2 had additive effects with those of ISI, suggesting that response selection constituted a bottleneck (McCann & Johnston, 1992). Similarly, additive effects were found when S2 required retrieval of a well-learned paired associate.

Earlier, Posner and Boies (1971) had arrived at a similar conclusion on the basis of probe studies in which S1 consisted of two successively presented visual letters requiring a same–different response on the basis of either physical or name identity. On a small proportion of the trials, a tone was presented during, before, or following the response to S1; the tone required an immediate response. When presented at the same time as the first letter of S1, RT to the tone was not delayed; it was delayed, though, when presented with the second letter. This suggests that encoding the first letter could occur in parallel with a response to the tone, whereas RT was delayed when the tone coincided with the decision about the same–different response. Later studies suggested that the delay may not occur when the response to the visual and the auditory stimulus stem from different effectors (McLeod & Posner, 1984). Yet, different effectors do not appear to eliminate the delay in a traditional PRP setting (Pashler, 1993).

Other instances of underadditive interactions of effects in the dual and single reaction have been found with other perceptual variables, among which is display density in visual search. Again, van Selst and Jolicoeur (1994) found evidence for a small underadditive interaction in the case of mental rotation. Consistent with the presumed perceptual locus of mental rotation (Fig. 3.2), this suggests that processes involved in mental rotation precede those of response selection. However, Ruthruff, Miller, and Lachmann (1995) failed to confirm the results of van Selst and Jolicoeur and found additive effects of mental rotation and ISI. Moreover, McCann and Johnston (1989) observed additive effects of stimulus discriminability (by distorting uppercase "A" and "H"). Together, these results suggest either that mental rotation and stimulus discriminability affect response selection as well as perceptual identification[44] or that the bottleneck is not limited to response selection and extends to perceptual discrimination.

In another study, Pashler (1991) used covert orienting in S2. A display of eight letters and a probe were presented, with the probe indicating which letter should be reported. The presentation was followed by a mask in order to avoid iconic persistence. If a shift of attention to the probed letter was delayed by processing S1, identification of the probe should be less accurate as ISI becomes smaller. The results show that completion of the first response did not affect probe identification. This suggests that covert orienting did not suffer from the bottleneck responsible for limitations in concurrent responding. These results provide additional evidence against a unitary concept of attention. Selective attention in covert orienting and in response selection seem to be different mechanisms. Changes in response modality—manual–manual versus manual–vocal—for S1 and S2 had little effect on the delay of CRT2, which argues against the potential use of multiple resources in executing responses in the PRP paradigm.

In almost all studies by Pashler and colleagues S1 consisted of one out of two tones requiring a manual choice reaction. Hence, their finding that encoding S2 may occur in parallel with S1 does not mean that encoding can always occur in parallel with processing another stimulus. For example, processing two successive stimuli in the same modality may lead to a loss of peripheral acuity of either one. Moreover, when S1 and S2 are similar, they may interfere on a perceptual level; interference may arise as well when the demands on S1 and S2 are increased at the same time.

Osman and Moore (1994) measured LRPs connected to the first and second reaction in a PRP paradigm. One major result was that the delay of CRT2 was accompanied by an equal delay of its LRP, suggesting that the bottleneck concerns processes that precede LRP onset. Thus, given that the bottleneck is on the level of response selection, the LRP would not reflect response selection per se but the outcome of response selection. Again, given that the bottleneck is on the level of response initiation, this process should precede the start of the LRP. The findings of Osman and Moore seemed to argue against a peripheral motor locus of the bottleneck, in

---

[44]From the perspective of stage analysis, the loci of these variables have not yet been sufficiently established. Most studies on mental rotation used mirror-normal responses in that participants decided whether a rotated letter had been in a normal or in a mirrored position. The bulk of the effect may be due to this decision and could reflect response selection rather than perception.

particular because the start of the LRP to the second reaction did not always wait for completion of CRT1. The LRP to the first stimulus was neither affected by the second reaction nor by ISI. This seems to argue against capacity sharing and response conflict in the conditions of the Osman and Moore study.

The revival of a single-channel bottleneck at the level of response selection does not mean that this notion has now been generally accepted. Thus, de Jong (1993) argued in favor of a double bottleneck, one at response selection and another at response initiation. This received support from the results of Sanders and Keuss (1969) that suggested that PRP effect extends to overt motor execution (Keele, 1973). In de Jong's studies, the first stimulus was one out of two tones, one of which served as go stimulus and the other as no-go stimulus (*c*-reaction). The second stimulus required either a simple or a choice reaction. As in Sanders and Keuss, the PRP effect was larger in the case of the go than of the no-go trials, which suggests that response execution played a part in the PRP delay. In addition, the effect of a choice versus a simple reaction increased as a function of ISI in go but not in no-go reactions. Following Pashler's logic, this provides additional support for a bottleneck on the level of response initiation. The problem may center around emitting independent discrete responses, a view that comes close to Neumann's (1987) effector recruitment as main performance constraint.

Meyer et al. (1995) recently developed a symbolic-theoretical model (EPIC) that accounts for many PRP results without claiming any structural bottleneck at all, although, at close scrutiny, there still may be one at response initiation. Meyer et al. noted that despite various attractive features, the single-channel bottleneck has problems in explaining some PRP results, among which is the finding that the slope relating RT2 and ISI is sometimes much less and on other occasions much steeper than one. Again, within an experiment, there appear to be quite consistent, individual differences, with some participants showing a much flatter slope and others a much steeper slope than predicted by single-channel response selection. Moreover, in one study, more processing demands on S2 by increasing the number of alternatives had the effect that the slope flattened. Thus, the main effect of the increased demands on S2 was at a long ISI rather than at a short ISI (Fig. 8.20).

Meyer et al. (1995) suggested that responding in the PRP is a matter of strategic control, for example, when deciding to group rather than to process in succession. In addition, they argued that performance limits might primarily be due to structural interference (Kahneman, 1973) or to constraints in effector recruitment (Neumann, 1987). In other words, the nature of performance limits are thought to be much more peripheral than assumed by a single-channel decision mechanism. The EPIC simulation model consists of perceptual processors, a cognitive processor, and motor processors. The perceptual processors detect and identify stimuli in various sensory domains; they work

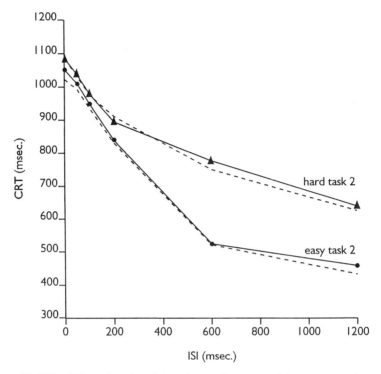

FIG. 8.20. RT2 as a function of ISI with an auditory-manual first reaction and a visual-manual second reaction in the case of easy (circles) and hard (triangles) demands on response selection. The dashed lines are predictions from the EPIC model. Adapted from Meyer, D. E., Kieras, E., Lauber, E. H., Schumacher, J., Glass, E., Zurbriggen, L., & Apfelblat, D. (1995). Adaptive executive control: Flexible multiple task performance without pervasive immutable response-selection bottlenecks. *Acta Psychologica, 90,* 163–190. Copyright © 1995 with kind permission of Elsevier Science-NL, Sara Burgerhartstraat 25, 1055 KV, Amsterdam, The Netherlands.

in parallel and deposit an outcome—for example, "there is an 800 Hz tone"—in a declarative working memory, which is one of the three structures of the cognitive processor. The other two are production memory and a production-rule interpreter. The production memory consists of a set of "if–then" rules that enable translation of stimuli into responses—for example, "if there is an 800 Hz tone, then respond with the left hand"—and that also stipulate strategic performance aspects. For example, if, as is common in a PRP study, the instruction asks for a fast response to S1, this instruction is included in the production rules for the S1 S–R rules, for example, "if there is an 800Hz tone, respond with the left hand with absolute priority."

The production-rule interpreter checks all task-relevant rules in working memory and determines which rules match those that have currently been established. The next step is that the matches are executed. It is relevant that the interpreter has no central bottleneck because it can forward several matches to the motor level at the same time. At the motor level, finally, the details of the response are further specified. There are different motor structures, such as verbal and manual ones, that operate in parallel. Yet, the motor structures have a single-channel constraint in that they can only prepare and initiate one response movement at a time. Thus, when instructed, one may carry out a combined movement with two hands, but when instructed to respond with one hand, one cannot initiate another movement with the other hand at the same time. This constraint is consistent with de Jong's (1993) plea for a bottleneck at response initiation. It is unclear how it can be reconciled with the LRP findings of Osman and Moore (1994), an issue that certainly deserves further consideration.

Aside from the three processors, EPIC has a supervisory control structure that coordinates processing S1 and S2. Depending on instructions and on constraints, the controller defines lockout points. For instance, when the instruction stresses absolute priority of processing S1, the controller blocks processing S2 beyond a certain point until S1 enters a done state indicating that the response has been completed. The main reason for blocking S2 is that in line with the instructions, a reponse to S2 should never preceed a response to S1. Consistent with discrete-stage models of CRT, blocking may occur either (a) prior to, (b) after identification, or (c) after response choice, with the specific properties of tasks 1 and 2 determining at which point a lockout actually occurs. For example, when there is a danger of cross-talk or of perceptual confusion, one may block S2 earlier in the process than when stimuli and responses of S1 and S2 can be easily distinguished. On the other hand, when the instruction requires response grouping, S1 may be blocked until the S2 processes have proceeded to a point where the grouped response can be carried out. The fact that the controller can choose different lockout points means that the CRT2—ISI function will vary in steepness.

Thus, EPIC rejects structural bottlenecks except for a peripheral[45] limit in effector recruitment. The PRP is supposed to be largely a matter of task-determined blockades, so bottlenecks are due to software rather than to hardware. They are not limited to a particular stage but can occur anywhere when competing processes are too loading.

Comments

The story of the PRP clearly illustrates that issues are studied in the context of a theoretical *Zeitgeist*. The loss of interest during the 1970s was due to

---

[45]One may doubt, though, whether EPIC's manual constraint of only one overt response at a time is a more *peripheral*—on the level of motor adjustment—or a more *central*—on the level of motor programming—bottleneck.

the dominance of the limited-capacity concept. Yet, this could not appropriately account for the data. Capacity theory tended to consider the PRP paradigm as an artifact and shifted attention to complex dual tasks in which time sharing was more common. However, there remains the well-established finding that independent successive decisions are hard to complete in parallel. It remains a matter of debate whether this reflects a centrally located bottleneck or peripheral motor interference. One of the issues is whether EPIC can account for data, like Sanders' (1967a) on grouping incompatible reactions, which suggest strong interference between production rules when more than one incompatible response command is issued. At first sight, this seems not strategic but reminds of a central bottleneck.

SUMMARY

One general conclusion of this chapter is that capacity theory does not fare well in its homeland of dual-task performance. The approach is too molar and insufficiently detailed. Moreover, the main predictions from the single-resource model failed to be confirmed. The problem with multiple resources is their ad hoc and faculty-like character and their lack of theoretical underpinning. In addition, the evidence on instances of interference and time sharing in dual-task performance could not be summarized by a limited number of resources. These criticisms notwithstanding, multiple resources still have a heuristic value in applications and may capture some broad categories of cognitive processing. Different types of resources show less mutual interference; therefore, their combination often makes up a more efficient dual task. The rough classification in perceptual, central, and response resources is consistent with the results on stage analysis. The distinction between spatial versus verbal central resources, vocal versus manual output resources and visual versus auditory input resources carries the multiple-resource view beyond stage analysis.

Multiple resources are, at best, a rough categorization. There are additional differences in efficiency among dual tasks within a resource. Moreover, using different resources is not always a guarantee for better dual-task performance. Therefore, current descriptions stress notions, such as outcome conflict, preparation, interference, confusion, and cross-talk, sometimes framed in a connectionist structure. This coincides with a renewed interest in the PRP in which similar notions have been popular ever since the 1950s. One question of interest is the relation between the results in the simple setting of reacting to two successive, independent stimuli—with a response-related bottleneck, insensitivity to practice, and little evidence for multiple resources—and the more complex dual tasks that depend strongly on practice and that show evidence for multiple resources. It is clear that the PRP cannot be considered as a standard instance of dual-task performance. Yet, under what conditions may it play up in dual tasks? What are the essential additional features of more complex dual tasks? Is it a matter of more opportunity for the development of automaticity and chunking? The issue is returned to in the discussion on typing as a transcription skill.

The new interference theory of dual-task performance has, as yet, to make its promises true. After all, capacity theories were simplistic but had the advantage that they could be shown to be wrong on various critical issues. So far, the same cannot be said of the interference concepts, perhaps with the exception of the PRP, but as previously said, the PRP is not a standard dual task. Interference notions should be considerably more detailed in order to become testable. It does not suffice to build some neural network that fits a number of existing results. Instead, the network should be predictive and should suggest new experimental developments. Thus far, no major experimental impulses have emerged from the new approach, at least not in the area of divided attention. This judgement might be too hasty; new prospects may be on the horizon.

A final remark concerns a major feature of capacity theory, namely, the emphasis on allocation policy or, in other words, on the operation of a central executive. The information-processing tradition has not embraced, but still tolerates this homunculus notion. Connectionism is considerably less tolerant in this respect. The discussion on the central executive has led to the conclusion that even when tolerated, its powers should be limited as much as possible. The connectionist claim that a central executive is not needed when control is distributed throughout the network is an important future research issue.

Energetics, Stress, and Sustained Attention

This chapter is concerned with the energetics of human performance, often referred to as *intensity of attention* or *sustained attention*. Issues on sustained attention were among the applied interests of the new performance theory, particularly in regard to the problem of maintaining alertness in monotonous, watchkeeping tasks. It is remarkable that, their common themes notwithstanding, research on energetics and on selective attention and reaction processes has been carried out in almost complete isolation. One may safely say that the mainstream of performance research has been engaged with cognitive aspects of performance without any consideration of energetics. The dominant interest in computation rather than in energy may be due to the computer metaphor that is insensitive to emotions, motivation, and fatigue. The available research on alertness, fatigue, and the effects of stresses and psychotropic drugs has had little impact on cognitive performance models. In the same way, computational performance models have hardly inspired the performance tasks that were popular in the study of energetics. This has hampered progress because energetics and computation are fully intertwined.

It has been recognized for a long time that some concept of energy[1] is essential as a driving force to performance (van der Molen, 1996). It is of

---

[1]The term *energy* is merely used as a metaphor and does not refer to physical energy. Although on a local level, regional blood flow and glucose consumption depend on the neural structures involved in the ongoing mental activities (e.g., Posner, Peterson, Fox, & Raichle, 1988), the effects on oxygen and glucose consumption are negligible in comparison with those elicited by bodily activities.

interest in this respect that an integrated approach toward computational and energetic aspects of behavior was explicitly implied by the neobehaviorists (Hull, 1943). They saw behavior as a joint function of habit strength— i.e., the computational component—and of the excitatory potential of a specific or a generalized drive. A habit could not elicit behavior without an excitatory drive potential, and vice versa. The notion of a generalized drive state regulating energy and varying along a single dimension gained currency during the 1950s under the label of arousal. This was characterized by Hebb (1955) as an energizer, not a guide, a distinction that may well have contributed to the subsequent, isolated development. Admittedly, energetics played a prominent role in Broadbent's (1958, 1971) and Kahneman's (1973) views. Broadbent's selective filter could become satiated by selecting the same type of information again and again (Broadbent, 1958), thus leading to a bias against responding in monotonous conditions (Broadbent, 1971). Kahneman's capacity concept was also energetical, yet the energetical notions had little relation to the nature of cognitive processes.

The first part of this chapter outlines the traditional unidimensional-arousal view and its problems. This is followed by a discussion of resource-strategy views on energetics that emphasize the qualitative nature of cognitive-energetic processes. The next step is the description of a cognitive-energetic model of information processing that also aims at integrating computational and energetical components of performance but with roots in stage theory rather than in capacity theory (Sanders, 1983; van der Molen, 1996). The second part is concerned with research on traditional issues on energetics, among which are long-term performance, diurnal rhythms, sleep loss, and vigilance. A problem here is that the theoretical accounts are still often based on the traditional unidimensional-arousal view. This means that, albeit in more specific contexts, some of the arguments of the first part of the chapter recur when called for.

AROUSAL

Unidimensional Arousal

During the 1950s, the notion of a unidimensional-arousal system gained rapid acceptance. This was particularly due to studies on the relation between alertness and the state of the ascending pathways of the reticular formation in the brain. For example, cats with lesions in that area became extremely inactive. Moreover, there was the discovery of variations in EEG waves among levels of mental activity. Fast, low amplitude, desynchronized, and high-frequent β-activity proved typical for an alert state; slower α-activity was characteristic when the participant was passively awake; still slower and higher amplitude θ-activity was found in the case of near sleep; and very slow and high-amplitude δ-activity occurred in deep sleep. Together, these results suggested a single dimensional continuum varying from deep sleep, via a passive but awake condition, to a state of high alertness and excitement (Duffy, 1957; Malmo, 1959). Some features of a state of high arousal were already mentioned in the discussion on orienting reactions. However, in that context, arousal was merely viewed as a state and not as a continuum.

The theoretical relation between the level of arousal and that of perform-ance is given by the well-known "inverted-U" curve derived from early work by Yerkes and Dodson (1908) on the effects of electrical shocks on brightness discrimination learning by mice. They observed that mice learned slower when shocks were either weak or strong and faster when shocks had a moderate intensity, suggesting that the elicited drive level was optimal in that condition.[2] The inverted U was generalized from Yerkes and Dodson's learning study to a general performance principle and served for some time as the leading notion about the relation between energetic and cognitive factors in shaping performance, that is, that performance is poor when arousal is either too low or too high.

The inverted-U law relied on two major assumptions. The first was that energetics refer to a one-dimensional, biologically driven system, the level of which depends on a combination of internal biorhythms and outside stimulation. It was initially assumed that the level of arousal depends pri-marily on internal factors, but this changed because of the pronounced negative effect of sensory deprivation, a condition in which all outside stimu-lation is removed for a prolonged period of time, on the energetic state (Hebb, 1955). The second assumption was that the relation between arousal and cognition is aspecific, which was the main justification for separating cognitive and energetic aspects of information processing. The hypothesis was that the properties of arousal and cognition are independent, perhaps with the exception of a general complexity factor. The inverted-U model assumed that the optimal performance level of a more demanding cognitive task is somewhat lower, whereas an easier task is performed best at a somewhat higher arousal level.

An influential, theoretical account of the relation between complexity and arousal stemmed from Easterbrook (1959). He suggested that any object or situation and its environment emit cues that are either relevant or irrelevant to performance, an assumption that reminds of some of the single-process models of C(RT). As the level of arousal increases, intake of both task-rele-

---

[2]The results of the Yerkes-Dodson experiment and subsequent follow-up studies have not been replicated. There is little empirical evidence for an optimal drive level for discrimination learning (Bartoshuk, 1971); yet the law has a strong intuitive appeal.

vant and task-irrelevant cues narrows (narrowing). In contrast, as the level of arousal decreases, relevant and irrelevant cues are readily admitted (widening). Consequently, a low level of arousal performance would lead to blurred discrimination of task-irrelevant and task-relevant cues. At too high a level of arousal, task-irrelevant cues are hardly admitted. The same can be said for task-relevant cues, with the effect being that performance suffers from a lack of relevant cues. In other words, at a low level of arousal, the main problem is distractability and competing response tendencies due to irrelevant cues; at a high level of arousal, insufficient task-relevant information precludes reliable action. It follows that a more complex task, characterized by more task-relevant features, should suffer more from relatively high arousal than a less complex task. The interesting aspect of Easterbrook's hypothesis is that performance is supposed to decline when arousal is either too low or too high but for different reasons and in different ways.

This highly influential statement is still often referred to, but this does not mean that it has not been debated. In particular, M. W. Eysenck (1982) raised some major objections. First, the assumption that tasks are composed of cues, a certain number of which are admitted for processing, is speculative and cannot boast much support. Although not invariably, attentional narrowing is indeed observed in dual-task performance when arousal is presumably high. However, narrowing may well be strategical rather than determined bottom up by deficient cue utilization. Again, the suggestion that cue utilization widens in drowsy conditions should not be taken to imply more openness to experience. High arousal is sometimes thought to be related to high anxiety. It would follow from Easterbrook's (1959) view that high-anxiety participants are less distractible, but the available data suggest exactly the opposite. A drowsy state may lead to inactivity and slow responding, and a nervous state may lead to overactivity and dominance of speed at the cost of accuracy. However, this does not necessarily follow from variations in cue utilization. The influence of the Easterbrook hypothesis may have been largely due to the suggestion that high and low levels of arousal are connected with different patterns of performance decrement rather than to one general pattern, a notion that became current starting in the 1970s.

The unidimensional-arousal theory flourished during the early 1960s. It played an important part in theories on vigilance and could nicely account for a fair number of results on effects of environmental stresses. However, the notion was seriously challenged by subsequent physiological and behavioral evidence. The physiological and behavioral objections are certainly not independent but are distinguished to avoid the risk of committing a category error. It is conceivable that a unidimensional-arousal theory satisfactorily covers behavioral results but fails to account for neurophysiological data, or vice versa.

Psychophysiological Objections

Initially, the psychophysiological objections centered mainly on the failure to find convincing correlations among the various proposed psychophysiological indexes of energy mobilization (Lacey, 1967). Aside from EEG-derived measures of the central nervous system, popular arousal indexes were (a) on the somatic level, such as muscle tension and the galvanic skin response (GSR); (b) on the level of the autonomous nervous system, such as heart rate (HR), blood pressure, and pupil diameter; and (c) on the endocrine level, such as cathecholamine and cortisol excretion. Initially, low and high arousal were thought to be characterized by opposite, coherent syndromes of these measures, with the OR physiological pattern as a showcase of high arousal.

At the extremes of deep sleep and a state of nervous excitement, the opposite arousal syndromes have indeed been found, but the indexes appear to dissociate on less extreme occasions. For example, there is the case of paradoxical, or rapid eye movement (REM), sleep. Despite the fact that one is asleep, indexes such as HR, muscle activity, and EEG suggest a state of high arousal during REM. There is also a lack of correlation among psychophysiological indexes during performance. Lacey's (1967) prime example concerned HR deceleration during the foreperiod in a choice reaction. HR decelerated and muscle tension increased while preparing to respond.

The rebuttal from the unidimensional-arousal view was that low correlations among indexes are indecisive. Besides expressing arousal, physiological variables have functions such as pumping blood (the heart), regulating light (the pupil), and getting ready for action (the muscles). These functions are unrelated to arousal, but their uncontrolled variation may easily lead to low correlations (Duffy, 1972). Moreover, the indexes are sensitive to cognitive and perceptual–motor processing, so they always reflect a mixture of specific, perceptual–motor, and energetic effects. Yet, an unfortunate consequence of the low correlations has been that the term "arousal" is often used as a mere label for some physiological index. Examples are "cortical arousal" for EEG and "autonomous arousal" for HR, both of which are void of theoretical meaning.

Moreover, the unidimensional-arousal theory faced the problem of deviant psychophysiological patterns. For instance, Malmo and Surwillo (1960) found an increase rather than a decrease of HR and muscle activity as a function of time on task in a monotonous setting. Other studies on vigilance failed to show any regular pattern of physiological changes over time at all, not even in the presence of a performance decrement. It was suggested at the time that endocrine measures might suffer less from specific behavioral or cognitive factors and, therefore, might be a better index of arousal (Selye, 1979). Yet, there are various results that suggest that there are also specific connections between endocrine secretion and cognitive aspects of information processing. One example regards Mason's (1975) patterns 1 and 2, which relates to the extent to which a future event can be predicted. Mason found that cortisol and noradrenaline levels were elevated irrespective of whether an event was predictable, whereas the level of adrenaline was only elevated in the case of a low-predictable event and, presumably, reflects a response to an unexpected stimulus.

However, from a physiological perspective, the definitive blow to the unidimensional view on arousal was the accumulation of data suggesting that the ascending reticular formation consists of multiple neural systems that all have their own projections to the forebrain. There is also rapidly growing evidence for a variety of brain structure patterns and connected neurotransmitter functions with specific reference to energetics as well as to cognitive and perceptual–motor processes (e.g., Pribram & McGuinness, 1975; Robbins, 1986; Robbins & Everitt, 1995). In short, the evidence suggests distinct cognitive-energetic patterns rather than a relatively loose relation between separate energetic and cognitive systems as embodied in the in-verted-U model.

An early amendment to the unidimensional-arousal notion was the dis-tinction between tonic and phasic arousal. Tonic arousal was thought to reflect a stable and slowly changing energetic state and was supposed to depend on variables such as time of the day, psychotropic drugs, and sleep loss. In contrast, phasic arousal would be short lasting and foremost regulated by outside stimulation. As already discussed, ORs to novel, intense, complex, and deviant stimuli are prototypical for phasic arousal, whereas actively maintained response readiness is thought to rely on tonic arousal. Some psychophysiological measures such as GSR, background EEG, some patterns of endocrine secretion, and body temperature may reflect the slow-tonic component; other measures, such as the ERP, are more likely to reflect phasic arousal, whereas still other measures, such as HR, might be related to either system. The distinction between tonic and phasic arousal is still quite relevant in more recent formulations on energetics.

Behavioral Objections

The behavioral unidimensional-arousal concept was strongly connected with the inverted-U as an explanation of performance effects of presumably arousing or dearousing conditions such as noise, sleep loss, heat, incentives, and psychotropic drugs. Interestingly, the evidence of the 1960s on interac-tions among the effects of stresses was roughly consistent with the inverted-U model. A night's loss of sleep had a negative effect on performance, which further increased as a function of time on task but which was counteracted by an incentive as knowledge of results, stimulating psychotropic drugs, and even noise. A combination of noise and incentives had a positive effect on performance when participants suffered from sleep loss, but they had a negative effect after normal sleep. Again, together with arousing social stimulation, a small dosage of alcohol had a more pronounced negative-performance effect. This fits a unidimensional model of counteracting effects of arousing and dearousing variables (Broadbent, 1971).

Broadbent (1971) also noted problems with respect to the inverted-U model. One was that noise only had detrimental effects during the later part of a work spell, but arousal theory predicts a stronger effect at the beginning. Arousal is supposed to decrease as a function of time on task in a monotonous setting. Hence, if noise is overarousing, a negative effect of noise should occur at the start of a session when arousal is still supposed to be relatively high. Due to the decrease in arousal, performance might even be assumed to benefit from some noise later in the workspell. Another concern was that the effect of heat, which is supposed to be arousing as well, did not interact with the effects of the other energetic factors in the same way as noise. However, perhaps most importantly, the inverted-U pattern of interactions was only found in repetitive and monotonous tasks such as vigilance and self-paced serial reactions.[3] There are other, usually more complex, tasks that proved to hardly suffer from a night's loss of sleep or from noise. From the perspective of the inverted-U hypothesis, it may be suggested that more complex tasks have a lower optimal level of arousal and that interesting tasks are intrinsically arousing (Wilkinson, 1969), but this is, at best, a post hoc explanation.[4]

To study the relation between arousal and task complexity more directly, Sanders et al. (1982) varied stimulus quality and S–R compatibility in a CRT task. The four conditions were carried out in separate blocks for half an hour each, following a night's loss of sleep or after normal sleep. The prediction of the arousal theory is that the most complex condition, that is, the condition in which the stimuli were degraded and required an incompatible response, should suffer less from sleep loss than easier conditions such as the degraded–compatible and the intact–incompatible ones. In turn, these easier conditions should suffer less than the easiest condition, that is, the intact–compatible one. The results of this study show an interaction of the effects of sleep loss and stimulus quality. Sleep loss had a more pronounced negative effect on CRT when stimuli were degraded than when they were intact (Steyvers, 1991). In contrast, variation of S–R compatibility proved insensitive to sleep loss. Thus, the effect of sleep loss was not determined by complexity per se but by the nature of the cognitive demands. In terms of stage analysis, response selection appeared insensitive, whereas feature extraction was sensitive to sleep loss. The result suggests a much more intimate relation between cognitive and energetic processes than assumed by the inverted-U model and by Kahneman's (1973) capacity model.

---

[3]In a self-paced serial-reaction task, the reaction to a stimulus immediately elicits the next stimulus, followed by a new response, and so on.

[4]It is of interest to contrast this view—in which a more complex task is supposed to suffer less from sleep loss than an easier one—with Kahneman's (1973) energetic capacity theory. Kahneman's capacity view assumes that sleep loss has the effect of reducing arousal as well as capacity. A more complex task demands more capacity and because less capacity is available, it should suffer more from sleep loss than an easier task.

QUALITATIVE CHANGES IN ENERGETIC STATE

Some investigators argued in favor of a qualitative analysis of cognitive-energetic states (e.g., Hockey, 1986, 1993; Rabbitt, 1979). Stresses such as noise and sleep loss would not affect the level of arousal or the amount of capacity but would lead to a qualitatively different distribution of energetic resources needed to comply with the task demands. This way of theorizing is at the basis of the resource strategy approach as distinct from the resource volume approach. The emphasis is on tracing qualitative changes in loci of control, processing strategy, and coping with demands. The general aim of any human being is to restore an energetic equilibrium when disturbed by a stress. A perceived divergence between the actual energetic state and the equilibrium leads to measures to minimize the difference. The adaptation to the task demands is continuously traced in order to detect a potential divergence. A major element in this type of reasoning is that behavior is not simply determined by a combination of separate energetic forces and cognitive processes. The human organism is first and foremost viewed as a strategic, self-regulating system reacting to deviations in order to restore equilibrium and to cope with demands.

Proponents of the resource-strategy view do not deny that the properties of a task are vital to the effects of an environmental stress. Hockey (1986) suggested a set of important performance properties, namely, general alertness, selectivity, speed, accuracy, and short-term memory capacity. General alertness is reflected by performance variability, in that performance is less variable in an alert than in a nonalert state. For example, in a serial-reaction task, performance becomes more variable in conditions of low alertness induced by factors such as prolonged work, sleep loss, or a depressant drug. On the other hand, variability does not increase in conditions of high alertness induced by a stimulant drug, an incentive, or heat. The issue of performance variability is discussed in the context of mental blocks and reactive inhibition.

Hockey's (1986) second property, selectivity, is related to the relative priority of tasks in dual-task performance. In one of Hockey's own studies, participants carried out a tracking task, centrally located in the visual field, together with detection of peripherally presented stimuli. Central tracking suffered most from sleep loss, and peripheral stimulus detection suffered most from noise (Hockey, 1970a, 1970b).[5] Thus, participants tended to neglect the tracking task after sleep loss, whereas they tended to focus on tracking when performing under loud noise. Hence, narrowing of attention is supposed to be one of the qualitative changes in conditions of high

---

[5]Other studies failed to replicate this finding (e.g., Loeb & Jones, 1978). Hockey suggested that failures in replicating effects of stresses may be due to the fact that stress effects are concerned with motivation and strategic adaptation of resources, and this may not always lead to uniform performance effects.

arousal. This reminds one of Easterbrook's (1959) view, albeit in a theoretically different context, which is characterized by top-down strategical allocation of resources rather than by bottom-up limits of cue utilization.

Narrowing or widening attention is not viewed as a matter of central or peripheral location of stimuli in the visual field, but of relative strategic priority to either the central or the peripheral task. As an illustration, Hamilton, Hockey, and Quinn (1972) asked participants to detect stimuli that could occur with a certain probability at different spatial locations. The locations of the stimuli were occluded, but one could issue an observing response, that is, disclose a certain location in order to see whether a stimulus had been presented at that location. It is obvious that detection improves as the distribution of the observing responses agrees with the distribution of the probability of stimulus occurrence at the various spatial locations. After sleep loss, participants tended to be less selective; they did not disclose the most probable positions often enough. When exposed to noise, they were overselective; they disclosed the most probable positions too often.

Shifts in SAT toward speed in conditions of high and toward accuracy in conditions of low arousal is the next strategical element. Shifts in SAT have been found in studies on serial reactions after sleep loss and under noise. Sleep loss led to more missed stimuli and longer CRTs, whereas noise had the effect of a higher error rate (e.g., Rabbitt, 1979). Finally, evidence for stress effects on short-term memory (*STM*) stem from studies on running memory in which participants hear a sequentially presented list of items, for example, digits. The list stops abruptly, whereupon the participants must reproduce as many as possible from the more recently presented digits, in their correct order. One result (Hamilton, Hockey, & Reyman, 1977) was that after sleep loss, participants retrieved somewhat earlier presented items at the cost of more recent ones. In contrast, under noise, they tended to retrieve the most recent ones at the cost of somewhat earlier presented digits. This was interpreted as indicating that noise elicits "immediate throughputting," and sleep loss promotes "contemplacency." More readiness to respond in a high-arousal condition may underlie the shift in SAT as well.

In summary, the strategical resource view suggests that effects of stresses consist of strategical shifts in processing, the nature of which depend on the cognitive structure of a task. The aim is to maintain a cognitive-energetic equilibrium. When faced with adverse environmental or internal conditions, participants attempt to minimize the deviation from their optimal energetic state by adopting the most profitable strategy and the least damaging physiological arousal pattern. For instance, attentional narrowing in the case of high arousal may be a strategic adaptation aimed at reducing attentional demands and not an automatic consequence of the arousing stress (Hockey, 1993). The fact that the effects are strategic is the main reason that experimental results are not always easily replicated.

By emphasizing the intimate relation between cognition and energetic state, the resource-strategy view has undoubtedly delivered seminal insights and interesting experiments. Yet, it has always remained somewhat artistic and has never led to more rigid, falsifiable propositions. The suggestion that experimental results may not be replicable due to strategic changes in processing is a case in point. With this "emergency exit," one is obviously able to explain any result!

A COGNITIVE-ENERGETIC MODEL

The resource-strategy view emphasized the role of central control that aims at performance stability by comparing actual performance with internal reference values.[6] If performance falls short, it may be restored by effort. In principle, this view had been proposed earlier by Broadbent (1971), who distinguished both a lower and an upper arousal system. The lower one represented traditional unidimensional arousal and the upper system had the task of controlling the parameters of the lower one. The upper system is self-regulatory and minimizes the damage when the lower system deviates from its optimum.

Control of basal energetic systems by a strategic, superordinate principle is also central in Sanders' (1983) cognitive-energetic model (Fig. 9.1) that aimed at integrating the literature on energetics and processing stages, which was discussed in chapters 3 and 4. The model rejects the aspecificity hypothesis and assumes two basal energetic systems, labeled arousal and activation, which are uniquely linked to the input and output stages of information processing. There is a relation, though, between the arousal system in Fig. 9.1 and the earlier discussed phasic arousal because arousal is supposed to be a matter of rapid but transient reactions to outside stimulation. In the same way, activation in the cognitive-energetic model reminds one of tonic arousal, which varies more slowly and is primarily a function of the internal state of the organism. Arousal and activation interact because, although with a much reduced gain, changes in arousal may raise or lower the level of activation for a limited period of time.

The stages in Fig. 9.1 are derived from the AFM stage structure outlined in Fig. 3.1. The main extension is that the computational stages are supposed to receive, and cannot function without, energetic supply from two basal energetic systems. In normal operating conditions, energetic supply is assumed to be optimal, so computational processes can usually be studied without worrying too much about energetics. However, abnormal conditions

---

[6]Rabbit's (1986) tracking model of SAT is a good example of a control version of a resource-strategy model.

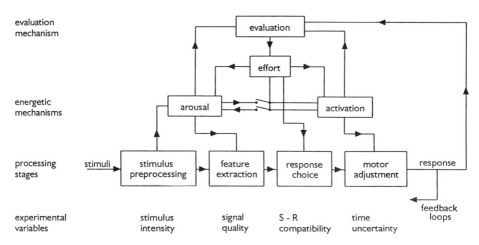

FIG. 9.1.   A cognitive-energetic model of human performance. Reprinted from
Sanders, A. F. (1983). Towards a model of stress and human performance. *Acta
Psychologica, 53,* 61–97. Copyright © 1983 with kind permission of Elsevier
Science-NL, Sara Burgerhartstraat 25, 1055 KV, Amsterdam, The Netherlands.

affect energetic supply because either too little or too much is supplied. Too
little supply from the arousal system affects the efficiency of perceptual
processing, moreso as the perceptual demands increase. Thus, the observed
interaction of the effects of a night's loss of sleep and stimulus quality on
CRT suggests that sleep loss impairs the supply of arousal: This is particularly
damaging when stimuli are degraded. A similar interaction of the effects of
arousal and stimulus quality was reported by Matthews, Jones, and Chamberlain (1989). In their study, participants were asked to give self-reports
about their experienced level of arousal and to carry out a rapidly paced
discrimination task with either intact or degraded stimuli. Performance deteriorated in a combination of degraded stimuli and low, self-reported
arousal, but reactions to degraded stimuli were unaffected when arousal
was reported to be high. Irrespective of experienced arousal, performance
was unaffected when stimuli were intact.

Similarly, too little supply of activation is supposed to be harmful to the
level of preparation and to readiness for action. In the framework of stage
analysis, this implies that the size of the effect of foreperiod duration on
CRT should covary with the level of activation and increase when participants
are drowsy. In support, Frowein, Gaillard, and Varey (1981) found a significant fourth-order interaction of the effects of foreperiod duration (TU), sleep
state, time of the day, and a stimulant drug. A night's loss of sleep had more
effect on CRT when the foreperiod was long. The effect was more pronounced in the afternoon than in the morning and largely disappeared after
administration of a stimulant drug (phentermine HCl; Fig. 9.2).

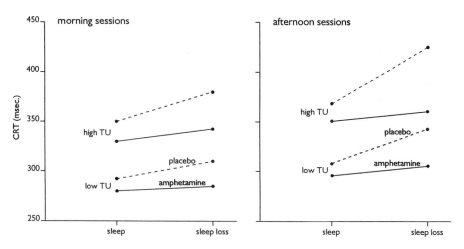

FIG. 9.2. Interaction of the effects of four energetic variables (stimulant, sleep loss, time of the day, time on task, and foreperiod duration (TU) on CRT. The stimulant eliminates most of the negative effects of the other energetic variables. From Frowein, H. W., Reitsma, D., & Aquarius, C. (1981). Effects of two counteracting stresses on the reaction process. In J. Long & A. D. Baddeley (Eds.), *Attention & Performance* (Vol. 9). Copyright © 1981 by Lawrence Erlbaum Associates, Hillsdale, NJ. Reprinted with kind permission of the publisher.

Hence, sleep loss seems to affect both arousal and activation. Yet, the effect of sleep loss is selective because it proved additive to that of S–R compatibility, suggesting that central stages, like response selection, are unaffected. This is supported by recent results from Humphrey, Kramer, and Stanny (1994), who found an almost equally strong effect of sleep loss in a visual-memory target-classification task, irrespective of whether VM or CM (cognitive memory) search was required. Other energetic variables appear to have a selective effect on either arousal or activation. Thus, Frowein et al. (1981) found an interaction of the effect of phentermine and that of foreperiod duration. However, the effect of phentermine was additive to those of variables affecting perceptual or central processing stages. In contrast, the effect of pentobarbital was found to interact with that of stimulus quality, suggesting an effect of that drug on feature extraction. Interestingly, the effect of pentobarbital was additive to those of experimental variables affecting central or motor stages. Thus, phentermine and pentobarbital appeared to have different points of application in the information flow. Selective effects of adverse conditions are an obvious prerequisite for distinguishing behavioral effects of arousal and activation.

Rather than provide too little energetic supply, arousal and activation may provide too much, which means that some computational systems may be flooded. This is likely to occur when facing emotional or threatening stimuli.

Due to ethical constraints, experiments on flooding are rare. Still, there are some classical studies on performance under stress. For example, in the isolation of the desert, soldiers were led to believe that a terrible disaster had occurred. This caused considerable performance decrement in tasks such as fault diagnosis of a failing radio or repair of some dysfunctioning device (Berkun, 1964). Again, Ursin, Baade, and Levin (1978) studied physiological state and performance of student paratroopers prior to their first jump and found pronounced effects on both hormonal levels and performance.[7] The aforementioned studies were not designed to test specific selective performance effects. They merely provide a hint about an important area of research. It is important that when under high stress, performance is least affected in well-practiced tasks, suggesting that too little as well as too much energetic supply is more disruptive as processing demands increase.

According to the inverted-U, noise and stimulant drugs are overarousing—provided that subjects are functioning at the optimal level—and they should affect performance negatively. The evidence is not convincing, though, and suggests that flooding is not brought about easily. Energetic effects of noise on performance are unsystematic, whereas a moderate dose of phentermine has clear effects on performance only when participants are underactivated, as after sleep loss. After normal sleep, the same dose of phentermine had, at best, a marginally positive effect on performance (Frowein et al., 1981).

Arousal and activation are supposed to be basal energetic mechanisms. Consistent with Broadbent's (1971) upper system, the cognitive-energetic model suggests a third superordinate-energetic mechanism that has the role of supervising and coordinating arousal and activation. The supervision consists of supplying additional energy to the arousal and activation systems when they fall short and of dampening these systems when they tend to flood. Thus, the third system, called effort, has the task of minimizing the damage of adverse conditions (Hockey, 1993). It is evident that the effort system should be kept informed about the state of the two basal systems in order to know whether any regulation is required. The model proposes an evaluation system that collects information about whether the flow of ongoing processes is proceeding satisfactorily. The evaluation mechanism receives its information through performance feedback as well as through internal feedback from the basal systems. It is clear that the criteria of the evaluation system are complex and vary as a function of motivational state. Thus, it would be unwise to supply additional energy to the arousal and activation mechanisms when retiring, whereas it is quite wise to invest effort when driving a car late at night!

---

[7]The effects were no longer found prior to the second jump.

Besides maintaining the optimal state of arousal and activation, the effort mechanism is supposed to regulate their mutual connection so that sudden changes in arousal do not propagate in an unrestrained way to the activation system and its connected motor stages. An example is the case of immediate arousal. It was argued previously that loud auditory and tactual stimuli create an increased readiness to respond that may be ascribed to propagation of arousal to activation. The effect disappeared in the case of a choice-reaction task with incompatible S–R relations (Sanders & Andriessen, 1978). The cognitive-energetic model suggests that because response selection is by-passed, propagation from arousal to activation leads to ill-considered reactions and, consequently, to a high error rate. As a result, the effort mechanism may disconnect arousal from activation, thereby preventing a behavioral effect of immediate arousal to occur. A combination of behavioral inhibition and high arousal may be responsible for some of the previously noticed dissociations of psychophysiological responses. Finally, the model proposes that response selection is not affected by the basal mechanisms but depends directly on effort. It should be noted that the evidence on this suggestion is scant and is the most speculative part of the model.

If effort restores the optimal state of arousal and activation, one may wonder why working under adverse conditions has any negative effect on performance at all. It should be noted in this regard that performance effects of adverse conditions are actually small and variable in the laboratory and are much smaller than one would intuitively expect (Hockey, 1993). This may be due to greater effort investment in the laboratory, presumably because the participants are aware that their performance is continually monitored. However, performance decrements do occur in the laboratory, suggesting that effort—or perhaps the criteria of the evaluation mechanism—wane(s) as a function of time on task. Either one of these options implies that without additional, motivational stimuli, a deficient state of the basal energetic mechanisms is compensated less as time on task goes on. Thus, at the start of a workspell in the laboratory, suboptimal arousal or activation may often, but not invariably, be compensated. However, as time proceeds, the contribution of effort is likely to diminish, and this means that performance declines to a level that can be handled by the available supply from the basal systems. This performance level can be maintained for a much longer period of time. Thus, diminishing effort rather than arousal or fatigue is proposed as the main reason for performance effects of time on task. The consequence is that when no effort is invested at the start of the work period, performance may be suboptimal from the very start, which may well be the case in many real-life settings. According to the cognitive-energetic model, effort is only invoked to force performance up and is not a normal condition.

Loci of the Effects

Thus far, the performance effects of adverse conditions were described as indirect effects of deficient energetic supply on cognitive processing. One may wonder, though, whether this assumption is really necessary because adverse conditions might also have direct effects on the computational processing stages. A distinction between direct computational effects and indirect energetic effects is only justified when they can be shown to be qualitatively different. There is actually the interesting possibility that additional demands on computation prolong the processing time of any individual trial, thus causing a shift of the whole density function and, perhaps, some increase in variance. In contrast, effects of low arousal or activation should be primarily evident at the upper tail of the distribution. The point is that a low state of arousal or activation does not imply that energetic supply is uniformly low but, rather, that it is more variable. In some trials, supply may be normal, in which cases CRT is not affected. In other trials, there is far too little supply, causing an inefficient and long CRT. In still other trials, supply may be less suboptimal, reflected by a somewhat longer CRT. Thus, the low end of the density function should hardly be affected by low arousal or activation.

A difference between this view and Bills' (1931) mental block, or lapse, hypothesis (to be discussed later in more detail), concerns the status of a long response time. Bills proposed that mental fatigue led to brief periods of inefficiency, enough for satiation to dissipate. During a lapse, performance is supposed to be fully blocked; otherwise it is supposed to be normal. This means that energetical supply is either normal or completely blocked. In contrast, the cognitive-energetic model assumes a gradually varying degree of energetic supply. The result is that low arousal and activation should increase the long tail of the distribution as well as the median response time, whereas only the fastest CRTs may remain unaffected (e.g., Dinges & Kribbs, 1991).

In conditions of too high a level of arousal and activation, the model suggests disorganization of performance when effort fails to dampen the oversupply. As said, experiments in this area are hard to realize, but in contrast to low arousal and activation, too much energetic supply may affect SAT and, perhaps, micro-SAT in particular. The occurrence of ill-considered reactions and errors may be followed by strong behavioral inhibition that could block any activity for some time. The net effect, then, could be an increase in errors together with a large variance in CRT, to which both the lower and upper tails of the density function would contribute. Yet, this reasoning is based on intuition and not evidence.

These criteria for distinguishing cognitive and energetic effects do not address the question about the relation between the basal mechanisms and effort. For example, the positive effect of phentermine was ascribed to restoring the optimal level of activation through effort. As an alternative, phentermine may not affect activation but, instead, may induce effort investment during the complete work period. In either case, performance remains optimal but, obviously, for different reasons. Again, when fully compensated by effort, a state of low arousal does not bring about a performance decrement either, which might lead to the incorrect conclusion that the level of arousal is normal. A decision between these two options awaits more research on which energetic variables are specifically related to the basal mechanisms and which are related to effort. The next section is devoted to knowledge of results (KR) as the prime candidate for a variable affecting effort. Moreover, research on the relative roles of effort and the basal mechanisms in shaping performance will obviously benefit from concurrent psychophysiological measures.

Knowledge of Results and Effort

KR is usually manipulated by online or offline evaluation of individual responses varying from "fine" to "poor," according to an individual criterion. The cognitive-energetic model states that KR has the function of updating the evaluation mechanism which, in turn, decides whether effort should be allocated. One prediction is that KR will only have an effect when effort is really needed, that is, under conditions of suboptimal arousal or activation. The experimental evidence generally supports this claim (Steyvers, 1991). Thus, effects of KR are virtually absent after normal sleep but prominent after sleep loss. Again, effects of KR increase as a function of time on task. This is consistent with the notion that effort declines as time on task goes on, but it may be maintained when providing KR. In a classic, self-paced serial-reaction study (Wilkinson, 1961), KR fully restored performance after sleep loss, although partial recovery is the more common finding. Figure 9.3 shows some results from Steyvers (1987, 1991) who tested participants in three successive sessions, one during the evening (19:30–1:00), one during the early morning (3:30–9:00), and a final one during the next day (11:30–17:00). Thus, the periods in Fig. 9.3 represent an increasing degree of sleep loss confounded with time of the day. The last data point (P) concerns CRT, that was measured a short time after completion of the final period of testing.

Steyvers (1991) used a discrete choice-reaction task and varied stimulus quality. His results confirmed the interaction of the effects of stimulus quality and sleep loss on CRT (Sanders et al., 1982). KR largely compensated for the effect of sleep loss and eliminated the effect of time on task. Figure 9.3 also suggests that the effect of KR was more pronounced when the stimuli were degraded. This was confirmed in a follow-up study. Finally, in the ECR, HR deceleration was more pronounced when KR was provided.

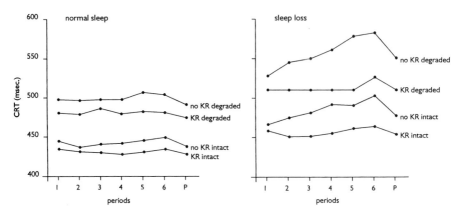

FIG. 9.3. Interaction of the effects of sleep loss, time on task, time of the day, stimulus quality, and KR. When stimuli are degraded CRT suffers more from cumulative sleep loss than when they are intact. KR diminishes the effect of sleep loss. From Steyvers, J. J. M. (1991). *Information processing and sleep deprivation. Effects of knowledge of results and task variables on choice reactions.* Doctoral dissertation. Tilburg University, Tilburg, The Netherlands. Reprinted with kind permission of the author.

In Steyvers' (1991) later studies, participants had one long session consisting of four successive half-hour blocks that were separated by brief breaks and that were carried out after a night's loss of sleep and after normal sleep. As usual, the effect of sleep loss increased as a function of time on task, the effect of which was partly eliminated by KR. As mentioned, KR was more beneficial when stimuli were degraded than when they were intact. It was of interest that both the effects of sleep loss and KR were marginal for the 25% fastest responses and strongest for the 25% slowest responses. This finding is consistent with the earlier outlined criteria for an energetic rather than for a computational effect. Together, the results suggest that effort compensates the effects of sleep loss on arousal at the beginning of a work period and wanes as time on task goes on. KR restores effort control of arousal to a considerable extent.

In a further study, Steyvers (1991) confirmed another result of Sanders et al. (1982), namely, that the effect of sleep loss is not sensitive to changes in S–R compatibility, nor did the effects of KR and S–R compatibility interact. Finally, Steyvers wondered whether the effect of KR was motivational— merely rewarding—or also informational because KR informs about how well one is doing. It turned out that attaching a real reward to KR did not change the size of its effect, nor did "faked" KR improve performance. Hence, Steyvers concluded that the informational aspect of KR was particularly relevant. This is consistent with an interpretation of KR in terms of a joint effect on evaluation and effort, but it argues against a direct effect of KR on arousal. The fact that the effects of KR, S–R compatibility, and sleep loss were additive may imply that, as such, effort is not affected by sleep loss.

Depression and Hyperactivity

As argued, the major prediction of the cognitive-energetic model is that energetic factors have selective effects rather than a general effect on a volume of available capacity, as implied by Kahneman (1973). This means that energetic factors should affect some computational processes but leave others unchanged, a situation that can be established by way of the AFM. So far, the discussion has been concerned with studies on effects of sleep loss, phentermine, pentobarbital, and KR. In addition, Brand and Jolles (1987) found that depressed patients differed from control participants in that they performed more slowly in regard to target classification and, more generally, to variables affecting central processing stages. This was confirmed by Azorin et al. (1995), who found an interaction of the effects of depressed state and of S–R compatibility. However, the effects of depression and visual stimulus intensity were additive. The implication could be that a depressed state affects effort. Sergeant and van der Meere (1990a) reviewed evidence on hyperactivity deficits from an AFM perspective. Clinical descriptions of the hyperactivity syndrome stress unrestrained overactivity, wide fluctuations in activity, and irritability, which should provide an excellent test case for the cognitive-energetic model.

Much research on information processing of hyperactive children has used some version of the so-called continuous performance test (CPT), a vigilance type of task in which a succession of letters is presented with the instruction to carry out an overt response whenever some specific letter or some combination of successive letters is presented. The general result has been that hyperactive children perform less well on the CPT than a control group of normal children, and that a stimulant drug improves performance of the hyperactive ones. Unfortunately, the CPT does not allow localization of the deficit in the information flow along the lines of stage analysis. This type of analysis was initiated, however, by Sergeant and van der Meere (1990b). First, they found that variation in encoding demands had almost the same effect on hyperactive and on normal children. Moreover, they reviewed studies on variations of encoding demands beyond the AFM paradigm, such as depth of processing by way of physical versus name matching (Posner, 1978), which did not differentiate between hyperactives and controls. They did not find a differential effect of hyperactivity on target classification either.

In contrast, hyperactives were particularly sensitive to variations in S–R compatibility and foreperiod duration. They performed less well than controls when S–R relations were incompatible and when foreperiods were long or variable. Sergeant and van der Meere (1990b) drew the tentative conclusion, therefore, that the problems of hyperactive chidren are related to the activation-effort axis of the cognitive-energetic model. Hyperactives may suffer from chronic underactivation, perhaps in combination with deficient control of the connection between arousal and activation (Fig. 9.1). Deficient control of this connection means an unrestrained flow from arousal to activation. In that case, hyperactives would suffer more from distraction and ill-considered action. The suggestion that hyperactives are underactivated is supported by evidence that stimulant drugs tend to improve their performance. The interaction with S–R compatibility suggests that they have problems with investing effort as well. Still, this might be indirect: They may continually need effort for monitoring the deficient arousal-activation connection which, in turn, could mean that less can be allocated to response selection. Alternatively, hyperactives may, indeed, have deficient effort allocation.

One implicit assumption underlying this interpretation is that as activation is less, it is more sensitive to changes in arousal. This is consistent with physiological data on enhanced autonomous effects after sleep loss, which indicate that after sleep loss, participants tend to react more strongly to intensive stimuli. In conclusion, then, the cognitive-energetic model provides tests and enables questions on behavioral functioning of hyperactives on a more detailed level. Aside from hyperactivity, Sergeant and van der Meere (1990b) considered as well the potential of the cognitive-energetic model for analyzing distorted information processing in other psychopathological syndromes.

Stress

The stress concept is another test case for the cognitive-energetic model. It was first introduced in physiology by Selye (1956) as a non-specific response of the body to any demand made upon it. Selye suggested that besides specific physiological reactions related to the nature of current behavioral demands, there is an aspecific physiological response pattern that is typical for stress and in which cortisol plays a prime part as stress hormone. In this definition, stress is a response to a stressor. When adopting a response definition, stress and "arousal"[8] are hard to distinguish because both concepts share the features of unidimensionality, aspecificity, and energy mobilization. There is a difference in research tradition in that stress has been mostly discussed in terms of hormonal responses, whereas "arousal" is more often related to autonomous or cortical indexes. However, this is a trivial distinction because both sets of measures are strongly interrelated.

---

[8]From now on, "arousal" (in quotes) refers to the unidimensional notion as outlined in the first section, whereas arousal (without quotes) refers to the more restricted meaning in the cognitive-energetic model.

In performance theory, stress is often defined as a stimulus. Thus, noise, heat, sleep loss, and psychotropic drugs belong to the category of stresses that elicit strain. In this definition, "arousal" may serve as an explanation for effects of noise, sleep loss, and other "stresses," thereby allowing Broadbent (1971) to discuss "the arousal theory of stress." It is clear that in a stimulus definition, the stress concept is atheoretical and serves only as label for an area of research. Aside from a response definition in physiology and a stimulus definition in performance theory, stress has an interactional definition that has been particularly popular in social and clinical psychology. It holds that stress arises from a divergence between perceived demands and perceived capabilities for adapting. A comparison between the perceived demands and the perceived quality of adaptation leads to both cognitive and physiological appraisal of the situation. A stress response occurs when in a subjectively relevant situation, the comparison between demands and adaptation is unfavorable and difficult to repair (Cox, 1978; Welford, 1973). One may cope by decreasing the perceived demands, by improving the quality of adaptation, or by combining these two factors. The interactional definition emphasizes the emotions, featured so prominently in the everyday meaning of stress.

The cognitive-energetic model is in line with the interactional definition but suggests multiple stress patterns rather than a single one. At least five patterns can be distinguished, depending on how the system fails to adapt to the task demands. They all reflect failures of the effort mechanism in maintaining optimal energetic supply. The first pattern arises when the arousal system is overstimulated and may relect Selye's (1956) shock phase of his general adaptation syndrome. In everyday life, it is found not only in panic caused by threatening stimulation but also in the less dramatic case of an unexpected loud noise. Stress arises when the effort mechanism fails to dampen overarousal and, hence, fails to prevent ill-considered action. Inappropriate action is perceived as a coping failure.

The opposite state, that is, underarousal, may correspond to habituation, which is a common phenomenon in repetitive and boring tasks (e.g., O'Hanlon, 1981). Habituation to stimuli and a reduced readiness to respond may be distinguished by the parameters (d', β) of signal detection theory. Whereas habituation to stimuli (a decrease in d') may reflect underarousal, a reduced readiness to respond (an increase in β) may reflect underactivation. Again, stress arises when a decrease in response to the outside world leads to unacceptable performance failures. Next, the case of overactivation reminds of the sensitive nervous state described by the "arousal" theory of the 1950s. It may occur particularly when anticipating a threatening situation such as an operation. A final state of stress may be related to failures of decision making and reasoning, as in the case of intolerable ambiguity when making a decision or solving a problem. Such ambiguities are supposed to need sustained high effort and, when faced with failure, can lead to the conflict type of stress.

As already briefly touched on, a multidimensional view on energetics has the advantage that it can account better for the discussed dissociations among psychophysiological measures. Aside from specific computational factors, the cognitive-energetic model acknowledges three energetic components that contribute to a current psychophysiological or hormonal response pattern. They are arousal and activation, effort, and potential stress reactions. As Hockey (1993) argued, the absence of performance impairment may well lead to an increase in compensatory physiological costs, thus expressing continued effort. One example is an increase in cathecholemine secretion and muscle tension for participants whose performance suffered the least from an adverse condition such as sleep loss. Along these lines, O'Hanlon (1965) found a decline in adrenaline and increased θ activity in the EEG of "decrementers" but not of "nondecrementers" in a vigilance task.

The costs of continuous effort may not be too high as long as the participants can meet the task demands, but they may rise sharply when coping fails (e.g., Frankenhaeuser, 1986). As an example, Wientjes, Grossman, Gaillard, and Defares (1986) had participants carry out a target classification task, with a monetary reward for "good" performance. In one condition, they received no KR; in another condition they had continuous KR; and in a final condition, continuous KR was combined with the requirement to improve on earlier performance in order to earn the reward. Each of these three conditions was run by two groups who had either many, or hardly any, psychosomatic complaints. As task demands increased, both groups showed similar physiological stress-like responses, but the high-complaints group experienced more psychosomatic symptoms when performing a more stressful condition. The frequency of experienced psychosomatic symptoms appeared to be related to hyperventilatory trends in respiration.

Comparisons With Other Models

The elements of the cognitive-energetic model remind of Posner's (1978) three components of attention. Thus, in regard to action, performance can be enhanced by preparation and by timing, both of which are related to presetting motor adjustment as closely as possible to the motor–action limit. Preparation is time consuming, voluntary (Sanders, 1972), maintained for only a limited period of time (Gottsdanker, 1975), and difficult to share with other processes (Posner & Boies, 1971). In fact, an optimal state of preparation comes close to what Posner has called alertness as a component of attention. The notion of alertness will be returned to in the discussion of vigilance; it corresponds to the activation mechanism in the cognitive-energetic model.

In view of the ample evidence for automatic and parallel perceptual processing, it may seem odd that encoding requires any energetic supply at all. However, perceptual processing is quite controlled in the case of unfamiliar or degraded stimuli. Moreover, there is growing evidence that encoding benefits from orienting and active search. Another major role of active encoding may be in separating relevant from irrelevant features, which comes close to Posner's (1978) orienting component of attention. Finally, the control function of effort in the cognitive-energetic model and its proposed relation to reasoning and decision making reminds of Posner's conscious processing as his third component of attention.

The cognitive-energetic model was completely derived from behavioral data. It is of great interest, though, to note the convergence with Pribram and McGuinness' (1975) neurophysiological argument. In their model, arousal expresses a phasic response to input, that is, orienting, which is presumably controlled by nuclei belonging to the amygdala. In turn, activation reflects a tonic readiness for action. Pribram and McGuinness proposed that this energetic system is controlled by the basal ganglia because the ability to maintain a state of alertness is greatly reduced in the case of a lesion in that region. As in the cognitive-energetic model, effort exerts supervisory control over arousal and activation, and it is thought to be controlled by hippocampal nuclei. Similarly, effort is supposed to play a role as well in reasoning and deciding. McGuinness and Pribram (1980) proposed that the three energetical mechanisms are related to different groups of endocrine and neurotransmitter systems, namely, serotenerg/noradrenergic (arousal), dopaminerg/cholinerg (activation), and ACTH-derived peptides (effort). The potential relation between corticoadrenal hormonal activity and effort underscores the connection between effort and stress.

It is also tempting to draw a comparison between effort and Gray's (1987) concept of behavioral inhibition. Like effort, this inhibition system is supposed to become active in the case of overarousal and serves the function of suppressing undesirable behavioral activity. The inhibition system is also supposed to counteract ill-considered reponding by disconnecting the shortcut between arousal and activation. Pribram and McGuinness' (1975) effort system and Gray's behavioral inhibition are both assumed to have the septohippocampal system as the underlying neural structure. In addition, Gray's proposal that activity in the behavioral inhibition system reflects anxiety corresponds directly to the presumed relation between effort and stress.

In view of the rapid progress on the more detailed functioning of brain structures, their interrelations, and their corresponding neurotransmitter systems, the aforementioned remarks are probably nothing but gross oversimplification. Thus, the neural substrate of the various forms of behavior consists presumably of complex interactions among several neurotransmitter systems rather than of a simple one-to-one connection. Combinations of neural structures and neurotransmitters are probably of greater interest than single neurotransmitters. Moreover, neural operations are obviously concerned with more than attention, among which are, most notably, memory and learning.

The simplification notwithstanding, the neurophysiological literature on attention suggests a relation between the central operations in motor behavior and striatal dopamine, between the central noradrenerg function and orienting, and between serotonine and behavioral inhibition (Robbins & Everitt, 1995). It is likely, though, that effort invested in either raising or dampening arousal and activation bears on different neurotransmitter systems.

A recent neuropsychological model of attention has emerged from the work of Posner and colleagues (e.g., Posner & Raichle, 1994). They observed that an alert state, referring to their previously discussed attention component, corresponded with increased blood flow in the right frontal and parietal lobes. The frontal lobe appeared particularly related to alertness because patients with lesions in that area had severe problems in maintaining vigilance. Another brain network was found to correspond to conscious attention, thought to be related to central executive attentional control in the organization of central processing and, presumably, to effort.[9] The connected brain structures centered around the anterior cingulate gyrus. This gyrus showed increased blood flow in tasks that required reasoning by way of generating a new word, by detecting the presence of a unique target, or by resolving conflict in a Stroop task. The activity of the anterior cingulate gyrus extended to other centers, in particular to those controlling working memory and visual orienting. A third attentional network in the brain proved to be more specifically related to orienting and had the posterior parietal lobe as its prime site. This network was already discussed in more detail in the section on covert orienting.

It is as yet unclear whether generalization from the cognitive-energetic model to the notions of Posner and Raichle (1994) is justified. The same may be said about the relations between Pribram's and Gray's predominantly limbic and Posner's cortical structures. Yet, it is interesting that evidence for a functional distinction between an input system (Posner's posterior structure), an output system (Posner's frontal lobe structure) and a central control system (Posner's anterior structure) reappears in all current descriptions of attentional mechanisms. The advent of advanced brain-imaging techniques underscores the need for much closer cooperation among performance theorists, neuropsychologists, and neurophysiologists in order to study the relations among the various notions.

COMMENTS

At this point, it is useful to reflect on the relative merits of resource strategy and stage analysis as different theoretical approaches to energetics. In brief,

---

[9]A relation with effort is suggested by the finding that patients with a frontal lesion have problems with sustained attention (e.g., Wilkins, Shallice, & McCarthy, 1987).

the resource approach emphasizes strategical changes in performance under adverse environmental or organismic conditions. Strategical changes are supposed to depend on the interaction between the participant's state and the nature of the task demands, the consequence of which was that the resource approach scrutinized energetic effects in a wide variety of fairly complex performances. The problem is that in the absence of process models for the complex tasks, the resource-strategy approach is less systematic and often has to resort to post hoc interpretation. In contrast, the stage analysis approach is limited to the analysis of choice reactions. This means a severe limitation, but within these limits, the stage approach is more predictive and explicit. Proponents of resource strategies have objected that merely using choice reactions restrains the variety of strategical processes to the rigid context of an artificial laboratory task. In this way, the two approaches are another reflection of the contrast between the total task and the small paradigm.

As repeatedly argued, generalization from theory on the basis of small paradigms to more complex situations is highly relevant, and back-to-back analysis serves the aim of assessing generalization gradients. A crude way of back-to-back analysis may be to compare the main conclusions of the more rigid but systematic stage approach and the more flexible but less systematic resource approach. Do their conclusions diverge or converge?

The first principle of the resource-strategy research concerned general alertness, that is, the changes in performance variability when performing under stress. Performance variability is an equally well-recognized principle in the cognitive-energetic model. It even served as a criterion for deciding whether an effect is computational or energetical. The second strategic principle concerned a shift in bias toward either storage of information in the case of sleep loss or immediate throughputting as a result of noise. In other words, this principle reflects a trend toward a relatively active or passive attitude. In the same way, AFM studies have suggested that sleep loss renders participants less responsive at both the perceptual and the motor level. Although this is viewed as a lack of energetic supply rather than as a change in strategy, either approach holds that SAT may vary. In the cognitive-energetic model, a change in strategy is primarily a matter of criteria, which belongs to the realm of the evaluation mechanism. In turn, the evaluation mechanism only regulates effort investment so that strategies are not operating on the perceptual or motor level per se.

There is hardly any research on the effects of loud noise in the context of the cognitive-energetic model, but if noise has the effect of enhancing arousal, it is likely to speed up perceptual–computational processes and lead to a higher error probability. One may be reminded, in this regard, of repeated findings that loud auditory or accessory stimuli[10] lead to faster

---

[10]An accessory stimulus is an irrelevant stimulus accompanying a relevant stimulus. Usually, the relevant stimuli are visual and the accessory stimuli auditory.

responses but at the cost of more errors, that is, to a shift in SAT (Sanders, 1980a). Yet, the effect of continuous and monotonous loud noise may be unrelated to immediate arousal but, instead, affect perceptual processing directly. This prediction is a refinement of the way in which noise may induce a shift in SAT, namely, on d' rather than on β.

The third suggestion from the resource-strategy approach concerns decreased cue selectivity after sleep loss in contrast to increased focusing on a narrow set after noise. Thus far, the stage approach may suggest one instance of decreased perceptual selectivity, namely, the negative effect of sleep loss on extracting relevant features from degraded stimuli. The effect may be due to a deficiency in separating relevant from irrelevant cues that is much along the lines of Easterbrook's (1959) cue utilization notion. Yet, the cognitive-energetic model would not ascribe this effect to a change in strategy but to a lack of energetic supply. Preliminary and incomplete as these three examples are, they do suggest that, although from different theoretical perspectives, the results from the stage and resource notions converge rather than diverge.

LONG-TERM PERFORMANCE AND FATIGUE

The previous sections outlined theoretical views on energetics, the experimental evidence of which spanned various traditional research topics. Now, the argument turns to a more systematic discussion of some traditional topics themselves. Whenever possible, the data are linked to the cognitive-energetic model, although most research has been carried out from other theoretical perspectives and from the dated "arousal" view in particular. The present section is devoted to long-term performance. It starts off with effects of time on task on active performance. There is special emphasis on the almost forgotten, albeit highly relevant and systematic, evidence on what the behaviorists called reactive inhibition. This is followed by a discussion of performance effects of diurnal rhythms and of sleep loss in which context the notion of fatigue is also scrutinized. The next section is concerned with effects of time on task on passive performance, which refers to supervisory control and monitoring of a system in order to detect rare targets. This area is usually called vigilance.

Continuous Performance and Reactive Inhibition

It was outlined previously that effects of time on task on CRT are mainly found under adverse conditions, such as sleep loss, and that the upper part of the CDF, in particular, is affected. Thus, the data in Fig. 9.3 show little effect of 30 minutes of continuous work on CRT after a night of normal

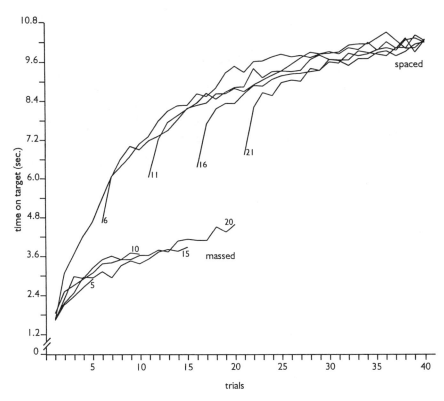

FIG. 9.4. The effects of massed and spaced practice on the development of skill acquisition in tracking. Practice mode (massed, spaced) has little effect on skill acquisition as is evident from the shifts from a massed to a spaced schedule. Yet, performance within massed and spaced sessions varies widely. From Adams, J. A. (1954). Psychomotor performance as a function of intertrial rest interval. *Journal of Experimental Psychology, 48,* 131–133.

sleep. In the same way, CRT, measured during a final isolated brief period of work, remained much the same after normal sleep (the last data point in Fig. 9.3), whereas it became much faster after sleep loss and without KR. The conclusion was that effort is restored when participants know that there is only going to be a brief test. The effect at the final brief test is only found after sleep loss; effort is either not needed or already optimal after a night of normal sleep.

However, the finding that when participants are tested under normal conditions, time on task has little effect on mean CRT may seem to be at odds with the classical results on reactive inhibition. This neobehavioristic concept refers to the well-established phenomenon in skill acquisition that performance hardly changes during a session of continuous (massed) practice, but improves considerably right at the start of the next massed session.

This is illustrated in Fig. 9.4 that depicts performance in a pursuit-tracking task. It is generally accepted that this so-called reminiscence effect is not due to learning during the rest interval, but that it reflects a performance effect. Thus, when participants carry out a few massed sessions and then continue with spaced practice, a schedule in which successive trials are always separated by brief rest intervals, it takes only a few trials to arrive at the same level of proficiency as reached by those who had spaced practice throughout and who showed the usual, gradual practice curve. The same is found with participants who shifted from a spaced to a massed practice schedule. They show a performance loss and continue to follow the pattern obtained with participants who had massed practice throughout (Adams, 1954; Denny, Frisbey, & Weaver, 1955).

The lack of improvement within a massed session was ascribed by the neobehaviorists to reactive inhibition, which refers to a decrease in drive potential as a consequence of habituation due to many repeated reactions. Thus, reactive inhibition is a negative effect that clouds practice effects. The processes underlying reactive inhibition have not been widely studied, but one suggestion is that it elicits resting responses that bring about partial dissipation of reactive inhibition (Kimble, 1949). Reactive inhibition is thought to fully dissipate during the interval between two massed sessions. This means that practice effects show up by a "jump" in performance at the start of the next session. There is a second phenomenon, called conditioned inhibition, which is held responsible for a second performance difference between massed and spaced practice and which occurs at the start of a session. When participants know that they are going to do a long massed session, they start less well than when they know that they will have spaced practice (Fig. 9.4). Reactive and conditioned inhibition obviously bear on time on task. It is noteworthy that either phenomenon vanishes as a function of practice.

The hypothetical resting responses remind one of the earlier mentioned mental blocks (Bills, 1931) that referred to incidental long reaction times in a self-paced serial-reaction task. Broadbent (1958) considered the mental block as "an interruption in the intake of information from one source to intake of information from another source" (p. 133). In line with reactive inhibition, the interruptions were thought to be due to satiation of selecting the same type of information over and over again. Blocks vanish also as a function of practice, although their frequency increases strongly again after sleep loss. The main theoretical difference between resting responses and blocks is that resting responses are ascribed to reactive inhibition of re-sponses, and blocks are seen as failures of perceptual selection. In terms of the cognitive-energetic model, resting responses suggest a deficiency in ac-tivation, and mental blocks suggest a deficiency in arousal.

Sanders and Hoogenboom (1970) had participants carry out an incom-patible six-choice, self-paced, serial-reaction task for seven sessions of 30 minutes each, with either a massed or a spaced schedule. During the last two sessions, the spaced group also changed to a massed schedule. The results show the usual evidence for reactive and conditioned inhibition. With the spaced schedule, CRT decreased gradually during a session, whereas CRT remained about the same during a massed session (reactive inhibition). Similarly, CRT was somewhat longer at the beginning of a new massed session than in the case of a comparable new spaced session (conditioned inhibition). Again, with a massed schedule, CRT was considerably faster at the start of a new session in comparison to the end of the previous one. The effects largely vanished at later sessions, all of which is perfectly consistent with Fig. 9.4. Thus, the same effects of time on task occur in pursuit tracking and in serial reactions.

Analysis of the CDFs in the Sanders and Hoogenboom (1970) experiment showed that (a) the massed and spaced schedules did not differ with respect to the first to third deciles of the distribution. In either case, they showed a gradually faster CRT as a function of practice; (b) throughout a session, the fourth to ninth deciles of the distribution were faster in the case of a spaced schedule; and (c) with a massed schedule, the tenth decile increased as a function of time on task, and this annihilated the practice effects at the fastest deciles. The long CRTs in the tenth decile were no outliers, as might be expected from mental blocks or from resting responses. Instead, mean CRT in the tenth decile increased gradually and was much less pronounced at later than at earlier massed sessions. Most of the increase in the tenth decile occurred within the first 10 minutes of a 30-minute spell. The observation that the effect of time on task usually arises during the first few minutes of work is actually a well-established finding (e.g., Bertelson & Joffe, 1963; J. F. Mackworth, 1964; Sanders et al., 1982). It will be recalled that sleep loss often has a similar effect during the first few minutes (Fig. 9.5).

Hence, the evidence on reactive and conditioned inhibition suggests subtle effects of time on task in normal conditions. The effect of reactive inhibition is presumably energetic because it is limited to the upper tail of the CDF. From its very start, a monotonous task may induce a somewhat suboptimal state of the basal energetic mechanisms—arousal, activation, or both—which brings about less regular energetic supply. As argued, effort is supposed to compensate for this lack at the beginning of a session but wanes as time goes on. Effort investment can also account for the effect of conditioned inhibition, that is, that participants tend to react somewhat more slowly at the start of a massed session. Less effort may be invested when they know that they are going to work for a long period. As a task is better practiced, processes run off more automatically and become less sensitive to suboptimal energetic supply. Hence, the effects of time on task are marginal once participants are well practiced and have had a normal night of sleep.

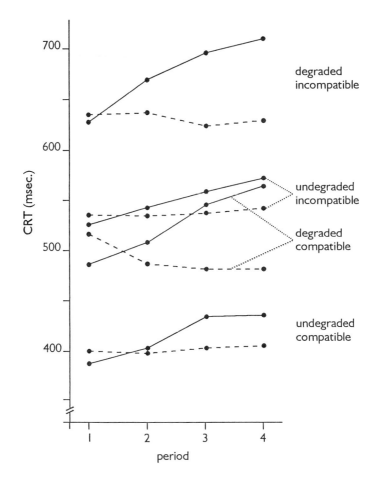

FIG. 9.5. Sleep loss has hardly an effect during the first few minutes of a 20-minute work period and builds up gradually afterward. The effect is more pronounced when stimuli are degraded. Reprinted from Sanders, A. F. (1983). Towards a model of stress and human performance. *Acta Psychologica, 53*, 61–97. Copyright © 1983 with kind permission of Elsevier Science-NL, Sara Burgerhartstraat 25, 1055 KV, Amsterdam, The Netherlands.

Sanders and Hoogenboom (1970) also found that when the participants changed from a spaced to a massed schedule, the first massed session showed a considerable effect of time on task that disappeared during the next massed session. This result suggests that the effect of time on task depends partly on the level of skill and partly on what may be called experience with performing a long session. This may be related to the skill of regulating effort throughout a session. It suggests that although effort may wane over time, its contribution does not disappear altogether.

The main difference between the cognitive-energetic and the resting response, or mental block interpretation, is that the former does not ascribe the effect of time on task to a decrease in activation or arousal, but to waning effort during the first few minutes of work (Dinges & Kribbs, 1991). In the same way, the cognitive-energetic account deviates from a mental fatigue interpretation. Mental fatigue suggests that at the start, performance is normal but deteriorates due to accumulating fatigue, which has the effect of reducing processing capacity. A major problem in this view is that it does not predict a decrement to occur during the very first few minutes, followed by a stable performance level during the remaining part of the spell. Instead, one would expect performance to decline progressively over time.

Fatigue and Diurnal Rhythms

Fatigue is a classical and intuitively appealing notion that assumes that performance deteriorates over time due to a gradually dissipating capacity of mental energy that can only be restored by sleep (Kraepelin, 1903). The previously discussed research does not fit this notion, but might meet the objection that the work periods were not long enough for fatigue to show up. Yet, studies in which the participants worked for a much longer period of time did not favor the hypothesis of a dissipating capacity either. This was already evident from early work (Musico, 1921) and was confirmed in studies in which the participants worked for long periods without showing any noticeable performance loss (e.g., I. D. Brown, 1967). In one unpublished trial, a participant drove 650 km without interruption from Amsterdam to Basel. Various behavioral and physiological measures were recorded, none of which showed any serious decrement. The trip was sponsored by a radio station in order to keep the public informed about the dangers of long-term driving. It was not successful.[11]

The single-capacity metaphor has evolved to the cognitive-energetic notion of mutually regulating energetic structures. As argued, arousal and activation may supply suboptimal energy. This does no harm as long as supply is still within limits and processing demands are low. Again, arousal and activation are supposed to be modulated by outside stimulation and by diurnal rhythm. Outside stimuli are supposed to affect arousal, and time of the day is supposed to modulate activation, and these effects may supersede those of a preceding period of continuous work. The consequence is that a before–after test usually shows little evidence for diminished energetic capacity. In a before–after test, participants receive a brief test before and after a prolonged demanding task in order to determine capacity depletion.

---

[11]It should be mentioned that this participant was a highly experienced driver. Moreover, the knowledge that he took part in an experiment was presumably motivating. Both moderators fit the cognitive-energetic model.

Once the demanding work has ended, the after-test may be sufficiently new to temporarily restore arousal to its optimal level. Moreover, the fact that the after-test will not take long offers an ideal opportunity for short-term effort investment.

Yet, Broadbent (1979) found that participation in earlier long-term work affected persistence in problem solving in an after-test. The longer and more demanding the main task had been, the less the participants were willing to continue analyzing an unsolvable puzzle afterwards. In the same way, Hockey and Wiethoff (1990) found an aftereffect on complex, self-paced decision making, which could be carried out with more or less sophisticated strategies. After a prolonged period on duty, participants opted for less sophisticated strategies in the after-task. The fact that more complex, effort-demanding, reasoning tasks prove more successful as after-task is of interest. It suggests unwillingness to invest effort in an after-task for more than a brief period.

Perhaps still more extreme situations should be considered in order to obtain fatigue-like performance decrements. Indeed, the most convincing evidence stems from studies "around the clock." In a classical study by Morgan, Brown, and Alluisi (1974), participants worked almost uninterruptedly on a number of tasks for 48 hours. One task was done without interruption and consisted of continuous monitoring of warning lights and pointer locations on dials. In addition, operators alternated half-hour periods of arithmetic work and visual pattern identification with an hour of a stimulus-encoding task. None of these tasks was really demanding, but because they were carried out in combination, the participants were always busy. Some results are shown in Fig. 9.6.

In line with the previously discussed data, there was little evidence for a decrement during the first day of work, with performance remaining at about 100% until late in the evening. Although decreasing during the course of the night, performance recovered during the next day to some 85% of the initial level. The decline was steeper during the second night, but again, there was a tendency toward recovery in the early morning of the following day. In brief, the data show pronounced effects of circadian changes on activation, especially following sleep loss. The effects seem fairly autonomous in that they may occur irrespective of how long the participants worked.

Similar results were found by Babkoff et al. (1988), who studied the effects of 72 hours' loss of sleep on a memory-search task. In each successive 3-minute trial, participants were presented with a matrix of 16 * 20 letters and instructed to cross out predefined target letters. The target set was varied within subjects and amounted to two, four, or six letters. As usual, the number of letters scanned per unit time decreased linearly as a function of target-set size. Forty-eight hours' loss of sleep caused a general decrease in scanning rate to about 70% of the initial level. Circadian effects were par-

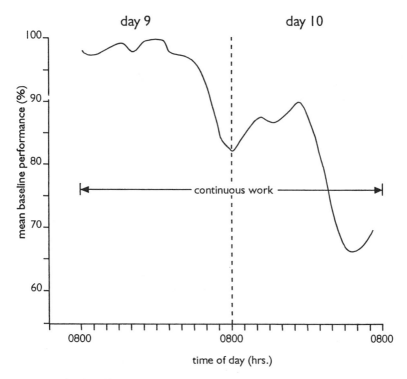

FIG. 9.6. The effect of "working around-the-clock" on continuous performance. The effects of diurnal rhythm are clearly visible. From Morgan, B. B.,
Brown, B. R., & Alluisi, E. A. (1974). Effects on sustained performance of 48
hours of continuous work and sleep-loss. *Human Factors, 16,* 406–414. Copyright © 1974 by the Human Factors and Ergonomics Society, Inc. Reproduced
by permission.

ticularly clear after 48 hours, in that a dip at 42 to 48 hours was followed
by a recovery around 55 to 60 hours. Because participants reacted only to
targets, the task was basically a c-reaction, which permits signal-detection
analysis. This showed that the effect of sleep loss and of circadian variation
on d' were stronger as target-set size was larger. Thus, even though scanning
rate was affected about equally for the various target-set sizes—even somewhat more pronounced for the set of two items—the accuracy of target
detection declined more for a larger target set, suggesting less thorough
memory scanning as sleep loss accumulated. Both d' and β had pronounced
circadian effects, with β becoming larger—less readiness to respond—at the
low points of the rhythm.

  In terms of the cognitive-energetic model, the interaction of d', sleep
loss, and target-set size suggests a relation between arousal and memory
search. The finding is consistent with the notion that energetic supply of

arousal and perceptual processing demands are related. The variation of β depended only on the circadian rhythm, which reflects the effect of accumulating sleep loss on activation.

In a study by Riemersma et al. (1977), participants drove along a highway for 8 hours during the night (from 22:00–6:00 hrs), with only one brief stop for refueling. The results of this study show a considerable performance decrement. Tracking accuracy decreased after 2 hours' driving, RT in a secondary task—noticing a change in color of a stationary light mounted in the periphery of the dashboard—increased, and instructed, regular routine checks tended to be forgotten. One conclusion was that driving changed from active, anticipatory search for relevant stimuli to passive reactions to what is actually occurring. It is interesting that, albeit not for long, performance recovered after the brief refueling stop. After the 8 hours' drive, participants had a 1-hour rest, during which period they had breakfast. Then, they drove for one additional hour, during which period performance did not significantly differ from that of control participants who had enjoyed normal sleep. This result reminds of the observation that participants may perform normally after a night's loss of sleep, provided that a task is intrinsically motivating or is carried out with an incentive.

In summary, a fatigue-like performance decrement is only found in the case of a combination of (a) prolonged performance, (b) late at night or early in the morning, (c) few incentives or little intrinsic interest, and (d) prolonged lack of sleep. These are precisely the conditions when a low state of arousal and activation are likely to be poorly compensated by effort. The willingness to invest effort is likely to decline as sleep loss accumulates, although investment may still occur as long as there are sufficiently strong incentives. Taking the evidence together, the cognitive-energetic model does well in accounting for the effects of fatigue and sleep loss, particularly in relation to CRT but also in tasks with measures beyond CRT. Yet, the more detailed predictions of the model in regard to the connections between arousal and perception and between activation and motor behavior have not been studied "around the clock" and await future research.

More on Time of Day and Night

Figure 9.6 shows an effect of time of the day and night on performance that becomes progressively stronger after sleep loss. The steep decrement late at night and early in the morning is invariably followed by (a) a recovery as the new day proceeds, (b) a temporary dip during the afternoon, (c) a further recovery and, finally, (d) another steep decrement during the late evening. This pattern suggests a contribution of sleep loss as well as of time of the day and night to performance. The latter category is usually called the circadian rhythm. It consists of a complex interplay of variations in physiological state, performance, and subjectively experienced sleepiness. The course of the body temperature is known the best, but there are also changes in the EEG and in endocrine secretion over time. Normally, the sleep–wake cycle is part of the general circadian rhythm as well, but rhythms of temperature and sleep–wake may dissociate in free-running tests. In such tests, participants are isolated and deprived of normal day–night cues. The sleep–wake cycle changes markedly without such cues, but the temperature cycle remains about the same. This suggests that they are under control of different processes (Monk, 1991). To further complicate the matter, the sleep–wake cycle may not consist of a single rhythm but, at least during the night, of 90-minute periods that all end in REM sleep. A similar 90-minute period may continue during the day as a short cycle superimposed on the much slower 24-hour cycle (P. Lavie, 1991).

Studies on day-to-day variation in sleeping and waking—for example, due to work shift—show that the rhythms are not only determined endogenously but also by the time elapsed since waking up (Spencer, 1987), with the rhythm rising the first few hours after awakening. This suggests that physiologically, diurnal effects cannot be ascribed to a single endogenous state of activation, yet most of the already discussed behavioral evidence is adequately accounted for by one single activation system. In particular, the aggravation of the effect of time of the day after sleep loss has been considered as positive evidence in this regard. For instance, Fig. 9.6 showed, at best, minor effects of time of the day during the first day of work, although in sensitive tests, effects of time of the day are found after normal sleep. It should be repeated that the time of the day effects do not appear to depend on long-term performance because they are equally found in relatively short-lasting tests. This renders these tests of particular interest for studying activation from a behavioral perspective.

Thus, research on tasks requiring immediate information processing, such as CRT, and visual search, has shown a rapid rise in efficiency during the early morning until 11:00, followed by a more gradual rise until 20:00, whereupon a decline sets in (Fig. 9.7).[12] In some studies, a postlunch dip, which is more pronounced after sleep loss (Fig. 9.6), has been found. Variations in performance and temperature appear to covary, and this agrees with what would be expected from variations in activation.

In contrast, studies on memory span and immediate retention of short stories show a reverse trend. Here, performance is best in the early morning and decreases gradually during the day. Still, this may not be a real problem

---

[12]This is only the trend for young, healthy participants and, in particular, for extraverts. For introverts, the performance function remains much more constant, whereas anxious, young participants and old people show a trend toward a decline of performance during the course of the day (Frewer & Hindmarch, 1988).

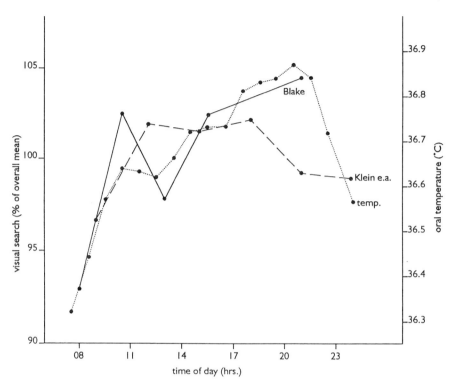

FIG. 9.7. Effects of time of the day on performance. The data are from Blake (1967) and from Klein et al. (1972) and appear to correspond to oral tempera-ture. Adapted from Folkard, S., & Monk, T. H. Carcadian rhythms in perform-ance. In S. Folkard & T. H. Monk (Eds.), *Hours of work: Temporal factors in work scheduling.* London: Wiley. Reproduced with permission.

because complex, short-term memory processes might do better at a some-what lower level of "arousal." This does not hold for long-term retention and, indeed, the evidence suggests that long-term retention is better if learn-ing takes place later in the day. Thus, the complication of memory is not necessarily at odds with the assumption of variations of a single "arousal" function (Folkard, 1983). The main exception concerns the earlier mentioned free-running conditions in which visual search and memory performance were affected in different ways, suggesting that they are controlled by dif-ferent processes (Folkard, Wever, & Wildgruber, 1983).

From the perspective of the cognitive-energetic model, the question is whether diurnal effects are exclusively limited to activation as a tonic ener-getic component—which seems the most natural candidate—or extend to arousal and effort. The critical studies have not yet been carried out—that is, the size of the effects of stimulus quality, S–R compatibility, and foreperiod duration as a function of time of the day—but some speculations may be made. First, the cognitive-energetic model holds that effort is particularly relevant to attentional control in memory and reasoning. In line with the evidence on fatigue, it could be that readiness to invest effort declines during the course of a day, thus causing a decline in performance on those tasks in which effort is most needed. Second, the suggestion of a short sleep–wake cycle superimposed on a long one might reflect a difference between arousal (the short cycle) and activation (the long one). As said, though, these are speculations that await future research.

Applications. Application of the results on fatigue, diurnal changes, and sleep loss may seem self-evident, but, in fact, its effects have been severely neglected. Thus, psychotropic drugs and alcohol usually show minor performance effects in laboratory tests, much less than the effects of sleep loss and time of the day. Still, drugs and alcohol are surrounded by many regulations, whereas sleep loss does not meet any, despite the strong, negative performance effects during the late night and the early morning, which agree with subjective reports of sleepiness and with increased α and θ activity in the EEG. For instance, the accident rate in flying, car driving, supervisory control, and bus driving was found to be relatively high late at night and early in the morning (Pokorny, Blom, & van Leeuwen, 1981). Again, the nuclear accidents at Chernobyl and Three Mile Island both occurred during the night (Akerstedt, 1991), and the doors of the "Harold of Free Enterprise" had not been closed because the operator on duty had fallen asleep. It is normal procedure to have junior physicians or surgeons on duty at night, without any serious consideration of negative effects of sleep loss. In a recent study by Pigeau et al. (1995), the time was measured for detecting the presence of a new aircraft on a radar screen. The results show little effect of time on task (60 vs. 20 min) except when tested late at night or in the early morning hours, thus suggesting that in these cases, a smaller, uninterrupted period of work really makes sense.

There are many other jobs that require work at unusual hours and for which similar questions can be raised. Following a night on duty, people usually drive home with an increased accident risk and without a clear recognition of their problem. Long-distance truck drivers are seriously at risk because their job often demands irregular hours of work. Drivers may be asleep at the wheel in at least 10% of collisions. It is of interest that the time spent at the wheel appears to have a relatively small effect on accident risk as long as duty periods are less than 12 hours and are restricted to daytime (I. D. Brown, 1994). The statutory regulations on drivers' work hours are inadequate, concerned as they are with the number of hours before taking a break, the maximum number of hours one may drive per day, and the minimum number of hours one may rest or sleep. These parameters fail to grasp the most important aspect of driver fatigue, namely, time of the day and night.

Some of these issues are summarized under the heading shiftwork, which refers to any arrangement of work hours that uses more than one team to cover the time needed for production. In the case of three shifts, the production is usually around the clock, with the nightshift working, for example, from 22:00 to 6:00 hours and the other shifts from 6:00 to 14:00 and from 14:00 to 22:00. A discussion of the extensive research on shiftwork is far beyond the scope of this book, in particular because the issues are not only limited to diurnal effects on performance but also extend to social relations. As far as performance is concerned, shiftwork has complex effects that depend on various interacting variables. One variable is the extent to which a person is capable of adapting to changes in sleep habits, which is, again, partly a social issue. Part of the problem is that nightshift workers appear to sleep the least.

Akerstedt (1991) summarized some major findings on shiftwork in a number of recommendations. First, the nightshift should be limited in time in order to allow for some sleep during the early morning hours and to prevent a late night's performance decrement (Fig. 9.6). Second, in the case of a rotating shift, the rotation should be clockwise. Thus, a night shift should be followed by an early shift and not by a late shift. The reason is that the sleep–wake cycle is slightly longer than 24 hours, so phase delays are easier to make than phase advances. Third, rotation should preferably be slow, that is, a nightshift should last for a number of successive nights. This is based on the observation that although far from optimal, there is still some adjustment in circadian rhythm across successive nights. From the perspective that effects of time on task are marginal in comparison with those of circadian rhythm, it is worth exploring the prospects of two 12-hour shifts instead of the traditional three 8-hour shifts (Duchon, Keran, & Smith, 1994).

VIGILANCE

Effects of time on task have been studied the most widely in the area of vigilance, whose main characteristic is that participants monitor a system for a prolonged period of time in an isolated cabin with their watches removed. The task is to detect rarely occurring, near-threshold target stimuli. For instance, N. H. Mackworth's (1950) clock test consisted of a disk with a pointer that jumped each second with a small step, but occasionally—24 times hourly—with a double step. Participants monitored the clock for 2 hours uninterruptedly and were required to detect the double jumps. The main result was that detection probability decreased as a function of time on task.

The motive for studying vigilance was the problem of undetected submarine contacts during World War II. Mackworth's (1950) research suggested that, indeed, an operator cannot remain fully alert under boring conditions. Whereas the double and single jump of the clock were detected almost perfectly in standard psychophysical conditions, participants detected some 80% of the 12 targets during the first half hour of vigilance. This leveled off to some 65% of the 12 targets presented in each of the three subsequent half hours. Thus, the vigilance function shows a decrement and an asymptote (Fig. 9.8).

N. H. Mackworth's (1950) monograph was followed by a large number of studies that used a variety of stimulus conditions. These included (a) detecting an increase in brightness or in pitch of a stationary stimulus, (b) near-threshold targets amidst noise on a simulated radar screen, and (c) successive presentations of letters or digits where some specific, temporal combinations served as target. The earlier work was extensively reviewed by Broadbent (1971). More recent summaries are in Loeb and Alluisi (1984) and in Parasuraman (1986). The present discussion is limited to a few highlights.

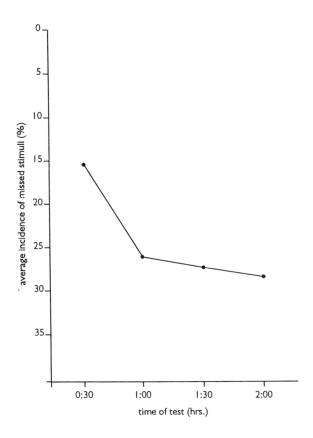

FIG. 9.8. The classical vigilance effect in the clock test. Reprinted from Mackworth, N. H. (1950). *Researches into the measurement of human performance.* Published with permission of Her Majesties Stationary Office.

A major problem in the study of vigilance is the lack of behavioral data, so measures have often been summarized over half-hour periods of time. However, Jerison (1959) concluded from a fine-grained analysis that, in line with the time-on-task effect in serial-reaction tasks, most of the vigilance decrement occurs during the first few minutes. A direct correspondence between passive vigilance and active serial reactions was demonstrated by Whittenburg, Ross, and Andrews (1956). They had participants carry out separate key-press reactions to the single and the double jump in the clock test and found results similar to when participants responded to the double jump only. When only responding to the double jump, participants missed targets; they erred more often when making choice reactions. Along the same lines, J. F. Mackworth (1964) proposed a negatively accelerated efficiency function for both active and passive monitoring tasks.

N. H. Mackworth's (1950) original experiments included some variables that effectively prevented a performance decrement. One was when KR was given after a correctly detected target; others were administration of dextroamphetamine and a motivating telephone call in the middle of the work spell.[13] The decrement was aggravated by sleep loss, which was fully restored by KR or by a stimulant drug. Together, these results added to the popularity of explaining the vigilance decrement by a decrease in "arousal." As already argued, though, a major problem for an "arousal" explanation is that the decrement occurs during the first few minutes, whereas performance remains relatively stable afterward. This is much less of a problem when assuming, as the cognitive-energetic model does, that participants invest effort at the start of a workspell that compensates for existing suboptimal arousal or activation.[14] KR may mean that effort is maintained for a much longer period, although at the price of physiological costs, whereas a stimulant drug may restore arousal or activation to its optimal level. In this view, arousal and activation are mainly relevant to the asymptote, whereas the initial level and the decrement are due to effort. Thus, the effect of sleep loss affects the asymptote rather than the course of the decrement (Wilkinson, 1969).

Why would arousal and activation be suboptimal in a vigilance task? Indeed, this question should be raised because, so far, it has been argued that arousal and activation are almost optimal in normal, daytime conditions. What, then, is so special to vigilance that the basal supply mechanisms fall short so soon? J. F. Mackworth (1969) proposed that the neutral stimulus, for example, the single jump of the clock, would rapidly habituate, irrespec-

---

[13]Relative target intensity, discriminability, and stimulus duration also affect detection rate. It is actually trivial that all targets may be detected when they are sufficiently discriminable from neutral stimuli or from noise. In that case, there still remains an effect on CRT, as was already discussed in the earlier section on time on task.

[14]This explanation was actually proposed for the first time by Buckner (1963). In the context of vigilance, effort belongs to the category of motivation-controlled concepts (Warm, 1984).

tive of whether it required an overt or a covert response. Hence, the repetitive neutral stimulus would dearouse and cause suboptimal arousal and a decline in d'. A telephone call or a short break would dishabituate and restore orienting to the stimulus.[15] Detecting a target would dishabituate as well, more so when KR is provided.[16] Habituation theory nicely explains the well-established result that the asymptote covaries with target probability because more targets lead to more dishabituation. In contrast, habituation should occur sooner if the rate of neutral stimuli is higher. In that case the decrement should be more pronounced which, indeed, has often been found (Parasuraman & Davies, 1977).

Unfortunately, however, other direct tests of habituation have failed to provide general support to the theory. For example, changing event rate[17] in the middle of a session should dishabituate and therefore have a positive effect on detection rate. Yet, detections decreased, in particular when going from a slow to a fast rate of neutral stimuli (Krulewitz, Warm, & Wohl, 1975). Again, Parasuraman (1985) compared passive habituation, in which case participants merely saw or heard stimuli without any task, with a vigilant target-detection task. Because detections dishabituate, ERPs should habituate less in the vigilant task than in the passive one. Furthermore, habituation of the ERP should be more pronounced at a higher event rate. The results of ERP studies confirmed that N1 amplitude was larger for the low event-rate than for the high one and also larger for the vigilant condition than for the passive one. Moreover, N1 amplitude declined over time, but the rate of the decline did not differ among event rates or between a passive and an active task. In conclusion, habituation may affect the asymptote but does not appear to offer an adequate explanation for the decrement. This agrees with the cognitive-energetic model, which holds that habituation affects the basal energetic mechanisms but not effort.

This is further underlined by the fact that habituation theory cannot account for some effects of cognitive factors on vigilance. Thus, there is virtually no performance decrement when targets occur at a strictly regular interval—for example, one every 2 minutes (Baker, 1963). This has led to a cognitive expectancy view that explains the decrement by assuming that initially,

---

[15]As discussed earlier, orienting is a behavioral orientation toward the source of stimulation, accompanied by a variety of physiological changes.

[16]It is curious that with the best traditions of behaviorism, N. H. Mackworth (1950) proposed extinction of the overt response to the target as explanation of the decrement.

[17]Event rate refers to the total number of events, neutral stimuli as well as targets, as a function of unit time. If the task is to detect a change in brightness or pitch of a stationary stimulus, the event rate is infinite. It is actually trivial that target detection and event rate are related, for the simple reason that participants *know* nothing will happen "in between" two discrete events. Thus, a low event-rate implies that continuous alertness is just no longer required (compare this reasoning with that on the condition in which targets occur at fully regular time intervals).

participants are alert because they expect targets to occur frequently, whereas expectancy and, hence, alertness, decline as time passes. Yet, expectancy theory has severe problems explaining the aforementioned habituation type of effects. It also faces the problem that a decrement appears to reoccur in successive vigilance sessions. The point is that a realistic expectancy about target frequency should be established during the first session. On the other hand, some contribution of expectancy to vigilance is evident from the results of Colquhoun and Baddeley (1967). They had participants perform a brief initial session in which one group received many targets and another group only a few. The "many-targets" group showed more decrement in a subsequent vigilance session than the "few-targets" group. This result suggests an effect of establishing a realistic expectancy about target frequency because members of the "many-targets" group were led to expect many targets in the vigilance session as well. From the perspective of the cognitive-energetic model, a state of high expectancy fosters effort investment because expectancy affects the criteria of the evaluation mechanism. However, there may well be various reasons other than expectancy that lead to effort investment.

Thus, expectancy affects, but does not exclusively determine, the initial detection level. If promoting effort investment, expectancy should play a role in the decrement but not in the asymptotic level of detection. Here, habituation may be the more relevant determinant (see Parasuraman, 1986, for a similar conclusion). The case in which targets occur at fully regular time intervals may eliminate the requirement of maintaining alertness because it is at odds with the basic prerequisite of a vigilance task that participants be unaware of the time at which a target will be presented.

Broadbent (1971) argued that concepts such as "arousal," habituation, and expectancy have little explanatory value—that is, *virtus dormitiva*—when not framed in an information-processing model. The filter theory of selective attention meant to provide such a frame. The filter becomes satiated, or habituated, when selecting the same type of information over and over again, and the efficiency of the filter diminishes as "arousal" is less. The filter is also sensitive to outside events, as implied by Berlyne's (1960) collative variables, but it is equally controlled by top-down cognitive expectancy. However, a major problem of filter theory is that it is merely concerned with sensory processing because the asymptotic level of detection is fully ascribed to deficient intake of information. Intuitively appealing as this may be, this view is at odds with the signal detection analysis of vigilance. The early vigilance studies had only considered detections and ignored false alarms, whereas, typically, both false alarms and detections tend to diminish during a prolonged spell (Colquhoun & Baddeley, 1967; Parasuraman & Davies, 1976). A decrease in both hits and false alarms implies a decrease in β rather than in d'. In turn, this suggests less readiness to respond rather than a reduction in sensitivity.[18] In terms of the cognitive-energetic model, the asymptote could be due to lack of readiness to respond (β; activation) rather than to deficient intake of information (d'; arousal).

In retrospect, some variables might have their effect foremost on d', and others might primarily affect β. In other words, arousal as well as activation deficits might contribute to the asymptote. For example, the effect of target frequency has been repeatedly shown to affect β. Indeed, along the lines of the AFM, variation of relative target frequency should affect response-related processs.[19] Similarly, the effect of expectancy, as brought about by pretraining, on the decrement appeared to be due to response set (Colquhoun & Baddeley, 1967; Craig, 1980) and changes in β. Other variables appear to have their primary effect on sensitivity. For example, habituation has been viewed as primarily affecting d'. Hence, the negative effect of a high event-rate on detection might be due to a lower d'.

A Taxonomy of Vigilance Tasks

Parasuraman (1986) proposed four categories of variables in vigilance with regard to the question of whether the sensitivity (d') or the criterion (β) is affected: (a) sensory modality (auditory–visual), (b) "source complexity" (monitoring a single-stimulus source as in the clock test or a single-stimulus intensity vs. multisource monitoring, such as simulated radar), (c) event-rate, and (d) presentation mode (simultaneous–successive presentation).[20]

From a review of the literature, Parasuraman (1986) concluded that d' is primarily affected in a vigilance task in the case of a combination of successive stimulus presentation and a high event-rate. A combination of these two conditions, of which the clock test is a perfect example, imposes the highest demands on encoding and would, therefore, affect d' in particular.

---

[18]There is the problem that false alarm rates are usually low, so a single false alarm has a disproportionate effect on β. It is also unlikely that noise and signal + noise are normally distributed with equal variance in vigilance tasks. Some studies used a rating procedure in which participants are asked to issue a rating about the presence of a target at the presentation of each new stimulus—targets as well as nontargets—or at specified intervals. This has the disadvantage that the vigilance task becomes much less passive. If one has only a single point on the ROC curve, sensitivity may be evaluated by way of P(A)—that is, the nonparametric equivalent of d'—but one should be particularly careful with estimates of β (e.g., Parasuraman, 1986).

[19]Broadbent (1971) proposed "response set" as the selective principle related to β. Response set supplemented "stimulus set," which represents the original filtering principle. As argued, response set refers to the state of activation of "dictionary units" which, if sufficiently high, may enable stimulus identification even when the corresponding outside stimulus is attenuated. This means that response set is still a matter of perceptual identification and not of readiness for action.

[20]Pairs of two stimuli were presented simultaneously or successively. A pair may consist of two neutral stimuli or of a neutral stimulus and a target.

A decrement in other combinations would usually reflect a shift in β (e.g., Parasuraman, 1984). Recently, Koelega (1991) and See et al. (1995) argued in favor of an additional sensory-cognitive dimension that would moderate the effects of event rate and presentation mode. In a meta-analysis of 138 vigilance studies, See et al. confirmed Parasuraman's conclusions. Moreover, they found evidence for a second-order interaction of the effects of event rate, presentation mode, and the sensory versus cognitive nature of the stimuli. Stimuli may be either sensory or cognitive in that they either require sensory detection (or discrimination) or ask for detecting the presence of a well-learned symbol, for example, a letter. In fact, sensory stimuli always do poorly except at a low event-rate and when successively presented. Cognitive stimuli do best in the case of simultaneous presentation (Fig. 9.9). For the present purpose, it is relevant to consider whether this pattern of results makes sense in the cognitive-energetic model as due to, respectively, arousal (d') and activation (β).

As mentioned, the effect of event rate may be perfectly trivial; as far as nontrivial, it is connected to habituation. Successive presentation of a stimulus pair requires individual comparisons of the stimuli with the internal codes of the target and of the neutral stimulus, whereas the neutral stimulus and the target can be directly compared with each other when they are presented simultaneously. Although this may be an advantage, simultaneous presentation has the disadvantage that both stimuli are either encoded or missed.

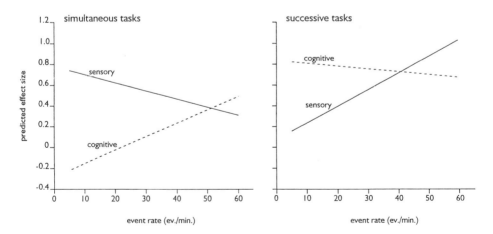

FIG. 9.9. Predicted effects of event-rate, simultaneous versus successive presentation and sensory vs. cognitive stimuli on the size of the vigilance effect. A larger effect is associated with a larger decrement in sensitivity. From See, J. E., Howe, S. R., Warm, J. S., & Dember, W. M. (1995). Meta-analysis of the sensitivity decrement in vigilance. *Psychological Bulletin, 117*, 230–249. Copyright © 1995 by the American Psychological Association. Reprinted with permission.

In contrast, successive presentation has the potential advantage that the first stimulus of a pair may be alerting. It follows that, particularly when targets are degraded, simultaneous presentation might overload encoding and, therefore, does poorly. Hence, the demands on encoding and not the simultaneous versus successive presentation mode might be decisive with respect to an effect on d' (Nuechterlein, Parasuraman, & Jiang, 1983). More recently, Parasuraman and Mouloua (1987) suggested that, when stimuli are degraded, a sensitivity decrement may occur, irrespective of presentation mode. Less familiar sensory stimuli always do poorly, with the exception of the low event-rate, successive-presentation condition. Here, monitoring may not suffer from habituation and, therefore, may profit from being alerted by the first stimulus. On the other hand, more familiar cognitive stimuli show less effect when presented simultaneously. This may be ascribed to the previously suggested advantage of direct comparisons between a target and a neutral stimulus. Thus, either effect may fit a perceptual habituation type of interpretation It is admitted that there is still a theoretical gap between these more detailed vigilance data and the inferences from the cognitive-energetic model. The reason is probably that the data are concerned with computational effects rather than with energetic ones.

The two other dimensions of Parasuraman's (1986) taxonomy are still harder to assess in terms of d' and β. For instance, various studies have shown that speed and accuracy of target detection is superior in the case of auditory vigilance than of visual vigilance (e.g., Colquhoun, 1975). This difference may vanish, however, when their discriminability and perceived intensity are standardized. "Normal" auditory and visual stimuli could differ in perceived intensity so that stimulus intensity, rather than modality, might underlie the better auditory detection. In addition, auditory stimuli may be better "coupled" than visual stimuli in that they suffer less from defocusing and blinking, factors that are likely to affect detection rate in visual tasks. There is some evidence (e.g., Beatty, 1982; Stern, Boyer, & Schroeder, 1994) that blinking and defocusing increase as a function of time on task. This would show up as an effect on β rather than on d' but would reflect an indirect motor effect rather than a shift in sensitivity or response bias.

The Effect of Task Complexity

The effects of task complexity on vigilance complicate the picture even more. Most vigilance studies have used a single-source task such as the clock test. It is of interest that research on monitoring more complex displays has often failed to find any decrement over time. Some studies on complex displays need not be considered because targets were easily discriminated or presented long enough to allow perfect detection throughout the whole spell. In other cases, however, the detection rate in the complex task proved to be low from the very start of a session (e.g., Warm & Jerison, 1984). The problem with a complex display, for example, a radar screen, is that various, additional factors may complicate the picture. For instance, participants may be asked to scan a radar display for the potential occurrence of a target. Suppose there is a vigilance decrement in the sense that the participants engage in active search—invest effort?—at the start of a session and become less active as time goes on. There is the well-established fact that detection is hardly possible during a saccade. This leads to the paradox that much eye activity may harm rather than promote detection at the beginning of a spell. Suppose, again, that there are fewer saccades later in the session, leading to predominant fixation of one part of the display, for example, the center, at the cost of neglect of the periphery. This would lead to a qualitatively different pattern of detections instead of fewer detections. Due to inter- and intraindividual differences, it will be hard to demonstrate consistent changes in detection pattern as a function of the area of the display. In all cases, though, the asymptotic detection rate will be less but may not decrease over time in comparison with a single-stimulus source.

Funneling of attention to the center of a display was proposed by Bartlett (1953) as a criterion for mental fatigue, but it has been difficult to really establish. There is evidence for a relative neglect of the edges of a display during free search, but evidence on a progression of peripheral neglect as a function of time on task is scant. Yet, one of the few studies in which eye movements were measured during a watch showed that fixations in the periphery of the screen were less frequent at the end of a work spell than at the beginning (Michon & Kirk, 1962).

Sanders (1963) had participants monitor 16 lights, with the task of detecting an occasionally occurring slight increase in brightness at one of the lights. The 16 lights were divided into a centrally located horizontal group of 8 and two groups of 4 lights that were located in the periphery at the left and at the right. The 8 lights were always in the same central position, but the position of the two groups of peripheral lights was either more-or-less peripheral. In the less peripheral case, participants could monitor the total display with eye movements (eye field condition), but they needed additional head movements in the more peripheral condition (head field condition). A target, that is, the increase in brightness, remained visible until it was detected. In the case of the eye field condition, RT for the peripheral lights was considerably longer than for the central lights throughout the 1-hour watch, reflecting a greater focus on the central lights. Irrespective of a central or a peripheral target, time on task increased RT by about 10%. In the case of the head field condition, the results were quite different. During the first half hour, RT for the central lights was almost equally as long as for the outer lights, suggesting frequent scanning and about equal emphasis on the central group and on the two peripheral groups of lights. During the second half hour, RT for the central lights decreased slightly and RT for the peripheral lights increased strongly, suggesting less frequent inspection of the peripheral lights. This is consistent with the hypothesis that scanning became less over time, with the effect of increasing neglect of the periphery. The results agree with the hypothesis that a head field condition is more loading than an eye field condition.

Such results underline that vigilant behavior in complex tasks may change in a subtle way that goes undetected by simple performance measures. They also suggest that a quest for the decrement and the asymptote, which has dominated research on vigilance, may not be appropriate in the case of more complex tasks. Instead, the results agree with the adage of the resource-strategy view about searching for qualitative performance changes. This does not mean that qualitative changes may not be ultimately due to a decrease in energetic supply, but these would be related to other processes simply than perceptual encoding and response readiness in a choice–reaction. This is precisely what the back-to-back strategy is meant for.

There are other differences in complexity that relate to cognitive rather than sensory stimuli. An example is the Bakan task (Bakan, 1959) in which participants watch a sequence of digits. Certain patterns of them are defined as targets, such as three successive odd and different digits, for example, . . . 7,3,9 . . . Normally, the results in a Bakan task do not strongly deviate from those in a sensory vigilance task, although there are indications that performance decrement is less as the cognitive operations become more complex (Loeb, Noonan, Ash, & Holding, 1987). The interpretation of this result is, as yet, unclear. It might reflect a practice effect in complex cognitive operations during a session, which counteracts a decrement. Alternatively, complex operations might be motivating, and lead to more sustained effort investment. Complex tasks might have intrinsic performance feedback that brings about KR. The same has been suggested to account for the observed absence of sleep-loss effects on motivating tasks (Wilkinson, 1969). It has little explanatory value, though, as long as the presumed intrinsic motivation is not independently assessed.

Psychophysiological Studies on Vigilance

As mentioned, the lack of observable data is the main weakness of the behavioral-vigilance measures. This is even more serious in view of the hypothesis that deficient energetic supply leads to a more variable information flow. The point is that subtle energetic effects cannot be analyzed when there are only a few overt reactions, which is enough reason for an interest in psychophysiological measures. The pertinent variables may be divided into two types, namely, those concerned with general state, such as background EEG, GSR, and HR on the one hand, and event-related variables, in particular the ERP, but also electrodermal habituation of the orienting response and task-evoked pupillary responses (TEPR).

Various studies have shown a relation between the speed of habituation of electrodermal responses and asymptotic vigilance performance. Slow habituators maintain a high level, whereas fast habituators do less well. The decrement over time appears much less related to electrodermal habituation (Koelega, 1990). This is consistent with the view that electrodermal responses may reflect activation or arousal but not effort. A relation between the decrement and effort investment was suggested by Beatty (1989) in a summary of his work on the TEPR. He reported that TEPR amplitude, that is, Kahneman's (1973) classic index of effort allocation, declined in the same way as d' did in an auditory vigilance task. In the same paper, Beatty reviewed the evidence on increased θ (4–7 Hz) and α (8–10 Hz) activity during a vigil. Other studies found HR to decrease and HR variability to increase as a function of time on task. Yet, the decrease in these electrocortical and autonomous measures occurred irrespective of decrement and asymptotic performance. The only prerequisite for reduced physiological activity appeared to be that the task lasts sufficiently long and is monotonous. The reasons for this dissociation are, as yet, unclear. From the perspective of the cognitive-energetic model, it could be that physiological measures reflect, for example, activation, whereas performance might be first and foremost sensitive to arousal. Alternatively, the decline in arousal or activation may have been too small to lead to a performance loss. Still another alternative is that the physiological indexes do not properly reflect the state of the basal energetic processes.

One of the first issues ever raised in research on ERP concerned the relation with vigilance. The decline of N1 amplitude as a function of time on task was among these early findings, but as already argued, this decline may not be typical for vigilance. Later studies were concerned with the modulation in amplitude of the N1 when attention is divided among different sensory channels, the phenomenon of mismatch negativity (MMN),[21] the P3, and the contingent negative variation (CNV). The problem is that only a very few studies have addressed the issue of changes in ERP as a function of time on task, but the ones that did reported a lack of correlation between performance decrement and changes in the ERP (Koelega & Verbaten, 1991). There is the problem that an ERP usually consists of an average of a number of trials, so a detailed relation between ERP and individual detections is hard to establish. However, Koelega et al. (1992) carried out a study on visual vigilance in which single-trial ERPs were meaured. They found sig-

---

[21]MMN is a negative shift of the total ERP between 100 and 250 ms after a deviant stimulus among a series of neutral stimuli has been presented and is supposed to be a "change-detector response" (Näätänen, 1992), comparable with an orienting response. CNV is a negative shift briefly before presentation of an expected stimulus and is supposed to reflect preparatory state (Näätänen & Gaillard, 1974).

nificant correlations between overall mean scores, for example, P3 amplitude and detection rate, but no evidence for a correlation with time on task. In brief, the difference in P3 between targets and neutral stimuli remained the same over time. They concluded that the correlation between the asymptotic level and P3 amplitude shows that P3 amplitude reflects resource investment, or the level of steady-state information-processing.

Individual Differences

There are relatively stable individual differences in the asymptotic level of performance but not in the decrement over time. Good and poor performers may show an about equal decrement or no decrement at all. The usual candidate for predicting the asymptotic level is the extraversion–introversion (E–I) dimension, with introverts performing better than extraverts. Indeed, there is a fair amount of evidence that this relation holds for simple vigilance tasks (e.g., M. W. Eysenck, 1982, 1988). The traditional explanation is that introverts habituate less rapidly than extraverts. In an earlier formulation, H. J. Eysenck (1967) related E–I to the development of reactive inhibition in monotonous–continuous reaction tasks. Extraverts would show a faster buildup of RI than introverts and would benefit more from outside stimulation. There is a fair amount of evidence that the superior performance of introverts concerns d' as well as β. In terms of the cognitive-energetic model, this could mean that introverts have a higher level of arousal and activation but do not differ from extraverts with regard to investing effort. Individuals may differ, though, in the quality of regulating effort that might be related to Eysenck's (1967) stability dimension rather than to E–I.

M. W. Eysenck (1988) proposed that "arousal" may include reacting effortful to compensate for a suboptimal state. This suggestion is at odds with the cognitive-energetic model and blurs the difference between cause and effect in compensatory energetic supply. According to Eysenck, introverts would make more use of effort. Yet, this should lead to a relation between E–I and the rate of decrement rather than the asymptotic level, but that has not been substantiated. Still, effort and E–I might be related in the case of overarousal and overactivation. If introverts usually have a higher level of arousal and activation, they may soon be in need of effort to compensate for too high a level. In turn, this would mean that introverts invoke behavioral inhibition more easily and suffer sooner from stress and anxiety, in particular when emotionally unstable with a deficient regulation of effort (Gray, 1987).

Vigilance and Stress

A high detection rate in vigilance may be achieved in either of two ways. As long as arousal and activation are adequate, the asymptote is at a high level, and little effort is needed to maintain it. This is not supposed to be stressful either. Alternatively, arousal and activation may be low, while per-formance is still maintained at a high level due to continuous effort. An example was the high asymptotic level when KR was provided after sleep loss. These two options are likely to be at the basis of the dissociations between behavioral and physiological data.

The cognitive-energetic model considers continuous effort investment as stressful. Hancock and Warm (1989) called it "adaptation to task demands," which has clear costs and limits. Indeed, there are various reports that suggest that maintaining perfect performance goes together with high physiological costs. According to the cognitive-energetic model, most stress is bound to arise in the case of performance loss together with failing attempts to compensate through effort. Hence, stress may arise irrespective of efficiency; therefore, vigilance tasks are far from benign. Evidence on stress may be derived from self-reports and from physiological measures, including muscle tension and catecholamine output. Thus, Galinsky et al. (1993) measured performance in an auditory and visual vigilance task, with event-rate as an additional variable. They obtained estimates of fatigue symptoms before and after and estimates of motor activity—restlessness—during a spell. The performance data are in Fig. 9.10. They show the typical effects of event-rate and of time on task, whereas the performance difference between sensory modalities was insignificant. However, fatigue symptoms increased more in the visual task than in the auditory one and were about the same for the two event-rates. In the same way, motor activity increased as a function of time in the visual task, again, irrespective of event-rate. Thus, stress symptoms were sensitive to modality, and performance was sensitive to event-rate. Due to better coupling, the auditory task may have demanded somewhat less effort than the visual task in order to maintain the same performance level.

Applications. Research on vigilance arose from problems in detecting critical stimuli during watchkeeping. It is still always an issue in any super-visory control task such as air-traffic control, quality inspection, monitoring of medical equipment, flying, and driving. Automation has increased rather than decreased the frequency of boring, supervisory tasks in which a human operator is completely passive but is still expected to be fully alert whenever a critical situation should arise. The question is, of course, the extent to which basic research has been helpful in suggesting improvements in shap-ing such tasks. In fact, there are many qualms about the results of basic research that, again, center around the traditional differences between labo-ratory and real life. Mackie (1987) listed five main differences, namely, (a) target frequency in the laboratory is usually much higher than in practice; (b) most operational tasks involve complex multidimensional discrimina-tions, whereas most laboratory tasks used simple sensory or cognitive stimuli; (c) potential defects in supervisory control are manifold and do not consist

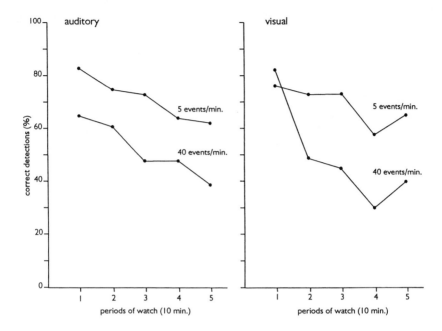

FIG. 9.10. Vigilance decrement as a function of sensory modality and event-rate. Performance depends on event-rate and not noticeably on sensory modality, whereas symptoms of fatigue and stress were more pronounced with visual stimuli. From Galinsky, T., Rosa, R. R., Warm, J. S., & Dember, W. N. (1993). Psychophysical determinants of stress in sustained attention. *Human Factors, 35*, 603–614. Copyright © 1993 by the Human Factors and Ergonomics Society, Inc. Reproduced by permission.

of a simple deviation from a neutral stimulus; (d) real-life tasks are carried out over long time periods rather than the usual 50′ to 100′ in the laboratory; and (e) differences in motivation may prevent generalization. Aside from these differences, there is the common qualm that 50 years of vigilance research has not produced a unified theoretical framework but, rather, a loose number of general concepts borrowed from other areas of performance research. It is evident that these remarks echo the debate between the small and simple paradigms and the richness of reality. This debate may be more vehement in vigilance than in some of the other information processing paradigms because, from an energetic perspective, vigilance research has always aimed at studying the total task.

It is undebated that demands on vigilance in the laboratory and in real life differ in many respects. It is equally obvious that it is impossible to carry out laboratory studies on vigilance with a real-life touch. It is hard to imagine an experiment which lasts for a number of days, and in which participants are passive because "nothing happens." To put the issue stronger: One should not even aim at such studies for the simple reason that they will turn out to be uninformative and have trivial outcomes, for example, that monotony leads to a suboptimal detection rate (Parsons, 1972)! Moreover, real-life tasks of supervisory monitoring differ widely in their microstructure. Supervisory control in an aircraft is quite different from controlling a nuclear energy plant, which differs, again, from long-term driving and quality inspection of sheet metal. The applied problems in these areas are concerned with much more than simply boredom and vigilance. Among others, the problems extend to issues of diagnosis, perceptual discrimination, and dual-task performance. Thus, even if "many-days-studies" on vigilance were designed, the results would not only be trivial but also not applicable beyond the particular setting in which it was tested.

A further problem with simulating real-life vigilance conditions concerns the prominent role of motivation. It is sometimes argued that participants are less motivated in the laboratory because the task has no "reality value"; others maintain that participants do better in the laboratory; they are more motivated there because they know that their performance is continuously measured and evaluated. An anecdote from an unpublished vigilance study by the author may illustrate the issue. The participants were volunteer soldiers who returned to the laboratory a few times to run vigilance sessions in a within-subjects design. One had been performing poorly, was unhappy, and objected to running his final session. The author's assistant tried to solve the problem by warning the soldier that another poor performance would jeopardize his upcoming leave. On hearing this, the soldier did the final session without any further complaint, and showed 100% detections without any false alarms throughout a 2-hour spell! The anecdote illustrates that, for unclear reasons, motivation may vary within and between conditions. Poulton's (1973) warning against the risks of a within-subjects design in stress studies should be well taken. Thus, one of the author's within-subjects studies on sleep loss was completely spoiled by the group of participants who had had the sleep-loss condition first and, then, did not take the subsequent normal night of sleep control condition seriously. Even within a session, participants may suddenly lose motivation or, on the contrary, decide to do better. All of this renders the outcome of vigilance studies much less reliable.

If, then, perhaps with the exception of some test trials for the purpose of demonstration, simulation of vigilance in real life is neither possible nor desirable, there only remains the option to derive applications from theory. This is actually a completely normal procedure in the natural sciences. Thus, various suggestions can be derived from the cognitive-energetic model, together with the many observations from accident analysis. Some are trivial, such as the warning with respect to an imperfect detection rate and a higher accident rate after prolonged work (Wiener, 1987). It is less trivial that current supervisory tasks usually require detecting qualitatively different types of targets from many simultaneous sources rather than a single type of target from a single source—like the double jump in the clock test. More complex targets from multiple sources are likely to decrease the rate of detection (e.g., Childs, 1976).

Another issue concerns the vigilance decrement, which is probably not common in real life and may appear to be an artifact of the laboratory (Adams, 1987). However, is it really an artifact? According to the cognitive-energetic model, a decrement reflects waning effort as a function of time. If no effort is invested at the start of a session, irrespective of a laboratory or a real-life setting, there is no decrement but, simply, a steady low detection-rate throughout the spell. Is it conceivable that awareness that performance is recorded leads to more initial effort investment that, then, wanes over time? When a personal interest is at stake, effort may be invested throughout a spell, again, both in the laboratory and in real life, the effect of which is that detection rate remains optimal throughout a workspell. As argued, however, maintaining effort over a longer period of time brings increasing physiological costs and is stressful. Even a strong, personal interest, such as staying alive on a ship during World War II, did not prevent a suboptimal rate of detection when a sonar-detection task was carried out over and over again. The conclusion is that the issue of performance decrement as a function of time is basically irrelevant. The really relevant problem is how to counteract a suboptimal detection rate. A number of propositions have emerged from the research.

First, target discriminability in a newly developed system cannot be evaluated by simply inserting a target at some known time and location followed by a demonstration "how well it can be seen."[22] Instead, it should be recognized that alertness declines in conditions of long-term, monotonous work. Unfortunately, this is not always recognized, which may be among the reasons that vigilance results are not applied as widely as they deserve. It is more common to blame operators for being inattentive.

Second, once the vigilance problem is recognized, there is the well-established finding that detection is better at a lower event-rate. Too high an event rate does not permit momentary variation in processing efficiency, for example, brief attentional lapses, which invariably leads to more missed targets. The issue of event rate is related to that of machine pacing. In machine-paced tasks, stimuli are presented at a fixed machine-determined rate and are only available for a short period. In contrast, a task is self-paced when the next stimulus is only presented after the response to the previous stimulus has been carried out. By their very nature, vigilance tasks are machine-paced, whereas continuous-reaction tasks may be either paced or self-paced.

---

[22]This is not far-fetched. I remember newly developed sonar equipment that was "tested" in this way. To the surprise and annoyance of the design engineer, the new system did not turn out to be superior to the existing one under vigilance conditions in trials at sea.

Studies in the laboratory have shown that a self-paced continuous-reaction task is carried out at a higher speed than a paced one, given that the pacing rate is adapted to the level of a participant's self-paced performance. Moreover, a paced condition appears to lead to more errors and response failures (Wagenaar & Stakenburg, 1975). The main problem with a high pacing rate is that each slow response leads to a backlog. This, in turn, leads to response failures and confusion, which propagate to the next responses. This means that paced performance is undesirable if only for the argument that errors induce unrewarded effort investment which, in turn, elicits stress. Thus, Johannson (1978) observed strongly elevated catecholamine levels in operators in an industrial sorting-task that had a high rate of machine pacing. At a slower pacing-rate, performance in machine-paced and self-paced tasks are more similar, and machine pacing may be even preferred. The point is that slow pacing imposes a brief rest between two responses which, among others, allows preparation for the next response. Decreasing the rate of pace is analogous to a lower event-rate in vigilance.

The third issue concerns the length of a spell. N. H. Mackworth's (1950) research had the effect that the watch of naval sonar and radar operators was reduced from 2 hours to 30 minutes. In other vigilance situations, such as air-traffic control, there are regular breaks, whereas uninterrupted periods of work in industrial inspections are often limited to some 20 minutes. Breaks are indeed important, but it is of interest that a brief rest appears to be equally as effective as a longer one. This is also the case for other tasks, such as truck driving, which have a much less fixed duration. Many countries have some official limit to total driving time but, as already argued, there are a number of factors that are more relevant to performance than the time spent at the wheel. As mentioned there, physiological indicators of alertness have been proposed for long-term driving, such as a warning when HR variability or θ activity increases beyond some critical level (O'Hanlon, 1971). This would certainly be useful, despite both individual differences in responsiveness and the absence of a well-established function relating the state of physiological parameters and driving performance.

A fourth suggestion concerns KR that can be achieved by feedback about detection of inserted artificial targets. It is possible that KR primarily affects readiness to respond (β); therefore, it might primarily have the effect of increasing the number of false alarms (Baker, 1961). Yet, KR about detecting artificial stimuli may have two positive effects, namely, the artificial stimuli increase the relative frequency of targets and operators receive performance feedback. Both variables are supposed to raise effort and keep performance optimal.

These suggestions were all concerned with keeping up motivation, which may also be achieved by background music (Fox, 1975) or appropriate social stimulation. Other suggestions about improving detections are concerned with target-to-noise ratio. The general tenet of the cognitive-energetic model is that as targets become more discriminable, they are less sensitive to the effects of low arousal and activation. Improving target discriminability has been a primary purpose in the development of new sonar and radar equipment. Thus, noise is suppressed by correlating the signals from successive broadcasts. In this way, a target can be considerably sharpened. However, the action radius of submarines has increased as well, so despite the improved signal-to-noise ratio, there remains the requirement that a target should be detected near threshold. Following each broadcast, computer calculations may suggest a location where the probability of a target is the largest. This means that the computer carries out a first selection that, aside from a potential target, will include a multitude of false alarms, the evaluation of which remains the main task of the operator. This procedure eliminates the traditional search of the sonar screen at each individual broadcast. It has the additional advantage that the operator is kept active, although evaluating the suggestions from the computer may increase the rate of reported false alarms.

Other attempts to improve the target-to-noise ratio are along the lines of Parasuraman's (1986) suggestion that it is better to present target and noise simultaneously than successively. For example, Lozzo and Drury (1980) presented an image of a good target prototype immediately before a stimulus. If prototype and stimulus were identical, they would fuse; if they deviated, the difference would be immediately visible through pop-out. In the same way, Fisk and Scerbo (1987) emphasized the relevance of pop-out to industrial inspection. When searching for complex targets, such as detecting critical deviations in a power plant, it may be helpful to have a general alarm telling the operator that "some location" needs attention. One should be certain, though, that the alarm will always occur in case of a deviation because, once introduced, only the alarm will alert operators. A target will almost certainly remain undetected when missed by the alarm. In other words, the alarm should have a small β, even at the cost of many false alarms.

SUMMARY

Research on energetics often suffers from inconsistent results. Some potential reasons were met throughout this chapter. First, it was argued that energetics are closely related to motivation, which is quite hard to control for (Hockey, 1993). Second, the effect of a stress is never an isolated affair but depends strongly on the momentary energetic state. Third, assessing stress effects in individual tasks, however popular, does not contribute to progress, at least not as long as the tasks have no proper process model as interpretative framework. Much of the research on, for example, psychotropic drugs has been carried out under industrial contract, which means that one should find an effect or, even better, show the absence of an effect when the contractor fears potential, undesirable side effects of a drug. It is evident that such research is always short term, and this means that many researchers just lack the opportunity to reflect on how to approach some of the afore-mentioned problems.

A major aim of this chapter was to present a few of such reflections. One concerned the emphasis on the interaction of cognitive and energetic factors, asking for a much closer cooperation between performance theorists inter-ested in computation and those interested in energetics. It was demonstrated that, thus far, there has hardly been any cooperation but, rather, a mutual neglect. Indeed, one may say that sustained attention has been the stepchild of most theorists on attention. The cognitive-energetic model was proposed as a research initiative more so than a ready-made model. A second reflection consisted of emphasizing what has actually been achieved. The point is that the many contradictory results notwithstanding, there are consistencies as well. Some, such as the evidence on reactive inhibition, represented half-forgotten but still quite relevant results. Others emerged from the plethora of research and led to, at least, a shortlist of recommendations for system design. Thus, in conclusion, it may be said that at present, there is a theo-retical alternative on the behavioral level for the dated, unidimensional "arousal" theory of the 1950s. Some may wonder whether this is a match for the rapidly expanding neurophysiological evidence on energetics. They may be reminded, though, of the category error and the problems involved in predicting behavior from neurophysiology. However primitive the theo-retical status on the behavioral level may be, it is the only match available for comparing the two levels of scientific enquiry.

EPILOGUE

Stages Versus Capacity: A Final Verdict

By way of epilogue, the discussion about the fields of reaction time and attention ends with a brief reflection on one of the aims of the book, namely, to contrast capacity- and processing-stage models in modulating the infor-mation flow through the organism. It was outlined that both models have deep classical roots that served as continuous threads throughout all previous chapters. It is evident, then, that the capacity notion faces considerable problems. First, their traditional starting point of a single, limited-processing capacity has appeared untenable. Second, a simple reference to capacity consumption fell short as a psychologically meaningful description of human information-processing. Multiple-resource theory has more psychological content and certainly has heuristic value but faces the objection that it merely deals with isolated faculties. The same might be said of Fleishman's (1984) catalogue of mental abilities, which is discussed in the next chapter and which may be conceived of as the most elaborate multiple-resource notion. They do not easily lead to a more detailed description of the processes that account for a resource or an ability. Neither does multiple-resource theory suggest a methodology for a more detailed inquiry. This is actually not surprising because the main emphasis has always been on hierarchically supraordinate strategic manipulation of resources rather than on a critical analysis of what a resource might actually entail. This is even more pronounced in the resource-strategy views with their emphasis on qualitative changes in performance as a result of energetic deficits and stress. It led to various seminal insights, but not to systematic progress.

The hope of some investigators that capacity consumption might be measured by means of autonomous, physiological indexes has not come through. For example, Kahneman's (1973) suggestion that capacity demands might correlate with pupil dilatation has hardly received any follow-up. It can be safely said that nowadays the main themes in cognitive psychophysiology are engaged with issues of specific localization of mental processes rather than with measuring general-capacity demands. This is clearly fostered by the rapid developments in brain-imaging techniques. The quest for specific localization is much more akin to a processing stage than to a capacity approach.

In research on focused attention (chapter 7), the limited-capacity concept has never been really crucial. It served as a general rationale for the existence of selective attention until it was realized that "explaining limits of selective attention by limited capacity" is an example of a *vertus dormitiva*. This may be the reason that the capacity notion has hardly stimulated research on focused attention. The emphasis was there on (a) early versus late selection, (b) the role of spatial localization on focusing, and (c) visual search strategies, which are all far beyond the capacity notion. It is of interest in this respect that in Broadbent's (1971) *Decision and Stress*, the argument was primarily based on signal-detection theory and not on capacity as the main conceptual principle. Since the failure of the serial dichotomization model, the capacity notion did not play a significant role in models of C(RT) either. In this area, the process models were largely inspired by decision theory (chapter 2).

The main, relevant research issue arising from the capacity concept was indeed the allocation policy (Kahneman, 1973) bearing on strategies and limits in dividing attention among tasks and, more generally, on the relative freedom of a central executive. Thus, the question whether reallocation of capacity between tasks can be gradual or only in rough steps could easily arise from a general capacity model. Allocation and reallocation are also main issues in the area of workload measurement, which explains that the capacity notion has enjoyed considerable popularity there. Moreover, a more general approach toward performance may have some appeal in the study of real-life tasks where more detailed architectural descriptions are lacking. In the end, however, an architectual approach to real-life tasks is indispensable. This is further elaborated in the discussion on simulation models and on measuring performance in dynamic simulators.

Most of the previous argument underscored the prospects of the processing-stage approach. It was prominent in the analysis of CRT, from where it fanned out to more general issues of information-processing, including the three varieties of attention. Its fan-out to attention was perhaps the most evident from the cognitive-energetic model. Although with fewer tight relations, issues of focused and divided attention also appeared to bear on stage concepts. One task for future research is to make this relation more explicit. The modern stage approach derives undoubtedly from the AFM which, despite its strong axioms, appeared to have a wider domain of application than might have been expected. Thus far, it led to a consistent description of processing stages in a traditional choice reaction, whereas its domain extended to response sequences, target classification, the psychological refractory period, visual fixation duration, and energetic variables. One important conulusion was that these extensions added to the basic structure of the traditional choice-reaction process without bringing about qualitative changes in that basic structure—as had been expected by proponents of capacity theory. The rather wide domain of the AFM is fostered by the fact that the logic appears to be less strictly tied to some of its axioms than originally thought. Moreover, when the AFM failed, as in the cases of immediate arousal and asynchronous discrete processing, it failed in interesting ways. The deviations were systematic, the conditions and reasons for the failure were delineated clearly, and, perhaps most importantly, the basic structure of the processing stages was left intact. In this way, the stage structure still proved to provide a solid basis for describing mental processing beyond the domain of the AFM. It is also undeniable that research on processing stages has been a valuable sparring partner for cognitive psychophysiology.

A major, future research effort should be devoted to more detailed process descriptions of the individual stages. Without process descriptions, the stages are void of content, in the same way as the factor analytic dimensions and the multiple resources. It is of interest to consider the prospects of single-process models as descriptors of what is going on in a particular stage. It is obviously relevant that stage models are not incompatible with the current connectionist Zeitgeist. In this regard, the capacity view is clearly fighting against odds! Both the stage view and the connectionistic view emphasize processing mechanisms by way of modular processing levels and of competing output codes within and between levels. This means that connectionist modeling on what is going on in a particular processing stage is an interesting avenue to process description. Although connectionist models assume massive parallel processing, they exclude neither constant stage output nor single-channel behavioral bottlenecks. Bottlenecks actually aid in suppressing interference and in guaranteeing stable behavior. Yet, from a connectionist perspective, bottlenecks are made up of software rather than hardware. Whenever interference, or competition among processes, has been eliminated by practice, a bottleneck will disappear because it has lost its function. The same may be valid for individual stages, which may be highly relevant in early practice but bypassed or take negligible time after extensive practice. Various instances of automatic processing proved to be related to such changes in the information flow.

Thus, delineation and localization of processing mechanisms are current passwords that directly correspond to the rapidly expanding potential of brain-imaging techniques, the development of which also does not favor the mass action type of capacity view. There remain a few issues, though, centered around the status of the central executive, which is quite akin to the capacity view, whereas its surmise should be impending from a connectionist perspective. Will it be possible to eliminate strategic performance control without impoverishing the scope of human performance analysis? Closely connected is the analysis of dual-task performance, where replacing limits of capacity sharing by patterns of interference does not mean a step ahead as long as the patterns of interference are not specified in considerably more detail. Thus far, stage analysis has had little to say about dual-task performance. Its experimental underpinning may well prove to be the Achilles' heel for present-day theoretical trends.

CHAPTER TEN

The Total Task:
Reversal of the Perspective

So far, the main concern of this book was a process-oriented discussion of reaction processes and attention. In this chapter, the perspective is task oriented, which means a focus on applied procedures in assessing human performance in real-life tasks, existing ones as well as those in the design phase. Real-life tasks are highly diverse and vary widely in nature and complexity. Some common elements notwithstanding, they are dominated by domain-specific features that require specialized expertise of a human-factors specialist. Examples include driving, flying, maneuvering a ship, supervising a nuclear or chemical control room, handling a text-processing system, carrying out a medical operation, and drilling teeth. Aside from questions about enhancing expert performance through better designs, there are human-factors issues with respect to training and instruction. The main question, then, is to what extent such specialized areas may benefit from evidence from small paradigms. What is the validity of the applied guidelines, as outlined in the previous chapters, for complex tasks? Is theory of any value? Is there actually any need for guidelines from basic research when designing a complex system?

Systems in their various phases of design can be developed and evaluated by analytical and behavioral procedures. The next two sections discuss analytical techniques of task description and task evaluation. They are labeled analytical because they are concerned with the relations between a total task and its elementary constituents. The first section is concerned with approaches "from the complex to the simple." A complex task is broken down into its simplest elements in order to list and check for potential ergonomic deficits of each element. Task analysis is the main password in

452

this approach. This is followed by a section on techniques "from the simple to the complex." Here, the purpose is to establish meaningful dimensions on which a taxonomy of tasks may be based. The quest is for a finite number of task dimensions that can be separately analyzed and accessed. Ideally, then, any task should be described in terms of a weighted combination of values on these dimensions. Performance limits in a complex task, then, would follow directly from limits of the individual dimensions. A third analytical approach is performance simulation by means of a computer model of the human operator. Domain-specific computer models describe performance in a specific skill; other computer models aim at establishing more general performance limits of the human operator. Examples of either category are discussed with the issue of application of basic research findings in mind.

Behavioral procedures are concerned with measurement of human performance either on the job or in a simulator in order to determine potential deficiencies. On-the-job measures are usually impractical and obviously impossible when a system is not yet operational. Although simulation studies are relatively recent, they are rapidly becoming relevant. In the case of a new system, a provisional simulation, either static or dynamic, may be achieved by way of rapid prototyping. The section on simulation is mainly concerned with problems and prospects of dynamic simulation. Is there any need for basic research findings in the simulation of complex tasks? The chapter and, actually, the book conclude with a scrutiny of the prospects of the back-to-back approach.

FROM THE COMPLEX TO THE SIMPLE: SYSTEM DESIGN

A system refers to any human–machine-based set of procedures that aim to accomplish a certain goal. For example, operating a spade in a garden is a system consisting of interplay between a human and a tool in order to, for example, plant roses. A system description entails all elements and their modes of operation in achieving the goals. It is common (Meister, 1985) to distinguish three types of systems: (a) manual systems in which the human operator carries out all actions and the tool provides more efficiency and precision. Examples are spade, knife, and drill; (b) mechanical systems, in which the tool performs its own actions that are dependent, though, on human input and control. Examples are rifle, car, and typewriter; (c) automated systems in which the tool achieves the full goal without any contribution of a human operator; there remains only supervisory monitoring of the machinery. A control room of a nuclear reactor or a chemical industry are among the common examples. Technological progress has caused an irreversible trend away from manual to mechanical systems and, from there, the advent of the computer has caused a further shift toward automated systems.

A system becomes more complex as achieving its goal—sometimes called its mission—entails cooperation among a larger number of components. When designing a complex system such as a submarine, a chemical plant, or an airport, it is common to distinguish a number of design phases, although their boundaries and procedures are fuzzy. A design starts with a mission analysis in which the operational requirements of the system are described. What is the system supposed to achieve, under which circumstances, in which environments, and with which limits? Thus, when designing an airport, safe and efficient handling of air transport is the widest but, of course, most unspecified description of the mission, which is then elaborated on in much greater detail by way of a list of statements. Examples may include (a) the type of transport, for example, passengers, freight, and so on, (b) types of aircraft to be handled, (c) air-traffic control services, (d) servicing aircraft, (e) immigration and customs services, (f) checking in, (g) safety measures, (h) inbound and outbound connections, (i) connections outside and inside the airport, (j) handling luggage, (k) restaurants and accommodations, (l) shops, (m) handling cargo, and (n) services to travel organizations. Aside from these examples, it is desirable to have an estimate of the total capacity of the airport and of the potential for future extension. It is relevant that the list of operational requirements is complete because it is usually difficult and expensive to add additional components after the system has been implemented. For instance, it took considerable time and effort to add a commodity to Schiphol airport that was capable of separating European-Union (EU) passengers from others. Increasing doubts are raised whether the location of Schiphol is appropriate in regard to a foreseeable need for future extension, a shortcoming that is, of course, almost impossible to repair.

Mission analysis is followed by function analysis. A function is defined as a logical unit of performance of the system. In the case of an airport, checking in, handling luggage, following emigration procedures, signaling the correct gate, making safety checks, and boarding passengers are among the functions that relate to the operational requirement of transport of passengers. It is evident that functions may be described on different levels of detail. For instance, handling luggage may be further subdivided into attaching the appropriate tag, transporting from the check-in desk, choosing the correct destination, transporting to the correct luggage area, transporting to the aircraft, and loading on the aircraft. Note that a function analysis merely lists functions—that is, what ought to be done—but does not specify how they should be realized. Hence, a function is not equal to a job. One function may consist of more than one job, whereas on other occasions, several functions may be combined into a single job.

The way in which functions are realized are of interest to the next design phase that is labeled *function allocation*. In this phase, the functions are analyzed; decisions are made about how the goal of each function will be achieved, about the desired hardware and software of the equipment, and about how to divide the work between machines and operators. Note that the operators are a crew. This means they do not only interact with equipment but also with each other in order to realize the goals of the system. In this phase, the actual jobs are shaped. There are usually different options for function allocation, which should all be described and subjected to task analysis, with the aim of scrutinizing the potential human–machine and human–human interactions. Each option leads to requirements for interfacing and workspace and to a prediction of system performance when a particular option is implemented. Sometimes, task analysis is limited to a detailed description of the human-factors problems associated with each of the options and how they might be avoided. Often, a task analysis includes recommendations about desired information exchange among the members of the crew. Ideally, a task analysis is supplemented by listing training needs and potential bottlenecks. These results are all fed back to function allocation as an aid for deciding which option to choose. Function allocation and task analysis may include rapid prototyping of the system, that is, a simulated, preliminary version of potential human–machine interactions through simulation.[1]

Research Techniques

Analytical methods are divided into macro- and micromethods. Macroanalysis is discussed in the context of task taxonomies. In a microprocedure, a task is decomposed into its most elementary operations. The smallest units are obtained by specifying inputs and outputs for any single action. Each action is analyzed on potential error sources, deficits, and performance limits. The results of a microanalysis are used for deciding about human factors, about work force allocation, and about function allocation.

A microanalysis entails (a) a relevant behavioral verb such as carry, store, inspect, search, react; (b) a stimulus that elicits the action of a verb; (c) a response in terms of equipment, such as switch, mouse, light pen, joystick; (d) the consequence of the action; (e) feedback; and (f) criteria for satisfactory performance. Unfortunately, there is no generally accepted and standardized description technique that systematically covers the preceding points (Meister, 1985). However, this is not felt to be a serious problem by practitioners as long as they feel that the aims of a task analysis are achieved.

---

[1]In the case of an existing system, task analysis is the main analytical method for deciding whether the system functions well.

There is no doubt, though, that it remains a serious shortcoming because only a well-researched, standard description technique guarantees that the essential elements of the system's actions have been accounted for. A standard technique is also indispensable for comparing the outcomes of different task analyses and for relating the individual actions to basic laboratory research. The issue deserves serious research effort, therefore, which may not be easily realized because it is neither of primary interest to the basic researcher nor directly cost effective to the practitioner.

Function Analysis

It is evident that both mission and function analysis do not apply to simple manual systems such as handling a rifle or operating a spade. Such systems can be directly subjected to task analysis to uncover potential problems in regard to, for example, a rifle's physical load, manual control, aiming precision, and cleaning. Mission and function analysis are essential steps, though, in the design of a more complex system. An important tool in function analysis is a flowchart that describes the successive steps of a process. Thus, in an airport, a departing passenger enters the airport area, finds an appropriate parking lot[2] (optional), carries the luggage, finds the way to the departure hall, finds the correct check-in desk, waits in line, checks in, stores papers, finds emigration (optional), visits shops (optional), finds the way to the correct gate, is subjected to a safety check, and boards the plane.[3] Together, the actions constitute a fixed sequence, or script. Each action is connected to issues of human factors and efficiency. For instance, some are concerned with visual search for appropriate signs, which bears directly on pop-out, as met in the discussion on focused attention (chap. 7).

In other applications, a flowchart may consist of a decision/action diagram in computer-program format. For instance, in sonar one may analyze the functions as shown in Fig. 10.1. The ensuing task analysis consists of listing potential human-factors problems arising from each individual step. Thus, "Is there a new contact?" raises the problem of detecting near-threshold signals. This was discussed at some length in chapter 9 in the context of vigilance. Matching the characteristics of the signal with known signatures is a matter of a same–different analysis of perceptual patterns (chap. 5), whereas classification of signals may benefit from research on target classification (chap. 5).

It is relevant to add time information to a flowchart, irrespective of whether a sequence of functions is one- or multidimensional. A multidimensional

---

[2]May not be needed if there is the option of coming by train or bus.

[3]At some airports, checking in is done at the gates. In that case, the sequence changes in that, on entering the departure hall, one has to find the appropriate gate number and the way leading to that gate. The optimal sequencing of functions is an obvious aspect in the design of an airport.

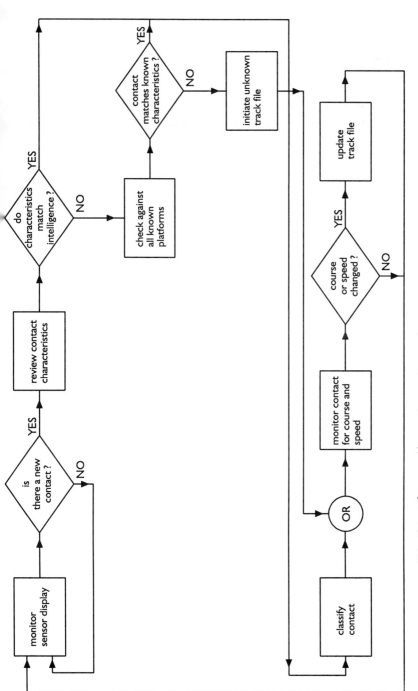

FIG. 10.1. Information/decision/action diagram for a sonar system concept (from Beevis et al., 1992). Reprinted from D. Beevis, J. P. Papin, B. Döring, H. Schuffel, E. Nordo, D. F. Streets, R. Bost, & F. R. Oberman (Eds.), *Analysis techniques for man-machine system design*. NATO document, 1992, AC/243 (panel 8) TR/7. Reprinted with permission of the editors.

457

sequence is common in more complex multihuman systems. Thus, in the case of an airport, take-off of aircraft depends, among others, on (a) availability of an aircraft, (b) maintenance and fueling, (c) a properly instructed crew, (d) loading luggage, (e) catering, (f) boarding passengers, and (g) clearance by air-traffic control. All these conditions have their own sequence of functions, many of which run off in parallel but should all be completed prior to take-off. The efficiency of a multidimensional sequence of functions is often represented by a PERT network.

Function Allocation

This may well be the most crucial phase in a design because it deals with options for concrete human–machine interactions. Examples are human–computer interaction at the check-in desk and signaling passengers how to get to the correct gate. Another example concerns the actions involved in finding one's way in an airport with an automatically operated ground transportation system. Given that airline and flight number are known, the task is to find the correct departure gate and the appropriate vehicle leading to that gate. A bulletin board at the entrance of the airport may inform the passengers that these data are dispayed on a set of three adjacent television screens. One screen describes which flight departs from which gate, another one describes which gates can be reached by which vehicle of the ground transportation system, and the third screen describes the routes of the vehicles by way of colored maps. Hence, the first screen informs about the desired gate, the second screen tells which vehicle to take, and the third screen indicates the route of that vehicle. When boarding a vehicle, the information about its route and stops is repeated. This provides a check whether the correct vehicle has been chosen (Laughery & Laughery, 1987). It is evident that this set of three television systems to guide the passengers to the correct departure gate is an example of function allocation. Ideally, the choice in favor of this solution should be based on task analysis of different options. Once a television-guiding system has been chosen, further task analyses are needed with respect to information presentation on those screens.

The basic questions of the stage of function allocation concern which tasks to assign to an operator and which to a machine, and how to achieve optimal communication among the elements of the system. With respect to the first question, Fitts (1951b) listed a number of relative strengths and weaknesses. Machines are better at performing repetitive, routine actions, are more precise, have a high speed, are capable of storing and retrieving large amounts of information, and have few limits in dividing attention among tasks. Machines also do not suffer from fatigue or loss of motivation and are relatively insensitive to adverse environmental conditions. In short, they are superior in most activities that bear on C(RT) and attention.

According to the same list, the human operator is better in performing input and output functions. Humans have excellent pattern perception, are sensitive to a wide variety of stimuli and have a highly elaborate and flexible motor system. In addition, humans are superior to machines in all situations that require knowledge-based behavior. This is among the major reasons for assigning supervisory control in automated systems to the human operator because machines may have trouble finding an adequate solution when an unforeseen error arises.[4]

It should be noted that the advent of parallel-distributed processors has greatly improved automatic pattern perception and that progress in artificial intelligence has led to expert systems on reasoning and fault diagnosis. Advances in robotics are impressive as well. Thus, although Fitts' (1951b) list is still correct in that humans excel in pattern perception, in complex motor behavior, and in adoption of flexible reasoning procedures, it is no longer valid that machines are necessarily inferior in these respects. This does not mean that whenever possible, tasks should be assigned to machines. The problem is that full automation is still always hard to accomplish, in particular, when the system's mission is not fully determined but probabilistic and somewhat domain aspecific. For example, thus far, expert systems have been the most successful in rather limited and well-structured domains. When automation is attempted in a somewhat more complex domain, the human often has the task of diagnosing errors as a leftover, that is hard to automatize. Incidentally, failing automated devices may actually lead to unsurmountable problems for the human operator as well. The point is that the leftovers of automation do not appeal to the strong side of a human operator either, which then leads to the frequent conclusion that an accident was due to human error (Reason, 1990). It is desirable, therefore, to aim at a balanced approach in system design and to divide the tasks in a way that optimally suits the capabilities of both human and machine (e.g., Kantowitz & Sorkin, 1987). Thus, function allocation requires a listing of all functions and an estimate of the relative advantages of allocating that function to human or machine. There are often various machine solutions to consider. The ultimate choice should depend on the outcome of a microtask analysis.

Task Analysis

As a simple example of a microanalysis, Drury (1983) analyzed port-of-entry operators who had the triple task of (a) taking cartons from a container and putting them on a conveyor belt, (b) entering appropriate shipping information into a computer, and (c) attaching a printed bar code to each carton

---

[4]It is well recognized that human operators are only superior if they have a thorough knowledge of the controlled processes. In order to get and maintain the necessary experience, they often practice by playing scenarios in dynamic system simulations.

in order to allow its automatic identification at a later stage. The task elements were (a) moving a pallet to the side of the conveyor belt, (b) entering shipping information from an invoice, (c) placing the first carton on the conveyor belt, (d) entering the code of the carton into the computer, (e) attaching the printed bar code, that is, the output of the computer, to the carton, (f) checking the bar code with the carton code, and (g) instructing the belt to start moving the carton.

As already indicated, task analysis emphasizes potential human-factors problems with respect to each individual task element. For instance, human–computer interfacing is relevant to entering shipping information into the computer, the code of a carton may exceed memory span, and moving the pallet may be physically hard to do. The same type of microanalysis can be applied to a variety of real-life tasks such as operating copying machines, desk calculators, video recorders, gas ovens, and text-processing systems as well as reading instruction manuals. As an example, the task of programming a future television broadcast on a video recorder requires a fixed sequence of actions, each of which involves identification and pressing of a correct button or switch. The switches usually have technical English names, often abbreviated, which are incomprehensible for nontechnical and nonnative English speakers. In addition, their close spacing on a small and crowded panel increases the probability of pressing an incorrect key. Finally, the instruction manual may be vague or obscure about the correct sequence of actions and about what to do in the case of an error. Many of these problems correspond to issues that are studied in small, basic paradigms. The example described the flow of a single sequence of actions that may be formalized by a standardized description format such as a timeline analysis, a flow-process chart, or an operational sequence diagram. Alternatively, one may list the tasks of an operator in a hierarchical, tabular format. Hierarchical task analysis (Annett & Duncan, 1967; Sheperd, 1989) is a prime example of this approach.

Timeline Analysis

Timeline analysis is a flowchart with listings of the times needed for completing all required actions in their correct sequence. It is often used for estimating work load. The first step is to develop a realistic scenario of a task, for example, a typical flight. The scenario defines flight segments and altitudes and speeds as well as key events and typical operations. A timeline relates the sequence of display-control operations to the scenario. The time taken by each operation is estimated and entered into the timeline. The major rationale is to estimate whether the sequence can be carried out within the time constraints that are available for the whole scenario (Parks & Boucek, 1989). The method derives from classical time and motion study aimed at estimating whether all required actions could be carried out when an assembly line had a given rate of pace.

MicroSAINT

MicroSAINT is a computer program that contains a network model of system performance. As usual, a potential system consisting of human and technical components is decomposed into its elementary functions that together make up a network. The functions, their interconnections in the network, and their time parameters are defined and entered into the MicroSAINT program. The total network consists of several relatively autonomous subnetworks affecting each other only through shared variables. For example, in a helicopter, the pilot, the cockpit, the helicopter hardware, and an alarm system, indicating threats from the environment, are relatively autonomous subnetworks but still share some common variables. Thus, a command to increase altitude changes the values of the corresponding controls; this has the effect that the hardware is activated to carry out its tasks. Moreover, once a certain altitude is exceeded, the threat alarm system may be alerted. One major function of MicroSAINT is to show the consequences of actions as they propagate through the system. In this way, it serves the function of a dynamic computer simulation of performance.

Another feature of MicroSAINT is that predictions about performance are calculated. For example, when one is flying a helicopter, the constant stream of information from the displays and from the outside world demands adequate responses. Any action takes time for initiation and completion; therefore, when too many actions are required at the same time, some desired responses may not be initiated. Instead, they queue, with the result that responses are aborted when the queue becomes too long.

It is evident that programming a system in MicroSAINT requires detailed assumptions about the time taken to initiate and complete each individual action and how well a pilot may divide attention among different activities. Again, some actions will be urgent, whereas others may be less bound to a specific response at a specific time. Does the pilot function as a single-channel processor, as in the case of the psychological refractory period, or can he carry out various actions in parallel? To what extent may parallel actions be a spin-off of automatic processing? To what extent is the system paced or self-paced? Is it useful to view the issue in terms of a central executive in the brain who plans the total activity and who decides about priorities with respect to which actions to abort when faced with overload?[5] These questions were all major issues in earlier chapters. Thus, performance

---

[5]One may distinguish a strategic planning level, a maneuvering level, and a control level in the execution of tasks such as driving a car or flying a helicopter. On the planning level, the ultimate goal is defined along with a sequence of subgoals—for example, route planning for a trip by car. The maneuvering level refers to interaction with other traffic in achieving the goals and subgoals. The control level, finally, is concerned with feedback-related corrections (Janssen, 1979). The time scales of these three levels are increasingly small and more paced.

predictions and workload estimates in MicroSAINT depend on the validity of the assumptions about processing speed and divided attention.

One extensive application of SAINT, of which MicroSAINT is a more simplified version, was maneuvering a submarine and, in particular, operating snort procedures (van Breda, 1989). The operator was simulated by a number of condition/action rules in which any specific action was appropriate as a specific response to a certain condition and took a fixed, estimated time. The operator was considered to be acting as a single channel, and the aim of the study was to determine the proportion of time that an operator was either idle, active with one operation, or faced with the requirement of simultaneous operations. A strict single-channel solution is obviously too simple and is likely to overestimate peak work load. In another application (Laughery, 1989), a helicopter pilot was modeled as a multiple-resource system consisting of an auditory and a visual resource, a cognitive-processing resource, and a psychomotor output resource. The times taken by the detailed operations in the network were estimated from the basic literature on CRT. The inputs for potential attack and defense actions consisted of information about the environment on displays and about outside threats via a threat alarm system. Additional actions were needed to fly correctly. The goal of the study was to evaluate alternative cockpit displays. The results show that overload—in the sense of the number of aborted responses—was primarily due to heavy demands on visual resources, which proved much reduced in the case of one of the potential displays.

Hierarchical Task Analysis

The tasks discussed previously shared the property that, although of varying complexity, they could be modeled as a PERT network of action sequences in which completion of one action or group of actions triggered the next one. There are other instances in which actions are less sequential, so a network analysis is less meaningful. Nor does a network analysis provide guidelines about how to decompose a total task into its constituent units. In those cases, a hierarchical, tabular format is more appropriate. Hierarchical task analysis (HTA) is a prime example. An HTA starts by defining the goals of a system. The way a task is carried out depends on constraints, available resources, and preferences as long as one has a choice among alternative actions. Any task is carried out by completing a number of operations. Although they all are meant to serve the final goal of the system, the effect of any particular operation may be fairly indirect, depending on the extent to which the ultimate goal is subdivided into a hierarchy of subgoals. Subgoals constitute an organized structure that is governed by the total plan (see footnote 5).

The major content of an HTA consists of decomposing a task into ever more refined subgoals. The ultimate goal is redescribed in greater detail until a satisfactory level of detail has been reached. The overall goal is usually trivial, for example, "safe and efficient traffic flow" in air-traffic control and "achieving economic stability" in a management game on controlling a simple economy. The first redescription lists a number of hierarchically subordinate but still quite abstract goals such as "know the features of the aircraft under present control" and "plan aircraft maneuvers," which is followed by further subdivision of the subgoals. Thus, the general features of controlled aircraft are listed in the next redescription, for example, identity, flight level, speed, present position, destination, and time of entering or leaving the airway. Again, "plan aircraft maneuvers" contains subgoals about sequencing aircraft and anticipating potential conflicts arising from descending and ascending traffic as well as general rules such as "maintain sufficient distance among aircraft" and "prevent aircraft from exceeding the airway." Each further redescription results in more and more concrete activities. Thus, at the next redescription the actual data for each aircraft may be described. Activities may sometimes have a fixed sequence but more typically, they may compete for priority. Thus, actions in air-traffic control often consist of informing and instructing pilots, the priority of which is partly determined by the operator but is also paced by the flow of incoming messages and by questions from pilots. A plan for optimal sequencing of activities should be added to each level of an HTA.[6] On completion of an HTA, the result may be modeled as a network.

An HTA needs a stopping rule for deciding whether a sufficiently fine level of subgoals has been reached. Annett and Duncan (1967) proposed the so-called P * C criterion, in which P refers to the probability of errors or of inefficient operations at a particular level of subgoals and C to the costs of inadequate performance at that level. If one of these two factors is sufficiently low, there is no reason for describing the goals in greater detail. It is evident that, viewed from this criterion, the preceding initial steps toward an HTA for air-traffic control should be elaborated into much greater detail. More concrete elaboration depends, of course, on the specific features of the ATC system as a whole. As a rule of thumb, though, the redescription of goals should proceed at least to the level of interface responses.

When to stop? One might imagine that at some level of an HTA, an operation may be "inform pilot about descent." An elaboration at the next level could be "choose the correct radio frequency," "call pilot," "inform pilot about the new flight level," "make sure that the message is understood," and "turn off radio." As mentioned, the probability of an error arising at each subgoal is of interest. At this particular level, there are potential errors arising from (a) the choice of the radio frequency, (b) the call sign of the aircraft, (c) the value of the new flight level, (d) the quality of the broadcast,

---

[6]It is evident that most of this could also be subsumed under function analysis.

(e) the intelligibility of speech, and (f) the use of standard terminology. It may be hard to estimate the error probabilities involved at each step; indeed, they may be considered negligible. Still, there is the example of the crash between the KLM and the Pan-American aircraft on the runway at Tenerife airport in 1977. The accident was at least partly the result of a misunderstanding between air-traffic control and the KLM pilot, who was under the impression that he had obtained clearance for take-off. The error was due to a combination of a bad communication line, problems of speech comprehension, and the fact that the pilot was eager to leave, all sufficient reasons to consider potential human-factors problems on this more detailed level. It is also evident that, when doing so, one immediately enters the realm of the small research paradigms such as a correct response, stimulus degradation, word identification, and short-term memory. The conclusion is that professional system evaluation by way of task analysis requires a thorough knowledge of the main trends of that basic literature.

FROM THE SIMPLE TO THE COMPLEX:
TASK TAXONOMY

Task decomposition via microanalysis is always going from the complex to the simple. In contrast, macroanalysis attempts to go from the simple to the complex. It aims at synthesis rather than analysis and consists of a list of characteristics and demands of a task. This may be achieved by a general questionnaire such as the Position Analysis Questionnaire (PAQ; McCormick, 1976) or by rating scales about an existing job or a set of coherent jobs that together make up the mission of a system. As always, the aim is to detect bottlenecks and shortcomings. The idea is to define a finite number of basic dimensions that, together, allow a taxonomic classification of real-life tasks. A taxonomy requires a descriptive system of well-defined behavioral or task-related categories and a set of criteria for determining whether, and to what extent, a particular category is relevant to a given task. For example, in zoology, the animal taxonomy is based on characteristics such as the mode of reproducing, breast feeding, flying, and swimming, with subdivisions such as gnawing and the structure of fins or hoofs. The zoological taxonomy has the obvious prerequisite that any individual animal can be unambiguously assigned to a particular cell. The advantages of a taxonomic classification system are obvious. For example, the position of a given task in the taxonomy provides an estimate of its demands structure.

The main research on a behavioral task taxonomy stems, undoubtedly, from the monumental project of Fleishman and colleagues (Fleishman & Quaintance, 1984), who described four potential taxonomic approaches: (a) behavior description, which derives from what operators actually do in terms of overt behavior; (b) behavior requirements, which describes tasks in terms of required mental processes such as stimulus identification and short-term memory; (c) the abilities approach, which is also based on behavioral attributes. However, in contrast to the two earlier approaches, abilities are not simply postulated but inferred from intertwining factor analyses; and (d) the task characteristics approach, in which performance is analyzed in terms of task dimensions without any reference to behavioral concepts.

The three behavioral approaches have in common that they all start from at least a rudimentary notion of information flow through processing stages. Performance is, invariably, supposed to proceed from perceptual input to central transmission of information and, finally, to motor output. Thus, in regard to behavior description, a taxonomic matrix has been proposed of four processes (perceptual, mediational, communication, and motor) and five activities (search, identification, information processing, problem solving, and discrete vs. continuous responding). Activities are descriptors of a task and should always be observable terms such as detects, scans, or reads as examples for search. Behaviors may be quantified by standard measures of frequency, CRT, and accuracy in order to assess the interplay between operator and equipment.

R. B. Miller's (1974) taxonomy is a typical example of the behavior-requirements approach. The goals of a task are achieved by a sequence of transactions that refer to the broad categories of input, memory, central processing, and motor output. A subdivision of each of these categories leads to transactions such as input selection, filtering, detecting, categorizing, storing, computing, and planning. Each of these functions has its specific strategic principles that enable an operator to complete a transaction more efficiently. In regard to task taxonomy, the task is to identify the main transactions and their connected strategies. This should enable task descriptions in terms of patterns of transaction demands.

Both approaches rely heavily on concepts from the basic literature. However, they fail to fill the gap between the small paradigms, in which these concepts are embedded, and the real-life tasks to which they should apply. The point is that with respect to real-life tasks, the concepts are always applied in an intuitive and haphazard way. Hence, one can never be sure whether the meaning of a concept, for example, detecting, is the same in the small paradigm and in the taxonomic scheme. It is equally dubious whether the meaning of a concept remains the same in different real-life tasks. In brief, the problem of either approach is that by introducing vaguely defined categories, one of the main prerequisites for a valid taxonomy is violated.

The Abilities Approach

Some of these problems are avoided in the abilities approach that, indeed, has much better prospects for bridging the gap between the large and the small. Abilities are at the basis of Fleishman's thirty-year taxonomy project.

The approach is, by far, the most sophisticated attempt toward a task taxonomy. The starting points are that an ability is a relatively enduring disposition of a person and that a particular task needs a subset of abilities so that it can be classified in terms of load on the required abilities. The first phase of the project determined a set of mental abilities via intertwining factor analytic studies concerned with a wide range of small laboratory tasks. In this way, Fleishman and Quaintance (1984) arrived at 52 abilities relating to (a) intellectual functions such as oral comprehension, fluency of ideas, mathematical reasoning, and problem sensitivity (Guilford, 1967; French et al., 1963); (b) information processing aspects of perception such as speed and flexibility of closure in pattern perception, visualization, and perceptual identification speed; (c) response selection; and (d) motor behavior. The motor abilities contain, among others, control precision, multilimb coordination, manual dexterity, and anticipatory movements in timing. As already briefly mentioned in chapter 8, the list of abilities contains three attention factors, namely, divided, focused, and sustained attention. A final number of abilities is concerned with peripheral sensory aspects and with physical proficiency aspects such as various forms of strength, bodily coordination, and bodily equilibrium.

Fleishman recognized the problem that assigning names to factors is hazardous and unwarranted. A considerable amount of research was devoted, therefore, to obtaining more precise descriptions of the verbal labels. For example, the motor factor "rate control" refers to the ability to adjust a control in response to changes in speed or direction of moving stimuli. In the pertinent research, the rate-control factor was found in compensatory as well as in pursuit tracking, and it also played a role when the task only required timing pursuit or compensatory movements. In contrast, rate control did contribute when the task was limited to a perceptual judgment about stimulus movements, such as when estimating a future stimulus location. The relevant specification is that rate control is only involved when controlling stimulus movements through manual motor activity. Again, the "reaction time" ability refers to RT and not to CRT, because it merely concerned the speed of a simple reaction. The factor "response orientation" carries the most weight in a choice reaction with poor S–R compatibility.

Fleishman also recognized that the factor structure of a task may not remain the same in the course of practice. In an early phase of the taxonomy project, Fleishman and Hempel (1955) studied a traditional choice–reaction task in which each response corresponded to a specific, spatial pattern of lights. In early practice, a spatial factor and a verbal factor were found, whereas the verbal factor vanished almost completely and the impact of the spatial factor strongly decreased late in practice. On the other hand, motor factors such as rate of movement and RT gained importance. Together, this result suggests controlled computational processes in order to identify the stimulus pattern in early practice whose processes automatize in due course (Fig. 10.2).

It is needless to say that the abilities approach is deeply rooted in the small, basic research paradigms. Some may even argue that factor analysis is nothing but another, and perhaps questionable,[7] approach toward investigating small paradigms. The essential question is, of course, whether Fleishman's abilities can be shown to play a part in complex, real-life tasks. This was primarily studied by way of rating procedures. After the specification of the abitities had been increasingly refined, samples of judges rated the extent to which they thought an ability would be relevant to a given laboratory task. Figure 10.3 illustrates the rating procedure with respect to the "verbal comprehension" ability. The construct validity of the rating scales was assessed by comparing the subjective ratings on the laboratory tasks with the corresponding factor analytic data. The point is that, ideally, the same factor structure should be found in either case. Following further adaptations, the comparisons were successful. Thus, as the next step, the rating scales were applied to requirements of jobs and professions such as air-traffic controller, sheet-metal worker, astronaut, helicopter pilot, and automobile driver. It was highly relevant that the ratings showed satisfactory interrater reliability, suggesting that the ability descriptions were sufficiently unambiguous and that they corresponded to what raters observed in the real world. In the meantime, scale values have been obtained for thousands of tasks that are included in a task bank and classified according to the ability taxonomy. For example, Fig. 10.4 lists the relations between specific tasks and the abilities "response orientation," "selective attention," "time sharing," and "reaction time."

It follows from Fleishman's project that, indeed, essential aspects of small paradigms generalize to the real world. Stated more strongly, laboratory tasks that draw on the same subset of abilities as a particular real-life task should be valuable predictors for successful performance in that real-life task. In other words, subsets of laboratory tasks should qualify as selection battery for real-life tasks. This deduction was confirmed in the BAT battery for fighter pilots. Evidence from small paradigms appeared to be valuable for assessing individual differences.

There are other potential applications as well. One is that the specific way in which practice affects a certain ability may serve as a guideline for constructing an adequate training program for real-life tasks in which that

---

[7]The common objection to the factor analytic approach is that it is atheoretical. Factors are merely a loose set of "faculties" that lack coherence and process description. Admittedly, the correlations have no direct theoretical implications, so much research is needed on the description of processes involved in any one. In this respect, there is clear analogy with stage analysis of CRT. The stages as inferred by the AFM remind of factors—they also need process models about their specific ways of operation.

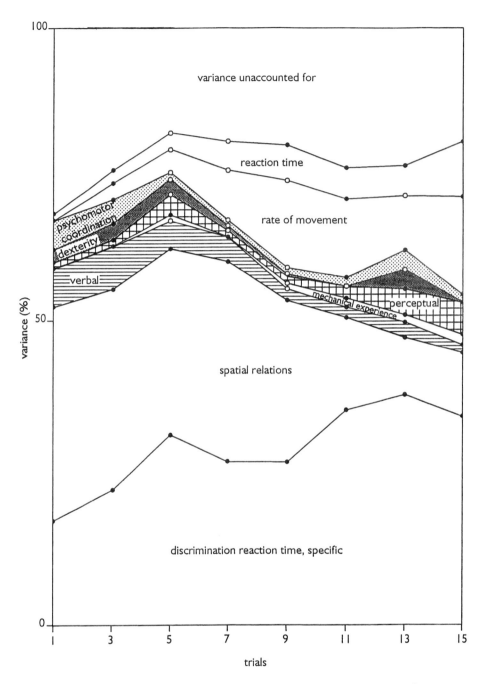

FIG. 10.2. Changes in the contribution of various abilities as a function of practice in a choice-reaction task. From Fleishman, E. A., & Hempel, W. E. (1953). The relation between abilities and improvement with practice in a visual discrimination task. *Journal of Experimental Psychology, 49,* 301–312.

> ## Verbal comprehension
> (the ability to understand English words and sentences)

Verbal comprehension: understand spoken or written English words and sentences.	V.S.	Verbal expression: speak or write English words or sentences so others will understand.

Requires understanding of complex, detailed information which contains unusual words and phrases and involves fine distinctions in meaning among words.

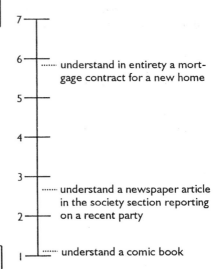

······ understand in entirety a mortgage contract for a new home

······ understand a newspaper article in the society section reporting on a recent party

······ understand a comic book

Requires a basic knowledge of language necessary to understand simple communications.

FIG. 10.3. Example of a rating scale for assessing abilities. Note the anchor points for the ability of verbal comprehension. From Fleishman, E. A., & Quaintance, M. K. (1984). *Taxonomies of human performance.* New York: Academic Press. Reprinted with kind permission of the publisher.

ability plays an essential part. Such training programs aim at eliminating the contribution of undesirable abilities that may dominate in early practice. Another application concerns system evaluation, in particular when norms can be formulated in regard to the desirability of certain abilities. Moreover, estimates of work load, of "weak spots," and of efficiency in a system may emerge from the ability assessment.

	Mean	σ

Response Orientation
-In a spacecraft out of control, quickly choose one of 5 possible corrections in 0.7. sec.	6.52	.74
-Operate a busy switchboard where you must plug in calls in and out quickly and accurately every few secs.	4.83	1.31
-When a doorbell and a telephone ring at the same time, select one to answer first in one sec.	2.93	1.22

Rate Control
-Operate aircraft controls to land a yet on an aircraft carrier in turbulent weather.	6.46	.92
-Keep up with a car you are following where the speed of the first car may vary.	3.64	1.22
-Ride a bicycle alongside a runner.	2.39	1.23

Reaction Time
- Hit back the ball which has been slammed at you in a ping-pong game	5.48	1.18
-Duck to miss being hit by a snowball thrown from across the street.	3.62	1.37
-Start to apply brakes on your car1 sec. after the light turns red.	2.28	1.13

Selective Attention
-Study for math exam in a house of noisy young children.	5.45	1.50
-Listen to news broadcast during a dinner conversation.	4.10	1.32
-Have a conversation with a friend at a noisy cocktail party	2.69	1.37

Time Sharing
-As air-traffic controller monitor a radar scpe to keep track of all inbound and outbound planes during a period of heavy and congested traffic.	6.07	.98
-Monitor several teletypes at the same time in a newsroom.	4.76	1.18
-Watch streetsigns and road while driving 50km/hr.	3.31	1.54

FIG. 10.4. Examples of ratings of anchor points for response orientation, rate control, reaction time, selective attention, and time sharing. From Fleishman, E. A., & Quaintance, M. K. (1984). *Taxonomies of human performance.* New York: Academic Press. Reprinted with kind permission of the publisher.

Task Characteristics

This approach differs from the three earlier ones in that tasks are only described in terms of objective task procedures, without any reference to behavioral concepts. It will not surprise, though, that the task characteristics and the ability approaches are strongly connected because abilities derive directly from task properties.[8] Farina and Wheaton (1973) constructed a taxonomy by decomposing tasks into components. This was followed by a description of the task characteristics of each component. The primary components of a task were goals, procedures, stimuli, responses, and S–R relations, all of which contained a number of specific characteristics. For example, the characteristics of the response component are (a) precision, (b) rate, (c) simultaneity of responses, and (d) degree of muscular effort. A rating procedure was used for assessing the relevance of any characteristic to particular real-life tasks. As in the abilities approach, a good interrater agreement was found after definitions of characteristics had been refined and proper scale anchors had been introduced.

A major criterion for the value of the task-characteristics approach is whether it predicts training and performance. This was studied by Farina and Wheaton (1973), who asked judges to rate tasks for which performance data were available. The results were promising because a selection of task characteristics proved to correlate with the performance data. Fleishman and Quaintance (1984) suggested that further refinement of this taxonomic approach may well lead to a common scheme of task characteristics and abilities.

By now, it is almost trivial to conclude that both the micro- and the macroapproach to system design cannot do without detailed knowledge of basic performance theory. It is the only way in which decomposed elements of real-life tasks can be related to corresponding performances, as studied in the basic literature. The abilities that have emerged from factor analytic studies on small paradigms appear to provide a suitable basis for the layout of a task taxonomy. This is relevant to bridging the gap between task and process orientation as well as to back-to-back analysis.

PROCESS SIMULATION

Performance research has not been exclusively concerned with small paradigms. Particularly in recent years, there have been many attempts to model more complex tasks. The example of visual monitoring was already discussed

---

[8]A nice example is actually the AFM, in which combinations of task variables define a behavioral processing stage such as feature extraction or response selection.

in chapter 7. Other examples include the MIXIC model (van Arem et al., 1994) that is concerned with car driving in a traffic stream—speed, lane changing, acceleration, and so on—and models on target search in natural scenes. There are also simulation models for skills such as typing and reading and for relevant components of verbal processing such as recognition of letters in words. In particular, the last mentioned models are theory driven and rely on data from basic research. In this way, they are between small paradigms and the richness of reality and, therefore, of considerable interest to the back-to-back approach.

There are also less domain-specific and less theory-based attempts toward modeling human performance, fostered by attempts toward computer simulation of a total system. It is now common to construct a computer model of a prospective system in an early phase of the design in order to evaluate its potential. The human operator is often the missing link in estimating system performance. Hence, there is a need for simulations of a human operator that can be plugged into any computer simulation of the technical part of a system. This simulation need not be a complete model of the human operator. Thus, there are standard programs—for example, SAMMIE (Bonney, Case, & Porter, 1989)—which simulate human anthropometric and biomechanical properties to aid design of appropriate workspace. Other simulations are concerned with signal detection, speed of responding, and dual-task performance. They are merely "intended to help remember facts and analyse human-machine interaction rather than intended as a statement of what is really in the head" (Card & Moran, 1986, p. 45-3). This aspect distinguishes simulation models of an operator from (a) simulations of skills such as scanning, typing, and reading, and (b) simulations of information processing in basic paradigms such as EPIC for the PRP and connectionist models on letter recognition in words.

Simulation of human information-processing is illustrated by (a) simulations of typing and MIXIC as domain-specific process models, and (b) the human operator simulator (HOS), GOMS, and the model human processor (MHP) as domain-aspecific aids to designers.

Typing

Studies on the PRP (chap. 8) have convincingly shown that human performance in serial responding has a limit of some two to three responses per sec. In contrast, rates of 8 to 12 responses per sec are normal in expert typing, and as many as 30 notes per sec may be produced by an expert pianist (Rumelhart & Norman, 1982). Moreover, typing has a large number of highly incompatible alternatives, whereas PRP studies have often used fairly compatible two-choice reactions. It is clear, therefore, that evidence on the PRP does not generalize to the transcription skill. How are these pronounced differences brought about?

The first point is that a fast typing-rate is only found when, indeed, a typist is highly skilled. Even after 4 weeks of practice, novices still show a variability in interstroke interval (II) ranging from 400 to 1,800 ms (Gentner, 1983), with a median of about one second. This does not essentially deviate from what is found in the PRP. An interesting difference between novices and experts concerns the so-called "double" that refers to repeated typing of the same letter. Doubles appear to be carried out relatively fast by novices and relatively slow by experts. This contrasts with the repetition effect in CRT, which is stronger for novices than for well-practiced participants. In typing, novices do relatively poorly on all other letter combinations such as successive responses with the same finger (one-finger digraphs), with different fingers of the same hand (two-finger digraphs), and with different fingers of different hands (two-hand digraphs). Experts do well on two-hand digraphs because they enable the almost simultaneous use of both hands, but they are also fast on two-finger digraphs as compared to one-finger digraphs. The point is that experts already start moving the appropriate finger for a next key press while still engaged with the preceding one. This explains that experts are relatively slow on one-finger digraphs because, there, advance motor activity of the finger is excluded (Viviani & Laissard, 1996).

In contrast, novices carry out key presses in strict succession. This has the paradoxical effect that they are less hindered by a double. In a PRP study, both novices and experts respond in strict succession simply because the situation forces them to do so. Advance processing of the second stimulus, while responding to the first one, is impossible in the PRP because the second stimulus has not yet been presented and is unrelated to the first stimulus. This is underlined by Salthouse's (1984) result that experienced typists, with a 177 ms median II, had 560 ms as median in a self-paced two-choice serial-reaction task. Yet, experts can also be forced to a strict, sequential performance in typing that was shown most clearly in Shaffer's (1973) classic research on the variation of the amount of preview and of the structure of the text. In one condition, typists were confronted with sequentially presented random letters, in which case the experts' II amounted to the same 500 ms as found in the PRP. The only advantage of the experts was that they had a thorough knowledge of the letter-position combinations. Therefore, the poor S–R compatibility of the typewriter had a less serious effect than it has on novices. Typing random letters with preview reduced the experts' II to some 200 ms, whereas typing a word in an unknown, foreign language took a II of about 150 ms.

It is highly interesting that the smallest II—some 100 ms—was obtained when typing meaningful words, irrespective of whether they were random or part of a meaningful sentence. Together, these results suggest that the word—and not the letter or the sentence—is the basic input in skilled typing and preview has a distinct effect. In another study, Shaffer (1973) found that preview has its maximal effect at about eight letters, which is in close agreement with the results on reading span. The relevance of preview is further underscored by the fact that saccade recordings show that typists are some five characters ahead of the letter they are actually typing (Salthouse, 1986). The perceived items are presumably stored and transformed into motor commands during previous key presses. In other words, there is evidence for a great deal of parallel processing in expert typing.

Most models on typing assume four processes. According to Salthouse (1986), a text is converted into chunks, presumably at the word level, followed by parsing, that is, decomposition of the chunk into a string of characters. As the next step, the characters are translated into movement specifications in their prescribed serial order, which is followed by motor implementation. Alternatively, one might assume that an identified word calls directly on a corresponding motor template that is, then, executed as a single burst of responses. An objection to this view is that, aside from endings such as "ing" or "the," there is no convincing evidence that IIs within a word differ in temporal structure from IIs between words (Gentner, 1987; Shaffer, 1975).[9] More specifically, a motor program may include a set of ratios between keystroke intervals that remain invariant, even when the sequence of keystrokes is carried out at different speed (proportionality hypothesis). Recently, Viviani and Laissard (1996) argued in favor of the proportionality hypothesis on the word level. This suggests the operation of hierarchically supraordinate rhythms in addition to biomechanical factors.

It is interesting to compare the aforementioned considerations with Verwey's (1994) results on generating response sequences in a small CRT paradigm (chap. 3). First, Verwey found evidence for motor chunks, but only after the same sequence had been repeated frequently. It is not surprising, therefore, that the status of motor chunks on the word level is debated in typing. In addition, Verwey's results suggest a sequencing stage in which successive elements of a key-press string are stored in a motor buffer in their correct serial order. Again, Verwey found concurrent processing in that new elements enter the motor buffer while completing earlier key presses. This greatly increased the net efficiency of the actions, despite the fact that entering new elements into the buffer slowed down the actual rate of key pressing. All in all, Verwey's account is fully consistent with those on expert

---

[9]This is in line with Logan's (1982) result that a signal to stop immediately is effective on the character level. Logan suggested that completing motor chunks is a ballistic process, whereas typing might be usually controlled on the character level (chap. 4 for the stop signal paradigm). However, a ballistic process need not be an essential element of a motor program (Viviani & Laissard, 1996).

typing and shows clearly the ways in which generalization from the PRP to typing fails. Verwey's sequencing stage did not play a role in early practice because novices handled individual responses in strict succession. It is relevant to repeat the evidence that the PRP effect is remarkably resistant to practice. As already reported (chap. 8), Sanders and Keuss (1969) practiced participants daily for some months without finding any qualitative changes in performance, suggesting again that PRP effects are only found with independent responses to uncorrelated, successively presented stimuli.

Salthouse's (1986) four hypothetical processes in transcription agree with Rumelhart and Norman's (1982) computer simulation model, which does not only claim to cover the previously discussed phenomena but also some typical typing errors. One frequent error is transposition, which refers to letter reversal (e.g., because > becuase). Another one is doubling. If a word contains a doubled letter, a wrong letter is prone to be doubled, as in look > lokk, or, more complex, in were > wrer.

The Rumelhart and Norman (1982) simulation is limited to movement specification and response initiation. This means that it neither addresses perceptual factors, nor word parsing, nor potential motor programs on the word level. Within these limits, the model has two major components. The first concerns sequencing of letter strings in a motor buffer, and the second motor execution. It is assumed that a letter sequence—the result of parsing a perceived word—activates an internal set of locations on the keyboard. A location is encoded by way of 2D coordinates, one on the upward–downward and another on the inward–outward dimension. The coordinates are sent to the response system that sets the palm and finger positions in order to press the keys at the encoded locations. An important feature of the simulation is that an earlier location code inhibits the following location codes. Thus, correct sequencing of key presses is achieved by the ordering of activation values of the location codes in the buffer. The current location of the fingers is fed back to the most strongly activated location code. If the appropriate finger—typists have learned that each finger controls a fixed number of keys—is within a criterion distance of the location, a response is triggered, and a movement is launched. This deactivates the location code that, in turn, releases inhibition of the next codes. In this way, the location code of the next letter gets the highest activation value, whereupon all processes are repeated.

The activation of the location codes is noisy, which accounts for transposition errors. Typing double letters (e.g., look) poses a problem, though, because one would expect that release of activation of the location code after a key press would render repetition of the same key press hard to do. To explain double letters, one might think of letter codes in terms of multiple instances. For example, the word "look" may be represented by location codes for l-o-o-k. Once the "l" has been typed, one instance of the location of the "o" has the highest activation and, on typing the "o," the other instance of the "o" location receives the highest activation. This view accounts for typing double letters but cannot account for the error of doubling another letter—e.g., pressing two "k"s instead of two "o"s—because only one instance of the "k" is activated. Rumelhart and Norman (1982) assumed, therefore, that there is only one code for each letter and an additional special code for a "double," for example, "l-o-double-k" if, on completing the "o," the code for "double" has the highest activation that triggers the second key press of the "o." Occasionally the "double" may become associated with a wrong letter, for example, "l-o-k-double," and the doubling error is a fact. Yet, this view faces the problem that if there is only a single-location code for a letter in a word, repeated letters, for example, in "perception," are not accounted for. Here, the solution may be that the parser detects repeated letters but blocks admittance of a repetition to the motor buffer until the first response has been executed. For example, in "perception," the parser may admit "p-e-r-c" to the buffer, but the other letters are only admitted when p-e- has been typed. Depending on the assumed speed with which the buffer is filled, the model may predict that a repeated letter in a word is executed somewhat slower than its first execution.

Motor execution is a matter of positioning hands and fingers. The palm and the fingers move in two dimensions, that is, up and down and inward and outward. The palm can move any distance in these two directions, whereas the different fingers all have a region of additional movement. For instance, the index finger can move 1.0 space inward and 0.8 space up or down but, due to its anatomical position, only slightly outward. The ultimate position of a finger on the keyboard depends on a combination of the position of palm and finger. A key assumption is that the movements of hands, palms, and fingers are determined by the activation of all the location codes in the buffer. This means that the code with the highest activation has the most effect on the motor system but that the next letters also exert some effect. When successive letters are typed by different fingers of the same hand, the palm is brought in a position that suits the first key-press the best, but at the same time, it anticipates the next responses. In this way, launching the next letter already starts during completion of the previous one, depending on the distance between the keys involved. It is obvious that anticipation is easier when successive key presses come from different hands. Thus, IIs between hands are faster than within hands. Again, typing double letters is slower because repeated launching of the same finger cannot occur in parallel.

The model also predicts that IIs are affected by context (Shaffer, 1978). For example, when all letters of a word require the palm of a hand to go upward, the locations of the individual letters can be reached faster than when some require the palm to go up, but other letters require it to go down.

The Rumelhart and Norman (1982) simulation was outlined in some detail because it is a beautiful example of a computer simulation of a complex skill. Programming the simulation demands that the variables and its parameter values are fully specified. This is the only way to obtain sufficiently detailed simulation data that can be compared with data from actual typing. As Rumelhart and Norman acknowledged, their model is incomplete because it does not cover all types of errors that humans commit, for example, typing "efficient" instead of "efficiency." Yet, such errors are presumably unrelated to location codes and response execution. In other respects, the model provides a fair approximation of how people carry out a real-life skill such as typing. Another positive aspect of the model is that it enables back-to-back comparison with data from simple paradigms. Thus, it confirms the earlier suggested difference between typing and the PRP. Indeed, the PRP is strictly limited to the case of uncorrelated, successively arriving stimuli. Simultaneously presented items, even when uncorrelated, allow parallel encoding followed by rapid emission of the responses, as illustrated by the findings on grouping in the PRP. Following Verwey (1994), processing efficiency would be enhanced considerably when the perceptual data allowed motor chunking, in which case loading the motor buffer and emitting responses occur concurrently.

MIXIC

This model simulates car driving in an ongoing traffic flow, with respect to both longitudinal control and overtaking. In each time-step, the model of the driver produces actions in regard to (a) the decision whether to change lanes and (b) longitudinal control through setting the steering wheel and the position of pedals and gears. For instance, when deciding to overtake, a combined maneuver of steering and acceleration is initiated. The actual implementation is calculated by the vehicle part of the model on the basis of how the controls are set. Thus, the model has a separate simulation of driver and vehicle, something that is not found in many earlier models but renders the model more interesting from a psychological perspective.

A wish to change lanes arises when the speed of a lead car is less than the desired speed of the driver. If so, the model determines whether a change of lanes is possible by considering whether traffic is approaching in the other lane. Information is required about the position and speed of potentially overtaking and oncoming cars in either lane, as well as about speed and accelerating power of one's own car. It is not surprising, therefore, that the decision criteria for changing lanes depend, among others, on the type of car. Once a positive decision has been reached, a time delay is inserted, in which the decision is reconsidered with regard to the safety of all time-steps that are involved in the maneuver. This provides the option of aborting the action when faced with a new or threatening element.

When following a lead car, the driver has to adjust his speed with respect to the traffic ahead. The model assumes optimal control, in that it aims at keeping a constant distance from the lead car. Information about this distance comes from the visual angle subtended by the lead car and from a threshold value for changes in visual angle. Once a deviation between the desired angle and the real visual angle is detected, the model needs 300 ms for initiating a pedal or gear correction. The model "knows" about the mutual effects of gear, braking, and accelerating in order to arrive at a desired speed. Shifting from the accelerator pedal to the braking pedal, and vice versa, takes the model a constant 150 ms of movement time (van Arem et al., 1994).

GENERAL PERFORMANCE SIMULATION

Human Operator Simulator (HOS)

Domain-aspecific computer simulation of the performance characteristics of a human operator cannot but rely on principles from basic performance theory, which renders the success of such simulations of particular interest. In regard to HOS, successive and increasingly complex versions have been launched, two of which are discussed in some more detail. The first version (HOS-1) was proposed by Lane et al. (1981) and had strict single-channel processing along the lines of Welford (1967) as its most salient characteristic. Thus, when engaged in any activity, a planned new activity had to queue up until completion of the earlier one. The queue was maintained in a short-term storage system that decayed over time. Thus, the probability of missing a planned activity increased sharply as a function of waiting time. Furthermore, the activities of HOS-1 consisted of a number of condition/action rules as correct responses to specific conditions. These rules were always available and, once elicited by the appropriate stimuli, were carried out error free. This means that processing occurred only bottom up because HOS-1 reacted to demands rather than taking an initiative. The role of energetic factors consisted of temporary and complete blocking of performance, the probability of which increased as a function of adverse conditions such as sleep loss or prolonged work.

In short, HOS-1 assumed that performance limits were equal to time limits. Changes in strategy or processing failures did not play a role. One may say that the model reflected the classical single-channel and filter notions that were rejected in the mid-1960s as too simplistic. HOS-1 is a conservative model in the sense that a strict single-channel notion underestimates performance limits. Yet, because operators can do better, a conservative model is never harmful. A more serious objection to HOS-1 is that no errors can be committed. This means that once the task demands are within its time limits, HOS-1 assumes perfect performance, with the only exception of incidental omissions due to failures of sustained attention. Also, HOS-1 does not have provisions for skill acquisition, that is, it cannot acquire additional command/action production rules.

HOS-4 (Harris, Iavecchia, & Dick, 1989) is a much extended and more flexible simulation. Although, when in an alert state, actions still take a fixed time, the simulation has many more complex process-models for perceptual processing (visual, auditory), cognitive processing (decision), motor processing (anatomy, movement), and energetics (fatigue). In HOS-4, information is specified in terms of objects, events, rules, and actions. Objects refer to important interfaces such as displays, controls, and sensors, all of which contain a list of features describing their status. Events refer to external occurrences that affect the simulation. They are defined by an event name, an event time, and the name of an action that is triggered by the event. Events usually consist of instructions about revision of features of objects; they may also indicate system failures that demand certain actions. The condition/action relations and their relative priorities are specified by production rules. Each rule has an IF clause, which specifies the initiation criteria (IF the color of an alerting light is yellow), a DO clause indicating the type of action, and an UNTIL clause indicating when to end the action. Rules are processed according to priority assignment. A total of 1,000 operator rules can be defined in HOS-4. Finally, the actions describe the contents of what to do. An action can be triggered by an event, a rule, or by another action. They update values of object characteristics and activate or suspend rules; they take time and have an error rate as specified in the perceptual, decisional, and motor modules of the system. As in HOS-1, actions are aborted when a queue lasts too long or when one is not reminded of a planned action in some other way.

HOS-4 is clearly more sophisticated than HOS-1. Actions do not only rely on information provided by objects but they can also be triggered by internal rules. This creates an opportunity for top-down processing. Processing times in HOS-4 are determined by micromodels about perception, decision, and motor activity that are much more detailed than in HOS-1. Moreover, the processing times of actions are derived from the basic performance literature, are probabilistic, and have associated error proportions because a rule may call on an inappropriate action. HOS-4 is also a less strict single-channel processor. Information from different senses is handled in parallel, and the simulation has a provision for rapid switching among ongoing actions. In addition, the priority assignments introduce a strategic element by way of allocating time to a planned action. Nevertheless, the database still consists of a set of disconnected rules and actions and, as yet, HOS-4 has nothing that reminds of the role of a mental model of a system. This means that it cannot handle knowledge-based problems, in which case simple application of condition/action rules does not suffice.

Goals, Operators, Methods, and Selection (GOMS) Rules. This model was proposed by Card et al. (1983) as a general conceptual framework for human–computer interaction. The operator's cognitive structure aims at achieving a set of goals by using a set of methods in combination with adequate operators and with an appropriate selection rule for choosing among competing goals and methods. As in a hierarchical task analysis, each goal has its subgoals. Thus, in the context of text processing, "edit manuscript" is a general goal, whereas the modification of a single line of text is a subgoal at a much lower level of the hierarchy. The operators are perceptual, cognitive, and motor acts, all of which are needed for accomplishing goals at the various levels of the hierarchy and for shifting from one subgoal to another. All operators are concerned with outputs that take a distinct time. Examples are to go to the next page, to operate a certain control, for example, a mouse or a keyboard, or to verify a result after correction. Operators at the higher levels of the hierarchy are concerned with more general aspects of the computer environment, such as "use the key commands." As they become lower in the hierarchy, the operators remind more and more of psychological mechanisms of perception, cognition, and action. GOMS is strictly single channel because it allows only one operation at a time.

The methods in GOMS describe acquired procedures that are needed to achieve a goal. For example, in text editing, the methods consist of a specific sequence of steps. When well-practiced and standard, methods may seem trivial because their success is certain. However, this changes in the absence of a standard solution for solving a problem. Here, the available methods may be applied but without guaranteed success. Finally, selection rules play a role in the case of competing methods or operators. When procedures have been sufficiently practiced, the activities are simulated by the MHP of information-processing.

The Model Human Processor (MHP)

GOMS is a description technique rather than a simulation. Instead, MHP is a serious attempt to construct a simulation on the basis of data from the literature on performance and problem solving (Card & Moran, 1986; Card, Moran, & Newell, 1983). The result is a collection of micromodels that, together, constitute MHP. Similar to HOS, it has the conventional three interacting subsystems, namely, perceptual, cognitive, and motor. Each subsystem consists of a set of memories and a processor and operates on a set of principles. All operations take a distinct time and are capacity limited. The chosen parameter values are particularly relevant to the simulation because they determine actual performance limits.

The perceptual processor translates information about the outside world into an internal code. First, a stimulus is detected by an auditory or visual module. Visual information is only obtained from an area around the fixation point, but MHP has the provision of eye movements in order to cover the complete visual field. Once a stimulus has been detected by a sensory module, it is transmitted to its corresponding sensory store. From there, it is encoded and stored in a cognitive working memory. As suggested by studies on iconic storage, the visual sensory store holds a trace of many stimuli for a very brief period of time only, so there is insufficient time for transferring all pertinent codes to the cognitive working memory. The cognitive processor decides which sensory traces will be transferred on the basis of some common physical, not semantic, feature. In addition, intense stimuli, moving stimuli, and stimuli with a low spatial frequency are more rapidly available for transfer to the cognitive system. The perceptual processor has a median cycle time of 100 ms, ranging between 50 and 200 ms. Events occurring within a single cycle are integrated into one percept. In this way, temporal summation and masking are simulated.

Movements are simulated as a series of discrete steps that take 30 to 100 ms each. There is a relatively time-consuming feedback loop from action to perception (200–500 ms). Thus, an action has to be executed as a single, preprogrammed burst of steps. The voluntary muscles of the arm-hand-finger system and of the eye-head system are simulated as well. Fitts' law is among the principles governing the motor system. The cognitive system connects inputs from the perceptual system with the motor system. Provisions for learning, retrieval of facts, and problem solving raise the system beyond a simple, rule-based level. MHP has two memories, namely, the earlier mentioned cognitive working memory and a long-term memory in the sense that—as is now commonly believed—working memory is an activated subset of long-term memory. Thus, working memory operates on chunks that are established as semantic nets in long-term memory. New chunks interfere with older ones. This has the effect that older chunks gradually fade from working memory. The long-term memory is the knowledge base of the system and consists of a network of related chunks. Incoming stimuli from the perceptual system receive codes on the basis of a successful match of the perceptual features with a long-term memory code. The model spells out principles for establishing new chunks in long-term memory, for retrieving nonactivated knowledge from long-term memory, and for generating hypotheses for problem solving. The cognitive aspects of the model are extremely relevant, but they are beyond the scope of this book.

Similar to the perceptual and the motor processors, the cognitive processor operates on the basis of a cycle that takes a median of 100 ms and ranges from 40–170 ms. During each cycle, the contents of working memory activate linked actions in long-term memory, among which are included recoding and response instructions that, in turn, give the contents more elaborate codes. For example, a digit may be recoded as a target or a nontarget during a cycle. This takes some 40 ms to complete. Deciding which finger to press in a CRT task is another example of a linked action in long-term memory. The time to complete the cycle depends on the amount of practice according to the power law[10] and on the principle of information theory that CRT increases as a linear function of the uncertainty about the decision. Once stored in working memory, an action command is issued to the motor system. Action commands are strictly serial, whereas, in contrast, the perceptual and motor systems operate in parallel.

An attractive property of MHP is that it generates recommendations for real-life issues on the basis of a relatively simple information-processing model. Moreover, it provides a set of values about cycle times, decay rates, and working memory capacity, all of which are derived from small paradigms. Thus, Card and Moran (1986) determined the maximal rate for receiving visual and auditory morse codes, the maximal rate for reading and for pressing buttons on a pocket calculator, and the maximal speed in operating different types of keyboards, all on the basis of MHP. Most calculations were in fair agreement with data from the actual tasks. The promising conclusion is that based on a limited set of basic performance principles, MHP provides a good first approximation for calculating the relative benefits of various proposed systems.

COMMENTS

All preceding examples agree that simulations bear heavily on outcomes and theoretical constructs from small paradigms. On almost all occasions and in accord with the information-processing approach, the simulation architectures assume a flow from perception to response selection and, from there, to motor behavior. Sometimes, the simulations relied directly on main performance principle such as the single-channel hypothesis in HOS-1. It is interesting that the hotly debated status of such notions in basic research notwithstanding, they do well as a first rough approximation in simulating complex, real-life tasks. This suggests that they capture at least some essential performance elements, thereby allowing simulation of various major behaviors.

On other occasions, as in GOMS and MHP, summary statements on basic research even constituted the main body of the simulation. A comparison

---

[10]According to the power law, the time $T(n)$ to complete a reaction on the nth trial equals:

$$T(n) = T(1) \ n^{-a}$$

in which $T(1)$ is the first reaction and a is a constant. CRT decreases as a negative exponential function of practice.

between HOS-1 and HOS-4 showed that a more detailed elaboration of basic principles adds to the power of the simulation. Yet, the generalizations remain an approximation and are undoubtedly wrong in many details. When such details are essential to a particular simulated task, the conclusions are bound to be incorrect. This means that when applying a human performance model to system design, one should not only be aware of the fact that the model has its limits but also of the nature of the limits in order to know the conditions under which the simulation may be taken more-or-less seriously. This requires knowledge about the current status of the basic performance literature.

Despite the apparent relevance of basic paradigms to process simulation, there were also instances in which generalization from basic research was unsuccessful. Examples included generalization from PRP to typing and from the functional visual field to reading. However, back-to-back comparison suggests the relevant differences between these simple and more complex tasks and proposes experiments to bridge the gap.

DYNAMIC SIMULATION

As outlined earlier, simulation has become a powerful tool for many applied purposes. The present discussion is mainly concerned with dynamic simulation, although there are also more simple and useful forms of simulation, among which a static mock-up of a work station and even pictures of a potential new design. A mock-up allows an advance impression of prospective locations of the various displays and controls, with the aim of eliciting a discussion about what should be the ultimate design. It may also serve as a 3D blueprint when the actual work station is being built. Pictures are particularly revealing in regard to visual effects. An example is the role of lampposts as a leading line on waterways or highways. When the lights are merely meant to indicate the borderlines of the road or of the waterway, lampposts appear less functional and more costly than simple circular lamps fixed at the sides or the edges. The difference is immediately evident from a static picture.

Yet, static simulation merely provides impressions, whereas dynamic simulation allows performance assessment. Dynamic simulation is most often used for training; it is relevant to system design, and it offers prospects for personnel assessment. The many prospects of simulators notwithstanding, two major problems should be discussed. The first concerns measurement of performance output, and the second simulator validation. Finally, the three areas of application, that is, training, design, and selection, have their own specific themes that will be briefly addressed.

The Measurement Problem

This problem has been most clearly raised by Vreuls and Obermayer (1985) in their statement that performance measures in otherwise sophisticated training simulators are so poorly designed that they are virtually useless. Indeed, performance measures have been notoriously absent in recent simulations regarding orientation in space, antitank gunnery and air-traffic control, all of which I happened to become acquainted with during recent years. Does this mean that performance measurement is irrelevant? By no means! In training, it provides feedback about current performance, errors, and how to correct errors; in system design, measures are essential for detecting potential system deficiencies; in personnel selection, they may provide quantitative predictors of success. Moreover, without performance assessment, it is hard to establish criteria with regard to expert performance. Therefore, expertise in many complex skills cannot be properly assessed. For example, Kelly (1988) concluded that the U.S. Air Force was not able to obtain an objective evaluation of the skill of its pilots from simulator performance. The same can probably be said about the quality of decision making in command and control situations in which objective performance measures are equally lacking.

Vreuls and Obermayer (1985) argued that the main problem in regard to measuring complex performance is that it is unclear what should be measured. A lack of consensus about the validity of potential measures for the achieved level of a skill would be the main reason for the deplorable situation. This lack of consensus would be due to a lack of basic performance theory. Yet, this may be too simple a view. Rather, it has been the problem that performance measures of complex skills can only be obtained by considering mutual relations among a wide range of standard behavioral measures that are usually not provided by the simulator. One reason for poor performance measures might be that most simulations are designed by engineers who typically show little interest in performance measurement. They are often satisfied when the simulation has an adequate physical fidelity— that is, when it intuitively corresponds to the real task—whereas performance assessment is often viewed as belonging to the expertise of instructors.

It is striking that in their discussion on the functional definition of training simulators, Flexman and Stark (1987) covered aspects such as data storage and system dynamics as well as issues on displays and controls, whereas performance measurement was only mentioned in passing, nor did Flexman and Stark's contribution have a single reference to performance theory. On the other hand, current volumes on human factors (Hancock, 1987; Wickens, 1992) contain much performance theory but hardly any discussion on simulation, a clear sign of the lack of cooperation between basic and applied interests! Task-analytical techniques would be a good starting point for bridging the gap.

In conclusion, appropriate measurement of human performance in simulations requires cooperation between simulation design and basic performance theory. In the present context, the issue of performance measures cannot be discussed in great detail but has to be limited to making a few remarks about potentially promising output measures and to delineating some issues that should not be confused.

First, then, there is the nature of the simulated skill. The measurement problem is different for speeded perceptual–motor activities on the skill-based and rule-based levels (Rasmussen, 1986) than for cognitive skills on the knowledge-based level. Air-to-air combat, finding one's way during a space walk, and maneuvering a car in heavy traffic belong to the first category, whereas supervision and decision making in command and control are usually knowledge based. Perceptual–motor skills are characterized by a continuous interplay between human actions and ongoing, outside events. Cognitive skills do not show much overt activity, and when an action is carried out, it is usually not strongly related to immediately preceding stimuli.

The second issue concerns the extent to which responses are time locked to specific, outside events. The strength of traditional S–R measures, practiced throughout this book, concerns the clear relations between overt, human activities and well-defined, outside events. The disadvantage is, of course, that behavior is not studied in real time but as "a sequence of stranded episodes" (Shaffer, 1980). The problem is that in many real-life simulations, the relations between stimuli and responses cannot be easily established.

The third issue is concerned with the definition of optimal performance, which is a problem in any setting in which performance outcomes are affected by a combination of random factors and intentional actions. It is also a problem in situations in which normatively defined, optimal performance, in terms of some mathematical model, turns out to be an unsuitable norm for a human operator.

Perceptual–Motor Measures

The compelling issue of how to link stimuli and responses in more complex perceptual–motor skills notwithstanding, traditional measures of CRT and accuracy and their derivates have been quite successful in skills such as typing, piano playing, car driving, reading, and speech production (e.g., Gopher et al., 1985; Shaffer, 1982). The examples of typing and aspects of driving were discussed earlier in this chapter. Car driving is, obviously, a more composite skill because it consists of a large variety of subtasks. Next to standard measures of speed, acceleration, and braking, it is possible to measure the quality of course keeping in simulations as well as in on-the-road tests. This is achieved by measuring the variance of the lateral distance from the car to the borderline of the traffic lane. Among others, this measure has been used for assessing effects of drugs and long-term driving on keeping a straight course and for establishing the validity of driving simulators (O'Hanlon et al., 1986; Riemersma et al., 1977; Riemersma et al., 1990). The variance in lateral distance is analogous to integrated error in manual tracking.

Another relevant chronometric measure in traffic research which, among others, has been applied to road design, is time-to-line crossing as an index of anticipatory activity (Godthelp, Milgram, & Blaauw, 1984). This measure is the time that remains until crossing a borderline, given that all relevant parameter remain the same. For instance, how much time is left until hitting a wall or a crossing without changing the speed and the direction? Does the available time-to-line crossing leave sufficient opportunity for preventing a crash? Research has been particularly concerned with the role of visual cues in estimating time-to-line crossing or time to collision (e.g., Bootsma & Oudejans, 1993; Sidaway, Fairweather, Sekiya, & McNitt-Gray, 1996). Thus, one may show an approach to a stationary target, occlude the scene, and ask participants to press a key when they estimate that the collision occurred. The accuracy of the estimate appears to increase at a higher velocity, suggesting a role of global, optic flow rate in the judgment of time to collision. A variation on time to collision is time headway, which refers to the time interval between two vehicles in car following, calculated as the distance between the cars divided by the speed of the following car (van Winsum & Heino, 1996).

The aforementioned measures are still quite close to standard CRT, but there are various, more novel measures as well. One concerns the dynamic window technique in research on reading, as discussed in chapter 5. This technique has contributed considerably to the knowledge on information processing in reading, and it is also promising for visual search and detection. Again, the technique clearly supersedes "stranded episodes" because reading is not disrupted. Another promising measure is occlusion during intake of visual information, which derives from the observing response technique in instrumental conditioning. Occluding a driver's outside view means that uncertainty about the state of the world grows over time, analogous to what happens when delaying inspection of an instrument on a panel. At some point, the uncertainty exceeds a threshold that marks the need of disclosing and inspecting the environment in regard to potential targets. Uncertainty grows more rapidly as the environment contains more information; hence, the occlusion technique can be used as a measure of visual information load in operational situations (Blaauw, 1982). It was first used for this purpose by Senders et al. (1967), whereas the occluding device has been refined by Milgram, Godthelp, and Blaauw (1982). It has been also used in tests of effects of stimulus expectancy and habituation in vigilance (Jerison, Pickett, & Stenson, 1965).

The preceding measures are all general performance indexes. The situation becomes more complex when performance cannot be simply characterized by a single measure but requires some combination of different measures. Evaluating performance in *Space Fortress*, a difficult video game developed for research purposes, is a case in point. The goal of the game is to destroy an enemy space fortress by using one's own spacecraft, the movements of which are controlled by a joy stick. In addition, the player is operating other controls in order to destroy enemy mines, to carry out attacks on the fortress, and to defend against counterattacks. The game has the interesting feature that all stimuli and responses stem from widely studied small paradigms such as the carrying out of responses in rapid succession, target classification, stimulus discrimination and C(RT). All in all, the measured performance output of the game consists of an array of 150 data variables with the purpose of carrying out a fine-grained analysis of how the game is mastered and which strategies are used (Mane & Donchin, 1989). Yet, 150 measures are impractical for assessing progress and strategies; the prime question is which combination of measures should be used. Measuring 150 data variables is a soluble technical problem but does not provide a simple answer to questions such as the optimal priority of handling events during the game.

One possible approach is through microtask analysis, the outcome of which could be a computer program that optimizes the action sequence both in order and in time. Such a program could simulate the skill of playing *Space Fortress* and, at the same time, assess the relative merits of the 150 dependent variables. An example in which such a task-analytical approach proved successful stems from Donk (1995a), who attempted to assess optimal performance in a management game. In this game, participants had the task of controlling a small-scale economy by measures such as founding a new factory, growing more wheat, increasing income, or raising taxes. The measures should aim at a stable economy in which people are optimally happy. The question was, of course, which measures are the most appropriate. The actual outcome is not a good criterion because participants may make good decisions but find themselves fighting against odds. Donk composed a computer program on the basis of a hierarchical task analysis that achieved a stable economy by means of a minimal number of measures. Proceeding from there, Donk evaluated the measures taken by participants in terms of deviations from the computer at any stage of the game.

A special problem arises when mathematically defined optimal performance conflicts with human performance limits. A simple illustration is the case of navigating a ship to a new, parallel course. The mathematically optimal way is through continuous adaptation that has the effect that the new course is reached smoothly. The problem is that humans are incapable of continuous adaptation but, instead, change the rudder at a few discrete moments in time. They overshoot when changing the rudder too much, too long, or too often. The good performers start off with a few small and brief

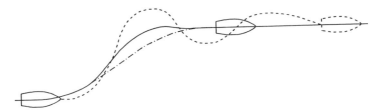

FIG. 10.5. Examples of possible tracks when instructed to reach a new course that runs parallel to an earlier course of a ship. The interrupted line is mathematically optimal but is risky because it requires continuous revision of the rudder angle. The dashed line shows the effect of changing the rudder angle too much and too long. The solid line is the optimal strategy. It consists of a few discrete changes leading to a slight overshoot that can be easily corrected. From Sanders, A. F. (1991). Simulation as a tool in the measurement of human performance. *Ergonomics, 34,* 995–1025.

rudder changes that lead to a slight overshoot that can be easily compensated during the final stage of the maneuver (Fig. 10.5).

This example illustrates the relevance of knowledge about the dynamics of human performance when deciding which elements to measure in a complex system. It is even more indispensable when designing a new system. Thus, there are two central human-factors issues when simulating a complex task. One is whether a potential design meets human performance limits; the other is which output measures are required in the operational system.

Finally, what can a practitioner still achieve when a simulator has no performance measures at all? There remain some rude forms of observation and subjective assessment that may still be worthwhile. For example, during the 1970s, air-traffic control at Schiphol airport had a simulator without any output measures. Work load was manipulated by varying the number of aircraft to be controlled during a half-hour period. Two objectives could be achieved without having any output measure: First, workload was increased until experienced operators started to commit grave errors that were diagnosed by simple observation. This provided an estimate of the capacity of the system. Second, operators gave introspective descriptions of their strategies about spatial and temporal sequencing of aircraft, which could then be used for training purposes. Yet, this remains a rude approach. Output measurement would have enabled a more fine-grained analysis of actions and their temporal structure as well as a more quantitative assessment of a trainee's performance, and it would have augmented feedback to enhance skill acquisition.

Simulator Validation

It may seem commonplace that a simulator must be validated in order to find out how well it reflects reality. Yet, validation is often completely ignored. For instance, a "simulation of driving skills" that merely consists of a compensatory tracking task together with a measure of CRT to unexpected stimuli (e.g., Willumeit, Ott, & Neubert, 1984)[11] may be advertised. The need for validation is gradually being accepted, though, both for training and design simulators. The issue should not be taken lightly because a poor simulation may produce negative effects rather than benificial ones. A well-known example from the early days was the Esso training simulator for maneuvering a supertanker. Trainees maneuvered a 1:25 scale model of a tanker in a pond near Grenoble, France. It had the obvious deficiency that rudder commands are implemented much faster in the model than in reality. Wagenaar and Michon (1968) studied the effect of the rate of implementing a rudder command in a computer-based maneuvering simulator. A control group of participants practiced maneuvering with slow implementation throughout all trials, whereas the experimental participants started with more rapid implementation, whereupon they were transferred to slow implementation. The results show negative transfer of training in that the transfer group performed less well at the slow implementation trials than the control group during their initial practice. This result suggests that participants in the transfer group had acquired an incorrect model that degraded rather than improved performance at slow implementation.

A common engineer's approach to validation is to duplicate reality within close tolerance limits in order to arrive at a near-perfect physical correspondence. Yet, this is neither a necessary nor a sufficient criterion for validity. Close physical similarity notwithstanding, a simulation may still lack some essential feature that renders it useless. On the other hand, complete physical fidelity may not always be needed to fulfil the purpose of a simulator (e.g., Allen, Hays, & Buffardt, 1986) and, in particular, not when the simulator is meant for training. For instance, there is wide evidence that complex skill acquisition benefits from partial-task training. A task component may be practiced in isolation or with priority within the complete skill (e.g., Gopher, Weil, & Siegel, 1989). Hence, a simulation of an isolated component may well show some positive transfer. The issue is, of course, to determine the relevant components. This may be achieved through task analysis or perhaps through insights from basic research via back-to-back analysis. The ultimate proof consists of a successful validation study.

The most common validation methods are transfer of training from simulator to the real task and planned comparisons between behaviors in the simulator and in the real task. Transfer is the most common when the primary interest is in training, whereas planned comparisons are the dominant technique when the simulator is used for design purposes. Once a simulator

---

[11]Note that from a back-to-back perspective, this combination of tasks might well be worthwhile. It may have functional fidelity with respect to driving, but this should be proven rather than postulated.

has been validated, it can be used, in turn, for studying effects of deviations from full physical fidelity or the effect of simulation of a component of a skill. In this way, dynamic simulation is highly relevant in the chain of back-to-back studies.

Transfer

When the formal training procedure of a skill consists of real-life trials, as is the case in driving or flying, one may determine the extent to which simulator training reduces the number of real-life trials needed to reach some proficiency criterion. As an example, pronounced positive transfer was found by Moraal and Poll (1979) from a moving-base tank simulator to actual tank maneuvers in regard to features such as changing gear, steering, and avoiding obstacles. The simulator consisted of a combination of a computer-monitored television system, a mathematical model of the dynamic properties of the tank, and a cabin that moved by way of three rotations brought about by sensor systems on terrain unevenness. The results suggest that a moving base pays off in simulating driving.

One should be careful, though, because results on a more recent tank simulator based on computer-generated terrain images failed to show any positive transfer, presumably due to a critical deviation between visual and motion information (Padmos, 1988). Conceivably, a simulation with deviant visual and motion information is worse than one with no information on motion at all. Koonce (1979) observed that the absence of motion cues in a flight simulator affected simulator performance negatively. Yet, it did not affect the amount of transfer from the simulator to subsequent real-life trials, the quality of which was judged by experts. This illustrates, again, that full simulation is not always needed. It is remarkable in this regard that Gopher (1992; Gopher, Weil, & Bareket, 1994) found positive transfer of varied priority training in the Space Fortress video game to pilot training. Evidence for a divided-attention skill also stems from studies that showed that the efficiency of switching from one ear to the other in dichotic listening is correlated with success in pilot training and in performance of bus drivers (Kahneman, Ben Ishai, & Lotan, 1973). This suggests that the skill of flexible scheduling and attention control is less domain specific than one might imagine and can be transferred from the laboratory to a complex real-life task such as flying. Apparently, laboratory tasks are not far removed from reality in these cases.

There is divergent evidence on the question of whether simulation of complex visual details is needed for achieving positive transfer. For example, Lintern, Thornley-Yates, Nelson, & Roscoe (1987) studied the effects of the amount of visual detail on a simulated air-to-ground attack and found that realistic visual scenes had more positive transfer than a schematic grid pattern. This result suggests that detailed visual cues are indeed relevant. Presenting a larger number of different visual scenes in the practice phase had little additional effect on training whereas, not surprisingly, augmented[12] feedback was a very potent variable. However, it would be wrong to generalize from this result to other visual tasks. Thus, earlier work by Lintern (1980) showed that practice with a schematic scene of a horizon, a runway outline, and a center line transferred to landing an aircraft. Hence, different visual tasks appear to require different degrees of visual similarity between simulation and real life. High physical fidelity may be needed when, as in the case of an air-to-ground attack, a range of visual cues is used when aiming at a target.

Transfer studies have their limitations. First they are always post hoc, so they only add to simulator design after the fact. Second, there is a criterion problem that is well known from the validation of mental tests. Performance measures in real-life trials are usually subjective in that they consist of expert judgments that are often biased by the instructor's attitude toward the simulation. Finally, there are conditions in which results from real trials are simply not available, such as in war games, emergencies, and air-to-air combat.

Behavioral Correspondence

As an alternative to transfer, it is sometimes possible to compare simulator and real-life behaviors directly. For instance, the helmsman of a ship approaches a barrier, for example, a bridge over a river, at a certain angle that depends, among others, on wind and current. From a valid simulator one would expect that participants should produce about the same angles in the simulator as in reality. This approach was taken to validate the former navigation simulator of the TNO Human Factors Institute at Soesterberg, The Netherlands.[13] The angles between ship and barrier were hard to determine in actual maneuvers; hence, they were derived from judgments of four experienced captains of container barges who judged 32 scenarios of an existing, regularly passed setting near a crossing of fairways. Then, each captain had 16 trials in the simulator on a subset of the scenarios. The results showed a 0.61 correlation between the estimated angles and those produced in the simulator (Truijens & Schuffel, 1978).

---

[12]*Augmented feedback* refers to a condition in which participants do not only receive knowledge of results about the quality of their performance, but also about how and in which way their actions should change in order to improve. Augmented feedback may contain additional visual aids that are not available in practice, but are still beneficial to acquiring the proper action patterns.

[13]This simulator was based on a television projection system that moved around in a scale model. The shots of the environment were projected on a large screen and perceived by the participants who, in turn, carried out control actions such as moving a rudder. The control actions were entered into the mathematical model of a ship, which was stored in a computer. The output of the computer instructed the movements of the TV system in which way the loop was closed. The present navigation simulator uses computer-generated images.

The same technique was used for validating a fixed-base driving simulator that was also based on a television projection of a scale model. Blaauw (1980, 1982) compared performance with respect to longitudinal and lateral control[14] in the simulator and in an experimental car on the road, with experienced and novice drivers as participants. Longitudinal control was similar in either condition but lateral control was superior in actual driving, presumably due to lack of kinesthetic feedback in the simulator. Yet, the effects of experimental variables such as a sudden disturbance affecting lateral control were similar in the simulator and in the experimental car.[15] The conclusion was that the lack of motion information in the simulator affected performance but did not distort its relative validity. Yet, in particular for experienced drivers, relative validity broke down in the case of high task demands. Under such conditions, novices showed no difference between performance in the simulator and in actual driving, but experienced drivers tended to behave as novices in the simulator. A more recent fixed-base simulator with computer-generated images did better in this regard. This suggests that the breakdown of relative validity might not have been due to the absence of motion cues. Other studies showed relative validity of the driving simulator in regard to lane width, presence of chevrons on the road surface, and curve characteristics (Kaptein et al., 1996, for a review). Together, this suggests that, at least for straight road driving, a fixed-base simulator is quite useful. A moving-base simulator is superior but, as argued, only when its characteristics fully correspond to reality.

Perhaps the most powerful and advanced moving-base simulator for car-driving is the Daimler-Benz simulator in Berlin. In a validation study on behavioral correspondence, Riemersma, van der Horst, Hoekstra, Alink, and Otten (1990) repeated an earlier real-world study in this simulator to find out whether similar results would be obtained. The real-world study had been concerned with the effect of measures to reduce driving speed on a straight main road in a village. Among others, the measures had consisted of a change in lane width and in surface color and/or of disruption of the appearance of the straight road. In real-life trials, these measures had the effect that average speed reduced some 8 km/hr, whereas fast-moving cars slowed down relatively more. The same study was carried out in the Daimler-Benz simulator, with about equal results. This shows that the simulator is valid for evaluating the effects of road characteristics on driving speed. The fact that the simulator did well in those conditions suggests, at the same time, that there were no serious deviations in visuomotion correspondence.

---

[14]Lateral control refers to the moment-to-moment variation of the distance of the car to the borderline of the road. Longitudinal control refers to the extent one is driving straight ahead.

[15]This is sometimes labeled "relative validity" as distinct from "absolute validity," in which case the absolute parameter values of simulator and reality converge.

Effects of deviations among information from different senses are usually quite serious. A discrepancy among information from various sensory modalities leads to misorientation, simulator sickness, and suboptimal performance. A discrepancy within the visual modality may raise problems as well. For example, a basic problem in helmet-mounted virtual environments is alignment of visual coordinates with the normal ones. The effect of pitching a visual environment in both a normal and a simulated condition may, again, be assessed by measuring behavioral correspondence. Thus, Nemire, Jacoby, and Ellis (1994) measured perceived eye-level as a function of a pitched optical array rotated in the sagittal plane. Normally, perceived eye-level is biased into the direction of the pitch (Matin & Fox, 1989). In the simulation, this bias was less unless longitudinal, parallel lines were added to the optical array, which might have the effect of improving perceived perspective in the simulator. The result suggests that valid simulation of visual and gravitational information may be feasible but requires detailed consideration of visual perception and balancing.

As already noted, the validation problem may be the most serious in the case of complex, multisensory environments and of fine-grained, visual scenes. The issues always center around realistic and sufficiently high-resolution display of complex visual patterns and around proprioceptive motion characteristics. The advance of computerized real-life tasks tends to ease this problem. For example, changing from a raw display to a synthetic one—as has occurred in air-traffic control—eliminated most of the display problems. Thus, raw radar or sonar is hard to simulate due to the complex visual properties of clutter, whereas simulation of present-day synthetic radar displays is simple. The trend toward presenting information on computer screens and the discussions about diagnostic object displays in process control are other examples. In those cases, simulation is easy because information from the real-life task and from the simulation are both presented on a computer screen and, therefore, converge completely.

Training Complex Skills

As mentioned on various occasions, training in a highly validated simulator has pronounced advantages. One may provide augmented feedback about performance and errors, one may train through practicing examples of relevant performance strategies, and one may drill on task components in partial-task training. All of this is not feasible or is impractical when training on the job. Trivial and self-evident as these advantages may sound, they are often poorly implemented in training programs. All too often, the incorrect principle that repetitive "practice makes perfect" is adopted. This is bluntly wrong whenever a skill requires acquisition of composite strategies (e.g., Schneider, 1985). For example, in air-traffic control, training programs in a simulator usually consist of having trainees control aircraft, the number of which is gradually increased. When faced with a larger number of aircraft, many trainees fail to fulfil the course requirements for the simple reason that strategies of sequencing and other economizing principles in organizing air traffic have not been taught in any systematic way. An example of the benefits of teaching strategies stems from Schuffel's (1986) findings on the positive effects of installing perceptual reference-signals, or even a complete leading line, when maneuvering vessels. The general finding that knowledge of results contributes little as long as it does not contain indications about the correct performance strategy is, of course, at the basis of augmented feedback and feedforward.

Simulation also offers the opportunity of practicing procedures that are rare in real life. It is often said that process controllers of automated systems run the risk of losing their diagnostic and problem-solving skills because problems rarely arise (Bainbridge, 1979). A simulator offers excellent opportunities for practicing emergency procedures and is, therefore, widely used by nuclear plant operators and by aircraft pilots. The problem remains that one can never be sure whether one has scenarios for any possible emergency. Recently developed error analysis techniques may be useful for improving existing sets (Reason, 1990).

Equipment Design

Simulators are used less frequently for design than for training, despite the fact that it enables advance evaluation of a system. For example, a design of a road intersection or a tunnel can be simulated by computer-generated images and can be approached or traversed by a car together with other simulated traffic. In the same way, one may determine the most appropriate location of road signals well as the amount of preview that a designed road provides at any point of its course. Again, simulator studies are highly useful when studying dangerous situations. In navigation, there are comparable applications with respect to the design of fairways and, indeed, of complete harbors from the perspective of safe maneuvering. Schuffel (1986) reported that in navigation, radar and outside viewing are differentially sensitive to information. Radar proved to provide more precise distance information, whereas outside viewing was better in regard to detecting changes in the relative position of a moving ship. It is obvious that this type of study requires a full-task simulation.

The considerable potential of simulation in system design notwithstanding, performance analysis should always be reminded of the pitfalls described by Parsons (1972) on the mammoth simulation studies of the 1950s. A system such as the bridge of a ship, is highly complex and may be varied in countless ways. Because simulation experiments are expensive, one should carefully consider which display options should be compared in an experimental test. In fact, the full simulation might be an ultimate test—a demonstration of the suitability of a new design rather than an open-ended trial. Again, the best strategy is to break a system down into manageable components through task analysis and to aim at optimal design of these components. This may be achieved by means of partial simulation but, preferably, from evidence from small paradigms prior to testing on how the components interact.

Personnel Assessment

Researchers on personnel selection have shown a traditional interest in partial simulation of complex skills in that a simplified miniature of a real-life task may predict a person's proficiency in that task. Miniature-situation tests, in which only a few symbols are learned, have been successful as predictors for skills such as telegraphy and morse coding, both of which have perceptual speed as the dominant ability. However, miniature-situation tests may be only successful when training consists of doing the same over and over again at an increasingly faster pace and with a gradually more extended vocabulary. The point is that miniature-situation tests have not shown much promise in regard to training more complex skills such as car driving, air-traffic control, or flying.

However, this does not mean that a simplified simulation may not be predictive at all. Thus, the Häkkinen (1976) test battery consists of a combination of paper-and-pencil and psychomotor performance tests but has criterion-related validity in regard to the accident rate of bus drivers in heavy traffic. Equally promising results have been obtained with the basic-attributes test battery (BAT) for fighter pilots (Imhoff & Levine, 1981). It should be kept in mind, though, that tests included in a successful battery are usually not constructed on an intuitive basis. Thus, the BAT derives from Fleishman and Quaintance's (1984) factor-structure of human cognitive and perceptual–motor abilities. The construction of predictive batteries for complex tasks is a painstaking affair that requires long-term research.

As an alternative to a selection battery or a miniature situation, measures of initial performance level have been proposed as a predictor of final skilled performance. The rationale is that if a student cannot cope with the task demands in early practice, problems will only increase at a later stage. In fact, an early stage of training may be viewed as a somewhat extended miniature-situation test. This reasoning was tested by Damos (1978) and by Crosby and Parkinson (1979), who measured secondary task performance at the initial level of pilot training. Actual performance in the simulator could not be measured—that is, no performance measures were available—and, moreover, potential measures might suffer from data limits. Thus, determining spare capacity was more informative. They found that as trainees did

CHAPTER 10

better on the secondary task during early training, they were also more likely to complete the course. In other words, although all might perform the early task level equally well, the good trainees had more spare capacity than the poor ones. Similar data were obtained by Jorna (1981), who found that more proficient divers performed better on a secondary continuous-memory test[16] during deep sea diving. It should be noted that such results are at odds with Schneider's (1985) view that performance in early training is not predictive for ultimate success. His rationale was that the many changes in strategies and demands in the course of acquiring a complex skill cannot be estimated during early training.

One might equally consider the value of popular video games as simplified simulations of a skill. Despite a general skepticism, there are various positive outcomes. Thus, Lintern and Kennedy (1984) found a correlation between performance in landing an aircraft in a video game and glide scope tracking performance in simulated carrier landings. Ohde and Sanders (1988) studied an air-traffic-control simulation game and found a correlation between early and later performance levels on that game. Moreover, they found a positive correlation between later performance and performance on a secondary continuous-memory test during an early trial. Again, the better performers had more spare capacity.

CONCLUSIONS

From the perspective of back-to-back studies, simulation is becoming *the* essential link between simple paradigms and real life. Yet, it should not be concluded that simulation may replace the simple paradigm. This is even less so in low-cost simulation, in which case theoretical considerations are decisive to the question as to which components should be simulated. Task analysis is a major tool, but the quality of a task analysis also depends on theory based on small paradigms. Again, simulation is usually impractical when designing a new system, in particular when there are still many potential options. In that case, the designer has to rely largely on analytical procedures. As argued, theoretical views on human performance dominate such procedures and they, again, stem largely from small paradigms.

Hence, the general tenet is that applied procedures and basic research are strongly intertwined in both analytical and behavioral procedures. Microanalysis is aimed at breaking down a task into elementary steps, which directly leads to questions on the level of the small paradigm. Attempts

---

[16]In a continuous-memory task, a running account is kept of the frequency of occurrence of four different target letters among a continuous stream of auditorily presented letters, targets as well as nontargets.

toward task taxonomies all started from the distinction among perceptual, mediational, and motor variables, which implies a stage-type concept of information flow. The most successful task taxonomy, that is, Fleishman's, was even based on factor analytic dimensions derived from research on small paradigms. It is promising that his abilities were useful as taxonomic dimensions for real-life tasks. The measurement problem in dynamic simulation illustrated, in particular, the adverse effects of the lack of cooperation between basic and applied research. Such cooperation should aim at concepts about how an appropriate measure should look. Basic research results appeared equally essential to deciding how low-cost simulators may be developed. All in all, the impending schism between basic and applied research appears highly detrimental to either side.

BACK-TO-BACK ANALYSIS: AN INTERIM EVALUATION

There is no need repeating the many instances highlighting the relevance of wide interaction between basic and applied research. These instances suggest some essential issues as well. Thus, throughout this book frequent mention was made of applied potential of basic data but only occasionally of applied prospects of theory emerging from these data. As an example, it is easy to imagine that a practitioner realizes that the effect of visual pop-out is relevant to system design, but may fail to see the relevance of the many subtle differences among the various theoretical stands about visual selective attention. One may even maintain that theory is not needed for applying the pop-out effect. The argument, as developed here, takes strong issue with that position. Admittedly, most present generalizations stem from experimental data, but ultimate generalizations to real life should come from theory, and theory can never be sufficiently subtle or detailed. In regard to pop-out, indeed, elementary forms may be directly applicable and may even seem trivial and self-evident, but this changes rapidly in more complex cases.

As basic research advances, theory should become better equipped to generate options for improving existing real-life tasks and for designing new ones. A comparison between the argument in this volume and similar ones of, for example, 30 years ago, shows that the painstaking effort of dealing with increasingly complex questions has not been in vain. The research is clearly on a much more detailed and conceptually advanced level than at the time of the first meeting on Attention and Performance in 1966.

A key question of this book concerned the extent to which results—data as well as theory—from small paradigms generalize to real life. Generalization proved to be not self-evident. Various degrees of correspondence between laboratory and real-life tasks were met in the discussion of the basic literature. Are there any rules about when generalization has better prospects?

To illustrate the issue, some examples of theory-driven design (Card, 1989) are briefly considered.

The Example of Sensory Psychophysics

This is a nice illustrative example because it is often taken for granted that there the data can be easily generalized. One instance concerns visual acuity, which is usually measured by having people look at Landolt rings—"c"-types of symbols of varying size, with the opening in one out of four directions—in order to determine the marginally visible opening of the "c" in terms of visual angle. A correction is based on detection accuracy that is generalized to a wide variety of real-life conditions.

The generalization from Landolt rings to real life has its limits because the paradigm fails to capture the role of spatial frequency. Hence, psychophysical measurement of contrast sensitivity as a function of spatial frequency has been proposed as a better test of visual acuity, in particular when monitoring computer or television screens (Sanders & McCormick, 1992). Yet, in spite of the fact that neither Landolt rings nor spatial-frequency patterns are close to any real-life task, there is little debate about their generalization gradient to real-life situations such as reading, car driving, and looking at computer screens. One would not be tempted to replace the preceding tests by field trials in more ecologically valid situations, for example, having participants read a passage from a book or have them find their way in twilight. The success of small laboratory tasks in sensory perception is based on a fairly detailed theory on sensory processing, which is even capable of indicating the applied limits of the Landolt ring task.

The same seems to hold as well for other sensory phenomena such as dark adaptation, color vision, and glare. Thus, poor color vision in the dark follows directly from knowledge about the relative sensitivity of rods and cones. The use of blue light in command and control rooms is based on laboratory studies on the role of blue-sensitive cones. Blue light guarantees optimal contrast on a radar screen while also providing acceptable viewing conditons for reading and writing. The recommendation to use fluorescent orange jackets for road workers stems from laboratory evidence on relative strength of contrast among colors (Michon, Eernst, & Koutstaal, 1965).

In the same way, hearing damage is estimated from auditory intensity thresholds for simple tones as a function of frequency, a raised threshold indicating a hearing loss for that frequency. In light of the many complaints about hearing aids, this procedure may not always be successful, though. The complaints are still occasionally ascribed to a lack of adaptation rather than to failures in generalizing from simple sounds to speech (Kryter, 1985), but it is evident that theories on speech and hearing will be able to delineate the limits of the audiogram.

Still, these restrictions suggest that even in relatively well-developed areas of research, one should be careful in generalizing to real life. One failure concerned the deduction that hemianopia—that is, the loss of the peripheral half field in both eyes—precludes safe driving. The deduction is based on the consideration that peripheral stimuli remain undetected, which is intuitively harmful to driving. Yet, in one case, a hemianopic truck driver had driven accident free for many years (Vos & Riemersma, 1976). Another failure concerned crane operators with deficient binocular vision. A lack of binocular vision was taken to imply that one would have problems in aiming a crane at some exact spatial location. Yet, individual crane drivers with deficient binocular depth perception had been among the most proficient operators.

Principles About Generalization

These cases suggest two important principles about generalizing laboratory data to real life. First, when generalizing, a laboratory task should capture the main aspects of a real-life task. In other words, the laboratory task should be a valid simulation of at least some major aspects of a real-life task. Thus, a Landolt ring may be sufficiently "letter-like" to generalize to reading, whereas it does less well when the visual task requires analysis of spatial frequencies such as when inspecting pictures. In contrast, sensitivity to tones of different frequencies such as those measured in an audiogram may not do well enough as a simulation of the more complex speech sounds. It is evident that the limits should follow from theory and not from intuition or from trial-and-error type of correlations between real life and a small task.

Second, generalization is limited when participants may use strategies or different ways of processing in the real-life task that were not captured by the small paradigm. Thus, the hemianopic truck driver had an obvious deficiency in peripheral vision. However, he fully and satisfactorily compensated his deficit by making additional eye and head movements.[17] Again, depth is inferred from many outside cues, and binocular vision appears to contribute primarily to performance at a short distance. In the same way, one might compensate deficient visual acuity by adapting reading distance or by accommodation. In this way, people may postpone wearing or changing correcting glasses at the cost of unpleasant visual strain. In these examples performance was not simply limited by the quality of sensory processing. Hence, simple application of the theory of sensory processing failed to predict performance of the hemianopic truck driver and the crane operator. The moral is that other areas of research, which go beyond stimulus pre-processing and take account of strategic aspects of performance, should get

---

[17]In fact, the person was unaware of his hemianopia, which was discovered in an optometrist's office.

involved. Indeed, one of the shortcomings of many simple paradigms may be that one is forced to act in a prescribed and reduced way and cannot employ strategic compensations, which one has available in real life.

The back-to-back approach is aware of this problem by stressing the relevance of studies between the simple paradigm and real life—for example, by using a simulation—with the purpose of delineating the limits of domain-specific theories and by uncovering and explaining gaps in the transition from small paradigms to real-life performances.

Two Examples of Intended Back-to-Back Studies

Thus far, explicit attempts to bridge the gaps between laboratory and real life are rare. In other words, there are hardly any studies in which the back-to-back approach was intentionally implemented. Yet, two examples are described here in greater detail by way of illustration how one may proceed. One stems from Schuffel's (1986) dissertation.

Schuffel carried out two types of experiments back to back, with a different level of "reality value," in order to get a better theoretical underpinning of phenomena that had been observed in real life. In natural studies, participants sailed a 40,000 ton vessel in the highly validated TNO maneuvering simulator in order to assess total system performance. Coupled with the natural studies, there were experiments that were less natural but better controlled enabling more detailed questions about human information-processing while handling this type of ship. Schuffel wondered whether, while maneuvering, pilots primarily rely on open-loop preprogrammed actions or on feedback control by continually comparing the changes in the course of the ship to an internal or external perceptual reference of the desired course.

In the natural experiment, participants carried out a zig-zag maneuver, as illustrated in Fig. 10.6. The track-to-be-"sailed" consisted of passing through successive gates. In some conditions, two gates were close together, so the participants could only issue a single, supposedly open-loop, rudder command to achieve a correct passage. In other conditions, there was sufficient time to carry out further corrections while approaching a gate. The results clearly show that performance in the case of a single rudder command was inferior. This could suggest that feedback-based corrections are benificial to performance.

Yet—as not uncommon in real-life conditions—the results might be interpreted equally well otherwise. For instance, they could reflect a difference in task difficulty rather than a difference in operating strategy. In the more unnatural conditions, therefore, participants sailed with the instruction to issue one, and only one, rudder command in order to pass a gate, which led to deficient performance for all forcing functions. Knowledge of results had only a positive effect when participants received information about what would

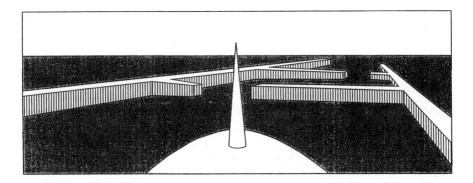

FIG. 10.6. A forcing function viewed from the windows of the bridge. The top of the forcing function is in the center of a 200 m opening in a dike perpendicular on the fareway axis. In the foreground the mast and deck of the ship are shown. From Schuffel, H., *Human control of ships in tracking tasks.* Doctoral dissertation, University of Tilburg, Tilburg, The Netherlands. Reprinted with kind permission of the author.

have been the correct rudder command at the particular forcing function of that trial. In contrast, knowledge of results had no effect when it indicated the position error resulting from the rudder command that had actually been issued. Schuffel (1986) argued that when learning consisted of acquiring an open-loop rule—relating the forcing function to the rudder command—either type of knowledge of results should have been equally efficient.

In another study, Schuffel (1986) confirmed the positive effect of perceptual references on maneuvering in a study in which visual reference points indicated the moments that the track should be corrected. The positive effect on skill acquisition remained when the references were omitted in a later stage of practice. Together, these results provide support for the hypothesis that maneuvering did not rely on open-loop internal rules but on feedback control by way of comparisons with perceptual reference points.

Thus, the results in the unnatural one-rudder command conditions aided the interpretation of the results in the more natural condition. Yet, either condition was still carried out in a simulator. One additional back-to-back study would be to further reduce the situation to a condition of simple pursuit tracking and aiming in order to find out whether the main conclusions about feedback control would still hold. Another back-to-back study would be to find out whether the observed lack of evidence for open-loop control in zig-zag maneuvering might be due to the nature of this maneuver. Zig-zag maneuvers might be too little practiced and need feedback, whereas extensively practiced, real-life maneuvers might actually occur through open-loop control. Again, Schuffel's (1986) results may change if the same set of zig-zag maneuvers were intensively practiced under identical conditions. This last option would be in line with evidence from automatic versus controlled processing. It could be reasoned that (a) automatic processing implies acquisition of open-loop control, (b) experienced pilots develop automatic processing, and (c) hence, they should be capable of completing the task in an open-loop way. The finding that the zig-zag maneuvers benefited from feedback is at odds with this reasoning. Perhaps the second assumption was wrong. The skill of piloting may not be simply a matter of acquiring automatic processing. It could be that pilots acquire sets of rules enabling efficient but controlled adaptation to a variety of maneuvering conditions. As shown in chapter 8, automatic processing develops mainly in conditions of consistent mapping—that is, repetitions of a set of identical domain-specific situations. Zig-zag maneuvers are unusual in navigation; therefore, pilots may not have developed consistent mapping in a zig-zag task. Transferred to real life, a pilot may develop open-loop control in the standard situation of the port in which he has worked for a long time. This would agree with the observation that pilots may issue rudder commands after casual, or almost without any, inspection of the perceptual environment.

The second example comes from Fröhlich's (1994) dissertation on the effect of drugs and tracking. The point is that it has been repeatedly found that a small dose of a tranquilizer, for example, diazepam, degrades course keeping during highway driving in real-life trials with an experimental car (O'Hanlon, Haak, Blaauw, & Riemersma, 1982). On the other hand, the effects of a similar dose of diazepam are quite unreliable in tests of manual tracking in the laboratory (Sanders & Wauschkuhn, 1988). The question, then, is whether potential differences between the demands of manual tracking in the laboratory and those of course keeping on the road may explain the divergence. Fröhlich reasoned that one difference concerns the quality of performance feedback. Error feedback is immediate and implicit in manual tracking, and it is, actually, the only information on which a corrective movement can be based. In contrast, feedback is much less immediate on the road because the painted side and middle lines provide much less precise indications about the lateral and longitudinal position of the car. Fröhlich hypothesized that the more precise feedback in the laboratory could counteract the performance effect of a sedating drug. This would be consistent with evidence on the effects of knowledge of results on performance in conditions of low arousal or activation. It is obvious that, if a manual-tracking task would be carried out for a long time or if a larger dosage of diazepam would be administered, the effect of the drug may show up in spite of the counteracting effect of feedback.

Fröhlich's (1994) reasoning was confirmed by a set of studies in which he found no effect of an antihistamine on manual pursuit tracking in the laboratory, with common, immediate feedback, whereas an effect appeared when feedback was made less precise. This last condition were constructed in order to achieve closer correspondence to what is observed from the front window of a car. Thus, this back-to-back study shows evidence for a relevant variable that accounted for the divergent findings in the laboratory and in real life. At the same time, it suggests that driving safety may benefit from more precise feedback about the optimal lateral track.

The preceding examples are illustrative for the back-to-back approach because they addressed different levels of approximation to real life and considered theoretical arguments about convergence and divergence among these levels. The examples also demonstrated relative strengths and weaknesses. One may be reminded of the fact that real tasks consist of a set of specific conditions, the combination of which is hard to interpret and analyze. The laboratory is incomplete, and generalization may lead astray, but results can be more easily analyzed; they are more appropriate as a starting point for theory, and ultimately, they are more suitable for generalization across conditions. The availability of more complex laboratory conditions—as in present-day simulators—is an important step toward bridging the gap. It is apparent, though, that research is needed on all levels. A great danger of the potential schism between basic and applied research is that the different levels grow apart and lose contact. The consequence is a neglect of back-to-back research because the need for that would neither be felt by basic nor applied researchers. Unfortunately, the conclusion that a schism is detrimental does not automatically imply that the danger has disappeared.

A Reiteration of Some Back-to-Back Options

As said, Schuffel's (1986) and Fröhlich's (1994) studies are rare examples of a planned back-to-back approach. Most of the evidence in this book was more indirect and on divergent levels. Together, they may still illustrate the basic principles of back-to-back from the small to complex, and vice versa. To conclude, a few prime examples are briefly reiterated.

Compatibility. Basic research on compatibility in its various manifestations has, undoubtedly, been a major applied success story. As discussed in chapter 4, principles of S–S, S–R, and R–R compatibility find wide application, ranging from S–R relations in the operation of gas stoves to the construction of keyboards and to "cursor up" and "cursor down" instructions on computer screens. The wide potential for generalization suggests that the basic paradigm is a perfect simulation of the principles governing deterministic S–R relations. Moreover, one has no strategical tricks available for overcoming the negative effects of poor S–R compatibility. The only way is through extended practice. The inefficiency of poor S–R compatibility is clearly demonstrated by the absurdly long time needed to become a skilled typist and to master key command-relations in most text-processing systems.

Fitts' Law. A similar case can be made for Fitts' law about the time to complete an aiming movement. In human–computer interfacing, a device was needed to operate directly on the screen. Handling a mouse appears to obey Fitts' law, with similar parameter values as in the laboratory (Card et al., 1983). This suggests that aiming by way of potential other devices, for example, a light pen, should not be more efficient. This was instrumental in deciding on the commercial introduction of the mouse.

Time Uncertainty. As mentioned in chapter 4, effects of time uncertainty in the laboratory are directly relevant to response speed in traffic. It has been repeatedly found that the effect of time uncertainty on CRT interacts with the effects of time on task and of stressors such as sleep loss and sedative drugs (chap. 9). This suggests traffic conditions, which are particularly sensitive to sleep loss and sedatives. For example, when driving home after a night shift, one is likely to have an increased risk of neglecting or reacting too slowly to the brake lights of a lead car, with the effect being a head–tail collision.

Separable Versus Integral Dimensions. The laboratory distinction between separable and integral stimulus dimensions is essential background information for the development of object displays. Here, theoretical developments clearly preceded applications. An example is the notion of emergent features such as further specification of integrality. In general, designing an integrated display and testing its usefulness is best done in the laboratory prior to operational tests in a simulator or in real life.

The Functional Visual Field. Generalization of the findings and, in particular, of the theoretical statements on the functional visual field to optimal display size was discussed in chapter 5. Among others, the evidence was instrumental in improving the design of periscopes in tanks and was in line with results on the effect of the optimal position of side mirrors in cars. Another generalization concerned the maximal, permissible visual angle between the location of written text and of a typewriter. Moreover, there are potential generalizations to reading that await further research. Visual-fixation duration depends on perceptual demands in either case, although the comparison is complicated by the fact that in contrast to the functional visual field, reading requires rapid alternation between saccades and fixations. This seems to mark the point at which generalization of the evidence on the functional visual field has its limits.

Memory Span. Data on memory span and, more generally, on limits of working memory generalize as well to a variety of conditions ranging from identification codes on cars, to secret codes of bank passes, and to telephone and bank account numbers. For instance, AHT397 is easier to retain than A3H9T7. This follows directly from basic theory on working memory. At the same time, data on memory span are highly domain specific in that they cannot be taken to imply that "7 plus-or-minus-two" items can be readily retained. This error was committed when on introduction, the four-digit "secret number" of bank passes, many users proved incapable of producing the number when required. In the meantime, this has improved for the simple reason that a four-digit number can be learned by heart. One should not raise the idea of changing all numbers, though!

Pop-Out. Pop-out in visual search is another principle that generalizes widely beyond the laboratory. The rapid theoretical developments during the last decades have brought much more detailed knowledge of the conditions under which pop-out occurs. For example, it used to be popular to attempt improving target detection on a screen through adding colored stimuli. We now know that in many cases, adding color has a negative effect on detection. Recent studies have been engaged in studying pop-out in conditions of divided and focused attention. This enables a more detailed specification of the conditions under which variants of search studies are a satisfactory simulation of, for example, searching a computer screen for new information.

Legibility of Print. At first sight, principles of visual discrimination and word perception were thought to generalize readily to recommendations on legibility of print. Indeed, there is reasonable evidence for the relevance of discrimination of spatial positions, letter and word similarity, and the use of uppercase versus lowercase letters. On the other hand, the lack of correlation among the various measures of legibility of print (Chapanis, 1971) suggests that no single laboratory measure generalizes to the variety of reading conditions in real life. There seem to be different requirements for reading lines of text, reading single words as in advertisements, reading traffic signs on the road, and searching for information on a screen. These conditions need their own task analysis and consideration of the critical processses contributing to the ultimate performance. The situation is more complex than envisaged.

PRP and Typing. The reasons behind the failure to generalize from the PRP to more complex transcription skills are highly illustrative. The two major differences concerned preview and sequential redundancy, the combination of which appears to allow a fair deal of concurrent input and output processing. It is noteworthy that a novice on typing behaves in about the same way as a participant in the PRP and that, in the absence of preview and sequential redundancy, an expert typist does not do better than about two decisions per second. This back-to-back comparison proved quite useful for uncovering the relevant differences between the involved skills. It implies that when participants react to uncorrelated stimuli, they tend to behave as a single-channel processor. In real-life conditions, for example, driving, this is liable to create sudden, dangerous situations. Hence, it would be absolutely incorrect to consider the PRP as nothing but an artifact of the laboratory.

Vigilance. This is an area in which there are strong complaints about a lack of consistent laboratory results as well as about the value of laboratory studies for real life. It is interesting to note that the dim views concern an area in which performance is strongly affected by motivation. Applications from basic research in such areas may never be through direct transfer of results but are bound to be largely theory driven. It is relevant in this respect to trace the potential of the cognitive-energetic model to real-life instances of performance under stress. Are effects of sleep loss in real life also more pronounced in the case of degraded perceptual conditions? Is there supporting evidence from real life for the five variants of stress, as suggested by the model? These are merely two out of the many back-to-back issues arising from that model.

The aforementioned reiteration concerned but a small sample of fruitful interplay between the small paradigm and real life. It could be extended with various other themes that were discussed in this book, including mental load, situational awareness, motor sequences, training skills, and so on. The present sample may suffice, though, as an incentive to fight the imminent schism by improving the image of applied issues to the basic researcher as well as the image of basic research to the practitioner.

References

Abrams, R. A., & Balota, D. A. (1990). Mental chronometry: Beyond reaction time. *Psychological Science, 2*, 153–157.

Abrams, R. A., & Dobkin, R. S. (1994). Inhibition of return: Effects of attentional cuing on eye movement latencies. *Journal of Experimental Psychology: Human Perception & Performance, 20*, 467–477.

Adams, J. A. (1954). Psychomotor performance as a function of intertrial rest interval. *Journal of Experimental Psychology, 48*, 131–133.

Adams, J. A. (1971). A closed loop theory of motor learning. *Journal of Motor Behavior, 3*, 111–150.

Adams, J. A. (1987). Criticisms of vigilance research: A discussion. *Human Factors, 29*, 737–740.

Akerstedt, T. (1991). Sleepiness at work: Effects of irregular working hours. In T. H. Monk (Ed.), *Sleep, sleepiness and performance.* New York: Wiley.

Alegria, J. (1975). Sequential effects of foreperiod duration: Some strategical factors in tasks involving time uncertainty. In P. M. A. Rabbitt & S. Dornic (Eds.), *Attention & Performance* (Vol. 5). London: Academic Press.

Alegria, J., & Bertelson, P. (1970). Time uncertainty, number of alternatives and particular signal-response pair as determinants of CRT. *Acta Psychologica, 30*, 36–44.

Allen, J. A., Hays, R. T., & Buffardt, C. L. (1986). Maintenance training, simulator fidelity and individual differences in transfer of training. *Human Factors, 28*, 497–509.

Allport, A. (1980a). The state of cognitive psychology: A critical note of W. G. Chase: Visual information processing. *Quarterly Journal of Experimental Psychology, 31*, 141–152.

Allport, A. (1980b). Attention and performance. In G. Claxton (Ed.), *Cognitive psychology: New directions.* London: Routledge.

Allport, A. (1987). Selection for action: Some behavioral and neurophysiological considerations of attention and action. In H. Heuer & A. F. Sanders (Eds.), *Perspectives on perception and action.* Hillsdale, NJ: Lawrence Erlbaum Associates.

Allport, A. (1993). Attention and control: Have we been asking the wrong questions? A critical review of twenty-five years. In D. E. Meyer & S. Kornblum (Eds.), *Attention & Performance* (Vol. 14). Cambridge, MA: MIT Press.

Allport, A., Antonis, B., & Reynolds, P. (1972). On the division of attention: A disproof of the single channel hypothesis. *Quarterly Journal of Experimental Psychology, 24*, 225–235.

Allport, A., Styles, E. A., & Hsieh, S. (1994). Shifting intentional set: Exploring the dynamic control of tasks. In C. Umilta & M. Moscovitch (Eds.), *Attention & Performance* (Vol. 15). Cambridge, MA: MIT Press.

Andersen, G. J., & Kramer, A. F. (1993). Limits of focused attention in three-dimensional space. *Perception & Psychophysics, 53,* 658–667.

Annett, J., & Duncan, K. D. (1967). Task analysis and training design. *Occupational Psychology, 41,* 211–221.

Annlo-Vento, L., & Hillyard, S. A. (1996). Selective attention to the color and direction of moving stimuli: Electrophysiological correlates of hierarchical feature selection. *Perception & Psychophysics, 58,* 191–206.

Antes, J. R., & Penland, J. G. (1981). Picture context effects on eye movements. In D. F. Fisher, R. A. Monty, & J. W. Senders (Eds.), *Eye movements, cognition and visual perception.* Hillsdale, NJ: Lawrence Erlbaum Associates.

Anthony, B. J., & Graham, F. K. (1983). Evidence for sensory-selective set in young infants. *Science, 220,* 742–744.

Aretz, A. J. (1991). The design of electronic map displays. *Human Factors, 33,* 85–102.

Ashby, F. G. (1982). Deriving exact predictions from the cascade model. *Psychological Review, 89,* 599–607.

Attneave, F. (1955). Symmetry, information and memory for patterns. *American Journal of Psychology, 68,* 209–222.

Attneave, F. (1959). *Applications of information theory to psychology: A summary of basic concepts, methods and results.* New York: Holt, Rinehart & Winston.

Attneave, F. (1961). In defense of homunculi. In W. Rosenbliftt (Ed.), *Sensory communication.* New York: Wiley.

Audley, R. J. (1960). A stochastic model for individual choice behavior. *Psychological Review, 67,* 1–15.

Averbach, E., & Coriell, A. S. (1961). Short-term memory in vision. *Bell System Technical Journal, 40,* 309–328.

Azorin, J. M., Benhaïim, P., Hasbrouck, T., & Possamaï, C. A. (1995). Stimulus preprocessing and response selection in depression: A reaction time analysis. *Acta Psychologica, 89,* 95–100.

Babkoff, H., Mikulincer, M., Caspy, T., Kempinski, D., & Sing, H. (1988). The topology of performance curves during 72 hours of sleep loss: A memory and search task. *Quarterly Journal of Experimental Psychology, 40,* 737–756.

Baddeley, A. D. (1966). The capacity for generating information by randomisation. *Quarterly Journal of Experimental Psychology, 18,* 119–129.

Baddeley, A. D. (1986). *Working memory.* Oxford: Oxford University Press.

Baddeley, A. D. (1993). Working memory or working attention? In A. D. Baddeley & L. Weiskrantz (Eds.), *Attention: Selection, awareness and control.* Oxford: Clarendon.

Baddeley, A. D. (1996). Exploring the central executive. *Quarterly Journal of Experimental Psychology, 49,* 5–28.

Baddeley, A. D., & Ecob, J. R. (1973). Reaction time and short-term memory: Implications of repetition effects for the high-speed exhaustive scan hypothesis. *Quarterly Journal of Experimental Psychology, 25,* 229–240.

Baddeley, A. D., & Hitch, G. (1974). Working memory. In G. A. Bower (Ed.), *Recent advances in learning and motivation.* New York: Academic Press.

Badia, P., & Defran, R. H. (1970). Orienting responses and GSR conditioning: A dilemma. *Psychological Review, 77,* 171–181.

Bainbridge, L. (1979). Verbal reports as evidence of the operator's knowledge. *International Journal of Man-Machine Studies, 11,* 411–436.

Bakan, P. (1959). Extroversion–introversion and improvement in an auditory vigilance task. *British Journal of Psychology, 50,* 325–332.

Baker, C. H. (1961). Maintaining the level of vigilance by means of knowledge of results about a secondary vigilance task. *Ergonomics, 4,* 311–316.

Baker, C. H. (1963). Further towards a theory of vigilance. In D. Buckner & J. J. McGrath (Eds.), *Vigilance: A symposium.* New York: McGraw-Hill.

Ball, K. K., Beard, B. L., Roenker, D. L., Miller, R. L., & Griggs, D. S. (1988). Age and visual search: Expanding the useful field of view. *Journal of the Optical Society of America, 5,* 2210–2229.

Ballard, D. H. (1986). Cortical connections and parallel processing: Structure and function. *The Behavioral and Brain Sciences, 9,* 67–120.

Bamber, D. (1969). Reaction times and error rates for "same–different" judgments of multidimensional stimuli. *Perception & Psychophysics, 6,* 169–174.

Barber, P. J. (1988). *Applied cognitive psychology.* London: Routledge.

Barnett, B. J., & Wickens, C. D. (1988). Display proximity in multicue information integration: The benefit of boxes. *Human Factors, 30,* 15–24.

Bartlett, F. C. (1943). Fatigue following highly skilled work. *Proceedings of the Royal Society, B–131,* 247–257.

Bartlett, F. C. (1953). Psychological criteria of fatigue. In W. F. Floyd & A. T. Welford (Eds.), *Symposium on fatigue* (pp. 1–5). London: Lewis.

Bartoshuk, A. K. (1971). Motivation. In J. W. Kling & L. A. Riggs (Eds.), *Experimental psychology.* New York: Holt, Rinehart & Winston.

Bashinsky, H. S., & Bacharach, V. R. (1980). Enhancement of perceptual sensitivity as a result of selectively attending to spatial positions. *Perception & Psychophysics, 28,* 241–248.

Bashore, T. R. (1990). Stimulus–response compatibility viewed from a cognitive psychophysiological perspective. In R. W. Proctor & T. G. Reeve (Eds.), *Stimulus–response compatibility* (pp. 183–223). Amsterdam: North-Holland.

Bashore, T. R., Osman, A., & Heffley, E. F. (1989). Mental slowing in elderly persons: A cognitive psychophysiological analysis. *Psychology and Aging, 4,* 235–244.

Beatty, J. (1982). Task-evolved pupillary responses, processing load and the structure of processing resources. *Psychological Bulletin, 91,* 276–292.

Beatty, J. (1989). Neurophysiology of sustained attention. In A. Coblentz (Ed.), *Vigilance and performance in automatized systems.* Dordrecht, The Netherlands: Kluwer.

Becker, C. A., & Killion, T. H. (1977). Interaction of visual and cognitive effects in word recognition. *Journal of Experimental Psychology: Human Perception & Performance, 3,* 389–401.

Beevis, D., Papin, J. P., Döring, B., Schuffel, H., Nordo, E., Streets, D. F., Bost, R., & Oberman, F. R. (1992). *Analysis techniques for man-machine system design.* (NATO document No. AC/243, panel 8, TR/7)

Bennett, C., Chitlangia, A., & Pangrekar, A. (1977). Illumination levels and performance of practical visual tasks. *Proceedings of the 21st Meeting of the Human Factors Society,* St. Louis, MO.

Bennett, K. B., Toms, M. L., & Woods, D. D. (1993). Emergent features and graphical elements: Designing more effective configural displays. *Human Factors, 35,* 71–93.

Bentin, S., Kutas, M., & Hillyard, S. A. (1995). Semantic processing and memory for attended and unattended words in dichotic listening: Behavioral and electrophysiological evidence. *Journal of Experimental Psychology: Human Perception & Performance, 21,* 54–67.

Berger, G. O. (1886). Über den Einfluss der Reizstärke auf die Dauer einfacher psychischer Vorgänge mit besonderer Rücksicht auf Lichtreize [On the effect of stimulus intensity on the deviation of simple mental events with special emphasis on visual stimuli]. *Philosophische Studien, 3,* 38–93.

Berkun, M. M. (1964). Performance decrement under psychological stress. *Human Factors, 6,* 21–30.

Berlyne, D. E. (1960). *Conflict, arousal and curiosity.* New York: McGraw-Hill.

Bernstein, A. S. (1969). To what does the orienting response respond? *Psychophysiology, 6,* 338–350.

Bernstein, A. S. (1981). The orienting response and stimulus significance: Further comments. *Biological Psychology, 12,* 171–185.

Bernstein, I. H., Chu, P. K., Briggs, P. B., & Schurman, D. L. (1973). Stimulus intensity and foreperiod effects in intersensory facilitation. *Quarterly Journal of Experimental Psychology, 25,* 171–181.

Bernstein, P. S., Scheffers, M. K., & Coles, M. G. H. (1995). Where did I go wrong? A psychophysiological analysis of error detection. *Journal of Experimental Psychology: Human Perception & Performance, 21,* 1243–1258.

Bertelson, P. (1961). Sequential redundancy and speed in a serial two-choice responding task. *Quarterly Journal of Experimental Psychology, 13,* 90–102.

Bertelson, P. (1963). S–R relationships and reaction times to new versus repeated signals in a serial task. *Journal of Experimental Psychology, 65,* 478–488.

Bertelson, P. (1965). Serial choice reaction time as a function of response versus signal-and-response repetition. *Nature, 206,* 217–218.

Bertelson, P. (1967a). The refractory period of choice reactions with regular and irregular interstimuli intervals. *Acta Psychologica, 27,* 45–56.

Bertelson, P. (1967b). The time course of preparation. *Quarterly Journal of Experimental Psychology, 19,* 272–279.

Bertelson, P., & Barzeele, J. (1965). Interaction of time uncertainty and relative signal frequency in determining choice reaction time. *Journal of Experimental Psychology, 65,* 478–488.

Bertelson, P., & Joffe, R. (1963). Blockings in prolonged serial responding. *Ergonomics, 6,* 109–116.

Besson, M., & Macar, F. (1987). An event-related potential analysis of incongruity in music and other non-linguistic contexts. *Psychophysiology, 24,* 14–25.

Bevan, W., Hardesty, D., & Avant, L. (1965). Response latencies with constant and variable interval schedules. *Perceptual & Motor Skills, 20,* 969–972.

Biederman, I. (1972). Perceiving real-world scenes. *Science, 77,* 77–80.

Biederman, I. (1987). Recognition-by-components: A theory of human image understanding. *Psychological Review, 94,* 115–147.

Biederman, I., & Kaplan, R. (1970). Stimulus discriminability and stimulus response compatibility: Evidence for independent effects on choice reaction time. *Journal of Experimental Psychology, 86,* 434–439.

Biederman, I., Mezzanotte, R. J., & Rabinowitz, J. C. (1982). Scene perception: Detecting and judging objects underlying relational violations. *Cognitive Psychology, 14,* 143–177.

Bills, A. G. (1931). Blocking: A new principle of mental fatigue. *American Journal of Psychology, 43,* 230–254.

Blake, M. J. F. (1967). Time of day effects on performance in a range of tasks. *Psychonomic Science, 9,* 349–350.

Blaauw, G. J. (1980). Driving experience and task demands in simulator and instrumented car: A validation study. IZF Report 1980–9. The Netherlands: Soesterberg.

Blaauw, G. J. (1982). Driving experience and task demands in simulator and instrumented car: A validation study. *Human Factors, 24,* 473–486.

Boer, L. C., & Jorna, P. G. A. M. (1987). Taskomat: Een batterij voor informatieverwerkingstaken [Taskomat: A battery for information-processing tasks]. IZF Report 1987–2. The Netherlands: Soesterberg.

Boer, L. C., & van der Weygert, E. C. M. (1988). Eye movements and stages of processing. *Acta Psychologica, 67,* 3–17.

Bonney, M., Case, K., & Porter, M. (1989). Applications of SAMMIE and the development of man-modelling. In G. R. McMillan, D. Beevis, E. Salas, M. H. Strub, R. Sutton, & L. van Breda (Eds.), *Applications of human performance models to system design.* New York: Plenum.

Bootsma, R. J. (1988). *The timing of rapid interceptive actions.* Doctoral dissertation, Free University, Amsterdam.

Bootsma, R. J., & Oudejans, R. R. D. (1993). Visual information about time-to-collision between two objects. *Journal of Experimental Psychology: Human Perception & Performance, 19,* 1041–1052.

Bouma, H. (1978). Visual search and reading: Eye movements and the functional visual field. In J. Requin (Ed.), *Attention & Performance* (Vol. 7). Hillsdale, NJ: Lawrence Erlbaum Associates.

Boyce, P. R. (1981). *Human factors in lighting.* New York: Macmillan.

Brainard, R. W., Irby, T. S., Fitts, P. M., & Alluisi, E. A. (1962). Some variables affecting the rate of gain of information. *Journal of Experimental Psychology, 70,* 448–451.

Brand, N., & Jolles, J. (1987). Information processing in depression and anxiety. *Psychological Medicine, 17,* 145–154.

Briand, K. A., & Klein, R. M. (1987). Is Posner's beam the same as Treisman's glue? On the relation between visual orienting and feature integration theory. *Journal of Experimental Psychology: Human Perception & Performance, 13,* 228–241.

Broadbent, D. E. (1952). Listening to one of two synchronous messages. *Journal of Experimental Psychology, 44,* 51–55.

Broadbent, D. E. (1956). Successive responses to simultaneous stimuli. *Quarterly Journal of Experimental Psychology, 8,* 145–152.

Broadbent, D. E. (1958). *Perception and communication.* London: Pergamon.

Broadbent, D. E. (1959). Information theory and older approaches in psychology. *Acta Psychologica, 15,* 111–115.

Broadbent, D. E. (1971). *Decision and stress.* London: Academic Press.

Broadbent, D. E. (1979). Is a fatigue test now possible? *Ergonomics, 22,* 1277–1290.

Broadbent, D. E. (1982). Task combination and selective intake of imformation. *Acta Psychologica, 50,* 253–290.

Broadbent, D. E. (1984). The maltese cross: A new simplistic model for memory. *Behavioral & Brain Sciences, 7,* 55–68.

Broadbent, D. E., & Broadbent, M. H. (1980). Priming and the passive/active model of word recognition. In R. S. Nickerson (Ed.), *Attention & Performance* (Vol. 8). Hillsdale, NJ: Lawrence Erlbaum Associates.

Broadbent, D. E., & Gregory, M. H. (1962). Donders' B and C reaction and S–R compatibility. *Journal of Experimental Psychology, 63,* 575–578.

Brookhuis, K. A., Mulder, G., Mulder, L. J. M., & Gloerich, A. B. M. (1981). Late positive components and stimulus evaluation time. *Biological Psychology, 17,* 277–296.

Brooks, L. R. (1968). Spatial and verbal components of the act of recall. *Canadian Journal of Psychology, 22,* 349–368.

Brooks, B. A., Yates, J. T., & Coleman, R. D. (1980). Perception of images moving at saccadic velocities during saccades and during fixation. *Experimental Brain Research, 40,* 71–78.

Brown, I. D. (1967). Measurement of control skills, vigilance and performance on a subsidiary task during 12 hours of car driving. *Ergonomics, 10,* 665–673.

Brown, I. D. (1978). Dual task methods of assessing workload. *Ergonomics, 21,* 221–224.

Brown, I. D. (1994). Driver fatigue. *Human Factors, 36,* 298–314.

Brown, J. (1959). Some tests of the decay theory of immediate memory. *Quarterly Journal of Experimental Psychology, 10,* 12–21.

Brunia, C. H. M. (1993). Waiting in readiness: Gating in attention and motor preparation. *Psychophysiology, 30,* 327–339.

Buckner, D. N. (1963). An individual-difference approach to explaining vigilance performance. In D. N. Buckner & J. J. McGrath (Eds.), *Vigilance: A symposium*. New York: McGraw-Hill.

Campbell, F. W., & Wurtz, R. H. (1978). Saccadic omission: Why we do not see a grey-out during a saccadic eye movement. *Vision Research, 18*, 1297–1303.

Campbell, K. C., & Proctor, R. W. (1993). Repetition effects with categorizable stimulus and response sets. *Journal of Experimental Psychology: Learning, Memory and Cognition, 19*, 1345–1362.

Canic, M. J., & Franks, I. M. (1989). Response preparation and latency in patterns of tapping movements. *Human Movement Science, 8*, 123–139.

Carbonell, J. R. (1966). A queuing model of visual sampling: Experimental validation. *IEEE Transactions on Man-Machine Systems* MMS-9, 82–87.

Card, S. K. (1989). Theory-driven design research. In G. R. McMillan, D. Beevis, E. Salas, M. H. Strub, R. Sutton, & L. van Breda (Eds.), *Applications of human performance models to system design*. New York: Plenum.

Card, S. K., & Moran, T. P. (1986). An engineering model of human performance. In K. R. Boff, L. Kaufman, & J. P. Thomas (Eds.), *Handbook of perception & human performance* (chap. 45). New York: Wiley.

Card, S. K., Moran, T. P., & Newell, A. (1983). *The psychology of human-computer interaction*. Hillsdale, NJ: Lawrence Erlbaum Associates.

Carpenter, P. A., & Just, M. A. (1978). Eye fixations during mental rotation. In J. W. Senders, D. F. Fischer, & R. A. Monty (Eds.), *Eye movements and the higher psychological functions*. Hillsdale, NJ: Lawrence Erlbaum Associates.

Carpenter, P. A., & Just, M. A. (1983). What your eyes do while your mind is reading. In K. Rayner (Ed.), *Eye movements in reading: Perceptual and language processes*. New York: Academic Press.

Carr, T. H. (1986). Perceiving visual language. In K. R. Boff, L. Kaufman, & J. P. Thomas (Eds.), *Handbook of perception & human performance* (chap. 29). New York: Wiley.

Carr, T. H., Posner, M. I., Pollatsek, A., & Snyder, C. R. R. (1979). Orthography and familiarity effects in word processing. *Journal of Experimental Psychology: General, 108*, 389–414.

Carswell, C. M., & Wickens, C. D. (1987). Information integration and the object display: An interaction of task demands and display superiority. *Ergonomics, 30*, 511–527.

Carswell, C. M., & Wickens, C. D. (1990). The perceptual interaction of graphical attributes: Cofigurality, stimulus homogeneity and object integration. *Perception & Psychophysics, 47*, 157–168.

Carswell, C. M., & Wickens, C. D. (1996). Mixing and matching lower-level codes for object displays: Evidence for two sources of proximity compatibility. *Human Factors, 38*, 1–22.

Cattell, J. M. (1886). The time taken by cerebral operations. *Mind, 11*, 202–242.

Cave, K. R., & Wolfe, J. M. (1990). Modeling the role of parallel processing in visual search. *Cognitive Psychology, 22*, 225–271.

Cerella, J. (1990). Aging and information processing rate. In J. Birren & K. Schaie (Eds.), *Handbook of the psychology of aging* (pp. 201–221). San Diego: Academic Press.

Chapanis, A. (1971). The search for relevance in applied research. In W. T. Singleton, J. G. Fox, & D. Whitfield (Eds.), *Measurement of man at work*. London: Taylor & Francis.

Chase, W. G. (1986). Visual information processing. In K. R. Boff, L. Kaufman, & J. P. Thomas (Eds.), *Handbook of perception & human performance* (chap. 28). New York: Wiley.

Chen-Hui, L., & Proctor, R. W. (1995). The influence of irrelevant location information on performance: A review of the Simon and spatial Stroop effects. *Psychonomic Bulletin & Review, 2*, 174–207.

Cherry, E. C. (1953). Some experiments on the recognition of speech with one and with two ears. *Journal of the Acoustical Society of America, 25*, 975–979.

Childs, J. M. (1976). Signal complexity, response complexity and signal specification in vigilance. *Human Factors, 18*, 149–160.

Chocholle, R. (1940). Variations de temps de reaction auditifs en fonction de l'intensite a diverses frequences [Variation in auditory reaction time as a function of intensity at different frequencies]. *L'Annee Psychologique, 41,* 5–124.

Churchland, P. M. (1981). Eliminative materialism and the propositional attitudes. *Journal of Philosophy, 72,* 741–760.

Clark, F. C. (1958). The effect of deprivation and frequency of reinforcement on variable-interval responding. *Journal of the Experimental Analysis of Behavior, 1,* 221–228.

Cohen, A. (1993). Asymmetries in search for conjunctive targets. *Journal of Experimental Psychology: Human Perception & Performance, 19,* 775–797.

Cohen, A., & Ivry, R. (1991). Density effects in conjunction search: Evidence for a coarse location mechanism of feature integration. *Journal of Experimental Psychology: Human Perception & Performance, 17,* 891–901.

Colavita, F. B. (1971). Human sensory dominance. *Perception & Psychophysics, 16,* 409–412.

Coles, M. G. H., & Gratton, G. (1986). Cognitive psychophysiology and the study of states and processes. In G. R. J. Hockey, A. W. K. Gaillard, & M. G. H. Coles (Eds.), *Energetics and human information processing.* Dordrecht, The Netherlands: Nijhoff.

Coles, M. G. H., Gratton, G., Bashore, T. R., Eriksen C. W., & Donchin, E. (1985). A psychophysiological investigation of the continuous flow model of human information processing. *Journal of Experimental Psychology: Human Perception & Performance, 11,* 529–553.

Colquhoun, W. P. (1975). Evaluation of auditory, visual, and dual mode displays for prolonged sonar monitoring in repeated sessions. *Human Factors, 17,* 425–437.

Colquhoun, W. P., & Baddeley, A. D. (1967). Influence of signal probability during pretraining on vigilance decrement. *Journal of Experimental Psychology, 73,* 153–155.

Coltheart, M., Cutris, B., Atkins, P., & Haller, M. (1993). Models of reading aloud: Dual route and parallel distributed processing approaches. *Psychological Review, 100,* 589–608.

Comstock, E. (1973). Processing capacity in a letter-matching task. *Journal of Experimental Psychology, 100,* 63–72.

Cooke, N. J., Durso, F. T., & Schvaneveldt, R. W. (1994). Retention of skilled search after nine years. *Human Factors, 36,* 597–605.

Cooper, L. A. (1980). Recent themes in visual information processing: A selected overview. In R. Nickerson (Ed.), *Attention & Performance* (Vol. 8). Hillsdale, NJ: Lawrence Erlbaum Associates.

Cooper, L. A., & Podgorny, P. (1976). Mental transformations and visual comparison processes: Effects of complexity and similarity. *Journal of Experimental Psychology: Human Perception & Performance, 2,* 503–514.

Cooper, L. A., & Shepard, R. N. (1973). Chronometric studies of the rotation of mental images. In W. G. Chase (Ed.), *Visual information processing* (pp. 75–176). San Diego: Academic Press.

Corballis, M. C. (1986). Is mental rotation controlled or automatic? *Memory & Cognition, 14,* 124–128.

Corballis, M. C., Zbrodoff, N. J., Shetzer, L. I., & Butler, P. B. (1978). Decisions about identity and orientation of rotated letters and digits. *Memory & Cognition, 6,* 98–107.

Cordo, P., Schieppati, M., Bevan, L., Carlton, L. G., & Carlton, M. J. (1993). Central and peripheral coordination in movement sequences. *Psychological Research, 55,* 124–130.

Courtney, A. J., & Chan, H. S. (1986). Visual lobe dimensions and search performance for targets on a homogeneous background. *Perception & Psychophysics, 40,* 39–44.

Coury, B. G., & Boulette, M. D. (1992). Time stress and the processing of visual displays. *Human Factors, 34,* 707–725.

Cox, T. (1978). *Stress.* London: Macmillan.

Craig, A. (1980). Effect of prior knowlege of signal probabilities on vigilance performance. *Human Factors, 22,* 361–371.

Craik, K. J. W. (1948). Theory of the human operator in control systems: Man as an element in the control system. *British Journal of Psychology, 39,* 142–148.

Crosby, J. V., & Parkinson, S. (1979). A dual task investigation of pilots' skills level. *Ergonomics, 22,* 1301–1313.

Crossman, E. R. F. W. (1953). The measurement of discriminability. *The Quarterly Journal of Experimental Psychology, 5,* 41–52.

Crowder, R. G. (1982). The demise of short-term memory. *Acta Psychologica, 50,* 291–323.

Dallenbach, K. M. (1920). Attributive and cognitive clearness. *Journal of Experimental Psychology, 3,* 183–230.

Damos, D. (1978). Residual attention as a predictor of pilots' performance. *Human Factors, 20,* 435–440.

Davis, H., & Zerlin, S. (1966). Acoustic relations of the human vertex potential. *Journal of the Acoustical Society of America, 39,* 109–116.

Davis, R. (1959). The role of "attention" in the psychological refractory period. *The Quarterly Journal of Experimental Psychology, 11,* 211–220.

Davis, R. (1967). Intermittency and selective attention. *Acta Psychologica, 27,* 57–63.

de Jong, F., & Sanders, A. F. (1986). Relative signal frequency imbalance does not affect perceptual encoding in choice reactions. *Acta Psychologica, 62,* 211–223.

de Jong, P. F. (1991). Het meten van aandacht [The measurement of attention]. Doctoral dissertation, Free University, Amsterdam.

de Jong, R. (1991). Partial information or facilitation? Different interpretations of the results from speed–accuracy decomposition. *Perception & Psychophysics, 50,* 333–350.

de Jong, R. (1993). Multiple bottlenecks in overlapping task performance. *Journal of Experimental Psychology: Human Perception & Performance, 19,* 965–980.

de Jong, R. (1995). Strategical determinants of compatibility effects with time uncertainty. *Acta Psychologica, 88,* 187–207.

de Jong, R., Coles, M. G. H., Logan, G. D., & Gratton, G. (1990). Searching for the point of no return: The control of response processes in speeded choice reaction performance. *Journal of Experimental Psychology: Human Perception & Performance, 16,* 164–182.

de Jong, R., Liang, C. C., & Lauber, E. H. (1994). Conditional and unconditional automaticity: A dual process model of effects of spatial stimulus–response correspondence. *Journal of Experimental Psychology: Human Perception & Performance, 20,* 731–750.

de Jong, R., Wierda, M., Mulder, G., & Mulder, L. J. M. (1988). Use of partial information and responding. *Journal of Experimental Psychology: Human Perception & Performance, 14,* 682–692.

de Klerk, L. F. W., & Oppe, S. (1970). Subjective probability and choice reaction time. *Acta Psychologica, 33,* 243–251.

Denny, M. R., Frisbey, N., & Weaver, J. (1955). Rotary pursuit performance under alternate conditions of distributed and massed practice. *Journal of Experimental Psychology, 49,* 48–59.

Detweiler, M. C., & Lundy, D. H. (1995). Effects of single and dual-task practice on acquiring dual-task skill. *Human Factors, 37,* 193–211.

Detweiler, M., & Schneider, W. (1991). Modelling the acquisition of dual task skill in a connectionist/control architecture. In D. L. Damos (Ed.), *Multiple task performance.* Philadelphia: Taylor & Francis.

Deutsch, J. A. (1977). On the category effect in visual search. *Perception & Psychophysics, 21,* 590–592.

Deutsch, J. A., & Deutsch, D. (1963). Attention: Some theoretical considerations. *Psychological Review, 70,* 80–90.

DeValois, R. L., Albrecht, D. G., & Thorell, L. G. (1982). Spatial frequency selectivity of cells in macaque visual cortex. *Vision Research, 22,* 545–559.

DeValois, R. L., Yund, E. W., & Hepler, N. (1982). The orientation and direction sensitivity of cells in macaque visual cortex. *Vision Research, 22,* 531–544.

Dillon, P. J. (1966). Stimulus versus response decisions as determinants of the relative frequency effect in disjunctive reaction time performance. *Journal of Experimental Psychology, 71,* 321–330.

Dinges, D. F., & Kribbs, N. B. (1991). Performing while sleepy: Effects of experimentally induced sleepiness. In T. H. Monk (Ed.), *Sleep, sleepiness and performance.* New York: Wiley.

Donchin, E. (1981). Surprise! . . . Surprise? *Psychophysiology, 14,* 456–467.

Donchin, E., & Coles, M. G. H. (1988). Is the P300 component a manifestation of context updating? *The Behavioral and Brain Sciences, 11,* 357–374.

Donchin, E., Kramer, A. F., & Wickens, C. D. (1986). Applications of brain event-related potentials to problems in engineering psychology. In M. G. H. Coles, E. Donchin, & S. W. Porges (Eds.), *Psychophysiology: Systems, processes and applications.* New York: Guilford.

Donders, F. C. (1868). Over de snelheid van psychische processen: Onderzoekingen gedaan in het physiologisch laboratorium van de Utrechtse Hoogeschool [On the speed of mental processes: Research from the physiological laboratory of the University of Utrecht]. Tweede Reeks, *11,* 92–130.

Donk, M. (1993). On the measurement of conspicuity and visibility for a feature and a conjunction target. In G. d'Ydewalle & J. van Rensbergen (Eds.), *Perception & Cognition: Advances in Eyemovement Research.* Amsterdam: North-Holland.

Donk, M. (1994a). Human monitoring behavior in a multi-instrument setting: Independent sampling, sequential sampling or arrangement dependent sampling? *Acta Psychologica, 86,* 31–55.

Donk, M. (1994b). The effect of secondary task load on visual sampling behaviour. *Ergonomics, 37,* 1089–1096.

Donk, M. (1995a). Nadiros: Ein computergestütztes Management Planspiel zur Auslese von Offizierbewerbern der Bundeswehr [Nadiros: A computerized management game for the selection of officers for the German army]. *Untersuchungen des psychologishen Dienstes der Bundeswehr 1993/1995.* Band 1. 215–381.

Donk, M. (1995b). Some evidence for unequal loss of location and feature information as a function of retinal eccentricity in visual search. *Visual Cognition, 2,* 201–220.

Donk, M., & Hagemeister, C. (1994). Visual instrument monitoring as affected by simultaneous self-paced card-sorting. *IEEE Transactions on Systems, Man and Cybernetics, 24,* 926–931.

Donk, M., & Sanders, A. F. (1989). Resources and dual task performance: Resource allocation versus task integration. *Acta Psychologica, 72,* 221–232.

Dornier, L. A., & Reeve, T. G. (1996). Evaluation of mental representation for same and mixed compatibility assignments. *Perception & Psychophysics, 58,* 47–55.

Dosher, B. A. (1979). Empirical approaches to information processing: Speed–accuracy tradeoff functions of reaction time—a reply. *Acta Psychologica, 43,* 347–359.

Dosher, B. A. (1981). The effects of delay and interference: A speed–accuracy study. *Cognitive Psychology, 13,* 551–582.

Downing, C. J. (1988). Expectancy and visual-spatial attention: Effects on perceptual quality. *Journal of Experimental Psychology: Human Perception & Performance, 14,* 188–202.

Downing, C. J., & Pinker, S. (1985). The spatial structure of visual attention. In M. I. Posner & O. M. Marin (Eds.), *Attention & Performance* (Vol. 11). Hillsdale, NJ: Lawrence Erlbaum Associates.

Driver, J., MacLeod, P., & Dienes, Z. (1992). Motion coherence and conjunction search: Implications for guided search theory. *Perception & Psychophysics, 51,* 79–85.

Drury, G. C. (1983). Task analysis methods in industry. *Applied Ergonomics, 14,* 19–28.

Drury, G. C. (1990). Visual search in industrial inspection. In D. Brogan (Ed.), *Visual search*. London: Tayler & Francis.

Duchon, J. C., Keran, C. M., & Smith, T. J. (1994). Extended workdays in an underground mine: A work performance analysis. *Human Factors, 36*, 258–268.

Duffy, E. (1957). The psychological significance of the concept of arousal or activation. *Psychological Review, 64*, 265–275.

Duffy, E. (1972). Activation. In R. S. Greenfield & R. A. Sternbach (Eds.), *Handbook of Psychophysiology*. New York: Holt, Rinehart & Winston.

Duncan, J. (1978). Response selection in spatial choice reaction: Further evidence against associative models. *Quarterly Journal of Experimental Psychology, 30*, 429–440.

Duncan, J. (1980). The locus of interference in the perception of simultaneous stimuli. *Psychological Review, 87*, 272–300.

Duncan, J. (1983). Perceptual selection based on alphanumerical class: Evidence from partial reports. *Perception & Psychophysics, 33*, 533–547.

Duncan, J. (1989). Boundary conditions on parallel processing in human vision. *Perception, 18*, 459–467.

Duncan, J., & Humphreys, G. W. (1989). Visual search and stimulus similarity. *Psychological Review, 96*, 433–458.

Duncan, J., & Humphreys, G. W. (1992). Beyond the search surface: Visual search and attentional engagement. *Journal of Experimental Psychology: Human Perception & Performance, 18*, 578–588.

Easterbrook, J. A. (1959). The effect of emotion on cue utilisation and the organisation of behaviour. *Psychological Review, 66*, 183–201.

Easterby, R. (1970). The perception of symbols for machine displays. *Ergonomics, 10*, 195–205.

Eberts, R. E., & Posey, J. W. (1990). The mental model in stimulus–response compatibility. In R. W. Proctor & T. G. Reeve (Eds.), *Stimulus–response compatibility* (pp. 389–425). Amsterdam: North-Holland.

Edwards, W. (1961). Costs and pay-offs are instructions. *Psychological Review, 68*, 275–284.

Edwards, W. (1966). Optimal strategies for seeking information: Models for statistics, choice reaction times and human information processing. *Journal of Mathematical Psychology, 2*, 312–329.

Eernst, J. T., & ter Linden, W. (1967). De invloed van de omvang van het gezichtsveld en van beeldvergroting op de rijprestatie in leger voertuigen [The effect of the size of the visual field and of image magnification on driving performance in military vehicles]. IZF report 1967–12.

Egeth, H., Jonides, J., & Wall, S. (1972). Parallel processing of multielement displays. *Cognitive Psychology, 3*, 674–698.

Egeth, H. E., Virzi, R. A., & Garbart, H. (1984). Searching for conjunctively defined targets. *Journal of Experimental Psychology: Human Perception & Performance, 10*, 32–39.

Egly, R., & Homa, D. (1984). Sensitisation of the visual field. *Journal of Experimental Psychology: Human Perception & Performance, 17*, 142–159.

Eichelman, W. H. (1970). Simulus and response repetition effects for naming letters. *Perception & Psychophysics, 7*, 94–96.

Eimer, M. (1994). An ERP study on visual-spatial priming with peripheral onsets. *Psychophysiology, 31*, 154–163.

Eimer, M. (1995). Stimulus-response compatibility and automatic response activation: Evidence from psychophysiological studies. *Journal of Experimental Psychology: Human Perception & Performance, 21*, 837–854.

Eimer, M., Hommel, B., & Prinz, W. (1995). S–R compatibility and response selection. *Acta Psychologica, 90*, 301–313.

Eimer, M., Nattkemper, D., Schröger, E., & Prinz, W. (1996). Involuntary attention. In O. Neumann & A. F. Sanders (Eds.), *Handbook of perception & action: Vol. 3. Attention.* London: Academic Press.

Elithorn, A., & Lawrence, C. (1955). Central inhibitions—some refractory observations. *Quarterly Journal of Experimental Psychology, 7,* 116–127.

Elliott, E. (1957). Auditory vigilance task. *Advancement of Science, 33,* 393–399.

Elliott, R. (1968). Simple visual and simple auditory reaction time: A comparison. *Psychonomic Science, 10,* 335–336.

Ellis, S. R., McGreevy, M. W., & Hitchcock, R. J. (1987). Perspective traffic display format and air pilot traffic avoidance. *Human Factors, 29,* 371–382.

Engel, F. L. (1976). *Visual conspicuity as an external determinant of eye movements and selective attention.* Doctoral dissertation, University of Eindhoven, The Netherlands.

Enns, J. T. (1990). Three dimensional features that pop out in visual search. In D. Brogan (Ed.), *Visual search.* London: Taylor & Francis.

Enns, J. T., & Rensink, R. A. (1992). A model for the rapid interpretation of line drawings in early vision. In D. Brogan, A. Gale, & K. Carr (Eds.), *Visual search: Vol. 2. Proceedings of the second international conference on visual search.* London: Taylor & Francis.

Eriksen, B. A., & Eriksen, C. W. (1974). Effects of noise letters upon the identification of a target letter in a non-search task. *Perception & Psychophysics, 16,* 143–149.

Eriksen, C. W., O'Hara, W. P., & Eriksen, B. A. (1982). Response competition effects in "same–different" judgements. *Perception & Psychophysics, 32,* 261–270.

Eriksen, C. W., & Rorbaugh, J. W. (1970). Some factors determining efficiency of selective attention. *American Journal of Psychology, 83,* 330–342.

Eriksen, C. W., & St. James, J. D. (1986). Visual attention within and around the field of focal attention: A zoom lens model. *Perception & Psychophysics, 40,* 225–240.

Eriksen, C. W., & Schultz, D. W. (1979). Information processing in visual search: A continuous flow conception and experimental results. *Perception & Psychophysics, 25,* 249–263.

Eriksen, C. W., & Webb, J. M. (1989). Shifting of attentional focus within and about a visual display. *Perception & Psychophysics, 45,* 175–183.

Eriksen, C. W., & Yeh, Y. Y. (1985). Allocation of attention in the visual field. *Journal of Experimental Psychology: Human Perception & Performance, 11,* 583–597.

Everett, B. L., Hochhaus, L., & Brown, J. R. (1985). Letter naming as a function of intensity: Degradation, S–R compatibility and practice. *Perception & Psychophysics, 37,* 467–470.

Exner, S. (1873). Experimentelle Untersuchung der einfachsten psychischen Prozesse [Experimental study of the simplest mental processes]. *Pflüger's Archiv der gesammten Physiologie, 7,* 601–660.

Eysenck, H. J. (1967). *The biological basis of personality.* Springfield: Thomas.

Eysenck, M. W. (1982). *Attention and arousal.* Berlin: Springer.

Eysenck, M. W. (1988). Individual differences, arousal and monotonous work. In J. P. Leonard (Ed.), *Vigilance: Methods, models and regulation.* Frankfurt: Lang.

Falkenstein, M., Hohnsbein, J., & Hoorman, J. (1993). Late visual and auditory components and choice reaction time. *Biological Psychology, 35,* 201–224.

Falmagne, J. C., Cohen, S. P., & Dwivedi, A. (1975). Two-choice reactions as an ordered memory scanning process. In P. M. A. Rabbitt & S. Dornic (Eds.), *Attention and Performance* (Vol. 5). London: Academic Press.

Farell, B. (1985). "Same–Different" judgments: A review of current controversies in perceptual comparisons. *Psychological Bulletin, 98,* 419–456.

Farina, A. J., & Wheaton, G. R. (1973). Development of taxonomy of human performance: The task characteristics approach to performance prediction. *JSAS Catalog of Selected Documents in Psychology, 3,* 323.

Finke, R. A., & Shephard, R. N. (1986). Visual functions and mental imagery. In K. R. Boff, L. Kaufman, & J. P. Thomas (Eds.), *Handbook of perception & human performance* (chap. 37). New York: Wiley.

Fisher, B., & Breitmeyer, B. (1987). Mechanisms of visual attention revealed by saccadic eye movements. *Neuropsychologia, 25*, 73–83.

Fisher, D. L., & Tan, K. C. (1989). Visual displays: The highlighting paradox. *Human Factors, 31*, 17–30.

Fisk, A. D., Ackerman, P. L., & Schneider, W. (1987). Automatic and controlled processing theory and its applications to human factors problems. In P. A. Hancock (Ed.), *Human factors psychology*. Amsterdam: North-Holland.

Fisk, A. D., & Hodge, K. A. (1992). Retention of trained performance in consistent mapping search after extended delay. *Human Factors, 34*, 147–164.

Fisk, A. D., & Jones, C. (1992). Global vs local inconsistency: Effects of degree of within-category inconsistency on performance and learning. *Human Factors, 34*, 693–705.

Fisk, A. D., & Scerbo, M. W. (1987). Automatic and controlled processing approach to interpreting vigilance performance: A review and re-evaluation. *Human Factors, 29*, 653–660.

Fisk, A. D., & Schneider, W. (1981). Controlled and automatic processing during tasks requiring sustained attention: A new approach to vigilance. *Human Factors, 23*, 737–750.

Fisk, A. D., & Schneider, W. (1983). Category and word search: Generalising search principles to complex processing. *Journal of Experimental Psychology: Learning, Memory & Cognition, 9*, 177–195.

Fitts, P. M. (1951a). *Human engineering for an effective air navigation and traffic control system*. Washington, DC: National Research Council.

Fitts, P. M. (1951b). Engineering psychology and equipment design. In S. S. Stevens (Ed.), *Handbook of experimental psychology* (pp. 1227–1340). New York: Wiley.

Fitts, P. M. (1966). Cognitive aspects of information processing. III: Set for speed versus accuracy. *Journal of Experimental Psychology, 71*, 849–857.

Fitts, P. M., & Deininger, R. L. (1954). S–R compatibility: Correspondence among paired elements within stimulus and response codes. *Journal of Experimental Psychology, 48*, 483–492.

Fitts, P. M., Jones, R. E., & Milton, J. L. (1950). Eye movements of aircraft pilots during instrument landing operations. *Aeronautical Engineering Review, 9*, 1–5.

Fitts, P. M., & Peterson, J. R. (1964). Information capacity of discrete motor responses. *Journal of Experimental Psychology, 67*, 103–112.

Fitts, P. M., Peterson, J. R., & Wolfe, G. (1963). Cognitive aspects of information processing: Adjustments to stimulus redundancy. *Journal of Experimental Psychology, 65*, 423–432.

Fitts, P. M., & Seeger, C. M. (1953). S–R compatibility: Spatial characteristics of stimulus and response codes. *Journal of Experimental Psychology, 46*, 199–210.

Flach, J. M. (1990). The ecology of human-machine systems. I Introduction. *Ecological Psychology, 2*, 191–205.

Fleishman, E. A., & Hempel, W. E. (1955). The relation between abilities and improvement with practice in a visual discrimination task. *Journal of Experimental Psychology, 49*, 301–312.

Fleishman, E. A., & Quaintance, M. K. (1984). *Taxonomies of human performance*. New York: Academic Press.

Flexman, R. E., & Stark, E. A. (1987). Training simulators. In G. Salvendy (Ed.), *Handbook of human factors*. New York: Wiley.

Fodor, J. A. (1975). *The language of thought*. Cambridge, MA: Harvard University Press.

Folkard, S. (1983). Diurnal variation. In G. R. J. Hockey (Ed.), *Stress and fatigue in human performance*. New York: Wiley.

Folkard, S., & Monk, Th. (1985). Circadian performance rhythms. In S. Folkard & Th. Monk (Eds.), *Hours of work: Temporal factors in work scheduling*. London: Wiley.

Folkard, S., Wever, R. A., & Wildgruber, C. M. (1983). Multioscillatory control of circadian rhythms in human performance. *Nature, 305,* 223–226.

Forrin, B., & Morin, R. (1966). Effect of contextual associations upon selective reaction time in a numeral naming task. *Journal of Experimental Psychology, 71,* 40–46.

Forster, K. I. (1994). Computational modeling and elementary process analysis in visual word recognition. *Journal of Experimental Psychology: Human Perception & Performance, 20,* 1292–1310.

Fowler, B. (1994). P300 as a measure of workload during a simulated aircraft landing task. *Human Factors, 36,* 670–683.

Fox, J. G. (1975). Vigilance and arousal: A key to maintaining inspector's performance. In C. G. Drury & J. G. Fox (Eds.), *Human factors in quality control.* London: Taylor & Francis.

Fracker, M. L., & Wickens, C. D. (1989). Resources, confusions and compatibility in dual axis tracking: Displays controls and dynamics. *Journal of Experimental Psychology: Human Perception & Performance, 15,* 80–96.

Fraisse, P. (1969). Why is naming longer than reading? *Acta Psychologica, 30,* 96–104.

Francolini, C. M., & Egeth, H. E. (1979). On the non-automaticity of "automatic" activation: Evidence of selective seeing. *Perception & Psychophysics, 25,* 99–110.

Frankenhaeuser, M. (1986). A psychobiological framework for research on human stress and coping. In R. H. Appley & R. Trumbell (Eds.), *Dynamics of stress: Physiological, psychological and social perspectives* (pp. 101–116). New York: Plenum.

Freeman, G. L. (1940). The relationship between performance level and bodily activity level. *Journal of Experimental Psychology, 27,* 602–608.

Freeman, G. L., & Kendall, W. E. (1940). The effect upon reaction time of muscular tension induced at various preparatory intervals. *Journal of Experimental Psychology, 27,* 136–148.

French, J. W., Ekstrom, R. B., & Price, L. A. (1963). *Kit of reference tests for cognitive factors.* Princeton, NJ: Educational Testing Service.

Frewer, L. J., & Hindmarch, I. (1988). The effects of time-of-the-day, age and anxiety on a choice reaction task. In I. Hindmarch, B. Aufdembrinke, & H. Ott (Eds.), *Psychopharmacology and reaction time.* New York: Wiley.

Fröhlich, J. (1994). *Vorhersage pharmakologischer Leistungsbeeintrachtigung des Fahrverhaltens im Strassenverkehr aufgrund von Labortests* [Prediction of pharmacological effects on driving performance on the basis of laboratory tests]. Doctoral dissertation, RWTH Aachen, Germany.

Frowein, H. W. (1981). Selective effects of barbiturate and amphetamine on information processing and response execution. *Acta Psychologica, 47,* 105–115.

Frowein, H. W., Gaillard, A. W. K., & Varey, C. A. (1981). EP components, visual processing stages and the effect of a barbiturate. *Biological Psychology, 13,* 239–249.

Frowein, H. W., Reitsma, D., & Aquarius, C. (1981). Effects of two counteracting stresses on the reaction process. In J. Long & A. D. Baddeley (Eds.), *Attention & Performance* (Vol. 9). Hillsdale, NJ: Lawrence Erlbaum Associates.

Frowein, H. W., & Sanders, A. F. (1978). Effects of visual stimulus degradation, S–R compatibility and foreperiod duration on choice reaction time and movement time. *Bulletin of the Psychonomic Society, 12,* 106–108.

Galinsky, T., Rosa, R. R., Warm, J. S., & Dember, W. N. (1993). Psychophysical determinants of stress in sustained attention. *Human Factors, 35,* 603–614.

Gardner, G. T. (1973). Evidence for independent parallel channels in tachistoscopic perception. *Cognitive Psychology, 4,* 130–155.

Garner, W. R. (1962). *Uncertainty and structure as psychological concepts.* New York: Wiley.

Garner, W. R. (1974). *The processing of information and structure.* Hillsdale, NJ: Lawrence Erlbaum Associates.

Garner, W. R. (1988). Facilitation and interference with a separable redundant dimension in stimulus comparison. *Perception & Psychophysics, 44,* 321–330.

Garner, W. R., & Felfoldy, G. L. (1970). Integrality of stimulus dimensions in various types of information processing. *Cognitive Psychology, 1,* 225–241.

Gehring, W. J., & Knight, R. T. (in preparation). An electrophysiological study of prefrontal executive control. Manuscript in preparation.

Geissler, W. S., & Chou, K-L. (1995). Separation of low-level and high-level factors in complex tasks. *Psychological Review, 102,* 356–378.

Gentner, D. R. (1983). The acquisition of typewriting skill. *Acta Psychologica, 54,* 233–248.

Gentner, D. R. (1987). Timing of skilled motor performance: Tests of the proportional duration model. *Psychological Review, 94,* 255–276.

Gibson, J. J. (1950). *The perception of the visual world.* Boston: Houghton Mifflin.

Gladstones, W. H., Regan, M. A., & Lee, R. B. (1989). Division of attention: The single channel hypothesis revisited. *Quarterly Journal of Experimental Psychology, 41,* 1–17.

Glaser, M. O., & Glaser, W. R. (1982). Time course analysis of the Stroop phenomenon. *Journal of Experimental Psychology: Human Perception & Performance, 8,* 875–894.

Glencross, D., & Barrett, N. (1992). The processing of visual feedback in rapid movements revisited. In J. J. Summers (Ed.), *Approaches to the study of motor control and learning.* Amsterdam: North-Holland.

Godthelp, H., Milgram, P., & Blaauw, G. J. (1984). The development of a time-related measure to describe driving strategy. *Human Factors, 26,* 257–268.

Gopher, D. (1982). A selective attention test as a predictor of success in flight training. *Human Factors, 24,* 173–183.

Gopher, D. (1984). On the contribution of vision-based imagery to the acquisition and operation of a transcription skill. In W. Prinz & A. F. Sanders (Eds.), *Cognition and motor behavior.* Heidelberg: Springer.

Gopher, D. (1986). In defense of resources: On structures, energies, pools and the allocation of attention. In G. R. J. Hockey, A. W. K. Gaillard, & M. G. H. Coles (Eds.), *Energetics and human information processing.* Dordrecht, The Netherlands: Nijhoff.

Gopher, D. (1992). The skill of attention control: Acquisition and execution of attention strategies. In D. Meyer & S. Kornblum (Eds.), *Attention & Performance* (Vol. 14). Cambridge, MA: MIT Press.

Gopher, D., Brickner, M., & Navon, D. (1982). Different difficulty manipulations interact differently with task emphasis: Evidence for multiple resources. *Journal of Experimental Psychology: Human Perception & Performance, 8,* 146–157.

Gopher, D., & Donchin, E. (1986). Work load: An examination of the concept. In K. R. Boff, L. Kaufman, & J. P. Thomas (Eds.), *Handbook of perception & human performance* (chap. 41). New York: Wiley.

Gopher, D., Karis, D., & Koenig, W. (1985). The representation of movement schemas in long-term memory: Lessons from the acquisition of a transcription skill. *Acta Psychologica, 60,* 105–134.

Gopher, D.; & Sanders, A. F. (1984). S-Oh-R: Oh stages! Oh resources! In W. Prinz & A. F. Sanders (Eds.), *Cognition and motor behavior.* Heidelberg: Springer.

Gopher, D., Weil, M., & Bareket, T. (1994). Transfer of skill from a computer game trainer to flight. *Human Factors, 36,* 387–405.

Gopher, D., Weil, M., & Siegel, D. (1989). Practice under changing priorities: An approach to training of complex skills. *Acta Psychologica, 71,* 147–179.

Gottsdanker, R. (1975). The attaining and maintaining of preparation. In P. M. A. Rabbitt & S. Dornic (Eds.), *Attention and Performance* (Vol. 5, pp. 33–49). London: Academic Press.

Gottsdanker, R., & Shragg, G. P. (1985). Verification of Donders' subtraction method. *Journal of Experimental Psychology: Human Perception & Performance, 11,* 765–776.

Gottsdanker, R., & Stelmach, G. E. (1971). The persistence of psychological refractoriness. *Journal of Motor Behavior, 3,* 301–312.

Gottsdanker, R., & Way, T. C. (1966). Varied and constant intersignal intervals in psychological refractoriness. *Journal of Experimental Psychology, 84*, 392–398.

Gould, J. D., & Dill, A. (1969). Eye movement patterns and pattern recognition. *Perception & Psychophysics, 6*, 311–320.

Grainger, J., & Jacobs, A. M. (1994). A dual read-out model of word context effects in letter perception: Further investigations of the word superiority effect. *Journal of Experimental Psychology: Human Perception & Performance, 20*, 1158–1176.

Gratton, G., Coles, M. G. H., & Donchin, E. (1992). Optimizing the use of information: Strategic control of activation of responses. *Journal of Experimental Psychology: General, 121*, 480–506.

Graves, M. K., Ball, K. K., Cissell, G. M., West, R. E., Whorley, K., & Edwards, J. D. (1993). Auditory distraction results in functional visual impairment for some older drivers. *Investigative Opthalmology and Visual Science, 34*, 1418.

Gray, J. A. (1987). *The neuropsychology of anxiety.* Oxford: Oxford University Press.

Gray, J. A., & Wedderburn, A. A. I. (1960). Grouping strategies with simultaneous stimuli. *Quarterly Journal of Experimental Psychology, 12*, 180–184.

Greany, J., & MacRae, A. N. (1996). Diagnosis of fault location using polygon displays. *Ergonomics, 39*, 400–411.

Green, C. A., Logie, R. H., Gilhooly, K. J., Ross, D. G., & Ronald, A. (1996). Aberdeen polygons: Computer displays of physiological profiles for intensive care. *Ergonomics, 39*, 412–428.

Green, D. M., & Swets J. A. (1966). *Signal detection theory and psychophysics.* New York: Wiley.

Greenwald, A. G. (1970). Sensory feedback mechanisms in performance control: With special reference to the ideomotor mechanism. *Psychological Review, 77*, 73–99.

Greenwald, A. G., & Shulman, H. G. (1973). On doing two things at once: II Elimination of the psychological refractory period effect. *Journal of Experimental Psychology, 101*, 70–76.

Grice, G. R. (1968). Stimulus intensity and response evocation. *Psychological Review, 75*, 359–373.

Grice, G. R. (1972). Application of a variable criterion model to auditory reaction time as a function of the type of catch trial. *Perception & Psychophysics, 12*, 103–107.

Grice, G. R., Hunt, R. L., Kushner, B. A., & Morrow, C. H. (1974). Stimulus intensity, catch trial effects and the speed–accuracy trade-off in reaction time. *Memory & Cognition, 2*, 758–770.

Grice, G. R., & Hunter, J. J. (1964). Stimulus intensity effects depend on the type of experimental design. *Psychological Review, 71*, 247–256.

Grice, G. R., Nullmeyer, R., & Spiker, V. A. (1982). Human reaction times: Towards a general theory. *Journal of Experimental Psychology: General, 111*, 135–153.

Grossberg, S. (1987). Competitive learning: From interactive activation to adaptive resonance. *Cognitive Science, 11*, 23–63.

Guilford, J. P. (1967). *The nature of human intelligence.* New York: McGraw-Hill.

Haber, R. N. (1983). The impending demise of the icon: A critique of the concept of iconic storage in visual information processing. *The Behavioral & Brain Sciences, 6*, 1–54.

Hake, H. W., & Garner, W. R. (1951). The effect of presenting various numbers of discrete steps on scale reading accuracy. *Journal of Experimental Psychology, 42*, 358–366.

Häkkinen, A. (1976). Traffic accidents and psychomotor performance. *Modern Problems of Psychopharmacology, 11*, 51–87.

Hamilton, P., Hockey, G. R. J., & Quinn, J. G. (1972). Information selection, arousal and memory. *British Journal of Psychology, 63*, 181–189.

Hamilton, P., Hockey, G. R. J., & Reyman, R. (1977). The place of the concept of activation in human information processing. In S. Dornic (Ed.), *Attention & Performance* (Vol. 6). Hillsdale, NJ: Lawrence Erlbaum Associates.

Hancock, P. A. (Ed.). (1987). *Human factors psychology.* Amsterdam: North-Holland.

Hancock, P. A., & Warm, J. S. (1989). A dynamic model of stress and sustained attention. *Human Factors, 31,* 519–537.

Hansen, W., & Sanders, A. F. (1988). On the output of encoding during stimulus fixation. *Acta Psychologica, 69,* 95–107.

Hansen, R. S., & Well, A. D. (1984). The effects of stimulus sequence and probability on perceptual processing. *Perception & Psychophysics, 35,* 137–145.

Harm, O. J., & Lappin, J. S. (1973). Probability, compatibility, speed and accuracy. *Journal of Experimental Psychology, 100,* 416–418.

Harman, H. H. (1961). Simulation: A survey. (*Report No. SP-260*). Santa Monica, CA: System Development Corporation.

Harpster, J., Freivalds, A., Shulman, G., & Leibowitz, H. (1989). Visual performance on CRT screens and hard-copy displays. *Human Factors, 31,* 247–257.

Harris, R., Iavecchia, H. P., & Dick, A. O. (1989). The human operator simulator (HOS-4). In G. R. McMillan, D. Beevis, E. Salas, M. H. Strub, R. Sutton, & L. van Breda (Eds.), *Applications of human performance models to system design.* New York: Plenum.

Hawkins, H., & Presson, J. (1986). Auditory information processing. In K. R. Boff, L. Kaufman, & J. P. Thomas (Eds.), *Handbook of perception & human performance* (chap. 26). New York: Wiley.

Heathcote, A., Popiel, S. J., & Mewhort, D. J. K. (1991). Analysis of response time distributions: An example using the Stroop task. *Psychological Bulletin, 109,* 340–347.

Hebb, D. O. (1949). *The organisation of behavior: A neurophysiological theory.* New York: Wiley.

Hebb, D. O. (1955). Drives and the C.N.S. (Conceptual Nervous System). *Psychological Review, 62,* 243–254.

Hedge, A., & Marsh, N. W. A. (1975). The effect of irrelevant spatial correspondence on two-choice response time. *Acta Psychologica, 39,* 427–439.

Helmuth, L. L., & Ivry, R. B. (1996). When two hands are better than one: Reduced timing variability during bimanual movements. *Journal of Experimental Psychology: Human Perception & Performance, 22,* 278–293.

Hendrikx, A. J. P. (1984). Temporal aspects of retrieval in short-term serial retention. *Acta Psychologica, 57,* 193–214.

Henning, H. (1925). Die Untersuchung der Aufmerksamkeit [Research on attention]. In E. Abderhalden (Ed.), *Handbuch der biologischen Arbeitsmethoden* (Abschnitt 3). Berlin: Urban & Schwarzenberg.

Henry, F. M., & Rogers, D. E. (1960). Increased response latency for complicated movements and a "memory drum" theory of neuromotor reaction. *Research Quarterly for Exercise and Sport, 31,* 448–458.

Heuer, H. (1984). Motor learning as a process of structural constriction and displacement. In W. Prinz & A. F. Sanders (Eds.), *Cognition & motor behavior.* Heidelberg: Springer.

Heuer, H. (1985). Some points of contact between models of central capacity and factor-analytic models. *Acta Psychologica, 60,* 135–155.

Heuer, H. (1990). Rapid responses with the left or right hand: Response–Response compatibility effects due to intermanual interactions. In R. W. Proctor & T. G. Reeve (Eds.), *Stimulus–response compatibility.* Amsterdam: North-Holland.

Heuer, H. (1996). Dual task performance. In O. Neumann & A. F. Sanders (Eds.), *Handbook of perception & action: Vol. 3. Attention.* London: Academic Press.

Hick, W. E. (1952). On the rate of gain of information. *Quarterly Journal of Experimental Psychology, 4,* 11–26.

Hillyard, S. A., & Münte, T. F. (1984). Selective attention to color and location: An analysis with event-related brain potentials. *Perception & Psychophysics, 36,* 185–198.

Hirst, W., & Kalmar, D. (1987). Characterising attentional resources. *Journal of Experimental Psychology: General, 116,* 68–81.

Hirst, W., Spelke, E. S., Reaves, C. C., Caharack, G., & Neisser, U. (1980). Dividing attention without alternation and automaticity. *Journal of Experimental Psychology: General, 109,* 98–117.

Hockey, G. R. J. (1970a). Effect of loud noise on attentional selectivity. *Quarterly Journal of Experimental Psychology, 22,* 28–36.

Hockey, G. R. J. (1970b). Changes in attention allocation in a multicomponent task under loss of sleep. *British Journal of Psychology, 61,* 473–480.

Hockey, G. R. J. (1986). Operator efficiency as a function of effects of environmental stress, fatigue and circadian rhythm. In K. R. Boff, L. Kaufman, & J. P. Thomas (Eds.), *Handbook of perception & human performance* (chap. 44). New York: Wiley.

Hockey, G. R. J. (1993). Cognitive-energetical control mechanisms in the management of work demands and psychological health. In A. D. Baddeley & L. Weiskrantz (Eds.), *Attention: Selection, awareness and control* (pp. 36–52). Oxford: Clarendon.

Hockey, G. R. J., & Wiethoff, M. (1990). Assessing patterns of adjustment to the demands of work. In S. Puglisi-Allegra & A. Oliverio (Eds.), *Psychobiology of stress.* Dordrecht, The Netherlands: Kluwer.

Hoffman, J. E. (1986). Spatial attention in vision: Evidence for early selection. *Psychological Research, 48,* 221–229.

Hoffman, J. E., & Subramaniam, B. (1995). The role of visual attention in saccadic eye movements. *Perception & Psychophysics, 57,* 787–795.

Hohle, R. H. (1965). Inferred components of reaction times as functions of foreperiod duration. *Journal of Experimental Psychology, 69,* 382–386.

Holender, D., & Bertelson, P. (1975). Selective preparation and time uncertainty. *Acta Psychologica, 39,* 193–203.

Hommel, B. (1995). Stimulus–response compatibility and the Simon effect: Toward an empirical clarification. *Journal of Experimental Psychology: Human Perception & Performance, 21,* 764–775.

Houtmans, M. J. M., & Sanders, A. F. (1983). Is information acquisition during large saccades possible? *Bulletin of the Psychonomic Society, 21,* 127–130.

Houtmans, M. J. M., & Sanders, A. F. (1984). Perception of signals presented in the periphery of the functional visual field. *Acta Psychologica, 55,* 143–155.

Hughes, T., & MacRae, A. W. (1994). Holistic peripheral processing of a polygon display. *Human Factors, 36,* 645–651.

Hull, C. L. (1943). *Principles of behavior.* New York: Appleton-Century-Crofts.

Humphrey, D. G., & Kramer, A. F. (1994). Towards a psychophysiological assessment of dynamic changes in mental workload. *Human Factors, 36,* 3–26.

Humphrey, D. G., Kramer, A. F., & Stanny, R. R. (1994). Influence of extended wakefulness on automatic and non-automatic processing. *Human Factors, 36,* 652–669.

Humphreys, G. W., & Müller, H. J. (1993). Search via recursive rejection (SERR): A connectionist model of visual search. *Cognitive Psychology, 25,* 43–110.

Humphreys, G. W., Quinlan, P. T., & Riddoch, M. J. (1989). Grouping processes in visual search: Effects with single and combined feature targets. *Journal of Experimental Psychology: General, 118,* 258–279.

Humphreys, G. W., Riddoch, M. J., & Quinlan, P. T. (1985). Interactive processes in perceptual organisation: Evidence from visual agnosia. In M. I. Posner & M. Marin (Eds.), *Attention & Performance* (Vol. 11). Hillsdale, NJ: Lawrence Erlbaum Associates.

Hyman, R. (1953). Stimulus information as a determinant of reaction time. *Journal of Experimental Psychology, 45,* 188–196.

Ilan, A. B., & Miller, J. (1994). A violation of pure insertion: Mental rotation and choice reaction time. *Journal of Experimental Psychology: Human Perception & Performance, 20,* 520–536.

Imhoff, D. L., & Levine, J. M. (1981). Perceptual-motor and cognitive performance task battery for pilot selection. *AFHRL TR 80–27.* Brooks AFB, Texas.

Inhoff, A. W., & Rayner, K. (1986). Parafoveal word processing during eye fixations in reading: Effects of word frequency. *Perception & Psychophysics, 40,* 431–439.

Irwin, D. E. (1991). Information integration across saccadic eye movements. *Cognitive Psychology, 23,* 420–456.

Irwin, D. E. (1992). Memory for position and identity across eye movements. *Journal of Experimental Psychology: Learning, Memory & Cognition, 18,* 307–317.

Irwin, D. E., Carlson-Radvansky, L. A., & Andrews, R. V. (1995). Information processing during saccadic eye movements. *Acta Psychologica, 90,* 261–273.

Israel, J. B., Chesney, G. L., Wickens, C. D., & Donchin, E. (1980). P300 and tracking difficulty: Evidence for multiple resources in dual task performance. *Psychophysiology, 17,* 259–273.

Israel, J., Wickens, C. D., & Donchin, E. (1980). The event-related brain potential as a selective index of display monitoring load. *Human Factors, 22,* 211–224.

Ivry, R. B. (1986). Force and timing components of the motor program. *Journal of Motor Behavior, 18,* 449–474.

Jacobs, A. M. (1987). Towards a model of eye movement control in visual search. In J. K. O'Regan & A. Levi-Schoen (Eds.), *Eye movements: From physiology to cognition.* Amsterdam: North-Holland.

Jacoby, L. L. (1991). A process dissociation framework: Separating automatic from intentional uses of memory. *Journal of Memory and Language, 30,* 513–541.

James, W. (1890). *Principles of psychology.* New York: Holt, Rinehart & Winston.

Janssen, W. H. (1979). Route planning en geleiding [Planning and leading the course of a trip]. IZF 1979–C13. TNO, Soesterberg, The Netherlands.

Jerison, H. J. (1959). Effects of noise on human performance. *Journal of Applied Psychology, 43,* 96–101.

Jerison, H. J., Pickett, R. M., & Stenson, H. H. (1965). The elicited observing rate and decision processes in vigilance. *Human Factors, 7,* 107–125.

Johannson, G. (1978). Social, psychological and neuroendocrine stress reactions in highly mechanical work. *Ergonomics, 21,* 583–599.

Johnson, D. N., & Yantis, S. (1995). Allocating visual attention: Tests of a two-process model. *Journal of Experimental Psychology: Human Perception & Performance, 21,* 1376–1390.

Johnston, J. C. (1978). A test of the sophisticated guessing theory of word perception. *Cognitive Psychology, 10,* 123–154.

Johnston, W. A., & Dark, V. J. (1986). Selective attention. *Annual Review of Psychology, 37,* 43–75.

Jonides, J. (1981). Voluntary versus automatic control over the mind's eye movement. In J. Long & A. D. Baddeley (Eds.), *Attention & Performance* (Vol. 9). Hillsdale, NJ: Lawrence Erlbaum Associates.

Jonides, J. (1983). Further towards a model of the mind's eye movement. *Bulletin of the Psychonomic Society, 21,* 247–250.

Jonides, J., & Gleitman, H. (1976). The benefit of categorisation in visual search: Target location without identification. *Perception & Psychophysics, 20,* 289–298.

Jonides, J., & Mack, R. (1984). On the cost and benefit of cost and benefit. *Psychological Bulletin, 96,* 29–44.

Jonides, J., & Yantis, S. (1988). Uniqueness of abrupt visual onset in capturing attention. *Perception & Psychophysics, 43,* 346–354.

Jorna, P. G. A. M. (1981). Stress, information processing and diving. *IZF 81–4,* TNO, Soesterberg, The Netherlands.

Jorna, P. G. A. M. (1992). Spectral analysis of heart rate and psychological state: A review of its validity as a workload index. *Biological Psychology, 34*, 237–258.

Juola, J. F., Koshino, H., & Warner, C. B. (1995). Tradeoffs between attentional effects of spatial cues and abrupt onsets. *Perception & Psychophysics, 57*, 333–342.

Juola, J. F., Bouwhuis, D. G., Cooper, E. E., & Warner, C. B. (1991). Control of attention around the fovea. *Journal of Experimental Psychology: Human Perception & Performance, 17*, 125–141.

Just, M. A., & Carpenter, P. A. (1976). Eye fixations and cognitive processes. *Cognitive Psychology, 8*, 441–480.

Just, M. A., & Carpenter, P. A. (1980). A theory of reading: From eye fixations to comprehension. *Psychological Review, 87*, 329–354.

Just, M. A., & Carpenter, P. A. (1985). Cognitive coordinate systems: Accounts of mental rotation and individual differences in spatial ability. *Psychological Review, 92*, 137–171.

Kahneman, D. (1973). *Attention and effort.* Englewood Cliffs, NJ: Prentice-Hall.

Kahneman, D., Ben Ishai, R., & Lotan, M. (1973). Relation of a test of attention to road accidents. *Journal of Applied Psychology, 58*, 113–115.

Kahneman, D., & Chajczyk, D. (1983). Tests of automaticity of reading: Dilution of Stroop effects by color-irrelevant stimuli. *Journal of Experimental Psychology: Human Perception & Performance, 9*, 497–509.

Kahneman, D., & Henick, A. (1981). Perceptual organization and attention. In M. Kubovy & J. R. Pommerantz (Eds.), *Perceptual organization.* Hillsdale, NJ: Lawrence Erlbaum Associates.

Kahneman, D., & Treisman, A. (1984). Changing views on attention and automaticity. In R. Parasuraman & R. Davies (Eds.), *Varieties of Attention.* New York: Academic Press.

Kail, R. (1991). Controlled and automatic processing during mental rotation. *Journal of Experimental Child Psychology, 51*, 337–347.

Kalsbeek, J. W. H. (1967). *Mentale belasting [Mental Load].* Doctoral dissertation. University of Amsterdam.

Kantowitz, B. H. (1974). Double stimulation. In B. H. Kantowitz (Ed.), *Human information processing: Tutorials in performance and cognition.* Hillsdale, NJ: Lawrence Erlbaum Associates.

Kantowitz, B. H., & Sorkin, R. D. (1987). Allocation of functions. In G. Salvendy (Ed.), *Handbook of human factors.* New York: Wiley.

Kantowitz, B. H., Triggs, T. J., & Barnes, V. E. (1990). Stimulus–response compatibility and human factors. In R. W. Proctor & T. G. Reeve (Eds.), *Stimulus–response compatibility.* Amsterdam: North-Holland.

Kaptein, N. A., Theeuwes, J., & van der Heijden, A. H. C. (1995). Search for a conjunctively defined target can be selectively limited to a color-defined subset of elements. *Journal of Experimental Psychology: Human Perception & Performance, 21*, 1053–1069.

Kaptein, N. A., Theeuwes, J., & van der Horst, R. (1996). Driving simulator validity: Some considerations. Seventy-fifth annual meeting of the Transportation Research Board, Washington, DC.

Karlin, L. (1959). Reaction time as a function of foreperiod duration and variability. *Journal of Experimental Psychology, 58*, 185–191.

Karlin, L., & Kestenbaum, R. (1968). Effects of number of alternatives on the psychological refractory period. *Quarterly Journal of Experimental Psychology, 20*, 167–178.

Keele, S. W. (1973). *Attention and human performance.* Pacific Palisades, CA: Goodyear.

Keele, S. W. (1986). Motor control. In K. R. Boff, L. Kaufman, & J. P. Thomas (Eds.), *Handbook of perception & human performance* (chap. 30). New York: Wiley.

Keele, S. W., Pokorny, R. A., Corcos, D. M., & Ivry, R. (1985). Do perception and motor production share common timing mechanism? A correlational analysis. *Acta Psychologica, 60*, 173–191.

Kelly, M. J. (1988). Performance during simulated air-to-air combat. *Human Factors, 30,* 495–506.

Kimble, G. A. (1949). An experimental test of a two factor theory of inhibition. *Journal of Experimental Psychology, 39,* 15–23.

Kimchi, R. (1992). Primacy of wholistic processing and global/local paradigm: A critical review. *Psychological Bulletin, 112,* 24–38.

Kinsbourne, M., & Hicks, R. (1978). Functional cerebral space. In J. Requin (Ed.), *Attention & Performance* (Vol. 7). Hillsdale, NJ: Lawrence Erlbaum Associates.

Kirby, N. H. (1980). Sequential effects in choice reaction time. In A. T. Welford (Ed.), *Reaction times* (pp. 129–172). New York: Academic Press.

Kirby, N. H. (1976a). Sequential effects in an eight-choice serial reaction time task using compatible and incompatible stimulus–response relations. *Acta Psychologica, 40,* 207–216.

Kirby, N. H. (1976b). Sequential effects in two-choice reaction time: Automatic facilitation or subjective expectancy? *Journal of Experimental Psychology: Human Perception & Performance, 2,* 567–577.

Klapp, S. T. (1981a). Motor programming is not the only process which can influence RT: Some thoughts on the Martiniuk & MacKenzie analysis. *Journal of Motor Behavior, 3,* 320–328.

Klapp, S. T. (1981b). Temporal compatibility in dual motor tasks: II. Simultaneous articulation and hand movements. *Memory & Cognition, 9,* 398–401.

Klapp, S. T. (1995). Motor response programming during simple and choice reaction time: The role of practice. *Journal of Experimental Psychology: Human Perception & Performance, 21,* 1015–1027.

Klapp, S. T., & Erwin, C. I. (1976). Relation between programming time and duration of the response being programmed. *Journal of Experimental Psychology: Human Perception & Performance, 2,* 591–598.

Klein, K. E., Wegmann, H. M., & Hunt, B. I. (1972). Desynchronization of body temperature and performance circadian rhythm as a result of outgoing and homegoing transmeridian flights. *Aerospace Medicine, 43,* 119–132.

Klein, R. M., & Farrell, M. (1989). Search performance without eye movements. *Perception & Psychophysics, 46,* 476–482.

Klein, R. M., & Posner, M. I. (1974). Attention to visual and kinesthetic components of skill. *Brain Research, 71,* 401–411.

Kline, D. W., & Fuchs, P. (1993). The visibility of symbolic highway signs can be increased among drivers of all ages. *Human Factors, 35,* 25–34.

Knowles, W. B. (1963). Operator loading tasks. *Human Factors, 5,* 151–161.

Koch, R. (1993). *Die Psychologische Refraktärperiode* [The psychological refractory period]. Frankfurt/Main: Lang.

Koelega, H. S. (1990). Vigilance performance: A review of electrodermal predictors. *Perceptual & Motor Skills, 70,* 1011–1029.

Koelega, H. S. (1991). *Studies of human vigilance performance.* Doctoral dissertation, University of Utrecht, The Netherlands.

Koelega, H. S. (1996). Sustained attention. In O. Neumann & A. F. Sanders (Eds.), *Handbook of perception & action: Vol. 3. Attention.* London: Academic Press.

Koelega, H. S., Brinkman, J. A., Hendriks, L., & Verbaten, M. N. (1989). Processing demands, effort and individual differences in four different vigilance tasks. *Human Factors, 31,* 45–62.

Koelega, H. S., & Verbaten, M. N. (1991). Event-related potentials and vigilance performance: Dissociations abound. A review. *Perceptual & Motor Skills, 72,* 971–982.

Koelega, H. S., Verbaten, M. N., van Leeuwen, T. H., & Kenemans, J. L. (1992). Time effects on event-related potentials and vigilance performance. *Biological Psychology, 34,* 59–86.

Kohfeld, D. L. (1971). Simple reaction time as a function of stimulus intensity in decibels of light and sound. *Journal of Experimental Psychology, 88,* 251–257.

Kohfeld, D. L., Santee J. L., & Wallace N. D. (1981). Loudness and reaction time. *Perception & Psychophysics, 29,* 535–549.

Köhler, W. (1925). Gestalttheorie und Komplextheorie [Gestalt theory and complex theory]. *Psychologische Forschung, 6,* 358–416.

Köhler, W. (1947). *Gestalt psychology.* New York: Liveright.

Kok, A. (1986). Effects of degradation of visual stimuli on components of the event-related potential in go/no-go reactions. *Biological Psychology, 23,* 21–38.

Kok, A., & Looren de Jong, H. (1980). Components of the event-related potential following degraded and undegraded visual stimuli. *Biological Psychology, 11,* 117–133.

Kooi, F. L., & Valeton, J. M. (1997). Quantifying the conspicuity of objects in real scenes. TM 97. TNO, Soesterberg, The Netherlands.

Koonce, J. M. (1979). Predictive validity of flight simulators as a function of simulator motion. *Human Factors, 21,* 215–223.

Koriat, A., & Norman, J. (1988). Frames and images: Sequential effects in mental rotation. *Journal of Experimental Psychology: Learning, Memory and Cognition, 14,* 93–111.

Kornblum, S. (1967). Choice-reaction time for repetitions and non-repetitions: A reexamination of the information hypothesis. *Acta Psychologica, 27,* 178–187.

Kornblum, S. (1969). Sequential determinants of information processing in serial and discrete choice reaction time. *Psychological Review, 76,* 113–131.

Kornblum, S. (1973). Sequential effects in choice reaction time: A tutorial review. In S. Kornblum (Ed.), *Attention and Performance* (Vol. 4). New York: Academic Press.

Kornblum, S. (1975). An invariance in choice reaction time with varying numbers of alternatives and constant probability. In P. M. A. Rabbitt & S. Dornic (Eds.), *Attention and Performance* (Vol. 5). London: Academic Press.

Kornblum, S., Hasbroucq, T., & Osman, A. (1990). Dimensional overlap: Cognitive basis for stimulus–response compatibility. A model and taxonomy. *Psychological Review, 97,* 253–270.

Kornblum, S., & Ju-Whei, Lee (1995). Stimulus–response compatibility with relevant and irrelevant stimulus dimensions that do and do not overlap with the response. *Journal of Experimental Psychology: Human Perception & Performance, 21,* 855–875.

Korteling, J. E. (1994). *Multiple task performance and aging.* Doctoral dissertation, University of Groningen.

Kosslyn, S. M., & König, O. (1992). *Wet mind: The new cognitive neuroscience.* New York: The Free Press.

Kraepelin, E. (1903). Über Ermüdungsmessungen [On measures of fatigue]. *Archiv für die gesammte Psychologie, 1,* 9–30.

Kramer, A. F., Sirevaag, E. J., & Braune, R. (1987). A psychophysiological assessment of operator workload during simulated flight missions. *Human Factors, 29,* 145–160.

Kramer, A. F., & Spinks, J. (1991). Capacity views of human information processing. In R. Jennings & M. G. H. Coles (Eds.), *Handbook of cognive psychophysiology: Central and autonomic nervous systems approaches.* London: Wiley.

Kramer, A. F., Strayer, D. L., & Buckley, J. (1990). Development and transfer of automatic processing. *Journal of Experimental Psychology: Human Perception & Performance, 16,* 505–522.

Kristofferson, A. B. (1990). Timing mechanisms and the threshold for duration. In H-G. Geissler (Ed.), *Psychophysical explorations of mental structures.* Stuttgart: Hogrefe & Huber.

Krueger, L. E. (1978). A theory of perceptual matching. *Psychological Review, 85,* 278–304.

Krueger, L. E. (1984). The category effect in visual search depends on physical rather than conceptual differences. *Perception & Psychophysics, 35,* 558–564.

Krulewitz, J. E., Warm, J. S., & Wohl, T. H. (1975). Effects of shifts in the rate of repetitive stimulation on sustained attention. *Perception & Psychophysics, 18,* 245–249.

Kryter, K. (1985). *The effects of noise on man.* Orlando, FL: Academic Press.

Külpe, O. (1905). *Outlines of psychology.* New York: Macmillan.

Kundul, H. L., & La Follette, P. S. (1972). Visual search patterns and experience with radiological images. *Radiology, 103,* 523–528.

Kwak, H. W., Dagenbach, D., & Egeth, H. (1991). Further evidence for a time-independent shift of the focus of attention. *Perception & Psychophysics, 49*, 473–480.

LaBerge, D. A. (1962). A recruitment theory of simple behavior. *Psychometrika, 27*, 375–396.

LaBerge, D. A.(1973). Attention and the measurement of perceptual learning. *Memory & Cognition, 1*, 268–276.

LaBerge, D. A., Brown, V., Carter, M., Bash, D., & Hartley, A. (1991). Reducing the effect of adjacent distractors by narrowing attention. *Journal of Experimental Psychology: Human Perception & Performance, 17*, 65–76.

LaBerge, D. A., & Tweedy, J. R. (1964). Presentation probability and choice time. *Journal of Experimental Psychology, 68*, 477–481.

Lacey, J. I. (1967). Somatic response patterning and stress: Some revisions of activation theory. In M. H. Appley & R. Trumbull (Eds.), *Psychological stress: Some issues in research.* New York: Appleton-Century-Crofts.

Lamb, M. R., & Robertson, L. C. (1988). The processing of hierarchical stimuli: Effects of retinal locus, locational uncertainty, and stimulus identity. *Perception & Psychophysics, 44*, 172–181.

Laming, D. R. J. (1968). *Information theory of choice reaction times.* London: Academic Press.

Laming, D. R. J. (1979). Choice reaction performance following an error. *Acta Psychologica, 43*, 199–224.

Lane, N. E., Strieb, M. I., Glenn, F. A., & Wherry, R. A. (1981). The human operator simulator: An overview. In J. Moraal & K. F. Kraiss (Eds.), *Manned System Design: Methods, Equipment & Applications.* New York: Plenum.

Lange, L. (1888). Neue Experimente über den Vorgang der einfachen Reaktion auf Sinnesreize [New experiments on the event of a simple reaction to sensory stimuli]. *Philosophische Studien, 4*, 479–510.

Larish, D. D. (1986). Influence of stimulus–response translations on response programming: Examining the relationship of arm, direction, and extent of movement. *Acta Psychologica, 61*, 53–70.

Larish, I., & Wickens, C. D. (1991). Attention and HUD's: Flying in the dark? *Proceedings of the Society of Information Display*, Playa del Rey, CA.

Lashley, K. S. (1929). *Brain mechanisms and intelligence.* Chicago: University of Chicago Press.

Latour, P. L. (1962). Visual threshold during eye movements. *Vision Research, 2*, 261–262.

Laughery, K. R. (1989). Microsaint: A tool for modelling human performance in systems. In G. R. McMillan, D. Beevis, E. Salas, M. H. Strub, R. Sutton, & L. van Breda (Eds.), *Applications of human performance models to system design.* New York: Plenum.

Laughery, K. R., Sr., & Laughery, K. R., Jr. (1987). Analytic techniques for function analysis. In G. Salvendy (Ed.), *Handbook of human factors.* New York: Wiley.

Lavie, N. (1995). Perceptual load as a necessary condition for selective attention. *Journal of Experimental Psychology: Human Perception & Performance, 21*, 451–468.

Lavie, P. (1991). The 24-hour sleep propensity function (SPF): Practical and theoretical implications. In T. H. Monk (Ed.), *Sleep, sleepiness and performance.* New York: Wiley.

Leeuwenberg, E. L. J. A. (1971). A perceptual coding language for visual and auditory patterns. *American Journal of Psychology, 84*, 307–349.

Leonard, J. A. (1959). Tactual choice response time. *Quarterly Journal of Experimental Psychology, 11*, 76–83.

Lindsay, D. S., & Jacoby, L. L. (1994). Stroop process dissociations: The relationship between facilitation and interference. *Journal of Experimental Psychology: Human Perception & Performance, 20*, 219–234.

Lintern, G. (1980). Transfer of landing skill after training with supplementary visual clues. *Human Factors, 22*, 81–88.

Lintern, G., & Kennedy, R. S. (1984). Videogame as a covariate for carrier landing research. *Perceptual & Motor Skills, 58*, 167–172.

Lintern, G., Thornley-Yates, K. E., Nelson, B. E., & Roscoe, S. N. (1987). Content variety and augmentation of simulated visual scenes for teaching air-to-ground attack. *Human Factors, 29*, 45–59.

Lima, S. D. (1987). Morphological analysis in sentence reading. *Journal of Memory and Language, 26*, 84–99.

Liu, Y. (1996). Interactions between memory scanning and visual scanning in display monitoring. *Ergonomics, 39*, 1038–1053.

Loeb, M., & Alluisi, E. A. (1984). Theories of vigilance. In J. S. Warm (Ed.), *Sustained attention in human performance* (pp. 179–205). New York: Wiley. ·

Loeb, M., & Jones, P. D. (1978). Noise exposure, monitoring and tracking performance as a function of signal bias and task priority. *Ergonomics, 21*, 265–272.

Loeb, M., Noonan, T. K., Ash, D. W., & Holding, D. H. (1987). Limitations of the cognitive vigilance increment. *Human Factors, 29*, 661–674.

Logan, G. D. (1978). Attention in character classification: Evidence for the automaticity of component stages. *Journal of Experimental Psychology, General, 107*, 32–63.

Logan, G. D. (1979). On the use of a concurrent memory load to measure attention and automaticity. *Journal of Experimental Psychology: Human Perception and Performance, 5*, 189–207.

Logan, G. D. (1980). Attention and automaticity in Stroop and priming tasks: Theory and data. *Cognitive Psychology, 12*, 523–533.

Logan, G. D. (1982). On the ability to inhibit complex actions: A stop signal study of typewriting. *Journal of Experimental Psychology: Human Perception & Performance, 8*, 778–792.

Logan, G. D. (1988). Toward an instance theory of automatisation. *Psychological Review, 95*, 492–527.

Logan, G. D. (1995). On the ability to inhibit thought and action: A users' guide to the stop signal paradigm. In D. Dagenbach & T. H. Carr (Eds.), *Inhibitory processes in. attention, memory and language.* New York: Academic Press.

Logan, G. D., & Cowan, W. B. (1984). On the ability to inhibit thought and action: A theory of an act of control. *Psychological Review, 91*, 295–327.

Logan, G. D., & Etherton, J. L. (1994). What is learned during automatization? The role of attention in constructing an instance. *Journal of Experimental Psychology: Human Perception & Performance, 20*, 1022–1050.

Logie, R., Baddeley, A. D., Mane, A., Donchin, E., & Sheptak, R. (1989). Working memory in the acquisition of complex cognitive skills. *Acta Psychologica, 71*, 53–87.

Logsdon, R. L., Hochhaus, H. L., Williams, H. L., Rundell, O. H., & Maxwell, D. (1984). Secobarbital and perceptual processing. *Acta Psychologica, 55*, 179–193.

Looren de Jong, H., & Sanders, A. F. (1991). Stratification in perception and action. *Psychological Research, 52*, 216–228.

Los, S. A. (1994). Procedural differences in processing intact and degraded stimuli. *Memory and Cognition, 22*, 145–156.

Los, S. A. (1996). On the origin of mixing costs: Exploring information processing in pure and mixed blocks of trials. *Acta Psychologica, 94*, 145–188.

Loveless, N. E., & Sanford, A. J. (1974). Effects of age on the contingent negative variance and preparatory set in a reaction time task. *Journal of Gerontology, 29*, 52–63.

Lovie, A. D. (1983). Attention and behaviorism—fact and fiction. *British Journal of Psychology, 74*, 301–310.

Lozzo, J., & Drury, G. C. (1980). An evaluation of blink inspection. *Human Factors, 22*, 201–210.

Luce, R. D. (1986). *Response times.* New York: Oxford University Press.

Mackie, R. R. (1987). Vigilance research: Are we ready for counter measures? *Human Factors, 29*, 707–723.

MacMillan, N. A., & Creelman, C. D. (1991). *Detection theory: A user's guide.* Cambridge, England: Cambridge University Press.

Mackworth, J. F. (1959). Paced memorizing in a continuous task. *Journal of Experimental Psychology, 58*, 206–211.

Mackworth, J. F. (1964). Performance decrement in vigilance, thresholds and high-speed perceptual-motor tasks. *Canadian Journal of Psychology, 18*, 209–223.

Mackworth, J. F. (1969). *Vigilance and habituation.* London: Penguin.

Mackworth, N. H. (1950). *Research in the Measurement of Human Performance.* MRC Special Report Series. London: Her Majesty's Stationery Office.

Mackworth, N. H. (1976). Stimulus density limits in the useful field of view. In R. A. Monty & J. W. Senders (Eds.), *Eye movements and psychological processes.* Hillsdale, NJ: Lawrence Erlbaum Associates.

Mackworth, N. H., Kaplan, I. T., & Metlay, W. (1964). Eye movements during vigilance. *Perceptual & Motor Skills, 49*, 315–318.

Mackworth, N. H., & Morandi, A. J. (1967). The gaze selects informative details within pictures. *Perception & Psychophysics, 2*, 547–552.

MacLeod, C. M. (1991). Half a century of research on the Stroop effect: An integrative review. *Psychological Bulletin, 109*, 163–203.

Malmo, R. B. (1959). Activation: A neuropsychological dimension. *Psychological Review, 66*, 367–386.

Malmo, R. B., & Surwillo, R. B. (1960). Sleep deprivation: Changes in performance and physiological indicants of activation. *Psychological Monographs, 74*, 502.

Malone, T. B. (1986). The centered-high mounted brake light: A human factors success story. *Human Factors Society Bulletin, 29*, 1–3.

Mane, A., & Donchin, E. (1989). The Space Fortress game. *Acta Psychologica, 71*, 17–22.

Mangun, G. R., & Hillyard, S. A. (1990). Electrophysiological studies of visual selective attention in humans. In A. Scheibel & A. Wechsler (Eds.), *The neurobiological foundations of higher cognitive functions.* New York: Guilford.

Mangun, G. R., & Hillyard, S. A. (1991). Modulations of sensory-evoked brain potentials indicate changes in perceptual processing during visual-spatial priming. *Journal of Experimental Psychology: Human Perception & Performance, 17*, 1057–1074.

Mansfield, R. W. J. (1973). Latency functions in human vision. *Vision Research, 13*, 2219–2234.

Marcel, A. J., & Forrin, B. (1974). Naming latency and the repetition of stimulus categories. *Journal of Experimental Psychology, 103*, 450–460.

Marocco, R. T. (1976). Sustained and transient cells in monkey lateral geniculate nucleus: Conduction velocities and response properties. *Journal of Neurophysiology, 39*, 340–353.

Mason, J. W. (1975). Emotion as reflected in patterns of endocrine integration. In L. Levi (Ed.), *Emotions, their parameters and measurement.* New York: Raven.

Massaro, D. W. (1988). Some criticisms of connectionist models of human performance. *Journal of Memory and Language, 27*, 213–234.

Massaro, D. W., & Cohen, M. M. (1994). Visual, orthographic, phonological and lexical influences in reading. *Journal of Experimental Psychology: Human Perception & Performance, 20*, 1107–1128.

Matin, E. (1974). Saccadic suppression: A review and an analysis. *Psychological Bulletin, 81*, 899–917.

Matin, L., & Fox, C. R. (1989). Visually perceived eye level and perceived elevation of objects: Linearly additive influences from visual field pitch and from gravity. *Vision Research, 29*, 315–324.

Matthews, G., Jones, D. M., & Chamberlain, A. G. (1989). Interactive effects of extroversion, and arousal on attentional task performance—multiple resources or encoding processes. *Journal of Personality and Social Psychology, 56*, 629–639.

Maylor, E. A., & Rabbitt, P. M. A. (1989). Relationship between rate of preparation for and processing of an event requiring a choice response. *Quarterly Journal of Experimental Psychology, 41A*, 47–62.

McCann, R. S., & Johnston, J. C. (1989). *The locus of processing bottlenecks in the overlapping task paradigm*. Paper presented at the thirty-third annual meeting of the Psychonomics Society, Denver.

McCann, R. S., & Johnston, J. C. (1992). Locus of the single channel bottleneck in dual task interference. *Journal of Experimental Psychology: Human Perception & Performance, 18,* 471–484.

McCarthy, G., & Donchin, E. (1981). A metric for thought: A comparison of P300 latency and reaction time. *Science, 211,* 77–80.

McClelland, J. C., & Rumelhart, D. (1981). An interactive activation model of context effects in letter perception. Part 1: An account of basic findings. *Psychological Review, 88,* 375–407.

McClelland, J. L. (1979). On the time relations of mental processes: An examination of systems of processes in cascade. *Psychological Review, 86,* 287–330.

McClelland, J. L. (1987). The case for interactionism in language processing. In M. Coltheart (Ed.), *Attention & Performance* (Vol. 12). Hillsdale, NJ: Lawrence Erlbaum Associates.

McComas, J. C. (1922). A measure of attention. *Journal of Experimental Psychology, 5,* 1–18.

McConkie, G. W. (1983). Eye movements and perception during reading. In K. Rayner (Ed.), *Eye movements in reading: Perceptual and language processes.* New York: Academic Press.

McConkie, G. W., Underwood, N. R., Zola, D., & Wolverton, G. S. (1985). Some temporal characteristics of processing during reading. *Journal of Experimental Psychology: Human Perception & Performance, 11,* 168–186.

McCormick, E. J. (1976). Job and task analysis. In M. E. Dunnette (Ed.), *Handbook of industrial and organisational psychology.* New York: Wiley.

McGehee, D. V., Dingus, T., & Horowitz, A. D. (1992). *The potential value of a front-to-rear-end collision warning system based on factors of driver behavior, visual perception and brake reaction time.* Proceedings of the thirty-sixth annual meeting of the Human Factors Society, Atlanta.

McGill, W. J. (1963). Stochastic latency mechanisms. In R. D. Luce, R. R. Bush, & E. Galanter (Eds.), *Handbook of mathematical psychology: Vol. 1.* New York: Wiley.

McGuinness, D., & Pribram, K. (1980). The neuropsychology of attention: Emotional and motivational controls. In M. C. Witrock (Ed.), *The brain and psychology.* New York: Academic Press.

McKnight, A. J., & Shinar, D. (1992). Brake reaction time to center high-mounted stop lamps on vans and trucks. *Human Factors, 34,* 205–213.

McLeod, P., & Posner, M. I. (1984). Privileged loops from percept to act. In H. Bouma & D. G. Bouwhuis (Eds.), *Attention & Performance* (Vol. 10). London: Lawrence Erlbaum Associates.

Meister, D. (1985). *Behavioral analysis and measurement methods.* Chichester: Wiley.

Merkel, J. (1885). Die zeitliche Verhältnisse der Willenstätigkeit [The temporal relations of activities of the will]. *Philosophische Studien, 2,* 73–127.

Metzger, W. (1954). *Psychologie* [Psychology]. Darmstadt, Germany: Huber.

Meulenbroek, R. G. J., & van Galen, G. P. (1988). Foreperiod duration and the analysis of motor stages in a line drawing task. *Acta Psychologica, 69,* 19–34.

Mewhort, D. J. K., Butler, B. E., Feldman-Stuart, D., & Tramer, S. (1988). "Iconic memory" location information and the bar-probe task: A reply to Chow. *Journal of Experimental Psychology: Human Perception & Performance, 14,* 729–736.

Mewhort, D. J. K., Campbell, A. J., Marchetti, F. M., & Campbell, J. I. D. (1981). Identification, localisation and iconic memory: An evaluation of the bar-probe task. *Memory & Cognition, 9,* 50–67.

Mewhort, D. J. K., Johns, E. E., & Coble, S. (1991). Early and late selection in partial report: Evidence from degraded displays. *Perception & Psychophysics, 50,* 258–266.

Meyer, D. E., & Kieras, D. E. (1997). A computational theory of executive cognitive processes and multiple task performance, part 1: Basic mechanisms. *Psychological Review, 104,* 3–65.

Meyer, D. E., Kieras, E., Lauber, E. H., Schumacher, J., Glass, E., Zurbriggen, L., & Apfelblat, D. (1995). Adaptive executive control: Flexible multiple task performance without pervasive immutable response-selection bottlenecks. *Acta Psychologica, 90,* 163–190.

Meyer, D. E., Osman, A. M., Irwin, D. E., & Yantis, S. (1988). The dynamics of cognition and action: Mental processes inferred from speed–accuracy decomposition. *Psychological Review, 95,* 183–237.

Meyer, D. E., Schvaneveldt, R. W., & Ruddy, M. (1975). Loci of contextual effects in visual word recognition. In P. M. A. Rabbitt & S. Dornic (Eds.), *Attention & Performance* (Vol. 5). London: Academic Press.

Meyer, D. E., Yantis, S., Osman, A. M., & Smith, J. E. K. (1985). Temporal properties of human information processing: Tests of discrete vs continuous models. *Cognitive Psychology, 17,* 445–518.

Michon, J. A. (1966). Tapping regularity as a measure of perceptual motor load. *Ergonomics, 9,* 401–412.

Michon, J. A., Eernst, J. Th., & Koutstaal, G. A. (1965). Onderzoek veiligheidskleding op de weg [*Study on safety clothing on the road*]. IZF 1965–C7. TNO, Soesterberg, The Netherlands.

Michon, J. A., & Kirk, N. S. (1962). Eye movements in radar watchkeeping. IZF 1962–17. TNO, Soesterberg, The Netherlands.

Milgram, P., Godthelp, J., & Blaauw, G. J. (1982, June). An investigation of decision-making criteria adopted by drivers while monitoring vehicle state in the temporary absence of visual input. *Proceedings of the second annual Conference on Human Decision-Making and Manual Control.*

Miller, G. A. (1956). The magical number seven plus or minus two: Some limits on our capacity for processing information. *Psychological Review, 63,* 81–97.

Miller, G. A., & Selfridge, J. A. (1950). Verbal context and the recall of meaningful material. *American Journal of Psychology 63,* 176–185.

Miller, J. (1982). Discrete versus continuous stage models of human information processing: In search of partial output. *Journal of Experimental Psychology: Human Perception & Performance, 8,* 273–296.

Miller, J. (1987). Evidence of preliminary response preparation from a divided attention task. *Journal of Experimental Psychology: Human Perception & Performance, 13,* 425–434.

Miller, J. (1988). Discrete and continuous models of human information processing: In search of partial output. *Acta Psychologica, 67,* 191–257.

Miller, J. (1989). The control of attention by abrupt visual onsets and offsets. *Perception & Psychophysics, 45,* 567–571.

Miller, J. (1991). The flanker compatibility effect as a function of visual angle, attentional focus, visual transients and perceptual load: A search for boundary conditions. *Perception & Psychophysics, 49,* 270–288.

Miller, J. (1993). A queue-series model for reaction time with discrete stage and continuous flow models as special cases. *Psychological Review, 100,* 702–715.

Miller, J., & Bauer, D. W. (1981). Irrelevant differences in the "same–different" task. *Journal of Experimental Psychology: General, 110,* 39–55.

Miller, J., & Hackley, S. A. (1992). Electrophysiological evidence for temporal overlap among contingent mental processes. *Journal of Experimental Psychology: General, 121,* 195–209.

Miller, J., Riehle, A., & Requin, J. (1992). Effects of preliminary perceptual output on neuronal activity of the primary motor cortex. *Journal of Experimental Psychology: Human Perception & Performance, 18,* 1121–1138.

Miller, J., van der Ham, F., & Sanders, A. F. (1995). Overlapping stage models and the additive factor method. *Acta Psychologica, 90,* 11–28.

Miller, R. B. (1974). *A method for determining task strategies.* AFHRL Report TR-74–26.

Milliken, B., Tipper, S. P., & Weaver, B. (1994). Negative priming in a spatial localisation task: Feature mismatching and distractor inhibition. *Journal of Experimental Psychology: Human Perception & Performance, 20,* 624–646.

Modigliani, V., Wright, R. D., & Loverock, D. S. (1996). Inattention and perception of visual feature conjunctions. *Acta Psychologica, 91,* 121–129.

Monk, T. H. (1984). Search. In J. S. Warm (Ed.), *Sustained attention in human performance.* New York: Wiley.

Monk, T. H. (1991). Circadian aspects of subjective sleepiness: A behavioural messenger? In T. H. Monk (Ed.), *Sleep, sleepiness and performance.* New York: Wiley.

Moraal, J., & Poll, K. J. (1979). De Links-Miles rijsimulator voor pantservoertuigen: Verslag van een veld onderzoek [The Links-Miles driving simulator for tanks: Report of a field study]. *IZF 1979-23,* TNO, Soesterberg, Netherlands.

Moraglia, G., Maloney, K. P., Fekete, E. M., & Albasi, K. (1989). Visual search along the colour dimension. *Canadian Journal of Psychology, 43,* 1–12.

Morawski, T. B., Drury, C. G., & Karwan, M. H. (1980). Predicting search performance for multiple targets. *Human Factors, 22,* 707–718.

Moray, N. H. (1959). Attention in dichotic listening: Effective cues and the influence of instructions. *Quarterly Journal of Experimental Psychology, 11,* 56–60.

Moray, N. H. (1967). Where is capacity limited? A survey and a model. *Acta Psychologica, 27,* 84–92.

Moray, N. H. (1975). A data base for theories of selective listening. In P. M. A. Rabbitt & S. Dornic (Eds.), *Attention and Performance* (Vol. 5, pp. 669–682). London: Academic Press.

Mordkoff, J. T., & Yantis, S. (1991). An interactive race model of divided attention. *Journal of Experimental Psychology: Human Perception & Performance, 17,* 520–538.

Morgan, B. B., Brown, B. R., & Alluisi, E. A. (1974). Effects on sustained performance of 48 hours of continuous work and sleep-loss. *Human Factors, 16,* 406–414.

Morin, R. E., & Forrin, B. (1962). Mixing of two types of S–R associations in a choice reaction time task. *Journal of Experimental Psychology, 64,* 137–141.

Morton, J. (1969). Interaction of information in word recognition. *Psychological Review, 76,* 165–178.

Mowbray, G. H. (1960). Choice reaction times for skilled responses. *Quarterly Journal of Experimental Psychology, 12,* 193–203.

Mowbray, G. H. (1962). Some remarks concerning Brebner & Gordon's paper "Ensemble size and selective response time with a constant signal rate." *Quarterly Journal of Experimental Psychology, 14,* 117–118.

Mowbray, G. H., & Rhoades, M. V. (1959). On the reduction of choice reaction time with practice. *Quarterly Journal of Experimental Psychology, 11,* 16–23.

Mozer, M. C. (1991). *The perception of multiple objects.* Cambridge, MA: MIT Press.

Mulder, G. (1980). *The heart of mental effort.* Doctoral dissertation. University of Groningen, The Netherlands.

Mulder, G., Gloerich, A. B. M., Brookhuis, K. A., Dellen, H. J., & Mulder, L. J. M. (1984). Stage analysis of the reaction process using brain-evoked potentials and reaction time. *Psychological Research, 46,* 15–32.

Mulder, G., Smid, H. G. O. M., & Mulder, L. J. M. (1993). On the transfer of partial information between perception and action. *Attention & Performance, 14,* 567–588.

Mulder, G., Wijers, A. A., Brookhuis, K. A., Smid, H. G. O. M., & Mulder, L. J. M. (1994). Selective visual attention: Selective cueing, cognitive processing and response processing. In H. J. Heinze, T. F. Münte, & G. R. Mangun (Eds.), *Cognitive Electrophysiology.* Boston: Birkhhäuser.

Mulder, G., Wijers, A. A., Lange, J. J., Buijink, B. M., Mulder, L. J. M., Willemsen, A. T. M., Paans, A. M. J. (1995). The role of neuroimaging in the discovery of processing stages: A review. *Acta Psychologica, 90,* 63–79.

Müller, G. E. (1923). *Komplexteorie und Gestalttheorie: Ein Beitrag zur Wahrnemungspsychologie* [Complex theory and Gestalt theory: A contribution to the psychology of perception]. Göttingen: Ludwig.

Müller, H. J., Heller, D., & Ziegler, J. (1995). Visual search for singleton feature targets within and across feature dimensions. *Perception & Psychophysics, 57*, 1–17.

Müller, H. J., & Humphreys, G. W. (1991). Luminance increment detection: Capacity-limited or not? *Journal of Experimental Psychology: Human Perception & Performance, 17*, 107–124.

Müller, H. J., Humphreys, G. W., & Donnelly, N. (1994). Search via recursive rejection (SERR): Visual search for single and dual form-conjunction targets. *Journal of Experimental Psychology: Human Perception & Performance, 20*, 235–258.

Müller, H. J., & Rabbitt, P. M. A. (1989). Reflexive and voluntary orienting of visual attention: Time course of activation and resistance to interruption. *Journal of Experimental Psychology: Human Perception & Performance, 15*, 315–330.

Murray, H. G. (1970). Stimulus intensity and reaction time: Evaluation of a decision theory model. *Journal of Experimental Psychology, 84*, 383–391.

Musico, B. (1921). Is a fatigue test possible? *British Journal of Psychology, 12*, 31–46.

Näätänen, R. (1971). Non-aging foreperiods and simple reaction time. *Acta Psychologica, 35*, 316–327.

Näätänen, R. (1982). Processing negativity: An evoked potential reflection of selective attention. *Psychological Bulletin, 92*, 605–640.

Näätänen, R. (1990). The role of attention in auditory information processing as revealed by event-related potentials and other brain measures of cognitive function. *The Brain & Behavioral Sciences, 13*, 201–288.

Näätänen, R. (1992). *Attention and brain function.* Hillsdale, NJ: Lawrence Erlbaum Associates.

Näätänen, R., & Gaillard, A. W. K. (1974). The relationship between the contingent negative variation and the reaction time under prolonged experimental conditions. *Biological Psychology, 1*, 277–291.

Näätänen, R., & Gaillard, A. W. K. (1983). The N2 deflection of the ERP and the orienting reflex. In A. W. K. Gaillard & W. Ritter (Eds.), *EEG correlates of information processing theoretical issues.* Amsterdam: North Holland.

Näätänen, R., Gaillard, A. W. K., & Mäntysalo, S. (1978). Early selective attention effect on evoked potential reinterpreted. *Acta Psychologica, 42*, 313–329.

Näätänen, R., & Merisalo, A. (1977). Expectancy and preparation in simple reaction time. In S. Dornic (Ed.), *Attention & Performance, 6*, 115–138. Hillsdale, NJ: Lawrence Erlbaum Associates.

Näätänen, R., Muranen, V., & Merisalo, A. (1974). The timing of the expectancy peak in a simple reaction time situation. *Acta Psychologica, 38*, 461–470.

Nasman, V. T., & Rosenfeld, J. P. (1990). Parietal P3 response as an indicator of stimulus categorisation: Increased P3 amplitude to categorically deviant target and non-target stimuli. *Psychophysiology, 27*, 338–350.

Nattkemper, D., & Prinz, W. (1984). Costs and benefits of redundancy in visual search. In A. Gale & F. Johnson (Eds.), *Theoretical and applied aspects of eyemovements research.* Amsterdam: North Holland.

Nattkemper, D., & Prinz, W. (1990). Local and global control of saccade amplitude and fixation duration in continuous visual search. In R. Groner, G. d'Ydewalle, & R. Parham (Eds.), *From eye to mind: Information acquisition in perception.* Amsterdam: Elsevier.

Navon, D. (1977). Forest before trees: The precedence of global features in visual perception. *Cognitive Psychology, 9*, 353–383.

Navon, D. (1984). Resources: A theoretical soupstone. *Psychological Review, 91*, 216–234.

Navon, D. (1985). Attention division or attention sharing? In M. I. Posner & O. M. Marin (Eds.), *Attention & Performance, 11.* Hillsdale, NJ: Lawrence Erlbaum Associates.

Navon, D. (1989). The importance of being visible: On the role of attention in a mind viewed as an anarchic intelligence system: (1) Basic tenets (2) Application to the field of attention. *European Journal of Cognitive Psychology, 1,* 191–213, 215–238.

Navon, D., & Gopher, D. (1979). On the economy of processing systems. *Psychological Review, 86,* 214–255.

Navon, D., & Miller, J. (1987). The role of outcome conflict in dual task interference. *Journal of Experimental Psychology: Human Perception & Performance, 13,* 435–448.

Navon, D., & Norman, J. (1983). Does global precedence really depend on visual angle? *Journal of Experimental Psychology: Human Perception & Performance, 14,* 89–100.

Nazir, T., O'Regan, J. K., & Jacobs, A. M. (1991). On words and their letters. *Bulletin of the Psychonomic Society, 29,* 171–174.

Neisser, U. (1963). Decision time without reaction time: Experiments on visual search. *American Journal of Psychology, 76,* 376–395.

Neisser, U. (1976). *Cognition and reality.* San Francisco: Freeman.

Nemire, K., Jacoby, R. H., & Ellis, S. R. (1994). Simulation fidelity of a virtual environment display. *Human Factors, 36,* 79–93.

Netick, A., & Klapp, S. T. (1994). Hesitations in manual tracking: A single channel limit in response programming. *Journal of Experimental Psychology: Human Perception & Performance, 20,* 766–782.

Neumann, O. (1984). Automatic processing: A review of recent findings and a plea for an old theory. In W. Prinz & A. F. Sanders (Eds.), *Cognition and motor behavior.* Heidelberg: Springer.

Neumann, O. (1987). Beyond capacity: A functional view of attention. In H. Heuer & A. F. Sanders (Eds.), *Perspectives on perception and action.* Hillsdale, NJ: Lawrence Erlbaum Associates.

Neumann, O. (1991). *Konzepte der Aufmerksamkeit: Enstehung, Wandlungen und Funktionen eines psychologischen Begriffs* [Concepts of attention: Origins, changes, and functions of a psychological concept]. Habilitationsschrift. Ludwig Maximilian Universität, München.

Neumann, O., & Prinz, W. (1987). Historical approaches to perception and action. In O. Neumann & W. Prinz (Eds.), *Relationships between perception and action: Current approaches.* Heidelberg: Springer.

Neumann, O., Niepel, N., & Tappe, T. (1994). *Stimulus modality effects on RT and the limits of direct parameter specification.* Unpublished manuscript, University of Bielefeld, Germany.

Neumann, O., Tappe, T., & Niepel, M. (1995). *The effect of stimulus intensity and sensory modality on reaction time and temporal order judgment: A survey and an appraisal.* Unpublished manuscript, University of Bielefeld, Germany.

Newell, A. (1974). You can't play twenty questions with nature and win. In W. G. Chase (Ed.), *Visual information processing.* New York: Academic Press.

Newell, A. (1980). Physical symbol systems. *Cognitive Science, 4,* 135–183.

Nickerson, R. S. (1967). Expectancy, waiting time and the psychological refractory period. *Acta Psychologica, 27,* 23–34.

Nickerson, R. S. (1973). Intersensory facilitation of reaction time: Energy summation or preparation enhancement? *Psychological Review, 80,* 489–509.

Nickerson, R. S. (1975). Effects of correlated and uncorrelated noise on visual pattern matching. In P. M. A. Rabbitt & S. Dornic (Eds.), *Attention & Performance* (Vol. 5). London: Academic Press.

Niemi, P. (1979). Stimulus intensity effects on auditory and visual reaction processes. *Acta Psychologica, 43,* 299–312.

Niemi, P., & Lehtonen, E. (1982). Foreperiod and visual stimulus intensity: A reappraisal. *Acta Psychologica, 50*, 73–82.

Niemi, P., & Näätänen, R. (1981). Foreperiod and simple reaction time. *Psychological Bulletin, 89*, 133–162.

Nissen, M. J. (1977). Stimulus intensity and information processing. *Perception & Psychophysics, 22*, 338–352.

Nissen, M. J., Posner, M. I., & Snyder, C. R. R. (1978). *Relationships between attention shifts and saccadic eye movements.* Unpublished paper to the Psychonomic Society.

Noble, M. E., & Sanders, A. F. (1980). Searching for traffic signals while engaged in compensatory tracking. *Human Factors, 22*, 89–102.

Noble, M. E., Sanders, A. F., & Trumbo, D. A. (1981). Concurrence costs in double stimulation tasks. *Acta Psychologica, 49*, 141–158.

Norman, D. A., & Bobrow, D. G. (1975). On data-limited and resource-limited processes. *Cognitive Psychology, 7*, 44–64.

Norman, D. A., & Shallice, T. (1986). Attention to action: Willed and automatic control of behavior. In R. J. Davidson, G. E. Schwartz, & D. Shapiro (Eds.), *Consciousness and self regulation.* New York: Plenum.

Norris, D. (1990). How to build a connectionist idiot. *Cognition, 35*, 277–291.

North, R. A. (1977). Task components and demands as factors in dual task performance. Technical report ARL77–2, Aviation Research Laboratory, University of Illinois, Urbana, Ill.

North, R. A., & Riley, V. A. (1989). A predictive model of operator workload. In G. R. McMillan, D. Beevis, E. Salas, M. H. Strub, R. Sutton, & L. van Breda (Eds.), *Applications of human performance models to system design.* New York: Plenum.

Nuechterlein, K., Parasuraman, R., & Jiang, Q. (1983). Visual sustained attention: Image degradation produces rapid sensitivity decrement over time. *Science, 83*, 220, 227–229.

O'Donnell, R. D., & Eggemeier, F. T. (1986). Workload assessment methodology. In K. R. Boff, L. Kaufman, & J. P. Thomas (Eds.), *Handbook of perception & human performance* (chap. 42). New York: Wiley.

O'Hanlon, J. F. (1965). Adrenaline and noradrenaline: Relation to performance in a visual vigilance task. *Science, 150*, 507–509.

O'Hanlon, J. F. (1971). Heart rate variability: A new index of driver alertness/fatigue. HFR Technical Report 1712–1. Goleta, CA.

O'Hanlon, J. F. (1981). Boredom: Practical consequences and a theory. *Acta Psychologica, 49*, 53–82.

O'Hanlon, J. F., Brookhuis, K. A., Louwerse, J. W., & Volkerts, E. R. (1986). Performance testing as a part of drug registration. In J. F. O'Hanlon & J. J. de Gier (Eds.), *Drugs and Driving.* London: Taylor & Francis.

O'Hanlon, J. F., Haak, T., Blaauw, G. J., & Riemersma, J. B. J. (1982). Diazepam impairs lateral position control in highway driving. *Science, 217*, 79–82.

Ohde, H., & Sanders, A. F. (1988). *Further evidence in favor of a second task as predictor of later performance in a complex skill.* Master's thesis. Institut für Psychologie, RWTH, Aachen.

Ollman, R. T. (1966). Fast guesses in choice reaction time. *Psychonomic Science, 6*, 155–156.

O'Regan, J. K. (1990). Eye movements and reading. In E. Kowler (Ed.), *Eye movements and their role in visual and cognitive processes.* Amsterdam: Elsevier.

O'Regan, J. K., & Levi-Schoen, A. (1987). Eye movements strategy and tactics in word recognition and reading. In M. Coltheart (Ed.), *Attention & Performance* (Vol. 12). Hillsdale, NJ: Lawrence Erlbaum Associates.

Osman, A., Bashore, T. R., Coles, M. G. H., Donchin, E., & Meyer, D. E. (1988). A psychophysiological study of response preparation based on partial information [Abstract]. *Psychophysiology, 25*, 426.

Osman, A., Bashore, T. R., Coles, M. G. H., Donchin, E., & Meyer, D. E. (1992). On the transmission of partial information: Inferences from movement-related brain potentials. *Journal of Experimental Psychology: Human Perception & Performance, 18*, 217–232.

Osman, A., Kornblum, S., & Meyer, D. (1986). The point of no return in choice reaction time: Controlled and ballistic stages of response preparation. *Journal of Experimental Psychology: Human Perception & Performance, 12*, 243–258.

Osman, A., & Moore, C. M. (1994). The locus of dual task interference: Psychological refractory effects on movement-related brain potentials. *Journal of Experimental Psychology: Human Perception & Performance, 19*, 1292–1312.

Paap, K. R., & Johansen, L. S. (1994). The case of the vanishing frequency effect: A retest of the verification model. *Journal of Experimental Psychology: Human Perception & Performance, 20*, 1129–1157.

Paap, K. R., Newsome, S. L., McDonald, J. E., & Schvaneveldt, R. W. (1982). An activation-verification model for letter and word recognition: The word superiority effect. *Psychological Review, 89*, 573–594.

Pachella, R. G. (1974). The interpretation of reaction time in information processing research. In B. Kantowitz (Ed.), *Human information: Tutorials in performance and cognition.* Hillsdale, NJ: Lawrence Erlbaum Associates.

Padmos, P. (1988). Visual modelling errors in the Leopard 2 driving simulator. *IZF Report 88–12.*

Parasuraman, R. (1984). The psychobiology of sustained attention. In J. S. Warm (Ed.), *Sustained attention in human performance.* New York: Wiley.

Parasuraman, R. (1985). Sustained attention: A multifactorial approach. In M. I. Posner & O. M. Marin (Eds.), *Attention & Performance* (Vol. 11). Hillsdale, NJ: Lawrence Erlbaum Associates.

Parasuraman, R. (1986). Vigilance, monitoring and search. In K. R. Boff, L. Kaufman, & J. P. Thomas (Eds.), *Handbook of perception & human performance* (chap. 43). New York: Wiley.

Parasuraman, R., & Davies, D. R. (1976). Decision theory analysis of response latencies in vigilance. *Journal of Experimental Psychology: Human Perception & Performance, 2*, 569–582.

Parasuraman, R., & Davies, D. R. (1977). A taxonomic analysis of vigilance performance. In R. R. Mackie (Ed.), *Vigilance: Theory, operational performance, and physiological correlates.* New York: Plenum.

Parasuraman, R., & Mouloua, M. (1987). Interaction of signal discriminability and task type in vigilance decrement. *Perception & Psychophysics, 41*, 17–22.

Park, J., & Kanwisher, N. (1994). Negative priming for spatial locations: Identity mismatching, not distractor inhibition. *Journal of Experimental Psychology: Human Perception & Performance, 20*, 613–623.

Parks, D. L., & Boucek, G. P. (1989). Workload prediction, diagnosis and continuing challenges. In G. R. McMillan, D. Beevis, E. Salas, M. H. Strub, R. Sutton, & L. van Breda (Eds.), *Applications of human performance models to system design.* New York: Plenum.

Parsons, H. M. (1972). *Man-machine system experiments.* Baltimore, MD: Johns Hopkins University Press.

Paschal, F. C. (1941). The trend in theories of attention. *Psychological Review, 48*, 383–403.

Pashler, H. (1984). Processing stages in overlapping tasks: Evidence for a central bottleneck. *Journal of Experimental Psychology: Human Perception & Performance, 10*, 358–377.

Pashler, H. (1987). Target-distractor discriminability in visual search. *Perception & Psychophysics, 41*, 285–292.

Pashler, H. (1988). Cross-dimensional interaction and texture segregation. *Perception & Psychophysics, 43*, 307–318.

Pashler, H. (1991). Shifting visual attention and shifting motor responses: Distinct attentional mechanisms. *Journal of Experimental Psychology: Human Perception & Performance, 17*, 1023–1040.

Pashler, H. (1993). Dual-task interference and elementary mental mechanisms. In D. Meyer & S. Kornblum (Eds.), *Attention & Performance* (Vol. 14). Cambridge, MA: MIT Press.

Pashler, H. (1994a). Dual-task interference in simple tasks: Data and theory. *Psychological Bulletin, 116*, 220–244.

Pashler, H. (1994b). Graded capacity sharing in dual-task interference? *Journal of Experimental Psychology: Human Perception & Performance, 20*, 330–342.

Pashler, H., & Baylis, G. (1991a). Procedural learning: Locus of practice effects in speeded choice tasks. *Journal of Experimental Psychology: Learning, Memory & Cognition, 17*, 20–32.

Pashler, H., & Baylis, G. (1991b). Procedural learning: Intertrial repetition effects in speeded-choice tasks. *Journal of Experimental Psychology: Learning, Memory & Cognition, 17*, 33–48.

Pashler, H., Carrier, M., & Hoffman, J. (1993). Saccadic eye movements and dual task interference. *Quarterly Journal of Experimental Psychology, 46*, 51–82.

Payne, S. J. (1995). Naive judgments of stimulus–response compatibility. *Human Factors, 37*, 495–506.

Peterson, M. A., & Gibson, B. S. (1991). Directing spatial attention within an object: Altering the functional equivalence of shape descriptions. *Journal of Experimental Psychology: Human Perception & Performance, 17*, 170–182.

Pew, R. W. (1969). The speed–accuracy operating characteristic. *Acta Psychologica, 30*, 16–26.

Pew, R. W. (1984). A distributed processing view of human motor control. In W. Prinz & A. F. Sanders (Eds.), *Cognition and motor behavior.* Heidelberg: Springer.

Phaf, R. H., van der Heijden, A. H. C., & Hudson, P. T. W. (1990). SLAM: A connectionist model for attention in visual selection tasks. *Cognitive Psychology, 22*, 273–341.

Philips, R. J. (1979). Why is lower case better? *Applied Ergonomics, 10*, 211–214.

Picton, T. W., Goodman, W. S., & Brice, D. P. (1970). Amplitude of evoked response to tones of high intensity. *Acta Otolaryngology, 70*, 77–82.

Pieron, H. (1920). Nouvelles recherches sur l'analyse du temps de latence sensorielle et sur la loi qui relie le temps a l'intensité d'excitation [New studies on sensory latency and on the law that relates latency to stimulus intensity]. *L'Annee Psychologique, 22*, 58–142.

Pieters, J. P. M. (1983). Sternberg's additive factor method and underlying psychological processes. *Psychological Bulletin, 93*, 411–426.

Pigeau, R. A., Angus, R. G., O'Neill, P., & Mack, I. (1995). Vigilance latencies to aircraft detection among NORAD surveillance operators. *Human Factors, 37*, 622–634.

Pike, A. R. (1973). Response latency models for signal detection. *Psychological Review, 91*, 384–388.

Poffenberger, A. T. (1912). Reaction time to retinal stimulation with special reference to the time lost in conduction through nerve centers. *Archives of Psychology, 23*, 1–73.

Pokorny, M. L. I., Blom, D. H. J., & van Leeuwen, P. (1981). Analysis of traffic accident data from bus drivers. In A. Reinberg, N. Vieux, & P. Andauer (Eds.), *Night and shiftwork: Biological and social aspects.* Oxford: Pergamon.

Pollack, I. (1952). The information of elementary auditory displays: One. *Journal of the Acoustical Society of America, 24*, 745–749.

Pollack, I. (1953). The information of elementary auditory displays: Two. *Journal of the Acoustical Society of America, 25*, 765–769.

Pollatsek, A., Rayner, K., & Balota, D. A. (1986). Inferences about eye movement control from the perceptual span in reading. *Perception & Psychophysics, 40*, 123–130.

Polson, M. C., & Friedman, A. (1988). Task sharing within and between hemispheres: A multiple resource approach. *Human Factors, 30*, 633–643.

Pomerantz, J. R. (1986). Visual form perception: An overview. In H. C. Nusbaum & E. C. Schwab (Eds.), *Pattern recognition by humans and machines: Vol. 2. Visual Perception.* Orlando, FL: Academic Press.

Ponsford, J., & Kinsella, G. (1992). Attentional deficits following closed head injury. *Journal of Clinical and Experimental Neuropsychology, 14*, 822–838.

Posner, M. I. (1964). Information reduction in the analysis of sequential tasks. *Psychological Review, 71*, 491–504.

Posner, M. I. (1978). *Chronometric explorations of mind*. Hillsdale, NJ: Lawrence Erlbaum Associates.

Posner, M. I. (1980). Orienting of attention. *Quarterly Journal of Experimental Psychology, 32*, 3–25.

Posner, M. I., & Boies, S. J. (1971). Components of attention. *Psychological Review, 78*, 391–408.

Posner, M. I., & Cohen, Y. (1984). Components of visual orienting. In H. Bouma & D. Bouwhuis (Eds.), *Attention & Performance* (Vol. 10). Hillsdale, NJ: Lawrence Erlbaum Associates.

Posner, M. I., & Keele, S. W. (1968). On the genesis of abstract ideas. *Journal of Experimental Psychology, 77*, 353–363.

Posner, M. I., Nissen, M. J. , & Klein, R. M. (1976). Visual dominance: An information processing account of its origins and significance. *Psychological Review, 83*, 157–171.

Posner, M. I., Nissen, M. J., & Ogden, W. C. (1978). Attended and unattended processing modes: The role of set for spatial location. In H. L. Pick & E. J. Saltzman (Eds.), *Modes of perceiving and processing information*. Hillsdale, NJ: Lawrence Erlbaum Associates.

Posner, M. I., & Petersen, S. E. (1990). The attention system of the human brain. *Annual Review of Neuroscience, 13*, 25–42.

Posner, M. I., & Rafal, R. D. (1987). Cognitive theories of attention and the rehabilitation of attentional deficits. In M. I. Meier, A. L. Benton, & S. Diller (Eds.), *Neuropsychological rehabilitation*. New York: Guilford.

Posner, M. I., Rafal, R. D., Choate, L. S., & Vaughan, J. (1985). Inhibition of return: Neural basis and function. *Cognitive Neuropsychology, 2*, 211–228.

Posner, M. I., & Raichle, M. E. (1994). *Images of the mind*. New York: Scientific American Library.

Posner, M. I., & Snyder, C. R. R. (1975). Facilitation and inhibition in the processing of signals. In P. M. A. Rabbitt & S. Dornic (Eds.), *Attention and Performance* (Vol. 5, pp. 669–682). Hillsdale, NJ: Lawrence Erlbaum Associates.

Posner, M. I., Snyder, C. R. R., & Davidson, B. J. (1980). Attention and detection of signals. *Journal of Experimental Psychology: General, 109*, 160–174.

Posner, M. I., Walker, J. A., Friedrich, F. J., & Rafal, R. D. (1987). How do the parietal lobes direct covert attention? *Neuropsychologia, 25*, 135–145.

Potter, M. C., & Faulconer, B. A. (1975). Time to understand pictures and words. *Nature, 253*, 437–438.

Poulton, E. C. (1950). Perceptual anticipation and reaction time. *Quarterly Journal of Experimental Psychology, 2*, 99–112.

Poulton, E. C. (1967). Searching for newspaper headlines printed in capitals or lower case letters. *Journal of Applied Psychology, 51*, 417–425.

Poulton, E. C. (1973). Unwanted range effects from using within subject experimental designs. *Psychological Bulletin, 80*, 113–121.

Poulton, E. C. (1974). *Tracking skills and manual control*. New York: Academic Press.

Pribram, K. H., & McGuinness, D. (1975). Arousal, activation and effort in the control of attention. *Psychological Review, 82*, 116–149.

Prinz, W. (1972). Reaktionszeit-Fraktionierung durch Varianzanalyse? [Fractination of reaction time through analysis of variance?]. *Archiv für Psychologie, 124*, 240–252.

Prinz, W. (1987a). Continuous selection. *Psychological Research, 48*, 231–238.

Prinz, W. (1987b). Ideomotor action. In H. Heuer & A. F. Sanders (Eds.), *Perspectives on perception and action* (pp. 47–77). Hillsdale, NJ: Lawrence Erlbaum Associates.

Prinz, W., Tweer, R., & Feige, R. (1974). Context control of search behavior: Evidence from a hurdling technique. *Acta Psychologica, 38*, 72–80.

Proctor, R. W. (1981). A unified theory for matching task phenomena. *Psychological Review, 88*, 291–326.

Proctor, R. W., & Reeve, T. G. (Eds.). (1990). *Stimulus–response compatibility.* Amsterdam: North-Holland.

Quinlan, P. T., & Bailey, P. J. (1995). An examination of attentional control in the auditory modality: Further evidence for auditory orienting. *Perception & Psychophysics, 57*, 614–628.

Rabbitt, P. M. A. (1967). Learning to ignore irrelevant information. *American Journal of Psychology, 80*, 1–13.

Rabbitt, P. M. A. (1968). Two kinds of error-signalling responses in a serial choice task. *Quarterly Journal of Experimental Psychology, 20*, 179–188.

Rabbitt, P. M. A. (1979). Current paradigms and models in human information processing. In V. Hamilton & D. M. Warburton (Eds.), *Human stress and cognition.* New York: Wiley.

Rabbitt, P. M. A. (1981). Visual selective attention. In C. R. Puff (Ed.), *Handbook of research methods in human memory and cognition.* New York: Academic Press.

Rabbitt, P. M. A. (1986). Models and paradigms in the study of stress effects. In G. R. J. Hockey, A. W. K. Gaillard, & M. G. H. Coles (Eds.), *Energetics and human information processing.* Dordrecht, The Netherlands: Nijhoff.

Rabbitt, P. M. A. (1988). The faster the better? Some comments on the use of information processing rate as an index of change and individual differences on performance. In I. Hindmarch, B. Aufdembrinke, & H. Ott (Eds.), *Psychopharmacology and reaction time.* New York: Wiley.

Rabbitt, P. M. A., & Rogers, B. (1977). What does a man do after he makes an error? An analysis of response programming. *Quarterly Journal of Experimental Psychology, 29*, 232–240.

Rabbitt, P. M. A., & Vyas, S. M. (1970). An elementary preliminary taxonomy for some errors in laboratory tasks. *Acta Psychologica, 33*, 56–76.

Rafal, R., Calabresi, P., Brennan, C., & Sciolto, T. (1989). Saccade preparation inhibits reorienting to recently attended locations. *Journal of Experimental Psychology: Human Perception & Performance, 15*, 673–685.

Ragot, R. (1990). Cerebral evoked potentials: Early indexes of compatibility effects. In R. W. Proctor & T. G. Reeve (Eds.), *Stimulus–response compatibility* (pp. 225–240). Amsterdam: North-Holland.

Rasmussen, J. (1986). *Information processing and human-machine interaction: An approach to cognitive engineering.* Amsterdam: North-Holland.

Ratcliff, R. (1978). A theory of memory retrieval. *Psychological Review, 85*, 59–108.

Ratcliff, R. (1985). Theoretical interpretations of speed and accuracy of positive and negative responses. *Psychological Review, 92*, 212–225.

Ratcliff, R. (1988). Continuous versus discrete information processing: Modeling accumulation of partial information. *Psychological Review, 95*, 238–255.

Ratcliff, R. (1993). Methods for dealing with reaction time outlyers. *Psychological Bulletin, 114*, 510–532.

Ratcliff, R., & Hacker, M. J. (1981). Speed and accuracy of same and different responses in perceptual matching. *Perception & Psychophysics, 30*, 303–307.

Rayner, K. (1978). Foveal and parafoveal cues in reading. In J. Requin (Ed.), *Attention & Performance, 7*, 149–161. Hillsdale, NJ: Lawrence Erlbaum Associates.

Rayner, K., & Duffy, S. A. (1986). Lexical complexity and fixation times in reading: Effects of word frequency, verb complexity and lexical ambiguity. *Memory & Cognition, 14*, 191–201.

Rayner, K., & Pollatsek, A. (1981). Eye movement control during reading: Evidence for direct control. *Quarterly Journal of Experimental Psychology, 33A*, 351–373.

Rayner, K., & Pollatsek, A. (1989). *The psychology of reading.* Englewood Cliffs, NJ: Prentice-Hall.

Reason, J. (1990). *Human error.* Cambridge, England: Cambridge University Press.

Reeve, T. G., & Proctor, R. W. (1990). The salient features coding principle for spatial and symbolic compatibility effects. In R. W. Proctor & T. G. Reeve (Eds.), *Stimulus–response compatibility.* Amsterdam: North Holland.

Reeve, T. G., Proctor, R. W., Weeks, D. J., & Dornier, L. (1992). Salience of stimulus and response features in choice-reaction tasks. *Perception & Psychophysics, 52,* 453–460.

Reicher, G. M. (1969). Perceptual recognition as a function of meaningfulness of stimulus material. *Journal of Experimental Psychology, 81,* 274–280.

Remington, R. J. (1969). Analysis of sequential effects in choice reaction times. *Journal of Experimental Psychology, 82,* 250–257.

Rensink, R. A., & Enns, J. T. (1995). Preemption effects in visual search: Evidence for low level grouping. *Psychological Review, 102,* 101–130.

Requin, J., Riehle, A., & Seal, J. (1993). Neuronal networks for movement preparation. In D. E. Meyer & S. Kornblum (Eds.), *Attention & Performance* (Vol. 14). Cambridge, MA: MIT Press.

Ridderinkhof, K. R., van der Molen, M. W., & Bashore, T. R. (1995). Limits on the application of the additive factors logic: Violations of stage robustness suggest a dual-process architecture to explain flanker effects on target processing. *Acta Psychologica, 90,* 29–48.

Riemersma, J. B. J., Sanders, A. F., Wildervanck, C., & Gaillard, A. W. K. (1977). Performance decrement during prolonged night driving. In R. R. Mackie (Ed.), *Vigilance: Theory, operational performance and physiological correlates.* New York: Plenum.

Riemersma, J. B. J., van der Horst, A. R. A., Hoekstra, W., Alink, G. M. M., & Otten, N. (1990). The validity of a driving simulator in evaluating speed-reducing measures. *Traffic Engineering & Control, 9,* 416–420.

Robbins, T. W. (1986). Psychopharmacological and neurobiological aspects of the energetics of information processing. In G. R. J. Hockey, A. W. K. Gaillard, & M. G. H. Coles (Eds.), *Energetics and human information processing.* Dordrecht, The Netherlands: Nijhoff.

Robbins, T. W., & Everitt, B. J. (1995). Arousal systems and attention. In M. S. Gazzaniga (Ed.), *The cognitive neurosciences.* Cambridge, MA: MIT Press.

Roberts, S. (1987). Evidence for distinct serial processes in animals: The multiplicative factors method. *Animal Learning & Behavior, 15,* 135–173.

Roberts, S., & Sternberg, S. (1993). The meaning of additive reaction-time effects: Tests of three alternatives. *Attention & Performance, 14,* 611–653.

Robertson, L. C., Egly, R., Lamb, M. R., & Kerth, L. (1993). Spatial attention and cuing to global and local levels of a hierarchical structure. *Journal of Experimental Psychology: Human Perception & Performance, 19,* 471–487.

Rogers, R. D., & Monsell, S. (1995). Costs of a predictable switch between simple cognitive tasks. *Journal of Experimental Psychology: General, 124,* 207–231.

Rogers, W. A., Lee, M. D., & Fisk, A. D. (1995). Contextual effects on general learning, feature learning, and attention strengthening in visual search. *Human Factors, 37,* 158–172.

Rollins, R. A., & Hendricks, R. (1980). Processing of words presented simultaneously to eye and ear. *Journal of Experimental Psychology: Human Perception & Performance, 6,* 99–109.

Roscoe, S. N. (1981). *Aviation psychology.* Iowa City: University of Iowa Press.

Rosenbaum, D. A. (1980). Human movement initiation: Specification of arm, direction and extent. *Journal of Experimental Psychology: General, 109,* 444–474.

Rosenbaum, D. A. (1987). Successive approximations to a model of human motor programming. In G. H. Bower (Ed.), *The psychology of learning and motivation* (Vol. 21). New York: Academic Press.

Rosenbaum, D. A. (1991). *Human motor control.* New York: Academic Press.

Rosenbaum, D. A., Hindorff, V., & Munro, E. M. (1987). Scheduling and programming of rapid finger sequences: Tests and elaborations of the hierarchical editor model. *Journal of Experimental Psychology: Human Perception & Performance, 13,* 193–203.

Rösler, F., Clausen, G., & Sojka, B. (1986). The double priming paradigm: A tool for analysing the functional significance of endogenuous brain potentials. *Biological Psychology, 22,* 239–268.

Rösler, F., Hasselmann, D., & Sojka, B. (1987). Central and peripheral correlates of orienting and habituation. *EEG Supplement 40: Current trends in event-related potential research,* 366–372.

Rubin, E. (1921). Die Nicht-Existenz der Aufmerksamkeit [The non-existence of attention]. *Bericht über das neunten Kongress für experimentelle Psychologie,* Jena.

Rumelhart, D. E., & McClelland, J. L. (1981). An interactive activation model of context effects in letter perception. Part 2: The contextual enhancement effect and some tests and extensions of the model. *Psychological Review, 88,* 375–407.

Rumelhart, D. E., & McClelland, J. L. (1986). PDP models and general issues in cognitive science. In D. E. Rumelhart & J. L. McClelland and the PDP research group (Eds.), *Parallel distributed processing: Explorations in the microstructure of cognition: Vol. 1: Foundations.* Cambridge, MA: MIT Press.

Rumelhart, D. E., & Norman, D. (1982). Simulating a skilled typist: A study of skilled cognitive-motor performance. *Cognitive Science, 6,* 1–36.

Russo, J. E. (1978). Adaptation of cognitive processes in the eye movement system. In J. W. Senders, D. F. Fisher, & R. A. Monty (Eds.), *Eye movements and the higher psychological functions.* Hillsdale, NJ: Lawrence Erlbaum Associates.

Ruthruff, E. (1996). A test of the deadline model for speed-accuracy tradeoffs. *Perception and Psychophysics, 58,* 56–64.

Ruthruff, E., Miller, J., & Lachmann, Th. (1995). Does mental rotation require central mechanisms? *Journal of Experimental Psychology: Human Perception & Performance, 21,* 552–570.

Sagi, D., & Julesz, B. (1985). Detection versus discrimination of visual orientation. *Perception, 14,* 619–628.

St. James, J. D., & Eriksen, C. W. (1991). Response competition produces a fast same effect in same-different judgments. In J. R. Pomerantz & G. R. Lockhead (Eds.), *The perception of structure.* Washington, DC: American Psychological Association.

Salame, P., & Wittersheim, G. (1978). Selective noise disturbance of the information input in short-term memory. *Quarterly Journal of Experimental Psychology, 30,* 693–704.

Salthouse, T. A. (1984). Effects of age and skill in typing. *Journal of Experimental Psychology: General, 113,* 345–371.

Salthouse, T. A. (1986). Perceptual, cognitive and motoric aspects of transcription typing. *Psychological Bulletin, 99,* 303–319.

Salthouse, T. A. (1991). *Theoretical perspectives on cognitive aging.* Hillsdale, NJ: Lawrence Erlbaum Associates.

Sanders, A. F. (1963). *The selective process in the functional visual field.* Assen, Netherlands: Van Gorcum.

Sanders, A. F. (1964). Selective strategies in the assimilation of successively presented signals. *Quarterly Journal of Experimental Psychology, 16,* 378–372.

Sanders A. F. (1967a). Some aspects of reaction processes. *Acta Psychologica, 27,* 115–130.

Sanders, A. F. (1967b). The effect of compatibility on grouping successively presented signals. *Acta Psychologica, 26,* 373–382.

Sanders, A. F. (Ed.). (1967c). Attention & Performance. *Acta Psychologica, 27.*

Sanders, A. F. (1970a). Some aspects of the selective process in the functional visual field. *Ergonomics, 13,* 101–117.

Sanders, A. F. (1970b). Some variables affecting the relation between relative signal frequency and choice reaction time. *Acta Psychologica, 33,* 45–55.

Sanders, A. F. (1971). Probabilistic advance information and the psychological refractory period. *Acta Psychologica, 35,* 128–137.

Sanders, A. F. (1972). Foreperiod duration and the time course of preparation. *Acta Psychologica, 36,* 60–71.

Sanders, A. F. (1975a). The foreperiod effect revisited. *Quarterly Journal of Experimental Psychology, 27,* 591–598.

Sanders, A. F. (1975b). Some remarks on short-term memory. In P. M. A. Rabbitt & S. Dornic (Eds.), *Attention & Performance* (Vol. 5). London: Academic Press.

Sanders, A. F. (1977). Structural and functional aspects of the reaction process. In S. Dornic (Ed.), *Attention & Performance* (Vol. 6). Hillsdale, NJ: Lawrence Erlbaum Associates.

Sanders, A. F. (1979). Some remarks on mental load. In N. Moray (Ed.), *Mental workload: Its theory and measurement.* New York: Plenum.

Sanders, A. F. (1980a). Stage analysis of reaction processes. In G. E. Stelmach & J. Requin (Eds.), *Tutorials in motor behavior.* Amsterdam: North-Holland.

Sanders, A. F. (1980b). Some effects of instructed muscle tension on choice reaction time and movement time. *Attention & Performance, 8,* 59–74.

Sanders, A. F. (1983). Towards a model of stress and human performance. *Acta Psychologica, 53,* 61–97.

Sanders, A. F. (1984). Ten symposia on attention and performance: Some issues and trends. In H. Bouma & D. Bouwhuis (Eds.), *Attention & Performance* (Vol. 10, pp. 1–10). Hillsdale, NJ: Lawrence Erlbaum Associates.

Sanders, A. F. (1987). Problems of a novice: Some introspective observations. In G. Salvendi (Ed.), *Social, ergonomic and stress aspects of work with computers.* Amsterdam: Elsevier.

Sanders, A. F. (1990). Issues and trends in the debate on discrete vs. continuous processing of information. *Acta Psychologica, 74,* 1–45.

Sanders, A. F. (1991). Simulation as a tool in the measurement of human performance. *Ergonomics, 34,* 995–1025.

Sanders, A. F. (1993a). Processing information in the functional visual field. In G. d'Ydewalle & D. van Rensbergen (Eds.), *Perception & cognition: Advances in eye movement research.* Amsterdam: North-Holland.

Sanders, A. F. (1993b). Performance theory and measurement through chronometric analysis. In D. E. Meyer & S. Kornblum (Eds.), *Attention & Performance* (Vol. 14). Cambridge, MA: MIT Press.

Sanders, A. F. (1993c). On the output of a visual fixation. In A. D. Baddeley & L. Weiskrantz (Eds.), *Attention: Selection, awareness and control.* Oxford: Clarendon.

Sanders, A. F. (1995). Discrete vs. continuous processing: The fate of an incompletely processed perceptual dimension. *Acta Psychologica, 90,* 211–227.

Sanders, A. F., & Andriessen, J. E. B. (1978). A suppressing effect of response selection on immediate arousal in a choice reaction task. *Acta Psychologica, 42,* 181–186.

Sanders, A. F., & Donk, M. (1996). Visual search. In O. Neumann & A. F. Sanders (Eds.), *Attention.* New York: Academic Press.

Sanders, A. F., & Hoogenboom, W. (1970). On the effects of continuous active work on performance. *Acta Psychologica, 33,* 414–431.

Sanders, A. F., & Houtmans, M. J. M. (1985a). There is no central stimulus encoding during saccadic eye shifts: A case against general parallel processing notions. *Acta Psychologica, 60,* 323–338.

Sanders, A. F., & Houtmans, M. J. M. (1985b). Perceptual processing modes in the functional visual field. *Acta Psychologica, 60,* 251–262.

Sanders, A. F., & Keuss, P. J. G. (1969). Grouping and refractoriness in multiple selective responses. *Acta Psychologica, 30,* 177–194.

Sanders, A. F., & Rath, A. (1991). Perceptual processing and speed-accuracy trade-off. *Acta Psychologica, 77,* 275–291.

Sanders, A. F., & Reitsma, W. D. (1982). Lack of sleep and covert orienting of attention. *Acta Psychologica, 52,* 137–145.

Sanders, A. F., & Schroots, J. J. F. (1968). Cognitive categories and memory span: The effect of temporal vs categorical recall. *Quarterly Journal of Experimental Psychology, 20,* 373–379.

Sanders A. F., & Schroots, J. J. F. (1969). Cognitive categories and memory span: Effects of similarity on recall. *Quarterly Journal of Experimental Psychology, 21,* 21–28.

Sanders, A. F., & Terlinden, W. (1967). Decision making during paced arrival of probabilistic information. *Acta Psychologica, 27,* 170–177.

Sanders A. F., & Wauschkuhn, C. H. (1988). Drugs and information processing in skilled performance. In I. Hindmarch & H. Ott (Eds.), *Benzodiazepine, receptor ligands, memory and information processing.* Heidelberg: Springer

Sanders, A. F., & Wertheim, A. (1973). The relation between physical stimulus properties and the effect of foreperiod duration on reaction time. *Quarterly Journal of Experimental Psychology, 25,* 201–206.

Sanders, A. F., Wijnen, J. L. C., & van Arkel, A. E. (1982). An additive factor analysis of the effects of sleep-loss on reaction processes. *Acta Psychologica, 51,* 41–59.

Sanders, A. F., & Willemse, E. (1978). The course of proactive interference in immediate probed recall. *Acta Psychologica, 42,* 133–144.

Sanders, M. S., & McCormick, E. J. (1992). *Human factors in engineering and design.* New York: McGraw-Hill.

Sanocki, T. (1988). Font regularity constraints on the process of letter recognition. *Journal of Experimental Psychology: Human Perception & Performance, 17,* 924–941.

Santee, J. L., & Egeth, H. E. (1980). Selective attention in the speeded classification and comparison of multidimensional stimuli. *Perception & Psychophysics, 28,* 191–204.

Schmidt, R. A. (1987). *Motor control and learning: A behavioral emphasis.* Champaign, IL: Human Kinetics.

Schmidt, R. A. (1988). Motor and action perspectives on motor behaviour. In O. G. Meijer & K. Roth (Eds.), *Complex movement behaviour: The motor-action controversy.* Amsterdam: North-Holland.

Schmitter-Edgecombe, M. E., Marks, W., Fahy, J. F., & Long, C. J. (1992). Effects of severe closed head injury on three stages of information processing. *Journal of Clinical and Experimental Neuropsychology, 14,* 717–737.

Schneider, W. (1985). Training high performance skills: Fallacies and guidelines. *Human Factors, 27,* 285–300.

Schneider, W., & Fisk, A. D. (1982). Concurrent automatic and controlled search: Can processing occur without resource costs? *Journal of Experimental Psychology: Learning, Memory and Cognition, 8,* 261–278.

Schneider, W., & Fisk, A. D. (1984). Automatic category search and its transfer. *Journal of Experimental Psychology: Learning, Memory and Cognition, 10,* 1–15.

Schneider, W., & Shiffrin, R. M. (1977). Controlled and automatic human information processing: Detection, search and attention. *Psychological Review, 84,* 1–66.

Schneider, W., Vidulich, M. A., & Yeh, Y. Y. (1982). Training spatial skills for air-traffic control. *Proceedings of the twenty-sixth annual meeting of the Human Factors Society.*

Schouten, J. F., & Bekker, J. A. M. (1967). Reaction time and accuracy. *Acta Psychologica, 27,* 143–153.

Schuffel, H. (1986). *Human Control of Ships in Tracking Tasks*. Doctoral dissertation, University of Tilburg, Tilburg, The Netherlands.

Schvaneveldt, R. W., & McDonald, J. E. (1981). Semantic context and the encoding of words. *Journal of Experimental Psychology: Human Perception & Performance, 7*, 673–687.

Schweikert, R. (1978). Critical path generalisation of the additive factor method: Analysis of a Stroop task. *Journal of Mathematical Psychology, 18*, 105–139.

Schweikert, R. (1985). Separable effects of factors on speed and accuracy: Memory scanning, lexical decision and choice tasks. *Psychological Bulletin, 97*, 530–546.

Schweikert, R., & Townsend, J. T. (1989). A trichotomy: Interactions of factors prolonging sequential and concurrent mental processes in stochastic discrete mental (PERT) networks. *Journal of Mathematical Psychology, 33*, 328–347.

See, J. E., Howe, S. R., Warm, J. S., & Dember, W. M. (1995). Meta-analysis of the sensitivity decrement in vigilance. *Psychological Bulletin, 117*, 230–249.

Seibel, R. (1963). Discrimination reaction time for a 1023 alternative task. *Journal of Experimental Psychology, 66*, 215–226.

Seibel, R. (1972). Data entry devices and procedures. In H. P. van Cott & R. G. Kinkade (Eds.), *Human engineering guide to equipment design*. Washington, DC: U.S. Government Printing Office.

Seidenberg, M. S., & McClelland, J. L. (1989). A distributed developmental model of word recognition and naming. *Psychological Review, 96*, 523–568.

Selye, H. (1956). *The stress of life*. New York: McGraw-Hill.

Selye, H. (1979). The stress concept and some of its implications. In V. Hamilton & D. M. Warburton (Eds.), *Human stress and cognition*. New York: Wiley.

Senders, J. W. (1983). *Visual sampling processes*. Hillsdale, NJ: Lawrence Erlbaum Associates.

Senders, J. W., Kristofferson, A. B., Levison, W. H., Dietrich, C. W., & Ward, J. L. (1967). The attentional demand of automobile driving. *Highway Research Record, 95*, 15–33.

Semjen, A., Requin, R., & Fiori, N. (1978). The interactive effect of foreperiod duration and response movements characteristics upon choice reaction time in a pointing task. *Journal of Human Movement Studies, 4*, 108–118.

Sergeant, J., & van der Meere, J. (1990a). Convergence of approaches in localizing the hyper-activity deficit. In B. B. Lahey & A. E. Kazdin (Eds.), *Advances in clinical child psychology: Vol. 13*. London: Plenum.

Sergeant, J., & van der Meere, J. (1990b). Additive factor method applied to psychopathology with special reference to childhood hyperactivity. *Acta Psychologica, 74*, 277–295.

Shaffer, L. H. (1973). Latency mechanisms in transcription. In S. Kornblum (Ed.), *Attention & Performance* (Vol. 4). New York: Academic Press.

Shaffer, L. H. (1975). Multiple attention in continuous verbal tasks. In P. M. A. Rabbitt & S. Dornic (Eds.), *Attention & Performance* (Vol. 5). London: Academic Press.

Shaffer, L. H. (1978). Timing in the motor programming of typing. *Quarterly Journal of Experimental Psychology, 30*, 333–345.

Shaffer, L. H. (1980). Book review. *Quarterly Journal of Experimental Psychology, 32*, 174–176.

Shaffer, L. H. (1982). Rhythm and timing in skill. *Psychological Review, 89*, 109–122.

Shallice, T., & Burgess, P. (1993). Supervisory control of action and thought selection. In A. D. Baddeley & L. Weiskrantz (Eds.), *Attention: Selection, awareness and control*. Oxford: Clarendon.

Shallice, T., & Vickers, D. (1964). Theories and experiments on discrimination times. *Ergonomics, 7*, 37–49.

Shepard, R. N., & Metzler, J. (1971). Mental rotation of three-dimensional objects. *Science, 171*, 701–703.

Sheperd, A. (1989). Analysis and training in information technology tasks. In D. Diaper (Ed.), *Task analysis for human-computer interaction*. Chichester: Horwood.

Shepherd, M., Findlay, J. M., & Hockey, R. J. (1986). The relationship between eye movements and spatial attention. *Quarterly Journal of Experimental Psychology, 38,* 475–491.

Shiffrin, R. M. (1975). The locus and role of attention in memory systems. In P. M. A. Rabbitt & S. Dornic (Eds.), *Attention and Performance* (Vol. 5). London: Academic Press.

Shiffrin, R. M. (1988). Attention. In R. C. Atkinson, R. J. Herrnstein, G. Lindzey, & R. D. Luce (Eds.), *Stevens' handbook of experimental psychology: Vol. 2. Learning and cognition.* New York: Wiley.

Shiffrin, R. M., & Schneider, W. (1977). Controlled and automatic human information processing: perceptual learning, automatic attending and a general theory. *Psychological Review, 84,* 127–190.

Shingledecker, C. A. (1984). A task battery of applied human performance assessment. *Airforce Aeromedical Research Laboratory.* Report AFAMRL-TR-84–071.

Shingledecker, C. A., Acton, W. A., & Crabtree, M. S. (1983). *Development and application of a criterion task set for workload metric evaluation.* (SAE technical paper series, 831419)

Shiu, L., & Pashler, H. (1994). Negligible effect of spatial precuing on identification of single digits. *Journal of Experimental Psychology: Human Perception & Performance, 20,* 1037–1054.

Shulman, G. L., Sheehy, J. B., & Wilson, J. (1986). Gradients of spatial attention. *Acta Psychologica, 61,* 167–181.

Shulman, G. L., Sullivan, M. A., Gish, K., & Sakoda, W. J. (1986). The role of spatial frequency channels in the perception of local and global structure. *Perception, 15,* 259–273.

Shulman, H. G., & McConkie, A. (1973). S–R compatibility, response discriminability and response codes in choice reaction time. *Journal of Experimental Psychology, 98,* 375–378.

Shwartz, S. P., Pommerantz, J. R., & Egeth, H. E. (1977). State and process limitations in information processing: An additive factor analysis. *Journal of Experimental Psychology: Human Perception & Performance, 3,* 402–410.

Sidaway, B., Fairweather, M., Sekiya, H., & McNitt-Gray, J. (1996). Time-to-collision estimation in a simulated driving task. *Human Factors, 38,* 101–113.

Siegel, A. I., & Wolf, J. J. (1969). *Man-machine simulation models: Performance and psychosocial interaction.* New York: Wiley.

Simon, J. R. (1969). Reactions towards the source of stimulation. *Journal of Experimental Psychology, 81,* 174–176.

Simon, J. R. (1990). The effects of an irrelevant directional cue on human information processing. In R. W. Proctor & T. G. Reeve (Eds.), *Stimulus–response compatibility.* Amsterdam: North-Holland.

Simon, J. R., & Baker, K. L. (1995). Effect of irrelevant information on the time to enter and retrieve relevant information in a Stroop-type task. *Journal of Experimental Psychology: Human Perception & Performance, 21,* 1028–1043.

Simon, J. R., & Berbaum, K. (1988). Effect of irrelevant information on retrieval time for relevant information. *Acta Psychologica, 67,* 33–57.

Simon, J. R., & Small, A. M. (1969). Processing auditory information: Interference from an irrelevant cue. *Journal of Applied Psychology, 53,* 433–435.

Simon, J. R., & Wolf, J. D. (1963). Choice reaction time as a function of angular stimulus–response correspondence and age. *Ergonomics, 6,* 99–105.

Smets, G. J. F., & Stappers, P. J. (1990). Do invariants of features determine the conspicuity of forms? In D. Brogan (Ed.), *Visual search.* London: Taylor & Francis.

Smid, H. G. O. M., Bøcker, K. B. E., van Touw, D. A., Mulder, G., & Brunia, C. H. M. (1996). A psychophysiological investigation of the selection and the use of partial stimulus information in response choice. *Journal of Experimental Psychology: Human Perception & Performance, 22,* 3–24.

Smid, H. G. O. M., Lamain, W., Hogeboom, M. M., Mulder, G., & Mulder, L. J. M. (1991). Psychophysiological evidence for continuous information transmission between visual search and response processes. *Journal of Experimental Psychology: Human Perception & Performance, 17*, 696–714.

Smid, H. G. O. M., Mulder, G., & Mulder, L. J. M. (1990). Selective response activation can begin before stimulus recognition is complete: A psychophysiological and error analysis of continuous flow. *Acta Psychologica, 74*, 169–201.

Smid, H. G. O. M., Mulder, G., Mulder, L. J. M., & Brands, G. J. (1992). A psychophysiological study of the use of partial information in stimulus–response translation. *Journal of Experimental Psychology: Human Perception & Performance, 18*, 1101–1119.

Smith G. A. (1977). Studies of compatibility and a new model of choice reaction time. In S. Dornic (Ed.), *Attention & Performance* (Vol. 6). Hillsdale, NJ: Lawrence Erlbaum Associates.

Smith, G. A. (1980). Models of choice reaction time. In A. T. Welford (Ed.), *Reaction times.* London: Academic Press.

Smith, P. L. (1995). Psychophysically principled models of visual simple reaction time. *Psychological Review, 102*, 567–593.

Smith P. L., & Vickers, D. (1988). The accumulator model of two-choice discrimination. *Journal of Mathematical Psychology, 32*, 135–168.

Smith, S. W., & Rea, M. S. (1979). Relationships between office task performance and ratings of feelings and task evaluation under different light sources and level. *Proceedings of the nineteenth session of the Commission Internationale d'Eclairage*, Publication 50.

Smolensky, P. (1988). On the proper treatment of connectionism. *Behavioral and Brain Sciences, 11*, 1–74.

Smulders, F. (1994). The selectivity of age effects on information processing. Doctoral dissertation, University of Amsterdam.

Smulders, F. T. Y., Kok, A., Kenemans, J. L., & Bashore, T. R. (1995). The temporal selectivity of additive factor effects on the reaction process revealed in ERP component latencies. *Acta Psychologica, 90*, 97–109.

Soetens, E., Boer, L. C., & Hueting, J. E. (1985). Expectancy or automatic facilitation? Separating sequential effects in two-choice reaction time. *Journal of Experimental Psychology: Human Perception & Performance, 11*, 598–616.

Sokolov, E. N. (1963). Higher nervous functions: The orienting reflex. *Annual Review of Physiology, 25*, 545–580.

Sokolov, E. N. (1975). The neuronal mechanisms of the orienting reflex. In E. N. Sokolov & O. S. Vinogradova (Eds.), *Neuronal mechanisms of the orienting reflex*. Hillsdale, NJ: Lawrence Erlbaum Associates.

Sollenberg, R. L., & Milgram, P. (1993). Effects of stereoscopic and rotational displays in a three-dimensional path-tracing task. *Human Factors, 35*, 483–499.

Sorkin, R., Kantowitz, B., & Kantowitz, S. (1988). Likelihood alarm displays. *Human Factors, 30*, 455–459.

Spencer, M. B. (1987). The influence of regularity of rest and activity on performance: A model based on time since sleep and time of day. *Ergonomics, 30*, 1275–1286.

Sperling, G. (1960). The information available in brief visual presentations. *Psychological Monographs, 74*, 11.

Sperling, G. (1984). A unified theory of attention and signal detection. In R. Parasuraman & R. Davies (Eds.), *Varieties of attention*. New York: Academic Press.

Sperling, G., Budiansky, J., Spivak, J. G., & Johnson, M. C. (1971). Extremely rapid visual search: The maximum rate of scanning letters for the presence of a numeral. *Science, 174*, 307–311.

Sperling, G., & Dosher, B. A. (1986). Strategy and optimization in human information processing. In K. R. Boff, L. Kaufman, & J. P. Thomas (Eds.), *Handbook of perception & human performance*. New York: Wiley.

Sperling, G., Wurst, S. A., & Lu, Z. (1993). Using repetition detection to define and localize the processes of selective attention. In D. E. Meyer & S. Kornblum (Eds.), *Attention & Performance* (Vol. 14). Cambridge, MA: MIT Press.

Spijkers, W. A. C. (1987). Programming of direction and velocity of an aiming movement: The effect of probability and response specificity. *Acta Psychologica, 65*, 285–304.

Spijkers, W. A. C. (1990a). The relation between response specificity, S–R compatibility, foreperiod duration and muscle tension in a target aiming task. *Acta Psychologica, 75*, 261–277.

Spijkers, W. A. C. (1990b). Response selection and motor programming: Effects of compatibility and average velocity. In R. W. Proctor & T. G. Reeve (Eds.), *Stimulus–response compatibility* (pp. 297–310). Amsterdam: North-Holland.

Spijkers, W. A. C., & Sanders, A. F. (1984). Spatial accuracy and programming of movement velocity. *Bulletin of the Psychonomic Society, 22*, 531–534.

Spijkers, W. A. C., & Spellenberg, S. (1995). On-line visual control of aiming movements? *Acta Psychologica, 90*, 333–348.

Spijkers, W. A. C., & Steyvers, J. J. M. (1984). Specification of direction and duration during programming of discrete sliding movements. *Psychological Research, 46*, 59–71.

Spijkers, W. A. C., & Walter, A. (1985). Response processing stages in choice reactions. *Acta Psychologica, 58*, 191–204.

Stankov, L. (1983). Attention and intelligence. *Journal of Educational Psychology, 4*, 471–490.

Stankov, L. (1988). Aging, attention and intelligence. *Psychology and Aging, 3*, 59–74.

Stanners, J. E., Jastrzembsky, J. E., & Westbrook, A. (1975). Frequency and visual quality in a word–non-word classification task. *Journal of Verbal Learning and Verbal Behavior, 14*, 259–264.

Stanovich, K., & Pachella, R. (1977). Encoding, stimulus–response compatibility and stages of processing. *Journal of Experimental Psychology: Human Perception & Performance, 3*, 411–421.

Stark, L., & Ellis, S. R. (1981). Scan path revisited: Cognitive models direct active looking. In D. F. Fisher, R. A. Monty, & J. W. Senders (Eds.), *Eye movements, cognition and visual perception*. Hillsdale, NJ: Lawrence Erlbaum Associates.

Stein, W., & Wewerinke, P. W. (1983). Human display monitoring and failure detection: Control theoretic models and experiments. *Automatica, 19*, 711–718.

Stern, J. A., Boyer, B., & Schroeder, D. (1994). Blink rate: A possible measure of fatigue. *Human Factors, 36*, 285–297.

Sternberg, S. (1969). The discovery of processing stages: Extensions of Donders' method. *Acta Psychologica, 30*, 276–315.

Sternberg, S. (1975). Memory scanning: New findings and current controversies. *Quarterly Journal of Experimental Psychology, 27*, 1–42.

Sternberg, S., Knoll, R. L., Monsell, S., & Wright, C. E. (1988). Motor programs and hierarchical organisation in the control of rapid speech. *Phonetica, 45*, 175–197.

Sternberg, S., Monsell, S., Knoll, R. L., & Wright, C. E. (1978). The latency and duration of rapid movement sequences. In G. E. Stelmach (Ed.), *Information processing in motor control and learning*. New York: Academic Press.

Steyvers, F. J. J. M. (1987). The influence of sleep deprivation and knowledge of results on perceptual encoding. *Acta Psychologica, 66*, 173–187.

Steyvers, F. J. J. M. (1991). *Information processing and sleep deprivation: Effects of knowledge of results and task variables on choice reaction.* Doctoral dissertation, Tilburg University, Tilburg, The Netherlands.

Stoffels, E. J. (1988). *Reactions towards the stimulus source: The locus of the effect.* Doctoral dissertation, Free University, Amsterdam.

Stoffels, E. J. (1996). On stage robustness and response selection routes: Further evidence. *Acta Psychologica, 91*, 67–88.

Stoffels, E. J., van der Molen, M. W., & Keuss, P. J. G. (1985). Intersensory facilitation and inhibition: Immediate arousal and location effects of auditory noise on visual choice reaction time. *Acta Psychologica, 58*, 45–62.

Stokx, L. C., & Gaillard, A. W. K. (1986). Task and driving performance of patients with a severe concussion of the brain. *Journal of Clinical and Experimental Neuropsychology, 8*, 421–436.

Strayer, D. L., & Kramer, A. F. (1990). Attentional requirements of automatic and controlled processing. *Journal of Experimental Psychology: Learning, Memory and Cognition, 16*, 67–82.

Stroop, J. R. (1935). Studies of interference in serial verbal reactions. *Journal of Experimental Psychology, 18*, 643–661.

Sugg, M. J., & McDonald, J. E. (1994). Time course of inhibition in color-response and word-response versions of the Stroop task. *Journal of Experimental Psychology: Human Perception and Performance, 20*, 647–675.

Summers, J. J. (1989). Motor programs. In D. H. Holding (Ed.), *Human skills* (pp. 49–69). Chicester: Wiley.

Swensson, R. G., & Edwards, W. (1971). Response strategies in a two-choice reaction task with a continuous cost for time. *Journal of Experimental Psychology, 88*, 67–81.

Tanner, W. P., & Swets, J. A. (1954). A decision making theory of visual detection. *Psychological Review, 61*, 401–409.

Teichner, W. H., & Krebs, M. J. (1972). Laws of the simple visual reaction time. *Psychological Review, 79*, 344–358.

Teichner, W. H., & Mocharnuk, J. B. (1979). Visual search for complex targets. *Human Factors, 21*, 259–275.

ten Hoopen, G. (1996). Auditory attention. In O. Neumann & A. F. Sanders (Eds.), *Attention*. New York: Academic Press.

Tent, L. (1962). Untersuchungen zur Erfassung des Verhältnisses von Anspannung und Leistung bei vorwiegend psychisch beanspruchenden Tätigkeiten [Studies on the relation between effort and performance in primarily mentally loading tasks]. *Archiv für die gesammte Psychologie, 115*, 106–172.

Theeuwes, J. (1989). Effects of location and form cuing on the allocation of attention in the visual field. *Acta Psychologica, 72*, 177–192.

Theeuwes, J. (1990). Perceptual selectivity is task-dependent: Evidence from selective search. *Acta Psychologica, 74*, 81–99.

Theeuwes, J. (1991a). Center high-mounted stop light: An evaluation. IZF 1991-C3, TNO, Soesterberg, The Netherlands.

Theeuwes, J. (1991b). Categorisation and identification of simultaneous targets. *Acta Psychologica, 76*, 73–86.

Theeuwes, J. (1991c). Exogenous and endogenous control of attention: The effects of visual onsets and offsets. *Perception & Psychophysics, 49*, 83–90.

Theeuwes, J. (1991d). Visual selection: Exogeneous and endogenous control. In A. G. Gale (Ed.), *Vision in vehicles* (Vol. 3). Amsterdam: North-Holland.

Theeuwes, J. (1992). Perceptual selectivity for color and form. *Perception & Psychophysics, 51*, 599–606.

Theeuwes, J. (1993). Visual selective attention: A theoretical analysis. *Acta Psychologica, 83*, 93–154.

Theeuwes, J. (1995). Abrupt luminance change pops out; abrupt color change does not. *Perception & Psychophysics, 57*, 637–644.

Theeuwes, J., & Hagenzieker, M. P. (1993). Visual search of traffic scenes: On the effect of location expectations. In A. G. Gale (Ed.), *Vision in vehicles* (Vol. 4). Amsterdam: North-Holland.

Theios, J. (1973). Reaction time measurements in the study of memory processes: Theory and data. In G. H. Bower (Ed.), *The psychology of learning and motivation* (Vol. 7). New York: Academic Press.

Theios, J., & Amrhein, P. C. (1989). Theoretical analysis of the cognitive processing of lexical and pictorial stimuli: Reading, naming and conceptual comparisons. *Psychological Review, 96,* 5–24.

Tipper, S. P. (1985). The negative priming effect: Inhibitory effects of ignored primes. *Quarterly Journal of Experimental Psychology, 37A,* 571–590.

Tipper, S. P., Brehaut, J. C., & Driver, J. (1990). Selection of moving and static objects for the control of spatially-directed action. *Journal of Experimental Psychology: Human Perception and Performance, 16,* 492–504.

Tipper, S. P., Driver, J., & Weaver, B. (1991). Object-centered inhibition of return of visual attention. *Quarterly Journal of Experimental Psychology, 43A,* 289–298.

Tipper, S. P., Weaver, B., Jerreat, L., & Burak, A. (1994). Object-based and environment-based inhibition of return of visual attention. *Journal of Experimental Psychology: Human Perception and Performance, 20,* 478–499.

Titchener, E. B. (1910). *A textbook of psychology.* New York: Macmillan.

Tolhurst, D. J. (1975). Sustained and tranient channels in human vision. *Vision Research, 15,* 1151–1155.

Townsend, J. T., & Ashby, F. G. (1983). *Stochastic modelling of elementary psychlogical processes.* Cambridge, England: Cambridge University Press.

Townsend, J. T., & Nozawa, G. (1995). Spatio-temporal properties of elementary perception: An investigation of parallel, serial and coactive theories. *Journal of Mathematical Psychology, 39,* 321–359.

Townsend, J. T., & van Zandt, T. (1990). New theoretical results on testing self-terminating vs exhaustive processing in rapid search experiments. In H. G. Geissler (Ed.), *Psychophysical explorations of mental structures.* Stuttgart: Hogrefe & Huber.

Travis, L. E. (1929). The relation of voluntary movements to tremors. *Journal of Experimental Psychology, 12,* 515–524.

Treisman, A. M. (1960). Contextual cues in selective listening. *Quarterly Journal of Experimental Psychology, 12,* 242–248.

Treisman, A. M. (1970). Perception and recall of simultaneous speech stimuli. *Acta Psychologica, 33,* 132–148.

Treisman, A. M. (1988). Features and objects: The fourteenth Bartlett memorial lecture. *Quarterly Journal of Experimental Psychology, 40,* 201–237.

Treisman, A. M. (1993). The perception of features and objects. In A. D. Baddeley & L. Weiskrantz (Eds.), *Attention: Selection, awareness and control* (pp. 5–35). Oxford: Clarendon Press.

Treisman, A. M., & Davies, A. (1973). Divided attention to eye and ear. In S. Kornblum (Ed.), *Attention & Performance* (Vol. 4). New York: Academic Press.

Treisman, A. M., & Gelade, G. (1980). A feature integration theory of attention. *Cognitive Psychology, 12,* 97–136.

Treisman, A. M., & Gormican, S. (1988). Feature analysis in early vision: Evidence from search asymmetries. *Psychological Review, 95,* 15–48.

Treisman A. M., & Riley, J. (1969). Is selective attention selective perception or selective response? A further test. *Journal of Experimental Psychology, 79,* 27–34.

Treisman, A. M., & Sato, S. (1990). Conjunction search revisited. *Journal of Experimental Psychology: Human Perception and Performance, 16,* 459–478.

Treisman, A. M., & Schmidt, H. (1982). Illusory conjunctions in the perception of objects. *Cognitive Psychology, 14,* 107–141.

Truijens, C. L., & Schuffel, H. (1978). Ergonomisch onderzoek "Open Hartel kanaal". Deel 3: Validering van de simulatie van duwvaart in het Hartelkanaal ["Open Hartel fairway." Part 3: Validation of the simulation of pusher tug shipping in the Hartelkanaal]. *IZF 1978-C6.* TNO, Soesterberg, The Netherlands.

Trumbo, D. A., & Milone, F. (1971). Primary task performance as a function of encoding, retention and recall in a secondary task. *Journal of Experimental Psychology, 91,* 273–279.

Tsang, P. S., Shaner, T. L., & Vidulich, M. A. (1995). Resource scarcity and outcome conflict in time-sharing performance. *Perception & Psychophysics, 57,* 365–378.

Umilta, C., & Nicoletti, R. (1990). Spatial stimulus–response compatibility. In R. W. Proctor & T. G. Reeve (Eds.), *Stimulus–response compatibility.* Amsterdam: North-Holland.

Umilta, C., Riggio, L., Dascola, I., & Rizolatti, G. (1991). Differential effects of central and peripheral cueson the reorienting of spatial attention. *European Journal of Cognitive Psychology, 3,* 247–267.

Underwood, G. (1982). Attention and awareness in cognitive and motor skills. In G. Underwood (Ed.), *Aspects of consciousness* (Vol. 3). London: Academic Press.

Unger, S. M. (1964). Habituation of the vasoconstrictive orienting reaction. *Journal of Experimental Psychology, 67,* 11–18.

Ursin, H. E., Baade, E., & Levine, S. (1978). *Psychobiology of stress: A study of coping man.* New York: Academic Press.

van Arem, B., Hogema, J. H., de Vos, A. P., Janssen, W. H., Zegwaard, G. F., van der Horst, A. R. A. (1994). The microscopic traffic simulation model MIXIC 1.1. (Report INRO-VVG 1994–21)

van Breda, L. (1989). Analysis of a procedure of multiple operator task performance on submarines using a network model. In G. R. McMillan, D. Beevis, E. Salas, M. H. Strub, R. Sutton, & L. van Breda (Eds.), *Applications of human performance models to system design.* New York: Plenum.

van Delft, J. H. (1987). The development of a response sequence: A new description of human sampling behaviour with multiple independent sources of information. *Proceedings of the thirty-first annual meeting of the Human Factors Society,* New York.

van Dellen, H. J., Brookhuis, K. A., Mulder, G., Okita, T., & Mulder, M. J. M. (1985). Evoked potential correlates of practice in a visual search task. In D. Papakoustopoulos, S. Butler, & E. Martin (Eds.), *Clinical and experimental neurophysiology.* Dover, NH: Croom Helm.

van der Heijden, A. H. C. (1992). *Selective attention in vision.* London: Routledge.

van der Heijden, A. H. C., Brouwer, R. F. T., & Serlie, A. W. (1992). Single letter recognition and position information: Benefits with a symbolic cue. *Psychological Research, 54,* 182–186.

van der Heijden, A. H. C., Malhas, M. S. M., & Roovaart, B. P. (1984). An empirical inter-letter confusion matrix for continuous line capitals. *Perception & Psychophysics, 35,* 85–88.

van der Heijden, A. H. C., Schreuder, R., De Loor, M., & Hagenzieker, M. (1987). Early and late selection: Visual letter confusions in a bar-probe task. *Acta Psychologica, 65,* 75–89.

van der Heijden, A. H. C., Schreuder, R., Maris, L., & Neerincx, M. (1984). Some evidence for correlated separate activation in a simple letter-detection task. *Perception & Psychophysics, 36,* 577–585.

van der Molen, M. W. (1996). Energetics and the reaction process: Running threads through experimental psychology. In O. Neumann & A. F. Sanders (Eds.), *Attention.* New York: Academic Press.

van der Molen, M. W., Bashore, T. E., Halliday, R., & Callaway, E. (1991). Chrono-psychophysiology: Mental chronometry augmented with psychophysiological time-markers. In J. R. Jennings & M. G. H. Coles (Eds.), *Handbook of cognitive psychophysiology: Central and autonomic nervous system approaches.* Chichester, UK: Wiley.

van der Molen, M. W., & Keuss, P. J. G. (1979). The relationship between reaction time and auditory intensity in discrete auditory tasks. *Quarterly Journal of Experimental Psychology, 31,* 95–102.

van der Molen, M. W., & Keuss, P. J. G. (1981). Response selection and the processing of auditory intensity. *Quarterly Journal of Experimental Psychology, 33,* 177–184.

van der Molen, M. W., Somsen, R. J. M., Jennings, J. R., Nieuwboer, R. T., & Orlebeke, J. F. (1987). A psychophysiological investigation of cognitive-energetic relations in human information processing: A heart rate/additive factors approach. *Acta Psychologica, 66,* 251–289.

van Duren, L. L. (1993). Central stimulus processing during saccadic eye movements. In G. d'Ydewalle & D. van Rensbergen (Eds.), *Perception & cognition: Advances in eye movement research*. Amsterdam: North-Holland.

van Duren, L. L. (1994). *Signal processing during eye fixations and saccades*. Doctoral dissertation, Free University, Amsterdam.

van Duren, L. L., & Sanders, A. F. (1988). On the robustness of the additive factors stage structure in blocked and mixed choice reaction designs. *Acta Psychologica, 69*, 83–94.

van Duren, L. L., & Sanders, A. F. (1995). Signal processing during and across saccades. *Acta Psychologica, 89*, 121–147.

van Galen, G. P., & Teulings, H. L. (1983). The independent monitoring of form and scale factors in handwriting. *Acta Psychologica, 54*, 9–22.

van Mier, H., & Hulstijn, W. (1993). The effect of motor complexity and practice on initiation time in writing and drawing. *Acta Psychologica, 84*, 231–251.

van Selst, M., & Jolicoeur, P. (1994). Can mental rotation occur before the dual task bottleneck? *Journal of Experimental Psychology: Human Perception and Performance, 20*, 905–921.

van Winsum, W., & Heino, A. (1996). Choice of time-headway in car-following and the role of time-to-collision information in braking. *Ergonomics, 39*, 579–592.

van Zomeren, A. H., & Brouwer, W. H. (1994). *Clinical neuropsychology of attention*. Oxford: Oxford University Press.

van Zomeren, A. H., Brouwer, W. H., & Deelman, B. G. (1984). Attentional deficits: The riddles of selectivity, speed and alertness. In D. N. Brooks (Ed.), *Closed head injury: Psychological, social and family consequences*. Oxford: Oxford University Press.

Velden, M. (1978). Some necessary revisions of the neuronal model concept of the orienting response. *Psychophysiology, 15*, 181–185.

Veltman, J. A., Gaillard, A. W. K., & van Breda, L. (1995). Physiological reactions to workload peaks. *TM 1995-A33*. TNO, Soesterberg, The Netherlands.

Venturino, M. (1991). Automatic processing, code dissimilarity, and the efficiency of successive memory searches. *Journal of Experimental Psychology: Human Perception and Performance, 17*, 677–695.

Vervaeck, K. R., & Boer, L. C. (1980). Sequential effects in two-choice reaction time: Subjective expectancy and automatic after-effect at short response-stimulus intervals. *Acta Psychologica, 44*, 175–190.

Verwey, W. B. (1994a). *Mechanisms of skill in sequential motor behavior*. Doctoral dissertation, Free University, Amsterdam.

Verwey, W. B. (1994b). Evidence for the development of concurrent processing in a sequential keypressing task. *Acta Psychologica, 85*, 245–262.

Verwey, W. B. (1996). Buffer loading and chunking in sequential keypressing. *Journal of Experimental Psychology: Human Perception and Performance, 22*, 544–562.

Vidulich, M. A. (1988). Speech responses and dual task performance: Better time-sharing or asymmetric transfer. *Human Factors, 30*, 517–534.

Virzi, R. A., & Egeth, H. E. (1985). Toward a translational model of Stroop interference. *Memory & Cognition, 13*, 304–319.

Vitu, F., O'Regan, J. K., Inhoff, A. W., & Topolski, R. (1995). Mindless reading: Eye movement characteristics are similar in scanning letter strings and reading texts. *Perception & Psychophysics, 57*, 354–362.

Viviani, P., & Laissard, G. (1996). Motor templates in typing. *Journal of Experimental Psychology: Human Perception and Performance, 22*, 417–445.

Viviani, P., & Swensson, R. G. (1982). Saccadic eye movements to peripherally discriminated visual targets. *Journal of Experimental Psychology: Human Perception and Performance, 8*, 113–126.

von Helmholtz, H. L. F. (1850). Messungen über den zeitlichen Verlauf der Zuckung animalischer Muskeln und die Fortplanzungsgeschwindigkeit der Reizung in den Nerven. *Archiv für Anatomie und Physiologie*, 276–364.

Von Wright, J. M. (1970). On selection in visual immediate memory. *Acta Psychologica, 33*, 280–292.

Von Wright, J. M., Anderson, K., & Stenman, U. (1975). Generalisation and conditional GSR in dichotic listening. In P. M. A. Rabbitt & S. Dornic (Eds.), *Attention and Performance* (Vol. 5). London: Academic Press.

Vos, J. J., & Riemersma, J. B. J. (1976). On the behavior in traffic of a homonymous hemianope. *Opthalmologica, 173*, 427–428.

Vreuls, D., & Obermayer, R. W. (1985). Human system performance measurement in training simulators. *Human Factors, 27*, 241–250.

Wagenaar, W. A. (1972). *Sequential response bias.* Doctoral dissertation, University of Leyden, The Netherlands.

Wagenaar, W. A. (1973). The effect of fluctuations of response criterion and sensitivity in a signal detection experiment. *Psychological Research, 36*, 27–37.

Wagenaar, W. A., & Michon, J. A. (1968). The effect of contracted time-scales in scale model maneouvring. *IZF 1968 C-3*, TNO, Soesterberg, The Netherlands.

Wagenaar, W. A., & Stakenburg, H. (1975). Paced and self-paced continuous reaction time. *Quarterly Journal of Experimental Psychology, 27*, 559–563.

Wallace R. J. (1972). Spatial S–R compatibility effects involving kinesthetic cues. *Journal of Experimental Psychology, 93*, 163–168.

Warm, J. S. (1984). An introduction to vigilance. In J. S. Warm (Ed.), *Sustained attention in human performance.* New York: Wiley.

Warm, J. S., & Jerison, H. J. (1984). The psychophysics of vigilance. In J. S. Warm (Ed.), *Sustained attention in human performance.* New York: Wiley.

Warrick, M. J. (1947). Direction of movement in the use of control knobs to position visual indicators. In P. M. Fitts (Ed.), *Psychological research on equipment design.* Research Report 19, Aviation Psychology Program.

Watson, A. B. (1986). Temporal sensitivity. In K. Boff, L. Kaufman, & J. Thomas (Eds.), *Handbook of perception and performance: Vol. 1.* Chapter 6. New York: Wiley.

Watson, D. G., & Humphreys, G. W. (1995). Attention capture by contour onsets and offsets: No special role for onsets. *Perception & Psychophysics, 57*, 583–597.

Watson, J. B. (1917). An attempted formulation of the scope of behavior psychology. *Psychological Review, 24*, 329–352.

Weijers, A. A., Mulder, G., Okita, T., & Mulder, L. J. M. (1989). Attention to color: An analysis of selection, controlled search, and motor activation, using event-related potentials. *Psychophysiology, 26*, 89–109.

Welford, A. T. (1952). The psychological refractory period and the timing of high speed performance—a review and a theory. *British Journal of Psychology, 43*, 2–19.

Welford, A. T. (1967). Single channel operation in the brain. *Acta Psychologica, 27*, 5–22.

Welford, A. T. (1973). Stress and performance. *Ergonomics, 16*, 567–580.

Welford, A. T. (1976). *Skilled performance: Perceptual and motor skills.* Glenview, IL: Scott, Foresman.

Welford, A. T. (1980). The single channel hypothesis. In A. T. Welford (Ed.), *Reaction times.* London: Academic Press.

Wells, F. L., Kelly, M., & Murphy, G. (1921). On attention and simple reactions. *Journal of Experimental Psychology, 4*, 391–398.

Wertheim, A. H. (1979). *Information processed in ocular pursuit.* Doctoral dissertation, University of Groningen, Groningen, The Netherlands.

Wertheim, A. H. (1989). A quantitative index for visual conspicuity: Theoretical background and experimental validation of a measuring method. IZF 1989 C-20, TNO, Soesterberg, Netherlands.

Whitaker, L. (1979). Dual task interference as a function of cognitive processing load. *Acta Psychologica, 43,* 71–84.

Whittenburg, J. A., Ross, S., & Andrews, T. G. (1956). Sustained perceptual efficiency as measured by the Mackworth clock test. *Perceptual and Motor Skills, 14,* 211–215.

Wickelgren, W. A. (1977). Speed–accuracy trade-off and information processing dynamics. *Acta Psychologica, 41,* 67–85.

Wickens, C. D. (1980). The structure of attentional resources. In R. Nickerson (Ed.), *Attention & Performance* (Vol. 8). Hillsdale, NJ: Lawrence Erlbaum Associates.

Wickens, C. D. (1984). Processing resources in attention. In R. Parasuraman & R. Davies (Eds.), *Varieties of attention.* New York: Academic Press.

Wickens, C. D. (1991). Processing resources and attention. In D. L. Damos (Ed.), *Multiple task performance.* Washington: Taylor & Francis.

Wickens, C. D. (1992). *Engineering psychology and human performance.* New York: Collins.

Wickens, C. D., & Carswell, C. M. (1995). The proximity compatibility principle: Its psychological foundation and relevance to display design. *Human Factors, 37,* 473–494.

Wickens, C. D., Derrick, W. A., Gill, R., Donchin, E. (1981). *The processing demands of higher order control: Converging evidence from event-related brain potentials and additive factors methodology.* Unpublished manuscript, University of Illinois.

Wickens, C. D., & Liu, Y. (1988). Codes and modalities in multiple resources: A success and a qualification. *Human Factors, 30,* 599–616.

Wickens, C. D., Moody, M. J., & Vidulich, M. (1985). Retrieval time as a function of memory set size, type of probes, and interference in recognition memory. *Journal of Experimental Psychology: Learning, Memory and Cognition, 11,* 154–164.

Wickens, C. D., & Sandry, D. L. (1982). Task-hemispheric integrity in dual-task performance. *Acta Psychologica, 52,* 227–248.

Widdel, H. (1983). A method for measuring the visual lobe area. In R. Groner, C. Mentz, D. F. Fisher, & R. A. Monty (Eds.), *Eye movements and psychological functions.* Hillsdale, NJ: Lawrence Erlbaum Associates.

Wiener, E. L. (1987). Application of vigilance research: Rare, medium or well done? *Human Factors, 29,* 725–736.

Wientjes, C. J. E., Grossman, P., Gaillard, A. W. K., & Defares, P. B. (1986). Individual differences in respiration and stress. In G. R. J. Hockey, A. W. K. Gaillard, & M. G. H. Coles (Eds.), *Energetics and human information processing.* Dordrecht, The Netherlands: Nijhoff.

Wijers, A. A., Lamain, W., Slopsema, S., Mulder, G., & Mulder, M. J. M. (1989). An electrophysiologic investigation of the spatial distribution of attention to colored stimuli in focused and divided attention conditions. *Biological Psychology, 29,* 213–245.

Wilkins, A. J., Shallice, T., & McCarthy, R. (1987). Frontal lesions and sustained attention. *Neuropsychologia, 25,* 359–365.

Wilkinson, R. T. (1961). Interaction of lack of sleep with knowledge of results, repeated testing and individual differences. *Journal of Experimental Psychology, 62,* 263–271.

Wilkinson, R. T. (1969). Some factors influencing the effects of environmental stressors upon performance. *Psychological Bulletin, 72,* 260–272.

Williams, L. G. (1967). The effect of target specification on objects fixated during visual search. *Acta Psychologica, 27,* 355–360.

Willows, D. M., & McKinnon, G. E. (1973). Selective reading: Attention to the unattended lines. *Canadian Journal of Psychology, 27,* 292–304.

Willumeit, H. P., Ott, H., & Neubert, W. (1984). Simulated car driving as a useful technique for the determination of residual effects and alcohol interaction after short-and long-acting benzodiazepines. *Psychopharmacology, 1*, 182–192.

Wittenborn, J. R. (1943). Factorial equations for tests of attention. *Psychometrika, 8*, 19–35.

Wolfe, J. M. (1994). Guided search 2.0: A revised model of visual search. *Psychonomic Bulletin and Review, 1*, 202–238.

Wolfe, J. M., Cave, K. R., & Franzel, S. L. (1989). Guided search: An alternative to the Feature Integration model for visual search. *Journal of Experimental Psychology: Human Perception and Performance, 15*, 419–433.

Wood, C. C., & Jennings, J. R. (1976). Speed–accuracy trade-off functions in choice reaction time: Experimental designs and computational procedures. *Perception & Psychophysics, 9*, 93–102.

Wood, J. M., & Troutbeck, R. (1994). Effect of visual impairment on driving. *Human Factors, 36*, 476–487.

Woodhead, M. M. (1964). The effects of bursts of noise on an arithmetic task. *American Journal of Psychology, 77*, 627–633.

Woods, D. D. (1991). The cognitive representation of problem representations. In G. R. S. Weir & J. R. Alty (Eds.), *Human computer interaction and complex systems* (pp. 169–188). London: Academic Press.

Woods, D. D., Wise, J. A., & Hanes, L. F. (1981). An evaluation of nuclear power plant safety parameter display systems. *Proceedings of the twenty-fifth annual meeting of the Human Factors Society*, Rochester, NY.

Woodworth, R. S. (1938). *Experimental psychology.* New York: Holt, Rinehart & Winston.

Wright, R. D., Katz, A. N., & Hughes, E. A. (1993). Inattention and the perception of visual features. *Acta Psychologica, 83*, 225–235.

Wundt, W. (1883). Über psychologische Methoden [On psychological methods]. *Philosophische Studien, 10*, 1–38.

Wundt, W. (1896). *Grundrisz der Psychologie* [Basics of psychology]. Leipzig, Engelmann.

Yantis, S., & Hilstrom, A. P. (1994). Stimulus-driven attentional capture: Evidence from equiluminant visual objects. *Journal of Experimental Psychology: Human Perception and Performance, 20*, 95–107.

Yantis, S., & Johnston, J. C. (1990). On the locus of visual selection: Evidence from focused attention tasks. *Journal of Experimental Psychology: Human Perception and Performance, 16*, 135–149.

Yantis, S., & Jonides, J. (1984). Abrupt visual onsets and selective attention: Evidence from visual search. *Journal of Experimental Psychology: Human Perception and Performance, 10*, 601–621.

Yarbus, A. L. (1967). *Eye movements and vision.* New York: Plenum.

Yeh, Y. Y., & Eriksen, C. W. (1984). Name codes and features in the discrimination of letter forms. *Perception & Psychophysics, 39*, 225–233.

Yeh, Y. Y., & Wickens, C. D. (1988). The dissociation of subjective measures of mental workload and performance. *Human Factors, 30*, 111–120.

Yellott, J. I. (1967). Correction for guessing in choice reaction time. *Psychonomic Science, 8*, 321–322.

Yellott, J. L. (1971). Correction for guessing and the speed-accuracy trade-off in choice reaction time. *Journal of Mathematical Psychology, 8*, 159–199.

Yerkes, R. M., & Dodson, J. D. (1908). The relation of strength of stimulus to rapidity of habit formation. *Journal of Comparative Neurology and Psychology, 18*, 459–482.

Yntema, D. B., & Trask, F. P. (1963). Recall as a search process. *Journal of Verbal Learning and Verbal Behavior, 2*, 65–74.

Zacks, J. L., & Zacks, R. T. (1993). Visual search times assessed without reaction times: A new method and application to aging. *Journal of Experimental Psychology: Human Perception and Performance, 19,* 798–813.

Zeitlin, L. R. (1995). Estimates of driver mental workload: A long-term field trial of two subdsidiary tasks. *Human Factors, 37,* 611–621.

Zelasnik, H. N., & Franz, E. (1990). Stimulus–response compatibility and the programming of motor activity: Pitfalls and possible new directions. In R. W. Proctor & T. G. Reeve (Eds.), *Stimulus–response compatibility.* Amsterdam: North-Holland.

Zelaznik, H. N., & Hahn, R. (1985). Reaction time methods in the study of motor programming. *Journal of Motor Behavior, 17,* 190–218.

Author Index

557

Subject Index